THE ILLUSTRATED ENCYCLOPEDIA OF
CLASSIC COCKTAILS
MIXED, BLENDED AND FRUIT DRINKS

THE ILLUSTRATED ENCYCLOPEDIA OF
CLASSIC
COCKTAILS
MIXED, BLENDED AND FRUIT DRINKS

Over 750 all-time favourite drinks using spirits, liqueurs, wine, beer, mixers and fresh juices

Stuart Walton • Suzannah Olivier • Joanna Farrow

LORENZ BOOKS

This edition is published by Lorenz Books

Lorenz Books is an imprint of Anness Publishing Ltd
Hermes House, 88–89 Blackfriars Road, London SE1 8HA
tel. 020 7401 2077; fax 020 7633 9499
www.lorenzbooks.com; info@anness.com
© Anness Publishing Ltd 2005

UK agent: The Manning Partnership Ltd, tel. 01225 478444;
fax 01225 478440; sales@manning-partnership.co.uk

UK distributor: Grantham Book Services Ltd, tel. 01476
541080; fax 01476 541061; orders@gbs.tbs-ltd.co.uk

North American agent/distributor: National Book Network,
tel. 301 459 3366; fax 301 429 5746; www.nbnbooks.com

Australian agent/distributor: Pan Macmillan Australia, tel. 1300
135 113; fax 1300 135 103; customer.service@macmillan.com.au

New Zealand agent/distributor: David Bateman Ltd,
tel. (09) 415 7664; fax (09) 415 8892

Publisher: Joanna Lorenz
Editorial director: Judith Simons
Project editor: Felicity Forster
Photographers: Frank Adam, Steve Baxter, Gus Filgate,
    Janine Hosegood, Craig Robertson and Simon Smith
Designer: Nigel Partridge
Editorial reader: Jay Thundercliffe
Production controller: Pedro Nelson

Previously published in two separate volumes, *The Complete Guide to
Cocktails and Drinks* and *Juicing, Smoothies and Blended Drinks*

10 9 8 7 6 5 4 3 2 1

NOTES

Bracketed terms are intended for American readers.
Standard spoon and cup measures are level.
1 tsp = 5ml, 1 tbsp = 15ml, 1 cup = 250ml/8fl oz
The very young, elderly and those in ill-health or with
a compromised immune system are advised against
consuming juices or blends that contain raw eggs.
American readers should note that the mixer known as
Club soda is referred to throughout as soda or soda water.

CONTENTS

JUICES AND SMOOTHIES 272

INTRODUCTION

At what point in history someone first used an alcoholic substance to fulfil what would become its time-honoured role as intoxicant is a question that may never be answered. What is certain is that the first such use arose from the discovery of the effects of fermentation on either fruit, honey or sticky-sweet palm sap.

First alcohol

The ancient Egyptians used fermented grains for making prototype forms of beer. These grains also enabled them to refine the techniques for producing raised breads. They found that adding beer sediment – which was still full of live yeasts – was the quickest and easiest method of encouraging the start of fermentation in a new batch of dough.

Below: This Egyptian figure dates from c.2450–2290 BC, and shows a woman at a mixing tub making beer.

Wine came after beer, but was to become of crucial cultural and religious importance to the civilizations of Egypt, and classical Greece and Rome. It was used as a sacrament in orgiastic celebrations of the festivals of Dionysos, the Greek god of nature (Bacchus to the Romans). From such ancient rituals, the first public performances recognizable as drama are said to have evolved.

In addition to its ceremonial and cultural role, wine was also used for culinary purposes. Not only was it capable of making tough meat more supple, but wine marinades would have removed excess salt from meats that had been encrusted with salt, or soaked in brine, for preservation. Wine vinegar, its alcohol lost to acetic acid, may have been the first recourse, but wine itself appears in sauce recipes in the historically important late Roman cookbook of Apicius (3rd century AD). The wine itself was commonly infused with spices to mask the rank flavours of oxidation or acetification.

The discovery of distillation

The next important step was the discovery of the art of distilling. Distillation (from the Latin *destillare*; to drip) is the use of vaporization, by heat, to produce a drink higher in alcohol than the naturally fermented liquid. High levels of alcohol kill yeast and thus stop fermentation. The process is easier to control than fermentation. Whereas freshly pressed grape juice needs the right ambient temperature to begin the process of turning into wine, a spirit can be produced from wine simply by applying heat to it.

Alcohol has a lower boiling point than water (about 78°C/172°F, compared to 100°C/212°F), so it vaporizes into steam some time before the water content in the wine starts to boil. When the alcohol-laden steam hits a cool surface, it forms a dripping condensation, and reverts to a liquid with a much higher proportion of alcohol than the wine. Boil that liquid

up again, and the same procedure will yield an even higher alcohol, and so on.

Much academic debate has been generated in the last 30 years or so as to when and where distillation was first discovered. The Greek philosopher Aristotle, who lived in the 4th century BC, writes of distillation as a way of purifying seawater to make it drinkable. He comments in passing that the same treatment can be given to wine, which is reduced thereby to a sort of "water". He was tantalizingly close to a breakthrough, but his experiment did no more than prove that wine is just a form of modified water, and that a liquid can only derive flavour from whatever happens to be mixed with the water that forms its base.

The documented beginnings of systematic and scientifically founded distillation, at least in Europe, come from the celebrated medical school at Salerno around AD 1100. Wine itself was held to have a range of medicinal properties (a view that found favour again in the 1990s), and the extraction of what was held to be the soul or spirit of the wine, through distillation, is what led to the naming of distillates as "spirits".

Alcohol and alchemy

Alcohol was believed to be the active ingredient in the healing powers of wine. Up to that time, the word "alcohol" was applied as a generic term to any product derived through vaporization and condensation. Its origin from the Arabic word *al-kuhl* refers to the Arab practice of producing a black powder by condensing a vapour of the metal antimony. The powder was then used as eye make-up, which is why eye-liner is still occasionally known as kohl. It was not until some time during the 16th century that "alcohol" was used specifically in reference to distilled spirits.

Not only medicine but the ancient practice of alchemy were involved in the European origins of distillation. Alchemy was a respected branch of the physical

Above: A vase painting from c.460–450 BC, showing Greeks sharing a drink at a banquet. Note the flat drinking vessel.

sciences, and was chiefly concerned with finding a means of transforming ordinary metals into gold. People wholeheartedly believed that if such a process could be discovered, it might well be possible to apply it to the human body and extract the essential life force from its mortal shell, thus guaranteeing eternal youth. With the realization that alcohol could be repeatedly distilled to ever-greater levels of purity, people came to believe that spirits could be the Holy Grail.

It can't have taken long for the Salerno doctors to ascertain that, whatever other remarkable properties distilled spirit had, the power to confer everlasting life wasn't one of them. However, the medical applications of spirits were to endure for hundreds of years. It was Arnaldo de Vilanova, a Catalan physician of the 13th century,

Right: This 15th-century English illustration shows scientists preparing for an alchemical experiment.

who first coined the Latin term *aqua vitae*, "water of life", for distilled spirits, indicating that they were associated with the promotion of vitality and health. (That term lives on in the Scandinavian *aquavit* and the French *eau de vie*, as well as the names of various other spirits.)

The first distillates

Undoubtedly, the earliest distillates were of wine, since it had a more salubrious and exalted image than beer; grain distillation to produce the first whiskies and neutral spirits followed in the Middle Ages. Many of these prototypes contained herb and spice extracts, or were flavoured with fruit, in order to enhance the medicinal properties of the preparation. The additives also conveniently masked what must have been the fairly raw taste and off-putting aroma of the unadulterated liquor.

Anyone who has smelt and tasted clear spirit dripping off the still in a brandy distillery (or, for that matter, has had a brush with illicit Irish poteen or American moonshine) will know how far removed untreated spirit is from the welcoming smoothness of five-star cognac or single malt Scotch. The infused distillates were the antecedents of many of the traditional aromatic liqueurs and flavoured vodkas of today.

Such, for centuries, was the official account of the birth of distilled spirits. In 1961, however, an Indian food historian, O. Prakash, argued that there was evidence that distillation of rice and barley beer was practised in India as early as 800 BC. Others have argued that, if this was so, then distillation probably arrived there from China even

Above: This late 14th-century Italian manuscript shows people enjoying their wine in an upper room, with the cellarman hard at work in the wine cellar below.

earlier. Thus, current theory cautiously credits the Chinese as the discoverers of the art.

It seems unusual that distilled alcohol was not remarked on or, apparently, even encountered by soldiers engaged in the European invasion of India, led by Alexander the Great in 327 BC. His campaign is reliably credited with having brought rice back to Europe, but any rice spirit appears to have been overlooked. Perhaps, if it was drunk at all by the invaders, it was in a diluted form, and was therefore not perceived to be any higher in alcohol than the grape wine with which they were familiar. Then again, it may just have been rejected as smelling or looking unclean. Whatever the explanation, if the Chinese or Indians did practise distillation as long ago as is claimed, the expertise they had stumbled on centuries before the Europeans remained specific to that part of the world. Thus did the course of history remain tantalizingly unchanged.

Distillation methods

The original and widespread distillation vessel, still used in the Cognac region of France and by the whisky distillers of Scotland, is the pot still. It consists of the only three elements absolutely essential to the process: a pot in which the fermented product (malted grains, wine, cider, etc.) is heated; the alembic, or tube, through which the alcohol vapour driven off is sucked up; and the condenser, where the steam is cooled and reliquefied. To obtain a better quality product, spirits are generally distilled at least twice for greater refinement, so the still has to be started up again.

Not all the condensed vapour is suitable for use in fine liquor. The first and last of it to pass through (known as the "heads" and "tails") are generally discarded, because of the relatively high level of impurities they contain. The invention of the continuous still in the early 19th century, in which the process carries on to a second distillation uninterrupted, made spirit production more economical and easier to control. This is the method used in France's other classic brandy, armagnac, and the continuous still is now the preferred apparatus for the production of most spirits worldwide.

Below: Distillation in Strasburg, Germany, during the 16th century.

Spirits

Probably the first spirit to be taken seriously as an object of connoisseurship, as distinct from being purely medicinal or just a method of using up surplus grape or grain production, was the brandy of the Cognac region of western France. People noticed that the superior, mellower spirit produced by the light wines of Cognac responded particularly well to ageing in oak casks. The casks were traditionally fashioned out of wood from the Limousin forests of the region. The manufacture and preparation of brandy casks demands particular care. After 25 years in a cask, a brandy loses about one-third of its original volume.

Cask-aged spirits derive every aspect of their final character – from the precise shade of tawny in the colour to their richness and roundness of flavour – from the maturation period they undergo in wood. They will not continue to develop in the bottle. The complex classification system in operation today for cognac is based on the length of time the spirit has been aged. It is testimony to a reputation for painstaking quality that dates back to around the end of the 17th century.

Scottish and Irish whiskies rose to similar prominence soon after this date. Their differing production processes resulted in quite distinct regional styles, depending on the quantities of peat used in the kilns where the malted grain is dried, on the quality of the spring water used in the mash and, some have claimed, on the shape of the still. Varieties of whisky are made across the world these days, from North America to Japan, but all attempts to replicate the precise taste of great Scotch – despite the use of identical ingredients and procedures – have somehow inexplicably foundered.

The distilled grain of cereals yields other spirits, such as Kornschnaps. Sometimes it is flavoured with juniper berries to produce gin. In Mexico the fermented juice of the agave cactus is distilled to produce mescal and the rather more refined tequila.

Spirits are also distilled from many other fruits as well as the grape. These include apricots, cherries, figs, plums, pears, peaches, raspberries, bilberries, mulberries, mirabelles and greengages. The fruit is first fermented, as for cider and wine. True rum is distilled from fermented sugar cane juice, but nowadays a molasses-based version, once known as tafia, is also called rum.

Liqueurs

Where a distilled drink stops being a spirit and turns into a liqueur is something of an elusive question. The one constant is that, to be a liqueur, a drink should have some obvious aromatizing element (perhaps even a hundred or more in the case of certain celebrated products). This doesn't mean that all flavoured distillates are liqueurs – flavoured vodkas are still vodka – but there are no neutral liqueurs. Some of these products have

Below: Cognac ageing in barrels at Courvoisier in Jarnac.

Right: Modern whisky stills at the Glenfiddich distillery in Scotland.

histories at least as venerable as those of cognac and Scotch. The most notable are those produced by the old French monastic orders. Bénédictine, the cognac-based, herb-scented potion that originated at the monastery in Fécamp, in Normandy, can convincingly lay claim to a lineage that rolls back to the beginning of the 16th century. Chartreuse – another famous liqueur flavoured with a complex combination of herbs – is named after the monastery of Grande-Chartreuse, where it is still made by the monks.

The first and greatest cocktail era, which arrived with the advent of the Jazz Age in the 1920s, rescued many of the traditional liqueurs from the niches of obscurity into which they had been relegated by popular taste. The Benedictine monks may have been a little shocked to hear that their revered creation was being mixed with English gin, American applejack, apricot brandy

and maple syrup, and then shaken to within an inch of its life and renamed the Mule's Hind Leg, but at least it was drunk – as were the giggling flappers after recklessly knocking back three or four of them.

Classic cocktails

A cocktail is a drink consisting of two or more ingredients, stirred or shaken. It can be a short aperitif type of cocktail for serving before a meal, such as a Dry Martini or a Gin Cocktail, or a longer drink in the style of a Tequila Sunrise or Sunset, to be drunk at any time of day or night. It may contain ice – "on the rocks" – and fruits to add colour, flavour and visual interest. Or it may contain cream and liqueur, such as Dizzy Dame or Grasshopper – rich, sweet cocktails traditionally served after dinner.

In the past all cocktails had a spirit as their base. The five main spirits that provided the different characters of these "true" cocktails are vodka, gin, rum, whisky and brandy. The spirits that are most suitable for making drinks with fruit are rum and brandy. Both are renowned for their fieriness and yet provide a perfect base for blended fruit. Rum is perhaps the most obvious of the two to use as it comes from the Caribbean, well-known for its tropical fruits and delicious drinks such as Piña Colada and Zombie. Because rum is available in white, light and dark varieties, it can be used for a wide range of different cocktails.

Nowadays, with the increase in the number and popularity of mixed drinks of all kinds, cocktails include both wine-

Above: Luigi is a classic short drink that is popular as a before-dinner aperitif. It has equal measures of gin and dry vermouth, with a little grenadine.

based and non-alcoholic mixed drinks. Wine concoctions, whether called cups, punches or cocktails, are refreshing, easy to make, and can be very varied. The most luxurious are those based on champagne, of which the most famous is Buck's Fizz, a mixture of two-thirds champagne to one-third orange juice. Champagne Cocktail, a slightly stronger drink, was first made in the 19th century – its origins are uncertain, but one story is that a prominent member of the English court was the first to discover its delights.

Above: Gin, dry vermouth and sweet red vermouth wtih a dash of orange bitters make up the RAC, which is shaken with ice and then strained.

More popular than ever nowadays, cocktails without alcohol can be just as tantalizing in appearance and taste as their alcoholic equivalents. As well as fruits, juices and syrups, these can be created using lemonade, ginger ale, tonic and soda water, coffee and tea.

The garnish or decoration of a cocktail is very much a personal thing and provides a wonderful opportunity for individual flair and invention. Although there are no hard and fast rules with garnishes, there are certain cocktails, for example the Martini, which call for a particular type, such as a twist of lemon, an olive or, as in the case of a Gibson, a cocktail onion. Slices of orange and lemon and a cherry on a stick are the most frequently used garnishes, but with the availability of more exotic fruits, such as kumquats, mangoes and physalis, many more variations are possible. And there are now so many different types of novelty decoration that even the most simple cocktail can be transformed into an outrageous creation. Let your imagination run wild with parasols, sparklers and personalized cocktail sticks.

Left: Stocking up with a selection of spirits, liqueurs, fortified wines and bitters is a vital part of the preparation for cocktail making.

Above: This fruit punch made with papaya, passion fruit and lychees has quite a kick to it from the addition of Grand Marnier liqueur.

Juices and smoothies

These two types of drink are very similar, and there is no precise dividing line between them. Juicing is the extraction of the juice from a fruit or vegetable, leaving behind the fibre and pulp in the juicer. The vitamins, minerals, sugars, starches and enzymes form a concentrate of almost all the plant's nutrients, without the fibrous plant cell walls. The juice is absorbed quickly and easily by the body. Almost all fruits and vegetables are suitable for juicing. The best of them all are apples and carrots, which produce wonderful juices on their own but are also subtle enough to be mixed with any other fruit or vegetable that you may choose.

Smoothies are usually made in a blender, simply by chopping the fruit and blending it all to a pulp. In this way the whole fruit can be consumed, fibre, juice and all. In addition to the health-giving vitamins and enzymes, you will also consume the fruit's fibre, which is excellent for the health of the colon and bowel. Bananas are particularly good for blending rather than juicing,

Right: Iron Crazy and Body Builder are super healthy juices that are highly nutritious and ideal choices for the seriously health-conscious.

as are soft exotic fruits such as peaches, mangoes, papaya and pineapple. Smoothies are especially good when blended with milk, cream, ice cream or yogurt, which give them a delicious thick consistency with the texture of milkshakes.

Both juices and smoothies can be flavoured with herbs and spices, such as ginger, cinnamon, cardamom, mint, parsley or rosemary. They can also incorporate other healthy ingredients, including brewer's yeast, wheatgrass, kelp, ginseng, aloe vera, nuts and seeds. Honey, fructose or molasses may be added for sweetness.

Juices are a key ingredient in many cocktails. The juices used in most cocktail bars come out of a carton and are rarely fresh, but you can set up a raw juice bar to make drinks that taste superb and are nourishing as well as intoxicating. Raw juice is especially useful for mixing with the clear spirits, particularly vodka, but be careful how much you add, as raw juice cocktails are deceptively easy to drink.

How to use this book

The book begins with a section on bartending techniques, including what equipment is needed for making cocktails, juices and smoothies, which glasses to use, and how to make decorative garnishes. There is practical advice on how to prepare for a party, plus useful information about alcohol and health, including tips for safe drinking and avoiding hangovers.

Above: Blueberries and vanilla-flavoured buttermilk are the main ingredients in this Purple Haze smoothie, which looks and tastes utterly divine.

Whether you are throwing a cocktail party or just want to know how to make cocktails as good as – if not better than – those you have tasted in a bar, all the information you need is here.

The main part of the book is divided into two sections, Classic Cocktails and Juices and Smoothies. The first section looks at all the categories of alcoholic drink: spirits, liqueurs, fortified wine, beer and cider. This is followed by a guide to the non-alcoholic ingredients with which they can be mixed: fruit juices, syrups, sparkling beverages, coffee, chocolate or simply water. The recipe section describes more than 500 cocktail recipes, arranged by type, so that you can expand your repertoire. These include classics from the 1920s and trendsetting new concoctions available in bars today.

In the second section you will find advice on buying and preparing ingredients for juices and smoothies, and on how to get your daily dose of essential vitamins. More than 160 recipes include fresh juices made with fruit and vegetables, traditional milkshakes and exciting party tipples. That drink after work or on Saturday night need no longer be the same old bottle of beer, glass of wine or G&T. The drinking world is your oyster. Do it wisely, and have fun.

bartending techniques

In this part of the book, we shall find out what props and paraphernalia are needed to set up your own professional-looking bartending operation at home. After useful advice on planning a successful cocktail party and avoiding or mitigating the unwanted after-effects of such an occasion, we'll learn about the bartender's equipment – from cocktail shakers and muddlers through to swizzle-sticks and types of glasses. There are also helpful tips on how to garnish your creations with salt, sugar, citrus twists, soft fruits and green olives. The section concludes with tricks and techniques of the trade, including how to make decorative ice cubes and melon balls, how to frost glasses, make basic sugar syrup and steep spirits.

Professional bartending

There is much more to becoming a successful bartender than being able to whip up a few cocktails at home. The job has something of the nature of a true vocation about it, with national and international professional associations for working bartenders, and a constant interchange of information taking place via trade journals and the internet. Educational courses, in both the theory and practice of what has come to be known quite seriously as "mixology", are organized, and the crowning events of each year are the cocktail competitions, at which aspiring grand masters produce their latest new creations for an international panel of judges.

While there is inevitably an air of commodious bonhomie about such occasions, that does not mean they are not taken extremely seriously. The fact that, when all is said and done, you are dealing in strong alcoholic drink is never forgotten, and there is a focus on encouraging responsible drinking as well as dispensing enjoyment. Achieving a full understanding of the raw materials of your trade – learning the history of each drink, gaining familiarity with its range of flavours and its potential in the mixed drink repertoire – is absolutely essential. New products are coming on to the market at a faster rate than ever before. Some are likely to be here today and gone tomorrow; others are of more lasting importance. They must all become familiar to you.

The approach to cocktail creation must be taken as seriously and as studiously as learning to become a chef, and indeed there are obvious connections between the two professions. You don't just suddenly become a bartender overnight because you can make a Brandy Alexander that your friends like without spilling anything. The skills you will acquire will

Above: A good bartender needs to know his or her way around a bewildering array of products these days.

Below: Dealing with a press of thirsty customers can be a thoroughly daunting business.

include consistency (making sure the same drink turns out tasting the same way each time), dexterity (shaking up one cocktail after another for a bar full of thirsty customers is necessarily lightning-quick and exhausting work), and what is known in the educational courses as "flair training".

Putting it very roughly, flair training will enable you to withstand comparison to Tom Cruise in the famous, although universally derided, 1988 motion picture *Cocktail* (for which the tagline was "When he pours, he reigns"). Believe it or not, they really do teach aspiring young mixologists how to juggle with bottles, create pyrotechnical effects with flaming alcohol, and even set up little brain-teasers with matchsticks for those, perhaps sitting with their elders in a hotel bar, not quite old enough to drink.

Most countries have their own professional organizations. The American Bartenders' Guild, and its British equivalent the UKBG, are among the longest-established, and many now belong to an umbrella group called the International Bartenders Association.

Below: A professional barman at work is something of a showman too.

Above: The movie Cocktail *stars Tom Cruise as the flamboyant, bottle-throwing barman who tries to make it big in his own top-class bar.*

The IBA was founded with a meeting at the Grand Hotel in Torquay, south-west England, in 1951. Just seven European countries were represented at that inaugural gathering – Denmark, France, Italy, the Netherlands, Sweden, Switzerland and the UK – but the group now claims members from all around the world. It held its first cocktail competition at its 1955 conference, the prize being carried off by an Italian bartender, Giuseppe Neri. In 1975, the IBA took the revolutionary step of admitting female members, and at the beginning of the new century, 50 years after its foundation, it now boasts over 50 international affiliates.

If you should feel yourself drawn to this very singular vocation, the first step is to acquire the skills and techniques we look at in this book. Hosting even a small cocktail party, and keeping things flowing without either major spillages or (even worse) running out of ice, is almost as challenging as organizing army manoeuvres. Only when you have reached an elevated level of aptitude in

that department should you go on to the really fun side of the business, namely, inventing your own cocktail recipes.

Useful professional publications to help get you started are the UKBG's *International Guide to Drinks*, or, in the United States, *The Original Guide to American Cocktails and Drinks (The Bartender's Companion)*. The UKBG also publishes a magazine, *Spirit*, which is packed with news from the frontline, features and reports of tastings; *Class*, "the magazine of bar culture", is a vibrant and entertaining consumer journal that keeps tracks of what's going on in fashionable bars around the world. Good websites that are worth a look include *www.cocktailtimes.com* and *www.webtender.com*. Both are full of recipes, as well as containing plenty of invaluable reference information.

Planning a party

The key to planning and carrying out your first successful cocktail party is to start small. Inviting the entire neighbourhood to a riotous bash might sound rather tempting, but you will only come unstuck by overreaching your own resources. A small group of old friends – say, half a dozen – is a good starting point.

Browse through the recipes in this book, try out for yourself a few of the recipes that appeal to you, and whittle them down to two or three that you think will prove popular with guests whose tastes are familiar to you. A pleasing balance of sour and sweet, or sour, sweet and fizzy, drinks will make for a satisfying evening. Choosing one cocktail that can be made in the liquidizer, one that is made in the shaker and one that is mixed in a pitcher would make logistical sense, so that you are not frantically rinsing out the shaker as guests move from one cocktail to another.

State your start and end times in advance when you invite people. That way, you can ensure that you are not still dealing with thirsty stragglers at one o'clock in the morning.

Provide food, but make it clear that this is a cocktail evening, not a dinner

Below: Champagne chilling in a bucket of iced water needs about 15 minutes.

Above: Nibbles will help absorb some of the alcohol consumed.

party. You are going to be quite busy enough with drink preparation, without having to cook. However, the more guests are encouraged to eat, the slower the intoxication effect will set in. Little salty and cheesy nibbles, tortilla chips with dips, and nuts are always popular. If you really want to splash out, you could make or buy some canapés ahead of time as well.

Decide on which glasses you are going to use for which cocktail, and make sure there is one of each for each guest. Go through your checklist of vital equipment several times, to be certain you haven't forgotten anything: shaker (with measures), liquidizer, pitcher, glasses, fruit for garnishing (remember that citrus fruit slices and twists can be prepared in advance before anyone arrives), a knife for last-minute slicing, bags of ice, and any special opening implements for flipping off bottle-tops or pulling corks. Serving each drink on a little folded paper napkin is the kind of touch that really impresses.

Quantities will depend on how many people you invite, but it is worth doing some initial calculations. A standard measure in these recipes is 25ml/1fl oz,

of which there are 28 in a standard bottle of spirits and 20 in a 50cl bottle of liqueur. Divide each bottle not by single measures, but by the number of measures in each recipe, which may be higher or lower than one. For some drinks, you may find a half-bottle will be quite enough to be going on with.

If there is one golden rule, it has to be that you can never have too much ice. Cocktail-making uses an enormous amount, as each batch is used for the few seconds it takes you to shake the cocktail, and is then thrown away. But ice is only water after all, so be extravagant, and if you aren't sure you have enough ice trays or bags to cope, then buy one of those industrial-sized bags of ice from the supermarket. Better still, buy two or three, which shouldn't set you back too much. They aren't very cost-effective, I admit, but at some late stage in the evening, you'll be mighty glad it's there, if only to clamp firmly on your head as you see the last happy guests away.

So good luck, and have fun!

Alcohol and health

It has now been established that a glass of wine a day is probably good for you. It is a bulwark in the body's defence against coronary heart disease because its antioxidants help to break down bad cholesterol in the arteries. To some extent, ethanol (alcohol) itself in any of its forms can assist in this, as has been found by scientists in Denmark, but there are obviously limits. Alcohol is virtually worthless in terms of nutritional value and, if drunk in excess, is positively harmful.

Heavy drinking damages the liver, possibly irreparably, and puts strain on its normal day-to-day functioning. It also depletes nutrients, such as vitamins A and C, the B vitamins, magnesium, zinc and the essential fatty acids, and leads to severe dehydration.

Modern methods of producing alcoholic drinks often mean that your average glass of wine, beer or spirit will contain chemical pesticides, colourants

Below: Nuts and fruits are efficient sources of protein and vitamins to replace essential nutrients.

and other noxious additives, which you might be a lot more circumspect about if you found them in food products.

Each drinker famously has his or her own limit. What may be no more than a convivial evening's imbibing to one would have the next person sliding under the table. As a very general rule, an adult woman's capacity is thought to be about two-thirds that of a man's, so women shouldn't feel under any pressure to keep pace.

It would be disingenuous to pretend that you won't at some stage wake up feeling so unutterably lousy that you'll swear to forgo all strong liquors forever more. Welcome to the wonderful world of the alcohol hangover, caused by dehydration and too much toxin in the bloodstream. Everybody has his or her own best cure, whether it be milk, fried foods, black coffee, the rather dubious hair-of-the-dog approach (i.e. another small drink) or my own indispensable standby: aspirin.

Far smarter than a hangover cure, though, is knowing how to avoid such a ghastly outcome in the first place. Ways

Above: Fruit juices will help to make life fun during periods of abstinence.

of doing this include: lining the stomach with lactic fat (300ml/½ pint whole milk) before you embark on the evening's drinking; taking 500mg of aspirin beforehand; downing a glass of water between drinks to rehydrate; and (most important of all) slowly drinking a pint of water before falling into bed.

Treat yourself to a break from it all periodically. Non-alcoholic juices made from fruits and vegetables stimulate the body, speed up metabolism, encourage the elimination of toxins via the lymphatic system, and strengthen the body's overall immunity. They play a vital role in detoxing – everyone's favourite pastime in January – and should be drunk fresh. When making juices at home, choose ripe fruits and fresh vegetables. Juices can be very strong, so dilute with filtered or mineral water to taste. They should always be drunk as soon as they are made.

Health-food stores and pharmacies sell a natural remedy called milk thistle in capsule form, which has been clinically proven to assist in liver cell regeneration. Take it in doses of up to 200mg per day, especially during periods of abstinence. It really will make you feel better.

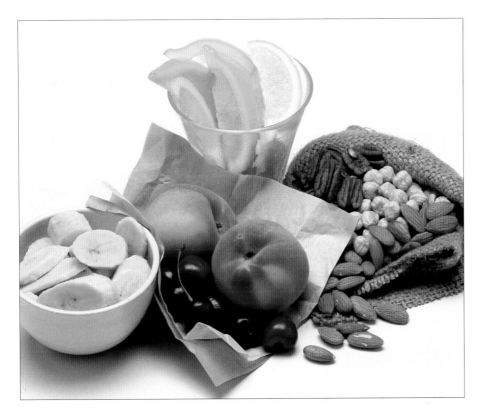

Bartending equipment

To make a successful cocktail bartender, you will need a few essential pieces of equipment. The most vital and flamboyant is the cocktail shaker, but what you have on hand in the kitchen can usually stand in for the rest. After a while, though, you may feel an urge to invest in more of the following specialist pieces of equipment.

Cocktail shaker

The shaker is used for drinks that need good mixing, but don't have to be crystal-clear. Once the ingredients have been thoroughly amalgamated in the presence of ice, the temperature clouds up the drink. Cocktail shakers are usually made of stainless steel, but can also be silver, hard plastic or tough glass. The Boston shaker is made of two cup-type containers that fit over each other, one normally made of glass, the other of metal. This type is often preferred by the professional

Below: Measuring jug and spoon measures.

Left: Cocktail shakers now come in various shapes and sizes but the classic shaker remains unchanged.

Below: Measure.

bartender. For beginners, the classic three-piece shaker is easier to handle, with its base to hold the ice and liquids, a top fitted with a built-in strainer and a tight-fitting cap. Make sure you hold on to that cap while you are shaking. As a rough rule, the drink is ready when the shaker has become almost too painfully cold to hold, which is generally not more than around 15–20 seconds.

Measure

Most cocktail shakers come with a measure, known in American parlance as a "jigger". They usually come as a single-piece double cup, with one side a whole measure and the other a half. This is an invaluable little piece of equipment, providing the easiest way of measuring standard quantities of ingredients, as well as helping to add a professional-looking touch.

Measuring jug and spoons

For some recipes, the most convenient way to measure ingredients will be in a measuring jug, measuring cup, or standard-size spoons for smaller quantities. If you need to measure standard bar measures in a jug, cup or spoons, remember that one measure is 25ml/1fl oz. When following the cocktail recipes, you should stick to either the bar measures or the spoons; don't switch from one to the other within the same recipe.

Blender or liquidizer

Goblet blenders are the best shape for mixing cocktails that need to be aerated, as well as for creating frothy cocktails or ones made with finely crushed ice. Attempting to break up whole ice cubes in the blender may

Below: Blender.

very well blunt the blades. Opt for an ice bag or dishtowel, a rolling pin and plenty of brute force, or better still, use an ice crusher. These feature a plastic or glass jug (pitcher) placed on top of a motorized base, which powers blades inside the jug.

Blenders work best with soft fruit, such as bananas, peaches and berries, to which you add a liquid ingredient, such as water, milk or juice, to create delicious smoothies and shakes. Some can also be used to crush ice, but always check the instructions.

Food processor

These multi-functional machines comprise a main bowl and a variety of attachments, some of which are supplied with the original purchase; others can be bought individually. For making juices and blends, the most important attachments are:
• A strong blade that blends medium-hard or soft fruit and vegetables.
• A centrifugal juicing attachment that turns your food processor into a juicer. This is not as efficient as a dedicated juicer, but is a good option if you juice only occasionally or have limited storage space.
• A citrus press attachment.
• Whisking attachments.
• Ice crushing attachments.

Centrifugal juicer

These come in a variety of different designs. They are the least expensive type of electric juicer, yet are perfectly adequate for most juices. They have a pulp collector into which the fibre and pulp residue is ejected. Some come with a jug (pitcher) attachment that collects the juice; others require a separate container to be placed under the spout. Centrifugal juicers work by finely grating vegetables and fruit, and spinning them at great speed, which separates the juice from the pulp. Juicers are used to extract juice from hard vegetables and fruit, such as carrots and apples, and from leafy vegetables such as cabbage.

Masticating juicer

These are more high-tech than centrifugal juicers, and also more expensive. Instead of shredding the produce they finely chop it and then force the pulp through a mesh to separate out the juice. Electric or manually operated, masticating juicers produce a greater volume of juice than centrifugal models and, because of the method of extraction, the juice contains more live enzymes. In addition to using masticating juicers to make juices you could also use them to make delicious nut butters, ice cream from frozen fruit ingredients and healthy baby foods. Some masticating juicers come with useful attachments for milling grains, otherwise you can buy the attachments separately.

THE FIBRE ISSUE
Both smoothies and juices enable you to consume fresh produce in its raw state with the valuable nutrients intact. However, smoothies made in a blender are different from juices made in a juicer in one important way: they retain the fibre of the fruits. Fibre is not only important for healthy digestion, but also for cardiovascular health and helping to balance blood-sugar levels. When choosing equipment, bear in mind that fibre is valuable in the diet and, while juicing will not replace eating whole fruits and vegetables, smoothies and other blended drinks are nutritionally equivalent to eating the whole fruit. However, nutritional guidelines state that one glass of juice does count towards the recommended total daily intake of five portions of fruit and vegetables.

Above: Centrifugal juicers are quick, easy to use and relatively cheap.

Above: Melons are easy to blend, but harder fruits need a machine with a strong blade.

Above: Whichever type of juicer you use, prepare the fruit just before pressing for maximum freshness and flavour.

Electric wand

These handheld electric mixers are good for no-fuss blending. Some models come with a variety of attachments for blending and whisking. You need to use an electric wand with a deep bowl, or a flask (which is sometimes supplied). If you are going to blend on a regular basis it is much more practical to buy a proper blender, although handheld wands can blend soft fruit and liquid, syrup or powdered ingredients well. Creamy whipped toppings can be made with the whisk attachment.

Citrus juicers

There are three main types of citrus juicers available. You can buy electrically operated machines, which extract citrus juice into a container; hand-operated presses, which squeeze the juice down into a container; and hand-operated squeezers, which catch the juice in the base and collect the pips in a ridge. The simple, traditional squeezers, where the halved fruit is pushed down and twisted over a ridged mound-shape, are the cheapest and also the easiest

to clean, but more laborious when making large quantities of juice. You may occasionally want to use a blender or food processor instead, so that you retain the fibre and pulp of the fruit.

Right: Hand-operated citrus squeezers strain the pips and collect the juice.

Below: Handheld blender wands are easy to use and very effective.

BUYING TIPS

When deciding what equipment to buy, think about what you will be using it for. Will you be making fresh fruit juices for cocktails, or is blending ingredients for smoothies a priority? Juicers are best for firm fruits and vegetables, such as apples and carrots, but they are not good for soft fruit, such as bananas and mangoes, which clog up the machine and do not provide much juice. On the other hand, blenders are ideal for soft fruit and allow you to retain all the fibre. Before buying, ask yourself the following questions.

• Is it easy to feed the fruit and vegetables into the machine?
• If you are going to make large quantities, does the machine allow you to do this? How much pulp residue is collected?

• Are there any awkward corners to get into when cleaning the equipment? Round containers are usually easier to clean.
• Is the machine easy to assemble and take apart?
• Are any parts easily breakable? Make sure that removable parts are easy to replace if necessary.
• Is a jug (pitcher) provided or will you need to get hold of a container to collect the juice?
• Does the machine have a see-through container or lid so you can see what is happening inside?
• Is the power of the motor suitable? Some models have two-speed motors; others just have one speed. Decide which you need.
• Do you need to be able to crush ice? If so, check that the machine is suitable for this purpose.

Above: Use a larger knife for halving bigger items such as grapefruit and melons. A smaller knife is better for peeling fruit.

Sharp knives
Whether cutting lemons for garnishing drinks, or chopping vegetables for juicing, sharp knives make the job easier.

Apple corer
These make quick work of coring apples or pears before you blend them. Place over the core at the stem end and push down firmly right through the fruit, then twist slightly and pull out the core and pips. There is no need to core apples or pears if you are putting them through a juicer.

Chopping board
Some fruit and vegetables will have to be chopped up in order to fit them into the juicer's feeder tube. A large chopping board is most useful. Plastic boards are easier to keep clean than wooden ones. To clean chopping boards, scrub with washing-up liquid (dishwashing detergent), then allow them to air dry – drying with a cloth often leads to recontamination. To avoid contamination, use one chopping board for fruit, vegetables and bread, and keep another for meat; a third for onions and garlic is also a good idea.

Below: Always use a good sharp knife to peel and chop fruit and vegetables.

Below: Chopping boards with handles are easier to manipulate when you are feeding chopped fruit or vegetables into a blender.

Right: Apple corer.

Zester and canelle knife

These are used for presenting fruit attractively to garnish glasses. If you don't already have them, don't feel obliged to run out and buy them, as drinks can look equally attractive with simply sliced fruit. The zester has a row of tiny holes that remove the top layer of skin off a citrus fruit when dragged across it (although the finest gauge on your multi-purpose grater was also designed for just this job). A canelle knife (from the French word for a "channel" or "groove") is for making decorative stripes in the skins of a whole fruit. When sliced, they then have a groovy-looking serrated edge. It is, in effect, a narrow-gauged version of a traditional potato peeler, but is purely for decorative purposes.

Vegetable peeler

For preparing some root vegetables, such as potatoes and carrots, you will need a sturdy vegetable peeler. There are two main types available: straight blade or swivel blade. Experiment with each before choosing the one you feel most comfortable with, as this can make the job much easier.

USING A ZESTER

Hold the citrus fruit firmly in one hand and the zester in the other. Peel away short or long strips of the skin as desired. The pared-away skin makes a delicate garnish that floats on the surface of a drink.

Cherry stoner

This simple tool takes the hard work out of pitting cherries and makes the job much quicker. The bowl of the implement has a hole through which the cherry stone (pit) is ejected when the fruit is pressed.

Melon baller

Insert this small round scoop into the melon flesh and twist to remove neat balls of fruit.

Above: Cherry stoner and melon baller.

Below: Citrus zesters and canelle knives are useful for preparing fruit.

Below: There are many different types of vegetable peeler.

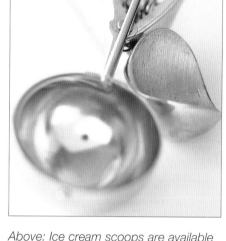

Above: Ice cream scoops are available in many different shapes and styles.

Ice cream scoops

These are useful for scooping ice cream, frozen yogurt or sorbet into milkshakes or smoothies. Choose from half-moon-shaped stainless-steel scoops with sleek steel handles, simple spoon-shaped scoops with metal handles or easy-grip moulded plastic handles, or brightly coloured plastic scoops with quick release levers. For smaller rounds of sorbet or frozen yogurt, try using a melon baller as a scoop.

Plastic spatula

These are handy for scraping thick blends out of a blender or food processor, and the plastic will not scratch the equipment.

Ice bags

These plastic bags that can be filled with water and frozen are a kind of disposable ice tray. You simply press each piece of ice out of them, tearing through the plastic as you go. They also have the advantage of making a more rounded piece of ice, as opposed to the hard-angled cube that an ice tray produces.

Wooden hammer

Use a wooden hammer for crushing ice. If you don't have a special hammer, the end of a wooden rolling pin works just as well.

Ice bag or towel

A towel or bag is essential for holding ice cubes when crushing, whether

Below: Wooden hammer and towel.

you are creating roughly cracked lumps or a fine snow. It must be scrupulously clean and fresh for each repeated use.

Ice crusher

If the prospect of breaking up ice with a hammer and dish towel comes to seem almost as much of a penance as working on a chain gang, an ice-crushing machine is the answer. It comes in two parts. You fill the top with whole ice cubes, put the lid on and, while pressing down on the top, turn the gramophone-type handle on the side. Take the top half off to retrieve the crystals of ice "snow" from the lower part. Crushed ice is used to fill the glasses for drinks that are to be served frappé. It naturally melts very quickly, though, compared to cubes.

Ice bucket and chiller bucket

An ice bucket with a close-fitting lid is useful if you are going to be making several cocktails in quick succession. They are not completely hermetic though, and ice will

eventually melt in them, albeit a little more slowly than if left at room temperature. It should not be confused with a chiller bucket for bottles of champagne and white wine, which is bigger and has handles on the sides, but doesn't have a lid. A chiller bucket is intended to be filled with iced water, as opposed to ice alone.

Left: Ice crusher.

Right: Chiller bucket.

Above: Mixing jug and muddlers.

Above: Bar spoon.

and looks like a flat spoon with holes and a curl of wire on the top. It is held over the top of the glass to keep the ice and any other solid ingredients back.

Sieve

This can be useful when you want to strain juices to remove seeds and pips for fussy children, or if you just want a thinner juice.

Corkscrew

The fold-up type of corkscrew is known as the Waiter's Friend, and incorporates a can opener and bottle-top flipper as well as the screw itself. It is the most useful version to have to hand as it suits all purposes. The spin-handled corkscrew with a blade for cutting foil is the best one for opening fine wines.

Right: Corkscrew.

Mixing jug or bar glass

It is useful to have a container in which to mix and stir drinks that are not shaken. The glass or jug (pitcher) should be large enough to hold two or three drinks. This vessel is intended for drinks that are meant to be clear, not cloudy.

Muddler

A long stick with a bulbous end, the muddler is used for crushing sugar or mint leaves, and so is particularly useful when creating juleps or smashes. A variety of sizes are available. It should be used like a pestle; large ones are needed for a mixing jug, smaller ones for individual glasses. At a pinch, a flattish spoon can be used instead of a muddler, but then you will

Right: Strainer.

find it more awkward to apply sideways rather than downward pressure when trying to press those mint leaves.

Bar spoon

These long-handled spoons can reach to the bottom of the tallest tumblers and are used in jugs, or for mixing the drink directly in the glass. Some varieties look like a large swizzle-stick, with a long handle and a disc at one end. They also look considerably more elegant than a dessert spoon.

Strainer

Used for pouring drinks from a shaker or mixing jug into a cocktail glass, the strainer's function is to remove the ice with which the drink has been prepared. Some drinks are served with the ice in (or "on the rocks") but most aren't, the reason being that you don't want the ice to unhelpfully dilute the drink. The best strainer, known professionally as a Hawthorn strainer, is made from stainless steel

Below: Sieves can be used to strain thick blends or to remove large seeds.

Nutmeg grater

A tiny grater with small holes, for grating nutmeg over egg-nogs, frothy and creamy drinks. If this sounds too fiddly, buy ready-ground nutmeg instead. It's almost as good.

Below: Nutmeg grater.

Egg whisk

Use a whisk to beat a little frothy texture into egg white before you add it to the shaker. It helps the texture of the finished drink no end. An ordinary balloon whisk will do the trick, although for culinary uses, a rotary whisk with a handle (or the electric specimen) is best.

Straws, swizzle-sticks and cocktail sticks

These decorative items are used to add the finishing touches to a cocktail. It was once considered axiomatic to drink all cocktails through straws. They tend now to be the exception rather than the rule. The flavours of the drink are better appreciated if it is poured directly into the mouth, as opposed to being sucked up in a thin stream. A mythical belief that the alcohol took effect more quickly if taken through straws was responsible for their popularity in the 1980s.

A swizzle-stick is a stirring aid used to mix and aerate a drink. It is often used for champagne, to give it extra sparkle, although overuse will flatten any carbonated drink. A swizzle-stick may be replaced by such food items as a stick of celery in a Bloody Mary, or a length of whole cinnamon for a short creamy cocktail or a hot, spicy drink such as mulled wine or ale.

Cocktail sticks (toothpicks) are used for holding ingredients such as cherries or other items of fruit that would otherwise sink to the bottom of the glass. And if you intend to eat the cherry or olive, it's handier if it's already speared, so that you don't have to commit the appalling faux pas of dipping a finger into the drink to catch it.

Storage jug or vacuum flask

Choose a storage jug (pitcher) with a close-fitting lid or place clear film (plastic wrap) over the opening before securing the lid. Covering the juice or blend securely limits its exposure to oxygen and prevents it from oxidizing. Even better, use a wide-necked vacuum flask.

Serving jugs and bowls

Buy different shapes and colours and have some fun with these, contrasting them with the colour of the cocktail, juice or smoothie you are serving. Ideally, punch should be served from a punch bowl. A good punch set is expensive, but will include a ladle and special glasses. Hot punches are traditionally served in a silver bowl and ladle, if you are fortunate enough to own them. For cold punches, a crystal or glass bowl with matching ladle is appropriate.

Above: Have a large glass jug for serving your drinks. Both the jug and the glasses will look more attractive (and be more hygienic) if they are really clean and sparkling. Wash them in hot water, rinse, and then dry with a clean, lint-free glasscloth.

Above: Egg whisk.

Right: Cocktail sticks.

Left: Swizzle-sticks.

Glasses

To ensure that glasses are sparkling clean, they should always be washed and dried with a glass cloth. Although some recipes suggest chilled glasses, don't put best crystal in the freezer; leave it at the back of the refrigerator instead. An hour should be enough.

Cocktail glass or Martini glass

This elegant glass is a wide conical bowl on a tall stem: a design that keeps cocktails cool by keeping warm hands away from the drink. It is by far the most widely used glass, so a set is essential. The design belies the fact that the capacity of this glass is relatively small (about three standard measures). Uses: the classic Martini and its variations, and almost any short, sharp, strong cocktail, including creamy ones.

Collins glass

The tallest of the tumblers, narrow with perfectly straight sides, a Collins glass holds about 350ml/12fl oz, and is usually used for serving long drinks made with fresh juices or finished with a sparkling mixer such as soda. This glass can also stand in as the highball glass, which is traditionally slightly less tall. Uses: Tom Collins, and all drinks that are to be "topped up" with anything.

Old-fashioned glass, tumbler or rocks glass

Classic, short whisky tumblers are used for shorter drinks, served on the rocks, and generally for drinks that are stirred rather than shaken. They should hold about 250ml/8fl oz. Uses: Old-Fashioned, Manhattan, Sours, etc.

Liqueur glass

Tiny liqueur glasses were traditionally used to serve small measures of unmixed drinks, and hold no more than 80ml/3fl oz. They are a good alternative for making a pousse-café or layered cocktail. They are best not used for serving measures of fortified wines such as sherry, port and madeira, where they will look ridiculously mean.

Above: Tumbler.   *Above: Liqueur glass.*

Brandy balloon or snifter

The brandy glass is designed to trap the fragrance of the brandy in the bowl of the glass. Cupping the glass in the palm of the hand further helps to warm it gently and release its aromas. Not now considered the thing to use for best cognac, it nonetheless makes a good cocktail glass for certain short, strong drinks that have been stirred rather than shaken. The wide bowl makes them suitable for drinks with solids floating in them.

Below: Large cocktail glass.

Below: Collins glass.

Below: Cocktail glass.

Below: Brandy balloon.

Above: Champagne flute.   *Above: Champagne saucer.*   *Above: Red wine glass.*   *Above: White wine glass.*

Large cocktail goblet or poco

Available in various sizes and shapes, large cocktail goblets are good for serving larger frothy drinks, or drinks containing puréed fruit or coconut cream. Classically, they are the glasses for Piña Coladas. The wider rims leave plenty of room for flamboyant and colourful decorations.

Champagne flute

The champagne flute is the more acceptable glass to use for quality sparkling wines. It is more efficient at conserving the bubbles since there is less surface area for them to break on. It should be used for champagne cocktails too. Always choose one with good depth, as the shorter ones look too parsimonious.

Champagne saucer

The old-fashioned saucer glass may be frowned on now for champagne, but it is an attractive and elegant design and can be used for a number of cocktails, particularly those that have cracked ice floating in them. Because of the wider surface area, there is plenty of scope for fruity garnishes too.

Red wine glass

The most useful size of wine glass, the red wine glass holds about 500ml/ 16fl oz. It should only be filled about a third full to allow the wine to be swirled around, so that it releases its bouquet. It can be used for long wine cocktails too, and will do at a pinch as a stand-in for the large cocktail goblet.

White wine glass

A long-stemmed, medium-sized glass of about 250ml/8fl oz capacity, a white wine glass should be held by the stem so as not to warm the chilled wine or cocktail with the heat of the hand. Use it for short wine cocktails such as spritzers and wine-based punches.

Pousse-café

A thin and narrow glass standing on a short stem, a pousse-café is used for floating or layering liqueurs one on top of the other. If you haven't got one, use a liqueur glass or even an old-fashioned sherry schooner instead. This is not a type of drink you are likely to be making very often. Although they look impressive, the novelty does rather wear off.

Shot glass

A tiny glass with a capacity of no more than 50ml/2fl oz, the shot glass is used for those very short, lethally strong cocktails known as shooters. If you're going to make a shooter, this is absolutely the only glass to use. No substitute will be accepted. The glass itself is usually extremely thick, as these drinks are intended to be thrown back in one, and then the glass slammed down fairly peremptorily on the bar counter. Go for it.

Below: Pousse-café.

Below: Shot glass.

Garnishes

It is far more elegant not to overdress cocktails, otherwise they all too quickly turn into a fruit salad with a drink attached. Less is best. The edible extras suggested on these pages add colour, flavour and visual interest to any glass.

Frosting
Frosting glasses with salt, sugar or cocoa is a simple but effective touch. It is extremely quick and easy, and means that the drink needs no other decoration.

Salt is absolutely indispensable for frosting the rim of a textbook Margarita, and is normally done with lime juice. For a sweet drink, sugar frosting makes for an appealingly festive look. It is appropriate for drinks such as Royal Silver, Golden Start and Brandy Crusta.

Left: Many kinds of sugar can be added to drinks: soft brown, demerara, dark muscovado, sugar cubes, cane sugar and caster (superfine) sugar.

SALT

A traditional Margarita should always have salt around the rim of the glass. To do this, rub the rim of the glass with a wedge of fresh lime and then dip the glass in fine salt. This example has an additional twist of cucumber rind as a garnish – but try not to over-garnish your drinks. Less is more.

SUGAR AND SYRUP

This champagne saucer was dipped into a shallow bowl of grenadine, then dipped into caster (superfine) sugar to create a frosted rim. The grenadine makes the sugar go bright pink. The glass was then placed in the refrigerator so that it was well chilled before being filled.

SUGAR AND FRUIT JUICE

It is possible to frost a glass with any fruit that goes with the drink. For example, this drink consists of Galliano mixed with a variety of fruit juices and coconut cream. The rim of the glass has been dipped in pineapple juice, then covered in a fine coating of caster (superfine) sugar.

Alternatively, a dark brown frosting of cocoa powder can be applied to a glass for Brandy Alexander, Cara Sposa or any other creamy cocktail flavoured with chocolate, coffee or orange.

To frost a glass, tip the rim of the glass in water, egg white, citrus juice or one of the syrups, and then dip it again in the chosen frosting. The garnish will take on the colour of the liquid.

Citrus fruits

Edible garnishes should reflect the various contents of the cocktail. Citrus fruit is widely used because it is appetizing to look at, and can

be cut in advance and kept covered in the refrigerator for a day until needed. Whole slices cut halfway through can be balanced on the rim of a highball glass, while half-slices are best used for floating in a cocktail glass. Apple, pear and banana are also suitable, but they do discolour on exposure to the air; dip them in lemon juice first to preserve colour and flavour.

Lemon is probably the most important fruit of all for the bartender. It is handy in everything from a simple gin and tonic to almost any cocktail.

A lime is small enough for you to be able to use whole slices to garnish a sharp-tasting cocktail containing its juice, such as a Moscow Mule.

Orange is indispensable for garnishing not just orange-flavoured drinks, but old-time mixtures of vermouth and spirit, such as Negroni.

Kumquats are bitter little citrus fruits, which are eaten with the skin on. Use half of one on a stick to garnish a cocktail that has some bitter orange flavour in it.

Above: Oranges.

Left: Kumquats.

Left: Limes.

Left: Lemons.

USING CITRUS FRUITS

A twisted half-slice of lemon adds an elegant decoration to any cocktail containing lemon juice.

A simple twist of lime looks effective and adds to the taste of a tequila, banana and lime cocktail.

Grated orange rind goes well with drinks containing orange, such as this creamy chocolatey-orange Tuaca and orange curaçao cocktail.

Soft fruits

Fresh soft fruit such as strawberries, cherries, peaches, apricots, blackberries and redcurrants make fabulous splashes of colour and add a delicious flavour, although they still tend to be mainly available in the summer.

Quartered large strawberries or, better still, the whole, small, wild variety, such as the French *fraises des bois*, would look good on a Strawberry Kiss.

Whole fresh cherries, particularly the black varieties, can be used in place of standard cocktail cherries from a jar to adorn a drink containing cherry brandy or kirsch. Singapore Sling contains the former, Rose the latter. The maraschino cherry is a popular option too, even though it is seen as something of a cliché these days.

A thin slice of very ripe peach is appropriate for a drink containing peach schnapps or peach brandy, such as Sparkling Peach Melba. White peach is best.

If there's apricot brandy in the drink (for example, Festival), a thin slice of apricot will work well. Use only juicy-ripe fruits though. The French Bergeron is a good variety.

Blackberries are the only garnish to use for a Blackberry and Champagne Crush, so long as they're in season.

The endless supply of tropical fruits available all year long, such as mango, pineapple, star fruit, papaya, physalis and the various types of melon, offers numerous decorative ideas and combinations for garnishing. A twiglet of redcurrants, perhaps with a little sugar frosting, makes a rather Christmassy-looking garnish. Physalis is a favourite garnish for modern desserts. Bring it into the cocktail repertoire too for exotically flavoured drinks.

Below: Cherries.

Below: Strawberries.

Above: Peaches.

Left: Apricots.

Below: Blackberries.

USING SOFT FRUITS
A cherry and an apricot slice can be skewered with a cocktail stick to make a stylish, fruity garnish.

Below: Physalis.

Above: Redcurrants.

Above:
Chocolate.

Above: Nutmeg.

Below: Cherry
tomatoes.

Above: Red
chillies.

Above: Green and black olives.

Right:
Mint.

Above: Celery.

USING OTHER GARNISHES

A sprig of fresh mint adds
freshness to drinks such as this
Long Island Iced Tea, or anything
containing crème de menthe.

Grated dark chocolate adds flavour
to sweet cocktails such as this gin,
banana and cream mixture.

Whole cinnamon sticks can be
used as stirrers for hot drinks such
as coffee or hot chocolate.

Other garnishes

Not all garnishes and decorations need
be fruit, however. A block of chocolate
can be grated over a drink, or melted
and scraped into chocolate curls, to
decorate a cocktail such as Iced Mint
and Chocolate Cooler.

Ground (or whole) cinnamon makes
an appropriate garnish for hot mulled
wine or punch.

Nutmeg goes well with egg-nogs
and flips. Either grate whole nutmegs,
or add the powdered version to the
surface of cream cocktails containing
chocolate or coffee flavours. A Brandy
Alexander cries out for nutmeg.

To some, green olives are
indispensable in a Dry Martini; to others,
they are anathema. When Martinis do
call for a green olive, always opt for
those packaged in brine, not in oil.

Plain or chilli-pepper vodka can
stand up to pickled chillies, while the
Martini variant known as a Gibson
would not be a Gibson without a white
pearl onion.

Red chillies should certainly set
the palate alight in a drink already
containing pepper vodka.

Cherry tomatoes are an interesting
alternative for garnishing a Bloody Mary,
while celery is the Bloody Mary's very
own swizzle-stick.

As well as forming an integral
ingredient in some cocktails, a sprig
of fresh mint makes an appealing
garnish, perhaps to the creamy,
mint-flavoured Grasshopper.

Tricks and techniques of the trade

It is worth mastering the techniques for the preparation of good-looking drinks. The following pages give you precise directions for some of the essential procedures, such as crushing ice, as well as some not-so-essential skills, such as making decorative ice cubes. Mastering these tricks of the trade is what will distinguish the dedicated bartender from the amateur dabbler.

Crushing ice

Some cocktails require cracked or crushed ice for adding to glasses, or a finely crushed ice "snow" for blending. It isn't a good idea to break ice up in a blender or food processor as you may find it damages the blades. Instead:

1 Lay out a cloth, such as a clean glass cloth or dishtowel, on a work surface, and cover half of it with ice cubes. (If you wish, you can also use a cloth ice bag.)

2 Fold the cloth over and, using the end of a rolling pin, or better still a wooden mallet of the sort used for tenderizing meat, smash down on the ice firmly several times, until you achieve the required fineness.

3 Spoon the ice into glasses or a pitcher. Fine ice snow must be used immediately because it melts away like morning mist, but cracked or roughly crushed ice can be stored in the freezer in plastic bags. Stay up all night with a sledgehammer, and you should have enough to do a moderate-sized social gathering. Alternatively, just buy an ice crusher.

Making decorative ice cubes

Decorative ice cubes can instantly jolly up the simplest of cocktails. Flavour and colour the water with fruit juices or bitters, and freeze in three stages.

1 Half-fill each compartment of an ice cube tray with water and place in the freezer for 2–3 hours, or until the water has frozen.

2 Prepare the fruit, olives, mint leaves, lemon rind, raisins or borage flowers and dip each briefly in water. Place in the ice-cube trays, put in the freezer and freeze again.

3 Top up the ice-cube trays with water and return to the freezer to freeze completely. Use as required, but only in one drink at each session.

Frosting glasses

The appearance and taste of a cocktail are enhanced if the rims of the glasses are frosted. Use celery salt, grated coconut, grated chocolate, coloured sugars or cocoa for an eye-catching effect. Once it is frosted, place the glass in the refrigerator to chill until needed, if you have time.

1 Hold the glass upside down, so the juice does not run down the glass. Rub the rim of the glass with the cut surface of a lemon, lime, orange or even a slice of fresh pineapple.

2 Keeping the glass upside down, dip the rim into a shallow layer of sugar, coconut or salt. Redip the glass, if necessary, and turn it so that the rim is well-coated.

3 Stand the glass upright and let it sit until the sugar, coconut or salt has dried on the rim, then chill.

Bartending know-how
Instead of using fruit juice as the frosting liquid, you can rub a glass rim with egg white instead.

Shaking cocktails

Cocktails that contain sugar syrups or creams require more than just a stir; they are combined and chilled with a brief shake. Remember that it is possible to shake only one or two servings at once, so you may have to work quickly in batches. Always use fresh ice each time.

1 Add four or five ice cubes to the shaker and pour in all the ingredients.

2 Put the lid on the shaker. Hold the shaker firmly in one hand, keeping the lid in place with the other hand.

3 Shake vigorously for about 15 seconds to blend simple concoctions, and for 20–30 seconds for drinks with sugar syrups, cream or egg. By this time, the shaker should feel extremely cold.

4 Remove the small cap and pour into the prepared glass, using a strainer if the shaker is not already fitted with one.

Bartending know-how
Never shake anything sparkling, whether lemonade or best champagne. It will flatten it.

Making twists

As an alternative to slices of the fruit, many drinks are garnished with a twist of orange, lemon or lime rind. The most famous one is Horse's Neck, but twists are useful in many other recipes. They should be made before the drink itself is prepared, so that you don't keep a cold cocktail waiting. Here's how:

1 Choose a fruit with an unblemished skin and a regular shape.

2 Using a canelle knife or potato peeler, start at the tip of the fruit and start peeling round, as though you were peeling an apple.

3 Work slowly and carefully down the fruit, being sure to keep the pared-away rind in one continuous strip.

4 Trim it, if necessary, to a length that suits the glass.

Melon balling

A gadget exists for producing perfect little balls of melon that can be used to decorate a cocktail.

1 Cut the ripe melon in half, and scoop out the seeds with a dessert spoon.

2 Push the baller deeply into the flesh of the fruit, and then turn it through 360° to extract as near to a perfect sphere as you can.

3 Thread balls of different-coloured melon (e.g. Galia, Charentais and watermelon) on to a cocktail stick for full visual impact.

Bartending know-how
Choose ripe melon by its fully developed skin colour, which should be properly deep.

Muddling

A muddler – a long stick with a bulbous end – is the only thing to use for pressing the juice out of mint leaves for use in cocktails in which the mint is an ingredient, rather than just a garnish.

1 Put the mint leaves and caster (superfine) sugar or sugar syrup in the bottom of your glass.

2 Give the leaves an initial twist and turn to break them up and mix them into the sugar.

3 Press them forcefully, with repeated turns of the wrist, to extract their juices.

Bartending know-how

Muddling is a vigorous process that involves more force than any other technique, apart from ice-smashing.

Flaming sugar for absinthe

This technique of adding sugar to your absinthe is favoured by the Czechs. It is more dramatic than simply pouring water over it in the Parisian fashion, and is more efficient anyway.

1 Put a sugar cube on a perforated spoon and immerse it in a generous shot of absinthe until it is saturated.

2 Balancing the spoon across the top of the glass, use a match to set fire to the sugar cube.

3 As the sugar cooks, the flame will gradually die down, and when it does, gently lower the melting cube once more into the drink, and stir it in to dissolve it.

4 Add the same quantity of cold water as absinthe, and stir the drink once more. It's all a bit of a fuss, but worth it.

Making basic sugar syrup

A sugar syrup is sometimes preferable to dry sugar for sweetening cocktails, since it blends immediately with the other ingredients. This recipe makes about 750ml/1¼ pints.

350g/12oz sugar
60cl/1 pint water

1 Place the sugar in a heavy pan with the water, and heat gently over a low heat. Stir the mixture with a wooden spoon until all of the sugar has dissolved completely.

2 Brush the sides of the pan with a pastry brush dampened in water, to remove any sugar crystals that might cause the syrup to crystallize.

3 Bring to the boil for 3–5 minutes. Skim any scum away and when no more appears, remove the pan from the heat. Cool and pour into clean, dry, airtight bottles. Keep in the refrigerator for up to one month.

Bartending know-how

Homemade sugar syrup is a useful standby ingredient, and cheaper than buying sirop de gomme.

Making flavoured syrup

Syrup can be flavoured with anything: a split vanilla pod, mint leaves or citrus rind. Simply boil, and then bottle with the syrup. This recipe makes about 450ml/¾ pint syrup.

900g/2lb very ripe soft or stone fruit, washed
350g/12oz sugar

1 Put the washed fruit of your choice in a bowl and, using the bottom of a rolling pin, a wooden pestle or a potato masher, crush the fruit to release the juices.

2 Cover and allow to sit overnight to concentrate the flavour.

3 Strain the purée through a cloth bag or piece of muslin (cheesecloth). Gather the corners of the cloth together and twist them tight, to remove as much juice as possible.

4 Measure the amount of juice and add 225g/8oz sugar to every 300ml/½ pint fruit juice.

5 Place the pan on a low heat, and gently stir until all the sugar has dissolved. Continue as for basic sugar syrup. The syrup will keep in the refrigerator for up to one month.

Making flavoured spirits

Gin, vodka and white rum can be left to steep and absorb the flavours of a wide variety of soft fruits. This recipe makes about 1.2 litres/2 pints.

450g/1lb raspberries, strawberries, or pineapple
225g/8oz sugar
1 litre/1¾ pints gin, vodka or light rum

1 Put the fruit in a wide-necked jar, and add the sugar.

2 Add the spirit. Cover tightly. Leave in a cool, dark place for a month, shaking gently every week.

3 Strain through clean muslin (cheesecloth) or a cloth bag, and squeeze out the rest of the liquid from the steeped fruit. Return the flavoured liquor to a clean bottle and seal. Store in a cool, dark place. It will happily keep for a year.

Steeping spirits

The process of steeping any spirit with a flavouring agent, such as chillies, creates a whole new sensation. This recipe makes about 1 litre/1¾ pints.

25–50g/1–2oz small red chillies, or to taste, washed
1 litre/1¾ pints sherry or vodka

1 Using a cocktail stick, prick the chillies all over to release their flavours.

2 Pack the chillies tightly into a sterilized bottle.

3 Top up with sherry or vodka. Fit the cork tightly and leave in a dark place for at least ten days or up to two months.

Variations

Try the following interesting alternatives: gin with cumin seeds, star anise or juniper berries; brandy with 25g/1oz peeled and sliced fresh ginger, or 15g/½oz whole cloves; vodka with 50g/2oz washed raisins, or 15–30ml/1–2 tbsp cracked black peppercorns; rum with 2–3 pricked vanilla pods. The amount of flavouring used is of course a matter of personal taste.

CLASSIC COCKTAILS

Introduction

The word "cocktail" may conjure up a picture of pleasant surroundings, subdued lighting, quiet background music, and behind the bar a friendly barman who takes his task of mixing your drink seriously. Or you may imagine yourself beside the pool on a sunny tropical island, with a tall glass of exotic fruit juice, liqueur and crushed ice in your hand. Whatever fantasy comes to mind, these pages will go some way towards fulfilling it.

The history of the cocktail

How the cocktail got its name, and by whom it was first created, is a subject of considerable debate. One theory is that an American barman had a large container in the shape of a cockerel into which he poured leftover drinks. Hard-up customers could buy this cheap mixture, and were served from a tap at the tail, hence a "cocktail". A different story comes from the time of the American Revolution. A Frenchman, after seeing bottles decorated with cocks' tails in Betsy's Tavern near Yorktown, gave the toast *"Vive le*

cocktail!" Yet another definition of the word refers to the special way of cutting a horse's tail – but the connection between a horse's tail and drinking a rather delicate blend of spirit, liqueur and fruit juice is not clear.

Above: Fresh soft fruits, skewered with a cocktail stick, make an elegant decoration and add a splash of colour to a cocktail.

Whatever the origin of the word, the creation of the cocktail can be traced back to the 19th century. One of the first cocktails was the Martini, whose origins come from an 1862 recipe for Martinez. This drink was created at the Occidental Hotel in San Francisco for a gold miner returning to his home in Martinez. By 1900 the Martini was known right across the United States and had spread to Europe. The Dry Martini, which was invented in 1910 at the Knickerbocker Hotel in New York, became even more famous, and around this time a growing number of basic cocktails emerged and steadily gained in popularity. The cocktail was given a boost when the Prohibition laws were enacted in the United States in

Left: The type of glass you choose for a cocktail is as important as the ingredients. A tumbler is ideal for shorter drinks, served with ice and stirred rather than shaken.

1920, making the manufacture or sale of intoxicating liquor illegal. This led to a healthy black market, with bootleggers such as Al Capone distributing moonshine nationwide. The quality of some of this moonshine was rather dubious and cocktails became very popular in the illegal bars and clubs that sprang up at the time, as a means of disguising its raw taste. Orange Blossom was the original gin and orange drink created at this time, to mask the ghastly flavour of bathtub gin.

Many of the classic cocktails we know today – Parisian, White Lady, Mayfair – were invented during the Depression in the 1920s. It is interesting to speculate whether the renewed interest in cocktails during the 1980s – another period of major recession – is simply coincidence. The champagne and orange juice mixture Buck's Fizz became hugely popular as a drink for all times of the day, including breakfast, and led the cocktail revival.

Below: Chartreuse liqueur gives this vodka cocktail its lovely green colour. The cocktail onion adds a sweet-and-sour twist.

Today, cocktails are as popular as they have ever been, and have become even more flamboyant and exotic. With the easy availability of equipment and the amazing range of spirits, liqueurs and exotic fruit juices from all over the world, there has never been a better time to try them out at home.

Naming cocktails

The names of the drinks themselves are much less of a mystery than the word "cocktail". Quite a few are named for people. In the golden age of cocktails in the 1920s the famous movie stars Mary Pickford and Charlie Chaplin were honoured by having drinks named after them, and later Marilyn Monroe received a similar accolade. Other famous people who are remembered in this way include Churchill, Rob Roy, Captain Kidd, Bonnie Prince Charlie and the Russian writer Pushkin. And one man actually became famous as a result of a cocktail being named for him. In the 1970s, a Californian surfer drank so much of a particular drink that as he found his way out of the bar, he bounced from one wall to the other – hence the name Harvey Wallbanger.

Above: There are no limits to the amount of decoration you can add to your creations. This punch is garnished with a peach slice and a physalis, complete with leaves attached.

Place names – often where the cocktail was first invented – are also a popular choice. One of the all-time greats, Singapore Sling, was created at the Raffles Hotel in Singapore, while the Savoy Hotel comes from the American bar of the famous London hotel. New York, Park Avenue, Princeton, Honolulu, Loch Lomond, Tipperary, Kowloon and Amsterdam are all names of classic cocktails.

Cocktails are sexy drinks, and not surprisingly some of them have sensual names. Between the Sheets is a 1920s recipe that became fashionable again in the 1980s, and has been joined by the seductively-named Sex on the Beach, Lady Killer, Kiss and Tell, and Slow Comfortable Screw.

The cocktail recipes included here should give you plenty of scope for experimenting with spirits and wines from all around the world. And who knows – that bottle of unfamiliar liqueur brought back from your travels could well be the basis of a new cocktail that will be the envy of bartenders in the world's leading bars and hotels. The possibilities for naming it are endless.

types of drinks

We begin our tour of the drinking world with spirits, which were the last of all the basic types of alcoholic drink to be invented. They are the products of distillation, made by heating fermented liquids until their vapours condense and form a much stronger drink. Following that, we delve into the weird and wonderful world of liqueurs, investigating their history and flavours, and suggesting some culinary uses along the way. A brief overview of wines (including champagne and fortified wines) comes next, and is followed by the other fermented drinks: beer and cider. We conclude the section with a comprehensive guide to the non-alcoholic ingredients used in mixed drinks.

SPIRITS

The earliest spirits were almost certainly fairly straightforward, rough-and-ready distillations of ordinary wine. For centuries, a form of distillation had been practised, using herbs and flowers infused in water, then cooked and condensed. The resulting essence was used medicinally, in cooking or just as a perfume. As we saw in the Introduction, the discovery in Europe of the art of distilling alcohol arose as a result of alchemical experiments designed to find the "elixir of life". The powerful brew that was created by distilling was thought to contain the "soul" or "spirit" of the wine.

When people realized that anything that had been fermented to produce alcohol could in turn be distilled into spirit, they began to ferment materials specifically for distillation. So, in regions that lacked the climate for winemaking, mashed malted grains were responsible for the first drinks definable as whiskies.

Below: Filling the mash tun at a single malt distillery in Dufftown, Scotland. Here, the two essential ingredients of malt whisky are brought together: finely ground malted barley and natural Highland spring water.

As wine itself was held in high esteem, and was imported in great quantity by the cooler countries of northern Europe, such as England and the Netherlands, the spirit produced from wine was the first to receive true acclaim. Traders on ships that arrived at La Rochelle and other ports in the Charente region of western France had no particular taste for the acidic, flavourless wines of the area, but the strong spirit made from these wines

Above: The Scottish Highlands at Lochnagar, north of Dundee.

was considered a lot better than other such distillates found elsewhere. Thus did cognac first come to prominence.

A memory of the alchemical quest to find the magic elixir was preserved in the Latin name first given to the product of distillation: *aqua vitae*, or water of life. That phrase has remained inseparable from spirits terminology: the French call their spirit *eau de vie*, the Scandinavians *aquavit*, and the Celts *uisge beatha*, which was eventually corrupted by non-Gaelic speakers into "whisky". In Russian, it became, more humbly, "little water" or vodka. The alternative medieval Latin name was *aqua ardens*, "burning water", for reasons that are not hard to fathom. The association with fieriness, both in the method used to extract the alcohol and in the sensation that drinking it produced, lived on in the naming of distilled wine *Gebranntwein* ("burnt wine") in German, *brandewijn* in Dutch, and eventually "brandy" in English.

Despite being highly prized at the time, these early spirits would not have tasted particularly pleasant to us. They would only have been distilled once and would therefore have contained

Right: The discovery of distillation provided the basis for all the classic spirits commonly in use today.

high concentrations of fusel oil, a group of compounds known in scientific parlance as the "higher alcohols", the "higher" referring to their greater acidity. It was only in 1800 that a physicist named Edouard Adam discovered the benefits of redistillation, or rectification. This dispensed with a large proportion, though not all, of the raw-tasting higher alcohols and resulted in a purer spirit. However, it also stripped away a lot of the positive by-products of distillation that gave the drink its character, and so for a while the infusions of herbs, spices and fruit extracts that had originally been used to disguise the roughness of the alcohol were reintroduced to give it flavour.

Eventually, the correct balance was struck. The products that needed some distillation character – brandies and

Below: Glenfiddich is distilled twice in traditionally shaped copper pot stills that are built and maintained by their own coppersmiths. The stills are unusually small, and have not changed size or shape since the distillery first started in 1887.

whiskies – retained it (undergoing a double distillation) and had it enhanced by ageing in wooden casks, while those that were intended to be as neutral as possible, such as vodka and gin, were subject to repeated redistillation. (In the case of gin and similar products, a neutral spirit base is created by prolonged rectification, so that the aromatic ingredients that are added can stand out more boldly.) Most commercial spirits produced today have been thoroughly rectified, which is not necessarily a blessing; for example, some brands of white rum can be extremely bland. The trend owes much to the fact that most of the white spirits are drunk with mixers these days.

When tasting a fine spirit – aged cognac, single malt whisky, sour-mash bourbon or old demerara rum, for example – the procedure that is used for tasting wine clearly won't do. Try rolling a liquid with 40% alcohol around your mouth and you'll soon wish you hadn't. Some tasters judge them on the nose alone; others add a similar quantity of water, which many feel emphasizes their aromatic subtleties. I prefer to be brave and taste them undiluted. If you adopt this technique, the trick is to take in only a very small amount of liquid, keep it at the front of

the mouth just behind the lips by lowering the head after sipping, draw some air over it quickly and spit it out before it starts burning. The whole exercise is much brisker than tasting a mouthful of wine.

Below: Classic cocktail recipes represent a fine way of bringing out the best in distilled spirits. In this drink – Paddy – Irish whiskey is mixed with sweet red vermouth and Angostura bitters.

Gin

Of the six essential spirits, gin is the only one that really has a reputation to live down. Over the years it has been the calamitous curse of the urban poor, the Mother's Ruin by which girls in trouble tried to induce miscarriages, the bathtub brew that rotted guts during American Prohibition, and the first resort of the miserable as the storm clouds of depression gathered. It was all so different in the beginning.

Although the English often claim to be the true progenitors of gin, its origins in fact go back to 16th-century Holland. Like many other distilled drinks, it was firstly medicinal. The blend of herbs and aromatics it contained was believed to guard against all the ills to which flesh was heir. Principal among these aromatics was the dark-berried plant juniper, the Dutch word for which – genever – is the linguistic root of the English word "gin".

The dark little fruits of the juniper tree contribute to the characteristic, strong perfume of gin. They are prized medicinally as a diuretic. Despite the predominance of juniper in the aroma and flavour of gin, however, there are other ingredients. Precise recipes vary according to the individual distiller, but other common components include angelica, liquorice, orris-root, dried citrus peel, caraway and coriander seeds, and many others.

It was probably British soldiers returning home from the Thirty Years War who first brought the taste for Dutch genever across the North Sea. In any case, a form of gin was being distilled in London by the 17th century, using the basic beer ingredients – hops and barley – and the essential juniper berries.

The rise in gin's popularity in Britain had two main causes. First, periodic hostilities with the French led to the application of punitive tariffs to their exports and, just as port came to be the wine of patriotic choice among the elite, so gin replaced cognac. To compound that, reform of the excise system resulted in beer being subjected to a much stricter levy than before, so that gin was

Left: The company of Booth's was established during the ban on gin in the UK.

actually cheaper. Not surprisingly, it became the staple drink of the poorest classes, who consumed it in much the same quantities as they had beer. Gin shops were born, and public drunkenness and alcohol-related illness soared.

So began gin's long association with gloom (which still persists today in the enduring myth that gin is more of a depressant than the other spirits). The purveyors of gin sold their wares in terms that no advertiser today could get away with: "*Drunk for a penny. Dead drunk for tuppence. Clean straw for nothing.*" In 1736, the purchase of small quantities was made illegal by Act of Parliament, but the law was hastily reversed six years later after it was predictably discovered that the contraband stuff then being drunk was considerably more toxic than the official spirit had been.

Far left: Belgravia London dry gin is one of the lesser-known London brands.

Left: Beefeater is one of the most famous London gins.

HOW TO SERVE

The age-old mixer for gin is, of course, Schweppes tonic, the production of which is almost exclusively sustained by gin drinkers. A gin and tonic is usually offered as a long drink with a slice of lemon and plenty of ice, but equal measures are a more sensitive way of treating the gin. Gin rubs along with any old mixer, though: orange juice, bitter lemon, ginger beer, whatever. (It isn't very nice with cola perhaps, but then few things are.)

HOW TO SERVE
Speciality gins can be served neat. Chill the bottle in the freezer, and serve the measures in small glasses. A taller, narrow-sided, stemmed glass – rather like a short champagne flute – is traditional in the Netherlands.

In 1750, the artist William Hogarth produced his famous engraving *Gin Lane*, depicting the degradation that was being wrought by the widespread consumption of gin. It was only in the late Victorian period that it began to regain a more dignified reputation, being seen as a usefully ladylike alternative to whisky and cognac. Finally, the gin and tonic, the world's favourite aperitif, was born, and a new era in gin's fortunes was ushered in. Gin has recently lost a lot of ground to vodka in the youth market, as its peculiar perfume is something of an acquired taste to untutored palates. Chic new brands may just reverse that trend.

Right: Dutch genever is the prototype for London gin.

Right: Bombay Sapphire is a more delicately aromatic gin than the commercial norm.

Far right: Gordon's is the brand leader among London gins.

Types of gin
English Gin There are two types. London dry gin is by far the more commonly known, although it doesn't have to be distilled in the capital. It is an intensely perfumed spirit, and varies greatly in quality between producers. Gordon's, Booth's and Beefeater are the most famous names. Speciality brands include Tanqueray and Bombay Sapphire in the pale blue, tinted bottle.

The other type is Plymouth gin, of which there is only one distiller, at the Blackfriars distillery not far from the city's waterfront. Plymouth gin is distinctly drier than the big London brands, and the aromatics used somehow give it a subtler bouquet than most gin-drinkers may be used to.

A very small amount of gin is cask-aged; this is referred to as golden gin, after the colour it leaches out of the wood.

Dutch Genever This is quite different from English gin, owing to the more pungently flavoured grain mash from which it is made. The mixture of barley, rye and corn (or maize) is often heavily malted, giving older spirits a lightly beery tinge. There are basically two grades: *oude* (old) or *jonge* (young), the latter looking more like

the English article. They frequently come in an opaque "stone" bottle, and have a more rustic flavour.

How it is made
Gin is an extremely simple drink, almost as elementary as vodka. A grain spirit is produced from rye and barley, although corn is commonly used in Dutch genever and American gin. For the English style, it is ruthlessly rectified through successive distillations until all the higher alcohols are driven off. After the aromatization process, which is carried out either by macerating the dry herbs, berries and spices in the alcohol or by running the spirit through them, the finished product is bottled for immediate release.

Tastes good with
The oily texture of gin complements the oiliness of certain fish reasonably well. Sip it with marinated herring covered in chopped raw onion – real Amsterdam street food. Even in this context, though, you may find its pungency easier to cope with if slightly diluted.

Vodka

In one sense, vodka is the closest thing to perfection ever conceived in the history of spirits. Had it been invented in the era of alcopops and ice beers, it would have been hailed as a supremely adept piece of marketing wizardry. Nobody, other than a confirmed teetotaller, could possibly dislike it, for the simple reason that it tastes of nothing whatsoever. It is pure, unadulterated, uncomplicated alcohol. At least, most of it is.

The word "vodka" is a Russian endearment meaning "little water", from their word for water, *voda*. That in turn derives from the widespread European practice of referring to all distillates originally as a form of water (as in *aqua vitae* or *eau de vie*).

Precisely because it is such a simple drink, it is almost impossible to pinpoint the origins of vodka. A potent spirit

Below: Blue label Absolut (left) is the unflavoured version. Absolut Kurant (middle) is solidly fruity and flavoured with blackcurrants. Absolut Citron (right) has a musky lemony tinge.

distilled from various grains has been made in Poland, Russia and the Baltic states since the very early days of distillation in Europe. But as to where a drink specifically recognizable as vodka first arose is a matter for the Poles and the Russians to sort out between themselves. (Most outsiders now tend to come down on the Polish side.) What is certain is that, by the time home distillation had become a favoured way of passing the long winters in Poland, peasant families were producing their own domestic vodkas extensively.

Rectification techniques having only been discovered at the beginning of the 19th century, these early distillates would have tasted fairly unclean. Any herbs, seeds or berries that were to hand would be steeped in the spirit to mask its rankness. So the first vodkas were not the

Left: This smooth Stolichnaya vodka should be sipped appreciatively.

anonymous products preferred today, but the true ancestors of the flavoured vodkas.

Nonetheless, it was the neutral, ultra-purified grain vodka – made from wheat or rye – that came to prominence in the West. So prevalent is it now, particularly among younger drinkers who have yet to appreciate the taste of unrectified spirits such as whisky and cognac, that it is hard to believe that barely anyone in western Europe or America had heard of it until the late 1940s. That all changed with the first stirrings of interest in California, during the period of the Beat Generation.

Vodka was seen as a provocatively dissident drink in the era of the onset of the Cold War. It was the

HOW TO SERVE

When serving vodka, everything should be almost painfully cold to the touch. The bottle should be kept in the freezer and the glasses should also be iced. If there isn't a heavy mist of condensation on the outside of the glass, it isn't cold enough. Some vodka shots are thrown back like schnapps, owing to an old folk belief that if you inhale the fumes for more than a split second, you will get too drunk too quickly. The aged vodkas, and specialities such as Zubrowka, are more often sipped slowly and appreciatively. A little shot glass is traditional, but in some homes a rather larger, narrow tumbler, or even something like a goblet wine glass, is used.

Above: Smirnoff, with its basic red label (left), is the market leader in vodka. Blue label (right) is a higher-strength version.

favoured "hooch" of the Soviet bloc, and in the witch-hunting atmosphere of 50s America, nothing was more guaranteed to inflame bourbon-drinking patriots than young folks gleefully imbibing the spirit of communism. The late Alexis Lichine, drink historian, attributes the start of vodka's meteoric rise in the West to the purchase by a US company of a recipe from a Russian refugee called Smirnoff, on the eve of the Second World War. The rest is history.

Vodka is still very much the drink of gastronomic choice in its native lands, drunk as aperitif, digestif and even as an accompaniment to food. It is nearly always taken icy-cold, preceded in Polish homes by the ritual wishing of good health – *na zdrowie* – to one's family and friends. The quantities

consumed may raise eyebrows in our Western unit-counting culture, but a vodka hangover is very rare, owing to the purity of the drink.

Perhaps the most celebrated flavoured product is Zubrowka, bison-grass vodka, which is generally sold with a blade of grass in the bottle, bison grass being the gourmet preference of the wild bison that roam the forests of eastern Poland.

Wisniowka (cherries), Limonnaya (lemon) and the Swedish Absolut company's Kurant (blackcurrant) are all appetizing drinks. Pieprzowka is infused with chilli peppers, and has a burning, spicy finish. Russia's Okhotnichya – "Hunter's Vodka" – is impregnated with orange rind, ginger root, coffee beans, juniper berries and even a drop of white port.

Neutral vodkas are produced all over the world now, although most grades are only intended to be served in mixed drinks. Russian Stolichnaya, particularly the Cristall bottling, is an honourable, silky-smooth exception. Smirnoff makes three types, in red, blue and black labels to denote varying strength. Scandinavian vodkas such as Finlandia and Absolut have their deserved followings, while most British vodka tends to be little more than patent alcohol. Also seen on the export markets is Polish Pure Spirit, bottled at around 70% ABV.

How it is made

Although potatoes and other vegetables have been used to make vodka at various times in its history, nowadays it is made virtually exclusively from grains, principally rye. A basic mash is made by malting the grains, and encouraging them to ferment with cultured yeasts. The resulting brew is then continuously distilled in a column still to increasing degrees of alcoholic strength, driving off nearly all of the higher alcohols. As a final insurance against flavour,

the spirit is filtered through a layer of charcoal, which strips it of any remaining character. It is then bottled at an average of 37.5% ABV.

In the case of flavoured vodkas, the aromatizing elements are added to the new spirit after rectification, and left to infuse over long periods – sometimes three years or more. Occasionally, a speciality vodka will be aged in cask and take on a tinge of colour; others derive their exotic hues from spices, flowers or nuts.

Tastes good with

Cold vodka is the classic accompaniment to Russian caviar, itself served on heaps of ice. In the Scandinavian countries, it is drunk, like aquavit, with marinated and smoked fish such as herring, mackerel and even salmon.

Below: This Pieprzowka vodka (left) has been coloured and flavoured with chillies. Cherry vodka (right) has a lustrous, deep red colour and is intensely fruity.

Rum

Probably the least understood of the five main spirits, rum is actually, in its white version, one of the biggest-selling of them all. Indeed, it is debatable whether many of those knocking back Bacardi-and-Cokes realize they are drinking some form of rum at all. To many, rum is inextricably associated with a rather antiquated pantomime idea of "Jolly Jack Tars" and a life on the ocean wave.

There is some uncertainty over the origin of the spirit's name, but the favourite theory is that it is a shortening of an old West Country English word "rumbullion", itself of unknown origin, but generally denoting any hard liquor.

The invention of rum dates from not long after the foundation of the sugar plantations in the West Indies, in the early 16th century. Until the voyages of Christopher Columbus, sugar was a luxury product, and much sought after in southern Europe, having originally

Left: Lamb's is one of the leading brands of dark rum.

been brought into Venice from India. When the Spanish explorers landed in Hispaniola and the neighbouring Caribbean islands, they saw promising environments for cultivating sugar cane for themselves. If yeasts need to feed on sugar in order to produce alcohol, then the sugar plant was always going to be an obvious candidate for distillation. When first pressed, cane juice is a murky, greenish colour and full of impurities. Boiled down, it crystallizes into sucrose and a sticky brown by-product, molasses, that would have fermented readily in tropical conditions. Rum is the result of distilling the fermented molasses.

Sugar soon became a widespread everyday product in Europe. The astronomical demand for it was serviced by the most notorious episode in European colonial history – the slave trade, in which rum played a crucial role. Settlers in New England financed their trips to West Africa by selling rum. A consignment of African slaves would be delivered to the

West Indies and sold for molasses, which would then be shipped back to New England to be turned into more rum, in a self-perpetuating cycle.

The association of rum with the British Navy arises from the fact that rum was provided to ordinary sailors as a daily ration from the 18th century. That tradition endured, basically because rum could withstand hot weather more sturdily than beer could. The initial allowance was a fairly rollicking half-pint a day, watered down eventually into the despised "grog", and then mixed with lemon juice to prevent scurvy. It was only in 1970 that the rum ration was abolished.

Today, rum is produced all over the West Indies and eastern South America, to a lesser extent in the Indian Ocean area – the Philippines and

HOW TO SERVE
The best dark rums, and aged rums in particular, should be served straight, unchilled, as digestifs. They make stimulating alternatives to malt whisky or cognac. Premium white rums from the independent producers are also best enjoyed neat, but they should be served cold, with a twist of lime.

Right: Wood's 100 is a particularly rich naval-strength dark rum.

Far right: Captain Morgan is the leading brand of dark rum.

Above left: Bacardi is the world's favourite white spirit brand.

Above right: Mount Gay Barbados is a major Caribbean brand of golden rum.

Mauritius – and in smaller quantities still in the USA and Australia. Inevitably, much of it is a by-product of the sugar-refining industry, but the best grades are made by smaller, independent companies growing sugar cane specifically for distillation.

Some rum is made from the pressed cane juice itself, but most is made from fermented molasses. In the former French colonies in particular, there is a distinguished tradition of *rhum agricole*, speciality products made on small sugar farms, produced with different strains of yeast.

Both methods of distillation are practised in the making of rum: the premium versions are double-distilled in a copper pot still, whereas continuous distillation and thorough rectification are used mainly by the bulk producers, particularly for the neutral-tasting white rums. Freshly distilled spirit from the pot still method is very high in impurities and must be allowed to mellow through a period of cask-ageing, which gives colour to the darker rums.

After white rum, dark rum is the next most important category commercially, and is certainly where the superior products are found. Leading brands are Captain Morgan and Lamb's. Some high-quality dark rums are bottled at the original naval strength of more than 50% ABV (Wood's Navy Rum, for example, is 57%); the traditional name for such strengths was "overproof". The everyday dark rums are a more standard 40%, while Bacardi is adjusted down to 37.5%, equivalent to the other white spirits.

Between the two styles is the increasingly popular golden or light rum, which is a particular speciality of Cuba and Puerto Rico, aged for less time in the barrel. The darkest and heaviest rums, some not far from the colour of black treacle, traditionally come from Jamaica. Good white rum, such as the white Rhum St James of Martinique, is full of burnt-sugar richness. Some exporters make a virtue of selling rums with 30 or 40 years of cask age, and there is even a tiny production of vintage-dated rum for the true connoisseur.

How it is made

Juice from the sugar cane is pressed and either fermented straight or boiled down to extract the molasses, which itself forms the basis of the ferment. It is either continuously distilled or, for speciality products, double-distilled in a pot still. For a headier product, some of the residue of the first distillation – known as "dunder" – may be added to the molasses during fermentation. Commercial white rums are rectified and bottled immediately. Coloured rums

HOW TO SERVE
Of the commercial products, white rum mixes famously well with cola, but also with orange juice or more tropical flavours such as pineapple or mango. Dark rum has traditionally been seen as compatible with blackcurrant or peppermint cordials, as well as the ubiquitous cola (as shown here).

are cask-aged, sometimes for decades, before they are bottled. The longer they are aged, the deeper the colour.

Tastes good with

More than any other basic spirit, rum makes an excellent accompaniment to fruits of all kinds. A "salad" of orange segments in golden rum was already a favoured dessert in the 18th century. Rum can be added to the syrup of all fruit salads, however, and works especially well with pineapple and banana. It is excellent for adding an enriching note to sponge-based desserts such as charlottes, as well as the famous rum baba – a soft rum-soaked sponge filled with raisins. Rum has a great natural affinity with that other celebrated Caribbean product, chocolate. Add dark or golden rum to the mixture for chocolate truffles, or the *ganache* mixture with which a chocolate gâteau may be glued together. In the Caribbean, they like a rum-based mixed drink with fish and meat dishes.

Whisky

One of the world's leading spirits, whisky (or whiskey, depending on where it hails from) boasts a history every bit as distinguished as that of cognac. Like the classic brandies of France, its spread around the world from its first home – the Scottish Highlands – has been a true testament to the genius of its conception. Tennessee sour mash may bear about as much relation in taste to single malt Scotch as Spanish brandy does to cognac, but the fact that they are all

Below left: Laphroaig is one of the richest of the peaty styles of Scotch produced in Islay.

Below right: This Glenlivet is a ten-year-old Speyside malt from the Scottish Highlands.

great products demonstrates the versatility of each basic formula.

Today, whiskies are produced all over the world. As the name is not a geographically specific one, all of these products may legitimately call themselves whisk(e)y. The five major producing countries are Scotland, the United States, Ireland, Canada and Japan.

The name "whisky" is yet another variant of the phrase "water of life". In translation, the Latin *aqua vitae* became *uisge beatha* in the Scots branch of Gaelic and *usquebaugh* in the Irish. The half-Anglicized "whisky" was in official use by the mid-18th century.

In countries that lacked the warm climate for producing fermented drinks from grapes, beer was always the staple brew and, just as brandy was the obvious first distillate in southern Europe, so malted grains provided the starting point for domestic production further north. Unlike brandy, however, which starts life as wine, whisky doesn't have to be made from something that would be recognizable as beer.

SCOTLAND

Home distillation in Scotland can be traced back to the 15th century, when the practice of distilling surplus grain to make a potent drink for clan chieftains was established.

Initially, the drink was valued for its medicinal powers, and early examples were no doubt infusions of herbs and berries rather than the pure grain product we know today. Although at first other cereals would have been used, malted barley became pre-eminent relatively early on.

Left: Whyte & Mackay whisky is re-blended for a second period of maturation.

Before the Act of Union of 1707, Scotch was hardly known in England. Gin was the national drink south of the border. Once the English laid their administrative hands on Scotland, they set about bringing whisky distillation under statutory control. Whisky-makers within striking distance of the border fled northwards with their stills into the Highlands, but by the 1870s, the number of convictions for illegal distilling was down to six (compared to nearly 700 only 40 years earlier).

In the early years of the 20th century, a Royal Commission was set up to determine the parameters for Scotch whisky production, i.e. the methods of distillation, rules on blending, minimum maturation times and, of course, the fact that Scotch could only be distilled and aged in Scotland, rather than anywhere south

HOW TO SERVE

The finest whiskies are not necessarily drunk neat. It is widely believed that taming some of the spirit's fire helps to bring up the array of complicated scents and flavours. A dose of water should be added, ideally the same spring water that goes into the whisky itself, otherwise any pure, non-chlorinated water. Half-and-half are the preferred proportions in Scotland and Ireland, while in Tennessee and Kentucky they add a little less than half.

Above left: The Famous Grouse is one of the leading brands of blended Scotch whisky.

Above right: J&B is a blended whisky that is popular in the American market; J&B stands for Justerini & Brooks.

of the border. These parameters remain in force today as the legal textbook for an industry that is a central part of the Scottish economy.

Types of Scotch
The most highly prized of Scotch whiskies are the single malts, which are produced entirely from malted barley, double-distilled, and made at a single one (hence the terminology) of Scotland's 100 or so working distilleries. Some of these products are aged for many years. Twenty-five-year-old Scotch will be shot through with all sorts of profoundly complex flavours and perfumes, from the cask and perhaps from the sea air that wafts around the coastal distilleries.

Some malts are the blended produce of several single malts, in which case they are known as vatted malts. Whiskies made from corn or unmalted barley are known as grain whiskies, and are always considerably lighter in style than malts. They could be described as beginner's Scotch, since they have far fewer of the aromatic components that account for the pedigree of great malt, although they should not be seen as worthless imitations.

Blended Scotch is made from a mixture of malt and grain spirits. This is the market-leading category, occupied by virtually all of the big brand names, such as Bell's, J&B, Johnnie Walker, Ballantine's, Whyte & Mackay, The Famous Grouse, White Horse and Teacher's. Most of these have fairly low concentrations of malt in the blend, although Teacher's and Johnnie Walker's Black Label are notable exceptions.

Scotch whisky is mostly retailed at the standard dark spirit strength of 40% ABV. A small proportion of the best grades are bottled from the barrel undiluted. These are known as "cask-strength" whiskies. You are not intended to drink them neat, but they should be diluted with water to the level of potency you prefer.

Areas of production
For the purposes of whisky production, Scotland is divided up into four broad regions: the Lowlands; Campbeltown; Islay and the Western Isles, including Jura, Mull and Skye; and the expansive Highlands region.

Lowland whiskies are generally the gentlest and sweetest styles of Scotch, while Campbeltown's are fresh and ozoney. Islay produces an instantly recognizable pungent spirit, full of seaweed and peat, while many Highland malts have a soft smokiness to them.

How it is made
In the case of malts, the grains of barley are soaked in water to encourage them to germinate. Soon after they have begun sprouting, the process is arrested by heating them in a kiln, in which variable quantities of peat will be added to the fuel, depending on the intended final flavour of the whisky. After kilning, the grain is mashed and drained and then poured into large tanks to begin fermentation, either with natural or cultured yeasts. The resulting brew is double-distilled in the traditional copper pot still.

The other factor in determining the character of a whisky is the maturation vessel. Scotch was traditionally aged in casks that had previously been used for shipping sherry, and some still is, but used bourbon casks from Kentucky are now quite common. In both cases, the wood is American oak, capable of imparting great richness to a whisky.

Tastes good with
Scotch is naturally the only accompaniment to the ceremonial haggis on Burns Night (January 25). Un-iced Scotch is also great with hearty soups, such as thick, barley-based Scotch broth or cock-a-leekie.

Right: Wild Turkey bourbon, which is aged in cask for eight years, comes from Lawrenceburg, Kentucky.

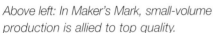

Above left: In Maker's Mark, small-volume production is allied to top quality.

Above right: Jim Beam is a particularly popular bourbon.

UNITED STATES

In North America, where whiskey is mostly spelled with an "e" as it is in Ireland, production of the drink dates back to the 18th century, in the era leading up to Independence. Before that, the staple spirit in America was dark rum. It was British and Irish settlers, bringing their own whisky with them from the old countries, who provided the impetus for the development of America's national spirit.

The first American whiskeys were made with malted barley and rye. Soon, however, a group of distillers in Bourbon County, Kentucky, began producing pure corn whiskey. By happy chance, from 1794 onwards their communities were infiltrated by droves of tax refugees who were fleeing from revenue officers in Pennsylvania. Suddenly, the Kentuckians had a ready-made new

market for their own product and, before too long, bourbon had established an illustrious reputation.

Rye whiskey is still made in Pennsylvania, Maryland and Virginia, but in ever-decreasing quantities.

Bourbon

Nowadays, most bourbon distilleries are concentrated not in Bourbon County, but around the towns of Louisville, Bardstown and Frankfort. Whiskeys from Kentucky are the only ones allowed to use the state name, alongside "bourbon", on the label.

Bourbon is not a straight corn whiskey, but is made from a mixture of not less than 51% corn with malted barley. Some may contain a little rye. The chief distinguishing taste of bourbon, however, derives from the barrels it matures in. These are made of new American oak, charred on the insides, which allows the spirit freer access to the vanillin and tannins in the wood.

There are two styles of bourbon: sweet mash and sour mash. The differences arise at the fermentation stage. For sweet mash, the yeasts are allowed to perform their work over a couple of days, while for sour mash, some yeast from the preceding batch augments the brew. This doubles the length of the fermentation and ensures that more of the sugars in the grain are consumed.

Most bourbon is labelled "Kentucky Straight Bourbon", which means it is made from at least 51% corn and is aged for a minimum of two years in charred new barrels.

The leading brand is Jim Beam, made at Bardstown. Other brands include Wild Turkey, Evan Williams, Early Times, Old Grand-Dad and Maker's Mark.

Tennessee

South of Kentucky, in Tennessee, a different but equally distinctive style of whiskey is made. Tennessee sour mash is represented by just two distilleries – Jack Daniel's in Lynchburg, and George Dickel in Tullahoma.

Whereas bourbon is matured in charred barrels, Tennessee takes the principle a stage further by actually filtering the newly-made spirit through a mass of charcoal. In the yards behind the distilleries, they burn great stacks of sugar maple down to ash, and then grind it all to powder. This is piled to a depth of around three metres or ten feet into so-called mellowing vats. The whiskey drips at a painfully slow rate from a gridwork of copper pipes above the vats, filtering gradually through the charcoal bed, prior to its period of cask maturation.

Jack Daniel's is one of the world's best-loved whiskey brands, led by its flagship Old No. 7 in the famous square bottle. Dickel (which spells its product "whisky" in the Scottish way), matures its No. 12 brand for several years longer, and the results are evident in a mellower nose and deeper colour. It is bottled at 45% ABV.

Tastes good with

There is a cultural affinity between bourbon and Tennessee whiskeys and the huge flame-grilled carpetbag steaks of Bardstown and Nashville. Add a little spring water to the spirit.

Left: Jack Daniel's is by far the bigger brand of the two Tennessee whiskeys.

Right: Paddy whiskey is distilled at Midleton, just outside the city of Cork in Ireland.

IRELAND

The origins of distillation in the Emerald Isle are lost in swathes of Irish mist, but are certainly of great antiquity. Irish whiskey once enjoyed an unrivalled reputation as a more approachable style of spirit than Scotch. It was only when blended Scotch began to be made on any significant scale towards the end of the 19th century that Irish whiskey was overshadowed.

The mellowness of Irish whiskey derives from its production process. No peat is used in the kilns, and Irish distillers use a mixture of malted and unmalted grain in their mash. It was a blended product long before today's standard Scotch blends were invented. It is then triple-distilled in a copper pot still, which results in a product with a softer palate that still retains all its complexity. The whiskey

Below: Crown Royal is a Canadian brand owned by Seagram's.

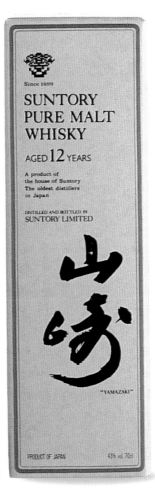

must then be cask-aged for a minimum of three years, although in practice most varieties are aged for two to three times longer. It is usually bottled at 40% ABV.

The brand leader on the export markets is Jameson's. Others include Bushmills, John Power, Murphy's, Paddy, Dunphy's and Tullamore Dew. All but one are made in the Irish Republic, the exception being Bushmills, which is made in County Antrim in the North.

CANADA

Canada's whiskies are made from blends of different grains, combining rye, corn and malted barley. They nearly always contain some spirit that is produced entirely from the heavier-tasting rye, but it usually accounts for less than a tenth of the final blend. As a result, they have the reputation of being among the lightest classic whiskies of all.

Distillation is by the continuous process, in gigantic column stills. Different spirits produced from different

Left: Suntory's 12-year-old Yamazaki is a kind of Japanese single malt.

mashes, or fermented from different yeast strains, are painstakingly blended by the distiller. All whiskies must spend at least three years in new barrels, but some are aged for 10, 12, even 18 years. The standard blends are sold at 40% ABV, but speciality aged bottlings may be stronger.

A curiosity of Canadian whisky is that the regulations permit the addition of a tiny quantity of other products, such as sherry or wine made from grapes or other fruits. While this may only account for 1% of the finished product, it makes its presence felt in the fleeting suggestion of fruitiness in some whiskies.

Most of the Canadian distilleries are situated in the eastern provinces of Ontario and Quebec. The leading label is Hiram Walker's Canadian Club, first blended in the 1880s, and is supported by the Burke's and Wiser's ranges from Corby's, McGuinness's Silk Tassel, Alberta Springs and Seagram's Crown Royal.

JAPAN

Of the leading five producers, Japan has by far the youngest whisky industry. The first distillery was established in 1923, and it is only in the last 30 years or so that its products have become known elsewhere.

The model for Japan's whiskies is single malt Scotch. They are made from a mash of malted barley, dried in kilns fired with a little peat. Distillation is by the pot still method. Some of the brands are aged in used sherry or bourbon casks, and others in heavily charred new American oak. The premium brands are generally bottled at around 43% ABV.

The giant drinks company Suntory is the biggest producer of Japanese whisky, accounting for 75% of the country's output. Behind Suntory comes the Nikka company, followed by the smaller producers Sanraku Ocean and Seagram's.

Tequila

Tequila is the national spirit of Mexico. It is one stage further down the road to refinement than its fellow cactus-based spirit, mescal, but several leagues ahead in terms of drinking pleasure. It starts life as *pulque*, the fermented beer-like juice of the agave plant, and is distilled twice before being aged in cask. It comes in two versions: silver is clear like vodka, and gold (or Oro) spends a longer period in contact with the barrels. Virtually unknown in Europe until comparatively recently, it made its first inroads into the world's drinks cabinet by travelling northwards to the USA, and it is now something of a cult drink in the youth market.

The name, tequila, is echoed in the full botanical name of the plant from which it is sourced: *Agave tequilana*. Perhaps what put everybody else off trying it for so long was the thought of a spirit made from cacti, and indeed even the finest grades don't actually smell particularly inviting. It has a sweaty, slightly muggy quality that must have come as something of a jolt at first to tastebuds honed on squeaky-clean vodka.

In recognition of its cultural importance, the production of tequila has been strictly delimited within Mexico. It may be distilled in only a handful of towns, including Tequila itself, and in the area immediately surrounding Guadalajara. Two of the brands most commonly encountered on the export markets are Cuervo and Montezuma, the latter usually in an engraved bottle.

Above left: Golden Montezuma is a gold tequila that has aged in cask for longer than the white variety.

Above right: Cuervo tequila is the white version of Mexico's national spirit.

HOW TO SERVE

Your drink is served to you cold and straight in a small shot glass. You then season your tongue with citrus and salt, by squeezing a wedge of lime (lemon for wimps) and pouring salt on to the back of the hand and then licking them up. To be anatomically precise, the hand should be held at a 45° angle away from the body, with the thumb extended downwards, and the juice and salt deposited along the groove between the bases of the thumb and forefinger. The tequila is then thrown back in one gulp like schnapps, carrying the seasonings with it. Repeat *ad infinitum*. Believe it or not, this really is how tequila is widely drunk on its native territory. If it sounds like a fiddly and indescribably messy procedure, the answer is that it is, but long practice induces a sort of head-tossing, devil-may-care sanguineness in experienced users.

How it is made

Like mescal, tequila is distilled from the chopped, pressed and fermented hearts of agave plants. The juice is quite high in acidity, which lends even the refined spirit a certain piquancy. It is distilled a second time in a pot still, and then matured in wooden casks, briefly for the silver version, and up to five years for the gold.

Tastes good with

The sharpness of the flavour of tequila is somehow appetizingly emphasized by the addition of salt, which is why tequila cocktails are often served in salt-rimmed glasses. In Mexico, they feel that their highly spiced food overwhelms the taste of most wines, so tequila is seen as a gastronomic drink. Otherwise, assuming you are not drinking a salted cocktail, or performing the salt-licking ritual, a tequila-based mixed drink is best accompanied by highly seasoned nibbles, such as salted nuts, marinated olives or Spanish-style tapas, including the likes of cured ham and brined cheeses. This is especially so if you have resorted to drinking Tequila Slammers.

Brandy

Strictly speaking, the term brandy applies to any grape-based spirit distilled from wine. There are "brandies" made from other fruits, but we shall deal with these under their own headings. The English name is a corruption of the Dutch *brandewijn*, meaning "burnt wine", an apt term for the product of distillation.

The most famous of all true brandies is cognac, named after a town in the Charente region of western France. It was to here that traders from northern Europe came in the 17th century, putting in at the port of La Rochelle to take delivery of consignments of salt. They inevitably took some of the region's thin, acidic wine with them as

Below left: The basic Rémy Martin is a VSOP grade of cognac.

Below right: Martell, the oldest house in Cognac, is still a brand leader.

well. Because of tax regulations, and to save space in the ships, the wines were boiled to reduce their volume and then reconstituted with water on arrival. It came to be noticed that the Charente wines positively benefited from the reduction process, and it was a short step from this to actual distillation.

Such was the fame and the premium paid for the distilled wines of the Charente that they came to have many imitators. None, however, could match the precise local conditions in which cognac is made. The chalky soils, maritime climate and ageing in barrels of Limousin oak were what gave it the pre-eminence it still enjoys.

France's other brandy of note, armagnac, is made in the south-west. Although not as widely known as cognac, it has its own special cachet, and is preferred by many as the better digestif.

There are grape brandies produced all over Europe and the Americas, the best of which are generally made by pot-still distillation.

Cognac

The Cognac region covers two *départements* in western France: inland Charente, and coastal Charente-Maritime. Cognac is a small town close to the border between the two. The vineyards are sub-divided into six areas, the best being Grande Champagne and Petite Champagne.

First among Cognac's entrepreneurs was Jean Martell, a Jersey-born

Left: Hennessy XO is a premium cognac in a singularly shaped decorative bottle.

opportunist who, in 1715, turned away from a life of crime (smuggling) in order to found the house that still bears his name. Other leading brands are Hennessy, Courvoisier, Hine, Otard and Rémy Martin.

The relative qualities of cognacs depend on the length of time they have been aged.

No *appellation contrôlée* cognac may be blended from spirits less than two years old. At the bottom rung of the classification is VS (designated by three stars on the label), which may contain brandies as young as three years old. ▶

HOW TO SERVE BRANDY

The finest, oldest brandies should not be mixed. Younger products mix reasonably well with soda; the vogue for brandy-and-tonic being assiduously promoted in Cognac, of all places, is not one that finds favour with the author. In the Far East, brandy is mixed with plenty of iced water and consumed in this denatured form with food.

HOW TO SERVE COGNAC

Fine cognac should be drunk just as it comes, without mixers and/or ice. It is traditionally served in balloon glasses that allow room for swirling. In fact, the aromas are better appreciated in something resembling a large liqueur glass, which mutes the prickle of the spirit. The bouquet is also encouraged by a gentle warming of the glass in the hand (for which the balloon was indisputably better designed), but not – as in former times – over a flame.

The next stage up is VSOP, Very Special (or Superior) Old Pale, a 19th-century British term. This is five-star cognac because the youngest spirit it contains has spent at least five years in wood.

Those cognacs blended from minimum six-year-old spirits may be entitled XO, or given one of the producers' own designations: Réserve, Extra, Cordon Bleu, Paradis or, classically, Napoléon – so named because the bottles once contained brandies aged since Bonaparte's day. The oldest cognacs generally come in something that looks like a giant

Right: The term "Hors d'Age" on an armagnac label denotes very long cask-ageing.

perfume bottle, fashioned in cut crystal and presented in a silk-lined box.

Armagnac

Once seen merely as France's "other brandy", armagnac is made in Gascony in the south-west. Of the three sub-regions – Bas-Armagnac, Ténarèze and Haut-Armagnac – the first is considered the best. Armagnac is a more venerable product than cognac, distillation in the region having been reliably dated back to the 1400s. While cognac is made largely from the Ugni Blanc grape, armagnac's base wine is made from a blend of several varieties. A local black oak (as distinct from Limousin) is used for the maturation, and the continuous still is widely used to distil the spirit.

So inextricably linked with armagnac was the continuous still that, for a long time, it was the only authorized apparatus. It yields a spirit rich in the aromatic impurities that promote character, which is why armagnac is noticeably more fragrant – biscuity, or even violetty – than cognac. The flavour tends to be drier because, unlike cognac, armagnac isn't adjusted with sugar, and the absence of caramel as a colouring matter leaves it paler.

The labelling system of armagnac (VS, VSOP, XO) is the

Left: Lepanto is Spain's leading brandy, made by Gonzalez Byass of sherry fame.

same as that of cognac, except that the very youngest armagnacs may be released after two years in cask rather than three. Vintage-dated armagnac – the unblended produce of a single year's harvest – has always been a local peculiarity (although vintage labelling has recently been relegalized in Cognac). If the label on, say, a 1959 armagnac looks suspiciously new, remember that it is because it has probably only recently been bottled. The ageing can only take place in wood, not glass. Prices for even the top armagnacs are considerably gentler than cognac.

Other European brandies

Spain The most significant producer of grape brandy outside France is Spain. There, premium products are accorded the same care as France's finest and, as a result, are comparable in quality.

Brandy production is concentrated in the southern, sherry-producing region of Jerez. Indeed, most Spanish brandy is distilled by the sherry houses. The grapes generally come from the huge central plain of La Mancha, but the wines are distilled and aged in Jerez. Look for "Brandy de Jerez" on the label, as it is a dependable indicator of quality.

Maturation is by a process known as fractional blending, or the *solera* system, which is also used for the finest sherries. The new spirit enters the top row of a stack of barrels and, at intervals of several months, a quantity of it is drawn off and added to the next row down, where it displaces a similar quantity into the row below, and so on. The bottom row contains the oldest brandies, which are drawn off in fractions for bottling. The brandy therefore gains greater age characteristics than it would if it were matured in the same barrel.

Top brands of Spanish brandy include Lepanto, made by Gonzalez Byass, Sanchez Romate's Cardinal Mendoza and Osborne's Conde d'Osborne, which comes in a bottle designed by Salvador Dali. The brand leader is Domecq's commendable Fundador. In Catalonia, the Torres winery makes its own excellent brandies.

Germany The best German offering seen on export markets is Uralt, an aged product made by Asbach in the Rheingau. It receives a maturation period of around 18 months.

Others Italy's brandies are fairly basic commercial spirits. Portugal makes a handful of good brandies, but its industry is heavily geared to supplying grape spirit for the port shippers. Cyprus makes some rough-and-ready brandies too.

Metaxa

Among Greek brandies, the abidingly popular Metaxa deserves a special mention. Despite the brouhaha with which it is treated in Greece itself, and a distinctly specious system of age-labelling, it is a fairly basic industrial product. The grape varieties that go into it are not generally held to be of sufficiently high acidity to produce a suitable base wine.

There are three grades of Metaxa, ascending in quality from three stars to seven. It is relatively pale in colour and much sweeter on the palate than cognac, with a highly moreish toffee flavour making it taste deceptively light.

American brandies

USA Brandy has been made in the United States since the days of the pioneers, mostly in California. At one

Left: Metaxa is the holidaymaker's favourite brandy.

time, brandy production was simply a convenient means of using up sub-standard grapes, but in the last 30 years or so, some finer aged spirits have been produced, and a number of these are capable of giving VSOP cognac a run for its money. Not all are made in the image of cognac; some are discernibly more Spanish in style. They are matured in American oak, which gives a more pronounced aroma to the spirit, accentuated by the charred inner surfaces of the barrels, and a great richness and complexity on the palate. Star names include Germain-Robin and RMS (the latter owned by Rémy Martin).

Latin America There is a long tradition of fiery spirits all over Central and South America, in which grape brandy plays its part – particularly in the areas where Spanish colonists first planted vines. Mexico is the most important producer. Its flagship is a big-selling global brand called Presidente, made in the light, simple style of basic Spanish brandy.

The peculiarly South American offering, however, is pisco. There is still much dispute over whether it originated in Peru or Chile, the two main centres of production. I shall forbear to come down on either side, except to say that the Pisco valley and its eponymous seaport are in Peru, although the Chileans simply insist that the port was one of the principal export destinations for their spirit, and that consequently the name just stuck.

Despite receiving some cask-aging, pisco is always colourless because the

barrels it matures in are so ancient that they can't tint the spirit. In Chile, the longer the maturation, the lower the dilution before bottling, so the finest grades (Gran Pisco is the best) are the strongest. Owing to widespread use of the Muscat grape, nearly all types and nationalities of pisco are marked by unabashed fruitiness.

Although it is technically a brandy, pisco should be treated more like the other white spirits – fine vodka and silver tequila. That is to say, it should be mixed, classically as a Pisco Sour, but also with any kind of fruit juice, and served over ice. I have tried it neat at room temperature, but it wasn't a particularly successful experiment.

Below left: Carneros Alambic comes from the Napa Valley, California.

Below right: This top-quality pisco hails from Peru.

Bitters

The term "bitters" refers to any of a number of spirits flavoured with bitter herbs or roots, which are generally held to have medicinal properties. They range from products such as Campari, which can be drunk in whole measures like any other spirit, to those that are so bitter that they are only added in drops to season another drink.

Bitterness is the last of the four main taste sensations (the others being sweetness, saltiness and sourness) that

Below left: Campari is Italy's most famous bitter aperitif. It also comes as a pre-mix, bottled with a crown cap.

Below right: The Italian bitter Fernet Branca is much prized as a hangover cure, and actually seems to work.

Left: Underberg is a pungent digestive bitter from Germany.

developing tastebuds learn to appreciate. A fondness for bitter flavours is often thought to be a sign of the palate having reached its true maturity.

The link between bitterness and health is evident in the fact that tonic water was originally conceived as an all-purpose pick-me-up containing the stimulant quinine, rather than as a mixer for gin, although these days its flavour tends to be drowned with artificial sweetening. The other unquestionably effective medicinal role of bitters is as an aid to digestion.

The origins of bitters lie in the flavouring elements that were commonly added to the very earliest spirits. These elixirs were taken as restoratives and remedies for a number of conditions, ranging from poor digestion to painful joints. The apothecaries who concocted them drew on the collected wisdom of herbal medicine, and added extracts of bark, roots, fruit peels, herbs and spices to enhance the healing powers of the drink.

Bitters are made all over the world. Perhaps the most famous of all is Angostura. An infusion of gentian root with herbs on a strong rum base, Angostura was invented in the 19th century by a German medic who was personal doctor to the South American revolutionary hero Simón Bolívar. It is named after a town in Venezuela, although today it is made exclusively in Trinidad, albeit still by the company founded by its inventor. Angostura is one of the few such medicinal drinks that can legitimately claim to have been formulated by a doctor.

In Europe the two major centres of production of bitters are Italy and France. Italy has Campari – a bright red

HOW TO SERVE

Campari is classically served with soda water and a twist of lemon peel, but don't drown it.

aperitif of uncompromising bitterness, made in Milan – and also Fernet Branca. Like Germany's Underberg, the latter is sold in little bottles as a hangover cure. France's bitters include Amer Picon (invented as an anti-malarial remedy by an army officer serving in Algeria). English fruit bitters, such as orange and peach, were widely used in the 1920s. Hungary's runner is Unicum, while the Latvians have their own treacle-dark dry tonic, Melnais Balzams (Black Balsam).

Below left: Angostura is the most widely used bitter in the cocktail repertoire.

Right: Unicum is a deeply coloured bitter speciality of Hungary.

Calvados

In areas where wine grapes could not be grown, other fruits were used in making distilled drinks. The most important as a source of alcohol, after grapes, is the apple. Apple trees are capable of fruiting in much more wintry conditions than the vine, and since many varieties of apple are too tart or bitter to be eaten, cider became an adjunct to beer in the cooler northern climates.

The distillation of cider is quite as old as the practice of distilling wine for grape brandy. In its heartland of Normandy in northern France, the earliest reference to an apple distillate dates from 1553, and the practice is probably older than that.

Calvados received *appellation contrôlée* status in 1942, soon after the introduction of the AC system. At the heart of the region is a particularly fine area called the Pays d'Auge, with its own designation. Both pot-still and

Left: The best calvados comes from the Pays d'Auge in Normandy, France.

continuous distillation are used, but the esteemed calvados of the Pays d'Auge area may only use the former.

Bitter-sweet apple varieties make up most of the blend in a typical calvados. After distillation, the spirit matures in French oak. The younger the calvados, the more likely it is to smell of apples; older ones take on the vanilla and spice tones of oak.

Age indications are similar to those of grape brandy. Three-star calvados spends a minimum of two years in cask; Vieux or Réserve three years; and Vieille Réserve or VSOP four years. Those aged for six or more years may be labelled "Hors d'Age" (beyond age!) If a calvados label describes it as, say, an eight-year-old product, the reference applies to the youngest spirit in it, rather than being the average. A small amount of vintage-dated calvados is made.

In the USA, an apple spirit has been made ever since the first British settlers found that apple trees proved hardier than grain crops in New England. Applejack is made in much the same way as calvados, starting with good cider, which is distilled twice in a pot still. It is then oak-aged for anything up to five years. The younger stuff is pretty abrasive, but on the eastern seaboard – as in

Right: Apple brandy is a fine, powerful apple spirit from Somerset, England.

Far right: Applejack is America's answer to calvados.

Normandy – they like it that way. Laird's is one of the bigger-selling brands, and gives a reliable introduction to this singular product.

Apple brandy, or cider brandy, is now being revived in the west of England, where Somerset is considered by many to produce the world's best ciders. Properly aged, such brandy can be quite impressive, although calvados aficionados would be unlikely to be fooled by it.

How it is made

Apples are harvested from September to December, depending on the variety. A blend of juices from different types is fermented into cider at about 5–6% alcohol. This is subjected to a double distillation (or continuous distillation, except in the Pays d'Auge). The spirit is then aged in cask for anything up to 40 years, and bottled at 40–45% ABV.

HOW TO SERVE
Younger calvados works surprisingly well with tonic, as long as you don't drown it. Varieties that have aged for longer, such as those labelled Hors d'Age, must be drunk unmixed.

Eau de vie

Eau de vie is the French phrase for the Latin *aqua vitae*, meaning "water of life". Strictly speaking, the term refers to all spirits distilled from fermented fruits, starting with wine-based cognac and armagnac. By the same token, calvados could therefore be considered an eau de vie of cider. Since the names of these individual spirits are legally protected by France's geographical *appellation contrôlée* regulations, they

Below left: Fraise is a popular eau de vie made from strawberries.

Below middle: Poire-Williams is an eau de vie flavoured with Williams pears.

Below right: Framboise Sauvage is an eau de vie intensely flavoured with wild raspberries.

have come to be known by those names instead of being referred to as eaux de vie.

Spirits can be produced from many other fruits as well as grapes or apples, however, and these are much less precisely defined. The term eau de vie, therefore, tends now to be reserved for these other fruit brandies. Apart from their basic ingredients, the main attribute that distinguishes eaux de vie from cognac and armagnac is that they are colourless because they haven't been aged in wood like their more famous cousins. The theory is that they develop in glass, which rather flies in the face of what is scientifically known about spirits – namely, that development stops once they are in the bottle.

Of the range of fruits used, the most often encountered – and those producing the most delicious eaux de vie – are the various soft summer berries. Alsace, a wine region of north-east France that has lurched from French to German domination and back again

since the late 19th century, is a particularly rich source of these spirits, although they are also made in Switzerland and Germany. Some of them are made by winemakers, others by specialist distillers. What they have in common is high alcohol (sometimes around 45% ABV), absence of colour and a clear, pure scent and flavour of the fruit from which they are made. They are not sweetened, and should not be confused with the syrupy liqueurs of the same flavours, which tend to be coloured anyway.

Tastes good with
Served very cold in small measures, eaux de vie can work well with certain desserts, particularly frangipane-based tarts topped with the same fruit as that used to make the spirit.

Left: Pascall makes the celebrated plum eau de vie, La Vielle Prune.

Kirsch

Kirsch is the original cherry spirit. It is a colourless pure distillate made from cherries, and has traditionally been seen as a distinctive product from the other fruit eaux de vie. It is principally made in the Alsace and Franche-Comté regions of eastern France, as well as in the Black Forest region of Bavaria in western Germany, its name being the German word for "cherry". It is also made in Switzerland and Austria.

When the cherry juice is pressed for the initial fermentation, the stones are ground up too and left to infuse in it, imparting a slightly bitter note to the spirit. It is generally given a short period of ageing in large earthenware vats. The true kirsch cherry is the black morello, but these days red varieties are often used instead.

Tastes good with

Use kirsch to add a touch of alcoholic richness to sweet desserts, whether for soaking the sponge base for a mousse, or moistening fresh fruit such as pineapple.

Left: Kirsch is a cherry eau de vie with an identity all of its own.

HOW TO SERVE
Lightly chilled in small glasses, kirsch makes a refreshing after-dinner tipple.

Slivovitz

True slivovitz is the local fruit brandy, or eau de vie, of Serbia and Bosnia-Herzegovina. The ravages of the war in the early 1990s in the former Yugoslavia, of which those countries were once part, put paid to a lot of the production capacity of the distilleries. A little did continue to be made, however, and with peace, production has risen once more.

At its best, slivovitz is one of the most distinguished eaux de vie made anywhere in Europe. The base fruit is a particular variety of black plum called Madjarka, which imparts a richly heady scent to the spirit. For the best grades, the spirit is cask-aged, and steeped in yet more whole fresh fruit during maturation to emphasize the flavour.

HOW TO SERVE
As with all such spirits, slivovitz is most commonly drunk unchilled, as a digestif.

It comes in a variety of weirdly shaped bottles, some tall and thin, some round and flask-shaped with bevelled edges, still others of faceted glass.

Slivovitz has always been made and drunk elsewhere in eastern and central Europe, notably in Bulgaria, Hungary, Germany, Austria and Italy. In the Balkans, it may also go by its other name of rakija. This name denotes its origin as one of the European fruit versions of the arak that originally came from the Far East.

How it is made

Black plums are crushed along with their stones and fermented very slowly over a period of around three months. A double distillation is carried out, and then the new spirit is aged in great casks of Slovenian oak. Sometimes, whole plums are thrown in to macerate in the spirit while it ages, further intensifying its ripe, musky flavour. It is generally bottled at about five years old and at 35–40% ABV.

Tastes good with

A little slivovitz added to stewed plums, or even to a traditional Christmas pudding, will enrich the dish no end.

Below: Sljivovica is a Croatian slivovitz in a flask-shaped bottle.

Marc

In European vineyards, winemakers have long had to accustom themselves to the precarious existence that nature imposes. A bumper harvest of healthy grapes means a reasonable income, but in the lean years, a by-product proves a valuable stand-by.

For many winemakers, marc is the answer. After grapes have been pressed for fermentation, a mass of skins and pips, itself capable of fermentation, is left. Marc is the distillate of this residue. In France, the most celebrated marc is made in Burgundy and Champagne, frequently by producers enthusiastic enough to buy other growers' leftovers, but it is also made in Alsace, Provence and the Jura.

In Italy, marc is known as grappa, and such is the connoisseurship surrounding it that varietal grappa, from the skins of single grape varieties, has become something of a fad. An indication of its trendiness is that several California producers (whose climate is sufficiently benign not to need such a stand-by) are making versions of grappa too. In all regions, the finer spirits may be treated to oak maturation, resulting in a golden colour, but most marc or grappa is clear.

Tastes good with

I once ate a sorbet in Reims that had been made with Marc de Champagne and anointed with yet more of it. It was acutely, if intriguingly, horrible. More palatable is the use of Marc de Bourgogne for marinating the rind of the pungently powerful soft cow's-milk cheese, Chambertin. It adds to the complexity of flavour of a mature specimen.

Left: This Marc de Champagne is made by the champagne giants Moët & Chandon.

HOW TO SERVE
Their strong tannins make marcs unsuitable for mixing. They are intended to be drunk neat, though their profoundly earthy flavour may come as a shock to the uninitiated. On the calvados principle that a strong spirit aids digestion, the Burgundians value them as after-dinner drinks.

Arak

Although the discovery of distillation is still hotly disputed, it is possible that some form of arak, or raki, was the very first spirit. There are even claims that it might have been made in India around 800 BC.

Arak is not really one drink, but a generic name for a group of clear distillates, for which the base material and method of production vary according to the region of origin. In Indonesia, the fermented juice of sugar cane provides the base, but there are also rice versions. The sap of palm trees is popular as a source of arak in India.

The drink came to the Middle East and the Mediterranean with the Arab spice trade; its name comes from the Arabic word for juice or sap, *araq*. Other easily fermentable products such as dates and figs were used, and still are in parts of North Africa and the Middle East. Finally, grape and raisin wine came to be used in the old winemaking cultures of Greece and Cyprus.

In the West today, arak is most commonly encountered in the form of raki, the aniseed-tasting spirit of Greece and Turkey. Some coloured, cask-aged raki is very fine, but most is a colourless and pretty raw-tasting spirit that can be anything up to 50% ABV.

Raki is an everyday product made virtually throughout all of the Balkan countries of south-east Europe.

Right: This simple Turkish raki has not been cask-aged.

HOW TO SERVE
Arak should be drunk fairly abstemiously. Owing to its rough potency, it isn't generally served chilled, and should be sipped slowly rather than downed in one.

Aquavit

Among the spirits whose names are derived from the phrase "water of life", Scandinavian aquavit or akvavit has a particularly ancient history. It is known to have been distilled in northern Europe since medieval times, and its use as a drink dates back as far as the 15th century.

Production is very similar to that of flavoured vodkas. Its base is a neutral grain and/or potato spirit, which is rectified to a high degree of purity and then aromatized, usually with spices. Scandinavia and Germany are the main production centres. Its alternative name, schnapps, derives from an old Nordic verb *snappen*, meaning to snatch or seize, denoting the way it is traditionally drunk – snatched down the throat in a single gulp.

How it is made

Potatoes are boiled in a contraption rather like a huge pressure cooker, and the resulting starchy mass is then mixed with malted grains. After fermentation with yeasts, it is double-distilled to obtain a neutral spirit. Dilution reduces it to a drinkable strength, and contact with charcoal, together with the approved flavouring elements, gives it its final character.

Right: Aalborg is a premium high-strength aquavit from Denmark.

Far right: Peach County Schnapps is a fruit-flavoured commercial "schnapps".

> **HOW TO SERVE**
> Aquavit should be served like good vodka – that is, ice-cold and neat from a receptacle no bigger than a shot glass. The bottle should be kept in the freezer prior to serving. It makes a superb winter aperitif.

Mescal

Mescal, or mezcal, is one of Mexico's indigenous drinks. It is a pale, yellowish spirit made from the juice of the agave cactus, like tequila.

It would be fair to say that mescal doesn't have a very salubrious image. It is the rapacious firewater drunk by the British Consul in Malcolm Lowry's alcohol-saturated novel, *Under the Volcano*. In the past, it was considered to be capable of inducing hallucinations, a feature Lowry's novel reports, but it is hard to account for this since the agave cactus is not one of the hallucinogenic species.

Mescal is often sold with a pickled white agave worm in the bottle. It is genuine, and is intended to be eaten as the last of the drink is poured out. Supposedly, ingestion of the worm encourages great heroism in those already brave enough to swallow it. Do try this at home.

Right: A little white worm lurks at the bottom of a mescal bottle.

How it is made

The unattractive agave plant has an enormous core, the shape of a pine cone, which is surrounded by great, spiny, fat leaves. This is hacked away and the expressed bitter, milky-white juice is fermented into pulque beer at around 5–6%. Mescal is the first rough distillation of this. It may be given a short period of wood-ageing.

> **HOW TO SERVE**
> If you want to tame its fire, mix mescal with a little lime juice and top it up with soda or tonic. In Mexico, they knock it back neat.

LIQUEURS

Since we are clearly distinguishing between spirits and liqueurs, it would be useful to arrive at a working definition of what constitutes a liqueur. Why is kirsch a spirit, for example, but cherry brandy a liqueur?

The distinction lies in the way that the various flavours of these drinks are obtained. Essentially, a liqueur is any spirit-based drink to which flavouring elements have been added, usually by infusion, and – in the vast majority of cases – enhanced by sweetening. Sometimes the flavourings are themselves subjected to distillation; sometimes they are merely soaked or macerated in an alcohol base. Although there are flavoured spirits, such as lemon vodka (or, for that matter, gin) there are no unflavoured liqueurs.

Below: Liqueurs play an indispensable part in the cocktail repertoire, usually sandwiched between one of the basic spirits and a non-alcoholic mixer or two.

Kirsch is a spirit because it is a straight, unsweetened distillate of cherries, whereas cherry brandy is a neutral spirit from other sources to which a cherry flavour is added by infusion of the fruit.

Liqueurs have their origins in the practice of adding aromatic ingredients, such as herbs, fruit extracts, seeds, spices, nuts, roots and flowers, to the earliest distilled spirits. This was done both to mask the unappealing flavour of the impurities that remained after rectification, and to endow the resulting potions with medicinal value. As long as basic spirits were available, a liqueur could and often would be concocted in a domestic kitchen for use in cooking as well as for drinking. As various proprietary liqueurs came on the market during the 19th century, so home liqueur-making declined.

When the science of distillation was still in its infancy in Europe, the Catalan physician Arnaldo de Vilanova advanced the theory that steeping

certain medicinal herbs in alcohol extracted the beneficial qualities. This was a logical progression of the non-alcoholic distillation of essential oils that had been practised in ancient Egypt and classical Greece. As an offshoot of the alchemical arts, distillation was intimately bound up with the doomed enterprise of attempting to turn base metals to gold, and so gold itself came to play a part in the formulation of alcohol-based remedies. (Arnaldo was saved from the Spanish Inquisition, it is said, because he had cured the Pope of a life-threatening illness by means of a tonic containing flakes of gold.) The tradition lives on today in the form of a drink called Goldwasser. Shake the bottle and it is suddenly alive with sparkling petals of gold leaf, like a child's snowstorm toy.

It was in the religious orders that many of the traditional liqueurs were first formulated, since the medicinal ingredients used were often grown in

*Above: The Grand Monastery of
Chartreuse in France, where the
famous Chartreuse liqueurs are made.*

the monastery gardens. By the late
Middle Ages, the Italians had become
the most celebrated practitioners of the
art of liqueur-making. In 1533, the
marriage of Catherine de Medici to
the future French King Henri II brought
a wave of Italians into France, and they
brought their expertise with them.
Some of the more notable products,
such as Bénédictine, were made by
French monastic orders until relatively
recently. Chartreuse still is.

In the 19th century, liqueurs had an
aura of being soothingly palatable after-
dinner digestifs for people, essentially
women, who were not fond of the
stronger alternatives, such as cognac.
Liqueurs were seen as more ladylike
drinks altogether, an image enhanced
by the introduction of the tiny glasses
that are still depressingly enough seen
as their appropriate receptacles. By
now, they had shed most of their
health-giving claims and become

honest-to-goodness drinks, although it
was still popularly believed by imbibers
that they had prophylactic properties.

The cocktail era of the 1920s and
30s that had doggedly to contend with
universal prohibition in the USA, but
suffered no such constraints in London,
Paris, Berlin and Venice, freed liqueurs
from the straitjacket of cultured
politeness in which the Victorian period
had imprisoned them. At a stroke, the
era transformed the old slings and
fizzes, fixes, sours, punches, cups and
smashes into drinks worthy of their
names. A mixture of gin with lemon
juice, sugar and soda may have been
a pleasant way of taking gin, but with a
slug of cherry brandy added, it became
an altogether more exciting and
hazardous proposition. That sense of
playing with fire is inscribed in many
of the most colourful names of the
great cocktail recipes of the 1920s, in
their evocations of gambling (Casino),
sex (Maiden's Blush), spiritual danger
(Hell, Little Devil) and even First World
War munitions (Whizzbang, Depth
Bomb, Artillery).

No drinking culture was ever happier
or more heedless than that of the
original and greatest cocktail era, and
it couldn't have happened without the
liqueurs. The following pages are a
taster's tour of the famous and the
not-so-famous.

*Below: The blue curaçao in this cocktail
certainly makes its presence felt.*

Cointreau

One of the most popular branded liqueurs of all, Cointreau is, properly speaking, a variety of curaçao. This means it is a brandy-based spirit that has been flavoured with the rind of bitter oranges. When it was launched in 1849 by the Cointreau brothers, Edouard-Jean and Adolphe, it was sold under the brand name Triple Sec White Curaçao, but so many other proprietary curaçaos began to be sold as triple sec that the family decided to give it their own name instead.

The centre of operations, as well as a distillery, are located in the French town of Angers, in the Loire valley, although Cointreau is also made in the Americas. A variety of different bottlings is available at different strengths, including a cream version, but the best-loved Cointreau is the one that comes in a square, dark-brown bottle at 40% ABV.

Despite its spirit strength, Cointreau tastes deliciously innocuous. It is sugar-sweet and colourless, but has a

powerful fume of fresh oranges, with an underlying, vaguely herbal note too. The oranges used are a clever blend of bitter, green, Seville-style varieties from the Caribbean (the island of Curaçao itself is close to Venezuela) and sweeter types from the south of France.

How it is made

Cointreau is a double distillation of grape brandy, infused with orange rind, and then sweetened and further aromatized with other secret plant ingredients.

Tastes good with

If the balance of other seasonings is right, Cointreau works admirably in the orange sauce that is classically served with duck. It is excellent in a range of desserts, particularly rich chocolate mousse.

Left: Cointreau is one of the best-loved liqueurs, and was one of the first of the orange-flavoured ones to achieve fame.

HOW TO SERVE

Absolutely everyone's favourite way of serving Cointreau is either on the rocks or frappé, depending on whether you like your ice in chunks or crystals. The cold then mitigates some of the sweetness of the liqueur, while the pure citrus flavour is exquisitely refreshing.

Cointreau can be mixed with virtually any spirit (except perhaps whisky) and a quantity of lemon juice, and shaken with ice. This is a Sidecar, made with cognac, Cointreau and lemon juice, one of the classic recipes of the original cocktail era.

Mix Cointreau with cognac, white rum and lemon juice to make another variation, Between the Sheets, a powerful, sharply flavoured cocktail from the 1920s. Whatever the formula, the pure orange flavour of the liqueur comes singing through.

Grand Marnier

Grand Marnier is another of the world's most popular orange-flavoured liqueurs. The original product is a little younger than Cointreau, its big French rival, but the style is quite different. In the sense that the oranges used in it are bitter varieties from the Caribbean, it may be classed as another type of curaçao, but it is a distinctly finer product than most ordinary curaçao.

The house that owns it was founded in 1827 by a family called Lapostolle. Louis-Alexandre Marnier later married into the family business and it was he who, in 1880, first conceived the liqueur that bears his name. Encountering the bitter oranges of Haiti on a grand tour, he hit upon the idea of blending their flavour with that of finest cognac, and then giving it a period of barrel-ageing that basic grades of curaçao never get.

Today, the production of the liqueur is split between two centres, one at Château de Bourg in the Cognac region, and the other at Neauphle-le-Château, near Paris. The initial blending is carried out at the former site, the ageing at the latter. What results is a highly refined, mellow, full-strength spirit that has a warm, amber colour and an intense, festive scent of ripe oranges.

It is sweet, but the distinction of the Fine Champagne cognac on which it is based prevents it from being in any way cloying when served straight.

The Marnier-Lapostolle company also tried cashing in on the mania for cream liqueurs that has arisen over the last 20 years by launching a Crème de Grand Marnier at a much lower strength, which I can't find it in my heart to recommend. On the plus side, it also makes a Cherry Marnier, from the *griotte* black cherry variety, naturally coloured a deep red and deeply delicious too.

How it is made

The distilled juice of Caribbean oranges is blended with top-quality cognac. After full amalgamation of the flavours, it is then re-distilled, sweetened and given a period of cask-ageing.

Tastes good with

Grand Marnier is the classic ingredient used in duck à l'orange.

Right: Grand Marnier is the equal of cognac.

HOW TO SERVE

Grand Marnier should be served with as much reverence as your best cognac would receive.

HOW TO MIX

Grand Marnier is mixed with curaçao, grenadine and lemon juice to make a Gloom Chaser.

The top layer of the pousse-café cocktail B52 is Grand Marnier.

Orange and coffee make a surprisingly successful combination in this Café à l'Orange.

Curaçao

First invented by the Dutch, curaçao was a white, rum-based liqueur flavoured with the peel of bitter green oranges found by the settlers on the Caribbean island of the same name, not far off the coast of Venezuela. Despite its geographically specific name, the liqueur has never been subject to anything like appellation regulations. It is made by many different companies in a number of countries, where brandy is used as the starter spirit instead.

A variant name in common use was triple sec, the most famous example being Cointreau, although confusingly curaçao is not at all *sec* (dry) but always sweet. The bitterness of the oranges – which are green simply because they are not quite ripe, not because they are some notably exotic variety – balances the sweetness, however, to the extent that drinkers may have been prepared to consider it relatively dry.

Curaçao comes in a range of colours in addition to the clear version. The orange curaçao, such as that made by Bols, is often particularly bitter, its colour a deep, burnished, tawny orange. Curaçao also comes in bright blue, dark green, red and yellow versions for novelty value, but the flavour is always of orange. The strength is generally somewhere between 25–30% ABV.

Below: All curaçao is flavoured with bitter oranges.

Below: The term triple sec tends to be used for the colourless curaçao.

The name of the island is not, of course, Dutch but Portuguese, after the original discoverers. There is more confusion over the correct way to pronounce "curaçao" than over the name of any other liqueur. It should properly be "coorashow" (to rhyme with "miaow"), but is corrupted by English speakers into something like "cura-say-oh".

These days it is probably the blue version that is most commercially popular, largely because it was for years the only blue alcoholic drink available. It added an unearthly hue to many cocktails, although the flavour – reassuringly enough – was only slightly bitter orange.

HOW TO SERVE
The bitterness of the fruit mixes well with other bitter flavours, so orange curaçao and tonic makes a particularly appealing long drink. Alternatively, use a not-too-sweet sparkling lemonade, if you can find one. Curaçao also works well when mixed in equal measures with either dry or sweet vermouth. It is not especially attractive taken neat.

How it is made
The blossom and dried peel of wild oranges are steeped in grape brandy or even neutral spirit, and the resulting infusion is sweetened, clarified and coloured according to style.

Tastes good with
Curaçao is indispensable in the classic crêpe suzette. In the recipe created by the great French chef Auguste Escoffier, pancake batter is flavoured with tangerine juice and curaçao, and the cooked crêpe sauced with butter, sugar and tangerine zests. These days, it is generally Grand Marnier that is used in this enduringly popular dessert, probably because it is a ritzier product.

Mandarine Napoléon

Mandarine is another type of curaçao, this time made with the skins of tangerines as opposed to bitter Caribbean oranges. By far the most famous brand is Mandarine Napoléon, the origins of which really do derive from the drinking preferences of the Emperor Napoleon I. The key figure in its history is a French chemist, Antoine-François de Fourcroy, who rose to prominence as a key figure in public administration after the French Revolution. Following the demise of the Jacobin regime, de Fourcroy found favour with Napoleon Bonaparte and was made a member of his Imperial State Council.

Left: Mandarine Napoléon is a French invention, which is now exclusively made in the Belgian capital, Brussels.

When the tangerine first arrived in Europe from China (hence its synonym, mandarin) at the end of the 18th century, there was something of a craze for it. The fashion was to steep the peel in cognac after eating the fruit, and Antoine-François records in his diary that many was the night he was called on to share such a convivial tot with Napoleon.

Mandarine Napoléon was launched in 1892 by a Belgian distiller, Louis Schmidt, who stumbled on the recipe in de Fourcroy's correspondence. It was only after the Second World War, when the distillery was relocated from Belgium to France, that the de Fourcroy family once again became involved with the liqueur, eventually taking on the worldwide distribution of Schmidt's preparation. As it became ever more successful, they moved the production back to Brussels, where it remains to this day – the primary Belgian liqueur.

The tangerines used in Mandarine Napoléon come exclusively from Sicily. Other companies make versions of tangerine liqueurs – Italians themselves make one from their Sicilian crop – but Mandarine Napoléon remains justifiably the pre-eminent example. Italian versions are named mandarinetto.

Van der Hum

Van der Hum is South Africa's equivalent of curaçao, made by several producers in the Cape, including the giant national wine consortium KWV. The whimsical name literally translates as "What's-his-name". Its base is Cape brandy, and the citrus fruit used is a tangerine-like orange variety locally known as *naartjies*. The rinds of the orange are infused in the brandy (as for Mandarine Napoléon) and supplemented with a herb or spice element, which generally includes nutmeg.

Like Mandarine Napoléon, the drink derives from the practice of steeping citrus rinds in the local brandy. It is a reliable and attractive liqueur, pale gold in colour and with a pronounced, bitter orange scent. The bottled strength is generally 25%-plus. Different brands have varying degrees of concentration.

Left: Van der Hum is South Africa's answer to orange curaçao.

Aurum

The name Aurum is Latin for "gold". Made in the Abruzzi mountains, on the Adriatic coast of Italy, Aurum is a brandy-based proprietary liqueur in which a mixture of orange rind and whole oranges is infused, its lustrous golden intensity enhanced by saffron. The basic formula is said to be of great antiquity. Aurum was given its name by the Italian writer Gabriele d'Annunzio.

The name hints that it may at one time have contained particles of genuine gold, harking back to the alchemical origins of distillation, and it has logically been argued that Aurum was the true forerunner of Goldwasser.

Left: Golden Aurum comes from Abruzzo, in eastern Italy.

How it is made

The brandy in Aurum is distilled by the makers from vintage Italian wines, and the distillate is cask-aged for around four years to take up colour. The oranges (and other citrus fruits) are infused separately in more brandy, and then the infusion is triple-distilled. This, and the first brandy, are then blended and allowed another period of oak maturation. The result is an impressively smooth liqueur, with a deceptive 40% alcohol.

Liqueur brandies

Some fruit liqueurs have traditionally been referred to as "brandies", even though they are properly nothing of the sort, in the sense that we now understand the term. There are essentially three fruit "brandies" – cherry, apricot and peach – and, although they are occasionally known by other names, it is as cherry brandy, etc. that drinkers know them best.

Strictly speaking, these products belong to the same large category as those liqueurs prefixed with the phrase "crème de", in that they are sweetened, coloured drinks, based on simple grape brandy that has been flavoured with the relevant fruits, as opposed to being primary distillates of those fruits themselves. The maceration of the fruit usually includes the stones or pips as well, for the bitter flavour they impart and, in the case of apricot kernels especially, the distinctive flavour of toasted almonds.

Of the three fruit brandies, the apricot variant has probably travelled the furthest. There are true apricot distillates made in eastern Europe, of which the Hungarian Barak Pálinka is

HOW TO SERVE
The best of these liqueur brandies make wonderful digestifs served in small quantities, provided they are not the very sweetest styles.

Right: Cusenier's liqueurs all come in distinctive bottles, such as this apricot brandy.

the most renowned, but they are dry like the fruit brandies of France. Good examples of sweet apricot liqueurs are Bols Apricot Brandy, Cusenier, and Apry, which is made by the Marie Brizard company of Bordeaux.

Cherry brandy is one of the few liqueurs that may have been invented by the English; the role of creator was claimed by one Thomas Grant of Kent. The original version was made with black morellos, although other cherry varieties may be used in modern products, depending on what is locally available. English cherry brandy contributed to the downfall of the dissolute King George IV, who consumed it in ruinous quantities, perhaps to get over the memory of his doomed affair with Mrs Fitzherbert in Brighton.

Among the more famous cherry liqueur brands are Cherry Heering, now properly known as Peter Heering Cherry Liqueur, which was first formulated in the mid-19th century by a Danish distiller of that name. The Heering company grows its own cherries to make this product, which is cask-aged. Others include Cherry Rocher, De Kuyper, Garnier and Bols, and there are brands produced in Germany and Switzerland.

Peach brandy is the one least frequently seen, its most famous manifestation probably being the one marketed by Bols. Its flavour is not quite as distinctive as the apricot.

Above right: Cherry brandy is crucial in the making of a Singapore Sling.

How they are made
The pressed juice and stones of the respective fruits are generally mixed with a neutral grape spirit (more rarely a grain spirit), sweetened with sugar syrup and macerated until the take-up of flavour is complete. If the fruit juice itself has a fairly high natural sweetness, correspondingly less syrup will be added. In some cases, the liqueurs may be treated to a period of cask-ageing, followed by adjustment of the colour with vegetable dyes. They are generally bottled at the standard liqueur strength of between 24% and 28% ABV.

Crème liqueurs

Liqueurs that use the prefix "crème de" may be bracketed together here. They are nothing at all to do with cream liqueurs, despite the terminology. They nearly always consist of one dominant flavour, which is indicated in the name. This is often, but not always, a fruit, and the liqueurs are usually appropriately coloured. In the main, they are bottled at 25–30% ABV, and may be considered among the more useful building-blocks of the cocktail-mixer's repertoire.

Originally, the term "crème" was used to indicate that these were sweetened liqueurs, as distinct from

Below left: Crème de Banane contains banana, a versatile flavour.

Below right: Crème de Cassis is a speciality of Burgundy.

dry spirits such as cognac or calvados. They were mainly French in origin, such as those produced by the 19th-century Bordeaux company Marie Brizard, but production soon spread to other specialist liqueur manufacturers such as Bols and De Kuyper of Holland.

Before the widespread availability of such products, the sweetening element in a cocktail used to be pure sugar, or perhaps a sugar syrup. The crème liqueurs had the advantage not only of providing that sweetness, but also of introducing another flavour into the cocktail mixture.

Most of these products are based on a neutral-tasting, un-aged grape brandy, and the various flavouring ingredients are either infused or macerated in the spirit rather than being subject to distillation themselves. The difference, essentially, between infusion and maceration is that the former involves some gentle heating action, while the latter is just a cold soaking of the flavouring element in the spirit. Maceration is obviously a considerably slower process than infusion. In both cases, the ingredient has to be rendered water-soluble.

Since they are intended to be rich but simple products, with one overriding flavour, crème liqueurs are not generally treated to ageing in wood. Oak maturation would interfere with the often bold primary flavours of the drinks.

How they are made

After the infusion or maceration, the aromatized spirit may then be strained to remove any solid particles caused by making the flavouring agent water-soluble. It is

HOW TO SERVE

These drinks were originally intended to be drunk as pleasant aids to digestion at the end of a grand dinner. As such, they are best served *frappé* (poured over shaved ice) rather than neat, to mitigate some of their sweetness.

then sweetened, usually by means of sugar solution. Unless it is possible to achieve a striking colour naturally (which is in fact quite rare), the colour is then created by the addition of vegetable-based colouring matter such as carotene or beetroot. Red colourings are often created by adding cochineal. The liqueur is then subjected to a heavy filtration to ensure a bright, crystal-clear product of unvarying consistency.

Tastes good with

The most obvious way to use crème liqueurs based on fruit is in desserts that are flavoured with the same principal ingredient. Enliven your strawberry mousse with crème de fraise, or your blackberry cheesecake with crème de mûre. Add crème de framboise to desserts based on raspberries, and crème de cassis to those made with blackcurrants. The flowery crème liqueurs, such as crème de violette and crème de roses, make exotic additions to the syrup for a simple fruit salad.

Maraschino

The original maraschino (which should be pronounced with a "sk" sound in the middle, not "sh") was a distilled liquor of some antiquity made from a sour red cherry variety called Marasca, which grew only on the Dalmatian coast.

When the Italian-speaking enclave of Dalmatia was incorporated into the then Yugoslavia, Italian production of maraschino was continued in the Veneto region of Italy.

Maraschino is a clear liqueur derived from an infusion of pressed cherry skins in a cherry-stone distillate. After further distillation to obtain a pure, clear spirit, it is aged, ideally for several years. It always remains colourless, and should have a pronounced aroma.

A number of Italian firms are especially associated with the production of maraschino, notably Luxardo, which traditionally sells its product in straw-covered flasks.

How it is made
The pomace of pressed cherries is infused over gentle heat in a cherry distillate for several months. It is then rectified and transferred to neutral maturation vessels to finish its aging.

Left: Luxardo's fine maraschino is traditionally sold in straw-covered bottles.

> **HOW TO SERVE**
> The best grades of maraschino should be smooth enough to drink on their own, but the sweeter it is, the more recourse to the ice-bucket you will need.

Poire William

Poire William is not to be confused with true pear brandy, also known as eau de vie de poire. Instead, it is a sweet, pear-flavoured liqueur, traditionally lightly coloured and made by the usual method of infusing crushed fruit in neutral grape spirit. The big liqueur companies nearly all make a version. Some may have a brief period of cask-aging, but most don't.

Pear-flavoured liqueurs are made in France (about the best brand is Marie Brizard), Italy (which has Pera Segnana), Germany and Switzerland. A novelty product is Poire Prisonnière, which comes with a whole pear in the bottle. The pears are grown in the bottles, which are attached to the tree, so that each fruit has its own private greenhouse. Before the bottles are filled with the liqueur, the pears are pricked in order to release their juices.

Right: Poire William is a delicately flavoured, French pear liqueur.

> **HOW TO SERVE**
> Served well chilled, or perhaps with a single piece of ice, it makes a good aperitif. Alternatively, Poire William is delicious with a splash of lemonade.

Tastes good with
Poire William is excellent poured over certain fresh fruits, notably pink grapefruit segments, pineapple and, of course, pear, when it subtly enhances the flavours.

Sloe gin

Sloe gin, and its French equivalent prunelle, are derived from a small, bitter-tasting plum, the fruit of a shrub called the blackthorn. English sloe gin is nothing more than sweetened gin in which sloes have been steeped and then strained out once they have stained it a deep red. The drink has a strong, rather medicinal taste.

Prunelle, from the French word for the fruit, is not red but green, and is made by macerating the fruit kernels in a grape spirit base. Although colour may be added, it does reflect the greenish flesh of the fruit. In Burgundy and Alsace, sloes are also used to make eau de vie.

Sloe gin is still made domestically in country areas of England, but only with commercial gin, of course. The picked fruits are left to macerate for several months.

Left: This sloe gin is made by one of the big names in gin.

> **HOW TO SERVE**
> Sloe gin is best served neat at room temperature. Alternatively, add ¼–½ measure/1–2 tsp to a glass of sparkling wine.

Midori

An instant hit when it was launched in 1978, Midori was another product from the giant Japanese drinks group, Suntory. It aimed for a slice of the cocktail action with this bright green liqueur in an idiosyncratic little bottle of textured glass. Originally a Japanese product, it is now made in Mexico.

The flavouring agent is melons, not a particularly common taste in the liqueur world, but the drink's vivid green colour is achieved by means of a dye. Indeed, its greenness is its principal sales pitch, since *midori* is the Japanese word for "green". The colour is perhaps intended to

Left: Bright green Midori has cornered the market in melon liqueurs.

evoke the skins of certain melon varieties, such as Cantaloupe or Galia, as opposed to the flesh that is actually used to flavour it. Its aroma is in fact much closer to banana. It is sweet and syrupy, and at the lower end of standard alcoholic strength for liqueurs: 20%.

Tastes good with

Midori was seized on by adventurous chefs for use in desserts that involve tropical fruit. Salads of mango, pineapple, melon, passion fruit and other tropical fruits are perfect choices, although the problem of the drink's unapologetic colour remains.

HOW TO SERVE

Midori is much better mixed than served straight, when its flavour quickly cloys. It blends beautifully with iced fruit juices, notably orange, except that the resulting colour is fairly lurid.

Midori can be treated in much the same way as the basic spirits to make a Sour, mixed with lemon juice and a dash of sugar syrup. It is always better shaken rather than stirred.

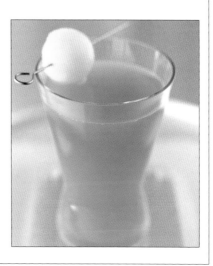

Pisang Ambon

An Indonesian liqueur made by the Dutch drinks company Bols, Pisang Ambon deserves its own separate entry. Ambon is the name of one of the many islands of Indonesia, in whose language *pisang* is the word for "banana". More than just another

HOW TO SERVE

Pisang Ambon is excellent topped up with good, sharply flavoured sparkling lemonade.

type of crème de banane, however, Pisang is made of green bananas and other tropical fruits, with a mixture of herbs thrown in for good measure. The formula is evidently based on an old local recipe.

The drink is a pronounced, deepish green colour, but nowhere near as vivid as Midori, and it is naturally very sweet. However, in comparison with the simplicity of other banana liqueurs, Pisang has an attractive savoury note of

cooked banana, making it a rather more versatile cocktail ingredient than a simple crème liqueur.

Tastes good with

It can be used to flavour desserts and pastries that use exotic fruits, including, of course, bananas.

Left: Pisang Ambon, Indonesia's contribution to the world of classic liqueurs.

Southern Comfort

The foremost American liqueur is Southern Comfort. Naturally, American whiskey is used as its starting point. The exact composition of Southern Comfort is of course a closely guarded secret, but what we do know is that the fruit flavouring it contains is peach, a fruit that grows in great quantities in the southern states.

The origins of Southern Comfort probably lie in the mixing of bourbon with peach juice as a traditional cocktail in the southern states. Down in Louisiana, close to New Orleans (as the song goes), there was once a mixed drink

Right: Southern Comfort is a fruity whiskey liqueur of the Deep South.

called Sazerac. It consists of a shot of rye whiskey, with a sprinkling of peach bitters, a lump of sugar and a dash of absinthe. So traditional is it that a New Orleans company has been producing a pre-mixed version of it since around the middle of the 19th century.

The Southern Comfort distillery is located in St Louis, Missouri. The drink comes in two strengths, 40% and 50% ABV, both of which have an appealing, fruity roundness of flavour and a mellow finish.

Tastes good with

Southern Comfort makes a good substitute for bourbon, poured over the traditional light fruitcake at Thanksgiving or Christmas. Quantities should be extremely generous.

HOW TO SERVE
Southern Comfort is intended to be meditatively sipped, like other fine American whiskeys, but you could try taming its fire and emphasizing its fruitiness with a mixer of peach nectar. It's also fine with orange juice on the rocks.

Sambuca

An Italian liqueur that became quite fashionable beyond its home region of Rome in the 1970s, Sambuca Romana is a clear, moderately sweet, quite fiery drink, flavoured with elderberries and aniseed. Its name is derived from the botanical name for elderberry, *Sambucus nigra*. Although it also contains many other herbs and roots, these are the two predominant flavours.

In the days when every drink had to be dignified with its own particular serving ritual, it was decreed that Sambuca was to be garnished with coffee beans and set alight. Aficionados of the custom differed quite sharply as to whether the correct number of beans was two or three. Such detail scarcely mattered, since what mostly preoccupied the

drinker was how to swallow it without singeing the nose.

To earn your Sambuca stripes, you have to blow out the flame on a glassful and then swallow the drink in one. In Rome, they will ask you whether you want it *con la mosca*, which literally means "with the fly" (i.e. with the coffee beans). There, they are not merely for garnish. If you say *si*, you will be expected to crunch the beans up as you drink.

Tastes good with

A chilled glass of Sambuca makes a good accompaniment to a genuine Italian torta, one of those heavenly sticky cakes of dried fruits, almonds and lemon rind.

Left: Sambuca is a fiery liqueur in more ways than one.

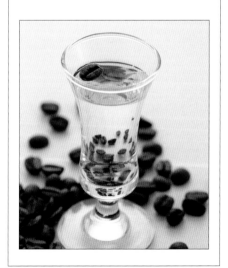

HOW TO SERVE
If you are going to try the flaming Sambuca trick, it helps to serve the liqueur in a narrow glass like an old-fashioned sherry schooner, because the flame will take more easily on a smaller surface.

Ratafia

Centuries ago, the term "ratafia" was used to describe fruits or nuts that were steeped in a sweetened spirit base. The term has now come to be applied mainly to a type of aperitif made in the brandy-producing areas of France. The brandy is mixed with fresh fruit juice.

Ratafia's name is not a geographical one. It derives from the old French practice of concluding any formal agreement, such a legal contract or business transaction, with a shared drink – a "ratifier", if you like. The original phrase is Latin: *rata fiat* (let the deal be settled).

There are also ratafias made in winemaking areas – particularly Burgundy and Champagne, in which the naturally sweet grape juice is mixed with some of the regional wine. The most celebrated ratafia, however, is Pineau des Charentes, made in the

Cognac region from grape juice fortified with cognac. It can't be considered a fortified wine, though, because the grape juice has not undergone fermentation. It comes in white and rosé versions, and always has the sweetness of ripe grape juice about it.

In Armagnac, not to be outdone, they make their own version of this drink by exactly the same method. Called Floc de Gascogne, its production, like that of armagnac itself, is on a much more modest commercial footing than its Charentais counterpart.

There is also a variant of this type of ratafia made in the Calvados region of Normandy, in which fresh apple juice is fortified with apple brandy. It is called pommeau, and is a considerably more palatable proposition (to the author's taste at least) than either Pineau or Floc.

Lesser-known variants of ratafia are made in most of the old wine-producing countries, wherever a grape spirit is produced. The Spanish drink, Moscatel de Valencia, should technically also be considered a type of ratafia, as it consists of grape spirit added to an unfermented, naturally sweet Moscatel grape juice.

How it is made

Grape brandy is added to unfermented grape juice, or apple brandy to apple juice. In each case the product is made to an average bottled strength of around 17% ABV, the same as a fortified wine.

Above left: Pineau des Charentes is the ratafia of the Cognac region.

Above right: Pommeau is an apple ratafia from Normandy.

Tastes good with

Ratafia works quite well, or at least better than most wine, as an accompaniment to a slice of aromatic melon. Because these drinks are all naturally sweet, they don't immediately appeal to all tastes as obvious aperitifs, where the preference is usually for something dry. They may work better as dessert wines for many, with fruit tarts, or a slice of sumptuously rich cake.

HOW TO SERVE

These drinks should be served, vigorously chilled, in wine glass quantities as aperitifs. In Armagnac, they mix the Floc with sparkling wine and call it a pousse-rapière (literally "rapier-pusher").

Amaretto

Of all the liqueurs that rely on almonds for their principal flavouring, amaretto is the most famous. It has become widely associated in people's minds with one particular Italian brand, Disaronno Originale, made by a company called Illva, although there are other liqueurs that may properly be called amarettos. The famous amaretto comes in a rectangular bottle, with a label in the form of an old scroll and a disproportionately large, square screwtop. The flavour is not entirely derived from almonds but from the stones of apricots too. Resembling a kind of liquid marzipan, the taste is strong and sweet and is quite assertive, even when mixed in a cocktail.

Legend has it that the recipe was given to an Italian painter of Leonardo da Vinci's school, Bernardino Luini, in 1525 by a young innkeeper. She had sat as the model for the Virgin Mary in his wall-painting of the Nativity at

Right: Casoni amaretto's flavour is like marzipan in a bottle.

Saronno, and taken rather a shine to him. Whether or not there is much truth in the tale, the original domestic concoction was probably grape brandy in which apricot kernels, with their strongly almondy flavour, had been left to infuse.

How it is made

Almond extracts, along with apricot kernels and seeds, are steeped in brandy, and the resulting drink is sweetened with sugar syrup and coloured to a deep brown.

Tastes good with

Just as a frangipane mixture, full of ground almonds, makes a good base for almost any fruit tart, so amaretto works well in the syrup for a fruit salad, or added to whipped cream or ice cream for most fruit-based desserts.

Left: Disaronno is the most famous brand of Italian amaretto.

HOW TO SERVE

The flavour of Disaronno Originale amaretto is quite complex enough for it to be enjoyable on its own, although it works better chilled. Serving it *frappé* (poured over crushed ice) is highly refreshing.

In a cocktail, amaretto mixes well with dry spirits such as cognac and gin, with perhaps some pure citrus juice (orange or lemon) to mitigate its sweetness.

It also marries deliciously with chocolate in the super-rich *pot au chocolat*. It is excellent in a liqueur coffee, and perhaps with cognac too. It pays to use the liqueur sparingly though, even in these culinary contexts, as its flavour is unignorably powerful. A little goes a long way.

Malibu

With the growth of tourism in the Caribbean islands, it was only a matter of time before liqueurs flavoured with coconut began to make their presence felt on the international market. Of these, the most famous is Malibu, made in Jamaica. Presented in an opaque white bottle, with a depiction of a tropical sunset on the front, it is a relatively low-strength (24% ABV) blend of rectified Barbados white rum with coconut extracts. The flavour is pleasingly not too sweet. Malibu was a better product than most of the liqueur concoctions with tropical names that bombarded the market during the cocktail renaissance of the early 1980s.

Another reasonably good product was Batida de Coco, a coconut-flavoured neutral spirit made in Brazil that was also exported in quantity to the holiday islands of the Caribbean. Cocoribe was similar.

All of these products are colourless, with an alcohol level slightly higher than that of fortified wine. Encouraged by the success of these proprietary products, some of the famous Dutch and French liqueur manufacturers have also marketed variants of crème de coco, although they aren't as good.

How they are made

Most of the coconut liqueurs are based on ultra-refined white rum, although one or two are made with a neutral grain alcohol. The dried pulp and milk of the coconut are used to flavour the spirit, which is then sweetened and filtered.

Tastes good with

A splash of coconut liqueur may productively be added to the sauces in Cajun or Far Eastern dishes, particularly those of Thai or Indonesian cuisine, where coconut itself figures strongly. Otherwise, it is splendid as a flavouring in a richly creamy ice cream, or poured over a salad of exotically flavoured tropical fruits.

Far left: Malibu is perhaps the best of the coconut liqueurs.

Left: Batida de Coco is Brazil's contribution to the coconut collection.

Bearing their tropical origins in mind, coconut rums mix well with other fruit-flavoured liqueurs from the hot regions. Crème de banane is an especially good partner for it.

Nut liqueurs

Liqueurs based on hazelnut, walnut and almond deserve to be considered separately, since they form quite a large sub-group.

In their French manifestations, hazelnut and walnut liqueurs are straightforward enough. They are named noisette and crème de noix, after the French words for hazelnut and walnut respectively. In the case of almonds, it all becomes a little more complicated, because the stones of certain fruit, such as apricots and cherries, have an almond-like taste. A liqueur that contains almonds themselves is called crème d'amandes. However, a liqueur called crème de noyau – *noyau* being the French term for the stone in which the almond-like kernel of a fruit is encased – will contain no

Left: Nocino is a strong walnut liqueur from Italy.

actual almonds, only an approximation of the flavour.

All nut liqueurs are brandy-based drinks in which the chopped nuts are steeped in a clear grape spirit and the resulting liqueur is clarified and bottled in a colourless state. The exception is crème de noyau, which more often than not has a faint, pinkish hue if it has been made from cherry stones. All of these liqueurs are sweet, with fairly syrupy textures, and make invaluable additions to the cocktail repertoire.

Italy produces a range of nut-based liqueurs, too. In addition to the distinctive almond-flavoured Disaronno Originale, there is also a walnut liqueur called Nocino. In the 1980s, a product called Frangelico was released. It was a delicate, straw-coloured liqueur flavoured with hazelnuts and herbs, dressed up initially in a faintly ridiculous, dark brown bottle designed to look like a monk. The large, brown, plastic top represented his cowl, and around the gathered-in waist, a length of white cord was knotted. It looked like a particularly embarrassing tourist souvenir, but the liqueur itself turned out to be delicious; it was not too sweet, and had an intriguing range of flavours.

How they are made

The nuts are crumbled up and left to infuse with the base spirit before sweetening and filtration. The liqueurs are bottled at the average liqueur strength, around 25%. In the case of the crème de noix of Gascony, the walnuts

are beaten off the trees while still green, and the spirit is sweetened with honey before being subjected to a further distillation. For crème de noyau, fruit stones are the infusion agent. They are usually either cherry or apricot, but peach and even plum may also be used, to much the same effect.

Taste good with

Nut liqueurs work well with nutty desserts, such as those containing almond paste or praline, but are also good in a chocolate mousse, or drunk alongside a piece of rich, dark fruitcake. Served chilled, Frangelico makes an unlikely table-fellow for a piece of mature Stilton.

Below left: Frangelico is a branded liqueur dressed up to look like a monk.

Below right: Eau de Noix is a rare French walnut liqueur.

HOW TO SERVE

These drinks are quite commonly taken with crushed ice as a digestif in France. Alternatively, they may be iced, slightly watered (using about the same amount of water as liqueur) and drunk as aperitifs.

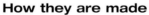

Tia Maria

Jamaica's contribution to the world of liqueurs, Tia Maria has turned into one of the best-loved of all such products in both America and Europe. It is a suave, deep brown coffee-flavoured drink, based on a recipe around three centuries old, that proves itself highly versatile on the cocktail circuit as well as for after-dinner sipping.

It is based, not surprisingly, on good, dark Jamaican rum of at least five-year-old standard and flavoured with the beans of the highly prized coffee variety, Blue Mountain. In addition to the coffee, the palate is further deepened by the addition of local

Right: Tia Maria is the world's most famous and best-loved coffee liqueur.

spices, including vanilla. Although the liqueur is sweet, the aromatic components in it prevent it from being cloying. This makes it one of the few such drinks that is actually quite acceptable to savour on its own.

One reason for the popularity of Tia Maria in Europe was the craze for the cocktail Black Russian, usually made with cola. Here, it provides a luxurious note of richness in what is otherwise a fairly prosaic mix.

How it is made

Coffee beans and various spices are infused in a base of cask-aged rum, which is then lightly sweetened. It is bottled at just under 27% ABV.

HOW TO SERVE

A pleasant way to enjoy Tia Maria as a digestif is to serve it on the rocks. Otherwise, it is one of the few liqueurs to make a successful mix with cola. Some people like it with orange juice, but the resulting colour is a little muddy.

Tastes good with

Tia Maria is brilliant for lacing chocolate desserts, and of course makes a good liqueur coffee – particularly when the coffee used is Blue Mountain. Although it isn't a strictly canonical ingredient in the original recipe, it also works well in the Italian dessert tiramisu, which is flavoured with coffee anyway. The essential alcohol ingredient of it is marsala, but a good slug of Tia Maria adds an extra-special kick.

Kahlúa

The only liqueur of any note to have been conceived in Mexico, Kahlúa is a dark brown, coffee-flavoured essence packaged in a round-shouldered, opaque bottle with a colourful label. Although some of it is still made in Mexico using home-grown arabica coffee beans, it is also made under licence in Europe. It is inevitably often compared to the other, more famous coffee liqueur, Tia Maria, but it is slightly thicker in texture and somewhat less sweet than its Jamaican counterpart. In addition to that, it has a more complex range of spice notes, including vanilla and nutmeg. The spirit base of the drink is a white cane rum, as opposed to the cask-aged base of Tia Maria, but the final strength is the same.

Right: Kahlúa is a liqueur with the stimulant properties of strong coffee.

Tastes good with

To enhance the flavour of a coffee dessert such as a soufflé or ice cream, Kahlúa somehow gives a smoother result than the more commonly used Tia Maria, probably on account of its noticeably more viscous texture. In a two-to-one mixture with warm full-cream (whole) milk, it makes a luxurious nightcap.

HOW TO SERVE

Kahlúa makes a very good chilled alternative to a liqueur coffee. Pour the Kahlúa over crushed ice in a tall glass and float some thick cream on top. Alternatively, add it to hot black coffee, top it with cream and a dusting of ground cinnamon.

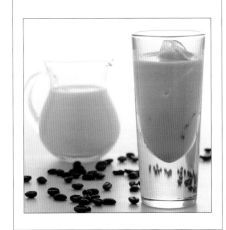

Crème de cacao

Endlessly useful in the cocktail repertoire, the world of chocolate-flavoured liqueurs begins with simple crème de cacao, which comes in two versions, brown or dark (which may also contain some vanilla flavouring) and white (which tends to be considerably sweeter). If the designation "Chouao" appears on the label, then the cocoa beans used have come from that particular district of the Venezuelan capital, Caracas.

Tastes good with

Use crème de cacao to boost the richness of your most chocolatey desserts, or add it to a cup of hot, strong coffee on a cold day.

HOW TO SERVE
Crème de cacao mixes well with coconut cream in a cocktail.

Right: Brown and white crème de cacao.

Sabra

This is Israel's entry in the liqueur stakes: a svelte concoction, flavoured with a clever mélange of Jaffa orange and chocolate, bottled at 26% ABV. Despite the gentle bitterness contributed by the orange peels, the resulting drink is exceptionally sweet. Try mixing it with cognac and ice to throw it into relief. The same company also makes a coffee liqueur called Sabra Café, which is a tiny bit less sweet.

Left: Sabra is a very sweet, but luscious, orange-chocolate liqueur from Israel.

Tastes good with

Sabra is an instant treat if poured over vanilla or chocolate ice cream, or it can be added to a chocolate mousse or ganache mixture for a particularly sumptuous dessert.

HOW TO SERVE
Sabra can be served as it comes, as its flavours are so indulgent.

Tuaca

An Italian liqueur reputed to be based on a 16th-century recipe created for Lorenzo de Medici, Tuaca is made by the resourceful Tuoni liqueur family of Livorno. It made its international debut in the 1950s after American servicemen stationed in Italy during the Second World War demanded that their local bars back home start stocking it. Its flavour is a beguiling mixture of orange

essence and vanilla on a base of Italian brandy. Because it is not excessively sweet and is bottled at almost spirit strength (35% ABV), it is

Right: Tuaca has become deservedly popular in recent years.

one of those liqueurs that makes an excellent single shot taken neat, as well being a good blending partner in the cocktail bar.

Tastes good with

Tuaca can be used to flavour desserts based on orange or chocolate, and is brilliant as an enriching ingredient in a chocolate sauce.

Cream liqueurs

Cream liqueurs are an ever-expanding category in the contemporary market. Whether the makers acknowledge it or not, cream liqueurs all owe something of their inspiration and appeal to the archetypal brand, Bailey's Irish Cream, made in Dublin. The manufacturers tend to push them particularly at Christmas, where they occupy a niche as the soft option for those who feel they need a spoonful of sugar and a dollop of cream to help the alcohol dose go down.

Bailey's itself is a blend of Irish whiskey and cream flavoured with cocoa, bottled at 17% ABV. It became suddenly chic after its invention in 1974, but was quickly saddled with the image of the kind of soft, svelte drink that unscrupulous boys plied unsuspecting girls with in nightclubs.

Left: Cadbury's Cream Liqueur can be substituted as a ready-made Brandy Alexander, at a pinch.

Right: Bailey's is the daddy of all cream liqueurs.

Since then, cream liqueurs have gone on relentlessly multiplying. Coffee and chocolate flavourings are particularly common, and indeed some cream liqueurs are made by confectionery companies, such as Cadbury's and Terry's. Then again, some of the more reputable liqueur-makers have produced cream versions of their own top products (such as Crème de Grand Marnier) in order to grab a share of this evidently lucrative market.

I have to say I decline to take these products seriously. At best, they are substitutes for real cream cocktails, but they are always sweeter and less powerful than the genuine home-made article, and many of them contain an artificial stabilizer to stop the cream from separating. In any case, why rely on somebody else's formula when you can follow your own specifications? Once you have made your own Brandy Alexanders, you won't want chocolate cream liqueur.

The extreme was reached when another Irish drinks company launched a product called Sheridan's Liqueur in 1993. It came in a bifurcated bottle with two tops, one half-filled with a dark chocolate and coffee liqueur, the other with thick, white, vanilla cream spirit. The idea was that you poured first from one side of the bottle and then from the other in order to simulate the appearance of a liqueur coffee. An even sweeter product is Dooley's, launched in 1999, a toffee-flavoured cream creation containing vodka, sugar, milk and cream, and with a quite

HOW TO SERVE
Both the sweetness and the texture of these products need the mitigating influence of ice to make them attractive. A brandy glass is the best receptacle.

A Brandy Alexander (equal measures of cognac, crème de cacao and thick cream) is the prototype cocktail upon which many of the cream liqueurs are based, and still manages to rise head and shoulders above them.

exceptionally cloying flavour. Some claim to find it intensely moreish and delicious, which only goes to show there's no accounting for taste.

Advocaat

Advocaat is a Dutch speciality. It is essentially a customized version of the humble egg-nog, without the milk: a mixture of simple grape brandy with egg yolks and sugar, as thick and as yellow as tinned custard. Most of it is sold in this natural form, although it is possible in the Netherlands to buy vanilla- and fruit-flavoured versions. As a result of its velvety texture and bland wholesomeness, advocaat is often thought of as a drink for the elderly, and is commonly added to mugs of hot chocolate or strong coffee.

The drink originated among Dutch settlers in South America, where its original main ingredient was the thick, fatty flesh of the avocado, hence its name. Attempting to replicate the recipe back home, the Dutch substituted egg yolk for the fruit.

There are a few widely available brands of advocaat on the market: the red-labelled Warninks is probably the most familiar, but Fockinks, and the liqueur specialists, Bols and De Kuyper, also make it. The standard bottled strength of around 17% ABV is quite low for a liqueur, and is about the same strength as the average fortified wine.

As well as the basic egg-and-sugar version, other variants of advocaat produced by the Dutch include orange, lemon and cherry versions. It isn't entirely surprising that these haven't much caught on among foreigners, as their sweetly fruity, eggy richness seems almost like too much of a good thing.

How it is made

Commercial grape spirit is sweetened with sugar syrup. Only the yolks of the eggs are added, along with an emulsifying agent to prevent the mixture from separating.

Tastes good with

As the ready-made basis of an egg-nog, advocaat can be made into a long drink by topping it up with full-cream (whole) milk and a sprinkling of nutmeg.

Below left: Warninks is probably the most famous advocaat brand.

Below right: Advocaat is the only manufactured drink in this book to contain egg yolk.

Absinthe and Pastis

Pastis is one of the most important traditional drinks of Europe, despite having only minority status in Britain and the other northern countries. Around the Mediterranean fringe of Europe, from south-east France to the Greek islands, pastis, in its various forms, functions as an everyday thirst-quencher, much as beer does in the northern European countries.

Drinkers the world over have, on first contact with pastis, usually been fascinated by its most famous property: it clouds up when mixed with water. This attribute is what gives the drink its name, "pastis" being a corruption of the French word *pastiche*, meaning a mixture.

The principal flavouring element in pastis is either liquorice or aniseed – more often the former – but there are other herbal

ingredients in it as well. Aniseed has been known as a digestive aid in medicine since the time of the Egyptians, and is still in use today.

The most famous pastis of them all is absinthe, which for a large part of the 20th century was illegal; since the 1990s, however, it has happily been restored to us. What originally doomed it was that it contained wormwood in concentrations held responsible for corroding the brain. During the late 19th century, it was the house drink of decadent Parisian artists and others, many of whom died the kinds of squalid deaths associated with laudanum use during the English Romantic period.

Although absinthe is being made in France again, it is still officially *persona non grata* there, and much is made in eastern Europe, especially the Czech Republic. Its flavour is hauntingly dense and concentrated, backed up by an incredible alcohol strength: it is at least 55% ABV, and more usually 65–70%. For the truly suicidal, there is even a Bulgarian product bottled at just a heartbeat under 90%.

When absinthe was given its marching orders in France by a governmental decree of 1915, other countries followed suit. One of its chief manufacturers, the firm of Henri-Louis Pernod, which had been making it for over a century, then turned to making a similar product without wormwood at a lower alcoholic strength. In effect, Pernod was the sanitized version of absinthe. The other main quality French brand, Ricard, is now part of the same group, although they are made at opposite ends of France.

Far left: Ricard is the famous pastis of southern France.

Left: Absinth made in eastern Europe is spelt without the "e".

The Spanish equivalent is *ojen* (pronounced "oh-hen"), named after the town where it is made, and sold in two versions, sweet and dry. Greece has ouzo, much beloved of holidaymakers on the Peloponnese and the islands. Its flavouring agent is anise and, like pastis, the drink turns milky-white when water is added. The bottled strength is around 35–40% ABV, which is similar to Pernod, but less than Ricard.

How they are made
The various herbs and plants are usually infused in a straight, highly purified vegetable spirit base, and essence of anise or liquorice is added. Further blending with rectified alcohol is followed by sweetening.

HOW TO SERVE
Absinthe should ideally be served in a small, thick-based glass with as much water as you feel you need. The water should be very cold, so as to obviate the need for ice. Those with slightly sweeter tastes may add sugar to it, classically by balancing a perforated spoon or metal tea-strainer with a sugar-cube on it across the top of the glass and then pouring the water over it.

Ouzo should be served cold in a small glass, either neat, with the equivalent amount of water, or with an ice cube or two.

Anis

Confusion reigns as to the precise differences between anis and pastis, and indeed whether there are any meaningful differences at all. They are both flavoured either with the berries of the aniseed plant, originally native to North Africa, or with Far Eastern star anise, and are popular all around the Mediterranean. They both turn cloudy when watered, and are both claimed as the respectable successor to the outlawed absinthe.

One august authority claims that pastis should be flavoured with liquorice rather than aniseed, although the two are very close in taste. Another claims that anis is simply one of the types of pastis. Still another claims that, whereas anis is a product of the maceration of aniseed or liquorice in spirit, pastis should properly be seen as a distillation from either of the two ingredients themselves.

These claims can't all be right of course, but for what it's worth, I incline to accept the last definition. For one thing, anis tends to be lower in alcohol than pastis, having the strength of a liqueur rather than a spirit. The one thing we can be sure of is that pastis is always French, whereas anis – particularly with that spelling – can also be Spanish. In Spain, there are sweet and dry varieties, whereas French anise tends mainly to be dry.

Ever since the days of the medical school of Salerno, and probably earlier, extract of anis has been seen as a valuable weapon in the apothecary's armoury. It is thought to be especially good for ailments of the stomach.

Anisette

Quite definitely a liqueur, anisette is French, sweetened, and usually somewhat stronger than anis. The most famous brand is Marie Brizard, from the firm named after the Bordelaise woman who, in the mid-18th century, was given the recipe by a West Indian sailor whom she had kindly nursed through a fever. The aromatizers in it include angelica, cloves, coriander and of course aniseed.

Far left: Dry and sweet, anis is made in Spain as well as in France.

Left: Anisette is a sweet liqueur form of anis, typified by this famed Marie Brizard version.

The only true way to serve anis is to take it ice-cold in a little, thick-based tumbler. The addition of a small amount of water – usually about as much again – turns it milky but with a faint greenish tinge. It is considered a great appetite-whetter.

Enhance the anise flavour in a cocktail in which either anis or anisette has been used by dropping in a whole star anise, the Far Eastern spice much used in Chinese and Thai cooking.

Chartreuse

Unlike Bénédictine, Chartreuse really is still made by monks, who make it at Voiron, near Grenoble, not far from the site of their Carthusian monastery, La Grande Chartreuse. Expelled from France at the time of the French Revolution, the order was allowed back into the mother country after the defeat of Napoleon, only to be kicked out again in 1903. It was then that a second branch of the operation was founded at Tarragona, in eastern Spain, and it continued as Chartreuse's second address until 1991, long after the production was finally re-established in France in 1932.

The Carthusians are a silent order, which has no doubt helped to keep the recipe a secret; like its Norman counterpart, it is known only to a lucky trio at any one time. Proceeds from the worldwide sales of Chartreuse are ploughed back into the order's funds, which pay for all kinds of charitable works.

There is a premium version of Chartreuse (the original recipe is said to date from 1605) called Elixir Végétal, which is sold in miniature bottles at a fearsome 71% ABV, but it is principally sold in two incarnations today: green (55%) and yellow (40%). The latter is a deep greenish-yellow hue, and is sweet, honeyed and slightly minty in flavour, while the green Chartreuse is a leafy colour, has a pungent herbal scent and is distinctly less viscous.

Additionally, the order produces a rare higher

Right: Green Chartreuse is intensely powerful and aromatic.

Far right: Yellow Chartreuse is sweeter than green Chartreuse and of normal spirit strength.

grade of each colour, labelled VEP, for *vieillissement exceptionnellement prolongé* (exceptionally long ageing).

How it is made

By varying processes of distillation, infusion and maceration, over 130 herbs and plants are used to flavour a base of grape brandy. They were all once gathered from the mountains surrounding the monastery, but some are now imported from Italy, Switzerland and further afield. Chartreuse is aged in casks for up to five years, except for the VEP, which is aged for at least eight.

Tastes good with

The French sometimes fortify their hot chocolate with a reviving splash of the green Chartreuse. The yellow is thought to be more suitable for coffee.

Above: Elixir Végétal is the original Carthusian elixir, bottled at very high strength: 71%.

HOW TO SERVE

If you find the flavour of Chartreuse overwhelming on its own, do as the French do and serve it mixed as a long drink with tonic or soda and plenty of ice. Alternatively, it mixes well (the yellow version especially) with gin in a cocktail, as below.

Bénédictine

"Deo optimo maximo" (To God, most good, most great), exclaimed the Benedictine monk, Dom Bernardo, who formulated the liqueur that now bears his order's name, on first tasting the results. Or so the story goes. It reputedly happened in 1510, so it isn't easy to verify. What is certain is that Dom Bernardo's monastery at Fécamp, in the Normandy region of northern France, produced this cognac-based herbal liqueur until the time of the French Revolution in 1789, when the monasteries were forcibly closed and production banned.

Bénédictine was officially extinct until the 1860s, when it was revived by a descendant of the monastery's lawyers, Alexandre Le Grand. On finding the secret recipe among a bundle of yellowing papers, he was inspired to build an extraordinary new distillery in the high Gothic style at Fécamp, and the now secularized liqueur, which was first christened Bénédictine by Le Grand, lived to fight another day.

Bénédictine is a bright golden potion of honeyed, spicy sweetness, containing a herbalist's pantheon of medicinal plants and spices. The exact formula is known only to three people at any given time, like Chartreuse, but it is thought to contain as many as 56 aromatizing ingredients. Its strength is 40% ABV.

While its flavour seems all honey at first, it develops very cleverly on the palate, and on the finish it is interesting to see how many of those herbs and spices you can correctly identify.

How it is made

The various herbs, spices, citrus peels etc. are left to infuse in a base of cognac, and then the resulting potion is re-distilled to concentrate the flavour.

Tastes good with

Because of its complex flavours, Bénédictine is not especially versatile in the culinary repertoire. It could perhaps be included in the syrup for a salad of citrus segments, and its honeyed roundness should work reasonably well with a honey-flavoured ice cream.

Left: Bénédictine is one of the old monastic liqueurs, still produced to a formula that reputedly dates back to the early 16th century. Its complex flavours result from a mixture of herbs, medicinal plants, spices and citrus fruit peels.

HOW TO SERVE

Bénédictine should ideally be served straight in a large liqueur glass at the end of a meal, but its makers clearly have no qualms about its use as a mixing ingredient by those who find the sweetness of classic liqueurs too much to take *au naturel*. Alternatively, try it with a dash of lemon juice and hot water, a comforting formula invented by English squaddies serving in wartime Normandy.

In cocktails, it rubs along nicely with the herbal fortified wine, vermouth, or with the other similarly flavoured liqueurs, such as Scotch-based Glayva or Drambuie (see entries on facing page).

Drambuie

Drambuie is Scotland's (and, for that matter, Britain's) pre-eminent contribution to the world's classic liqueurs. Hugely popular in the United States, it is a unique and inimitable concoction of Scotch whisky, heather honey and herbs. The story goes that the recipe was given as a reward to one Captain John Mackinnon in 1746, after the defeat at Culloden, by Charles Edward Stuart, or Bonnie Prince Charlie, as the pretender to the English throne became better known. The lad that was born to be king was of course ferried to Skye, and from thence to France, away from the clutches of the nefarious English. Captain Mackinnon was his protector.

That story has inevitably since been debunked by meticulous historians. The truth is almost certainly the other way round. It was the Mackinnons who revived the spirits of the fugitive Prince with their own Scotch-based home concoction, which was very much a typical blend of the period, an unrefined spirit disguised with sweet and aromatic herbal additives.

Today, the spirit is anything but unrefined, being a mixture of fine aged malt and straight grain whiskies, to which the flavourings are added. It is bottled at 40% ABV. The Mackinnon family still makes it, though near Edinburgh now rather than on Skye. They registered its name (from the Gaelic *an dram buidheach*, "the drink that satisfies") in 1892, but it was only launched commercially in 1906, with spectacular success.

HOW TO SERVE

Serve Drambuie as it comes, over ice, or mixed with plain Scotch as a Rusty Nail.

Tastes good with

A hunk of rich Dundee cake doused in Drambuie is a sumptuous cold-weather treat. It is also very good added to whipped cream and lemon zest to make a very grown-up syllabub.

Left: Drambuie is perhaps Britain's greatest contribution to the liqueur world.

Glayva

Like Drambuie, Glayva is a Scotch whisky-based liqueur made near Edinburgh, but it is of much more recent provenance. The drink was first formulated in 1947, its name a corruption of the Gaelic *glemhath*, or "very good". Its aromatizers are quite similar to those of Drambuie, although its flavour is intriguingly different. Heather honey and various herbs are used, and so is a quantity of orange peel, resulting in a noticeably fruitier attack on the palate. The strength is also slightly lower, at 35%.

The noble Scot commemorated in the case of Glayva is one

Right: The original formula for Glayva is much older than the product itself.

Master Borthwick, the phlegmatic 16-year-old credited with carrying Robert the Bruce's heart back to Scotland after the King's defeat at the hands of the Saracens. Not content with rescuing the regal heart, the indomitable lad cut off the head of a Saracen chieftain he had killed, impaled it on a spear, and brought that back too just to keep his spirits up. All those pubs named the Saracen's Head recall the event, as did the Moorish head once depicted on the Glayva label.

Tastes good with

Glayva is particularly good added to honey or orange ice cream.

HOW TO SERVE

Glayva should be served just as it is, in a standard whisky tumbler. Its fruitiness makes it slightly better for chilling than Drambuie, but don't overdo it. Alternatively, a dash of lemon juice and a squirt of soda won't go amiss.

Goldwasser

Goldwasser, or Danziger Goldwasser to give it its archetypal name, recalls the great Catalan physician Arnaldo de Vilanova who, in the 13th century, is reputed to have cured the Pope of a dangerous illness by giving him a herbal elixir containing specks of gold. In so doing, he also saved his own skin from the Inquisition.

The commercial prototype of the drink was first made in the Baltic port city of Danzig (now Gdańsk in Poland). Based on the drink kümmel, it is flavoured

Right: All Goldwasser originally came from Gdańsk, like this one.

with both aniseed and caraway seeds, is colourless, less sweet than many liqueurs, and it really does have a shower of golden particles added to it, in memory of Arnaldo. (There was also for a time a silver version, called Silberwasser.) Liqueur d'Or was a now-extinct French version of the same thing. Some brands also had a citric fruit flavour, which was sometimes lemon, sometimes orange.

Tastes good with

Soufflé Rothschild is a classic, hot dessert soufflé made from crème patissière and crystallized fruits that have been liberally macerated in Danziger Goldwasser.

HOW TO SERVE
The prettiness can be enhanced by serving Goldwasser in a little cut-crystal liqueur glass.

Galliano

One of Italy's liqueur specialities, golden-yellow Galliano is chiefly known on the international cocktail scene for its matchless role of livening up a vodka and orange in the Harvey Wallbanger cocktail, and for its tall, conical bottle.

It was invented in 1896 by one Arturo Vaccari, a Tuscan distiller who named his new creation in honour of an Italian soldier, Major Giuseppe Galliano. The previous year, Galliano had held out under siege at Fort Enda in Ethiopia for 44 days against vastly superior Abyssinian forces under the command of Haile Selassie's fearsome nephew.

The formula, as we are accustomed to hear in the world of liqueurs, is a jealously guarded secret, but is said to be based on over 30 herbs, roots, berries and flowers from the alpine

slopes to the north of Italy. Among its flavours is a strong presence of anise, and there is a pronounced scent of vanilla. It is also naturally very sweet. Despite the complexity of its tastes, it is a valuable addition to the bartender's battery, where it happily rubs shoulders with all of the white spirits, and is on nodding terms with cognac and even whisky as well.

How it is made

The various flavouring ingredients are steeped in a mixture of neutral spirit and water and then distilled; the resulting potion is then blended with refined spirits. It is bottled at 35% ABV.

Left: Galliano is an Italian classic that comes in a distinctive, conical bottle.

HOW TO SERVE
Galliano isn't particularly agreeable on its own, but makes a versatile cocktail ingredient, most notably with vodka and orange juice in the classic Harvey Wallbanger.

Kümmel

All we know of kümmel, one of the more ancient liqueurs, is that it originated somewhere in northern Europe, but precisely where isn't certain. The best guess is Holland, but the Germans have a respectable enough claim on the patent as well. Certainly, it was being made in Holland in the 16th century, and it very much fits the image of such drinks of the time, in that it would have been an unrefined grain spirit masked by an aromatic ingredient.

The ingredient in this case is caraway seeds. A certain amount of needless confusion is created by the fact that the name looks as though it has something to do with the more pungent cumin. This is only because, in certain European languages, caraway is often referred to as a sort of cumin. They have nothing to do with each other, the misleading nomenclature only arising because the seeds are supposed to look vaguely similar.

Left: Wolfschmidt is the leading brand of kümmel.

A key episode in kümmel's history occurred at the end of the 17th century, during Peter the Great's sojourn in Holland. He took the formula for the drink back home, and kümmel came to be thought of as a Russian product, or at least a Baltic one. The Baltic port of Riga, now capital of Latvia, was its chief centre of production throughout the 19th century, and some was also made in Danzig (now Gdańsk), where they eventually came to add flecks of gold to it and call it Goldwasser.

Versions of kümmel are today made not just in Latvia but also in Poland, Germany, Holland, Denmark and even the United States. One property of caraway, valued since Egyptian times, is its ability to counteract flatulence, which is why it was one of the traditional ingredients of gripe water for babies.

How it is made

The base is a pure grain distillate, effectively a type of vodka, in which the seeds are infused. Most brands are fairly heavily sweetened but they are always left colourless.

Tastes good with

Try adding kümmel to the mixture for old English seed cake, which is made with caraway seeds.

HOW TO SERVE

Kümmel is nearly always served on the rocks in its countries of origin.

Strega

The name Strega, a popular proprietary liqueur produced in Italy by the Alberti family since 1860, is Italian for "witch". It is so called because it is supposedly based on a witches' brew, an aphrodisiac love-potion guaranteed to unite in eternal togetherness any pair of lovers who drink it with each other. You have been warned.

It is a bright yellow concoction full of all sorts of complex flavours. The fruit base is a citrus blend and it reputedly also contains around six dozen

Right: Strega is an Italian liqueur that is full of complex flavours.

different botanical herbs, making it not dissimilar in style to the yellow version of Chartreuse. It has the same kind of syrupy texture, too, and is likewise considered an especially good digestif.

Although the colour resembles that of Galliano, Strega's flavour is quite different, more obviously herbal and minty, and with a stronger citrus element. It is also slightly stronger in alcohol, at 40% ABV. To my tastes at least, it is a more versatile mixing ingredient than Galliano, as its flavours blend more subtly with other drinks and mixers to create a pleasingly harmonious result.

How it is made

It is the product of a pot-still distillation, with the various aromatizers added separately before blending, after which it is aged in casks.

Tastes good with

Strega works particularly well as an accompaniment to freshly cracked nuts at the end of a meal, in particular walnuts and hazelnuts.

HOW TO SERVE

Strega is more appealing served frappé, on crushed ice, which takes the edge off its sweetness, than served on its own.

Parfait Amour

The long association of drinking and seduction is celebrated in the name of purple Parfait Amour, "perfect love". In the 18th century, particularly, the use of alcohol in amorous pursuits had less to do with getting your intended too stupefied to know what they were doing, than with stimulating the erotic impulses with artful concoctions of spices and flowers, mixed with alcohol.

Parfait Amour liqueur is really the only surviving link to that tradition. It is almost certainly Dutch in origin, a more exotic species of curaçao. Its name, as with all such potions, is French because that was considered the romantic language *par excellence*. As its (added) colour would lead you to expect, it is subtly scented with violets, but the flavour owes more to fruits and spices than to flowers, which marks it out quite distinctly from the colourless crème de violette. The main components are citrus fruits (usually lemons) and a mixture of cloves and other spices, including vanilla.

The drink enjoyed great popularity during the cocktail boom in the 1920s. Apart from anything else, no other liqueur is quite the same colour. There was once a red version of it too. Today, Parfait Amour is made not only by the Dutch liqueur specialists Bols, but by certain French companies as well. It has an average strength of around 30% ABV.

How it is made
The various aromatizing elements are macerated in grape spirit, which may then be re-distilled, and the purple colour is achieved by means of a vegetable dye.

Tastes good with
What else should be eaten with this purple liqueur but a box of violet creams?

Left: Parfait Amour is indelibly associated with romance on account of its singularly attractive colour, as well as the name.

HOW TO SERVE
It is best to serve Parfait Amour unmixed, or blended with something colourless such as lemonade, in order not to interfere with your beloved's enjoyment of the colour. It tastes better chilled.

Punsch

Although punsch is more familiarly known in English-speaking countries as Swedish punch, even then it isn't a drink many people have come across. Its lineage can be traced back to the 18th century, when Sweden's ocean-going trading vessels began doing business in the East Indies. Among the commodities they brought back was the local arak.

In its raw state, arak wasn't much to northern European tastes, and so a few drink companies took to blending it with grape brandy and various wines and cordials, in effect

Right: The real thing – Carlshamns, a cask-aged punsch from Sweden.

creating a kind of powerful punch in the process. Like a traditional punch, the mixture is also highly spiced.

The original punch was a British colonial invention, but by the 18th century, a vogue for it had spread not only to Scandinavia but into France as well. Rum was a favoured base ingredient, variously boosted with hot tea, lemon juice and sweet spices such as cinnamon. Punch was, in every way, the grand-daddy of the cocktail.

In an echo of the British habit, Swedish punsch was also usually served hot, at least until the end of the 19th century.

How it is made
These days, punsch is exclusively a rum-based drink, to which other forms of alcohol, including wine, are added, together with a quantity of fragrant spices, such as cinnamon and cloves. It is sweetened and then aged for several months in cask, before being bottled at around 26% ABV.

Tastes good with
Punsch works reasonably well with little salty nibbles made with strong cheese. In its native Sweden, it is often taken in liqueur quantities with marinated fish, typically herring, when it should be vigorously chilled. In this context, it is effectively a rather gentler alternative to aquavit.

HOW TO SERVE
To relive the old days, warm the punsch gently (without letting it boil) in a small saucepan and serve it in big, heatproof wine glasses.

Pimm's

Forever associated with the English summer, Pimm's No. 1 Cup is a proprietary version of a fruit cup created by James Pimm in the 1820s. He devised his recipe to mark out his own establishment in the City of London from the run of other oyster bars, which traditionally served stout ale to wash the bivalves down.

Pimm did such a roaring trade with his fruit cup that he began to market it ready-mixed in 1859, at a stiffish three shillings a bottle. Popular throughout the British Empire during colonial times, it came to enjoy a sudden vogue in France and Italy after the Second World War.

There were once six different versions of Pimm's, each based on a different

Left: Pimm's is the quintessential flavour of an English summer.

spirit. The market has since whittled these down to just two: Pimm's Vodka Cup and the original, which is still sold as No. 1 Cup, and is based on London gin, with an unmixed strength of 25% ABV. Pimm's has suffered somewhat from being seen as too fiddly to prepare. Its present owner has tried to combat that by launching little cans of pre-mixed Pimm's.

Tastes good with

Pimm's works well with classic English picnic foods, such as cucumber sandwiches, hard-boiled quail's eggs, crackers with cream cheese, and crudités. In this context, it's as well to make a fairly dilute mixture, so as not to overwhelm the food.

HOW TO SERVE

A double measure of Pimm's No. 1 should be poured over ice in a tall glass. (In Mr Pimm's oyster bar, it was knocked back by the pint.) It is then topped up with lemonade or soda, and garnished with slices of orange, lemon and lime, a wedge of apple and a dangling twist of pared cucumber rind. If you can find fresh borage, use some of its smaller leaves instead of the cucumber. Float a little bundle of mint leaves on top. If that sounds too much of a fandango, just throw in a slice of lemon and get on with it. It's just as nice.

Suze

If I had to nominate one other product to stand alongside champagne and fino sherry in a perfect trinity of aperitifs, it would unhesitatingly be Suze. It relies for its stimulating impact on gentian.

Gentian is a wild mountain plant found in the Alps and the mountains of the Jura. It has large yellow flowers, but is principally valued for its roots, which can grow up to a yard long and have an uncompromisingly bitter flavour. It was once the quinine of its day and, like quinine, is thought to be particularly good for ailments of the liver.

The Suze brand is owned by pastis manufacturers Pernod-Ricard, and it has a very delicate primrose colour. It is wine-based, and its

Right: It is well worth making a journey to France just to taste Suze.

flavour is so dry and bitter, even when mixed with a little water or served on ice, that it acts as an extraordinarily powerful appetite-rouser.

Other similar products may be labelled Gentiane in France and Switzerland, or Enzian in the German-speaking countries.

How it is made

An extract of gentian is steeped in a white wine base, imparting a little faint colour to the liquid. It is then clarified and bottled at 16% ABV.

Tastes good with

Suze is great served with any bitter nibbles, and combines extremely well with the more pungent varieties of green olive. Strong marinades, such as those made with garlic and chillies, won't faze it.

HOW TO SERVE

Pour a measure of Suze into a tumbler with either the merest splash of very cold water or a single cube of ice, just to freshen it up.

Cuarenta y Tres

Cuarenta is a sweet liqueur made in the Cartagena of eastern Spain, and based on a recipe that supposedly dates from classical times, when the Phoenicians founded Carthage, in North Africa, and introduced viticulture. Its name is Spanish for "forty-three" (it has the alternative name in English-speaking markets of Licor 43), and is so named because that is the number of herbs and spices it contains. Its strength is 31% ABV.

Cuarenta is concocted from a brandy base, with infusions of the various aromatizers, but has a noticeably predominant

Right: Cuarenta y Tres is supposedly based on a 2000-year-old recipe.

flavour of vanilla, which rather torpedoes the Carthaginian theory since vanilla was only discovered in the 16th century by Spanish explorers in Mexico. Not much seen outside its region of production, it is nonetheless held in high regard locally.

Tastes good with

A small chilled measure of Cuarenta is surprisingly good with hot desserts of stewed fruit and cream. It also has fleeting hints of chocolate and honey in the flavour, making it an ideal accompaniment to a light, chocolatey dessert – or try it with *crema catalana*, the citrussy Spanish answer to crème brûlée.

HOW TO SERVE
Cuarenta y Tres should be served either on the rocks, or mixed with a small quantity of freshly squeezed orange juice.

Cynar

A liqueur for the truly intrepid, Cynar is a soupy, dark brown potion made in Italy, the flavouring of which is artichoke leaves (its name derives from the Latin word for artichoke, *cynarum*). It contains all of the savoury bitterness of the globe artichoke, which is boldly illustrated on its label. If that sounds like fun, go ahead and try it. I once swallowed a modest measure of it in a little backstreet bar in Venice, and of all my shimmering memories of the watery city, Cynar is not, I have to say, the loveliest.

Great claims are made for Cynar as a health tonic as it contains herbs as well as artichoke, itself known to be good for the liver. First formulated in 1949, the brand is owned by Campari. It has

a bottled strength of 20% ABV, putting it at the upper end of the aperitif range for strength.

Tastes good with

It is often claimed that there is no wine in the world that makes a good gastronomic match for artichoke, when it is served as an hors d'oeuvre, partly because this vegetable has the peculiar property of making everything else alongside it taste a little sweeter than it naturally is. Cynar – with its syrupy texture helping it along – could just be the answer. Otherwise, it is probably best to forget the matchmaking.

Left: Cynar, the world's only artichoke drink.

HOW TO SERVE
As an aperitif, mix Cynar with tonic or soda water, add a slice of orange or lemon, and be very broad-minded. Served very well chilled, it can be drunk on its own – slowly.

Kikor

The first of three products on this page made by the Italian liqueur-makers, Tuoni and Canepa of Livorno, the family company that also created Tuaca, Kikor is the one with most obvious commercial appeal. It is a more complex chocolate liqueur than basic crème de cacao, made by a lengthy maceration of cocoa beans in a neutral alcohol base.

The flavour is an irresistible combination of slightly bitter dark chocolate, sugar and deceptive

hints of vanilla and coffee. It is thickly syrupy, but the bitterness of the cocoa used gives it exemplary balance. Its bottled strength is 30% ABV.

Tastes good with

The makers suggest pouring it over vanilla ice cream, and who am I to argue?

Left: Kikor is a sensuous liqueur flavoured with chocolate, vanilla and coffee.

HOW TO SERVE
Serve Kikor chilled with ice or mixed with cold full-cream (whole) milk.

Poncino Livornese

Poncino is a liqueur made for using in the classic Italian coffee preparation known as "ponch". This is basically a variant of the liqueur coffee procedure, in which sugar and lemon are added to a cup of hot, strong, boozy black coffee. It is an anis-based liqueur, infused with come-hither flavourings such as caramel, chocolate and coffee itself, and bottled at a fairly soul-stirring 47% ABV.

The aroma is a complex mixture of coffee, chocolate and a fleeting hint of citrus (either bitter orange or lemon),

underpinned by anis. When tasted, the anis comes through strongly, and adds its liquoricey depth to the chocolate aftertaste. This is an altogether less sweet liqueur than Kikor, but an equally appealing one.

Right: Poncino Livornese is an anis-based Italian liqueur.

HOW TO SERVE
Add a measure of Poncino to a small coffee cup. Pour in an espresso, sweeten to taste, and finish by squeezing a piece of lemon rind over the top and dropping it in. When cool enough, drink in one gulp. Alternatively, serve small measures of the liqueur well-chilled in a liqueur glass. With its anis content in mind, it makes a rather special digestif served neat.

Monasterium

A liqueur made in tribute to the celebrated monastic preparations of southern Europe, Monasterium is derived from an infusion of various Mediterranean citrus fruits with essential oils of a number of flowers and herbs. It is based on an old recipe handed down from Franciscan monks, and is affectionately – if rather alarmingly – known in Italy as the "Green Monster", although its colour is a delicate yellowy-green. Its alcohol strength is the same as Poncino, at 47% ABV, indicating that it is meant to be taken seriously.

Monasterium may, in time, come to be seen as one of the world's great liqueurs. It has something approaching the ineffable complexity of Chartreuse, perhaps without some of the bitterness of that monastic classic. Strong

Left: Monasterium is an extremely fine herbal liqueur in the monastic style of Chartreuse.

citrus notes of lemon (and possibly lime) mingle with medicinal herbal tones, and fill the mouth. It is sweetish, but not too syrupy, and leaves a clean, surprisingly subtle aftertaste for such a powerful liqueur.

HOW TO SERVE
Monasterium should be served in shot glasses, just as it is, or perhaps slightly chilled. It should certainly not be mixed.

WINE, CHAMPAGNE AND FORTIFIED WINES

Fermented drinks based on the wine grape, *Vitis vinifera*, are the most hugely varied of all drink categories.

Wine and champagne

At the heart of the enormous boom in wine consumption that has taken place in the English-speaking world over the last two decades or so is a fascinating, happy paradox. In the days when wine was exclusively the preserve of a narrow cultural elite, the ordinary drinker didn't get a look-in. Wine was considered a highly technical subject, in which anybody without the necessary ability could only fall flat on his or her face in embarrassment. It required an intimate knowledge of what came from where, and what it was supposed to taste like.

Those were times, however, when wine appreciation essentially meant a familiarity with the French classics, with perhaps a little sweet wine from Germany and a smattering of the traditional fortified wines: sherry, port and madeira. That was what the wine trade dealt in. These days, wine is bought daily in supermarkets to be consumed that evening; hardly anyone has a cellar

Below: Mature summer vines at the Robert Mondavi vineyard in the Napa Valley, northern California.

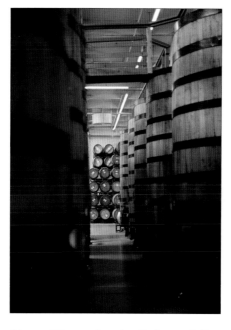

Above: Wine undergoing its fermentation in wooden vats.

to store it in and many don't even possess a decanter. Wines from dozens of countries cram the retail shelves.

It seems, in other words, that the commercial jungle that wine has now become has not deterred people in the slightest from plunging adventurously into the thickets. Consumers are no longer intimidated by the thought of needing to know their Pouilly-Fumé from their Pouilly-Fuissé, their Bardolino

Above: Champagne is the world's pre-eminent sparkling wine.

from their Brunello, just at the very moment when there is more to know than ever before.

The reason for this new mood of confidence is not hard to find. On virtually every wine label we come across is the name of the grape from which it is made. Consumers effectively recognize these as brand names, and have thus acquired a basic lexicon of wine that can serve them well.

In the wine heartlands of Europe, especially France, winemakers are scared to death of that trend. This is not because they think their wine isn't as good as the best from California or South Australia, but because they don't traditionally call their wines Cabernet Sauvignon or Chardonnay. They call them Château Ducru-Beaucaillou or Corton-Charlemagne, and they aren't about to change.

Wine consumption was also given a significant boost in the early 1990s by the pioneering work of Dr Serge Renaud, a nutritionist based at Lyon, who has spent many years investigating the reasons for the uncannily low incidence of coronary heart disease in the south of France. One of his findings is that the fat-derived cholesterol that builds up in the arteries can be dispersed by the antioxidants in wine.

Champagne has its own story, but where it once had the field almost to itself, with other sparkling wines being seen as cheap and usually nasty imitations, it must now try its luck in the marketplace against products that have, in recent years, improved beyond recognition.

Fortified wines

There is one important difference between fortified wines and ordinary table wines. The former have all been strengthened with spirit: usually grape spirit. None of these types of wine could have existed before the discovery of distillation.

In most cases, the creation of the classic fortified wines was a chance discovery made while trying to find ways of preserving ordinary wines. It wasn't that some bright spark in Portugal once thought, "Let's add some brandy to our wines and see what they taste like." The addition of spirit was

Below: Flor yeast growing on the surface of fino sherry. The yeast forms spontaneously and protects the wine from air. The yeast cells are nourished by oxygen, with new ones continuously being formed.

Above: Krug Grande Cuvée bottles, stored in candlelit cellars in Reims, France.

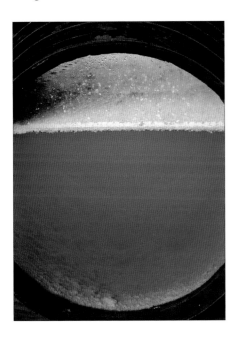

intended to keep wines on the arduous sea voyages they had to undergo to their customers abroad.

In the days when the chemistry of fermentation was not so well understood, wine was often shipped in a micro-biologically unstable state. Its fermentation may have been interrupted by a sudden drop in the cellar temperature, as opposed to having run its natural course. When such wines arrived at their destinations, it was found that they had begun re-fermenting or, worse, that they would re-ferment after being bottled.

The yeasts that ferment in grape juice can only work as long as the amount of alcohol generated doesn't exceed a certain level, which is usually estimated to be in the range of 16 to 17% ABV. After that, they die off, and the wine becomes stable. If you add a healthy dose of brandy or other spirit to wine that has apparently finished fermenting, you raise the alcohol level to such a degree that the yeasts are killed off.

The normal strength of unfortified table wines is in the region of 11 to 13% ABV. But 15% is the *starting* point for fortified wines, and they can be fortified to a maximum of 22%, putting them not far off the strength of the average liqueur.

Each of the world's classic fortified wines has its own particular method of production. The majority are made from white grapes, the most notable exception being port, most of which is red. They tend to be sweet, but don't have to be; fino and manzanilla sherry are the driest of the dry. Most of them contain only wine and grape spirit, but in the case of vermouth and related products, a whole bunch of aromatizing ingredients (familiar to us from some of the herbal liqueurs) creates a style that is halfway between a fortified wine and a liqueur.

By the time the 19th century dawned, most of these wines were seen as premium products. Vintage port and madeira, in particular, were as highly acclaimed as claret and burgundy. Since that time a progressive decline has taken place, as international tastes in wine have tended towards the dry and light end of the spectrum, and away from the sort of sinew-stiffening brew to be sipped by the fireside on winter nights.

Despite that, there will always be a place for the traditional fortified wines. They are unique styles of wine.

White, red and rosé wines

The three colours that unfortified table wines come in all require different production processes.

White wines

Of the three colours of wine, white is the simplest of all to make, precisely because it has no colour. When the ripe grapes are harvested, they are brought to the winery, and immediately de-stemmed and crushed to extract the first (and best) juice from them. After that, they are likely to be treated to a slightly heavier pressing, and then the juice is separated off from all the solid matter, such as skins, pips, leaves, etc.

The juice must be stored at low temperatures, to minimize the risk of spoilage through oxidation. While standing, any remaining minute, solid particles settle to the bottom and thus clarify the juice; the process can be speeded up artificially by subjecting it to centrifugal force. The fermentation of white wine takes place at much lower temperatures than that of reds, typically around 12–18°C/54–64°F, which means that it tends to be a fairly slow process.

At some stage, the wine may be encouraged to undergo a secondary type of fermentation to the sort that turns grape juice into alcohol. This is called the malolactic fermentation, and is useful for converting hard-tasting malic acid, with which grape juice is naturally abundant, into softer, creamier lactic acid. Some white wines are better off with a noticeable bite to them, and for those, the winemaker will take positive steps to avoid a malolactic fermentation, usually by keeping the temperature low.

The final decision is whether to bottle the wine as it is, or give it a period of ageing in oak barrels, which adds spiciness and richness to the finished product. If so, the wine may well be left on its lees (fermentation

Above left: Mâcon-Villages Chardonnay is a white wine from Burgundy.

Above middle: Orvieto Classico comes from Italy's Umbria region.

Above right: An Italian white wine from the Marches region.

sediments) to acquire extra character, and a periodic stirring up of the settled gunge with a wooden paddle helps to maximize that effect. Before bottling, the wine is generally subjected to a final filtration to ensure that it is absolutely bright and clear, but this has become a contentious issue in recent years, with some authorities feeling that it strips the wine of too much of its character.

Among the widely used international white grape varieties, whose names have become increasingly familiar, are: Chardonnay, Sauvignon Blanc, Sémillon, Riesling, Chenin Blanc, Gewürztraminer, Viognier and the various members of the Muscat family.

Left: Different styles of wine need different glasses, but the middle one here is the classic shape.

Below: Villa Montes Sauvignon Blanc from Chile is one of the band of southern hemisphere varietal wines that have taken Europe by storm.

Red wines

Making red wine is a more complicated process in that the grape juice has to be dyed. The skins of the grapes may be red (or deep purple, to be precise), but their juice is as colourless as that of white grapes. The colour has therefore to be put into the wine by leaching it out of the skins.

When the grapes have been de-stemmed and crushed, and perhaps pressed as well, the mass of smashed skins and pips is left sitting in the juice. A period of cold soaking before the fermentation begins is now common practice. It is thought to emphasize the wine's fruitiness, and to encourage the development of good, ripe fruit tannin which, together with acidity, will give the wine the structure to age well.

Red wine is fermented at higher temperatures than white: generally in the 25–30°C/77–86°F range, although some reds are allowed to go higher than this. The mass of skins, known as the pomace, is left in the fermenting juice. Of course, it's not doing any good merely floating on the surface, and so either the pomace is punched down manually a couple of times a day, or a device is used that pumps wine from the bottom of the vat over the floating cap of skins to give the fermenting juice the benefit of it. Malolactic fermentation is automatically carried out for the vast majority of red wines.

After the fermentation, the wine may be allowed a further few days of sitting in contact with the skins, before they are removed, and the wine transferred to its maturation vessel. This can be either stainless steel or oak, as in the case of white wine. Premium reds may be kept for a year or more in barrels in the winery cellar, during the course of which they may pick up more tannin (of a different kind, though, this time, from the wood) and undergo a very gentle process of oxygenation. Some reds are meant to be aged by the buyer; others, such as Spanish Reserva quality reds, have been aged for you by the winemaker, and are intended to be drunk on release.

Major international red grape varieties are: Cabernet Sauvignon, Merlot, Pinot Noir, Shiraz (or Syrah, as it is known in France) and Grenache. Grapes of importance in their homelands, but with international reputations, are the Gamay of Beaujolais, Spain's Tempranillo, Italy's Sangiovese and Nebbiolo, California's Zinfandel and South Africa's Pinotage.

Rosé wines

Rosé wine is basically a partially made red. It achieves its pale tint by virtue of the fact that the skins of the red grapes are only allowed a short maceration in the juice (usually less than 24 hours) before being removed. Some pink wine is made as an off-cut of a serious red, in that a little of the juice is siphoned off after the maceration has begun, with the rest going on to turn into fully fledged red.

In the case of pink champagne, a kind of cheat's approach has been sanctioned by the French wine authorities. The colour is attained by simply adding a slug of ready-made red wine to the finished white. If that sounds a little sloppy for a product as illustrious as champagne, rest assured that it is preferable to the colouring materials that were resorted to in the 19th century. The alternative method is to allow a short maceration period on the skins. Such a wine is said to have been *saignée*, or bled, but the technique is used for only about 2% of all pink champagne on the market. Although those who use it dispute the fact, the taste is essentially the same.

Below left: Chianti Classico comes from Tuscany in central Italy.

Below middle: Campo Viejo is a Rioja from northern Spain.

Below right: Château Saint-Maurice is from France's southern Rhône valley.

Champagne and sparkling wines

Although it was the winemakers of the Champagne region itself who perfected the various techniques indelibly associated with producing quality sparkling wines the world over, they would not have done so had the metropolitan English not developed a taste for deliberately spoiled wine. Effervescence in the wine was considered an exasperating liability in the cold, unforgiving northerly climate of Champagne.

The problem arose when the slow fermentation of the delicate and high-acid wines was interrupted by plummeting cellar temperatures as winter came on. When the time came

Below left: Moët & Chandon, from Epernay, is the world's most famous champagne.

Below right: Bollinger comes from the tiny Champagne village of Ay.

to bottle the wines the following spring, there was very often a certain amount of residual sugar left over from the uncompleted fermentation. As the weather warmed up again, the yeasts that had lain dormant in the wine over the winter now came back to life in the bottle and began feeding on the sugars once more. This time, however, the carbon dioxide gas that the fermentation process creates had no means of escape, so it dissolved into the wine until such time as the bottle came to be opened.

The British trade had, for sometime, been used to adding brandy and a little sugar to the wines it imported because it was the only way to save them from turning rank during the long sea voyages they had to endure. Champagne was the only wine, with the possible exception of burgundy, not to undergo this treatment as a matter of course, for the simple reason that, being the closest fine wine region to the British Isles, the journey was nowhere near as arduous as that made by other wines.

Since there was a marked British predilection, however, for sweetness and potency in wine, some merchants undoubtedly added a little sugar and a slug of spirit to the wines they brought in from Champagne as well. Given the fact that many of the wines were biologically unstable to begin with, this treatment, followed by early bottling, would have virtually assured anything from gentle *pétillance* to volcanic eruption when the bottle was broached.

Unbeknown to itself, the London demi-monde, having a rollicking good time drinking fashionable fizz in the cafés and playhouses, was assiduously

Left: Charles Heidsieck Brut Réserve is one of the richer and rounder styles of dry champagne.

developing the image that the champagne industry has traded on for most of the last three centuries. Fizzy wine is fun, and so champagne came to play a matchless role in partying and celebration.

If you visit the headquarters of the largest and most famous champagne producer of all, Moët & Chandon, in Epernay, you will encounter a rather stern-looking statue in the forecourt. It stands in commemoration of Dom Pérignon, a Benedictine monk who, in 1668, was appointed treasurer at the Abbey of Hautvillers near the town of Epernay, now the nerve centre of the region as a whole.

HOW TO SERVE

Champagne should be served in tall, narrow glasses known as flutes to minimize dispersal of its fizz, as the bubbles have a smaller surface area on which to break. Avoid the flat "saucer" glasses.

Among Dom Pérignon's formidable achievements were the perfecting of the technique of making a still white wine entirely from red grapes; the refinement of the art of blending wines from different vineyards in the region to obtain the best possible product from available resources; and advances in clarification treatments to ensure a brighter wine than was the turbid norm at the time.

Dom Pérignon also devoted much effort to researching ways of avoiding the dreaded re-fermentation that resulted in so many turbulent wines. His seminal place in the region's history is unquestionably merited, but not as the inventor of sparkling champagne.

As the process for making sparkling wines was rationalized, the inducement of the all-important second fermentation in the bottle was achieved by the addition of a little sugar solution to an already fully fermented wine. This then gave the surviving yeasts something more to chew over. The drawback to this was that the sediment of dead yeast cells then created remained trapped in the wine and gave it the cloudiness that Dom Pérignon had worked so hard to prevent. The house of Veuve Clicquot, founded in 1772, may take the credit for the solution to that particularly sticky problem.

Nicole-Barbe Clicquot-Ponsardin took over the running of the firm after her husband, the founder's son, left her widowed in her twenties. It was the development under her tutelage of the process of remuage that installed her unassailably in the region's hall of fame. By this method, the bottles are slowly tipped over a number of weeks, and the sediment gradually sinks

Right: Bluff Hill from New Zealand is typical of the sparklers now challenging French champagne.

towards the neck of the bottle until it all collects on the underside of the cap.

In time, the way to remove the accumulated deposit came to involve dipping the necks of the bottles in freezing brine so that the portion of wine containing the sediment is flash-frozen. When the metal cap is knocked away, the deposit flies out with it and the bottle is topped up and corked.

With the coming of prosperity after the Second World War, champagne began very gradually to trickle down the social scale and become less of a luxury. The industry lost its way somewhat in the 1980s when consumption in the UK reached unprecedented levels to coincide with relatively benign economic times. Some members of its controlling body felt that the wine was in danger of becoming too democratic and losing its aura of elite unaffordability. A more or less explicit attempt to ration consumption, using the sledgehammer of price inflation, was just beginning to work when the coming of severe recession did the job for them.

By the mid-1990s, champagne sales were once more on a gentle upward trajectory as prices moderated and a new quality charter came into effect to ensure that Champagne didn't just idly trade on its good name by selling wafer-thin, razor-sharp, watery wines as it had been tempted to do during the boom years. As a result, it is again possible to say that, when they play to the peak of their form, these are indeed the finest sparkling wines made anywhere.

Styles of champagne include: basic non-vintage (the flagship wine of each house); vintage-dated wine (the product of a single year's harvest); blanc de blancs (made only from Chardonnay grapes); blanc de noirs (made from either

Above left: Freixenet Cava comes from northern Spain, but is made by the same method as champagne.

Above right: Hardy's Nottage Hill Chardonnay Brut is a popular sparkling wine made in Australia.

or both the black grapes Pinot Noir and Pinot Meunier); and rosé. Brut is the classic ultra-dry style, Doux is distinctly sweet and Demi-Sec lies between the two.

Most champagne is released on to the market too young. In France, they rather like the rapier-like acidity of youthful champagne, but the British taste is for something softer and rounder. If you have the resources (a dark cupboard will do), it is always worth ageing it for some time. Six months will soften a non-vintage fizz considerably; a year is even better. Vintage-dated champagne should ideally not be breached at less than eight years old.

Port

Although it is one of the major fortified wines, port is the only example to be based on a red wine. True, there is such a thing as white port, but it accounts for only a fraction of the production. Port hails from only one delimited area, the Douro valley in northern Portugal. So popular has it traditionally been as a style of wine, that many non-European wine-making countries have been trying their hands at port lookalikes since the 19th century. The difference today is that, in the countries of the European Union at least, such products are no longer allowed to be called port.

The drink originated during one of the frequent periods of hostilities between the English and the French in the 17th century, as a consequence of which the English authorities declared a punitive tax levy on goods imported from France. This hit the wine trade hard. Wine shippers had to look to Portugal, England's oldest European ally, with whom there were preferential trade tariffs, to supply their customers. Journeying inland along the river Douro, the English merchants happened upon the fierce red wines of the region and found them pretty much to the domestic taste. As was common practice at the time, they fortified them with a little brandy for the sea voyage.

Thus was port born. Originally, it was of course a dry wine, since these were fully fermented wines that were being augmented with brandy. However, it took only the chance discovery of the effects of fortification on an extremely ripe, sweet wine to remodel port in the image with which we are familiar today. To preserve that sweetness, the wines would have their normal fermentation interrupted (or "muted") with brandy, so that some of the grape sugars would remain unconsumed by the yeasts.

Left: Cockburn's Vintage Port bears the year of its harvest on the label, and must be aged by the buyer.

Eventually, it was considered that using a simple, local grape spirit was cheaper than buying fine cognac for the fortification. Also, port was coming to be seen as a fine wine in its own right, and so it was desirable that the fortifying agent should be as neutral as possible, in order to allow the characteristics of the underlying wine to be shown off.

Port styles have since multiplied almost infinitely. At the top of the quality tree are the vintage ports, wines of a single year that must be bottled within two years of the harvest and are intended for long ageing. Late-bottled vintage (LBV) is also the product of a single year, but one that has been kept in cask in the shipper's premises for longer – around six years usually – in order to be more mature on bottling, and readier to drink on purchase. Vintage Character port is an everyday blended product and nothing special, while the fine old tawny ports are often aged for many years in barrel so that their initial full-blooded red fades to an autumnal brown.

Other countries producing good port-style fortified wines are Australia (where the favoured grape variety is the spicy Shiraz), South Africa and the United States. There is a very good

Right: Late Bottled Vintage Port matured in the cellars of the shipper.

Far right: Graham's Six Grapes is a sound blend of red wines from six different grape varieties.

Greek fortified red called Mavrodaphne that makes an agreeable alternative to the more basic offerings of the Douro.

How it is made
The fermentation of Douro wines is stopped part-way through by the addition of grape spirit, to produce a sweet, strong, liquorous wine. Various periods of cask-ageing are given to the various grades. The bottled strength is in the region of 18–20%, but can be as high as 22%.

Tastes good with
Port is excellent with nuts and with mature, strong hard cheeses, such as Cheddar, but less good with its traditional partner, Stilton, when the tannins in it always seem to me to clash. Some drink it with chocolate – I couldn't possibly comment.

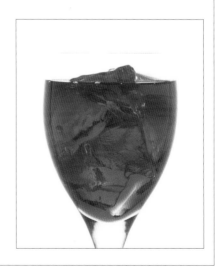

Far left: Taylor's 20 Years Old is a fine example of a cask-aged port, in which the average age of the wine in the blend is 20 years.

Second from left: Cockburn's Fine Ruby is a good, simple, everyday port from one of the most widely known of the English shippers.

Third from left: Quinta do Crasto is an LBV from a small Portuguese producer. Such ports will always have a vintage year on the label, but are released a few years later than true vintage ports.

Left: Quady's Batch 88 Starboard is a Californian fortified wine made in punning homage to port. It is sweet and fruity, and can be drunk in much the same way, with mature cow's-milk cheeses.

HOW TO SERVE

Good port should be served in wine glass quantities, rather than in silly little liqueur glasses. It should be served unchilled, except in the case of white port. Older wines that have thrown a sediment may need to be decanted.

Although it may seem to have an assertive (even, in the case of the basic grades, aggressive) flavour, port is surprisingly useful in the cocktail repertoire. It is inevitably best mixed with other grape products, perhaps with a dash of

best cognac for a simple digestif cocktail, or maybe with unfortified red wine and brandy for something a little racier, when it's best to throw in a lump or two of ice as well. If you can stretch to it, a good LBV is probably best for mixing.

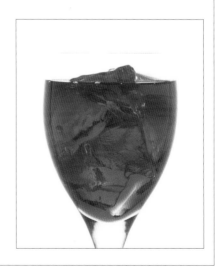

Sherry

Although fortified wines bearing the name of sherry have been produced around the world for well over a century, true sherry comes only from a demarcated region in the southern Spanish province of Andalucía. There are three main centres of production: Jerez de la Frontera, Puerto de Santa María and Sanlúcar de Barrameda. The last is the traditional home of a type of pale, delicate, notably tangy dry sherry called manzanilla.

The production process for sherry is one of the most complicated of any fortified wine. When the new white wine is made, it is fermented until fully dry, and then transferred into large butts. Some sherries, those that are destined

Below left: Tio Pepe's Muy Seco is the very driest style of sherry.

Below right: Harvey's Bristol Cream is a big-selling brown cream sherry.

HOW TO SERVE

Fino and manzanilla, and the sweetened pale sherries, should be served very well chilled, preferably from a freshly opened bottle. In Spain, they think nothing of drinking a bottle of dry sherry as we would a table wine. The other styles should be served at room temperature. Finos are brilliant aperitifs; old olorosos are best at the other end of the meal.

to end up as the pale dry styles known as fino or manzanilla, develop a film of yeast culture called *flor* on the surface of the wine. In some barrels, the layer of *flor* dies out because it has consumed all the remaining nutrients in the wine, whereupon it breaks up and sinks to the bottom of the butt. With the subsequent greater exposure to the air, the colour of the wine deepens through oxidation, and the style known as amontillado results.

Some wines develop no *flor* at all and go on to turn a deep, woody brown colour. These are oloroso sherries. The fortification of the wine varies according to the style. Fino may be fortified to only 15% ABV, whereas oloroso is generally bottled at around 20%. At this stage, all of the wines are naturally dry, and some – the true connoisseur's sherries – will be bottled in that condition after ageing in cask.

Many commercial sherries, however, are made sweet by the addition of a quantity of *mistela*, the juice of raisined

grapes to which grape spirit has been added. The best sweet sherries are sweetened with PX, which stands for Pedro Ximénez, the name of a grape variety whose berries are left to dry in the sun until loss of moisture has concentrated their sugars to an almost unbelievable degree. Some houses bottle some of their PX separately as a speciality product.

Other countries that produce sherry-style wines are Australia (which makes about the best outside Jerez), the United States, South Africa and Cyprus. Within Spain itself, there are two other regions near Jerez that produce similar fortified wines in the same range of styles, but they are not as distinguished as sherry. One is the distinctly cheaper Montilla-Morilés, the other the virtually forgotten Condado de Huelva.

Spain's other great, now sadly nearly extinct, fortified wine is Málaga, made around the Mediterranean port of that name. Its finest wines are deep brown, caramel-sweet creations of great power, once hugely popular in Britain, but now forsaken by the vagaries of fashion.

Tastes good with

Dry sherries are good with salted nuts such as almonds, piquant nibbles such as olives, salty fish like anchovies, and Serrano ham or its Mediterranean equivalents. The sweet old olorosos are wonderful with rich, dark fruitcake and hard Spanish sheep's-milk cheeses such as the tangily salty Manchego.

Right: Emva Cream is a Cypriot wine, no longer labelled as "sherry".

Madeira

Of all the classic fortified wines of southern Europe, madeira is the one with the most singular history. It comes from the island of the same name in the Atlantic Ocean, slightly nearer to the coast of North Africa than it is to that of Portugal, of which it is an autonomously governed region.

The evolution of this wine belongs to the days of the trading ships that plied the East India routes in the late 17th century. Madeira's geographical position made it a natural port of call for north European vessels on their way to Africa and the East Indies, and so they would load up with wine at the port of Funchal, the island

Right: Sercial is the palest and driest style of madeira.

Above: Verdelho is the second driest style; this five-year-old madeira is only very slightly sweet.

Left: Rich Malmsey is the sweetest style of madeira.

There are four basic styles of madeira, named after their grape varieties. The palest and driest style is sercial. Then comes verdelho, a little sweeter and darker, then bual, and finally malmsey (the last is an English corruption of the Portuguese name Malvasia). The wines are also graded according to how long they have been aged. This is generally given as a minimum age on the label (five-year-old, ten-year-old and so on). Some madeira is vintage-dated, meaning it is the unblended produce of the stated year's harvest.

How it is made

A light, white base wine is made from any of the four main varieties, perhaps supplemented with some juice from the local red grape Tinta Negra Mole. For the sweeter styles, the fermentation may be interrupted by the addition of grape spirit, meaning that some natural sugar remains in them; the drier wines are fermented until more of the sugar has been consumed before being fortified. The wines are then subjected to heat during the cask-ageing, either by one of the heating systems known as an *estufa* (stove), or by being left in the hottest part of the lodge, in which case it is known as a *vinho canteiro*.

Tastes good with

The driest styles present the answer to that age-old problem of what to drink with soup. They are particularly good with clear, meaty consommé. As you proceed to the richer end of the scale, drink them with mince pies, Christmas cake and other dense fruitcake mixes or, of course, madeira cake.

HOW TO SERVE

Serve madeira in a good-sized sherry glass or small wine glass. The drier styles may benefit from a little light chilling, but the richer, darker, sweeter styles, with their overtones of treacle toffee and Christmas cake, should be served at room temperature.

capital. It gradually came to be noticed that, whereas many more delicate table wines would be badly spoiled by the combination of violent shaking and the torrid heat in which they travelled the oceans, madeiras were eerily improved by the experience.

Eventually, it wasn't financially practical to keep treating the wine to a round-the-world cruise, and so the tortuous heat it endured at sea was recreated in the wineries or "lodges". Some madeira, known as *canteiro*, is heated simply by being left under the roof of the lodge to bake in the heat of the tropical sun. Some is stored in rooms where fat central-heating pipes radiate heat throughout the summer, and even the lowest grades are matured in vats that have hot-water pipes running through them.

Marsala

Sicily's very own fortified wine is named after the town of Marsala, in the province of Trapani at the western end of the island. Like many of the fortified wines of southern Europe, it has an English connection. It was effectively invented by a wine merchant, John Woodhouse, in 1773, in direct imitation of the sherry and madeira in which he was something of a specialist. He simply added a quantity of ordinary brandy to the traditional white wines of western Sicily, and found on shipping them that the result was a reasonably close approximation of the already established fortified wines.

Woodhouse founded a commercial operation on the island at the end of the 18th century, and won valuable orders from the British Royal Navy, among others. Marsala was carried on Nelson's ships during the hostilities with France, and the wine's reputation quickly spread. Although the early trade was dominated by English merchants, Italians themselves eventually got in on the act. The first significant house of Italian origin was Florio, founded in 1832.

The rules and regulations governing the production of marsala were only finally codified in 1969, and are considerably more flexible than those controlling the manufacture of the other famous fortified wines. Perhaps

Left: Terre Arse is a vintage-dated marsala from Florio.

Above left: Secco is the driest and lightest style of marsala.

Above right: Dolce is best suited for classic Italian desserts.

the least satisfactory aspect of them is the nature of the sweetening agent that may be added. It can be either a fortified grape juice, or just grape juice whose sweetness has been concentrated by cooking. This latter ingredient, known in Italian as *mosto cotto*, is not in itself alcoholic. The best marsalas have natural sweetness from ripe grapes, which is retained through interrupted fermentation.

Marsala is classified by age (Fine is one year old, Superiore two, Superiore Riserva four, Vergine five, Stravecchio ten), as well as by sweetness. Dry is labelled *secco*, medium-dry *semisecco* and the sweetest *dolce*. It also comes in three colours. The better grades are both shades of tawny, either amber (*ambra*) or golden (*oro*), but there is a red version too (*rubino*).

How it is made

Light white wines from local grape varieties Grillo, Inzolia and Catarratto are turned into marsala by one of three methods. They can be fortified with grape spirit in the traditional way, or sweetened and strengthened with either alcohol-boosted juice from ultra-sweet, late-ripened grapes or with cooked grape juice concentrate. Concentrate is only permitted in ambra marsala. The wines are then cask-aged for varying periods.

Tastes good with

Marsala has come to be seen as even more of a kitchen ingredient than madeira. It is indispensable as the alcohol element in both zabaglione and tiramisu, and makes a sticky brown sauce to go with scallopini of veal.

HOW TO SERVE

Dry and medium-dry marsala, of which there is a regrettably small amount, should be served chilled in generously sized sherry glasses as an aperitif. The sweetest styles should be served at room temperature as digestifs or with certain types of old, dry cheese.

Muscat and Moscatel

Sweet fortified wines are made from Muscat all over the world. It is easy to imagine Muscat as a single grape variety, but it is in fact a family. Some of its offshoots are of the highest pedigree, notably a type the French call Muscat Blanc à Petits Grains. Others, such as Muscat of Alexandria and Muscat Ottonel, are of humbler extraction, and give correspondingly less exciting wines. Moscatel is the name the family assumes on the Iberian peninsula, in Portugal and Spain.

Australian liqueur Muscats

These are hugely rich, strong, fortified Muscats made in and around the town of Rutherglen, in north-west Victoria. They are produced by a method that seems to combine a little of all the ways of making fortified wine. The grapes are

Left: A Moscatel de Valencia sold in a bottle that is highly ornate for a very simple drink.

left to overripen and shrivel on the vine, so that they are halfway to becoming raisins. After pressing, they ferment part-way, but the fermentation is arrested by fortification with grape spirit, keeping massive quantities of natural sugar in the wine. The cask-ageing they then receive combines elements of the *solera* system used in Spanish brandy and sherry, with the action of searing sunshine, as in the *canteiro* madeiras.

Vin doux naturel Muscats

A group of Muscat wines made in southern France are made by virtually the same method as port. Their collective name, *vins doux naturels*, means "naturally sweet wines". The grapes are picked very ripe and the normal process of fermentation is stopped by the addition of a powerful grape spirit, so the natural grapey sweetness of Muscat is retained. There are six appellations for this type of wine, the most famous of which is Muscat de Beaumes de Venise from the southern Rhône.

Four of the others – Muscat de Frontignan, de Lunel, de Mireval and de St Jean de Minervois – are in the Languedoc, while the sixth, Muscat de Rivesaltes, is grown even further south, in Roussillon near the Spanish border. De Rivesaltes does not have to be made from the noblest Muscat, and the quality varies hugely. The best are honeyed and orangey; the worst cloyingly sweet like barley sugar.

Left: This 20-year-old Moscatel is made on western Portugal's Setúbal peninsula.

Left: This Muscat de Beaumes de Venise is made by Domaine de Coyeux, one of the best producers of Muscat.

Setúbal Moscatel

This is a traditional fortified wine based on the Muscat of Alexandria grape, together with a couple of its more obscure cousins. It is made on the Setúbal peninsula in western Portugal, and was recognized as a regionally demarcated wine in the early 20th century. The process is the same as for *vin doux naturel*, except that after fortification, the grape skins are allowed to macerate in the finished wine for several months. Some Setúbal Moscatel is released after five years or so, when its colour is already a vivid orange from the wood. Other wines are aged for a couple of decades, deepening to burnished mahogany.

Moscatel de Valencia

Around Valencia, on the eastern coast of Spain, they make what the French would call a *vin de liqueur*, that is, an unfermented grape juice fortified with grape spirit. Moscatel de Valencia is not made from the most distinguished Muscat variety. When very well chilled, it can be a pretty refreshing drink, particularly in the stunning heat of a Spanish summer.

Jerepigo

Jerepigo is the South African version of Moscatel de Valencia, except that it uses the aristocratic Muscat Blanc à Petits Grains variety, here known as Muscadel or Muskadel. Otherwise, the production is the same, with grape spirit being added to the very sweet, freshly pressed grape juice. Vintages of Jerepigo are occasionally released at around 15 years old, and are found to retain much of their initial freshness. Don't expect great complexity though: because these aren't fermented wines, they don't mature in the same way.

Vermouth

As far removed from the natural produce of the vine as it is possible for a fortified wine to get, vermouth is not only strengthened with spirit, but also heavily aromatized with herbs and botanical ingredients. The result is a distinctive type of drink intended for drinking as an aperitif, either mixed or straight. It is an everyday product made to a consistent and unchanging recipe by each manufacturer.

The presence in vermouth of such a cocktail of herbs and roots alerts us to the fact that this was originally a

Below left: Noilly Prat is a bone-dry vermouth produced in the south of France.

Below right: Martini Extra Dry is the top brand of vermouth internationally.

medicinal drink. A popular early additive was wormwood, villain of the piece when absinthe was outlawed, yet much prized as a tonic for the stomach, from classical antiquity to medieval times and the beginnings of distillation in Europe.

To find a drink identifiable as the precursor of modern vermouth, we have to travel back to the 16th century to find a merchant called d'Alessio selling a wormwood wine in Piedmont (north-west Italy). The inspiration had come from similar German products, produced on a domestic scale, and it is from the German word for wormwood, *Wermuth*, that the modern English word is derived. It was already popular in England by the middle years of the following century.

Two centres of vermouth production came to be established. One was in d'Alessio's part of Italy, close to the alpine hills where the botanical ingredients that went into the wine were sourced, and the other over the border in south-east France. As the big commercial companies were founded, two distinct styles of vermouth emerged: one pale and dry with pronounced bitterness; the other red and sweet and not quite so bitter. The former was the style associated with France, the latter with Italy. So ingrained did these definitions become that, even now, drinkers still use the terms "French" and "Italian" to mean dry and sweet respectively, when these may not necessarily always be the geographical origins.

In fact, sweet and dry vermouths are made in both of these countries, as well as elsewhere, including the United States. Brands vary according to the number and type of the herbal ingredients added, but the basic style remains the same from one batch to the next. Cloves, cinnamon, quinine, citrus rinds, ginger, and perhaps a touch of wormwood are typical elements in the potpourri of

HOW TO SERVE
A drop or two only of dry French vermouth is needed for the perfect dry Martini or Vodkatini. All these drinks should be served as aperitifs or at the cocktail hour. Vermouth is not as fragile once opened as pale dry sherry tends to be. It doesn't have to be drunk within a few days, and is able to withstand extremes of temperature far more hardily than the other light fortified wines.

aromatizers that goes to create the distinctive flavours of modern vermouths.

As with many of the traditional liqueurs, the medicinal image of vermouth was, by the onset of the 20th century, something of an albatross around its neck, rather than a marketing opportunity. It was once again the cocktail era that rode to its rescue, finding multifarious uses for both styles of vermouth. After all, if the traditional dry Martini was destined to be the only use to which dry vermouth could be put behind the bar, one drop at a time, then it was not going to sell in very large quantities. Because it is quite as perfumed, in its way, as gin, vermouth proved hugely versatile in a range of mixed drinks, and the demand for it today, which is thanks in part to the big proprietary brands, remains reasonably steady.

The bulk-producing Italian firm of Martini e Rossi, based at Turin, is still the vermouth name that springs most readily to mind for consumers today. Other Italian producers are Riccadonna, Cinzano and Gancia. In France, the Marseillan producer Noilly Prat makes one of the more highly regarded dry vermouths, although it also has a sweeter style. The region of Chambéry in eastern France has been awarded the *appellation contrôlée* for its vermouths, which include a strawberry-flavoured fruit version called Chambéryzette. As well as red and white styles of vermouth, there is a golden or amber variant, and a rosé.

Other similar branded products include Lillet of Bordeaux, owned by one of the high-ranking claret châteaux, which blends a proportion of fruit juice with the wine base along with the customary herbs; the French Dubonnet, a red or white sweet vermouth also full of highly appetizing quinine bitterness; and Punt e Mes, a similar but dark-coloured Italian product that combines sweetening and bittering elements in an intriguing balance. These are all, without exception, products that deserve a wider audience. They are versatile cocktail ingredients that also happen to be supremely appetizing on their own.

Left: Cinzano Bianco is a hugely popular brand of sweet white vermouth.

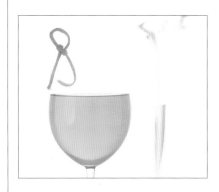

How it is made
A low-alcohol, and mostly white, wine is produced and may be allowed a short period of ageing. For the sweeter styles of vermouth, it then has a quantity of sugar syrup added to it before the fortification with spirit. This is usually grape spirit but may occasionally also be derived from vegetable sources such as sugar beet. The wine is then transferred into large barrels or tanks to which the dried aromatizing ingredients have already been added. From time to time, the mixture is stirred manually with wooden paddles. After the absorption of the flavourings, the vermouth will be bottled at around 17% ABV. Some producers insist that their vermouths will continue to age in the bottle for a couple of years if kept.

Tastes good with
Dry vermouths are particularly useful in the kitchen for adding to sauces to accompany fish. The herbal ingredients in the vermouth add an attractive savoury note to the dish. A seasoned reduction of Noilly Prat, lemon juice and single (light) cream is a fine way to treat good white fish such as sole or turbot. Try marinating chunks of monkfish in dry white vermouth.

Above left: A red version of vermouth, such as Dubonnet, mixes well with lemonade.

Above right: Carpano Punt e Mes is a deep red vermouth produced at Turin.

HOW TO SERVE
As one might expect, given the precedent of the classic Dry Martini, vermouth mixes superbly with gin in cocktails. It happily takes a dash of absinthe too, and gets along well with the herbal liqueurs such as Chartreuse, Glayva and Bénédictine.

BEER

An ancient drink with a chequered and varied history, beer has been used by preachers as a religious symbol, by doctors as a medicinal treatment and by workers as a means of relaxation after a hard day's toil. Throughout the ages, in different countries, beer has been both promoted as a health drink and reviled as the draught of the devil.

The brewing industry has changed fundamentally since the early medieval ale wives brewed in their kitchens, and it has been much affected by advances in technology. Now the centre of one of the largest multinational industries, beer is shipped around the globe, with large companies often producing their brews thousands of miles from home, but there is thankfully still room for the small-scale producer in today's richly varied marketplace.

The huge range of beers that is drunk all over the world is dazzling, as is the variety of customs associated with it. A glass of beer does not just mean a sparkling golden lager, familiar in every land. It could be a stout or a black beer, a weisse, a barley wine, a porter or a doppelbock.

Tasting beer

Good beer should never be rushed. Take the trouble to pour the beer carefully into a clean glass, ensuring a reasonable head, and then savour the aroma. Some have a subtle scent; others can be almost overpowering. When tasting, let the beer flow over your palate to pick up all the different taste sensations, savouring the flavours left behind after swallowing. A good beer should linger on the palate.

Generally, the best beer of most styles is hand-pumped, and the closer the pub or bar is to the brewery, the better the beer. It is at the heart of the community in many countries, whether it is served in a cosy English pub, a huge German beer cellar, a packed Czech bar or a roadside bar in Africa. Tasting local beer is often a good way to meet the locals, who will probably know where to find the best brews.

Styles of beer

It is only recently that beer has begun to be discussed with the same degree of attention that wine receives. Beer is at best a fine balance of malted grain and hops. There are different hop varieties, just as there are varieties of wine grapes, and there are many distinct styles of malt, as well as different cereal grains. Even spices are sometimes added.

There are basically two main beer categories: ale (or top-fermented beer, where the yeast rises to the top during fermentation) and lager (bottom-fermented, where the yeast eventually sinks). Within these, there are many different styles, ranging from dark, hearty ales to tangy, spritzy Belgian beers. Here is a lightning tour of some of the most famous varieties.

Abbey beers

Strong fruity ales, abbey beers are brewed in Belgium by commercial companies, sometimes under licence from religious communities. They copy the style of the surviving beers produced in monasteries, or name their brews after a church or saint.

Below: Ale is a convenient, catch-all term that is generally used to mean beer made using top-fermenting yeast. These are some of the many varieties.

Above: Examples of abbey beers – Leffe from Interbrew, Grimbergen from the Union Brewery and Maredsous from Moortgat. La Trappe is a Trappist beer.

Ale

Nowadays this is a vague term meaning any top-fermented beer. It is one of the two main branches of the beer family, the other being lager. Of the two, ale is the older, dating back thousands of years. England is the country where ales are now most commonly brewed.

Alt

This is the German word meaning "traditional" or "old", and in the context of Altbier it indicates a bitter-tasting brew produced by the ancient style of brewing using top-fermentation. Alt is a copper-coloured aromatic ale, made in the city of Düsseldorf and a few other cities in northern Germany. It is a firm-bodied but quite bitter beer that contains just over 4.5% alcohol.

Barley wine

A powerful, almost syrupy, strong ale, usually sold in small nip-size bottles, is known as barley wine in Britain.

These well-matured brews can be golden or dark in colour. The darker versions of barley wine were once called Stingo.

Berliner Weisse

A light, sharply acidic German wheat beer made predominantly in Berlin, this refreshing brew is relatively low in alcohol and is often laced with a dash of green woodruff or raspberry juice to add colour to its cloudy white (weisse) appearance. Bremer Weisse is a variation from the city of Bremen.

Bière de Garde

A top-fermenting "beer for keeping" from north-west France, this was originally made in farmhouses, but is now made by commercial breweries. This style produces medium to strong, spicy ales; some are bottle-conditioned, and many are sealed with champagne-style wired corks.

Right: Brands of German Altbier include Diebels, Rhenania and the organically produced Pinkus.

Above: Okells is a well-known brand of barley wine.

Bitter

The distinctive style of draught ale in England and Wales is generally served in pubs. It is usually dry and hoppy with an alcohol content of 3–5%. Traditionally reddish amber in colour, paler varieties are now proving popular in England. Stronger versions used to be called Best or Special.

Black beer

In Germany, Schwarzbier is a strong-tasting, bitter-chocolate lager. It is not a stout but a very dark lager and is a speciality of eastern Germany, particularly around Bernau. The town of Kostritz in the former East Germany is noted for its black lager, and Kulmbach and Erlangen are also known for their deep brown beers. This style is also made in Japan.

In England, especially Yorkshire, black beers are strong, pitch-black, treacly malt extracts, usually bottled for mixing with lemonade to make distinctive shandies.

Bock

A strong malty, warming German beer of about 6.5% alcohol, bock was originally brewed for the colder months. Traditionally dark in colour, today it is more likely to be golden-bronze. This powerful smooth brew originated in Einbeck in Lower Saxony, but is now more associated with Bavaria. Bock is also produced in Austria, the Netherlands and other countries surrounding Germany. The word bock means "billy goat", and a goat's head

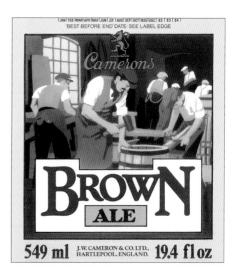

Above, above right and right: Some popular English brown ales – Old Ale from King & Barnes, Camerons, and Moonraker from Gibbs, Mew & Co.

often features on the label. The brew is sometimes linked with seasonal festivals, such as Maibock, which celebrates the arrival of spring. Extra-potent versions are called doppelbocks (and are chiefly associated with Bavaria), with more than 7% alcohol, such as Paulaner Salvator. Eisbocks, in which frozen water is removed from the beer, are even more powerful. This brew (10%) is the speciality of Reichelbrau of Kulmbach.

Brown ale

A sweetish, bottled mild ale, dark in colour and low in alcohol, from England, brown ale was once a popular workers' drink, although sales have declined heavily in recent years. The north-east of the country produces stronger, drier versions, such as the well-known Newcastle Brown Ale.

Left: Bocks were originally drunk by fasting monks because they were considered nutritious.

Belgium boasts its own sweet-and-sour brown ales from East Flanders. The main producer is Liefmans of Oudenaarde. The sour taste comes from a slow simmering rather than a boil, and from the addition of a lactic yeast. Other producers include Cnudde, also of Oudenaarde, the nearby Roman Brewery and Vanden Stock.

Chilli beer

Produced by only a handful of American breweries, this is an odd, slow-burning speciality. The Pike Place Brewery of Seattle produces an occasional Cerveza Rosanna Red Chilli Ale, while the hotter Crazy Ed's Cave Creek Chilli Beer of Phoenix, Arizona, has a whole chilli pod in each bottle. It reputedly goes well with Mexican food.

Cream ale

A sweetish, smooth, golden ale from the United States, cream ale was originally introduced by ale brewers trying to copy the Pilsner style. Some cream ales are made by blending ales with bottom-fermenting beers.

Diät pils

Nothing to do with dieting, diät pils is lager which undergoes a thorough fermentation which removes nearly all the sugars from the bottom-fermented, Pilsner-derived brew. This leaves a strong, dry-tasting beer, which is still packed with calories in the alcohol. It was originally brewed as a beer suitable for diabetics, rather than slimmers. Because it misled many, the word "diät" has now been removed.

Doppelbock

An extra-strong bock beer; doppelbock is not double in strength, but usually around 7.5% alcohol. It is rich and warming. The names of the leading Bavarian brands usually end in "ator", Salvator from Paulaner of Munich, for example.

Dortmunder

A strong, full-bodied export style of lager from Dortmund in Germany, the biggest brewing city in Europe, Dortmunder was originally brewed for export. It was once sold under this name across the globe, but is now declining in popularity. Malty, dry and full-bodied, these brews usually have an alcohol strength of around 5.5%, being firmer and less aromatic than a Pilsner. The leading examples include DAB, Kronen and DUB.

Dry beer

First produced in Japan by the Asahi Brewery in 1987, this is a super diät pils with a parching effect, which was widely adopted in North America. The beer taste is so clean it has been swept away almost entirely through further fermentation.

Above: The widely available and popular premium Pilsner from the Holsten brewery in Germany is one of the firm's famous dry, hoppy range.

Dry beer, in which more of the sugars are turned to alcohol leaving little taste, was developed in Japan and launched in America in 1988. After an initial surge in sales when Anheuser-Busch introduced Bud Dry, the market has faded almost completely away.

Dunkel

German lagers were traditionally dark, as "dunkel" indicates, and these soft, malty brown beers are associated with Munich, often being known as Münchner. Like the paler "hell", they contain around 4.5% alcohol. Most of the major Munich breweries produce a dunkel.

Duppel/Double

This term describes dark, medium-strength Trappist and abbey beers in Belgium, such as Chimay and Orval, which are now copied by some breweries and sold as abbey beers.

Eisbock

An extra-potent bock, eisbock is produced by freezing the brew and removing some of the frozen water to leave behind more concentrated alcohol. The most notable producer is Kulmbacher Reichelbrau in Northern Bavaria. Eisbock is the original ice beer.

Below: A selection of dunkel beers from the Munich area in Germany.

Export

This term was originally used to denote a better-quality beer, worth selling abroad. The Dortmunder style is also known as Dortmunder Export, since it became popular around the world. In Scotland, the term export is widely adopted for premium ales.

Left: Drybroughs Export from Edinburgh is one of the premium beers produced in Scotland.

Faro

Once the most common manifestation of Belgian lambic beer, faro is a weak lambic sweetened with sugar. Now this style has gone out of fashion and has largely disappeared.

Framboise/Frambozen

These are French and Flemish names for a Belgium fruit beer made by adding raspberries to a lambic. Framboise has a sparkling, pink champagne character and the raspberries impart a light, fruity flavour. Because the whole fruit is too soft, producers usually add raspberry syrup. In recent years a whole variety of other fruit juices have been tried, from peaches to bananas, with varying degrees of success.

Ginger beer

Despite its name, this is a refreshing, low- or no-alcohol soft drink flavoured with root ginger. However, long before the hop appeared, ginger was used in beer and some pioneering micro-brewers are trying it again: Salopian in England adds ginger to its dark wheat beer, Gingersnap.

Green beer

Any young beer which has not had time to mature is known as a green beer. The term is also used to denote a beer made with organic malt and hops. Organic green beer is known as biologique in France (where Castelain makes an organic beer called Jade) and biologisch in Germany. In Scotland, the Caledonian Brewery of Edinburgh has pioneered organic ale with Golden Promise.

Left: Several breweries have sprung up producing "green" beer using only organic ingredients.

Gueuze

This is a ripe blend of old and new Belgian lambics. By blending young and old lambics, a secondary fermentation is triggered. The resulting distinctive, sparkling beer, often sold in corked bottles like champagne to withstand the pressure, packs a fruity, sour, dry taste. Blending is such an art that some producers buy in their wort (the unfermented malt infusion). Often this beer is matured for many more months in the bottle. In some cases the secondary fermentation is triggered by the addition of various fruits. Traditionally gueuze should not be filtered, pasteurized or sweetened, though some commercial brands do all three.

Heavy

Scottish brewers use this term to describe a standard strength ale, between a Light and an Export. A "wee heavy" is a bottled strong ale, the wee referring to the small nip-size of the bottle.

Hefe

The German word for yeast is used to describe a beer that is unfiltered, with a sediment in the bottle. Draught beers "mit Hefe" are usually cloudy.

Hell

This word means pale or light in German and indicates a mild, malty golden lager, often from Munich. Notable examples include Hacker-Pschorr and Augustiner.

Honey beer

The Celts and other ancient peoples used to make mead from fermented honey. They also produced a beer, bragot, to which honey was often added as a soft sweetener. A hazy honey brew called Golden Mead Ale was produced in England by Hope & Anchor Breweries of Sheffield, and was widely exported until the early 1960s. Today, a few breweries have revived the style, notably Ward's of Sheffield with Waggle Dance and Enville Ales of Staffordshire. Some new American brewers also use honey, as do the innovative Belgian De Dolle Brouwers in their Boskeun beer.

Ice beer

A chilling innovation of the early 1990s; the brew is frozen during maturation to produce a purified beer, with the ice crystals removed to increase the strength.

Many ice beers were originally developed in Canada by Labatt and contain around 5.5% alcohol. Canadian brewers Labatt and Molson introduced the new beer style in 1993 in which the beer is frozen after fermentation, giving a cleaner, almost smoothed away flavour. Sometimes the ice crystals are removed, concentrating the beer. Most major US brewers have launched their own brands such as Bud Ice and Miller's Icehouse, but ice beer still accounts for less than 4% of the beer market.

In 1996, Tennent's of Scotland produced a Super Ice with a strength of 8.6%.

Imperial stout

See Stout.

IPA

The words behind the initials betray IPA's imperial origins – India Pale Ale. This strong, heavily hopped beer was brewed in Britain, notably in Burton-on-Trent by companies like Allsopp and Bass. The recipe was designed to withstand the long sea voyages to distant parts of the British Empire like India. According to legend, a cargo of 300 casks of Bass's East India Pale Ale was wrecked off the port of Liverpool in 1827. Some of the rescued beer was sold locally and won instant fame among English drinkers. Specialist American brewers

Left: US brewers have followed the Canadian innovation of ice beers and now most of them produce their own versions. Bud Ice is one of the best-known and most popular brands.

like Bert Grant's Yakima Brewing Company now probably produce the most authentic versions.

Irish ale

A soft, slightly sweet reddish ale from the "Emerald Isle". Top and bottom-fermenting versions are brewed commercially. This ale followed many of the Irish in migrating to other lands.

George Killian Letts, a member of the Letts family who brewed Ruby Ale in County Wexford until 1956, licensed the French brewery Pelforth to produce George Killian's Bière Rousse and the American brewers Coors to produce Killian's Irish Red. Smithwick's of Kilkenny (owned by Guinness) is the best-known ale produced in Ireland today.

Kölsch

The refreshing deep-golden sweetish beer from Cologne in Germany may look like a Pilsner (though it may sometimes be cloudy), but its light, subtle fruity taste reveals it to be a top-fermenting ale. Its fleeting aromatic nature masks an alcohol content of 4–5%.

Kölsch is produced only by some 20 breweries in and around the busy cathedral city of Cologne and it is usually served in small glasses. The leading producers include Kuppers and Fruh.

Right: A selection of IPAs.

Kriek

In this Belgian lambic beer, secondary fermentation is stimulated by adding cherries to give a dry, fruity flavour and deep colour. This is not a novelty drink, but draws on a long tradition of using local fruit to flavour an already complex brew, balancing the lambic sourness and providing an almond character from the cherry stones (pits). The kriek is a small dark cherry grown near Brussels. One of the best-known kriekbiers is produced by Liefmans brewery in Oudenaarde. It is a deep, cloudy, red-brown colour and has a strength of 6.5%. It is suitable for keeping for up to four years and will mature as it ages.

Kristall

This term, taken from the German word for a crystal-clear beer, usually indicates a filtered wheat beer or Weizenbier. Erdinger is one of the major producers.

Above: Apart from in Britain, the term lager is used generally for beer.

Lager

This is one of the two main branches of the beer family. The word lager is derived from the German word for "to store". In Britain it refers to any golden, bottom-fermented beer, but elsewhere it has little meaning, apart from a general word for beer.

Lambic

The wild beers of Belgium have their roots deep in history. One of the most primitive beers brewed on earth, these spontaneously fermenting beers are unique to Belgium, or to be more exact, to an area to the west of Brussels in the Senne Valley.

Lambic brewers use at least 30% unmalted wheat in order to produce a milky wort from the mash. Old hops are used, as they are only required for their preservative value, not their flavour or aroma. Unlike most other beer styles, in which a carefully cultivated yeast is used to ferment

the wort, the wheat brew used to produce lambic beer is left exposed to the air to allow spontaneous fermentation to happen from wild yeasts in the atmosphere. As in previous centuries, this beer is only brewed in the cooler months of the year, as the wild

HOW TO SERVE

Lager should be served well chilled as it is primarily about refreshment rather than connoisseurial flavour appreciation. It should be poured fairly quickly into a tall, tilted glass, which should then be righted once it is three-quarters full, so that the last complement of beer forms a luxuriant, feather-light, frothy head. Drink the first of the beer through the head rather than waiting for it to subside.

yeasts would be too unpredictable in summer. The fermenting wort is then run into large wooden casks and left to age in dark, dusty galleries from three months to many years.

The result is a unique, tart, sour beer, probably similar to the ales made in ancient times. The taste is almost like a flat, acidic cider, which attacks the tongue and sucks in the cheeks. It has an alcohol content of

Left: The term lambic means a Belgian wheat beer that is spontaneously fermented by wild, airborne yeast. Chapeau is a range of weak, lambic fruit beers including banana, strawberry and pineapple, and other brands are made with cherries or raspberries.

Above: In Miller Lite more of the sugar is turned to alcohol in the brewing process to produce a lower-calorie beer.

around 5%. This can be drunk young on its own, often on draught in cafés in the Brussels area, but it is usually blended with older lambics to produce gueuze. Sometimes fruit is added to create framboise (raspberry) or kriek (cherry) beers. The lambic range of beers is mainly produced by small, speciality brewers, like Boon, Cantillon, De Troch, Girardin and Timmermans. But there are a few more commercial brands, notably Belle-Vue (part of Interbrew) and St Louis.

Light ale

In England, this term indicates a bottled, weak bitter. In Scotland, it means the weakest brew, a beer light in strength although it may well be dark in colour.

Lite

In North America, this term is used to describe a thin, low-calorie beer, the best-known being Miller Lite. In some countries, Australia for instance, lite can mean low in alcohol.

Low alcohol

Since the late 1980s, many breweries throughout the world have added low- or no-alcohol brews to their beer range, usually in response to increasingly strict drink-driving laws. Low alcohol (or LA) can contain as much as 2.5% alcohol. Alcohol-free brews should contain no more than 0.05%. Some of these near beers are produced using yeasts which create little alcohol, or the fermentation is cut short. In others the alcohol is removed from a normal beer by distillation or reverse osmosis. It has proved difficult to provide an acceptable beer taste. Some of the more successful brews, such as Clausthaler from Frankfurt in Germany and Birell from Hürlimann of Zurich in Switzerland, now sell or license their low- or no-alcohol beers across many countries.

Malt liquor

In the United States, this term indicates a strong lager, often made with a high amount of sugar to produce a thin but potent brew. These beers are designed to deliver a strong alcoholic punch (around 6–8%) but little else. They are light beers with a kick, often cheaply made with a high proportion of sugar and using enzymes to create more alcohol. Sales of malt liquor account for about 4% of the total American beer market.

Right: Relatively low in alcohol, mild is usually a dark brown ale which was originally brewed for English workers. Hatters is from Robinson's in Stockport.

Märzen

A full-bodied copper-coloured lager, this beer style originated in Vienna, but developed in Munich as a stronger Märzen (March) brew (6% alcohol), which was laid down in March, to allow it to mature over the summer for drinking at the Oktoberfest after the harvest. It has largely been replaced in Germany by more golden "Festbiere". Smooth and malty, most are now stronger versions of the golden hell, containing more than 5.5% alcohol. Notable examples include Spaten Ur-Märzen and Hofbrauhaus Oktoberfest.

Mild

This was the dominant ale in England and Wales until the 1960s, and later in some regions. It is a relatively low-alcohol malty beer, usually lightly hopped, and can be dark or pale in colour. Mild was traditionally the workers' drink and would be sold on draught in the pub or club. Today, the style has vanished from many areas; it survives mainly in the industrial West Midlands and the north-west of England.

Milk stout
See Stout.

Münchner
The German name for a beer from Munich traditionally refers to the city's brown, malty lager style.

Oatmeal stout
See Stout.

Old ale
This strong, well-matured, rich, dark ale is usually sold as a seasonal beer in England as a winter warmer. Sometimes such ales are used as stock beers for blending with fresher brews.

Oud Bruin
Old Browns in the Netherlands are weak, sweetish lagers.

Oyster stout
See Stout.

Pale ale
An English bottled beer, pale ale is stronger than light ale and is usually based on the brewery's best bitter. See IPA.

Pilsner
Strictly speaking, Pilsner is a golden, hoppy, aromatic lager from the Bohemian Czech town of Plzen (Pilsen in German), where this classic style was first produced in 1842. The

Above: The Czech lager Pilsner has spawned many imitators.

original Pilsner Urquell (original source) is still brewed there. Czech Pilsner has a complex character with a flowery hop aroma and a dry finish.

This golden classic has spawned a thousand imitators, some excellent, others pale, lacklustre versions of the original. Variations on the style now dominate the world beer market.

Pilsner is now the predominant lager beer of Germany. German Pilsners are dry and hoppy with a light, golden colour. They contain around 5% alcohol and often lack the smooth maltiness of the original Czech version.

Leading German brands include Warsteiner, Bitburger and Herforder.

Porter
The origins of porter are shrouded in myths and legends. It was said to have been invented in London in 1722 by Ralph Harwood when he grew tired of making Three Threads,

Left: Palmers of Dorset is one of the many English breweries that produce a pale ale.

a popular drink of the day, by mixing strong, brown and old ales. He decided to brew one beer – or entire butt – combining the characteristics of all three.

In fact, porter was the product of the world's first major breweries, which were rising in London at this time. By brewing on a large scale with huge vessels, they were able to concoct a beer that was much more stable with far better keeping qualities than previous ales – porter.

The first porter was a traditional London brown mild ale which was much more heavily hopped than usual in order to improve its keeping qualities. The beer was then matured for months in vast vats, to increase its alcoholic strength. Older brews were then blended with fresher ones to produce an "entire" beer.

Only major brewers, such as Barclay, Truman and Whitbread, could afford to build the expensive plants that were necessary to produce beer on this scale and to tie up so much capital in maturing beer. In return for their investment, they captured the English capital's beer market, as porter was much more reliable than previous ales. The economies of scale in its production also made it cheaper. Porter proved so successful that it was widely distributed and exported.

Enterprising brewers elsewhere, like Guinness in Dublin, followed this example and began to brew their own porter. Sales gradually declined in the 19th century as it was replaced in popularity by paler ales and only the stronger or "stouter" porters survived. The name is still used around the world today to indicate a brown beer.

In the Baltic countries, strong porters are still made, based on the original export brews. Some new micro-brewers have also tried to revive the dark, dry style in England and North America.

Porter, however, was never a craft beer. It flowed from the Industrial Revolution. It was the first mass-produced beer.

Rauchbier
The intense smoky flavour of these German smoked beers from the region of Franconia comes from malt that has been dried over moist beechwood fires. There are nine breweries in the town of Bamberg that produce this dark, bottom-fermented speciality. Leading examples include Schlenkerla and Spezial.

Real ale
The British drinkers' consumer organization, CAMRA, the Campaign for Real Ale, devised this name for traditional cask-conditioned beer which continues to mature in the pub cellar. Real ale is not filtered or pasteurized.

Red beer
The reddish sour beers of West Flanders in Belgium are sometimes dubbed the Burgundies of Belgium. The colour comes from using Vienna malt. The prime producer is Rodenbach of Roeselare, who mature their beers in a remarkable forest of huge oak vats.

Younger brews are blended with old to create the distinctive Rodenbach brand. Some of the more mature beer is bottled on its own as the classic Grand Cru. Other brands include Petrus from Bavik and Duchesse de Bourgogne from Verhaeghe of Vichte.

Roggen
Only a few breweries make this German or Austrian rye beer. Some English and American breweries have started to use rye to add flavour to barley malt, and one American brewer produces its own Roggen Rye.

Left: Dark porters have diminished in popularity relative to when they were first introduced.

Above: CAMRA sparked a major revival of traditional cask beer in Britain.

Root beer
An American temperance soft drink, not a beer, it was originally flavoured with sassafras root bark. Root beer is boiled but not fermented.

Russian stout
See Stout.

Saison/Sezuen
This Belgian speciality beer is now hard to find. A refreshing, slightly sour summer style, saison (which means "season" in French) is mainly made in rural breweries in the French-speaking Wallonia region, some of which have closed in recent years. The orange, highly hopped, top-fermenting ales are brewed in winter and then laid down to condition for drinking in the hot summer months. They are sold in corked bottles after aging. Some contain added spices like ginger. Small producers include Silly, Dupont and Vapeur. The larger Du Bocq brewery makes Saison Régal, while in Flanders Martens of Bocholt produces Sezuens.

Above: The De Dolle brewery in Silly, Belgium, produces a strong, dark, Scotch-style ale.

Schwarzbier
See Black beer.

Scotch ale
Scotland's ales, brewed many miles from the nearest hop field, tend to be more malty in character than English beers. Bitters are called Light, Heavy, Special or Export in Scotland, depending on their strength, or are sometimes rated 60/-, 70/- or 80/- shillings according to an old pricing system.

Bottled Scotch Ale in Belgium is the name given to a powerful, rich ale, which is often brewed in Belgium itself.

Steam beer
An American cross between a bottom-fermented beer and an ale, steam beer was originally made in the Gold Rush days in California. It was brewed with lager yeasts at warm ale temperatures, using wide, shallow pans. Casks of this lively brew were said to hiss like steam when tapped. Now it is brewed only by the Anchor Steam Brewery of San Francisco.

Steinbier
German "stone beer" is brewed using a primitive method of heating, in which red-hot rocks are lowered into the brew to bring it to the boil. The sizzling stones become covered in burnt sugars and are then added back to the beer at the maturation stage to spark a second fermentation. This smoky, full-bodied brew is made only by Rauchenfels at Altenmünster near Augsburg.

Stout
One of the classic styles of ale, originally a stout porter, stout has survived and prospered thanks to its sharp contrast in taste and colour to the popular Pilsner – and also to the determined marketing and enterprise of one brewer, Guinness of Ireland.

This dry black brew is made with a proportion of dark roasted barley in the mash and is heavily hopped to give its distinctive taste. Draught stout tends to be much creamier and smoother than the more distinctive bottled beer, because it uses nitrogen gas in its dispenser. Guinness also produce a much heavier Foreign Extra Stout for export. Some other countries also produce dry stout, notably Australia, with fine examples from Cooper's of Adelaide and Tooth's of Sydney.

Besides dry or bitter stout, there are a number of variations of this dark style:

Milk or sweet stout
This is a much weaker and smoother bottled English stout, originally called Milk Stout because of the use of lactose (milk sugar). The name was banned in Britain in 1946 because of the implication that milk is added to the brew, though it is still used in some countries such as South Africa and Malta. The leading brand, Whitbread's Mackeson, still maintains a creamy connection through the sketch of a milk churn on the label. The Boston Beer Company in America produces a Samuel Adams Cream Stout. In addition, there are stronger tropical sweet stouts, notably Dragon brewed in Jamaica and Lion which comes from Sri Lanka.

Oatmeal stout
Many sweet stouts were sold as nourishing, restorative drinks for invalids. Some were further strengthened by the addition of oats. Once a popular bottled brew, most oatmeal stouts have vanished, but a few have been revived, including Sam Smith's Oatmeal Stout from Yorkshire in England and Maclay's Oat Malt Stout from

Left: Anchor Steam Beer was one of the pioneering brews of America's modern beer renaissance. Liberty Ale is one of the best IPAs available.

Scotland. The latter claims to be the only beer in the world to be brewed using malted oats, rather than oatmeal added to the mash.

Oyster stout

Stout has always been seen as an ideal accompaniment to a dish of oysters. Some brewers went further and added oysters to their beer. Famous examples from the past include Castletown on the Isle of Man and Young's of Portsmouth in England, who boasted that their oyster stout contained the "equivalent to one oyster in every bottle". The seaport brewers used concentrated oyster extract from New Zealand. Some American and English brewers have occasionally revived the style, but the main bottled oyster stout today from Marston's of Burton-on-Trent contains no oysters.

Russian or Imperial stout

Originally brewed in London in the 18th century as an extra-strong, export porter for the Baltic, this rich, intense brew with a fruit-cake character was reputed to be a favourite of the Russian Empress Catherine the Great, hence the

Russian Imperial title. Many Baltic breweries took up the style, including Koff in Finland, Pripps of Sweden (whose porter was sold under the Carnegie brand name) and Tartu in Estonia. In England, Courage still produces an occasional Imperial Russian Stout, which is matured for more than a year in the brewery. The nip-size bottles are year-dated, like vintage wines.

Tarwebier

This is the Flemish word for the Belgian style of wheat beer. (See Witbier.)

Trappist

This is a strict designation referring only to beers from the five Trappist monastery breweries of Belgium and one in the Netherlands. These silent orders produce a range of strong, rich, top-fermenting ales. The Chimay, Orval, Rochefort, Westmalle and Westvleteren breweries are in Belgium, while Koningshoeven (La Trappe) is Dutch. All the complex, spicy brews are bottle-conditioned. Some number their beers in strength, terming them dubbel or tripel.

Above: The characteristic dark, heavy, opaque hue of stout is unmistakable in the glass.

Commercial breweries that produce ales in the same style, or under licence from the religious communities, have to call their brews abbey beers.

Triple/Tripel

These are Flemish or Dutch terms, usually indicating the strongest brew in a range of beers, especially in Trappist or abbey beers. They are hoppy, golden brews, stronger than the darker doubles or dubbels.

Urquell

The German word for "original source", the term Urquell should be used to show that the beer is the first or original in its style, such as Pilsner Urquell from the Czech Republic. Often only Ur ("original") is used, as in Einbecker Mai-Ur-Bock.

Left: Stout is a derivative of porter. There are many varieties within the general category. Guinness and Murphy's are probably the best known. Oatmeal stouts include Scottish Oatmeal and Maclay's Oat Malt.

Above: A selection of German weisse, or wheat beers.

Vienna

The term Vienna indicates the amber-red lagers developed by the Austrian brewing pioneer Anton Dreher, but these beers now have little association with the city. The style is best found today in the Märzen beers of Germany.

Weisse or Weizen

This wheat beer style has grown from almost nothing in the early 1970s to a quarter of Bavaria's beer market today. The white or wheat beers of Bavaria are made with 50–60% malted wheat. These ghostly pale, often cloudy brews have become a popular summer refresher in Germany. They have the quenching qualities of a lager but, as they are top-fermented, all the flavour of an ale.

This is particularly true in the more popular unfiltered cloudy version containing yeast in suspension,

Hefeweizen. Filtered wheat beers are called Kristall, and dark ones are called Dunkelweizen. There is also a stronger Weizenbock at around 6.5% alcohol compared to Weissbier's usual 5%.

Notable Bavarian wheat beer brewers include Schneider and Erdinger. In north-eastern Germany, a weaker, sourer style made with about half the wheat is Berliner Weisse.

Fruit syrups are often added to Berliner Weisse by drinkers to provide a sweet and sour summer refresher. The leading brewers are Kindl and Schultheiss.

Right: Hoegaarden, first brewed by the Kluis brewery in 1966, is one of the best-known examples of Witbier or bière blanche. The chunky Hoegaarden glasses have become a familiar sight to drinkers in Belgian bars.

Witbier

The white wheat beers of Belgium are also known as "bières blanches" in French. These are brewed using around 50% wheat, but then a variety of spices are added, notably orange peel and coriander. This style is also known as tarwebier.

The witbier or bière blanche style has risen like a pale ghost from the dead to haunt every corner of the market, and the best-known example is the pioneering Hoegaarden. When Pieter Celis revived the art of brewing this spiced wheat beer in the small town of Hoegaarden in 1966, he could not have imagined how it would grow. Now many breweries in Belgium and other countries have copied the style.

Hoegaarden is brewed from roughly equal parts of raw wheat and malted barley. The cloudy top-fermented brew differs from German wheat beers through the use of coriander and curaçao (orange peel) to give a spicy, fruity flavour and enticing aroma. Other leading brands include Brugs Tarwebier (Blanche de Bruges) from the Gouden Boom brewery, Dentergems Witbier from Riva, and Du Bocq's Blanche de Namur.

CIDER

The fruitier alternative to grain beer, cider – fermented apple juice – has a long and distinguished history on both sides of the English Channel. It was introduced into England by the Normans of northern France during the conquests after the Battle of Hastings in 1066. Production gradually acquired momentum through the Middle Ages, and came to be concentrated in the West Country. Devon, Somerset and Herefordshire are the premium apple-growing counties.

Cider remained very much a local taste in those areas until the time of the Civil War in the 1640s, when soldiers of the Royalist and Parliamentary armies criss-crossing England to do battle with each other carried its reputation further afield. Eventually, as a contemporary agricultural writer John Worlidge noted, it was "valued above the wines of France". Particular varieties of apple, and especially the Redstreak, were held to make the best ciders, and were correspondingly the most prized.

In the 18th century, when it was the custom to part-pay agricultural labourers in cider, the reputation of the drink started sliding. It was now seen as the corrupting brew of lolling farm-workers too smashed to pitch hay, and nobody considering themselves to be of quality wanted to be seen drinking it. Mass production in the 20th century didn't help matters, but

Left: Aspall Dry Cyder, with the antique spelling, is made in Suffolk, England.

among Britain's 400 cider producers, there is still a handful of small farms making unfiltered real cider, including the famous "scrumpy", a hazy, potent brew over twice as strong as commercial lager. The UK industry accounts for around 65% of European output.

French cider, from Normandy, is a distinctly different style of drink to British. It tends to be thinner in texture and lower in alcohol, even though it is often produced by the champagne method of allowing a secondary fermentation in the bottle. Look for the wired cork that seals it.

Cider can be dry, medium-dry or sweet, depending on the types of apples used and the degree of fermentation the juice is permitted. There are hundreds of different varieties of cider apple, classified into four broad taste groups: sweet, bitter-sweet, bitter and acid. When the fruit is picked, it is first subject to a light crushing, which reduces it to a rough pulp. That pulp, known in England as "cheese", is then wrapped in hessian blankets, and it is these that go into the press to extract the juice.

Even the lowest grades of commercial cider are at the stronger end of the alcohol range associated with beer, i.e. 5–6% ABV. Premium brands may reach double figures. Some, such as the famous English brand Merrydown, make a virtue of only using dessert apples rather than cider apples in their products. The best ciders are vintage-dated like wines, indicating that what's in the bottle is the exclusive produce of that particular year's harvest. Unlike wine, however, there is no significant gain in quality to be had from keeping them.

Cider is another of those products in which England has a rich, distinguished heritage, but which it has allowed to decline. It deserves to be accorded the same dignity and legal protection that the French afford their wines under the *appellation contrôlée* system.

Above left: Premium organic cider from a Herefordshire specialist.

Above right: Westons cider is aged in oak casks for greater complexity.

HOW TO SERVE
Cider should be served well-chilled in tall glasses, or else in the earthenware cups traditional in northern France.

NON-ALCOHOLIC MIXERS

Although many of the alcoholic drinks talked about in this book are commonly drunk unmixed, such as single malt whiskies, aged brandies and rums, and the various wines and beers, the great majority of them would not be consumed at all were it not for non-alcoholic mixers. Some of these are so familiar as scarcely to need any explanation. Others may be used more rarely, but nonetheless constitute an important element in the mixed drink and cocktail repertoire.

The following pages provide a brief guide to the range of non-alcoholic ingredients you will need to assemble if you are intending to test the full range of alcoholic cocktails in this book. You may have expected to buy fruit juices, sparkling drinks and syrups such as grenadine, but coffee, cocoa and block chocolate also play their parts. Good mineral water is worth buying for mixing with fine Scotch, and you may decide to invest in a soda siphon.

Below: Fruit juices come in a huge variety of flavours these days, worth making the most of.

Right: Who would ever have thought that water would one day have its aficionados like wine? But it does.

Garnishing

As well as mixers, coffee and chocolate, there is the question of fruit garnishes. These are very much a matter of personal taste. The habit these days, and it is a wise one, is to keep garnishes nice and simple, and certain drinks don't need garnishing at all. Everybody remembers that first thrilling encounter in a cocktail bar with a drink that comes in a glass that looks like a flower vase, replete with slices of pineapple, wedges of citrus fruit and cherries on sticks, not to mention cocktail parasols and perhaps the odd fizzling sparkler. Apart from looking a trifle silly now, this over-the-top approach is not very sensible when making cocktails at home. If you've invited a few friends round, you'll spend the entire evening in the kitchen if you go to such extremes.

Slices and half-slices of citrus fruits are worth having to hand, as are twists of their peel pared off in spirals, and

you may want to invest in a jar of cocktail cherries (although even they aren't as popular now as they once were). That, apart from the odd Martini olive or slice of pineapple for the tropically inspired, rum-based recipes, is likely to be all you'll need. And perhaps coffee beans for the Sambucas.

Above: Coffee is the basis of many hot, alcohol-boosted after-dinner drinks, as well as being used iced in certain traditional cocktail recipes.

Water

The simplest of all mixers is the one that dilutes the strength of ardent spirits without altering the character of their basic flavour. Water is indispensable to whisky drinkers, who claim that it enhances rather than mutes the aromatic personalities of their favoured spirit. Water softens the olfactory impact of the alcohol, while allowing the complexities of grain, peat and wood to announce themselves. Pastis drinkers use plain water, too, since the cloudiness that gives the drinks their collective name can only be obtained by mixing. In all cases, good spring water or mineral water is preferable to heavily chlorinated tap water – especially so in the case of Highland and Lowland malts.

Below left: Badoit naturally sparkling mineral water comes from France.

Below right: Tŷ Nant is a Welsh mineral water that comes in a blue bottle.

Although the phenomenon would have been considered quite surreal a generation ago, something of a connoisseurship has arisen in the last few years with regard to bottled waters. Comparative tastings of spring waters and mineral waters from around the world are held, at which experts studiously roll one mouthful of water after another around their palates, looking for the telltale distinguishing characteristics in them, hoping to spot a slightly more obvious mineral content that would mark one sample out geographically from the next.

It is certainly the case that some waters have a distinctly higher presence of natural mineral salts than others. A celebrated example is the French mineral water Badoit, in such demand a few years ago that exports of it had to be rationed, and it is no longer available in retail outlets in the UK. It has a particularly salty, almost pungent flavour that is most definitely an acquired taste. Others occupy the other extreme of the spectrum, tasting as comfortingly neutral as one was always led to expect water to taste.

As a mixer for good spirits, completely neutral spring water should be used. In the case of single malt Scotch, the ideal water to choose is the one that the whisky itself was made with. Similarly, for a sparkling mixture, many people now prefer using a naturally effervescent, or even carbonated, water to the soda that was once traditional, and which is used extensively in the cocktail recipes that form the third part of this book. I still think soda has its place, but I can certainly see the attraction of sparkling spring water as an alternative. It definitely has a purer taste, by which I mean it has no taste at all.

Above left: Royal Deeside sparkling spring water is a Scottish product with an ultra-clean, pure taste.

Above right: Perrier from France is one of the most famous fizzy waters of them all, a superb palate-cleanser.

Should you doubt that different specimens of H_2O can taste different, try a comparative tasting of any bottled still spring water against what comes out of the kitchen tap. The presence of chlorine in the latter is quite a shock to the nose and tastebuds after the ethereal purity of the former.

Every now and then, some more or less alarming health hazard arises from tap water, which only goes to boost further the already explosively rising sales of bottled waters. Some authorities feel that if we carry on only drinking extremely pure water, we will dangerously lose much of our immunity to micro-organisms in the less pure variety.

Fruit juices

There are many different fruit juices, and blends of juices, on the market today, all of which can be pressed into service.

Orange juice

Of all the fruit juices, orange is probably the most important for mixing with single spirit shots, most notably with the white spirits that don't interfere with its colour. It is more versatile when used with more than one other ingredient in a cocktail, but when it does appear in a recipe, it will quite often be in conjunction with another fruit flavour, such as lemon or pineapple, or with a fizzy mixer. If you are buying commercial orange juice, the product to go for is the freshly squeezed or pressed article. The other stuff is made from concentrate, which is a dried fruit powder that has been reconstituted with tap water. All juices now are required to state on their packaging which kind they are.

Some squeezed orange juices make a virtue of having some fibrous fruit pulp left in them. From the cocktail point of view, these should be avoided, as pulp gets in the way of the correct composition of the drink. On the other hand, they do make for an extra-refreshing breakfast juice.

The best orange juice, as with all citrus juices, is the one you squeeze for yourself. It will have a noticeably thinner texture than packaged juice, but that is a welcome attribute to the cocktail maker. It makes for a less aggressive colour in the

Right: Orange juice labelled "squeezed" has not been reconstituted from powdered concentrate.

Above: Oranges are always best freshly squeezed at home, rather than coming from a carton.

mixture, and it also means that the juice blends in more subtly with the other ingredients, instead of overwhelming them.

If you are prone to heartburn, or acid reflux, then you need to be careful with orange juice. It is exceptionally high in acidity. Lemon, lime, grapefruit and the smaller orange varieties such as clementines, satsumas, tangerines and mandarins are less acidic, but the regular orange is not your friend. A lemon may be sourer, but it has balancing alkalinity in it, whereas an orange contains just too much roaring, unadulterated acidity.

Lemon juice

Freshly squeezed lemon juice is undoubtedly the most versatile ingredient in the cocktail repertoire. The juice of lemons has the uncanny ability to accentuate the flavours of other fruits, almost in the manner of a seasoning (try tasting a fresh fruit purée with and without lemon juice to demonstrate this point), and so it complements the

fruit-flavoured liqueurs very well. Additionally, its sourness mitigates the syrupy sweetness of the traditional liqueurs.

Many of the classic cocktail recipes, such as Sours and Daiquiris, rely on lemon juice for their bite. Not only does it provide that all-important sour edge, but it disguises itself very obligingly. A cocktail with lemon juice in it very rarely tastes particularly lemony unless a very generous measure has been used. It goes without saying that freshly pressed lemons are infinitely preferable to anything that comes in a bottle, or for that matter in a plastic container shaped like a lemon.

HOW TO SERVE

When drinking orange juice on its own, leave a little of the pulp to ensure a texturally interesting result. When mixing, it is better to strain the pulp out. Always drink fresh juice at once; don't keep it.

Right: Smooth-skinned lemons are best for juicing, as well as those with thin skins and relatively little pith.

Below: Limes have a sharper flavour than lemons. A little of their juice goes a long way.

Grapefruit juice

Grapefruit juice, with its bracing sourness, has more applications than you might anticipate in cocktail-making. Many of the modern recipes use it quite extensively. Pink grapefruit juice, with its slightly less acidic mien, is a particular boon, and should be used more often.

Other fruit juices

The more rarely encountered fruit juices, such as peach and apricot nectars, mango and passion fruit juice, diluted and sweetened cranberry drinks, and cherry and grape juices should all be used imaginatively in the cocktail repertoire. Tropical fruit flavours are especially good in rum-based cocktails.

In generous dilution and with plenty of ice, a lime and water (or soda) makes a fantastically thirst-quenching recourse on a hot day. It also serves its place with lager, adding a gentler note for palates that haven't quite got used to the bitter taste of the unmixed article.

Lime juice

Lime juice is even more sour, having a mere 0.5% natural sugar, and is used in drinks that should have a particularly biting tang. Unlike lemon, it advertises itself more assertively as a flavour, so that even half a measure in a welter of other ingredients makes its presence felt. Think of the limey tang in traditional Thai cooking, where it is one of the linchpins of the seasoning. To my mind, lime is a flavour that one can quickly have enough of, and if you are moving to a second cocktail after one that has had lime juice in it, it makes sense to choose a recipe without lime for the chaser.

As a cordial, lime is indelibly associated with one of the best-known British drink brands of all, Rose's.

Left: A bottle is the next best thing if fresh limes aren't available.

Pineapple juice

Pineapple makes a sweetly exotic element in some rum-based mixtures. Since the fruit itself is rather messy to prepare and so large, you will probably need to use packaged juice. Pineapple juice has breathtaking levels of natural sweetness, and it comes as something of a surprise to find 1920s cocktail recipes that use pineapple juice also adding a dash of sugar syrup. We rightly feel today that it doesn't need it.

Right: Pineapple juice is indispensable for many rum cocktails.

Above: A purée made of ripe apricots will work wonders with apricot brandy in a fruit Daiquiri, and bottled apricot nectar is a useful product too.

Tomato juice

The only juice that remains is tomato juice, which you may not find that useful. Until, that is, the morning comes when only a Bloody Mary will do, and then you'll be mighty glad you bought it. Only buy pure tomato juice, and not the varieties that have been pre-seasoned with Worcestershire sauce or salt, herbs or any sort of additive. Any seasoning you choose to add is up to you, the bartender.

Sparkling beverages

Fizzy drinks totally transform the character of a cocktail, whether they are neutral like soda, or assertively sharp like lemonade.

Soda water

To achieve the diluting effects of water without changing flavour, and to add a refreshing sparkle to a mixture, soda water is the required ingredient. At one time, no bar (or home, for that matter) was complete without a soda siphon. These were charged with tablets of sodium bicarbonate and dispensed a stream of bubbling water through a

Below left: Soda water in a bottle is the modern form of this staple cocktail ingredient.

Below right: A soda siphon was once an essential in all the best-equipped homes. They are efficient and fun to use.

pressurized nozzle. Nowadays, there is very little difference between bottled or canned soda and carbonated mineral water.

The siphon was an efficient means of keeping soda, as it allowed you to dispense it by one small squirt at a time. This was particularly useful for mixed drinks. Whisky and soda, Campari and soda, even a straightforward lime and soda, only needed a quick burst of the siphon. It came out fizzy and fresh, so that you didn't have to resort to the semi-flattened remains of an already opened bottle. The bicarbonate does give soda a slightly salty flavour, which was thought to add seasoning to a drink. Proprietary sparkling spring water really only introduces carbon dioxide and dilution.

If you are serious about testing out the full range of the cocktail repertoire, however, you will need to invest in some soda water. It is used widely, from old 19th-century recipes, through the Slings and Fizzes of the 1920s, and up to the more ostentatious creations of today.

Tonic water

Gin and tonic water go together like Fred Astaire and Ginger Rogers. A sweetened fizzy water flavoured with the bittering component, quinine, tonic is medicinally

Left: Tonic water isn't a very versatile cocktail ingredient, but many feel that gin would be nothing without it.

named for the anti-malarial properties it demonstrated in tropical climes. When first brought back to Europe from the Americas in the 17th century, quinine replaced the previously universal plant-derived liver tonic in European medicine, namely gentian. Tonic is useful not just with gin, but also with vodka and even calvados. Use it wherever the dryness of a drink can be made more appetizing with the addition of a little bitterness.

That said, tonic is probably the least useful of all the standard mixers when it comes to making cocktails, as its flavour is so assertive. Whatever bitterness it has also tends to be outweighed by the artificial sweeteners that are added to it, and to my tastebuds at least, these quickly cloy. One gin and tonic is usually enough. For that reason, you may find it as well to be fairly sparing when mixing with tonic. A half-and-half, or at a push two-thirds-to-one-third, mixture may be sufficient, as opposed to recklessly topping up a tall glass.

Lemonade

Far from being solely a children's drink, lemonade provides a useful way of administering citric sourness and fizz to a long drink. The best lemonades for bar use are not as sweet as the kids may like them. Some are actually still, in which case you may just as well use lemon juice and a pinch of sugar, or alternatively make your own still lemonade, following the recipe in this book.

Most of the recipes in which lemonade appears, though – and there are a surprising number of them – are

Above left: Lemonade adds sweetness, sharpness and fizz to a drink, but the home-made article is naturally still.

Above right: Coca-Cola is the first and most celebrated cola brand in the world, universally popular.

intended to be made with the fizzy variety. Go for one of those products that looks like the real thing, with an opaque, greyish-yellow appearance, rather than the crystal-clear products that just look like carbonated water.

Cola

All cola is derived from the invention of Coca-Cola in the United States in the late 19th century by one John Pemberton. The first version of a drink that was to become the most instantly recognizable multinational brand-name on the planet really was first mixed up in a tub in Mr Pemberton's back yard. There was very much a vogue for health-giving tonic beverages at the time, as indeed there is again today, and in some respects Coca-Cola can

be seen as the true forerunner of the isotonic sports drinks, vitaminized replacement drinks and energizing ginseng and guarana preparations of the modern era.

It was intended as a stimulating as well as a tonic drink, and included the ground nuts of the kola tree, along with crushed coca leaves. The latter are also the source of the drug cocaine, which was widely made illegal in the early years of the 20th century, and so the company removed them from the recipe. Rum and neutral vodka seem to be the main spirits with which cola mixes most happily, with coffee-flavoured Kahlúa and Tia Maria being its closest liqueur companions.

Cola is made by numerous rival companies today, and there is a kind of rudimentary connoisseurship among its drinkers, with some people, including children, genuinely able to tell one brand from another instantaneously. Not being able to get their preferred brand, and having to settle for another, causes as much distress to them as wine-drinkers face when confronted with the choice in the average pub or bar. Then there is a tiny minority of unusual people left in the world who can't stomach it in any form (the author, alas, included). Whether it's the sweetening, the aggressive carbonation, or just the flavour of the kola nut remains a mystery.

Right: Ginger ale is a traditional English summer concoction, working well as a mixer for basic Scotch, and with vodka and lime for a classic Moscow Mule.

Ginger ale

Also known as ginger beer, ginger ale also has its uses, with Scotch for example, and perhaps most famously with vodka and lime juice as a Moscow Mule. Vodka producer Smirnoff now makes a pre-mixed version of this drink, which appears to be a roughly reasonable approximation of the one you can make at home.

There is a long and distinguished folk history behind ginger ale in the English culinary tradition. It was brewed in country areas in centuries gone by not just as a refreshing summer tipple, but as a tonic remedy too. Ginger is good for aiding digestion, among a wide range of other medicinal applications, and as a spice it has always been held in great affection in the kitchen.

As with lemonade, there are both sparkling and still versions on the market. For cocktails, it's the sparkling you'll need, but go for one of the better brands. Fentiman's is a rightly celebrated example, full of the softly burning potency of this versatile spice. Some have a modicum of alcohol in them, which is not needed.

HOW TO SERVE
Ginger beer should be served on baking-hot summer days as an ice-cold drink in a tall glass. Some of the better brands will contain a little sediment, which is all to the good.

Syrups

Cocktail-making would not be quite what it is without the availability of a range of neutral or flavoured non-alcoholic syrups to add complexity and interest to a drink. Tastes in mixed drinks were often distinctly sweeter in the past than we might expect, and a dash, a teaspoon, even a half-measure of these products crops up quite regularly in older recipes.

Grenadine

The most famous of these syrups is grenadine, used to give a strong red colouring to otherwise clear mixtures, and to create the red-orange-yellow colour spectrum in the classic Tequila Sunrise. Grenadine is made principally from the juice of the pomegranate, the

Below: The principal flavour of grenadine is pomegranate.

peculiar Asiatic fruit that looks like a thick-skinned onion but, when cut, reveals a mass of jewel-like seeds within. It is thick, ruby-coloured and intensely sweet; some brands are made with a small alcohol quotient, but no more than about 3% ABV.

Grenadine, like all these products, should be used very sparingly, but it is an essential component of your starter kit, and you'll soon find that you won't get very far without it. Syrups are naturally loaded with sugar, so there is no need to worry about them going off. Even in the tiny measures in which it is used, you may be surprised how quickly you get through a bottle. Furthermore, grenadine is one of those ingredients for which there simply isn't any obvious alternative.

Orgeat

Orgeat is a much rarer syrup, although it was once used very widely in cocktails. It is flavoured with almonds and it adds that telltale taste of marzipan to a drink, even when used in very sparing quantities. Its name derives from the French word *orge*, meaning "barley", which was once one of its ingredients.

A few popular cockail recipes call for orgeat syrup. If you can't get hold of it, you can approximate the flavour of it by adding a similar quantity of amaretto, or other sweet almond liqueur. The only potential problem is that you will then be considerably increasing the quotient of alcohol in the drink, which in turn upsets the balance of flavours. The point of the syrups is that they added sweetness and flavour to a drink without strengthening the final mixture.

Left: Orgeat is an almond-flavoured syrup once widely used in cocktails.

Above left: Kiwi-flavoured syrup would make a fine addition to one of the exotic, rum-based cocktail recipes.

Above right: A syrup flavoured with passion fruit should be used sparingly, but proves to be a surprisingly versatile cocktail ingredient.

Fruit syrups

Other syrups, flavoured with a whole greengrocer's shop of exotic ingredients, are now available. Pineapple, peach, apricot, strawberry, banana, even kiwi fruit are produced, and can add an appetizing dash of fruit flavour to a mixed drink, without the extra alcohol that the equivalent liqueurs bring.

These products may come in handy when making a drink that is based on a liquidization of fresh fruit. They help to concentrate the flavour. I haven't by and large given indications for them in the cocktail recipes in the book, as they should be left very much up the the individual user's discretion. If you do resort to fruit syrups, though – perhaps because a particular batch of fruit is not quite as full-flavoured as you might have hoped – use them only in very small quantities. They really are extremely sugary.

Sirop de gomme

Sugar syrup was used quite widely in cocktail recipes in the era before the huge range of sweet liqueurs that we know today was generally available.

Below left: Peach and passion fruit is an enticing combination that would work well added to a summer fruit cup.

Below right: Summer berries cordial is just asking to be added to some light red wine in a summer punch concoction.

Left: Gomme is simply a straight sugar and water syrup.

It is possible to buy a bottled neutral sugar syrup called gomme (from the French word for "gum"), but as it consists only of sugar and water, it is easy to make your own. The sugar solution should be boiled briefly, just until the texture of it has begun to turn syrupy, and then removed from the heat and left to cool. Large quantities can then be bottled, and used as needed.

As it is only used in small doses, however, the neutral sweetening element that sugar syrup contributes can be just as easily derived from adding 2.5ml/½ tsp caster (superfine) sugar to a drink. Use caster sugar for its finer grains, which dissolve more readily. (It is possible to turn ordinary granulated sugar into something a little finer than commercial caster by whizzing it briefly in a dry liquidizer.)

Tinned fruits

Although health-conscious shoppers go for fruits in natural juices now, the sort that are canned in syrup ("light" or "heavy") are still of course widely available. Drain off some of these syrups as a more economical replacement for bottled syrups. The canning liquors from tinned peaches, apricots and pineapple are all very handy.

HOW TO SERVE
Grenadine not only adds a vivid red colour to a cocktail, but it was also one of the main sweetening agents in an otherwise dry, spirity cocktail.

The almond flavour of orgeat syrup works well with fruit juices. Use amaretto as a near substitute.

It isn't always necessary to buy a bottled syrup. The juice from a can of fruit in syrup will often do.

Coffee

Ever since its migration from Abyssinia (present-day Ethiopia) to Arabia many centuries ago, the coffee bean has played a multifaceted role in moulding history. That short hop across the Red Sea helped to alter social, political and economic life not only in Africa and the Middle East, but in mainland Europe, Britain and the Americas too. Coffee has made the fortunes and misfortunes of many, oiled the wheels of communication, inspired creative minds, stimulated the tired and, for countless imbibers the world over, become a daily necessity.

Coffee comes from the fruit of an evergreen shrub that flourishes in tropical and subtropical regions around the world. The trees produce delicate clusters of jasmine-scented blossoms, and fruit known as "cherries". Cocooned in each cherry, protected by pulp and parchment, are two coffee beans. Since around 4000 beans are needed to produce one pound of roasted coffee, few commodities require so much human effort.

Below: Colombian is one of the mildest and freshest varieties of coffee.

Right: Coffee beans are best bought whole, and freshly ground for each brew.

Below: A medium-grind coffee gives a smoother drink.

As with the discovery of the plant and its journey to Arabia, the process of development from food to hot beverage is a matter of historical speculation.

The comments of early European explorers and botanists indicate that the Ethiopians chewed raw coffee beans, obviously appreciative of their stimulating effect. They also pounded ripe coffee cherries, mixed them with animal fat and moulded the resulting paste into pellets. This powerful cocktail of fat, caffeine and meat protein was a vital source of concentrated energy. The cherries were probably eaten as a ripe fruit, too, since the pulp is sweet and contains caffeine.

It seems possible that coffee was treated as a food in Arabia, too, and only later mixed with water to make a drink. The earliest version of the beverage was probably a liquid produced by steeping a few whole hulls in cold water. Later, the hulls were roasted over an open fire, and then boiled in water for about 30 minutes until a pale yellow liquid was produced.

By about AD 1000, the drink was still a relatively crude decoction made with green coffee beans and their hulls. It was probably not until around the 13th century that the beans were dried before use. They were laid out in the sun, and, once dry, could be stored for longer periods. After that, it was a small step to roasting them over a charcoal fire.

Coffee as a stimulant

Once in Europe, coffee became a vital part of the pharmacopoeia used by 17th-century doctors, chemists, herbalists and even midwives. Caffeine's qualities as a stimulant did not go unnoticed, even then. One

Below: Coffee in a can from Japan, a very modern product.

Below: Illy is an internationally renowned Italian brand.

Dr Thornton was to assert: "A cup of Coffee strengthens and exhilarates our mental and bodily faculties; and nothing can be more refreshing either to the studious or the laborious."

Among coffee's opponents was an Italian medical writer, Sinibaldi. He stated: "[Coffee] has contributed most shockingly to the destruction of our constitutions... it produces debility, alters gastric juice, disorders digestion, and often produces convulsions, palsy of the limbs and vertigo."

The medical debate was to continue for many years, as doctors, pursuing new avenues of insight, argued the pros and cons of coffee, claiming it to be alternatively therapeutic and detrimental to the body and mind. This debate still continues today.

Coffee drinking today

Recent times have seen the development of speciality coffee shops, selling fine single-estate beans, treated as seriously as fine wine. Developing alongside them came a rash of modern coffee houses – the antithesis of the 1950s coffee bar – styled on minimalist lines and selling an extensive choice of coffee from around the world. Then there are the seemingly ubiquitous branches of American chains such as Starbucks, where coffee is sold in a variety of different presentations of Italian derivation, from long, hot, milky *latte* to small shots of black *ristretto*, the super-strength version of espresso.

The art of brewing coffee

From the moment coffee-drinking took hold, an enormous amount of ingenuity and effort went into perfecting the art of brewing. Not content with the simple act of pouring hot water over grounds and letting it sit, inventive minds in Europe and the United States managed to produce an astonishing variety of equipment: drips, filters, percolators and pressure machines, to name but a few.

One of the earliest devices was the cafetière, which made its debut in France around 1685. Its use became widespread throughout the reign of Louis XV. It was no more than a simple jug (carafe) with a heating plate warmed by a spirit lamp below. It was superseded in about 1800 by the first percolator, invented by Jean Baptiste de Belloy, the Archbishop of Paris. In Belloy's cafetière, the ground coffee was held in a perforated container at the top of the pot and hot water was poured over it. The water passed through the small holes in the container and into the pot below.

The cafetière still manages to produce a better cup of coffee than the elaborate coffee filter-machine that preceded it in British homes. Because the water only dribbles through it in a thin stream, a lot of the coffee in the filter paper doesn't get properly used, whereas in the cafetière, it is all sitting in the hot water. Not only that, but the filter machine doesn't boil the water properly, resulting in a

tepid brew. Going back for another cup from the jug after it has been sitting on the warm plate for an hour or so produces only a stewed, lukewarm drink. Note, however, that water should be allowed to come off the boil before adding to coffee beans; boiling water scalds them and spoils the taste.

Coffee mixes so very well with alcohol (and indeed makes the basis for some appetizing non-alcoholic mixtures) that we have included plenty of recipes for it. Dark-roast ground coffee is the best type for the great majority of these recipes.

Left: Lavazza is a good Italian arabica brand.

HOW TO SERVE

A cup of normal espresso laced with an alcoholic spirit or liqueur is a favoured preparation in Italy, where a little sugar and even lemon zest may also be added.

Above: Carte Noire Expresso is made exclusively from fine arabica beans.

Chocolate

One of the greatest discoveries in gastronomic history was the bean of the cocoa tree *Theobroma cacao*, the original source of chocolate. Smooth in texture, intense in taste, subtly perfumed and elegant to behold, chocolate is a rich source of sensory pleasure, adored by almost everyone.

It was Spanish colonists in the 17th century who, encountering chocolate use among the Aztecs in Mexico, first brought it back to Europe. It then followed the continental trade routes up to northern Europe, before making its way back across the Atlantic to the United States and Canada.

Initially known purely as a drink, as it had been among the Aztecs, chocolate soon became all the rage in the fashionable circles of most of the western European capitals. It made its debut as a hot beverage at almost exactly the same time as coffee and tea arrived, and speciality cafés and even gentlemen's clubs were established, specifically catering to a taste for one or the other of these beverages. The Cocoa Tree was the first London café establishment to specialize in hot chocolate.

Not only was chocolate valued for its stimulant properties (its essential alkaloid, theobromine, is a very efficient substance in this regard, and of course it also contains caffeine), it was also touted for a while as an aphrodisiac. Virtually all newly introduced foodstuffs following the discovery of the Americas, from the potato to the Jerusalem artichoke, were fanfared in this way at one time or another, but in chocolate's case, the image has never quite gone

Above: Chocolat Charbonnel is a premium French brand of instant drinking chocolate, with a particularly satisfying, rich flavour.

away. A box of chocolates is still seen as a romantic gift, and there is moreover a peculiar sensuousness to fine chocolate that no other confection can boast.

By the mid-18th century, chocolate had become more widely available and was often brought into Switzerland (eventually to become one of the great chocolate-producing nations of Europe) by travelling Italian merchants, known as *cioccolatieri*, who sold it at fairs and markets. A colourful American chocolate producer was Domingo Ghirardelli, an Italian confectioner with useful South American connections. The Ghirardelli company was the first in America to make easily dissolvable powdered cocoa, which was another landmark stage in the continuing commercialization of chocolate.

Above: Ghirardelli makes easily dissolvable powdered cocoa.

Cocoa

This rich, strong, dark powder is made by extracting some of the cocoa butter during chocolate production. What remains is a block containing around 20% cocoa butter, but this varies with each manufacturer. The cocoa is then ground and mixed with sugar and starch. The addition of starch means that cocoa needs to be cooked briefly

Left: Quality blocks of white, milk and dark chocolate.

*Above:
A layered bar
of plain, white
and milk chocolate.*

more expensive than some other brands, it is definitely worth using for chocolate-flavoured cocktails.

It is always worth using true cocoa in the chocolate drink recipes provided in the third part of this book. The alternative, drinking chocolate, is a vastly inferior product, contains a much higher ratio of sugar to cocoa solids, and is really only suitable for children.

HOW TO SERVE

Whole block chocolate can be melted with hot milk and brown sugar to make a highly refined hot chocolate drink. It is particularly popular in Spain and Mexico.

to remove the raw, floury taste. This can be done by mixing it to a paste with a little boiling water, which is the usual technique when making a hot drink with it. If a richer mixture is required, it will probably be mixed with hot milk.

The very best cocoa is produced in Holland. It is alkalized, a process that removes the acidity and produces a cocoa with a mellow, well-rounded flavour. The technique was devised by the manufacturer, Van Houten, some 150 years ago and this is still the very best cocoa available. Although it is

Garnishing with chocolate

As well as using cocoa as the basis for a chocolate drink, many of the cocktail recipes that use chocolate liqueurs are garnished with a sprinkling of grated chocolate. Always use a fine real chocolate for this purpose, and preferably one with a cocoa solids reading in the 60–70% range. Grate it roughly into coarse flakes so that its flavour is more readily appreciated. For more of a chocolate hit, pour a small quantity of good melted chocolate on to a baking tray, allow it to cool and then chisel it carefully away in long curls with the point of a knife.

Chocolate-coated coffee beans have become quite fashionable of late as an alternative to traditional petits fours. They too can be served on a chocolate cocktail, or perhaps as an exciting variation on the ordinary coffee beans served in a flaming Sambuca. They are naturally quite crunchy, but have the extra caffeine kick of the chocolate coating.

Below: These bars of Lindt chocolate have a very high cocoa content.

Left: Cadbury drinking chocolate is one of the most popular everyday brands for a sweet hot chocolate.

making cocktails

Now we can get down to business. The recipes in this part of the book are a mixture of old formulas that go back to the America of the 19th century; cocktails from the great jazz era of the 1920s; drinks that came to prominence in the cocktail revival of the 1980s; and new ones being drunk in trendsetting bars today. They are grouped into their basic drink categories in the same order that we encountered them in the first part of the book. For all recipes, 1 measure should be taken as the standard bar measure, that is 25ml or 1fl oz.

A "dash" is the amount that escapes from the bottle by tilting it and righting it again over the shaker in about half a second. Where orange, lemon and lime juices are specified, they should ideally be from the freshly squeezed fruit.

Gin

Of the six basic spirits that are used in cocktail-making, gin is the most versatile. That may seem strange in view of its assertively perfumed character, but it is precisely the herb and spice aromatics in its composition that enable it to blend well with a range of liqueurs and fruit juices, and even other spirits. In addition to that, it has in common with plain vodka, white rum and silver tequila the useful attribute of colourlessness, so that it makes a neutral background for some flamboyant-looking creations. Use a good brand of London gin in these recipes, except where one of the other types, such as Plymouth or Dutch genever, is specifically called for.

As with each section in this part of the book, we shall begin with the old classic recipes, which tend to do no more than slightly modify the flavour of the essential ingredient, before progressing on through the ages to today's more complex and challenging mixtures.

Gin Fizz

The combination of sourness and fizziness in this 19th-century recipe is what makes it so refreshing.

2 measures/3 tbsp gin
juice of half a large lemon
5ml/1 tsp caster (superfine) sugar
soda water

Shake the gin, lemon juice and sugar with ice until the sugar is properly dissolved. Pour out into a frosted, tall, narrow glass half-filled with ice, and top up with soda. Add two straws. There should ideally be a little less soda than the other combined ingredients, but it is very much a matter of personal taste.

Tom Collins

This is similar to a Gin Fizz, except that it isn't shaken and tends to be made with a little less soda. Originally known as John Collins, after the head waiter at a London hotel in the early 19th century, it changed its name when it began to be made with the Old Tom brand of gin.

2 measures/3 tbsp gin
juice of half a large lemon
5ml/1 tsp sugar
soda water

Pour the gin and lemon juice into a frosted, tall glass half-filled with ice. Add the sugar and stir to dissolve. Add roughly a measure and a half of soda, a slice of lemon and a couple of straws.

Gin Swizzle

The Swizzle dates from the early 19th century, and was originally a drink made frothy purely by energetic stirring. The implement used for this, the swizzle-stick, took its name from the drink.

2 measures/3 tbsp gin
¼ measure/1 tsp sugar syrup
juice of a lime
2 dashes Angostura bitters

Beat all the ingredients together (as if you were preparing eggs for an omelette) in a large jug, with ice. When the drink is good and foaming, strain it into a tall glass. Alternatively, make the drink in the tall glass, but remember to stir it up vigorously with a swizzle-stick. Some recipes add soda water to achieve the swizzle effect, but originally it was all done by elbow grease. The froth will subside fairly quickly anyway.

Bartending know-how

The invention of gin is apocryphally credited to one Franciscus de la Boë, a medical professor at the University of Leiden in the Netherlands, sometime in the mid-17th century. Even if he is the true progenitor of gin, however, he was almost certainly not the first to add juniper berries for medicinal reasons to a pure distilled spirit. The 12th-century monastery at Salerno, where European distillation was born, is the most likely origin of the basic recipe.

Gin Sling

Precursor of the Fizz, the Sling started life in the mid-18th century as a mixture of gin, lemon juice and sugar, but used plain water instead of sparkling. In later times, it also came to have a bittering element added to the sour, as here.

2 measures/3 tbsp gin
juice of half a lemon
5ml/1 tsp sugar
dash of Angostura bitters
still mineral water

Mix the gin, lemon juice, sugar and Angostura in a tumbler with plenty of ice until the sugar is fully dissolved. Top up the glass with cold water straight from the refrigerator. Add a twist of lemon rind and straws.

Gin Cocktail

A very simple preparation of fruity, bittered gin, this makes a highly sophisticated aperitif.

2 measures/3 tbsp gin
5 dashes orange bitters

Shake the ingredients well with ice and strain into a cocktail glass. This is one of those drinks that needs no garnish, but is perfect just as it is.

Gin Sour

The Sour dates from the 1850s, and can be made with any of the basic spirits. Fresh lemon juice is naturally the key to it, with the edge taken off it by means of a pinch of sugar. However, it should never taste at all sweet, otherwise it wouldn't be worthy of its name.

2 measures/3 tbsp gin
juice of half a large lemon
5ml/1 tsp caster (superfine) sugar

Shake all the ingredients together with ice and strain into a rocks glass or small tumbler. Some bartenders add the briefest squirt of soda just before serving for extra pep, but it is better served wholly still.

Dry Martini

No cocktail recipe is more energetically argued over than the classic dry Martini. It is basically a generous measure of virtually neat, stone-cold gin with a dash of dry white vermouth in it. But how much is a dash? Purists insist on no more than a single drop, or the residue left after briefly flushing the glass out with a splash of vermouth and then pouring it away. (They puzzlingly refer to such a Martini as "very dry", as if adding more vermouth would sweeten it. In fact, the terminology

harks back to the original recipe, when the vermouth used was the sweet red variety.) Some go for as much as half a measure of vermouth, which is guaranteed to send the purist into paroxysms of horror. If in doubt, it makes more sense to incline towards the purist philosophy: the vermouth should be added as if it were the last bottle in existence. Inevitably, individual preference remains the crucial factor.

The drink should properly be mixed gently in a large pitcher, with ice, and then strained into the traditional cocktail glass (the real name of which is a Martini glass), which should be straight out of the freezer. A twist of lemon rind should be squeezed delicately over the surface, so that the essential oil floats in globules on top of the drink, but don't put the lemon twist in the glass. The addition of a green olive to the glass is traditional, but definitely disliked by some for its salty pungency.

Orange Blossom

The original gin and orange, much drunk during the Prohibition era in the United States, where the fruit juice masked the ghastly flavour of bathtub gin. Note that the spirit isn't drowned with too much juice. Some recipes add a pinch of sugar, but it doesn't need it.

1½ measures/6 tsp gin
1½ measures/6 tsp freshly squeezed
  orange juice

Shake the ingredients with ice, and strain into a cocktail glass.

Clover Club

A traditional recipe from the 1920s cocktail era, named after a celebrated nightclub in Chicago.

2 measures/3 tbsp gin
juice of half a large lemon
1 measure/1½ tbsp grenadine
1 egg white

Shake all the ingredients with ice for at least 30 seconds to make sure the egg white is thoroughly incorporated. Strain into a rocks glass, and garnish with a half-slice of lemon.

Gibson

Well loved in Japan, this version of the Martini is named after one Charles Gibson, an American illustrator who found a cocktail onion in the drink more to his taste than the traditional olive. You can afford to be a little more generous with the vermouth.

½ measure/2 tsp dry white vermouth
2½ measures/3½ tbsp gin
2 cocktail onions

Pour the vermouth and gin into a large glass or pitcher with plenty of ice, and stir for at least 30 seconds to chill well. Strain into a Martini glass. Skewer the onions on to the end of a cocktail stick and add to the glass, so that they sit temptingly at the bottom. Better still, pour out the drink over the onions to release their flavours.

Gimlet

Like the Sour, the Gimlet is a small, sharply flavoured drink, but it is made with lime rather than lemon. As fresh lime juice is exceptionally sour, lime cordial is used, which is classically Rose's, as this was once the only brand available. The gin should ideally be Plymouth. The 1930 recipe in the *Savoy Cocktail Book* uses half-and-half proportions, but these days it is better adjusted to the quantities below so as not to be too syrupy. Some bartenders add a touch of soda.

2 measures/3 tbsp Plymouth gin
¾ measure/3 tsp Rose's lime cordial

Shake both ingredients well with ice and strain into a cocktail glass.

Bitter Gimlet

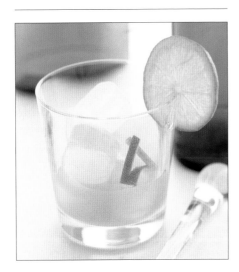

This is an old-fashioned aperitif, which could easily be turned into a longer drink by finishing it with chilled tonic or soda water.

1 lime, cut into wedges
1 measure/1½ tbsp gin
2 dashes Angostura bitters

Put the lime into a pitcher and, using a muddler, press the juice out of it. Add the cracked ice, gin and bitters and stir well until chilled. Strain the cocktail into a short tumbler over ice cubes. Add a triangle of lime rind to the drink.

Horse's Neck

The name derives from the shape of the lemon rind that hangs in the glass. There are various versions of this mix, the earliest using bourbon or brandy, but gin eventually became the most popular.

1 lemon
2 measures/3 tbsp gin
dry ginger ale

Cut the entire rind from a lemon, spiral-fashion, as in the recipe for Gin Crusta. Dangle it from the rim of a tall glass so that it hangs down inside. Add plenty of cracked ice and the gin, and then top up with ginger ale. You can also add a dash of Angostura bitters if the mood takes you, but it is by no means essential.

My Fair Lady

This frothy, fruity cocktail was invented at London's Savoy Hotel in the 1950s to coincide with a production of the much-loved Lerner and Loewe musical based on George Bernard Shaw's play *Pygmalion*.

1 measure/1½ tbsp gin
½ measure/2 tsp orange juice
½ measure/2 tsp lemon juice
¼ measure/1 tsp crème de fraise
1 egg white

Shake all the ingredients thoroughly with ice, and strain into a cocktail glass.

Gin and Lemon Fizz

If gin and tonic is your tipple, try this chilled alternative. The fruit and flower ice cubes make a lively decoration for any iced drink. This recipe serves two.

mixture of small edible berries or currants
pieces of thinly pared lemon or orange rind
tiny edible flowers
4 scoops of lemon sorbet
30ml/2 tbsp gin
120ml/4fl oz chilled tonic water

To make the decorated ice cubes, place each fruit, piece of rind or flower in a section of an ice-cube tray. Carefully fill with water and freeze for several hours until the cubes are solid. Divide the sorbet into two cocktail glasses or use small tumblers, with a capacity of about 150ml/¼ pint. Spoon over the gin and add a couple of the ornamental ice cubes to each glass. Top up with tonic water and serve immediately.

Bartending know-how
When making the ice cubes, choose small herb flowers such as borage or mint, or edible flowers such as rose geraniums, primulas or rose buds.

Gin Cobbler

The Cobbler is a very early drink, American in origin, that was served in the summer. It is basically sweetened spirit lavishly decorated with fruit. Brandy, whisky and dry sherry make popular alternatives to the gin version described here.

5ml/1 tsp caster (superfine) sugar
2 measures/3 tbsp gin
soda water
fruit, to garnish

Dissolve the sugar in a little water in a large goblet. Half-fill the glass with cracked ice and add the gin. Stir well and then double the quantity of liquid with soda water. The drink should then be adorned with slices of orange, lemon, pineapple, or whatever comes to hand, and drunk through straws.

White Lady

This is one of the classic cocktail recipes of the 1920s, and is still going strong today. The high strength of the alcohol ingredients and the sharpness of the lemon quite belie its innocuous reputation as a "lady's drink".

1 measure/1½ tbsp gin
1 measure/1½ tbsp Cointreau
1 measure/1½ tbsp lemon juice

Shake the ingredients with ice and strain into a frosted cocktail glass. Some recipes also add 5ml/1 tsp egg white. The *Savoy Cocktail Book* makes no mention of it. It simply gives the drink a frothier texture, if that's what you like. Garnish with a lime twist.

Perfect Lady

A blended cocktail with a nice sharp edge, given a frothy texture with a little egg white.

1 measure/1½ tbsp gin
½ measure/2 tsp peach brandy
½ measure/2 tsp lemon juice
1 measure/1½ tbsp egg white

Put all the ingredients into a liquidizer with a good handful of crushed ice, blend for a few seconds, and then pour into a champagne bowl. Garnish with a slice of juicy fresh peach.

Bartending know-how
When using eggs, always be sure that they are very fresh. The whites will whip better in this condition.

Tod's Cooler

The name of this cocktail refers to Tod Sloan, an American jockey of the era before the First World War, who invented this drink at one of his favourite haunts, the bar of the Palace Hotel in Brussels. Known to English racegoers as Toddy, his more famous nickname, coined in the States, was Yankee Doodle Dandy.

2 measures/3 tbsp gin
⅔ measure/1 tbsp crème de cassis
⅔ measure/1 tbsp lemon juice
soda water

Half-fill a tall glass with cracked ice, add the first three ingredients and then top up with soda. Garnish with a spiral twist of lemon rind.

Gin Smash

Try this cocktail with any fresh mint you can find: peppermint and spearmint would each contribute their own flavour to this simple and very refreshing summery drink.

15ml/1 tbsp sugar
4 sprigs fresh mint
2 measures/3 tbsp gin

Dissolve the sugar in a little water in the cocktail shaker. Add the mint and, using a muddler, bruise and press the juices out of the leaves. Then add plenty of crushed ice, and finally the gin. Shake for about 20 seconds. Strain into a small wine glass filled with crushed ice. If desired, add fresh mint sprigs and drinking straws.

Leap Year

The particular year in question was 1928, when Harry Craddock, a barman at the Savoy Hotel in London, created this drink for a party held there on February 29.

2 measures/3 tbsp gin
½ measure/2 tsp Grand Marnier
½ measure/2 tsp sweet red vermouth
dash lemon juice, plus lemon rind

Shake well and strain into a cocktail glass. Squeeze a bit of lemon rind over the surface of the drink so that a little of its oil sprays out.

Gin Rickey

The Rickey was invented in the last decade of the 19th century in the United States. It is almost the same as a Gimlet, only without the sweetening element of the cordial, which makes it a much more acerbic proposition. It can be made with any spirit, although gin is the original version.

juice and rind of half a lime
2 measures/3 tbsp gin
soda water

Half-fill a tall glass with ice. Squeeze the lime directly into the glass and then drop in the empty rind. Add the gin and stir vigorously, before topping with soda.

Gin Crusta

Prepare the glass in advance and keep it chilled in the refrigerator ready for instant use. The depth of pink colour will depend on the strength of the maraschino cherry juice you use.

1 lemon
25g/2 tbsp golden granulated sugar
3 dashes sugar syrup
2 dashes maraschino cherry juice
2 dashes Angostura bitters
1 measure/1½ tbsp gin

Cut both ends off the lemon and, using a canelle knife, peel it thinly in one long, continuous piece. Halve the lemon and rub the rim of a glass with the cut surface. Dip it into the sugar to create a decorative rim. Arrange the lemon rind in a scroll on the inside of a high-sided glass. Add the sugar syrup, cherry juice, Angostura, gin and juice of a quarter of the lemon to a cocktail shaker, half-filled with ice. Shake well and strain into the prepared glass.

Monkey Gland

From the classic cocktail era of the early 1920s, this drink was created at Ciro's Club in London, a legendary jazz nightspot just off the Charing Cross Road. Head bartender Harry McElhone later moved to Paris to run Harry's New York Bar, where he ascended to true international renown.

2 measures/3 tbsp gin
1 measure/1½ tbsp orange juice
½ measure/2 tsp grenadine
½ measure/2 tsp absinthe

Shake the ingredients with plenty of ice, and strain into a large wine glass. Garnish with a slice of orange.

Amsterdam

This deliciously orangey cocktail is unusual in having the ice left in it. It was invented in the city whose name it bears. Squeeze a fresh mandarin if you have one, or else use unsweetened juice from a can of mandarin segments.

1½ measures/6 tsp gin
½ measure/2 tsp Cointreau
¾ measure/3 tsp mandarin juice
1–2 mandarin segments

Shake the gin, Cointreau and mandarin juice with cracked ice and pour, without straining, into a rocks glass. Add a mandarin segment or two.

Lady Killer

A lusciously fruity, tropical-flavoured cocktail from a bar called the Wantagh Arms in New York State. It would make a good summer's afternoon cocktail.

1 measure/1½ tbsp gin
¾ measure/3 tsp apricot brandy
¾ measure/3 tsp Cointreau
2 measures/3 tbsp passion fruit juice
2 measures/3 tbsp pineapple juice

Shake all the ingredients together with ice, and strain into a highball glass half-filled with cracked ice. Garnish with a wedge of pineapple.

Pink Pussycat

An object-lesson in how easily gin takes to a range of tangy fruit flavours in a mixed drink, Pink Pussycat also has – as its name suggests – a most beguiling colour.

2 measures/3 tbsp gin
3 measures/4½ tbsp pineapple juice
2 measures/3 tbsp grapefruit juice
½ measure/2 tsp grenadine

Shake all the ingredients well with ice, and strain into a tall glass. Garnish with a segment of grapefruit.

Wilga Hill Boomerang

This sundowner is mixed in a large pitcher half-filled with ice cubes, and is served extremely cold.

1 measure/1½ tbsp gin
¼ measure/1 tsp dry vermouth
¼ measure/1 tsp sweet red vermouth
1 measure/1½ tbsp apple juice
dash Angostura bitters
2 dashes maraschino cherry juice

Pour the gin, dry and sweet vermouths and apple juice into a pitcher half-filled with cracked ice, and stir until the outside of the glass has frosted. Add the Angostura bitters and cherry juice to the bottom of a cocktail glass and add crushed ice, and then strain in the mixed cocktail. Prepare a strip of orange rind and a maraschino cherry to decorate the glass.

Arctic Summer

This is a very appealing, sunset-coloured cocktail. Don't stint on the ice.

1½ measures/6 tsp gin
¾ measure/3 tsp apricot brandy
¼ measure/1 tsp grenadine
4 measures/6 tbsp sparkling bitter lemon

Fill a highball glass with cracked ice, and add the ingredients one by one in the order above. Do not stir. Garnish with a slice of lemon and a cocktail cherry.

Vunderful

A long, lazy Sunday afternoon tipple, conjured up in the heat of southern Africa. Leave the fruits in the gin for as long as possible. This recipe contains 20 servings.

400g/14oz can lychees
2 peaches, sliced
¾ bottle gin

For each serving you will need:
1 measure/1½ tbsp Pimm's
2–3 dashes Angostura bitters
5 measures/120ml/4fl oz chilled tonic water
    or lemonade

Strain the lychees from the syrup and place them in a wide-necked jar with the peach slices and the gin. Let them sit overnight or for anything up to a month. For each serving, mix in a large pitcher a measure of the lychee gin with the Pimm's and the bitters to taste. Strain into tall tumblers filled with ice cubes. Add chilled tonic water or lemonade to top up. Put a couple of the drained gin-soaked lychees and peach slices into each glass, stirring and crushing the fruit into the drink with a muddler. Add a half-slice of lime to the rim of each glass.

Luigi

A 1920s classic, Luigi was created at the Criterion restaurant on London's Piccadilly Circus by one Luigi Naintré.

1½ measures/6 tsp gin
1½ measures/6 tsp dry vermouth
¼ measure/1 tsp grenadine
dash Cointreau
juice of half a tangerine or mandarin orange

Shake well with ice and strain into a glass. Add a segment of tangerine.

Bartending know-how
Mandarins and tangerines taste much the same, but the latter are full of pips.

Pink Lady

Yet another of the "Ladies", this one is more venerable than most. It dates from before the First World War, and was named after a now forgotten, hit stage play. The pink colour is achieved by means of a relatively large quantity of the pomegranite syrup, grenadine.

caster (superfine) sugar, for frosting
1½ measures/6 tsp Plymouth gin
½ measure/2 tsp grenadine, plus extra for frosting
½ measure/2 tsp double (heavy) cream
¼ measure/1 tsp lemon juice
1 measure/1½ tbsp egg white

Dip the rim of a champagne saucer or bowl-shaped cocktail glass into grenadine and then into caster sugar to create a bright pink, frosted rim. Shake the cocktail ingredients with ice and strain into the prepared glass. Garnish with a cherry.

Mistress

This is a long, delicately creamy cocktail. The Campari topping just gives it a tantalizing edge of bitterness.

1½ measures/6 tsp gin
1 measure/1½ tbsp white crème de cacao
2 measures/3 tbsp pineapple juice
1 measure/1½ tbsp passion fruit juice
1 measure/1½ tbsp whipping cream
¼ measure/1 tsp Campari

Shake all the ingredients except the last with ice, and then strain into a highball glass, half-filled with ice cubes. Drizzle the Campari on top.

Mayfair

Also dating from the 1920s, Mayfair was invented at the Embassy Club in that district of London. The recipe calls for syrup of cloves, which you may have difficulty tracking down, but its flavour is quite inimitable if you can. It has a sweetly floral quality.

1½ measures/6 tsp gin
¾ measure/3 tsp apricot brandy
¾ measure/3 tsp orange juice
¼ measure/1 tsp clove syrup

Shake all the ingredients well with ice, and strain into a cocktail glass.

Blue Star

The unearthly colour produced by mixing blue and orange in this drink is further enhanced by serving it frappé, over crushed ice.

1 measure/1½ tbsp gin
¾ measure/3 tsp Noilly Prat or other dry vermouth
⅓ measure/1½ tsp blue curaçao
1 measure/1½ tbsp orange juice

Shake all the ingredients well with ice, and strain into a cocktail glass full of finely crushed ice. Garnish with a half-slice of orange.

Jockey Club

This 1920s mixture of gin with dashes of this, that and the other came to Europe all the way from a nightclub in the Cuban capital, Havana.

2 measures/3 tbsp gin
⅓ measure/1½ tsp crème de noyau (or amaretto)
dash orange bitters (or orange curaçao)
dash Angostura bitters
⅓ measure/1½ tsp lemon juice

Shake all the ingredients well with ice and strain into a cocktail glass. Garnish with a half-slice of lemon.

RAC

This was created on the eve of the First World War by the barman of the Royal Automobile Club in London's Pall Mall.

1½ measures/6 tsp gin
¾ measure/3 tsp dry vermouth
¾ measure/3 tsp sweet red vermouth
¼ measure/1 tsp orange bitters

Shake well with ice, and strain into a glass. Squeeze a twist of orange rind over the top to release its oil.

Little Red Riding Hood

Vivid summery fruit flavours make a cocktail that tastes as innocent as Grandma, but has a bite more reminiscent of the Wolf!

1 measure/1½ tbsp gin
¾ measure/3 tsp crème de mûre
¾ measure/3 tsp crème de fraise
1½ measures/6 tsp orange juice

Shake the ingredients with ice and strain into a large cocktail glass filled with crushed ice. Garnish with a strawberry, a blackberry and a cherry.

Carla

This fruity concoction owes its character to Dutch genever, which should be used in preference to ordinary London gin.

1½ measures/6 tsp jonge genever
2 measures/3 tbsp orange juice
1 measure/1½ tbsp passion fruit juice
2 measures/3 tbsp lemonade

Shake the first three ingredients together with a couple of handfuls of crushed ice, and pour, unstrained, into a highball glass. Add the lemonade. You could garnish with a slice of orange.

Bartending know-how
In the Netherlands, genever is nearly always drunk neat, accompanied by a chaser of the local beer.

Bridesmaid

This drink sounds as though it would be perfect for a summer wedding, as long as the bridesmaids have fulfilled their duties by the time it's served.

2 measures/3 tbsp gin
1 measure/1½ tbsp lemon juice
¾ measure/3 tsp sugar syrup
dash Angostura bitters
4 measures/6 tbsp sparkling ginger ale

Add the first four ingredients to a tall glass filled with cracked ice, stir well and add the ginger ale. Garnish with a twist of lemon.

Bennett

Dating from the 1920s, this short drink is sometimes seen spelt with only one "t", and with a small quantity of sugar syrup added to it, but this is the original formula, which on the whole I prefer for its sharper edge.

César Ritz

Created at the Paris Ritz Hotel, this was named after the legendary chef of the 19th century.

2 measures/3 tbsp gin
⅔ measure/1 tbsp dry vermouth
⅓ measure/1½ tsp cherry brandy
½ measure/2 tsp kirsch

Stir the ingredients gently in a pitcher with ice cubes, until a frost of condensation mists the outside. Strain into a cocktail glass. Add a cocktail cherry that has been liberally dunked in kirsch.

1½ measures/6 tsp gin
½ measure/2 tsp lime juice
2 dashes Angostura bitters

Shake well with ice and strain into a cocktail glass.

Space

... the final frontier? Not quite, but this is a very moreish modern cocktail recipe made with hazelnut liqueur. A good aperitif.

1½ measures/6 tsp gin
1 measure/1½ tbsp Frangelico (or crème de noisette)
½ measure/2 tsp lemon juice

Shake all the ingredients well with ice, and strain into a rocks glass. Add a couple of pieces of cracked ice.

Bartending know-how
The monk after whom Frangelico is named, and who is credited with its recipe, lived as a hermit in north-west Italy in the 17th century.

Honolulu

This fruity little shooter should be served in a shot glass.

1 measure/1½ tbsp gin
¼ measure/1 tsp pineapple juice
¼ measure/1 tsp orange juice
¼ measure/1 tsp lemon juice

¼ measure/1 tsp pineapple syrup (from a can)
1 drop Angostura bitters

Shake all but the last ingredient with ice and strain into a shot glass. Add a single drop of Angostura to the drink, and knock back in one.

Caruso

Towards the end of his life, the celebrated Italian opera singer Enrico Caruso stayed at the Hotel Sevilla in Cuba, where an obliging barman created this cocktail in his honour.

1 measure/1½ tbsp gin
1 measure/1½ tbsp dry vermouth
1 measure/1½ tbsp green crème de menthe

Shake well with ice and strain into a cocktail glass. Some versions these days use a little less crème de menthe than a whole measure, as the flavour is so strong, but this is the original recipe.

Barbarella

This is a colourful drink named after the title character in the classic sci-fi movie, played by Jane Fonda.

1 measure/1½ tbsp Plymouth gin
1 measure/1½ tbsp dry vermouth
½ measure/2 tsp Galliano
¼ measure/1 tsp blue curaçao
2 measures/3 tbsp sparkling bitter lemon

Shake the first four ingredients well with ice, and strain into a rocks glass that has been half-filled with cracked ice. Add the bitter lemon, and garnish with a slice of lemon.

Damn the Weather

This cocktail has been around since the 1920s, and presumably commemorates a particularly persistent gloomy spell.

1 measure/1½ tbsp gin
½ measure/2 tsp sweet red vermouth
½ measure/2 tsp orange juice
¼ measure/1 tsp orange curaçao

Shake well with ice, and strain into a chilled whisky tumbler. Add a twist of orange wrapped around a cocktail stick.

Park Avenue

This sharp and fruity cocktail takes its name from one of the smartest thoroughfares in New York City.

1½ measures/6 tsp gin
½ measure/2 tsp cherry brandy
½ measure/2 tsp lime juice
¼ measure/1 tsp maraschino

Shake all the ingredients well with ice, and strain into a cocktail glass. Garnish with a cocktail cherry and add a thin slice of lime.

Derby

This classic, old, American short drink is just a barely modified gin. Instead of garnishing the glass with a mint leaf, you could add a couple of mint sprigs to the alcohol in the shaker, and then strain them out.

2 measures/3 tbsp gin
¼ measure/1 tsp peach bitters

Shake with ice and then strain into a liqueur glass. Garnish with a leaf of garden mint.

Red Cloud

Although red clouds at night were once said to be a sailor's delight, you don't have to be ocean-bound to enjoy one of these.

1½ measures/6 tsp gin
¾ measure/3 tsp apricot brandy
½ measure/2 tsp lemon juice
¼ measure/1 tsp grenadine
dash Angostura bitters

Shake all the ingredients well with ice, and strain into a champagne saucer or cocktail glass. Garnish with a half-slice of lemon and a cherry.

Bartending know-how
The oversized label around each Angostura bitters bottle was an administrative error that just stuck!

Maiden's Blush

There were two quite distinct recipes for Maiden's Blush, even in the 1920s. The first mixed gin with orange curaçao, lemon juice and grenadine. This one was a slightly more lethal proposition, and the blush effect in the colour is more apparent, if you need any excuse to up the ante.

2 measures/3 tbsp gin
1 measure/1½ tbsp absinthe
¼ measure/1 tsp grenadine

Shake all the ingredients well with ice, and strain into an ice-cold cocktail glass.

Bartending know-how
Cocktails containing absinthe should be served sparingly. Too many aren't necessarily very nice.

Bee's Knees

The name should give a clue as to the essential ingredient in this rather restorative mixture. The honey and lemon together give the drink a particularly comforting note.

1½ measures/6 tsp gin
¼ measure/1 tsp honey
¼ measure/1 tsp lemon juice

Shake the ingredients very well with ice to integrate the honey, and strain into a cocktail glass.

Cloister

A strong lemony/herbal flavour pervades the Cloister. It is a short drink that delivers a strong kick-start to the tastebuds.

1½ measures/6 tsp gin
½ measure/2 tsp yellow Chartreuse

Grapefruit Cocktail

If you have a grapefruit on the go after making a Cloister, it makes sense to move on to this classic preparation next. Waste not, want not.

1½ measures/6 tsp gin
1 measure/1½ tbsp grapefruit juice
¼ measure/1 tsp maraschino

Shake all the ingredients well with ice, and strain into a champagne saucer or cocktail glass. Garnish with a sliver of grapefruit and a cherry.

½ measure/2 tsp grapefruit juice
¼ measure/1 tsp lemon juice
¼ measure/1 tsp sugar syrup

Shake all the ingredients well with ice, and strain into a cocktail glass. Garnish with a twist of grapefruit rind.

Tangier

A four-city cocktail tour on this page starts in Morocco with this sweetly orangey number. The choice of city for the name distantly reflects the tangerines that go into Mandarine Napoléon.

1 measure/1½ tbsp gin
1 measure/1½ tbsp Cointreau
1 measure/1½ tbsp Mandarine Napoléon

Shake all the ingredients well with ice, and strain into a cocktail glass. Decorate the glass with a spiral twist of orange rind, wrapped around a cocktail stick.

Berliner

A dry, and very grown-up sort of drink, Berliner is full of herbal flavours from the vermouth and kümmel and has a finishing tang of lemon.

1½ measures/6 tsp gin
½ measure/2 tsp dry vermouth
½ measure/2 tsp kümmel
½ measure/2 tsp lemon juice

Shake all the ingredients well with ice, and strain into a chilled cocktail glass. Squeeze a bit of lemon rind over the top, and garnish with a half-slice of lemon.

Parisian

Another 1920s recipe that nicely balances the sweetness of blackcurrant liqueur with the acerbic dryness of good dry French vermouth.

1 measure/1½ tbsp gin
1 measure/1½ tbsp Noilly Prat
1 measure/1½ tbsp crème de cassis

Shake all the ingredients well with ice, and strain into a cocktail glass. Add three or four blackcurrants to the glass to add touches of sharpness to the drink. They can be eaten at the end.

Dundee

What else but Scottish ingredients (two of them, in fact) could give a drink a name like this? This is a dry, sour cocktail with quite a kick.

1 measure/1½ tbsp gin
¾ measure/3 tsp Scotch
½ measure/2 tsp Drambuie
½ measure/2 tsp lemon juice

Shake all the ingredients well with ice, and strain into a whisky tumbler. Squeeze a twist of lemon rind over the drink, and then drop it into the glass.

Juan-les-Pins

Once the preferred destination of the Mediterranean jet-set, the Riviera resort is fittingly honoured by this appetizing mixture of gin, an aperitif and a liqueur.

1 measure/1½ tbsp gin
¾ measure/3 tsp white Dubonnet

½ measure/2 tsp apricot brandy
dash lemon juice

Shake all the ingredients well with ice, and strain into a cocktail glass. Garnish with a slice of apricot and a cherry speared by a cocktail stick.

Bloodhound

The drink takes its name from the rather gory colour and texture produced by including whole strawberries in the blend.

1½ measures/6 tsp gin
½ measure/2 tsp dry vermouth
½ measure/2 tsp sweet red vermouth
¼ measure/1 tsp crème de fraise
6 strawberries

Put all the ingredients into a liquidizer with ice, and blend for about 20 seconds. Strain into a cocktail glass, and garnish with a final whole strawberry dipped in crème de fraise.

Princeton

This cocktail was created in the early 20th century to honour one of America's Ivy League universities. It was originally made with a sweet gin called Old Tom, but the drier version tastes better.

1½ measures/6 tsp gin
¾ measure/3 tsp ruby port
¼ measure/1 tsp orange bitters

Stir the ingredients together with plenty of ice in a large pitcher, and then strain into a rocks glass or cocktail glass. Squeeze a piece of lemon rind over the surface to release a spray of oil, and then drop it into the drink.

Whiteout

A highly indulgent preparation with which to conclude the gin collection, this is a sweet, chocolate cream cocktail that tastes far more innocuous than it actually is.

1½ measures/6 tsp gin
1 measure/1½ tbsp white crème de cacao
1 measure/1½ tbsp double (heavy) cream

Shake all the ingredients very well with ice to amalgamate the cream fully, and then strain into a chilled cocktail glass. Grate a small piece of white chocolate over the surface.

Bartending know-how
It is estimated that, at the time the Gin Act was introduced in 1736, average consumption in London had hit something like two-thirds of a bottle per head *per day*.

Vodka

Vodka may not seem the most obviously useful ingredient in the cocktail cupboard, in the sense that it is typically just a neutral, colourless spirit that at most can only add a further shot of alcohol to a mixed drink. However, many of the modern cocktails are based on the principle of blending a range of different, often exotic fruit flavours over an alcohol base that doesn't interfere with the taste of them. If there are surprisingly few vodka cocktails from the classic era, that is because vodka wasn't then generally commercially available. Some of the recipes here use one of today's ultra-fashionable flavoured vodkas.

Screwdriver

The Screwdriver is the original vodka and orange, so named – as the story has it – after an American oil-rig worker developed the habit of stirring his drink with a screwdriver. Presumably, swizzle-sticks are in rather short supply on oil-rigs. As a member of the classic cocktail repertoire, it probably only dates from the 1950s, which is when vodka made its first, tentative appearance on Western markets. The rest is history.

2 measures/3 tbsp vodka
4 measures/6 tbsp orange juice

Add the ingredients, spirit first, to a rocks glass or whisky tumbler loaded with ice cubes, and throw in a slice of orange. Made with freshly squeezed rather than commercial juice, the drink tastes more grown-up and appears to pack more of a punch, as the juice is naturally thinner than concentrate orange juice from a carton.

Moscow Mule

One of the classic American vodka-based cocktails, the Moscow Mule was invented at a Los Angeles restaurant in 1947 as part of the first US sales drive for the Smirnoff brand. It should contain enough vodka to give the drink a real kick, as befits a mule.

2 measures/3 tbsp vodka
¼ measure/1 tsp lime juice
3 measures/4½ tbsp sparkling ginger ale

Pour the vodka and lime juice into a highball glass half-filled with ice. Mix together well with a bar spoon. Top up the mixture with ginger ale, and add a few halved slices of lime to the cocktail.

Black Russian

The true Black Russian is simply equal measures of vodka and Tia Maria, or Kahlúa, mixed with ice cubes in a tumbler. However, the fashion in recent years has been to serve it as a long drink in a big glass, topped up with cola.

Proportions of the classic Black Russian vary according to taste. Two parts vodka to one part Tia Maria on ice, with no mixer, makes a very adult drink. Certain aficionados insist on Kahlúa rather than Tia Maria with the vodka. Either way, it is as well not to adulterate the drink with cola.

White Russian

The White Russian is a creamy version of the Black, which needs shaking rather than stirring, so as to incorporate the cream.

1 measure/1½ tbsp vodka
1 measure/1½ tbsp Kahlúa or Tia Maria
1 measure/1½ tbsp whipping cream

Shake all the ingredients well with ice, and strain into a cocktail glass.

Blenheim

A further twist on the basic Black Russian idea, Blenheim uses orange juice instead of cola, if you want a non-alcoholic mixer in there. The resulting colour is not the loveliest, but the flavour is better than it sounds.

1½ measures/6 tsp vodka
¾ measure/3 tsp Tia Maria
¾ measure/3 tsp orange juice

Shake all the ingredients well with ice, and strain into a cocktail glass.

Golden Russian

This is a quite distinct drink from the preceding two Russians, in which the vodka acts to take a little of the sweetness off the liqueur, while the lime sharpens it all up still further. It's a very ingenious (and powerful) mixture, and one that should not be taken lightly.

1½ measures/6 tsp vodka
1 measure/1½ tbsp Galliano
¼ measure/1 tsp lime juice

Pour all the ingredients into a rocks glass over plenty of cracked ice, and stir. Add a slice of lime.

Bullshot

The Bullshot is a sort of Bloody Mary, only with beef consommé replacing the tomato juice. It too is thought to have amazing restorative powers as a reviving breakfast drink after the previous night's indulgence. It can be handy if you really can't bear to eat anything, but drink some water first.

2 measures/3 tbsp vodka
4 measures/6 tbsp cold beef consommé
  (classically Campbell's)
½ measure/2 tsp lemon juice
¼ measure/1 tsp Worcestershire sauce
2 dashes Tabasco
pinch celery salt
pinch cayenne pepper

Mix all the ingredients with ice in a pitcher, and then strain into a highball glass half-filled with ice.

Bloody Mary

Everybody has his or her own recipe for the next best hangover cure after aspirin. Some strange people even put tomato ketchup into it. Others round out the alcohol with a splash of dry sherry. Here is my own formula.

Put a slice of lemon and 2–3 ice cubes in a tall glass, add 5ml/1 tsp Worcestershire sauce, 5ml/1 tsp freshly squeezed lemon juice, a pinch of celery salt, about six drops of Tabasco and six twists of the black pepper mill. Stir to coat the ice. Fill the glass to about 4cm/1½in from the top with tomato juice and pour in a generous measure of vodka. Stir well.

Dickson's Bloody Mary

This recipe has plenty of spicy character, with horseradish, sherry and Tabasco. Made with chilli or pepper vodka, it is a much hotter proposition than the standard recipe.

Gipsy

The ingredients in this recipe make for an exotically scented, and slightly bittersweet mixture. It would make a highly unusual digestif for the end of a grand dinner.

2 measures/3 tbsp vodka
1 measure/1½ tbsp Bénédictine
dash Angostura bitters

Add the ingredients to a whisky tumbler or Old-Fashioned glass half-full of cracked ice, and stir gently.

2 measures/3 tbsp chilli-flavoured
  vodka
1 measure/1½ tbsp fino sherry
7 measures/150ml/¼ pint tomato juice
1 measure/1½ tbsp lemon juice
2–3 dashes Tabasco
10–15ml/2–3 tsp Worcestershire sauce
2.5ml/½ tsp creamed horseradish
5ml/1 tsp celery salt
salt and ground black pepper
celery stalk, stuffed green olives and a
  cherry tomato, to decorate

Fill a pitcher with cracked ice and add the vodka, sherry and tomato juice. Stir well. Add the lemon juice, Tabasco, Worcestershire sauce and horseradish. Stir again. Add the celery salt, salt and pepper, and stir until the pitcher has frosted and the contents are chilled. Strain into a tall tumbler, half-filled with ice cubes. Add a stick of celery.

Mint Collins

The original Tom Collins recipe has been adapted since the 1950s to be made with vodka rather than gin. This refreshing, summery variation also adds the cool flavour of mint for extra class.

2 measures/3 tbsp vodka
⅓ measure/1½ tsp green crème de menthe
1 measure/1½ tbsp lemon juice
dash sugar syrup
5 measures/120ml/4fl oz soda water

Half-fill a highball glass with cracked ice, and then add the first four ingredients. Give the drink a good stir and then top up with the soda. Float a sprig of fresh mint on the top.

Chilli Vodkatini

Not quite a Vodkatini, but almost. This recipe produces a hot, savoury drink that is stirred in the manner of the original Dry Martini, and served with a couple of chilli peppers in it.

1 measure/1½ tbsp chilli or pepper vodka
¼ measure/1 tsp dry French vermouth
2 small pickled or vodka-soaked chillies and
   1 pitted green olive, to garnish

Vodkatini

This variation on a Dry Martini was popularized by James Bond. Famously, it should be "shaken, not stirred", which gives the drink a cloudiness not achieved in the classic recipe.

The mixture is basically that of a classic Dry Martini, but with vodka replacing the gin. Since vodka lacks the aromatic character of gin, it is generally served with a twist of lemon rind immersed in the drink, as well as being squeezed over it.

Add the chilli or pepper vodka to a bar glass of ice and mix for about 30 seconds, until the outside of the glass is frosted over. Add the vermouth to a chilled cocktail glass, swirl it around to wet the inside of the glass, and then pour it away. Cut one of the pickled chillies in half and discard the seeds. Thread it through the pitted green olive, and then thread the stuffed olive on to a cocktail stick with the other chilli. Strain the cocktail into the prepared glass. Add the olive and chilli decoration to the drink before serving.

Bartending know-how
There are two kinds of pepper vodka. Some is flavoured with red chillies, but most is spiced with crushed black peppercorns.

Après-Ski

Certainly not to be tried before skiing anyway. The intriguing mixture of aniseed, mint and lemon in this drink is quite a challenge. Somehow the mint emphasizes the flavour of the Pernod. One should be enough, not least because the drink has an exceedingly long aftertaste.

1 measure/1½ tbsp vodka
1 measure/1½ tbsp Pernod
½ measure/2 tsp green crème de menthe
5 measures/120ml/4fl oz sparkling lemonade

Shake the first three ingredients with ice, and then strain into a highball glass with a couple of ice cubes in it. Add the lemonade. Garnish the drink with a sprig of mint and a slice of lemon.

Harvey Wallbanger

This is the next step up from a Screwdriver, with a dash of Galliano added. It is a 1970s recipe that supposedly derives its name from having left a gentleman called Harvey, who had downed several of them, in the walking-into-walls state. There is no need to go quite that far, but it's easy to see why the formula became such a popular one in nightclubs.

2 measures/3 tbsp vodka
¾ measure/3 tsp Galliano
5 measures/120ml/4fl oz orange juice

Add the vodka and orange juice to a highball glass half-filled with cracked ice. Pour the Galliano carefully over the top so that it floats above the other ingredients. Garnish with a half-slice of orange, decorated with a canelle knife.

Kiss and Tell

A thoroughly exotic mixture of flavours goes into this modern cocktail, and the resulting throbbingly vibrant colour is something to be seen.

1 measure/1½ tbsp vodka
½ measure/2 tsp Galliano
¼ measure/1 tsp dry vermouth
¼ measure/1 tsp blue curaçao
2 measures/3 tbsp orange juice
1 measure/1½ tbsp passion fruit juice

Bartending know-how
The blue Bols curaçao is so popular that it is probably now the flagship product of their liqueur range.

Shake all the ingredients with roughly crushed ice and pour everything out into a tall glass. Garnish with a half-slice of orange and a cherry.

Liberator

Here is another of those cocktails full of blended, tropical fruit flavours, to which a vodka base lends itself so well.

1½ measures/6 tsp vodka
½ measure/2 tsp Midori or other melon liqueur
2 measures/3 tbsp mango juice
½ measure/2 tsp lime juice

Shake all the ingredients well with ice, and strain into a cocktail glass. Garnish with a neatly cut sliver of mango and a slice of lime.

Barbara

This is a variation on the White Russian, but with a chocolatey flavour replacing the original coffee.

1 measure/1½ tbsp vodka
1 measure/1½ tbsp white crème de cacao
½ measure/2 tsp double (heavy) cream

Shake all the ingredients well with ice, and strain into a cocktail glass. The surface of the drink can be sprinkled with grated chocolate.

Piranha

This is one of those deceptive cocktails that tastes relatively harmless, but in fact packs quite a bite, much like the predatory flesh-eating fish after which it is named.

1½ measures/6 tsp vodka
1 measure/1½ tbsp of brown crème de cacao
1 measure/1½ tbsp ice-cold cola

Pour the alcohol into a rocks glass containing plenty of cracked ice and stir vigorously, before adding the cola.

Bartending know-how
Brands of cola have proliferated like wildfire ever since the success of the original Coca-Cola. There are low-sugar and caffeine-free versions, and there is now a French brand aimed at the Muslim market.

Camshaft

I am not at all certain how this drink came to be named after part of a car engine. Perhaps the fruit juices in it act as sliding parts to facilitate the passage of the alcohol.

1 measure/1½ tbsp vodka
½ measure/2 tsp Campari
1 measure/1½ tbsp passion fruit juice
1 measure/1½ tbsp orange juice
1 measure/1½ tbsp sparkling lemonade

Pour the ingredients in this order into a rocks glass half-full of cracked ice. Stir briefly and gently, being careful not to neutralize the fizz in the lemonade. Garnish with a half-slice of orange and a half-slice of lemon.

Katinka

This fruity mixture achieves a nice balance of sweet and sour flavours, and is revved up with the added horsepower of the vodka. A good Russian brand such as Stolichnaya would be the optimum choice for the drink.

SOS

Lemon vodka is called for in this drink. Russian types are termed limonnaya and flavoured with natural lemon essence, or there is a mixed citrus version made by the Swedish Absolut company called Citron.

1 measure/1½ tbsp lemon vodka
1 measure/1½ tbsp peach schnapps
2 measures/3 tbsp unsweetened mandarin
   juice (from a can, if necessary)
¼ measure/1 tsp grenadine

Shake all the ingredients well with ice, and strain into a large cocktail glass. Garnish with a slice of lemon and a mandarin segment on a cocktail stick, and add a short straw.

1½ measures/6 tsp vodka
1 measure/1½ tbsp apricot brandy
½ measure/2 tsp lime juice

Shake all the ingredients well with ice, and strain into a cocktail glass heaped with slivered ice. Add a slice of lime.

Cooch Behar

This drink was supposedly created in an idle moment by the Maharajah of that eponymous part of India. It is basically a stripped-down, hot Bloody Mary.

2 measures/3 tbsp chilli or pepper vodka
4 measures/6 tbsp tomato juice

Add the ingredients to a rocks glass or whisky tumbler packed with ice cubes.

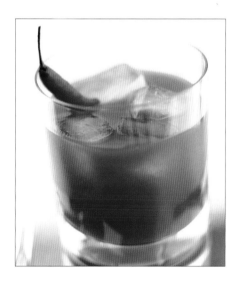

Czarina

A recipe from the age when vodka was still enough of a commercial novelty for a drink containing it to be given a name with glamorous Russian connotations.

1 measure/1½ tbsp vodka
½ measure/2 tsp apricot brandy
½ measure/2 tsp dry vermouth
dash Angostura bitters

Stir all the ingredients well with ice in a pitcher, and then strain into a chilled cocktail glass.

Graffiti

Grape juice isn't used that often in the cocktail repertoire, which is a pity, as its natural sweetness works well, particularly with the clear spirits.

1½ measures/6 tsp vodka
2 measures/3 tbsp white grape juice

Balalaika

My note on the Czarina applies equally here. The formula is basically a variation on the White Lady recipe, with vodka replacing the gin. As such, it has a slightly milder spirit flavour, but the sharp citrus flavours are still appetizingly apparent.

2 measures/3 tbsp sparkling cherryade

Pour the vodka and grape juice into a large wine goblet half-filled with cracked ice. Stir to combine, and then add the cherryade. Garnish with a green seedless grape and a cocktail cherry.

1½ measures/6 tsp vodka
¾ measure/3 tsp Cointreau
¾ measure/3 tsp lemon juice

Shake the ingredients well with plenty of ice, and strain into a cocktail glass. Add an orange-and-cherry garnish.

Kew Punch

This is a very drinkable concoction of vodka, sweet vermouth, curaçao, gin and cherry brandy served over fresh summer fruits.

1 measure/1½ tbsp vodka
1 measure/1½ tbsp sweet red vermouth
1 measure/1½ tbsp orange curaçao
⅔ measure/1 tbsp gin
⅔ measure/1 tbsp cherry brandy
assorted soft summer fruits, sliced
1–2 dashes Angostura bitters

2 measures/3 tbsp American dry ginger ale
2 measures/3 tbsp sparkling lemonade

Measure the vodka, vermouth, curaçao, gin and cherry brandy into a pitcher of ice and stir well to chill. Strain into a highball glass full of ice cubes and the sliced summer fruits (peach, apricot, strawberries, raspberries, etc). Add the bitters, and then pour in the chilled ginger ale and lemonade. Garnish with twists of lemon rind and leaves of lemon balm or mint.

Salty Dog

The name refers to the salt frosting that the glass is given. Otherwise, this is a bracingly sour and simple mixture of vodka and grapefruit juice that makes a good aperitif.

2 measures/3 tbsp vodka
5 measures/120ml/4fl oz grapefruit juice

Salt the rim of a highball glass by dipping it first in grapefruit juice and then in fine-ground sea salt. Half-fill it with cracked ice. Shake the liquid ingredients together with ice, and then strain into the prepared chilled glass. Add a decorative twist of grapefruit rind.

Black Cossack

You may think its presence will hardly be noticed, but the extra kick given to the beer by the slug of vodka in a Black Cossack is an appreciable one.

1 measure/1½ tbsp vodka
300ml/½ pint Guinness

Add well-chilled Guinness to a highball or half-pint glass into which a measure of ice-cold vodka has already been poured. Wait for the head on the beer to settle before drinking.

Ménage-à-Trois

Many modern cocktails have ice cream added to them. It gives a richer flavour and creamier texture, and makes for an altogether luxurious mixture. This is a particularly naughty example.

1 measure/1½ tbsp vodka
4 strawberries
1 measure/1½ tbsp coconut cream
30ml/2 tbsp rich chocolate ice cream

Add all the ingredients to a liquidizer with cracked ice and blend for 20 seconds or so, until the strawberries are quite pulverized. Strain into a chilled rocks glass. Garnish with another whole strawberry.

Slow Comfortable Screw

The 1970s idea of a joke in the drink's name may be a touch embarrassing now, but the mixture is a good one, and the drink was something of a modern classic a generation ago.

1 measure/1½ tbsp vodka
¾ measure/3 tsp Southern Comfort
¾ measure/3 tsp sloe gin
5 measures/120ml/4fl oz orange juice

Cosmopolitan

This drink has a similar bracing flavour to a Sea Breeze, but the sweet liqueur shows through the bitter juices.

1½ measures/6 tsp vodka
1 measure/1½ tbsp Cointreau
1 measure/1½ tbsp cranberry juice
½ measure/2 tsp lime juice

Shake all the ingredients well with ice, and strain into a large cocktail glass. Dangle a twist of orange in the drink.

Add the first three ingredients to a highball glass half-packed with ice. Stir to combine, and then top up with the orange juice. Garnish with a cocktail cherry on a stick for the essential seventies touch, and add two long straws. A plastic novelty will add that final note of sheer class, as will throwing back three of them and then slow-dancing with somebody ghastly.

Bailey's Comet

The spirit turns the popular creamy liqueur into a rather stiffer proposition.

1 measure/1½ tbsp vodka
1 measure/1½ tbsp Bailey's

Combine the ingredients with cracked ice in a rocks glass. The quantity can safely be doubled to save time, as you're bound to want another.

Sea Breeze

One of today's most requested cocktails, Sea Breeze was one of the first popular cocktails to use cranberry juice. Ocean Spray is one of the most famous brands, but the supermarkets nearly all have a proprietary version.

2 measures/3 tbsp vodka
2 measures/3 tbsp grapefruit juice
3 measures/4½ tbsp cranberry juice

Shake all the ingredients well with plenty of ice, and pour everything into a chilled highball glass. Add a wedge of lime and a few cranberries.

Bartending know-how
Cranberry juice is a sugar-and-water product. It is possible to buy apple juice with cranberry if you want neither sugar nor water.

Pompanski

This drink specifically calls for one of the premium Polish vodkas. Its soft texture and rounded feel in the mouth are a world away from neutral commercial vodka.

1 measure/1½ tbsp Wodka Wyborowa
½ measure/2 tsp dry vermouth
¼ measure/1 tsp Cointreau
1 measure/1½ tbsp grapefruit juice

Shake all the ingredients together with three or four ice cubes and then pour everything, unstrained, into a rocks glass. Add a twist of grapefruit rind.

Hammer Horror

Use the best vanilla ice cream you can find for this, and preferably one that is made with whole egg and real vanilla, for extra richness.

1 measure/1½ tbsp vodka
1 measure/1½ tbsp Kahlúa
60ml/4 tbsp vanilla ice cream

Add all the ingredients to a liquidizer with cracked ice, blend for a few seconds and then strain into a cocktail glass. Sprinkle the surface of the drink with grated dark chocolate.

French Horn

The drink is so called because it calls for a particular variety of French liqueur called Chambord, made from black raspberries. If you can't find it, substitute ordinary crème de framboise. Its sweetness is thrown into relief with the neutrality of the vodka and the sharpness of the lemon juice.

1 measure/1½ tbsp vodka
¾ measure/3 tsp Chambord (or crème de framboise)
½ measure/2 tsp lemon juice

Stir the ingredients in a pitcher with plenty of ice. Strain into a cocktail glass and garnish with a whole raspberry.

Hot Cherry

Solve the Russo-Polish dispute as to which of them originally invented vodka by combining both nationalities (in even-handed measure of course) in this exciting cocktail. The tonic water adds a pleasantly bitter note to the rich cherry fruitiness of the mixture.

1 measure/1½ tbsp Stolichnaya vodka
1 measure/1½ tbsp Wisniowka (Polish cherry vodka)
2 measures/3 tbsp tonic water

Shake the vodkas with plenty of cracked ice, strain into a rocks glass containing two ice cubes and add the tonic. Garnish with a cherry.

Kir Lethale

The raisins for this cocktail should be soaked overnight in vodka to give the drink that extra kick. This is a party recipe to serve six.

6 vodka-soaked raisins
30ml/2 tbsp vodka
3 measures/4½ tbsp crème de cassis
1 bottle brut champagne or dry sparkling wine, chilled

Place a vodka-soaked raisin at the bottom of each glass. Add ¼ measure/ 1 tsp plain vodka or the vodka from the steeped raisins, if using, to each glass. Add ½ measure/2 tsp crème de cassis to each and finish the drinks with the champagne or sparkling wine.

Pushkin's Punch

This powerful cocktail is named after the great Russian writer. Use a good sparkling wine from Australia or California.

1 measure/1½ tbsp vodka
1 measure/1½ tbsp Grand Marnier
dash lime juice
dash orange bitters (or orange curaçao)
dry sparkling wine

Shake the first four ingredients with ice, and strain into a chilled, large wine goblet. Top up with sparkling wine.

Soft Fruit and Ginger Cup

This colourful medley of soft fruits is steeped in vodka and served with an icy blend of sorbet and ginger ale. You will definitely need to use spoons. The recipe serves four, and can be used as a summer dinner-party dessert.

115g/4oz strawberries, hulled
115g/4oz raspberries, hulled
50g/2oz blueberries
15ml/1 tbsp caster (superfine) sugar
4 measures/6 tbsp vodka
600ml/1 pint still ginger ale
4 large scoops orange sorbet
1 measure/1½ tbsp grenadine

Cut the strawberries in half and put them in a bowl with the raspberries, blueberries and sugar. Pour over the vodka and toss lightly. Cover and chill for at least 30 minutes. Put the ginger ale and sorbet in a blender or food processor and process until smooth. Pour into four bowl-shaped glasses and

add a couple of ice cubes to each glass of sorbet mixture. Spoon ¼ measure/ 1 tsp grenadine over the ice cubes in each glass, then spoon the vodka-steeped fruits on top of the sorbet mixture and ice cubes. Garnish each glass with a physalis and serve.

Vodka and Kumquat Lemonade

This is a mild-sounding name for what is a strong concoction of kumquat and peppercorn-flavoured vodka and white curaçao. The recipe comfortably serves two, in long glasses.

90g/3oz kumquats
5 measures/120ml/4fl oz vodka
3 black peppercorns
⅔ measure/1 tbsp white curaçao
⅔ measure/1 tbsp lemon juice
7 measures/150ml/¼ pint sparkling mineral or soda water
fresh mint leaves

Thickly slice the kumquats and add to the vodka in an airtight jar with the cracked black peppercorns. Set aside for at least a couple of hours or overnight if possible. Fill a pitcher with cracked ice and then add the curaçao, the lemon juice and the kumquat-flavoured vodka with the sliced kumquats (but not the peppercorns). Using a long swizzle-stick, stir together well. Add the mineral or soda water and a few fresh mint leaves and gently stir everything together. Pour the drink into chilled glasses of ice. Add slices of kumquats to the glasses and garnish with extra mint sprigs.

Woo Woo

A creation of the 1980s, Woo Woo was one of the first cocktail recipes to use peach schnapps. Archer's Peach County was the brand preferred, and the recipe is still a popular one on today's cocktail lists.

1 measure/1½ tbsp vodka
1½ measures/6 tsp peach schnapps
4 measures/6 tbsp cranberry juice

Shake all the ingredients well with ice, and strain into a highball glass half-filled with cracked ice.

Bartending know-how
Peach schnapps is not really a true schnapps, but a sort of schnapps-based liqueur. Archer's now make lime and cranberry versions to supplement the original peach.

Nevsky Prospekt

The Russian reference here is to a boulevard in Moscow. You can add ¼ measure/1 tsp sugar syrup if you feel it needs a touch of extra sweetness, but I prefer it quite sour.

1½ measures/6 tsp Stolichnaya vodka
½ measure/2 tsp light rum
½ measure/2 tsp orange curaçao
¼ measure/1 tsp lime juice

Shake all the ingredients well with ice, and strain into a cocktail glass. Garnish with a half-slice of lime.

Green Dragon

You will find one glass of this dry, savoury and extremely strong cocktail is more than enough. Sip it slowly, or be brave and take it at a couple of gulps. Then lie down.

2 measures/3 tbsp Stolichnaya vodka
1 measure/1½ tbsp green Chartreuse

Shake the ingredients well with ice, and strain into a cocktail glass.

Blackhawk

A lustrous purple is more the colour here than black, and the combination of fruit flavours is quite enchanting. This is a very moreish short drink with an appealing balance of sweet and sour.

1½ measures/6 tsp vodka
½ measure/2 tsp crème de mûre
½ measure/2 tsp lime juice

Shake all the ingredients well with ice, and strain into a cocktail glass. Add a whole, perfectly ripe blackberry and a half-slice of lime.

Blue Shark

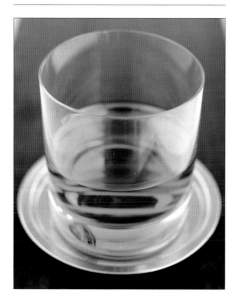

Blue curaçao mixes so well with clear spirits that it would seem a shame not to include a vodka-based recipe, and here is a popular American one.

1 measure/1½ tbsp vodka
1 measure/1½ tbsp tequila
½ measure/2 tsp blue curaçao

Shake all the ingredients well with ice, and strain into a small rocks glass. Squeeze a little orange rind over the drink to release the oil, but don't add the rind itself.

Bartending know-how
The kümmel you will buy for making a Boyar will most probably be the pre-eminent Wolfschmidt brand. It has been sold in the UK since the late Victorian era, having originally made its name in the Baltic state of Latvia.

Genoa

This is something like a strong Screwdriver with the bittering element of Campari adding savoury appeal.

1½ measures/6 tsp vodka
2 measures/3 tbsp orange juice
¾ measure/3 tsp Campari

Shake all the ingredients well with ice, and strain into a rocks glass containing a couple of cubes of ice. Add a twist of orange rind.

Boyar

This very dry and herb-tinged mixture would make a good appetite-whetter at a party where nibbles are going to be served. The tiny quantity of kümmel shines through, and leaves a very appetizing aftertaste in its wake.

Borodino

Let's get serious. This is a strong cocktail, with the ingredients in the 37.5% to 40% alcohol range, but the result is a virginal-looking white drink.

1 measure/1½ tbsp vodka
1 measure/1½ tbsp gin
1 measure/1½ tbsp Cointreau

Shake all the ingredients well with ice, and strain into a cocktail glass. Add a small piece of orange rind.

2 measures/3 tbsp vodka
½ measure/2 tsp dry vermouth
¼ measure/1 tsp kümmel

Shake with ice, and strain into a cocktail glass. The drink doesn't need a garnish.

Sex on the Beach

A variation on Woo Woo, this version has more fruit juice. The name has, not surprisingly, kept it popular in seaside resorts, as the next best resort after sex.

1 measure/1½ tbsp vodka
1 measure/1½ tbsp peach schnapps

3 measures/4½ tbsp cranberry juice
3 measures/4½ tbsp pineapple juice

Half-fill a highball glass with cracked ice, add all the ingredients in the above order, and stir vigorously. Garnish with pieces of pineapple and orange.

Kempinsky Fizz

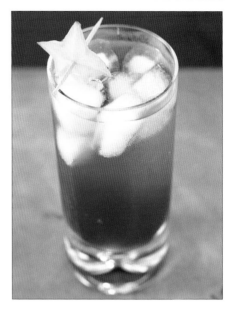

A luxuriously fruity, fizzy mixture with a delicate pinkish colour, this would kick off a dinner party in fine style.

1½ measures/6 tsp vodka
½ measure/2 tsp crème de cassis
¼ measure/1 tsp lemon juice
4 measures/6 tbsp sparkling ginger ale

Half-fill a chilled tall glass with ice, add the first three ingredients, stir briskly and then top up with ginger ale.

Soviet Cocktail

This is an American drink intended as a sort of grudging acknowledgement of its old adversary, the USSR.

1½ measures/6 tsp vodka
½ measure/2 tsp dry vermouuth
½ measure/2 tsp medium-dry (amontillado) sherry

Shake all the ingredients well with ice, and strain into a cocktail glass. Squeeze a twist of lemon rind over the top and drop it into the drink.

Prussian Salute

This is one of those hardcore cocktails that's all alcohol with no mixers. The sweet fruit notes in it help to soften its impact a little – but not much.

1½ measures/6 tsp vodka
½ measure/2 tsp crème de mûre
½ measure/2 tsp slivovitz
½ measure/2 tsp Cointreau

Shake all the ingredients well with ice, and strain into a cocktail glass. Garnish with a slice of lemon.

Bartending know-how
The original home of syrupy crème de cassis is Burgundy in eastern France, where much is made in Dijon. As a classic fruit liqueur, it dates back to the mid-19th century, and its principal export market today – somewhat surprisingly – is Japan, where they mix it with soda.

Rum

Before the advent of vodka cocktails, rum was the spirit with which all the exotic flavours were mixed. Coming from the tropical climates of the Caribbean and South America, it was felt to lend itself to all kinds of racy preparations, so unlike the comparative staidness of gin, whisky and brandy. There are basically three grades in the cocktail repertoire: white, light (or golden) and dark. The top-strength naval rums, known as "overproof", are sometimes added in droplets to a mixture: not just to fortify it, but to concentrate the flavour of what is still an under-appreciated spirit.

Tom and Jerry

A cold weather drink invented in the 1850s by the legendary Jerry Thomas of St Louis, Missouri, Tom and Jerry is one of the oldest cocktails in this book. It is said that Mr Thomas would serve these at the first snows of winter. This recipe serves four to six people.

For the batter:
3 eggs
45ml/3 tbsp caster (superfine) sugar
pinch bicarbonate of soda (baking soda)
1 measure/1½ tbsp dark rum
1.5ml/¼ tsp ground cinnamon
pinch ground cloves
pinch allspice

Separate the eggs and beat the whites into stiff peaks, adding 15ml/1 tbsp of the sugar with the bicarbonate. Mix the yolks separately with the rum, the rest of the sugar and the spices. Then fold in the whites with a metal spoon.

For each drink:
1 measure/1½ tbsp dark rum
1 measure/1½ tbsp brandy
4 measures/6 tbsp boiling milk

Using heatproof glasses, put in 15ml/1 tbsp of the batter and 1 measure/1½ tbsp each of rum and brandy, then top up with boiled milk. Dust with nutmeg.

Bacardi Cocktail

The original recipe, this must (legally, in the USA) be made with the world's biggest-selling white rum brand. It's short and sour and altogether perfect.

1½ measures/6 tsp Bacardi white rum
juice of half a lime
¼ measure/1 tsp grenadine

Shake all the ingredients well with ice, and strain into a cocktail glass. Add a slice of lime. (Add a measure of gin to turn it into a Bacardi Special, a variation created in the 1920s.)

Caribbean Breeze

This bang-up-to-date mixture of exotic fruit flavours will have party guests coming back for more.

1½ measures/6 tsp dark rum
½ measure/2 tsp crème de banane
3 measures/4½ tbsp pineapple juice
2 measures/3 tbsp cranberry juice
¼ measure/1 tsp lime cordial

Shake all the ingredients well with ice, and strain into a large wine goblet, generously filled with crushed ice. Garnish with a slice of pineapple and a wedge of lime.

Cuba Libre

This is a brand-specific cocktail if ever there was one. Created in Cuba – where Bacardi was then produced – in the late 19th century, the novelty value of Cuba Libre lay in its use of Coca-Cola, a newfangled tonic beverage, then less than ten years on the market.

juice and rind of half a lime
2 measures/3 tbsp Bacardi white rum
5 measures/120ml/4 fl oz Coca-Cola

Squeeze the juice directly into a highball glass half-filled with cracked ice, and then put the empty rind in too. Add the rum, stir, and finally top up with ice-cold Coca-Cola.

Ti Punch

This is a great favourite in the originally French Caribbean islands.

1 lime
2 measures/3 tbsp French Caribbean white rum
¼ measure/1 tsp sugar syrup

Cut the lime into wedges and put them in a wide-based rocks glass. Pound and crush them with a blunt instrument to release the juices, but leave all the residue in the glass. Add the syrup and the rum, and plenty of cracked ice.

Saoco

I have drunk this cocktail on Barbados served in half a hollowed-out coconut shell, but it does nearly as well served in a plain glass tumbler. Coconut milk is the watery liquid that is released from the centre of a coconut when the end is pierced, and not to be confused with canned coconut cream.

2 measures/3 tbsp white rum
4 measures/6 tbsp coconut milk

Shake both the ingredients well with ice, and then strain into a rocks glass that has been half-filled with finely crushed ice. Drink through two short straws.

Waikiki Beach

This creamy, nutty, exotic cocktail has the power to call up memories of Caribbean beach holidays gone by.

1½ measures/6 tsp white rum
½ measure/2 tsp amaretto
½ measure/2 tsp canned coconut cream
2 measures/3 tbsp pineapple juice
1 measure/1½ tbsp passion fruit juice
1 measure/1½ tbsp double (heavy) cream

Shake all the ingredients well with ice, and strain into a bowl-shaped cocktail glass half-filled with cracked ice. Garnish with a cube of pineapple and a cocktail cherry.

Mary Pickford

A 1920s recipe in tribute to one of the greats among the first generation of silent movie stars.

1½ measures/6 tsp white rum
1½ measures/6 tsp pineapple juice
¼ measure/1 tsp grenadine
dash maraschino

Shake all the ingredients well with ice, and strain into a cocktail glass filled with crushed ice. Garnish with a cocktail cherry.

Daiquiri

The Daiquiri is one of the most adapted and abused cocktails in the repertoire. Created in the 1890s, it is named after a town in Cuba and was originally nothing more than a white rum sour. Despite its extreme simplicity, this really is one of the all-time perfect cocktail recipes, standing proud above the fashionable fruit versions mentioned below.

2 measures/3 tbsp white rum
juice of half a lime or a quarter of a lemon
5ml/1 tsp caster (superfine) sugar

Fruit Daiquiri

The original Daiquiri recipe of white rum shaken with lemon or lime juice and a pinch of sugar can be adapted by adding a measure of any of the fruit liqueurs to it, with about 50g/2oz of the

Shake all the ingredients well with ice to dissolve the sugar, and strain into a well-chilled cocktail glass. Serve ungarnished.

equivalent puréed fruit as well. The sugar can then be left out. A strawberry version, made with crème de fraise and pulped fruit, is especially enticing, and banana is a crowd-pleaser too.

Presidente

Another 1920s Cuban recipe, this is named in honour of one of the island's old military rulers.

2 measures/3 tbsp white rum
1 measure/1½ tbsp orange curaçao
½ measure/2 tsp dry vermouth
¼ measure/1 tsp grenadine

Stir the ingredients with ice in a pitcher to chill them well, and then strain into a frozen rocks glass. Add a slice of lemon, decorated around the edges with a canelle knife.

Planter's Punch

This long, refreshing, old colonial drink originates from the sugar plantations that are dotted throughout the West Indian islands.

1 measure/1½ tbsp fresh lime juice
1 measure/1½ tbsp orange juice
2 measures/3 tbsp dark rum
½ measure/2 tsp grenadine
dash Angostura bitters
soda water or lemonade, chilled

Columbus

A simple and appealing mixture of sweet and sour, Columbus must absolutely be made with light rum, but if that's the only colour you haven't got, use a half-and-half mixture of dark and white.

1½ measures/6 tsp light rum
¾ measure/3 tsp apricot brandy
1 measure/1½ tbsp lime juice

Shake all the ingredients well with ice, and strain into a cocktail glass. Garnish with a slice of lime.

Squeeze the lime and orange juices and add them to a pitcher of ice. Add the dark rum and the grenadine, and mix them together well for about 20 seconds. Add a dash of Angostura bitters to the bottom of a wide tumbler filled with cracked ice cubes. Strain the rum and grenadine mixture into the chilled tumbler. Finish with plenty of chilled soda water or lemonade, according to taste.

Garnish with two skewered peach slices and a physalis, complete with its leaves attached.

Mai Tai

This is a very refreshing, long but strong party drink that slides down easily – just before you do!

1 measure/1½ tbsp light rum
1 measure/1½ tbsp dark rum
1 measure/1½ tbsp apricot brandy
3 measures/4½ tbsp orange juice
3 measures/4½ tbsp pineapple juice
1 measure/1½ tbsp grenadine

Shake the first five ingredients well with ice, and strain into a highball glass half-filled with cracked ice. Slowly pour the grenadine into the glass, letting it sink to the bottom of the drink to make a glowing red layer. The cocktail could be lavishly garnished with tropical fruits.

Monkey Wrench

Deliciously refreshing, despite its indelicate name, this makes a fine drink for a summer afternoon in the garden.

1½ measures/6 tsp white rum
3 measures/4½ tbsp grapefruit juice
3 measures/4½ tbsp sparkling lemonade

Half-fill a highball glass with roughly cracked ice, and add the rum and grapefruit juice. Stir briskly, before topping up with the sparkling lemonade. Decorate with intertwined twists of grapefruit and lemon rind in a suitably artistic arrangement.

Blue Hawaiian

This drink can be decorated as flamboyantly as Carmen Miranda's headdress with a mixture of fruits and leaves. It is an eye-catching, colourful cocktail that you'll find very drinkable.

1 measure/1½ tbsp blue curaçao
1 measure/1½ tbsp coconut cream
2 measures/3 tbsp light rum
2 measures/3 tbsp pineapple juice
leaves and wedge of pineapple, slice of
    prickly pear or orange, a wedge of lime and
    a maraschino cherry, to garnish

Escape Route

Punt e Mes, made by the Carpano company of Turin, is one of the classic vermouth brands, and is a must for this elegant cocktail.

1 measure/1½ tbsp light rum
1 measure/1½ tbsp Punt e Mes
½ measure/2 tsp crème de fraise
4 measures/6 tbsp sparkling lemonade

Half-fill a highball glass with cracked ice, and add the first three ingredients. Stir vigorously before topping up with the lemonade. Garnish with a slice of lemon and a couple of mint leaves.

Put the curaçao, coconut cream and light rum in a blender with a few cubes of ice. Process very briefly until the colour is even. Add the pineapple juice to the blender and process the mixture once more until frothy. Spoon crushed ice into a large cocktail glass or goblet until three-quarters full. Strain the cocktail from the blender over the crushed ice.

Garnish with a wedge of pineapple, a slice of prickly pear or orange, a wedge of lime and a maraschino cherry.

Zombie

This legendary 1930s recipe was created at Don the Beachcomber restaurant in Hollywood, reportedly as a hangover cure! It has everything but the kitchen sink in it, and yet is a harmonious (and dynamic) mixture.

1 measure/1½ tbsp light rum
½ measure/2 tsp dark rum
½ measure/2 tsp white rum
1 measure/1½ tbsp orange curaçao
¼ measure/1 tsp Pernod
1 measure/1½ tbsp lemon juice
1 measure/1½ tbsp orange juice
1 measure/1½ tbsp pineapple juice
½ measure/2 tsp papaya juice
¼ measure/1 tsp grenadine
½ measure/2 tsp orgeat (almond syrup)
¼ measure/1 tsp overproof rum

Blend all but the last ingredient with ice, and strain into an ice-packed highball glass. Sprinkle with overproof rum. Garnish with a slice of pineapple, a slice of lime and a mint sprig.

Piña Colada

This has to be one of the most popular cocktails worldwide, with a name meaning "strained pineapple". For that extra Caribbean touch, the drink may be served in a hollowed-out pineapple shell, which also means that you can liquidize the flesh for the juice in the recipe, but a bowl-shaped cocktail glass is the next best thing.

2 measures/3 tbsp white rum
2 measures/3 tbsp pineapple juice
1½ measures/6 tsp coconut cream
5ml/1 tsp caster (superfine) sugar (if freshly
    blended fruit is used)

Shake all the ingredients well with ice, and strain into a cocktail goblet. Garnish with a slice of pineapple and a cherry. (If you can't get hold of coconut cream, the equivalent quantity of any coconut liqueur such as Malibu may be used to good effect.)

Passion Punch

Although it is not really a punch at all, the combination of passion fruit and grape juices in this recipe is a winning one. The acidity of the one is mitigated by the sweetness of the other, with the pineapple syrup adding a viscous texture to the drink.

Hustler

This is a sharply tangy drink. I prefer it without sugar to emphasize its bite, but around 5ml/1 tsp will not go amiss, if you find it just too sour without.

1 measure/1½ tbsp light rum
1 measure/1½ tbsp white rum
1 measure/1½ tbsp passion fruit juice
juice of a lime
5ml/1 tsp caster (superfine) sugar (optional)

Shake all the ingredients well with ice (especially well to dissolve the sugar if you are using it), and strain into a large wine goblet. Add the empty shell of the lime to the drink.

1½ measures/6 tsp light rum
1 measure/1½ tbsp red grape juice
1 measure/1½ tbsp passion fruit juice
¼ measure/1 tsp pineapple syrup (from a can)

Shake all the ingredients well with ice, and strain into a rocks glass.

Sun City

A similar type of blend to the Mai Tai, and almost as lethal, this is a drink with plenty of personality.

1 measure/1½ tbsp white rum
½ measure/2 tsp dark rum
½ measure/2 tsp Galliano
½ measure/2 tsp apricot brandy
2 measures/3 tbsp pineapple juice
¼ measure/1 tsp lime juice
3 measures/4½ tbsp sparkling lemonade

Shake all but the last ingredient with ice, and then strain into a highball glass. Top up with the lemonade. Garnish with slices of lemon and lime.

Captain's Cocktail

This is named after Captain Morgan rum. Cocktail author Robert Cross suggests that the port be added to half of the drink's surface, so that it can be imbibed from the port side, as it were.

1 measure/1½ tbsp white rum
½ measure/2 tsp Captain Morgan spiced rum
1 measure/1½ tbsp lime juice
2.5ml/½ tsp caster (superfine) sugar
½ measure/2 tsp good ruby port

Shake the first four ingredients well with ice, and strain into a small tumbler. Sprinkle the port on top, and garnish with a slice of lime.

Costa del Sol

This is a light, sweet, fizzy drink with a gentle flavour, one of the less tastebud-startling rum cocktails.

2 measures/3 tbsp white rum
1 measure/1½ tbsp sweet red vermouth
1 measure/1½ tbsp sugar syrup
½ measure/2 tsp lemon juice
3 measures/4½ tbsp soda water

Half-fill a highball glass with cracked ice, and then add the first four ingredients. Stir, before adding the soda. Garnish with lemon pierced by a cocktail stick.

Beach Peach

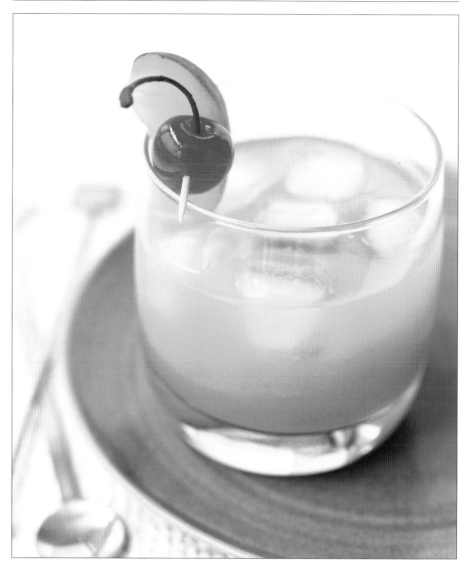

The flavour of this cocktail is largely derived from pure, thick peach nectar, and the drink has a nice balance of sweet and sharp flavours. It tastes alluring when sipped on the beach.

1½ measures/6 tsp white rum
¾ measure/3 tsp peach brandy
1 measure/1½ tbsp peach nectar
½ measure/2 tsp lime juice
¼ measure/1 tsp sugar syrup

Shake all the ingredients well with ice, and strain into a rocks glass half-filled with cracked ice. Garnish with a slice of ripe peach and a cherry.

Frozen Coconut

You may well have tasted something like this ice cream drink at a Thai restaurant with a cocktail list.

1½ measures/6 tsp white rum
1 measure/1½ tbsp Malibu or other coconut liqueur
45ml/3 tbsp coconut ice cream

Frost the rim of a large goblet by dipping it in coconut liqueur and then into grated or desiccated coconut. Half-fill it with finely crushed ice. Process all the ingredients thoroughly in a blender with plenty of ice, and strain into the prepared glass. Drink through a short straw, quickly.

Mulata

A Cuban creation of the 1940s, Mulata offers a beguiling combination of chocolate and lime flavours. It's a short but delicious drink that may well have you wanting a second one.

1¾ measures/2½ tbsp of light rum
¼ measure/1 tsp brown crème de cacao
juice of half a lime

Shake all the ingredients well with ice, and strain into a cocktail glass. Garnish with a half-slice of lime.

Jamaica Sunday

A spoonful of honey adds sweetness and an exotic note to this cocktail, the name of which indicates that it should specifically be made with a good Jamaican brand of rum. The darker and stronger the brand, the better.

2 measures/3 tbsp dark rum
¼ measure/1 tsp acacia honey

½ measure/2 tsp lime juice
2 measures/3 tbsp sparkling lemonade

In a separate glass, stir the honey into the dark rum until it is dissolved. Half-fill a rocks glass with cracked ice, and then add the honey-rum mixture and the lime juice, and stir again. Add the lemonade. Garnish with lime slices.

Goldilocks

The name is a rough approximation of the final colour of this appealing fruit-juice cocktail.

1 measure/1½ tbsp dark rum
1 measure/1½ tbsp Malibu
3 measures/4½ tbsp pineapple juice
2 measures/3 tbsp orange juice

Shake with ice, and strain into a tall glass half-filled with cracked ice. Garnish with slices of pineapple and orange.

Angel's Treat

The addition of cocoa powder to the mixture makes this an unusual but successful recipe. It should be sieved to remove any lumps, and combines very well with the almond-paste flavour of amaretto.

1½ measures/6 tsp dark rum
1 measure/1½ tbsp Disaronno Amaretto
1½ measures/6 tsp double (heavy) cream
2.5ml/½ tsp cocoa powder

Shake all the ingredients very vigorously with ice to dissolve the cocoa, and strain into a bowl-shaped cocktail glass. Sprinkle the surface with grated dark chocolate.

Arrowhead

The peachy flavour of Southern Comfort works well with fruity banana and lemon notes in this lightly fizzy rum cocktail.

1 measure/1½ tbsp dark rum
½ measure/2 tsp Southern Comfort
½ measure/2 tsp crème de banane
¼ measure/1 tsp lime juice
3 measures/4½ tbsp sparkling lemonade

Fill a rocks glass with ice nearly to the brim, and then add the ingredients in the order above. Give the drink a gentle stir without dispersing the fizz, and garnish with a half-slice of lemon.

Hurricane

There are almost as many different recipes for a drink called Hurricane as there are cocktail books, but this particular one, with its exuberantly fruity character, is my favourite.

1½ measures/6 tsp dark rum
1 measure/1½ tbsp white rum
1 measure/1½ tbsp lime juice
2 measures/3 tbsp passion fruit juice
1 measure/1½ tbsp pineapple juice
1 measure/1½ tbsp orange juice
½ measure/2 tsp blackcurrant syrup (from a can of fruit)

Shake all the ingredients well with ice, and strain into a highball glass. Decorate with slices of pineapple and orange and a cherry.

Chop Nut

An ingenious blend of coconut, chocolate and hazelnut flavours, all sharpened up with orange, this is a most satisfying drink.

1 measure/1½ tbsp white rum
¾ measure/3 tsp Malibu
½ measure/2 tsp white crème de cacao
¼ measure/1 tsp Frangelico
1½ measures/6 tsp mandarin juice

Shake all the ingredients well with ice, and strain into a bowl-shaped cocktail glass. For a slightly frothier texture, add 5ml/1 tsp egg white as well. Garnish with a twist of mandarin rind.

Emerald Star

Despite the presence of the green melon liqueur, the colour of this drink isn't exactly emerald. It's a pretty name nonetheless.

1 measure/1½ tbsp white rum
⅔ measure/1 tbsp Midori
⅓ measure/1½ tsp apricot brandy
⅓ measure/1½ tsp lime juice
1 measure/1½ tbsp passion fruit juice

Shake all the ingredients well with ice, and strain into a cocktail glass. Garnish with a slice of star fruit.

Bartending know-how
When the Japanese melon liqueur, Midori, was launched in New York in 1978, the party was held at the fabled Studio 54 nightclub. John Travolta, who had just made *Grease*, was among the guests.

Eye of the Tiger

This is another drink that has a dark rum float on top. It adds a suitably tigerish bite to what otherwise tastes like a rather innocent fruity mixture.

1 measure/1½ tbsp light rum
1 measure/1½ tbsp Malibu
1 measure/1½ tbsp cranberry juice
1 measure/1½ tbsp lemon juice
1 measure/1½ tbsp orange juice
1 measure/1½ tbsp sugar syrup
½ measure/2 tsp dark rum, preferably
   overproof

Shake all but the last ingredient well with ice, and strain into a highball glass half-filled with cracked ice. Sprinkle the dark rum on to the surface of the drink, and garnish with a slice of orange.

Petite Fleur

This tangy, refreshing cocktail makes a good aperitif. I'm not sure what flower is meant to be invoked by its name. Perhaps you can decide as you drink it.

1 measure/1½ tbsp white rum
1 measure/1½ tbsp Cointreau
1 measure/1½ tbsp grapefruit juice

Shake all the ingredients well with ice, and strain into a cocktail glass. Add a twist of grapefruit rind.

Rompope

Legend has it that this rich egg-nog was first made in the kitchens of a convent in Puebla, Mexico. It is traditional to seal bottles of Rompope with rolled corn husks, or corn cobs that have been stripped of their corn. The recipe makes 1.5 litres/2½ pints, and will keep for up to one week in the refrigerator.

1 litre/1¾ pints milk
350g/12oz sugar
2.5ml/½ tsp bicarbonate of soda (baking soda)
1 cinnamon stick
12 large egg yolks
300ml/½ pint dark rum

Pour the milk into a pan and stir in the sugar and bicarbonate of soda. Add the cinnamon stick. Place the pan over a medium heat and bring the mixture to the boil, stirring constantly. Immediately pour the mixture into a bowl and cool to room temperature. Remove the cinnamon stick, squeezing it gently to release any liquid.

Put the egg yolks in a heatproof bowl over a pan of simmering water and whisk until the mixture is very thick

Yum Yum

The name of this drink is an indication of most people's reactions to this exotically fruity recipe with a fleeting hint of coconut.

1½ measures/6 tsp white rum
½ measure/2 tsp Malibu
1 measure/1½ tbsp mango juice
1 measure/1½ tbsp peach juice
½ measure/2 tsp lime juice

and pale. Add the whisked yolks to the milk mixture a little at a time, beating after each addition.

Return the mixture to a clean pan, place over a low heat and cook until the mixture thickens and the back of the spoon is visible when a finger is drawn along it. Stir in the rum, pour into sterilized bottles and seal tightly with stoppers or clear film (plastic wrap). Chill until required, and serve very cold.

Shake all the ingredients well with ice, and strain into a highball glass half-filled with roughly cracked ice. Garnish with a slice of lime.

Bartending know-how
Malibu is from Jamaica, but its white rum base comes from Barbados.

Poker

Here is a simple cocktail from the 1920s. The preference now is for the proportions given below, although it was originally half-and-half. It may also be made with light rum instead of white, if you prefer.

1½ measures/6 tsp white rum
¾ measure/3 tsp sweet red vermouth

Shake the ingredients well with ice, and strain into a cocktail glass. Squeeze a twist of orange rind over the surface of the drink to release a spray of oil and then drop it in.

Bartending know-how
Recipes based on white rum are far more interesting if made with one of the small producers' island rums, rather than one of the big multi-national proprietary products.

Morning Joy

One wouldn't necessarily recommend making a habit of these, but the idea is of a more robust approach than usual to the glass of breakfast juice. How much joy it spreads over the morning may well depend on how joyful the night before was.

X.Y.Z.

The significance of its mysterious algebraic name escapes me, but this is a 1920s recipe that has survived the test of time. It's a strong one too.

2 measures/3 tbsp dark rum
1 measure/1½ tbsp Cointreau
1 measure/1½ tbsp lemon juice

Shake all the ingredients well with ice, and strain into a large cocktail glass. Add a half-slice of lemon.

1½ measures/6 tsp light rum
6 measures/135ml/4½ fl oz grapefruit juice
¼ measure/1 tsp sloe gin

Half-fill a highball glass with cracked ice, and then add the ingredients in this order, sprinkling the sloe gin on top as a float.

Trade Winds

The correct rum brand to use for this cocktail is Mount Gay, made on Barbados. It is properly served frappé.

2 measures/3 tbsp light rum
½ measure/2 tsp slivovitz
½ measure/2 tsp lime juice
½ measure/2 tsp orgeat (almond syrup)

Shake the ingredients well with ice, and strain into a cocktail glass filled with crushed ice. Add a half-slice of lime.

Kingston

This is named after the Jamaican capital, so it would be inappropriate to use rum from any other location.

1½ measures/6 tsp dark Jamaica rum
¾ measure/3 tsp gin

juice of half a lime
¼ measure/1 tsp grenadine

Shake all the ingredients well with ice, and strain into a cocktail glass. Garnish with a half-slice of lime.

Continental

An old-fashioned mixture of rum and peppermint cordial was once a popular drink. This cocktail presents a more adventurous spin on that formula. The colour is an attractive shade of tawny, and the mint flavour is agreeably set off by the piercing note of lime.

1½ measures/6 tsp light rum
½ measure/2 tsp green crème de menthe
½ measure/2 tsp lime juice

Shake all the ingredients well with ice, and strain into a cocktail glass. If available, add a sprig of mint to the drink.

Bolero

Here is one of those cocktails that's all alcohol and no mixers. Stirring the drink gently, as opposed to shaking it, emphasizes its strength, in the sense that the mixture doesn't become quite as chilled as it would in the shaker.

1½ measures/6 tsp light rum
¾ measure/3 tsp calvados
¼ measure/1 tsp sweet red vermouth

Mix the ingredients gently in a pitcher with a couple of ice cubes, and then strain into a pre-chilled rocks glass. Squeeze a twist of lemon over the drink, and then drop it in.

Pilot Boat

With its mixture of dark rum and banana, this is the most tropical-tasting cocktail imaginable. The relatively high proportion of citrus helps to sharpen it up most agreeably.

1½ measures/6 tsp dark rum, preferably Jamaica
1 measure/1½ tbsp crème de banane
2 measures/3 tbsp lemon juice

Shake all the ingredients well with ice, and strain into a bowl-shaped cocktail glass. Garnish with a slice of lemon.

Cantaloupe Cup

Another recipe containing puréed fruit. If a Cantaloupe melon isn't available, use any other sweet, green-fleshed variety. Note that the flavour of honeydew melon isn't strong enough for this drink.

1½ measures/6 tsp light rum
90g/3½oz ripe Cantaloupe melon, diced
½ measure/2 tsp lime juice
½ measure/2 tsp orange juice
dash sugar syrup

Process all the ingredients with smashed ice in the blender, and then strain into a goblet. Garnish with a thin slice of melon.

Strawberry and Banana Preparado

Similar to a smoothie, this is a thick, creamy fruit drink. You could leave out the alcohol if you prefer, but it would miss the point somewhat. The recipe serves four.

200g/7oz strawberries (plus a few extra to garnish)
2 bananas
115g/4oz block creamed coconut
120ml/4fl oz water
175ml/6fl oz white rum
60ml/4 tbsp grenadine

Pino Frio

Another in this mini-section of blended fruit cocktail recipes, this is a pineapple one with plenty of fruity zest to it.

1½ measures/6 tsp light rum
2 measures/3 tbsp pineapple juice
½ measure/2 tsp lemon juice
two slices of pineapple, about 2cm/1in thick, cut into chunks

Put all the ingredients into a blender with plenty of cracked ice, and whizz up until perfectly smooth. Pour the mixture into a chilled, tall glass, and garnish with a couple of extra chunks of fresh pineapple.

Hull the strawberries and chop them into halves, or quarters if they are large fruits. Peel the bananas and chop them into rough chunks. Put the fruit in a food processor or blender, crumble in the coconut and add the water. Process until smooth, scraping down the sides of the goblet as necessary. Add the rum, grenadine, and about ten ice cubes, crushing the ice first unless you have a heavy-duty processor. Blend until smooth and thick. Serve at once, garnishing the drink with the extra strawberries.

Bartending know-how
Creamed coconut not only makes for a luxuriously textured drink; it also has a wonderful concentrated coconutty flavour.

Havana Bandana

Use Cuban rum for this cocktail if you can get it. A drink full of liquidized banana makes for a very sumptuous and filling blend. Use one that has the mottled dark brown patches of a very ripe fruit.

2 measures/3 tbsp light rum
½ measure/2 tsp lime juice
1 ripe banana, sliced
¼ measure/1 tsp crème de banane

Add the first three ingredients to a blender with plenty of cracked ice, and process until the banana is fully incorporated into the liquids. Pour out into a chilled goblet, and spoon the banana liqueur on to the surface. Sprinkle some grated nutmeg over the top too, if desired.

Hot Tea Toddy

Rum isn't just a good partner for coffee. It also goes unexpectedly well with tea. Use a good Indian leaf such as Assam or Darjeeling in this recipe, and strain it.

1½ measures/6 tsp light rum
2.5ml/½ tsp clear honey
2.5ml/½ tsp ground cinnamon
slice of lemon
1 teacup hot black tea
piece of crystallized (candied) ginger

Add all but the last ingredient to a pan and gently warm until just about to boil. Pour out into a mug and add the ginger.

Bartending know-how
Hot tea cocktails are pretty few and far between. Use a fairly straightforward blend such as English Breakfast tea or perhaps Assam or Darjeeling. China teas will be too assertively flavoured to sit easily in the mix.

Jamaican Black Coffee

There are any number of combinations of alcohol with hot brewed coffee, some more successful than others. This delicious version of black coffee is in fact only slightly alcoholic but gains extra allure from the inclusion of citrus fruits. The recipe serves eight.

1 lemon and 2 oranges, finely sliced
1.5 litres/2½ pints black coffee (filter/cafetière brewed using 55g/2oz coffee per 1 litre/ 1¾ pints water)

Hot Buttered Rum

Another hot preparation for winter drinking, this will cheer the heart if you've just come in from the cold.

2 measures/3 tbsp dark rum
5ml/1 tsp light muscovado (raw) or demarara (brown) sugar
2.5ml/½ tsp ground cinnamon
15g/½oz unsalted butter

Mix the rum and sugar in a tall glass. Add the cinnamon and butter, and then fill with hot water. Remember to stand a spoon in the glass to conduct the heat if the water has just boiled. Stir well to dissolve the sugar.

2 measures/3 tbsp light rum
85g/3oz caster (superfine) sugar

Place the lemon and orange slices in a pan. Add the coffee and heat. When the mixture is about to boil, pour in the rum and sugar, stirring well until the sugar dissolves, then immediately remove from the heat. While the coffee is still very hot, pour or ladle into heatproof glasses, and garnish with a fresh lemon slice.

San Juan

A coconutty, fruity and strong cocktail seems the only fitting way to conclude our repertoire of rum recipes.

1½ measures/6 tsp light rum
1 measure/1½ tbsp grapefruit juice
1 measure/1½ tbsp lime juice
½ measure/2 tsp coconut cream
¼ measure/1 tsp overproof dark rum

Blend all except the last ingredient with cracked ice in the liquidizer, and then pour into a bowl-shaped cocktail glass. Sprinkle the surface of the drink with the overproof rum, and add a half-slice of lime.

Whisky

It is perhaps whisky that is the trickiest base ingredient to use in cocktails. Its flavour doesn't take quite as obligingly as the other spirits do to being mixed with liqueurs and fruit juices, although it is by no means bereft of its classic recipes. The rich, sweetly woody flavours of American whiskeys such as bourbon and rye, and the fruitiness of Canadian whisky, are better in this respect than Scotch. It is the iodiney pungency of much single malt Scotch that gets in the way. Perhaps these products really are best enjoyed on their own, or else with nothing more elaborate than fresh spring water.

Whisky Sour

Mix the juice of half a lemon with 5ml/ 1 tsp caster (superfine) sugar in a small tumbler with two or three cubes of ice. When the sugar is dissolved, add a generous measure of whisky and stir again – American whiskeys are best for this preparation. Some people add a brief squirt of soda. If you find this formula a little too sour, add a little more sugar, but this is the way I like it.

Perfect Manhattan

When making Manhattans it's a matter of preference whether you use sweet vermouth, dry vermouth or a mixture of the two. Both of the former require a dash of Angostura bitters. The last, given here, is such a harmoniously balanced mixture that it doesn't need it.

2 measures/3 tbsp rye whiskey
¼ measure/1 tsp dry vermouth
¼ measure/1 tsp sweet red vermouth

Pour the whiskey and vermouths into a bar glass half-full of ice. Stir well for 30 seconds to mix and chill. Strain on the rocks or straight up into a chilled cocktail glass. Pare away a small strip of lemon rind. Tie it into a knot to help release the oils from the rind, and drop it into the cocktail. Add a maraschino cherry with its stalk left intact. As any Manhattan drinker wil tell you, the cherry is essential.

Rob Roy

A further modification of the Perfect Manhattan recipe, Rob Roy is made with Scotch, and inclines very much to the sweeter end of the spectrum. It has traditionally been drunk on St Andrew's Day, November 30, but may with confidence be drunk all year round now.

1 measure/1½ tbsp Scotch
1 measure/1½ tbsp sweet red vermouth

Shake the ingredients well with ice, and strain into a cocktail glass. Some recipes add a dash of Angostura bitters to the mix as well, but I leave that to your discretion.

Mint Julep

One of the oldest cocktails of them all, this originated in the southern states of the USA, probably in the 18th century. It's the drink of tradition at the Kentucky Derby, the first Saturday in May, and is an incomparably refreshing mixture that has deservedly become a classic.

15ml/1 tbsp caster (superfine) sugar
8–10 fresh mint leaves
⅔ measure/1 tbsp hot water
2 measures/3 tbsp bourbon

Place the sugar in a mortar or bar glass. Tear the mint leaves into small pieces and add them to the sugar. Bruise them with a pestle or use a muddler to release their flavour and colour. Add the hot water and grind well together. Spoon into a highball glass and half-fill with crushed ice. Add the bourbon.
　Stir until the outside of the glass has frosted. Allow to stand for a couple of minutes until the ice melts slightly and dilutes the drink.

Whisky Mac

The classic cold remedy is half-and-half good Scotch and green ginger wine (preferably Crabbie's). These days, it is generally served over ice in a rocks glass, but traditionally it was taken straight up. Whether it actually gets rid of a cold must be open to doubt, but it certainly makes you feel better.

Canada Cocktail

An engagingly sweet and fruity cocktail that obviously has to be made with whisky from Canada. Canadian Club is a fine brand, and is generally available.

1½ measures/6 tsp Canadian whisky
¼ measure/1 tsp Cointreau
2 dashes Angostura bitters
5ml/1 tsp caster (superfine) sugar

Shake all the ingredients well with ice, and strain into a cocktail glass. Garnish with a twist of orange rind.

Bobby Burns

Similar to Rob Roy, but with the herbal tang of Bénédictine coming through it, this is a drink named after Scotland's national poet. It is best served on Burns Night, January 25.

1½ measures/6 tsp Scotch
¾ measure/3 tsp sweet red vermouth
¼ measure/1 tsp Bénédictine

Stir all the ingredients well with ice, and strain into a chilled cocktail glass. Squeeze a spray of oil from a piece of lemon rind over the surface, but in this case don't add the rind to the drink. In the 1920s, the cocktail was shaken, but it seems to work better stirred, which gives a less cloudy result.

Old-Fashioned

The Old-Fashioned is only a modified bourbon or rye whiskey, but quickly established itself as one of the all-time classic preparations. It is usually heavily garnished, and served in a particular kind of squat tumbler that is named after the drink.

¼ measure/1 tsp sugar syrup
2 dashes Angostura bitters
2 measures/3 tbsp bourbon or rye whiskey

Mix the sugar and Angostura in an Old-Fashioned glass until the sugar is dissolved. Add plenty of cracked ice and then the whiskey. Throw in a twist of lemon rind, a slice of orange cut laterally from the fruit and a cocktail cherry, and serve with a stirring implement in it. This is the most old-fashioned formula for an Old-Fashioned.

New York

This is another simple preparation for whisky that was made in the 1920s with Canadian whisky, despite its name. Scotch can also successfully be used, however, as can, seemingly, anything but American whiskey.

2 measures/3 tbsp Canadian whisky or Scotch
5ml/1 tsp caster (superfine) sugar
juice of half a lime
dash grenadine

Stir all the ingredients vigorously with ice in a pitcher, and then strain into a chilled cocktail glass. Squeeze a twist of lemon over the drink, but don't drop it in.

Bartending know-how
Bourbon and rye whiskeys have quite distinctive flavours. In each case, the chosen grain must constitute at least 51% of the mash (corn being used in bourbon). Rye results in a thicker, heavier-tasting whiskey with a rather more rustic appeal than classic bourbon.

Rusty Nail

A short, sharp drink, this is another classic half-and-half recipe, and one that still manages to do perfect justice to both ingredients.

1½ measures/6 tsp Scotch
1½ measures/6 tsp Drambuie

Pour both ingredients over crushed ice in a rocks glass or whisky tumbler, and stir gently. No garnish is necessary. Some prefer to leave the ice cubes whole so as not to dilute the drink too much. It should be drunk quickly.

Bartending know-how
A Rusty Nail is really *the* Drambuie cocktail. Attempts to make this fine Scottish liqueur blend with anything other than Scotch always seem to come to grief. It genuinely seems to be too good to mix.

Sea Dog

This is a long Scotch whisky drink with a citrus twist. For a sweeter drink, add a second sugar cube.

1–2 sugar cubes
2 dashes Angostura bitters
2 orange wedges
2 lemon wedges
⅔ measure/1 tbsp Scotch
1 measure/1½ tbsp Bénédictine
2 measures/3 tbsp soda water

Put the sugar cube at the bottom of a highball glass, add the bitters and allow to soak into the sugar cube. Add the orange and lemon wedges and, using a muddler, press the juices from the fruit. Fill the glass with cracked ice. Add the whisky and Bénédictine, and mix together well with a swizzle-stick. Add the chilled soda water. Serve with the muddler, so that more juice can be pressed from the fruit by the drinker. Garnish with a maraschino cherry.

Gall Bracer

Short and smart, this drink is served on the rocks in a tumbler, or in a long-stemmed glass with a maraschino cherry. It all depends on the drinker and the occasion.

2 dashes Angostura bitters
2 dashes grenadine
2 measures/3 tbsp bourbon or rye whiskey

Millionaire

Several cocktails have been recorded over the years under this name. The *Savoy Cocktail Book* lists two alternatives, one based on rum, the other on gin. This one is from roughly the same era, though.

1½ measures/6 tsp bourbon
¾ measure/3 tsp Cointreau
dash grenadine
½ egg white

Shake all the ingredients well with ice, and strain into a cocktail glass. Garnish with a half-slice of lemon.

Half-fill a bar glass with ice cubes. Add the Angostura bitters, grenadine and whiskey, and stir well to chill. Place some ice in a small tumbler and pour the cocktail over it. Squeeze lemon rind over the top and then discard. Garnish with a cherry, if desired. For a longer drink, finish with soda or sparkling mineral water.

Buckaroo

Not many cocktails work well with cola, but this is an honourable exception. The pronounced bittering note contributed by the Angostura is essential and should not be omitted.

1½ measures/6 tsp bourbon
2.5ml/½ tsp Angostura bitters
5 measures/120ml/4fl oz Coca-Cola

Add the first two ingredients to a highball glass containing plenty of cracked ice. Stir briskly and then top up with cola. Serve with a swizzle-stick for further stirring.

Loch Lomond

This is another very simple treatment for Scotch for those who are not quite up to taking it neat.

1½ measures/6 tsp Scotch
¼ measure/1 tsp sugar syrup
2 dashes Angostura bitters

Shake all the ingredients well with ice, and strain into a cocktail glass. Squeeze a piece of lemon over the surface and discard.

Bartending know-how
When Scotch is given as few additives as it is in the Loch Lomond cocktail, you can afford to be as choosy as any whisky connoisseur about which type you use. Even fine single malt will not suffer unduly in this simple preparation.

Duck Soup

A fruity preparation in which bourbon is given the treatment more normally accorded to rum. It works well, though, showing what a versatile drink American whiskey is.

2 measures/3 tbsp bourbon
½ measure/2 tsp apricot brandy
¾ measure/3 tsp lemon juice
¾ measure/3 tsp pineapple juice
5ml/1 tsp caster (superfine) sugar

Modern Cocktail

The meaning of "modern" here is not as in 21st century, but as in 1920s. There were two cocktails with this name even then. One had whisky and sloe gin in it, but this seems to have been the original. It has a strong and unusual flavour that is an acquired taste, but one that you may well find yourself acquiring.

2 measures/3 tbsp Scotch
⅓ measure/1½ tsp dark rum
¼ measure/1 tsp absinthe
¼ measure/1 tsp orange bitters (or curaçao)
⅓ measure/1½ tsp lemon juice

Shake all the ingredients well with ice, and strain into a cocktail glass. Garnish with a twist of lemon.

Shake all the ingredients well with ice, and strain into a rocks glass that is half-filled with cracked ice. Garnish with a slice of lemon and a cherry.

Bartending know-how
Bourbon can technically be made anywhere in the United States, as its name isn't a geographical designation. Its traditional home state, however, is Kentucky, which is the only one allowed to put its name on the label. Tennessee whiskey may not be called Tennessee bourbon because when the labelling laws were drawn up in the 19th century, Kentucky had more senators than its southern neighbour.

Brainstorm

Here is a recipe that specifically calls for Irish whiskey. Its smooth, triple-distilled flavour works exceptionally well with the other ingredients. Jameson's would be a particularly good brand to use.

2 measures/3 tbsp Irish whiskey
2 dashes dry vermouth
2 dashes Bénédictine

Half-fill an Old-Fashioned glass with cracked ice, and then add the ingredients in this order. Stir gently, add a twist of orange rind, and serve with a swizzle-stick for stirring.

Churchill

The British wartime leader is well-served by having this sophisticated and powerful cocktail named after him, even though Scotch wasn't his favourite tipple.

1½ measures/6 tsp Scotch
½ measure/2 tsp sweet red vermouth

½ measure/2 tsp Cointreau
½ measure/2 tsp lime juice

Shake all the ingredients well with ice, and strain into a chilled cocktail glass. Garnish with a half-slice of orange and a slice of lime.

Jack Frost

The Jack in the name refers to the ever-popular Tennessee whiskey brand, Jack Daniel's, and so that is the type that must be used. This is an exotic and highly appealing cocktail.

1 measure/1½ tbsp Jack Daniel's
¾ measure/3 tsp dry vermouth
⅓ measure/1½ tsp crème de banane

1 measure/1½ tbsp passion fruit juice
⅓ measure/1½ tsp pineapple juice

Shake all the ingredients well with ice, and strain into a large cocktail glass that has been half-filled with crushed ice. The drink could be garnished with a slice of lemon on a stick with a chunk of juicy, ripe pineapple.

Kentucky Kernel

The geographical reference of this drink indicates that it's a bourbon cocktail, and the second half of the name refers to the apricot kernels from which its other alcoholic ingredient is made. The grapefruit juice brings it all into focus.

1½ measures/6 tsp bourbon
½ measure/2 tsp apricot brandy
1 measure/1½ tbsp grapefruit juice
¼ measure/1 tsp grenadine

Shake all the ingredients well with ice, and pour the drink – ice and all – into a rocks glass.

Plank Walker

Another recipe that puns on a famous name, this one being the celebrated Scotch brand, Johnnie Walker. It's a hardcore, all-alcohol mixture.

1½ measures/6 tsp Johnnie Walker Red Label Scotch
½ measure/2 tsp sweet red vermouth
½ measure/2 tsp yellow Chartreuse

Shake all the ingredients well with ice, and strain into a rocks glass half-filled with roughly cracked ice. Add a wedge of lemon.

Pleasant Dreams

This fruity treatment for bourbon would make a very comforting nightcap – so long as you confine yourself to just the one, that is.

1½ measures/6 tsp bourbon
¾ measure/3 tsp crème de mûre
¼ measure/1 tsp peach schnapps

Shake all the ingredients well with ice, and pour without straining into a chilled rocks glass.

Artists' Special

This drink is so-named because it was invented at the Artists' Club in the rue Pigalle, Paris, in the 1920s. The red ingredient was originally redcurrant syrup, but grenadine can be used to perfectly good effect instead. The mixture of Scotch and sweet sherry at its heart is a very appealing one.

Algonquin

This is named after the elegant New York hotel where Dorothy Parker once ruled the roost. The types of whisky to be used are once again quite specific.

2 measures/3 tbsp rye or Canadian whisky
1 measure/1½ tbsp dry vermouth
1 measure/1½ tbsp pineapple juice

Shake all the ingredients well with ice, and strain into a rocks glass half-filled with cracked ice. Garnish with lemon.

1 measure/1½ tbsp Scotch
1 measure/1½ tbsp sweet brown sherry
½ measure/2 tsp lemon juice
½ measure/2 tsp grenadine

Shake all the ingredients well with ice, and strain into a cocktail glass. Add a half-slice of lemon.

Pamplemousse

The name is the French word for "grapefruit", and so it's not hard to work out what the principal flavour of this charming cocktail should be.

1½ measures/6 tsp Canadian whisky
½ measure/2 tsp Southern Comfort
2 measures/3 tbsp grapefruit juice
¼ measure/1 tsp pineapple syrup

Shake all the ingredients well with ice, and then strain into a rocks glass half-filled with cracked ice. Add a short twist of grapefruit rind and a cocktail cherry.

Bartending know-how
Both Southern Comfort and some Canadian whiskies have a fruity flavour, the former derived at least partly from the use of peaches. They work particularly well in fruity mixtures such as this one.

Rocky Mountain

Here is another of those cocktails that calls for three specific brands, and wouldn't be quite the same with substitutes. Its light, delicately herbal tinge is very attractive.

1½ measures/6 tsp Canadian Club
½ measure/2 tsp Glayva
¼ measure/1 tsp Punt e Mes

Shake all the ingredients well with ice, and pour without straining into a chilled rocks glass.

Bartending know-how
The Italian aperitif Punt e Mes, created in Turin in 1870, contains around four dozen herbs and spices on a white wine base. In Italy, it is traditionally accompanied by a piece of strong, dark chocolate.

Blizzard

The trick with this drink is to shake it for longer than normal with masses of ice until the mixture is extremely frosty-looking. That incidentally goes some way to disguise the high proportion of bourbon in it.

3 measures/4½ tbsp bourbon
1 measure/1½ tbsp cranberry juice

Grenoble

This is a superbly fruity cocktail with quite a kick, and one that demonstrates what a good mixer Kentucky whiskey is.

1½ measures/6 tsp bourbon
½ measure/2 tsp crème de framboise
½ measure/2 tsp Cointreau
1 measure/1½ tbsp orange juice
¼ measure/1 tsp orgeat syrup

Shake all the ingredients well with ice, and strain into a cocktail glass. Garnish with a half-slice of orange and a raspberry on a cocktail stick.

⅔ measure/1 tbsp lemon juice
30ml/2 tbsp sugar syrup

Shake all the ingredients extremely well with plenty of large ice cubes, and pour the mixture unstrained into a chilled highball glass. Garnish with a slice of lemon, and perhaps a couple of cranberries.

Tivoli

There is an Italian connection in this powerful little cocktail to reflect its name, but it comes by way of Scandinavia and Kentucky.

1½ measures/6 tsp bourbon
½ measure/2 tsp sweet red vermouth
½ measure/2 tsp aquavit
dash Campari

Shake all the ingredients well with ice, and strain into a chilled cocktail glass. Garnish the drink with a half-slice of lemon.

Paddy

Another traditional one, this was originally made with the Irish whiskey brand of the same name. In the 1920s, it had equal quantities of whiskey and vermouth and slightly less Angostura, which would obviously make for a sweeter result. This is today's drier and more sophisticated formula.

1½ measures/6 tsp Irish whiskey
¾ measure/3 tsp sweet red vermouth
3 dashes Angostura bitters

Shake all the ingredients well with ice, and strain into a chilled cocktail glass. Garnish with a half-slice of lemon.

Tipperary

You'll certainly know you've had one of these! Tipperary is an old 1920s mixture that's all alcohol, and packs the considerable punch of Chartreuse. If you're feeling brave, the Chartreuse was originally a whole measure too.

1 measure/1½ tbsp Irish whiskey
1 measure/1½ tbsp sweet red vermouth
½ measure/2 tsp green Chartreuse

Add the ingredients to a pitcher with plenty of cracked ice, and stir until cold enough to frost the sides of the glass. Strain into a pre-chilled cocktail glass.

Highland Morning

Although the name seems to be encouraging you to drink one of these for breakfast, a little later in the day might be wiser.

1 measure/1½ tbsp Scotch
¾ measure/3 tsp Cointreau
3 measures/4½ tbsp grapefruit juice

Loch Ness

A pair of Scottish and a pair of Irish cocktails rounds off with this tough cookie, which dates from the 1920s.

1½ measures/6 tsp Scotch
1 measure/1½ tbsp Pernod

Shake all the ingredients well with ice, and pour (unstrained if you really are having it in the morning) into a chilled rocks glass. The drink could be garnished with a twist of grapefruit rind and perhaps a half-slice of orange to reflect the presence of Cointreau in the mix.

¼ measure/1 tsp sweet red vermouth

Shake all the ingredients well with ice, and pour without straining into a chilled rocks glass or Old-Fashioned glass. Do not garnish.

Coffee Egg-Nog

This is a rather special coffee drink, particularly suitable for daytime summer-holiday festivities. The recipe serves six to eight.

8 eggs, separated
225g/8oz sugar
250ml/8fl oz cold strong coffee (espresso strength or filter/cafetière brewed at 75g/3oz coffee per 1 litre/1¾ pints water)
220ml/7½fl oz Scotch or bourbon
220ml/7½fl oz double (heavy) cream
120ml/4fl oz whipped cream
ground nutmeg, to decorate

Thoroughly beat the egg yolks, then add the sugar, mixing well. Heat gently in a pan over a low heat, stirring with a wooden spoon. Allow to cool a few minutes, stir in the coffee and whisky, and then slowly add the cream, stirring well. Beat the egg whites until stiff and stir into the egg-nog, mixing well. Pour into small round cups, top each with a small dollop of whipped cream and sprinkle nutmeg on top.

Jamaica Shake

Combining the best of both worlds, this cream cocktail brings together the complementary richnesses of American whiskey and Jamaica rum. It's a milkshake for adults.

1½ measures/6 tsp bourbon
1 measure/1½ tbsp dark Jamaica rum
1 measure/1½ tbsp double (heavy) cream

Shake all the ingredients well with ice to amalgamate the cream, and strain into a cocktail glass. Sift grated chocolate over the top.

Irish Chocolate Velvet

This is a luxurious creamy hot chocolate drink, with just a touch of alcohol to fortify it. It would be the perfect antidote to a winter morning spent working outdoors. The recipe serves four.

250ml/8fl oz double (heavy) cream
400ml/14fl oz milk
115g/4oz milk chocolate, chopped into small pieces
30ml/2 tbsp cocoa powder
60ml/4 tbsp Irish whiskey
whipped cream, for topping

Ring of Kerry

Since Irish whiskey lends itself so well to these creamy treatments, here is another one, in which it appears with its much-loved compatriot, Bailey's Irish Cream.

1½ measures/6 tsp Irish whiskey
1 measure/1½ tbsp Bailey's Irish Cream
½ measure/2 tsp Kahlúa

Shake all the ingredients well with ice, and strain into a chilled cocktail glass. Sprinkle 5ml/1 tsp grated chocolate over the top.

Whip half the cream in a bowl until it is thick enough to hold its shape. Place the milk and chocolate in a pan and heat gently, stirring, until the chocolate has melted. Whisk in the cocoa, then bring to the boil. Remove from the heat and stir in the remaining cream and the Irish whiskey. Pour quickly into four warmed heatproof mugs or glasses and top each serving with a generous spoonful of the whipped cream, finishing with a garnish of milk chocolate curls.

Tequila

Being even more of a recent commercial phenomenon than vodka, tequila has acquired correspondingly fewer recipes so far in the cocktail repertoire. That is gradually changing on modern bar menus as the salty, savoury, slightly feral aroma and flavour of the drink are appreciated. It mixes well with most fruit juices, and although combinations with liqueurs are still only at a fairly tentative stage, they are developing. There is therefore an experimental quality to some of the recipes that follow. Don't forget that, as well as basic, so-called "silver" tequila, there is also the richer and more complex oro, or "gold", style that has been aged in wooden casks.

Tequila Sunrise

This classic Mexican recipe of the 1930s takes its name from the way the grenadine – that bright red pomegranate cordial – first sinks in the glass of orange juice and then rises to the surface. Add it too slowly and it will simply blend into the drink, turning it a fetching (but totally incorrect) scarlet colour.

2 measures/3 tbsp gold tequila
4 measures/6 tbsp freshly squeezed orange
   juice
½ measure/2 tsp grenadine

Half-fill a highball glass with crushed ice. Pour in the tequila, then the orange juice, which must be freshly squeezed. Quickly add the grenadine, pouring it down the back of a spoon held inside the glass so that it sinks to the bottom of the drink. You could garnish the drink with a slice of orange and a cherry.

Tequila Sunset

This variation on the popular party drink can be mixed and chilled in a pitcher, ready to pour into glasses, and finished at the last minute with the addition of crème de cassis and honey.

1 measure/1½ tbsp gold tequila
5 measures/120ml/4fl oz lemon juice
1 measure/1½ tbsp orange juice
15–30ml/1–2 tbsp clear honey
⅔ measure/1 tbsp crème de cassis

Pour the tequila, and lemon and orange juices into a well-chilled cocktail glass. Using a swizzle-stick, mix the ingredients together well. Trickle the honey into the centre of the drink. It will sink and create a layer at the bottom of the glass. Add the crème de cassis, but do not stir. It will create a glowing layer above the honey at the bottom of the glass.

Margarita

With the Tequila Sunrise, Margarita (created in Tijuana in the late 1940s) is probably the best-known tequila cocktail of them all, and these days is a sight more popular. Its saltiness and sourness make it a great aperitif, and it is pleasingly strong too. Some recipes use lemon juice instead of lime, but lime juice sharpens its bite.

1½ measures/6 tsp silver tequila
½ measure/2 tsp Cointreau
juice of a lime

Rub the rim of a cocktail glass with a wedge of fresh lime, and then dip it in fine salt. Shake the tequila, Cointreau and lime juice with plenty of ice, and strain into the prepared glass. Garnish with a twist of cucumber rind or a half-slice of lime.

Iced Margarita

This smooth sorbet drink has all the punch of Mexico's renowned cocktail. This recipe makes two drinks.

2½ measures/3½ tbsp silver tequila
1¼ measures/5½ tsp Cointreau
1¼ measures/5½ tsp lime juice
6–8 small scoops lime sorbet
150ml/¼ pint chilled lemonade

Frost the rims of the glasses with cut lime and caster (superfine) sugar. Add lime and lemon slices to each. Mix the tequila, Cointreau and lime juice in a jug. Scoop the sorbet into the glasses. Pour an equal quantity of the drink into each glass. Top with lemonade and garnish with lemon balm.

Mango and Peach Margarita

Adding puréed fruit to the classic tequila mixture alters the consistency. This recipe serves four.

2 mangoes, peeled and sliced
3 peaches, peeled and sliced
5 measures/120ml/4fl oz silver tequila
2½ measures/3½ tbsp Cointreau
2½ measures/3½ tbsp lime juice

Blend the mango and peach slices in a liquidizer until a smooth paste is obtained. Add the tequila, Cointreau and lime juice, blend for a few seconds more, then add the ice. Blend again until the drink has the consistency of a milkshake. Pour into pre-chilled cocktail glasses, and garnish with slices of mango with the skin left on. Create other fruit variations on the basic Margarita, using this recipe.

Cactus Juice

In this modern recipe, the roundness of flavour of gold tequila is enhanced by marrying it with a little of the herb-flavoured Scotch liqueur, Drambuie.

2 measures/3 tbsp gold tequila
¼ measure/1 tsp Drambuie

1 measure/1½ tbsp lemon juice
5ml/1 tsp caster (superfine) sugar

Shake all the ingredients well with ice until the sugar is dissolved, and pour without straining into a rocks glass. Add a slice of lemon.

Pineapple Tequila

Flavours such as almond and quince have been added to silver tequila for some time. Many bars have developed unique flavours by combining ingredients such as chillies with tequila, and leaving them to infuse. The method below will make a smooth, fruity drink to serve six.

1 large pineapple
50g/2oz soft dark brown sugar
1 litre/1¾ pints silver tequila
1 vanilla pod

Rinse a large (about 2 litre/3½ pint) wide-necked bottle or demijohn and sterilize by placing it in an oven and then

turning on the oven and setting it at 110°C/225°F/Gas ¼. After 20 minutes remove the bottle from the oven with oven gloves and allow it to cool down.

Cut the top off the pineapple and then cut away the skin. Cut the flesh in half lengthways, then remove the hard centre core and discard it. Chop the rest of the pineapple into chunks, ensuring that they are small enough to fit in the bottle neck.

When the bottle is completely cold, put the pineapple into the bottle. Mix the sugar and tequila together in a pitcher until the sugar dissolves and then pour into the bottle. Split the vanilla pod and add it to the rest of the ingredients.

Gently agitate the bottle a few times each day to stir the contents. Allow the tequila to stand for at least a week before drinking with ice. (When all the tequila has been drunk, use the pineapple in desserts such as ice cream, or warm with butter and cinnamon and serve with cream.)

Home infusions of tequila like this are very popular in its native Mexico.

TNT

With a bit of twisting, the initials of the name just about indicate the ingredients of the drink: tequila, Napoléon and Tia (Maria). Rather more accurately, they mirror the effect of the drink, which is all alcohol with no mixers. The flavour is very satisfying, though.

1 measure/1½ tbsp gold tequila
½ measure Mandarine Napoléon
1 measure/1½ tbsp Tia Maria

Stir all the ingredients gently with ice in a pitcher until very cold, and then strain into a rocks glass half-filled with cracked ice. Suspend a twist of orange rind in the drink.

Tequila and Orange

Have done with the lemon-squeezing and salt-licking fuss associated with traditional tequila-drinking, and try tequila on the rocks with fresh orange juice and a half-slice of orange. It makes an enlivening change for those grown weary of vodka-and-orange. Silver tequila will do for this mix.

Mexican Chocolate

A chillier, and more inspiring, version of boozy hot chocolate, this makes a refreshingly original drink for a hot summer afternoon. It beats chocolate ice cream, anyway.

1½ measures/6 tsp gold tequila
1 measure/1½ tbsp Kahlúa
4 measures/6 tbsp prepared cocoa or drinking chocolate, made with full-cream (whole) milk

Shake all the ingredients well with ice, and strain into a large goblet. Drink through straws.

Tequila Slammer

The Slammer reflects something of the bravado with which tequila is traditionally drunk in Mexico. It is a drink in which one takes over the bartender's performance ethic for oneself, and it has not surprisingly become internationally practised among a certain age group.

1 measure/1½ tbsp silver or gold tequila
1 measure/1½ tbsp sparkling mixer (usually either lemonade or ginger ale, but can be sparkling wine)

Pour the two measures into a shot glass, cover with the palm of your hand (or a beer mat, if you don't fancy getting messy) and slam the glass down a couple of times on the bar counter. The drink will then fizz wildly up, and you have something less than a second to get it to your mouth, and down it in one.

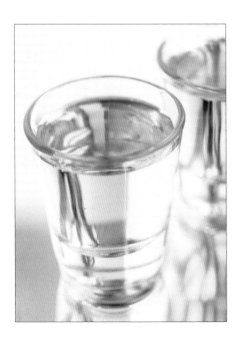

Bloody Maria

A close cousin of the original vodka-based Bloody Mary, this simple cocktail consists of tequila and tomato juice mixed together with spicy seasonings. The quantities here make two drinks, just in case that hangover is particularly persistent, or you have a fellow sufferer.

Bar Bandit

A long, fruity drink with a subtle, but nonetheless recognizable punch behind it. The inclusion of both types of vermouth proves once again the versatility of this style of fortified wine.

1 measure/1½ tbsp gold tequila
½ measure/2 tsp dry vermouth
½ measure/2 tsp sweet red vermouth
½ measure/2 tsp crème de framboise
¼ measure/1 tsp lime juice
4 measures/6 tbsp sparkling cherryade

Pack a highball glass with cracked ice, and add all but the last ingredient in the order above. Stir briskly with a swizzle-stick, and then top up with cherryade. Garnish with a slice of lime and a couple of cocktail cherries.

250ml/8fl oz tomato juice, chilled
2 measures/3 tbsp silver tequila
5ml/1 tsp Worcestershire sauce
few drops Tabasco
juice of half a lemon
pinch celery salt
salt and freshly ground black pepper

Pour the chilled tomato juice into a large pitcher and stir in the tequila. Add the Worcestershire sauce and stir the mixture well. Add a few drops of Tabasco and the lemon juice. Taste and season with celery salt, salt and pepper. Serve over ice cubes in highball glasses, with celery sticks standing in the drink for stirring it. The tequila naturally makes its presence felt in this mixture more obviously than vodka does.

Boomer

This is one of those recently popular drinks known as shooters, which are small, assertively flavoured preparations for downing at one gulp. It should be served either in a shot glass or small liqueur glass, when its short, sharp shock can be best appreciated.

⅔ measure/1 tbsp gold tequila
½ measure/2 tsp apricot brandy
½ measure/2 tsp orange juice
¼ measure/1 tsp lemon juice
¼ measure/1 tsp sugar syrup

Shake all the ingredients well with ice, and strain into a tiny glass.

Firebird

This is a fairly sweet, fizzy concoction that's shorter than most other sparkling cocktails.

1½ measures/6 tsp silver tequila
½ measure/2 tsp crème de banane
½ measure/2 tsp lime juice

2 measures/3 tbsp sparkling lemonade

Fill a rocks glass nearly to the brim with cracked ice. Add the first three ingredients, give them a quick stir and then add the lemonade. Garnish with a slice of lemon.

Sangrita

Sipping sangrita and tequila alternately is a taste sensation not to be missed, the warm flavours of the first balancing the strength of the second. The drinks are often served with *antojitos* (nibbles) as an appetizer. This recipe serves eight.

450g/1lb ripe tomatoes, or one 400g/14oz
    can chopped tomatoes
1 small onion, finely chopped
2 small fresh green chillies, seeded and
    chopped
120ml/4fl oz freshly squeezed orange juice
juice of 3 limes
2.5ml/½ tsp caster (superfine) sugar
pinch of salt
1 small shot glass gold or aged tequila per
    person

Cut a large cross in the base of each tomato. Place the tomatoes in a heatproof bowl and pour over boiling water to cover. Leave for 3 minutes. Lift the tomatoes out on a slotted spoon, and plunge them into a second bowl of cold water. Remove the skins, then cut the tomatoes in half and scoop out the seeds with a spoon. Chop the tomato flesh and put in a food processor. Add the onion, chillies, orange juice, lime juice, sugar and salt. Process until all the mixture is very smooth, then pour into a pitcher and chill for at least an hour before serving. Offer each drinker a separate shot glass of neat tequila as well. The drinks are sipped alternately.

Last Chance

A drop of honey makes a good companion for mellow, cask-aged tequila in this drink. It would make a rather comforting nightcap.

1¾ measures/2½ tbsp gold tequila
½ measure/1 tsp apricot brandy
1 measure/1½ tbsp lime juice
10ml/2 tsp clear honey

Shake all the ingredients very well with ice, ensuring that the honey is fully dissolved, and strain into a rocks glass. Garnish with a slice of lime.

Cherry Coco

Here is a sumptuously creamy, exotically flavoured cocktail that would look very elegant served in a champagne flute. It's both creamy and sour – a nice combination.

1½ measures/6 tsp silver tequila
¾ measure/3 tsp coconut cream
1 measure/1½ tbsp lemon juice
¼ measure/1 tsp maraschino

Shake all the ingredients well with ice, and strain into a tall, narrow glass. Drop a cocktail cherry into the drink.

Zorro

John J. Poister, author of *The New American Bartender's Guide*, has created this winning tequila recipe that uses the Balkan plum spirit, slivovitz.

1½ measures/6 tsp silver tequila
1 measure/1½ tbsp slivovitz
1 measure/1½ tbsp lime juice
¼ measure/1 tsp sugar syrup

Shake all the ingredients well with ice, and strain into a chilled cocktail glass. You could garnish with a slice of lime.

Bartending know-how
The best brands of slivovitz hail from Bosnia, Croatia and Serbia, and are made with a local plum variety called pozega, sourced from trees with a minimum age of 20 years.

Piñata

An odd name this, as you might think it contained pineapple, but no – banana and lime are the fruit flavours. It is, nonetheless, quite delicious enough to be going on with.

1½ measures/6 tsp gold tequila
1 measure/1½ tbsp crème de banane
1 measure/1½ tbsp lime juice

Shake all the ingredients well with ice, and strain into a cocktail glass. Dangle a twist of lime rind in the drink.

Rosita

A drink that bears some distant kinship to the Negroni, and is prepared in roughly the same way.

1½ measures/6 tsp silver tequila
1 measure/1½ tbsp Campari
½ measure/2 tsp dry vermouth
½ measure/2 tsp sweet red vermouth

Add the ingredients in this order to an Old-Fashioned glass or small rocks glass, half-filled with cracked ice. Stir. Squeeze a small twist of orange rind over the drink and then drop it in.

Mockingbird

A good balance of sweet and sour is achieved in this minty, but sharp-edged cocktail. It's one of those tastes of which one can say that a little goes a long way.

1½ measures/6 tsp silver tequila
¾ measure/3 tsp white crème de menthe
juice of half a lime

Shake all the ingredients well with ice, and strain into a chilled cocktail glass. Garnish with a half-slice of lime and a sprig of mint.

Brandy

In his strange, single-gendered world, Dr Johnson was quite clear about the status of brandy: "Claret is the liquor for boys; port for men; but he who aspires to be a hero must drink brandy." Indeed, fine cognac has for a long time been associated with a certain swaggering demeanour. Not for nothing is one of the top grades of cognac called Napoleon brandy. As well as cognac, there is armagnac from the south-west of France, and brandies from Spain, Germany, Mexico and the USA. They are good mixers in cocktails, and although, understandably, you wouldn't want to use your best Fine Champagne cognac in a mixed drink, it pays not to go for the cheapest grades either. They largely taste horrible, and will ruin the resulting cocktail.

Brandy Cocktail

Over time, this drink became modified to include Cointreau instead of curaçao, a little sugar syrup and a dash of Angostura. However, the earliest versions of it are nothing more than cognac with a soupçon of bitterness.

1½ measures/6 tsp cognac
2 dashes orange curaçao

Stir the ingredients gently with ice in a bar glass, and then strain into a brandy balloon. Do not garnish.

Brandy Fix

A Fix is a mixture of spirit with lemon juice, sweetening and in this case another alcohol flavour, with the shell of the lemon and a pile of ice left in the drink for good measure.

5ml/1 tsp sugar
juice and rind of half a lemon

1½ measures/6 tsp cognac
¾ measure/3 tsp cherry brandy

Dissolve the sugar in a little water in the bottom of a small tumbler, and then fill it with crushed ice. Add the lemon juice and alcohol and stir the drink well. Drop in the squeezed lemon rind.

Bonnie Prince Charlie

As its name indicates, this drink contains Drambuie, the liqueur that was given to Prince Charlie by the MacDonald family on his flight to Skye. The mixture is a strong one, but one that seems to do justice to the liqueur.

1 measure/1½ tbsp cognac
½ measure/2 tsp Drambuie
1 measure/1½ tbsp lemon juice

Shake all the ingredients well with ice, and strain into a cocktail glass. Garnish with a twist of lemon.

Brandy Blazer

A warming after-dinner tipple, this is ideally served with fresh vanilla ice cream or caramelized oranges.

½ orange
1 lemon
2 measures/3 tbsp cognac
1 sugar cube
½ measure/2 tsp Kahlúa

Pare the rind from the orange and lemon, removing and discarding as much of the white pith as possible. Put the cognac, sugar cube, lemon and orange rind in a small pan. Heat gently, then remove from the heat, light a match and pass the flame close to the surface of the liquid. The alcohol will burn with a low, blue flame for about a minute. Blow out the flame. Add the Kahlúa to the pan, and strain into a heat-resistant glass. Garnish with a cocktail stick threaded with orange rind, and serve warm.

B&B

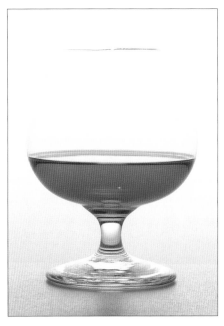

The traditional mix of this world-famous cocktail is half-and-half Bénédictine and good brandy (cognac for preference), stirred not shaken, and not usually iced. In fact, for true authenticity, you don't even need a stirrer. The two drinks are simply poured into a balloon glass, the brandy first, and the drink swirled in the hand before being passed to its recipient. No garnish is needed.

Brandy Smash

The excitingly named Smash is essentially a miniaturized julep (or Mint Julep). It may be made with any spirit, but is particularly successful with brandy.

5ml/1 tsp caster (superfine) sugar
4 mint leaves
2 measures/3 tbsp cognac
1 measure/1½ tbsp soda water

Dissolve the sugar in a little water in a tumbler. Add the mint leaves and press them into the sugar solution to express some of the juices. Put in a couple of ice cubes, and then add the brandy and stir vigorously. Add the soda. Squeeze a piece of lemon rind over the top of the drink, and decorate with a half-slice of orange.

Brandy Crusta

The sweet, frosted rim is all-important in this most appealing drink. It mitigates some of the sourness in the drink itself.

1½ measures/6 tsp cognac
½ measure/2 tsp Cointreau
¼ measure/1 tsp maraschino
dash Angostura bitters
¼ measure/1 tsp lemon juice

Frost the rim of a wide tumbler by dipping it first in lemon juice and then in caster (superfine) sugar. Hang a twist of lemon rind in it, and then fill it with cracked ice. Stir all the ingredients well with ice in a pitcher until the mixture is well-chilled, and then strain into the prepared glass. Garnish further with a half-slice of orange.

Brandy Alexander

One of the greatest cocktails of them all, Alexander can be served at the end of a grand dinner with coffee as a creamy digestif, or as the first drink of the evening at a cocktail party, since the cream in it helps to line the stomach. It was possibly originally made with gin rather than brandy, and the cream was sweetened, but the formula below is undoubtedly the best of all possible worlds.

1 measure/1½ tbsp cognac
1 measure/1½ tbsp brown crème de cacao
1 measure/1½ tbsp double (heavy) cream

Shake the ingredients thoroughly with ice, and strain into a cocktail glass. Scatter ground nutmeg, or grate a little whole nutmeg, on top. Alternatively, sprinkle with grated dark chocolate.

Corpse Reviver 1

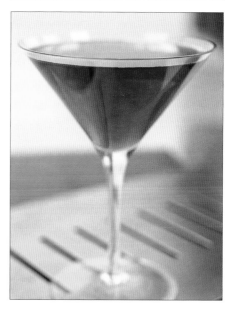

Not the most delicately named cocktail, this is a 1970s recipe intended of course as a morning-after remedy. I'm not sure I'd make quite that claim for it myself, but in its bitterly minty way, it tastes convincingly medicinal, which is what matters.

1 measure/1½ tbsp cognac
1 measure/1½ tbsp Fernet Branca
1 measure/1½ tbsp white crème de menthe

Shake all the ingredients well with ice, and strain into a cocktail glass. Do not garnish. If you really are taking it at 10 o'clock in the morning, you're not likely to care about twists of this and slices of that anyway.

Corpse Reviver 2

This was the 1920s idea of a morning-after remedy, and is probably the first recipe that can lay claim to this name. It looks much more like a night-before drink to me – and a good one at that.

1½ measures/6 tsp cognac
¾ measure/3 tsp calvados
¾ measure/3 tsp sweet red vermouth

Shake all the ingredients well with ice, and strain into a cocktail glass. Again, no garnish is required.

Morning Glory Fizz

A good early-morning drink, this should be consumed as soon as it is made, before it loses its bubbles.

⅔ measure/1 tbsp cognac
¼ measure/1 tsp orange curaçao
¼ measure/1 tsp lemon juice
dash anisette
2 dashes Angostura bitters
4 measures/6 tbsp soda water

Shake all but the last ingredient well with ice, and strain into a chilled highball glass. Finish with the soda water. Garnish the drink with a twist of lemon rind.

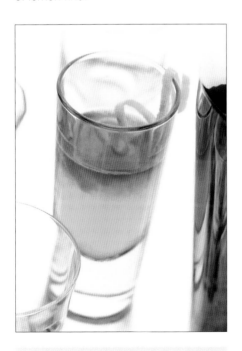

Bartending know-how
Always choose lemons that feel heavy for their size: they're the ones with the most juice.

Frozen Strawberry Daiquiri

This is a spinoff version of the rum original. When the fresh fruit isn't in season, use drained, canned strawberries instead, but wash off the sugar syrup.

4 strawberries
½ measure/2 tsp lime juice
1 measure/1½ tbsp cognac
1 measure/1½ tbsp light rum
dash grenadine

Put the strawberries, lime juice and brandy in a liquidizer and process to a purée. Add the light rum, grenadine and half a glass of finely crushed ice and process once more to a smooth slush. Pour the resulting mixture into a well-chilled cocktail glass. Garnish with a strawberry and a small sprig of fresh mint.

Vanderbilt

This cocktail was created in 1912 in honour of Cornelius Vanderbilt, member of one of America's great plutocratic families. The flavour is certainly rich enough to do justice to the name.

1½ measures/6 tsp cognac
½ measure/2 tsp cherry brandy
2 dashes Angostura bitters
¼ measure/1 tsp sugar syrup

Shake all the ingredients well with ice, and strain into a cocktail glass. Garnish with a twist of lemon, and a couple of cherries on a cocktail stick.

Connoisseur's Treat

Certainly a treat for somebody, this is a very strong, all-alcohol mix, not to be taken lightly. The flavour is a heady combination of herbs, vanilla and orange.

1½ measures/6 tsp cognac
½ measure/2 tsp Grand Marnier
½ measure/2 tsp Galliano

Stir the ingredients in a pitcher with ice until thoroughly chilled, and strain into a rocks glass. Garnish with a twist of orange rind.

Bombay

A very strong and challenging mixture, this is the kind of drink that comes in handy in situations where Dutch courage is called for. Or should that be Indian courage?

1½ measures/6 tsp cognac
¾ measures/3 tsp dry vermouth
¾ measure/3 tsp sweet red vermouth
¼ measure/1 tsp Cointreau
¼ measure/1 tsp absinthe

Shake all the ingredients well with ice, and strain into a cocktail glass or champagne saucer filled with crushed ice. Do not garnish.

East India

This short and elegant drink can be served as an aperitif, as it has a pleasantly bitter note to it.

⅔ measure/1 tbsp cognac
2 dashes white curaçao
2 dashes pineapple juice
2 dashes Angostura bitters

Stir all the ingredients well with ice in a pitcher until chilled, and strain into a small tumbler or Old-Fashioned glass, half-filled with broken ice. Garnish with a twist of lime and a cherry.

Apple Sour

For those who don't fancy swallowing raw egg, this drink can be made without the egg white. Applejack or apple schnapps also work well in place of the calvados.

1 measure/1½ tbsp cognac
1 measure/1½ tbsp calvados
⅔ measure/1 tbsp lemon juice
5ml/1 tsp sugar
dash Angostura bitters
1 egg white

Shake all the ingredients well with ice, and strain into a tumbler half-filled with cracked ice. Garnish the drink with slices of red and green apple dipped in lemon juice.

Brandy Punch

This old-fashioned punch recipe might have graced the table of an elegant Victorian party. It's a chilled punch as well, which tends to be a bit more popular these days than the hot version. The recipe should serve around 12 guests.

1 × 700ml/1 pint bottle of cognac
150ml/¼ pint orange curaçao
1 measure/1½ tbsp grenadine
juice of 5 lemons
juice of 2 oranges
250ml/8fl oz mineral water
orange and lemon slices
400ml/14fl oz sparkling ginger ale

Bartending know-how
Always ice the individual glasses rather than the punch bowl itself.

Mix all but the last ingredient in a punch bowl and add the ginger ale just before serving. Ladle into highball glasses packed with ice.

Lemon Lady

This is a delightful concoction that will have guests coming back for more. It could be served between courses as a more invigorating alternative to a straight sorbet.

1 measure/1½ tbsp cognac
½ measure/2 tsp Cointreau
3 measures/4½ tbsp light, partially melted lemon sorbet

Shake well with ice to combine the sorbet, and strain into a chilled cocktail glass. Garnish with a slice of lemon.

Never on Sunday

This recipe uses Metaxa, the softly caramelly Greek brandy, together with its compatriot, aniseedy ouzo, for a thoroughly Mediterranean experience.

1 measure/1½ tbsp Metaxa
½ measure/2 tsp ouzo
dash lemon juice

dash Angostura bitters
2 measures/3 tbsp dry sparkling wine
2 measures/3 tbsp sparkling ginger ale

Stir the first four ingredients in a pitcher with ice, strain into a tall glass and top up with the sparkling wine and ginger ale. Garnish with a slice of lemon.

Grenadier

This drink is a brandy variation on the Whisky Mac, and equally good at cheering up those suffering with a winter chill.

1 measure/1½ tbsp cognac
1 measure/1½ tbsp green ginger wine
5ml/1 tsp caster (superfine) sugar

Shake all the ingredients well with ice, and strain into a small tumbler. Drink quickly so that the warmth of the alcohol pervades the system in a comforting way.

Cranberry Kiss

In this delicious, full-flavoured cocktail, the tang of cranberry and pink grapefruit juices is balanced by the toffeeish sweetness of marsala.

redcurrants, to garnish
1 egg white, lightly beaten, and 15ml/1 tbsp caster (superfine) sugar, to garnish
1 measure/1½ tbsp cognac
2 measures/3 tbsp cranberry juice
2 measures/3 tbsp pink grapefruit juice
2 measures/3 tbsp marsala dolce

For the garnish, lightly brush the redcurrants with the egg white. Shake sugar over them to cover with a frosting. Set aside to dry. Shake the brandy, and cranberry and grapefruit juices with ice and strain into a well-chilled glass. Tilt the glass slightly before slowly pouring in the marsala down the side. Garnish with the frosted redcurrants.

Hard Case

For a small drink with a sharply fruity flavour, this is something of a misnomer. It's a (relatively) harmless customer.

1½ measures/6 tsp cognac
½ measure/2 tsp crème de cassis
¼ measure/1 tsp lemon juice

Shake all the ingredients well with ice, and strain into a cocktail glass. Garnish with a half-slice of lemon.

Champarelle

Dating from the late 19th century, this is one of the oldest recipes for the layered drink known as a pousse-café. It helps if the ingredients and the glass itself are pre-chilled, as they are not mixed in any way, and you can't put ice in the drink.

½ measure/2 tsp orange curaçao
½ measure/2 tsp yellow Chartreuse

Brandy Fino

The name tells you more or less what's in this, though the splash of Glayva may sneak craftily up on you.

1½ measures/6 tsp cognac
½ measure/2 tsp pale dry (fino) sherry
¼ measure/1 tsp Glayva

Stir all the ingredients well in a pitcher with ice until the mixture is properly chilled, and strain into a balloon glass. Do not garnish.

½ measure/2 tsp anisette
½ measure/2 tsp cognac

Carefully pour each of the ingredients in this order over the back of a large spoon into a liqueur glass or sherry schooner, ensuring that they remain in separate layers. Use a clean spoon for each ingredient.

Blackjack

Perhaps invented to steady nerves at the gaming table, this mix is more likely to impair concentration. It is a stimulating one nonetheless.

1 measure/1½ tbsp cognac
½ measure/2 tsp kirsch
½ measure/2 tsp Kahlúa
2 measures/3 tbsp cold black coffee

Shake all the ingredients well with ice, and pour without straining into a rocks glass. Do not garnish.

Bartending know-how
Kirsch made in Germany tends to be drier and higher in alcohol than the versions made in the Alsace region of France. The best French grade is labelled "pur". Avoid anything labelled "Kirsch de Cuisine".

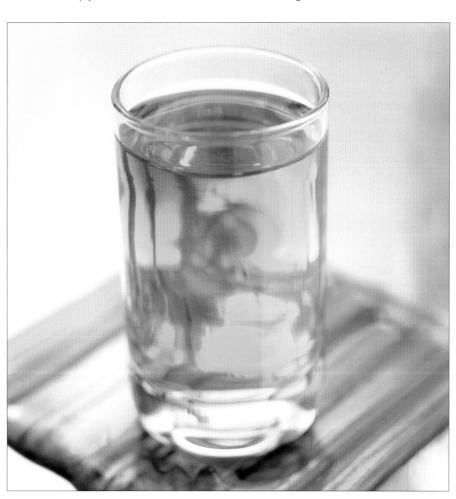

Arago

This delightful creamy creation is quite as irresistible as the Pompeii, below.

1½ measures/6 tsp cognac
1 measure/1½ tbsp crème de banane
1 measure/1½ tbsp double (heavy) cream

Shake all the ingredients well with ice, and strain into a cocktail glass. Sprinkle the surface of the drink with grated dark chocolate.

Pompeii

Here is a different spin on the Alexander formula, but with the chocolate component given a sweeter, nutty edge.

1 measure/1½ tbsp cognac
¾ measure/3 tsp white crème de cacao
½ measure/2 tsp amaretto
1 measure/1½ tbsp double (heavy) cream

Shake all the ingredients well with ice, and strain into a cocktail glass. Sprinkle the drink's surface with flaked almonds.

Last Goodbye

The flavours of cherry brandy and Cointreau are seen as being particularly compatible with cognac, and this is another appealing mixture.

1 measure/1½ tbsp cognac
¾ measure/3 tsp cherry brandy
¼ measure/1 tsp Cointreau
½ measure/2 tsp lime juice
¼ measure/1 tsp grenadine

Shake all the ingredients well with ice, and strain into a balloon glass. You could garnish with a lime slice and a cherry.

Incredible

Chartreuse doesn't often mix well with other spirits, but this is definitely worth a go, Incredible as it may seem.

1 measure/1½ tbsp cognac
½ measure/2 tsp green Chartreuse
½ measure/2 tsp cherry brandy

Stir all the ingredients gently with ice in a pitcher until well-chilled, and then strain into a rocks glass. Garnish with a cocktail cherry.

Missile Stopper

On a military hardware theme, this fruity little number should stop anyone in their tracks.

1 measure/1½ tbsp cognac
½ measure/2 tsp crème de fraise
1 measure/1½ tbsp grapefruit juice
1 measure/1½ tbsp pineapple juice
¼ measure/1 tsp grenadine

Shake all the ingredients well with ice, and strain into a chilled balloon glass. Garnish with a sliver of pineapple and a strawberry.

Port Side

The purply-red colour of this very sophisticated short drink looks very fetching sinking through a snowdrift of crushed ice.

1½ measures/6 tsp cognac
½ measure/2 tsp ruby port
½ measure/2 tsp crème de mûre

Stir all the ingredients with ice in a pitcher, and strain into a rocks glass half-filled with crushed ice. Garnish with a blackberry, if you happen to have one to hand.

Torpedo

I have come across various different mixtures going under this title. This seems to me to be the one most worthy of the name. It's very dry, spirity and strong, and its name reflects something of the force with which it will go through you.

1½ measures/6 tsp cognac
¾ measure/3 tsp calvados
dash gin

Shake all the ingredients well with ice, and strain into a pre-chilled cocktail glass. Garnish with a twist of lemon.

Coterie

Strong and sour, this is just the way a grown-up cocktail should be. Robert Cross's recipe suggests Chartreuse as an alternative to the hard-to-find, but similar, Basque liqueur, Izarra.

1 measure/1½ tbsp cognac
½ measure/2 tsp yellow Chartreuse
½ measure/2 tsp gin
¼ measure/1 tsp lemon juice
¼ measure/1 tsp sugar syrup

Stir all the ingredients well with ice in a pitcher, and strain the drink into a chilled small tumbler. Garnish with a half-slice of lemon.

Fighter

This combative mixture is rendered seemingly tamer by the sparkling top-up. Do not be deceived.

1 measure/1½ tbsp cognac
½ measure/2 tsp vodka
½ measure/2 tsp Mandarine Napoléon
4 measures/6 tbsp sparkling bitter lemon

Add the first three ingredients to a highball glass half-filled with cracked ice. Stir vigorously. Top up with the bitter lemon. Garnish with a slice of mandarin orange, clementine, satsuma or similar.

Pisco Sour

The origin of pisco, the colourless brandy of South America, is energetically disputed between Peru and Chile. This is the classic way of taking it locally.

juice of half a lime
5ml/1 tsp caster (superfine) sugar
2 measures/3 tbsp pisco

Half-fill a small tumbler with smashed ice. Squeeze the lime juice directly into the glass and drop in the wrung-out shell. Add the sugar and stir well to dissolve it. Now add the pisco, and give the drink a final stir. A dash of Angostura bitters can be added too, if desired, but it isn't essential.

Bayou

The peachiness of this cocktail evokes the southern United States, as does its name. It's rich and fruity, with a refreshing sour finish.

1½ measures/6 tsp cognac
½ measure/2 tsp peach brandy
1 measure/1½ tbsp peach juice
⅓ measure/1½ tsp lime juice

Shake all the ingredients well with ice, and strain into a rocks glass. Garnish with a slice of ultra-ripe white peach.

Apricot Bellini

This is a version of the famous aperitif served at Harry's Bar in Venice. Instead of the usual sparkling wine and peach juice, apricot nectar and apricot brandy make this a tempting, and stronger, variation. This recipe serves six to eight.

3 ripe apricots
½ measure/2 tsp lemon juice
½ measure/2 tsp sugar syrup
1 measure/1½ tbsp cognac
1 measure/1½ tbsp apricot brandy
1 bottle brut champagne or dry sparkling wine, chilled

Plunge the apricots into boiling water for 2 minutes to loosen the skins, then peel and pit them. Discard the pits and skin. Process the apricot flesh with the lemon juice until you have a smooth purée. Sweeten to taste with sugar syrup, then strain. Add the brandy and liqueur to the apricot nectar and stir together. Divide the apricot nectar among chilled champagne flutes. Finish the drinks with chilled champagne or sparkling wine.

Dizzy Dame

Well, she will be after drinking two or three of these. Another of those creamy cocktails full of rich, indulgent flavours (and calories).

1 measure/1½ tbsp cognac
¾ measure/3 tsp Tia Maria
½ measure/2 tsp cherry brandy
¾ measure/3 tsp double (heavy)
   cream

Shake all the ingredients well with ice, and strain into a cocktail glass. Garnish with a cherry.

Captain Kidd

Brandy and dark rum make a heady, but very successful mix in a powerful cocktail, and this one is further enhanced by the addition of strong chocolate flavour. There are no non-alcoholic ingredients, you'll notice, so watch out.

Mikado

This is a 1920s Savoy Hotel recipe of great charm. The Gilbert and Sullivan work of the same name was premiered at the Savoy Theatre in 1885.

1½ measures/6 tsp cognac
2 dashes orange curaçao
2 dashes crème de noyau
2 dashes orgeat syrup (or amaretto)
2 dashes Angostura bitters

Shake all the ingredients well with ice, and strain into a cocktail glass. Garnish with a half-slice of orange and a cherry.

1½ measures/6 tsp cognac
1 measure/1½ tbsp dark rum
1 measure/1½ tbsp brown crème de cacao

Shake well with ice, and strain into a chilled champagne saucer. Garnish with a physalis or a half-slice of orange.

Savoy Hotel

It's a short step from London's Savoy Theatre to the American Bar in the hotel itself, where this delightful cocktail (like many another) was created. It's a pousse-café or layered drink that requires a steady hand.

1 measure/1½ tbsp brown crème de cacao
1 measure/1½ tbsp Bénédictine
1 measure/1½ tbsp cognac

Carefully pour each of the ingredients, in this order, over the back of a spoon into a liqueur glass or sherry schooner to create a multi-layered drink. Serve immediately, while the effect is intact.

Harvard

This mixture was invented at the distinguished Ivy League university in the 1920s. It originally had equal quantities of brandy and vermouth and no lemon juice, but this is a less sweet and altogether more balanced mixture.

1½ measures/6 tsp cognac
½ measure/2 tsp sweet red vermouth
¼ measure/1 tsp lemon juice
¼ measure/1 tsp grenadine
2 dashes Angostura bitters

Shake all the ingredients well with ice, and strain into a cocktail glass. Garnish with a twist of lemon.

Brandy Melba

As might be expected, this is a very fruity cocktail that could almost pass as a sort of dessert. It uses the combination of peach and raspberry in the classic Peach Melba dessert.

1½ measures/6 tsp cognac
½ measure/2 tsp peach schnapps
¼ measure/1 tsp crème de framboise
½ measure/2 tsp lemon juice
¼ measure/1 tsp orange bitters (or curaçao)

Shake well with ice, and strain into a chilled cocktail glass. Garnish with a slice of ripe peach and a raspberry.

Lake Como

The geographical reference recalls the origins of the excellent Italian liqueur used in this recipe. You'll never want another Black Russian after tasting this.

1½ measures/6 tsp cognac
¾ measure/3 tsp Tuaca

Fjord

Good Scandinavian aquavit is needed for this recipe. The name suggests Norwegian, but Swedish or Danish would do quite as well.

1 measure/1½ tbsp cognac
½ measure/2 tsp aquavit
1 measure/1½ tbsp orange juice

Mix the ingredients well with ice in a large glass, and strain into an Old-Fashioned or small rocks glass. Squeeze a twist of lemon rind over the drink and then drop it into the glass. This is one for drinking quickly and confidently.

½ measure/2 tsp lime juice
¼ measure/1 tsp grenadine

Shake all the ingredients well with ice, and strain into a chliled rocks glass half-filled with cracked ice. Garnish the drink with half-slices of orange and lime.

Booster

This egg-white drink has a powerful kick. You may find it helps to whisk the egg white for a few seconds before adding it to the shaker, just to ensure the right kind of foamy texture in the finished drink.

2 measures/3 tbsp cognac
1 measure/1½ tbsp orange curaçao
½ egg white

Shake all the ingredients very thoroughly with ice, and strain into a cocktail glass. Sprinkle the surface with ground nutmeg.

Via Veneto

Named after the street in Rome that was once a scene of bohemian glamour, this cocktail contains the Italian elderberry-flavoured liqueur Sambuca Romana.

1½ measures/6 tsp cognac
½ measure/2 tsp Sambuca
½ measure/2 tsp lemon juice
¼ measure/1 tsp sugar syrup
½ egg white

Shake all the ingredients well with ice, and strain into a chilled rocks glass. Garnish with a slice of lemon.

Memphis Belle

One of the earliest cocktail recipes to use Southern Comfort, this may look an unlikely idea, in that it blends a whiskey-based liqueur with brandy, but in its dry, sharply sour way, it works.

1½ measures/6 tsp cognac
¾ measure/3 tsp Southern Comfort
½ measure/2 tsp lemon juice
¼ measure/1 tsp orange bitters (or curaçao)

Shake all the ingredients well with ice, and strain into a pre-chilled cocktail glass. Garnish with a twist of lemon.

Kiss the Boys Goodbye

As the name suggests, this is a cocktail with which American troops going off to serve in the Second World War were toasted. It seemed to do the trick.

1 measure/1½ tbsp cognac
1 measure/1½ tbsp sloe gin
¼ measure/1 tsp lemon juice
½ egg white

Shake all the ingredients well with ice, and strain into a rocks glass half-filled with cracked ice. Garnish with a wedge of lemon.

Coffee Cognac Cooler

This drink is unabashedly decadent, and not for those counting calories. The recipe serves two, so you can both feel guilty together.

250ml/8fl oz cold strong dark-roast coffee
80ml/3fl oz cognac
50ml/2fl oz coffee liqueur
50ml/2fl oz double (heavy) cream
10ml/2 tsp sugar
2 scoops coffee ice cream

Shake or blend all the ingredients except the ice cream, together with plenty of crushed ice. Pour into tall glasses and gently add a scoop of ice cream to each. Garnish with chocolate shavings, and serve with a long-handled spoon.

Coffee and Chocolate Flip

Use only the freshest egg in this recipe, as it isn't cooked. You could replace the Kahlúa with Tia Maria for a slightly sweeter version. The result is a smoothly frothy, intensely rich drink with a strong, beguiling coffee flavour. The chocolate element is confined to the garnish.

1 egg
5ml/1 tsp sugar
1 measure/1½ tbsp cognac
1 measure/1½ tbsp Kahlúa
5ml/1 tsp dark-roast instant coffee granules
3 measures/4½ tbsp double (heavy) cream

Separate the egg and lightly beat the white until frothy. In a separate bowl, beat the egg yolk with the sugar. In a small pan, combine the brandy, Kahlúa,

coffee and cream and warm over a very low heat. Allow the mixture to cool, then whisk it into the egg yolk. Add the egg white to the egg and cream, and pour the mixture briefly back and forth between two glasses until it is smooth. Pour into a tall glass over coarsely crushed ice and sprinkle the top with cocoa powder.

Café Royale

This is a highly sophisticated, and rather ostentatious digestif. The recipe serves four.

4 sugar cubes
300ml/½ pint hot, strong, black filter or cafetière coffee
4 measures/6 tbsp cognac

Rinse out four coffee cups with boiled water and pour away. Add a sugar lump to each cup and then fill with coffee to a little way below the rim. Float a measure of cognac on the surface, and then set it alight. Guests should allow the drink to flame for a few seconds, and then extinguish it by stirring with a spoon.

Alhambra Royale

We conclude our brandy repertoire with a hot chocolate mixture that tastes even more luxurious than the preceding coffee recipes.

hot chocolate, made up to just short of the cup's brim
1 small piece orange rind
1½ measures/6 tsp cognac
15ml/1 tbsp whipped cream

Drop the orange rind into the hot chocolate. Heat the cognac in a metal ladle over a gas flame or over boiling water, and set it alight. Pour it, flaming, into the chocolate. Stir it in, and spoon a blob of whipped cream on to the surface of the drink. Sprinkle with cocoa powder.

Bartending know-how
When using hot chocolate in a cocktail, it is always preferable to use proper cocoa with a good, high proportion of real cacao solids in it. The alternative – drinking chocolate – is mostly sugar and has a much less concentrated flavour.

Other spirits

In this section, we deal with those less well-known spirits that fall outside the main six. These will include the bitter aperitifs, such as Campari, as well as the concentrated bitters like Angostura; the apple brandies, such as France's calvados and America's applejack; and the traditional European fruit distillates, such as kirsch (made from cherries) and slivovitz (plums). Despite their minority status, these products have played an integral part in the cocktail repertoire, and will no doubt continue to do so.

Americano

A recipe going back to the early years of the 20th century, Americano was the one of the first to make a feature of the bitter red Italian *aperitivo*, Campari.

2 measures/3 tbsp sweet red vermouth
1 measure/1½ tbsp Campari
1 measure/1½ tbsp soda water

Add the first two ingredients to a rocks glass or Old-Fashioned glass with two or three cubes of ice in it. Stir, and add the soda. Squeeze a twist of orange rind over the drink and then drop it in.

Negroni

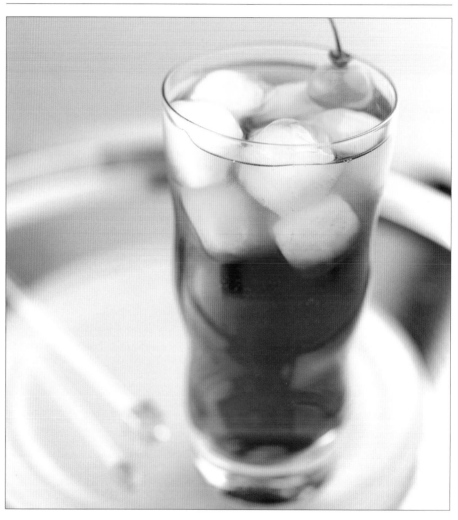

The Negroni is an Americano with gin, making an altogether drier drink. It is named after one Count Negroni who invented this formula at a bar in Florence just after the First World War. The addition of gin elevates the drink into a different class altogether. This is a brilliant aperitif.

2 measures/3 tbsp gin
1 measure/1½ tbsp sweet red vermouth
¾ measure/3 tsp Campari
1 measure/1½ tbsp soda water

Mix the first three ingredients in a tumbler with ice and then add the soda. Finish with orange, as for Americano.

Pink Gin

The famous tipple of British naval officers (the lower ranks drank rum), this is simply a neat, bittered gin. Classically, it should be made with Plymouth gin, for its milder aromatic quality and its naval associations.

Sprinkle about six drops of Angostura bitters into a goblet-shaped glass, roll it around to coat the inner surfaces, then dash it out. Add ice-cold gin, which will then take on the faintest pink tint.

Normandy Cooler

This refreshing summer drink is perfect for afternoons in the garden. It can be made with applejack instead of calvados and renamed a Harvard Cooler, in which it is as well to leave out the grenadine.

2 measures/3 tbsp calvados
1 measure/1½ tbsp lemon juice
¼ measure/1 tsp grenadine
½ measure/2 tsp sugar syrup
4 measures/6 tbsp soda water

Fill a highball glass with cracked ice and dangle a twist of lemon in it. Add the first four ingredients, give the drink a good stir, and then top up with the soda water.

Calvados Cream

The cheaper grades of calvados can be a little fiery. If that's what you have to hand, this should sort it out. It's a creamy, but sharply flavoured cocktail.

2 measures/3 tbsp calvados
½ measure/2 tsp lemon juice
1 measure/1½ tbsp double (heavy) cream
¼ measure/1 tsp pineapple syrup (from a can)

Shake the first three ingredients thoroughly with ice, and strain into a bowl-shaped cocktail glass. Sprinkle the pineapple syrup over the surface.

Depth Charge

This is one of several 1920s cocktails that owe their names to the World War then still fresh in everyone's memory.

1 measure/1½ tbsp calvados
1 measure/1½ tbsp cognac
½ measure/2 tsp lemon juice
¼ measure/1 tsp grenadine

Shake all the ingredients well with ice, and strain into a cocktail glass. Garnish with a twist of lemon.

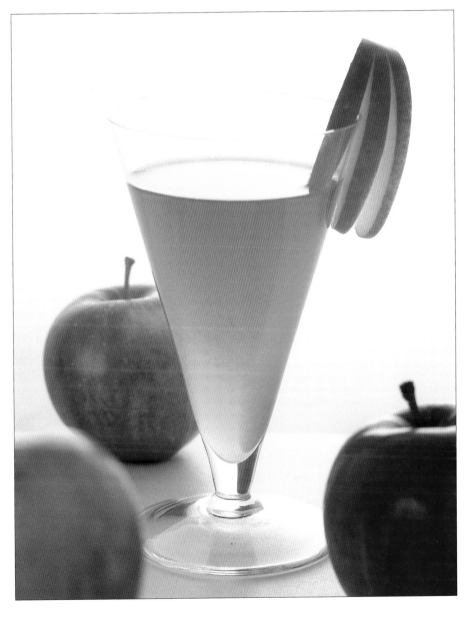

Calvarniac

The name of this drink is a combination of its three alcoholic ingredients. It is an impeccably French mixture, and a very fine one.

1 measure/1½ tbsp calvados
⅔ measure/1 tbsp Grand Marnier
⅓ measure/1½ tsp cognac
1 measure/1½ tbsp sparkling lemonade

Half-fill a rocks glass with cracked ice, and add the first three ingredients. Stir briskly, and then add the lemonade. Garnish with a slice of lemon.

French Toddy

This is a variation of a very old French recipe, said to have been a favourite of the novelist Gustave Flaubert, to which coffee and sugar have been added. This recipe serves two.

120ml/4fl oz calvados
50ml/2fl oz apricot brandy
20–30ml/4–6 tsp sugar, to taste
300ml/½ pint very strong coffee (filter/
    cafetière brewed at about 45g/8 tbsp
    coffee per 500ml/17fl oz water)

Applecart

This is another American recipe, but one that can just as easily be made with calvados as with applejack – or with home-grown Somerset cider brandy, for that matter.

1 measure/1½ tbsp applejack
¾ measure/3 tsp Cointreau
½ measure/2 tsp lemon juice

Shake all the ingredients well with ice, and strain into a chilled cocktail glass. Garnish the drink with a half-slice of lemon.

25ml/1½ tbsp double (heavy) cream

Very gently warm the calvados and apricot brandy together over a low heat, and transfer to large balloon glasses. Dissolve the sugar in the coffee and add to the liquor. Stir vigorously. While the contents are still rotating from the stirring, pour the cream over the surface in a circular motion. Do not stir further, just sip and savour.

Apple Blossom

The slightly sweeter finish of applejack is better suited than calvados in this American cocktail. Use ordinary sugar syrup if you can't get hold of maple, although it won't be quite the same.

1½ measures/6 tsp applejack
1 measure/1½ tbsp apple juice
½ measure/2 tsp lemon juice
¼ measure/1 tsp maple syrup

Shake all the ingredients well with ice, and strain into a cocktail glass or champagne saucer. Garnish with a wafer-thin slice of red apple with the skin left on, and a half-slice of lemon.

Bartending know-how
Applejack was the second-choice product of early American settlers. It was only when the hops they tried to make beer with failed that they turned to apples instead.

Rose

Although it looks delicately pink and sweet, the cocktail that this 1920s recipe actually produces is very dry, and would make a good aperitif.

1 measure/1½ tbsp kirsch
1½ measures/6 tsp dry vermouth
dash grenadine

Shake all the ingredients well with ice, and strain into a cocktail glass. You could garnish the drink with a cherry.

Bartending know-how
Kirsch and cherry brandy are not interchangeable, since the former is drier than the latter, and colourless. Cherry brandy is also lower in alcohol.

Vruiça Rakia

This is how slivovitz, the Balkan plum spirit, is often drunk in its regions of origin. It is a cold-weather preparation intended to insulate the outdoor worker. This recipe serves two.

4 measures/6 tbsp slivovitz
10ml/2 tsp soft brown sugar

Pit Stop

If Rose is too dry for you, this fizzy, fruity kirsch cocktail is definitely a more sweet-natured proposition.

1 measure/1½ tbsp kirsch
1 measure/1½ tbsp cherry brandy
¼ measure/1 tsp amaretto
2 measures/3 tbsp sparkling lemonade

Half-fill a rocks glass with cracked ice. Add the first three ingredients, stir and add the lemonade. Garnish with a twist of lemon and a couple of cherries on a cocktail stick.

4 measures/6 tbsp water

Put all the ingredients in a small pan and bring nearly to the boil, stirring to dissolve the sugar. Pour into mugs or heatproof glasses, and garnish with blueberries skewered on to a swizzle-stick. Drink while hot.

Slivovitz Fizz

A refreshing, cold, sparkling cocktail to complement the hot slivovitz above, this makes a original alternative to more mainstream long drinks.

2 measures/3 tbsp slivovitz
½ measure/2 tsp lime juice
¼ measure/1 tsp sugar syrup
4 measures/6 tbsp soda water

Shake the first three ingredients well with ice, and strain into a highball glass, half-filled with cracked ice. Top up with soda. Garnish with a slice of black plum.

Liqueurs

The world of cocktails would be virtually nothing without liqueurs. They are what give character and personality to many recipes. Sometimes they can be relied on to add sweetness as well as flavour to a drink, so that no other sugaring agent is needed, and sometimes – as in the case of the old herbal liqueurs like Chartreuse, Bénédictine and Strega – they add their peculiar aromatic quality to basic spirits. New liqueurs are being produced and included all the time (Malibu and Midori became firm cocktail flavourites in the 1980s), and, among the recipes that follow, you will find at least one or two appearances of nearly all the liqueurs discussed earlier.

Sidecar

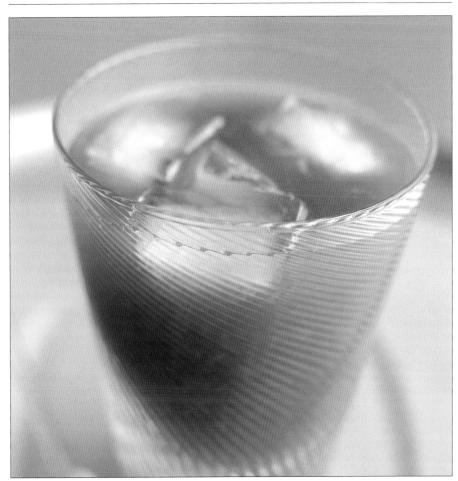

Cointreau can successfully be mixed with virtually any spirit (except perhaps whisky) and a quantity of lemon juice, and shaken with ice. Start with gin and you have a White Lady, vodka for a Balalaika and even tequila for a lemon Margarita. The brandy version is a Paris classic called Sidecar, after the preferred means of travel of a French army officer.

1½ measures/6 tsp cognac
¾ measure/3 tsp Cointreau
¾ measure/3 tsp lemon juice

Shake well with ice and strain into a rocks glass with a little cracked ice. Garnish with a half-slice of lemon.

Rum Sidecar

Just to complete the Sidecar repertoire, here's a version of the basic mix that uses light or golden rum. It produces a very slightly sweeter final result.

1½ measures/6 tsp light rum
¾ measure/3 tsp Cointreau
¾ measure/3 tsp lemon juice

Shake all the ingredients well with ice, and strain into a cocktail glass. Garnish with a half-slice of lemon.

Between the Sheets

A 1920s recipe that suddenly became very fashionable again in the 1980s, this is a powerful, sharply flavoured cocktail. Some recipes use light rum instead of white, but the resulting colour is inevitably slightly muddier.

1 measure/1½ tbsp Cointreau
1 measure/1½ tbsp cognac
1 measure/1½ tbsp white rum
½ measure/2 tsp lemon juice

Shake all the ingredients well with ice, and strain into a bowl-shaped cocktail glass. Garnish with a twist of lemon.

Bartending know-how
The principal flavouring element in crème de menthe – green or white – is peppermint. Its flavour is more subtly aromatic and refreshing than that of spearmint.

Stinger

The adaptable Stinger is simply a two-thirds-one-third mixture of any spirit with white crème de menthe, shaken with ice and served over smashed ice in a cocktail glass. The prototype version, dating from around the time of the First World War, is with cognac, as in the following recipe.

2 measures/3 tbsp cognac
1 measure/1½ tbsp white crème de menthe

Shake both the ingredients well with ice, and strain into a cocktail glass. You could garnish it with a tuft of mint, although it is fine without.

Grasshopper

This is a minted, creamy cocktail in an attractive shade of green. If you use dark crème de cacao, the cocktail will not be as vibrant a colour, but you'll find that it tastes just as good.

1 measure/1½ tbsp green crème de menthe
1 measure/1½ tbsp white crème de cacao
1 measure/1½ tbsp double (heavy) cream

Charlie Chaplin

The first, and in many ways the greatest, cocktail era was also the age of silent films, and it is no surprise to hear that, just as Mary Pickford was honoured with a cocktail named after her, so was the greatest silent comic of them all.

1½ measures/6 tsp sloe gin
½ measure/2 tsp apricot brandy
½ measure/2 tsp lime juice

Shake all the ingredients well with ice, and strain into a chilled cocktail glass. Garnish with a slice of lime, and perhaps a sliver of apricot.

Shake all the ingredients very well with ice, and strain into a cocktail glass. Sprinkle the surface with grated chocolate. Alternatively, decorate with chocolate curls, made by pouring melted chocolate on to a cold baking tray, allowing to harden and then scraping gently off with the point of a knife.

Snowball

This is the kind of cocktail generally considered safe to give to minors, since it resembles nothing so much as a particularly rich milkshake. It is almost the only thing worth doing with advocaat. If you require a bit more of a kick, add ½ measure/2 tsp sweet brown cream sherry as well.

2 measures/3 tbsp advocaat
5 measures/120ml/4fl oz ice-cold sparkling
   lemonade

Add to a highball glass half-filled with cracked ice, and stir gently. You could garnish with a cherry on a stick.

Bartending know-how
Snowball needs plenty of lemonade to avoid its texture being too cloying.

Hollywood Nuts

Almond and hazelnut are among the flavours in this cocktail. The original recipe has egg white in it too, but I don't tend to feel it needs it.

1 measure/1½ tbsp white rum
½ measure/2 tsp amaretto
½ measure/2 tsp brown crème de cacao
½ measure/2 tsp Frangelico
1 measure/1½ tbsp sparkling lemonade

Shake all but the last ingredient with ice, and strain into a rocks glass half-filled with cracked ice. Add the lemonade and stir. Garnish with a slice of lemon.

B52

This cocktail depends on the difference in specific weight or densities of each of the liqueurs to remain separated.

1 measure/1½ tbsp Kahlúa
1 measure/1½ tbsp Bailey's Irish Cream
1 measure/1½ tbsp Grand Marnier

Round the World

This cocktail certainly contains a cosmopolitan mix of ingredients. I can think of no other obvious explanation for its name.

1½ measure/6 tsp green crème de menthe
1 measure/1½ tbsp gin
2½ measures/3½ tbsp pineapple juice

Shake all the ingredients well with ice, and strain into a chilled wine goblet. Garnish with a chunk of pineapple on a cocktail stick.

Pour the ingredients in this order over the back of a cold teaspoon into a shot glass or liqueur glass, remembering to change the spoon between shots. If you can't get the hang of the layering, just shake it all up with ice and strain it into a cocktail glass.

Hooded Claw

Syrupy-sweet prune juice with amaretto and Cointreau makes a delicious digestif when poured over a snow of finely crushed ice. If you can't get it, you could try using the liquor from a can of prunes, although it may well be composed of other fruit juices. This recipe serves four people.

5 measures/120ml/4fl oz prune juice
2 measures/3 tbsp amaretto
1 measure/1½ tbsp Cointreau

Shake all the ingredients well with ice, and strain into four small liqueur glasses loosely filled with crushed ice.

Shamrock

Best described as something of an acquired taste, your view of this drink will depend crucially on how well you get on with the combination of green Chartreuse and mint. The Irish theme accounts for all the greenery. And it is, of course, an incredibly strong alcoholic drink.

1 measure/1½ tbsp Irish whiskey
1 measure/1½ tbsp dry vermouth
¼ measure/1 tsp green Chartreuse
¼ measure/1 tsp green crème de menthe

Stir all the ingredients well with ice in a pitcher, and strain into a cocktail glass. Garnish with a green olive.

Airstrike

This is a burning drink, similar to the Italian flaming Sambuca tradition.

2 measures/3 tbsp Galliano
1 measure/1½ tbsp cognac
1 star anise

Heat the Galliano and brandy in a small pan until just warm. Pour into a heat-resistant glass and add the star anise. Using a long match, pass the flame over the surface of the drink to ignite it, being careful not to burn yourself. Let it burn for a couple of minutes, until the star anise has begun to sizzle a little and released its aroma into the drink. Leave to cool slightly before drinking.

Bullfrog

This is a very simple mix for apricot brandy, in which the generous quantity of lemon juice takes all the sweetness off the liqueur.

1½ measures/6 tsp apricot brandy
juice of a lemon

Shake both the ingredients well with ice and strain into a cocktail glass. Garnish with a slice of lemon.

Long Island Iced Tea

This is a long, powerful drink with a rumbustiously intoxicating effect, its potency well disguised by the cola. For a simpler version, use equal quantities of rum, Cointreau, tequila and lemon juice, and top up with cola. The recipe does not contain tea. It's a facetious way of referring to the fact that it looks innocuously like a glass of non-alcoholic iced tea.

½ measure/2 tsp white rum
½ measure/2 tsp vodka

½ measure/2 tsp gin
½ measure/2 tsp silver tequila
½ measure/2 tsp Cointreau
juice of half a lemon
½ measure/2 tsp sugar syrup
4 measures/6 tbsp cola

Stir all but the last ingredient well with ice for about 30 seconds in a pitcher to chill. Strain into a highball glass filled with ice cubes and a twist of lemon. Add chilled cola, and finish with a sprig of fresh mint.

Old William

This is a gorgeously fruity mixture that brings out the best in the delightful liqueur Poire William. The citrus juices take the edge off its sweetness.

2 measures/3 tbsp Poire William
½ measure/2 tsp maraschino

½ measure/2 tsp orange juice
½ measure/2 tsp lemon juice

Add the ingredients in this order to a rocks glass half-filled with broken ice. Stir briskly, and garnish with half-slices of orange and lemon.

Las Hadas

This contemporary classic spin on the traditional Sambuca presentation is for those who aren't quite up to tackling a drink that's been set on fire.

1 measure/1½ tbsp Sambuca
1 measure/1½ tbsp Kahlúa

Stir both ingredients well with ice in a mixing glass, and strain into a pre-chilled wine goblet. Float a few coffee beans on the surface of the drink.

Alaska

This drink is intended to evoke the frozen wastes, so make sure it's shaken until the cocktail shaker is almost too cold to hold.

1½ measures/6 tsp gin
½ measure/2 tsp yellow Chartreuse

Shake both the ingredients very well with plenty of ice, and strain into a cocktail glass. No garnish is necessary.

Bijou

This recipe dates from the 1920s. The mix of Chartreuse and vermouth does indeed create a rather jewel-like colour. It must be Plymouth gin, by the way.

1 measure/1½ tbsp Plymouth gin
1 measure/1½ tbsp green Chartreuse
1 measure/1½ tbsp sweet red vermouth
dash orange bitters (or curaçao)

Stir all the ingredients well with ice in a pitcher, and then strain into a cocktail glass. Squeeze a twist of lemon over the drink, drop it in and add a cherry.

Frosty Amour

This drink would make a good tipple for a Valentine's Day evening in. Any frostiness will soon be dispelled after downing one.

1 measure/1½ tbsp vodka
1 measure/1½ tbsp apricot brandy
1 measure/1½ tbsp Southern Comfort
¼ measure/1 tsp Parfait Amour
¼ measure/1 tsp crème de banane
4 measures/6 tbsp 7-Up

Frost the rim of a highball glass with lemon juice and caster (superfine) sugar. Half-fill it with ice. Shake all but the last ingredient with ice, and strain into the prepared glass. Top with 7-Up. Garnish with a cherry and a slice of orange.

Fuzzy Navel

The evocative name of this drink plays on the ideas of the fuzzy-skinned peach and the navel orange. If it tastes a little too tame, add a measure of vodka to it and call it a Hairy Navel, a grown-up version of the same body part.

2 measures/3 tbsp peach schnapps
4 measures/6 tbsp orange juice

Add the ingredients to a highball glass half-filled with cracked ice, and stir well. Garnish with a slice of orange.

Singapore Sling

One of the all-time greats, Singapore Sling was created in 1915 at the world-famous Raffles Hotel in Singapore. Some recipes omit the soda for a slightly stronger drink. Some add a dash of grenadine just to deepen the pink colour, but it should nonetheless be no more than a fairly delicate blush.

2 measures/3 tbsp gin
⅔ measure/1 tbsp cherry brandy
⅔ measure/1 tbsp Cointreau
juice of 1 lemon
5ml/1 tsp caster (superfine) sugar
3 measures/4½ tbsp soda water

Shake all but the last ingredient well with ice, and strain into a highball glass. Add the soda, and decorate with a twist of lemon and a black cherry pierced with two cocktail sticks.

Zam

This is a very resourceful cocktail that uses no fewer than three liqueurs, without the need for a plain spirit base. This enhances the herbal flavours well, and the overall effect is nicely balanced between sweet and dry.

1 measure/1½ tbsp Glayva
½ measure/2 tsp Bénédictine
½ measure/2 tsp Sambuca
1½ measures/6 tsp orange juice
¼ measure/1 tsp sugar syrup
¼ measure/1 tsp lemon juice

Shake all the ingredients well with ice, and strain into a chilled champagne saucer or wine goblet loaded with crushed ice. Garnish with a strawberry.

Blanche

Another three-way liqueur blend, this one is fairly sweet, although the curaçao adds a balancing bitter note. To live up to its name, the curaçao really ought to be the white variety, but nobody will know if you use orange.

1 measure/1½ tbsp Cointreau
1 measure/1½ tbsp white curaçao
1 measure/1½ tbsp anisette

Shake all the ingredients well with ice, and strain into a cocktail glass. Emphasize the drink's purity of colour by refraining from any garnish.

Godfather

Like the Godmother, this drink uses amaretto, but substitutes Scotch for the vodka. This makes for a more complex flavour, and the drink would make a good aperitif.

Godmother

A very simple mixture, this is a formula to throw the sweetness of almond liqueur into relief for the more savoury-toothed. It should properly be made with the most famous brand of amaretto, Disaronno Originale, but won't come to any harm if you use another brand.

1½ measures/6 tsp amaretto
1½ measures/6 tsp vodka

Mix both ingredients well in a tumbler full of cracked ice. The drink does not need any garnish.

1½ measures/6 tsp amaretto
1½ measures/6 tsp Scotch

Mix both ingredients well in a tumbler full of cracked ice. Do not garnish.

Bunny Hug

This one is not for the novice cocktail drinker as it consists only of strong alcohol, and the flavour is very dry.

1 measure/1½ tbsp gin
1 measure/1½ tbsp Scotch
1 measure/1½ tbsp Pernod

Bartending know-how
Pernod and other forms of pastis will give an instant natural cloudiness to any mixture.

Shake all the ingredients well with ice, and strain into a pre-chilled cocktail glass. The drink can be garnished with a twist of lemon.

Festival

Strictly for the sweet and creamy brigade, this is the sort of drink that might well kick off a hen night, assuming the girls need any further egging on.

1 measure/1½ tbsp apricot brandy
¾ measure/3 tsp white crème de cacao

¼ measure/1 tsp grenadine
½ measure/2 tsp double (heavy) cream

Shake all the ingredients well with ice, and strain into a chilled cocktail glass. Garnish with a cherry or two speared on a cocktail stick.

Lost Bikini

The name seems to evoke memories of Ursula Andress emerging from the waves in the first James Bond movie, or is that just wishful thinking?

¾ measure/3 tsp Galliano
¾ measure/3 tsp amaretto
½ measure/2 tsp white rum
½ measure/2 tsp lime juice
2 measures/3 tbsp unsweetened mandarin juice (from a can)

Shake all the ingredients well with ice, and strain into a champagne saucer or cocktail glass. Garnish with a half-slice of orange and a cherry.

Kir

This world-famous gastronomic aperitif was created in Burgundy, and was originally named after a mayor of Dijon. It consists of a glass of light, dry, acidic white wine with a shot of crème de cassis stirred into it (¼–½ measure/ 1–2 tsp, depending on taste). The classic wine to use is a Bourgogne Aligoté of the most recent vintage, but any fairly neutral-tasting white wine will do, so long as it is sharp with acidity.

Add the cassis to a glass of non-vintage brut champagne and the drink becomes a Kir Royale.

Stratosphere

A few drops of crème de violette are added to a glass of champagne until a mauve colour is obtained. The scentedness is then enhanced by adding a whole clove to the glass.

Oracabessa

A recipe that will use your garnishing skills to the full. The more fruit it has piled on to it, the better, but the banana slices are essential.

1 measure/1½ tbsp dark rum
1 measure/1½ tbsp crème de banane
juice of half a lemon
thin banana slices
4 measures/6 tbsp sparkling lemonade

Shake the first three ingredients well with ice, and strain into a large cocktail goblet. Float some banana on the surface of the drink, and top it up with the lemonade. Garnish lavishly with fruits.

An American violet liqueur, Crème Yvette, was at one time the only correct product to use in this very ladylike aperitif. Parfait Amour might also do.

Blackout

The name of this cocktail does not mean it necessarily induces the said state, but is more of a description of the resulting colour of the drink. It is a very harmonious and appealing cocktail mixture.

1¾ measures/2½ tbsp gin
¾ measure/3 tsp crème de mûre
juice of half a lime

Shake all the ingredients well with ice, and strain into a cocktail glass. Garnish with a slice of lime and a couple of ripe blackberries threaded carefully on to a cocktail stick.

Silver Jubilee

This was created for Queen Elizabeth's Silver Jubilee in 1977. There is a tendency now to up the gin quotient to as much as double this quantity, but I find that these proportions work perfectly well.

1 measure/1½ tbsp gin
1 measure/1½ tbsp crème de banane
1 measure/1½ tbsp double (heavy) cream

Shake all the ingredients thoroughly with ice to amalgamate the cream, and strain into a chilled cocktail glass. Grate a little dark chocolate over the surface, if desired.

Bartending know-how
Cream cocktails should generally be made with double cream, as the single version tends to be too runny.

Oasis

Blue cocktails suddenly became all the rage during the cocktail boom of the 1980s. This is a particularly satisfying mixture that's not too sweet.

2 measures/3 tbsp gin
½ measure/2 tsp blue curaçao
4 measures/6 tbsp tonic water

Pour the gin into a highball glass half-filled with cracked ice. Add the curaçao, top up with the tonic and stir gently. Garnish with a slice of lemon and a sprig of mint.

English Rose

If you can find crème de roses, snap it up and use it in this very fetching cocktail that would make a fine Mother's Day toast. (Before you crack open the pink champagne, that is.)

1½ measures/6 tsp gin
¾ measure/3 tsp crème de roses
½ measure/2 tsp lemon juice
2.5ml/½ tsp caster (superfine) sugar
½ egg white

Shake all the ingredients thoroughly with ice, and strain into a wine glass. Alternatively, you can make this in the blender for that extra frothiness.

Olympic

Created for the 1924 Olympic Games in Paris, this is a gold medal-winning recipe.

1 measure/1½ tbsp cognac
1 measure/1½ tbsp orange curaçao

Whip

This lethally violent 1920s cocktail contains a lot of strong alcohol and no mixers. Caution is advised. One should be more than enough.

1 measure/1½ tbsp cognac
½ measure/2 tsp dry vermouth

1 measure/1½ tbsp orange juice

Shake all the ingredients well with ice, and strain into a cocktail glass. Garnish with a twist of orange rind.

½ measure/2 tsp sweet red vermouth
¼ measure/1 tsp orange curaçao
dash absinthe

Shake all the ingredients well with plenty of ice, and strain into a cocktail glass. You could garnish with a lemon twist.

Golden Tang

This recipe can be prepared short or long, depending on how the fancy takes you. If you serve it short, as here, use a wine glass. If you serve it long, increase the amount of orange juice to 4 measures/6 tbsp and serve it in a highball glass. The resulting drink is obviously more innocuous, but is an equally appealing aperitif long drink.

2 measures/3 tbsp vodka
1 measure/1½ tbsp Strega
½ measure/2 tsp crème de banane
½ measure/2 tsp orange juice

Shake all the ingredients well with ice, and strain into a large wine glass. Garnish with a twist of kumquat.

Golden Slipper

A group of "Golden" recipes continues with this American novelty drink from before the Second World War. I confess I haven't tried it; I suspect it may look rather prettier than it tastes.

1 measure/1½ tbsp yellow Charteuse
1 egg yolk
1 measure/1½ tbsp Goldwasser

Pour the yellow Chartreuse into a copita or sherry glass. Drop the egg yolk whole on to the surface, and then carefully pour the Goldwasser on top.

Golden Start

An ingenious mix of Galliano, fruit juices and coconut. It also works if the curaçao is replaced with white crème de cacao.

2 measures/3 tbsp Galliano
1 measure/1½ tbsp orange juice
1 measure/1½ tbsp pineapple juice
1 measure/1½ tbsp white or orange curaçao
1 measure/1½ tbsp coconut cream

Golden Dream

This fancifully named cocktail was created by the Galliano company itself in the 1960s. It's a sweetly delicious, creamy concoction.

1 measure/1½ tbsp Galliano
1 measure/1½ tbsp Cointreau
1 measure/1½ tbsp orange juice
1 measure/1½ tbsp whipping cream

Shake all the ingredients well with ice, and strain into a bowl-shaped cocktail glass. Decorate the surface with grated orange rind.

Process the Galliano, fruit juices and curaçao in a blender. Add the cream of coconut with 15ml/1 tbsp finely crushed ice, and process until smooth and frothy. Frost the rim of the cocktail glass by dipping it into pineapple juice and caster (superfine) sugar. Pour the cocktail into the prepared glass while still frothy.

Gloom Chaser

There was once a gin cocktail called Gloom Raiser, on account of the depressant qualities that spirit was mythically supposed to have. This, presumably, was intended as the antidote to it. I think we can safely say it works. Certainly, a couple of them will probably manage to dispel (temporarily) whatever it was that was bothering you.

1 measure/1½ tbsp Grand Marnier
1 measure/1½ tbsp orange curaçao
½ measure/2 tsp lemon juice
¼ measure/1 tsp grenadine

Shake all the ingredients well with ice, and strain into a chilled cocktail glass. Garnish the drink with a single slice of orange.

Paradise

A winning 1920s formula that should certainly waft you somewhere in the direction of paradise, however fleetingly.

1½ measures/6 tsp gin
¾ measure/3 tsp apricot brandy
¾ measure/3 tsp orange juice
dash lemon juice

Shake all the ingredients well with ice, and strain into a flared wine glass. Garnish with slices of orange, lemon and lime.

Alexander the Great

Another variation on the chocolate/coffee/cream combination, and distantly related to the classic Alexander, this drink is reputed to have been invented by the late Hollywood singing star Nelson Eddy. Indeed, in some quarters, he may well be more respectfully remembered for this recipe than for his films.

1½ measure/6 tsp vodka
½ measure/2 tsp Kahlúa
½ measure/2 tsp brown crème de cacao
½ measure/2 tsp double (heavy) cream

Tovarich

There are not many cocktail recipes with caraway-flavoured kümmel in them, but this one works very well, in its tartly bracing way.

1½ measures/6 tsp vodka
1 measure/1½ tbsp kümmel
juice of half a lime

Shake all the ingredients well with ice, and strain into a cocktail glass. Garnish the drink with a couple of rings of thinly sliced lime.

Shake all the ingredients well with plenty of ice, and strain into a cocktail glass. Add a couple of chocolate-coated coffee beans to the drink.

Bartending know-how
The liqueur components in Alexander the Great are Kahlúa and the brown version of chocolate liqueur. If your guests are sweeter-natured than this, substitute Tia Maria and white crème de cacao.

Batida Banana

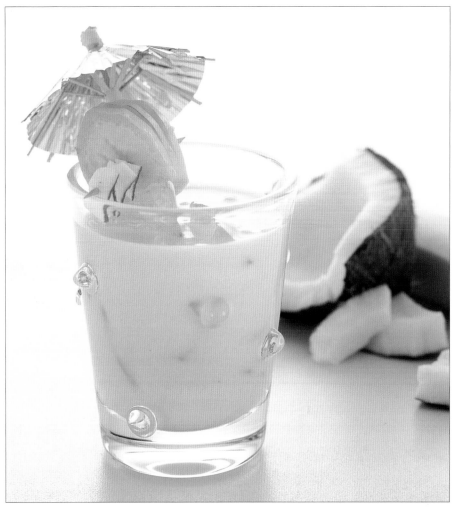

A recipe created specifically for the Brazilian coconut liqueur, Batida de Coco, this is dangerously moreish, and is effectively little more than a grown-up milkshake, but none the worse for that. The fact that it uses milk rather than cream means that the sweetness of its flavours is not as cloying as it might be.

1 measure/1½ tbsp Batida de Coco
1 measure/1½ tbsp crème de banane
5 measures/120ml/4fl oz full-cream (whole)
  milk

Mix the liqueurs with several ice cubes in a highball glass. Top with milk. Garnish with sliced banana and orange.

Pick-Me-Up

This is but one of the many recipes for pick-me-ups. As with all of them, it is intended to be drunk PDQ or, as Harry Craddock – Cocktail King of London's Savoy Hotel in the 1920s – used to put it, "while it's laughing at you".

1 measure/1½ tbsp dry vermouth
1 measure/1½ tbsp cherry brandy
2 dashes gin

Add the ingredients to a tumbler packed with cracked ice. Stir once, then drink.

Wally

This drink can be prepared with any apple spirit: calvados, applejack or English cider brandy. I have no idea who the gentleman was after whom it is named.

1 measure/1½ tbsp calvados
1 measure/1½ tbsp peach brandy
1 measure/1½ tbsp lime juice

Shake all the ingredients well with ice, and strain into a cocktail glass. Garnish with a thin slice of peach and a slice of lime on a cocktail stick.

Angel Face

To be dedicated to the one you love, perhaps, although after a couple of these, almost anyone will start to look good. It's another all-alcohol mix, and a pretty dry and bracing one at that, although the liqueur contributes a touch of almondy sweetness to the finish.

1 measure/1½ tbsp gin
1 measure/1½ tbsp apricot brandy
1 measure/1½ tbsp calvados

Shake all the ingredients well with ice, and strain into a cocktail glass. Garnish with a half-slice of lemon.

Tropical Cocktail

Not, as you might expect, a rum cocktail, this was the 1920s idea of tropical. In other words, it has a hint of chocolate in it. Use the brown version of crème de cacao for a less sweet result, but the attractively pale colour of the original will obviously be lost.

1 measure/1½ tbsp dry vermouth
1 measure/1½ tbsp maraschino
1 measure/1½ tbsp white crème de cacao
dash Angostura bitters
dash orange bitters (or curaçao)

Shake all the ingredients well with plenty of ice, and strain into a wine glass. Garnish with a slice of orange and a cherry.

Pink Almond

The colour of this isn't actually pink, more a sort of off-puce, but the flavour is indubitably of almond, so at least half the name is right.

1 measure/1½ tbsp Scotch
½ measure/2 tsp crème de noyau
½ measure/2 tsp kirsch
½ measure/2 tsp lemon juice
½ measure/2 tsp orgeat syrup

Shake all the ingredients well with ice, and strain into a wine goblet. Garnish with a twist of lemon and two or three slivers of flaked almond.

Green Caribbean

One of the 1980s creations that accompanied the launch of the delectable Japanese melon liqueur Midori, the name of which simply means "green". It's a supremely refreshing long drink with an appreciable kick.

Titanic

A modern recipe that should, not surprisingly, be served on a great heap of ice.

1½ measures/6 tsp vodka
1½ measures/6 tsp Mandarine Napoléon
3 measures/4½ tbsp soda water

Mix the vodka and Mandarine Napoléon with ice in a wide tumbler, and top up with soda water. Garnish with a twist of mandarin or tangerine rind.

1½ measures/6 tsp white rum
1½ measures/6 tsp Midori
4 measures/6 tbsp soda water

Shake the first two ingredients with ice, and strain into a highball glass. Add the soda and a slice of lemon.

Mad Monk

This is a cocktail I invented myself on first tasting the excellent hazelnut and herb liqueur, Frangelico, in its monk-shaped bottle.

1 measure/1½ tbsp gin
1 measure/1½ tbsp Frangelico
juice of half a lemon

Shake all the ingredients well with ice, and strain into a wine glass. You could garnish with a half-slice of lemon.

Bartending know-how
Yellow Chartreuse, formulated in 1840, is a more recent product than its green sibling. The colour of both is achieved by the natural colouring of their ingredients.

Walnut Whirl

This one sounds and, for that matter, tastes as though it ought to be lurking somewhere in the bottom layer of a box of fine chocolates.

1 measure/1½ tbsp cognac
1 measure/1½ tbsp crème de noix (walnut liqueur)
1 measure/1½ tbsp double (heavy) cream

Shake all the ingredients well with ice, and strain into a cocktail glass. Garnish with a sprinkling of grated dark chocolate and a walnut half.

Yellow Parrot

This is a powerful 1920s cocktail. It is essential to serve it over crushed ice, to mitigate a little of its firepower.

1 measure/1½ tbsp absinthe
1 measure/1½ tbsp yellow Chartreuse
1 measure/1½ tbsp apricot brandy

Shake all the ingredients well with ice, and strain into a cocktail glass filled almost to the brim with crushed ice. Do not garnish.

Eagle's Dream

The vanilla tones in purple Parfait Amour come through admirably in this foamy, gently flavoured 1920s cocktail. It should be served to your loved one on Valentine's Day, naturally.

1½ measures/6 tsp gin
1 measure/1½ tbsp Parfait Amour
juice of half a lemon
2.5ml/½ tsp caster (superfine) sugar
1 egg white

Whizz up all the ingredients with plenty of crushed ice in a blender, and strain into a large wine goblet. Garnish with a slice of lemon, or dangle a spiral twist of lemon or lime off the side of the glass, just to show you care.

Red Witch

In northern Europe and the United States, pastis is more often mixed with fruit juices than with water. Its colourlessness makes it a useful base; sharper flavours such as grapefruit are the most successful. A fashion for drinking it with blackcurrant cordial was quite the thing in Britain in the 1970s. It perhaps reminded the drinker of a certain type of childhood boiled sweet with a chewy centre that combined the flavours of liquorice and blackcurrant. Pernod and black in a tall glass topped up with sweet cider, known in the bars of the north of England as Red Witch, was a popular way of achieving oblivion in my own happily misspent youth.

Grand Slam

This is another recipe using punsch, which mixes very suavely with both shades of vermouth. Here is an aperitif cocktail, if ever there was one.

2 measures/3 tbsp punsch
1 measure/1½ tbsp dry vermouth
1 measure/1½ tbsp sweet red vermouth

Stir all the ingredients well with ice in a pitcher, and then strain over crushed ice in a wine glass. You could garnish the drink with a half-slice of orange.

Diki-Diki

I have no idea what the name of this cocktail refers to, but it was a very popular one in the Savoy American Bar in the 1920s. It is one of many from the period to use Swedish punsch.

2 measures/3 tbsp calvados
½ measure/2 tsp punsch
½ measure/2 tsp grapefruit juice

Shake all the ingredients well with ice, and strain into a cocktail glass. Add a small piece of pink grapefruit rind to the drink.

Rite of Spring

Green cocktails that don't somehow taste of mint are pretty few and far between. The relatively rare green version of curaçao is worth buying if you come across it, and here is a recipe of my own, tailor-made for it, if I say so myself.

2 measures/3 tbsp vodka
1 measure/1½ tbsp green curaçao
4 measures/6 tbsp sparkling lemonade

Mix the vodka and curaçao with ice in a pitcher until well-chilled. Pour without straining into a highball glass, and top up with the lemonade. Dangle a long twist of lemon rind in the drink.

Ojen Cocktail

This recipe was created specifically for the Spanish version of pastis, ojen. For that authentic touch, the twist should really be of the bitter Seville orange variety.

2 measures/3 tbsp dry ojen
5ml/1 tsp caster (superfine) sugar
½ measure/2 tsp still mineral water
dash orange bitters (or curaçao)

Shake all the ingredients well with ice, and strain into a small tumbler. Garnish with a twist of orange rind.

Absinthe Cocktail

This original 19th-century recipe could just be the most perfect cocktail in the world, for its simplicity and unforgettable power. Now that absinthe is widely commercially available again, it cries out to be tried. As a wise man once said, "Absinthe makes the heart grow fonder."

2 measures/3 tbsp absinthe
2 measures/3 tbsp still mineral water
dash sugar syrup
dash Angostura bitters

Shake all the ingredients well with ice, and strain into a cocktail glass. No garnish is needed. Sip slowly.

Matinée

In this nourishing, creamy, eggy mixture, the relatively small amount of Sambuca shines forth. Whip up the egg white a little before adding it to the shaker.

1 measure/1½ tbsp gin
½ measure/2 tsp Sambuca
½ measure/2 tsp double (heavy) cream
½ egg white
dash lime juice

Block and Fall

Cocktails that include pastis tend to be the most dramatic in the repertoire. Many of these contain no non-alcoholic ingredients. That is because a relatively small amount of pastis will have plenty to say for itself in even the most ferocious of mixes, concoctions that would drown the presence of many of the more delicate liqueurs.

Shake all the ingredients well with plenty of ice, and strain into a chilled cocktail glass. Sprinkle with finely grated nutmeg.

Bartending know-how
When three coffee beans are taken in a flaming Sambuca, they represent health, wealth and happiness.

1 measure/1½ tbsp cognac
1 measure/1½ tbsp Cointreau
½ measure/2 tsp Pernod
½ measure/2 tsp calvados

Stir all the ingredients together with ice in a pitcher, and then strain into a tumbler half-filled with cracked ice. Add a twist of lemon.

Drought

If you should bring back a bottle of delightful Suze from a trip to France, here is a good alternative to serving it neat. This is an unimaginably dry mixture, and a particular energizer to the appetite. It makes a fabulous lunchtime aperitif – or evening one, for that matter.

1 measure/1½ tbsp gin
1 measure/1½ tbsp Suze
dash orange juice

Shake all the ingredients well with ice, and strain into a small wine glass containing a single cube of ice. Add a little piece of orange rind.

Sundowner

This recipe uses the bitter, orange-flavoured South African liqueur, Van der Hum, in a variation on the formula for Sunburn (see below). Instead of using cognac, though, you could substitute a good South African brandy if you come across it. Many of them are surprisingly fine in quality.

1½ measures/6 tsp cognac
1 measure/1½ tbsp Van der Hum
½ measure/2 tsp orange juice
½ measure/2 tsp lemon juice

Shake all the ingredients well with ice, and strain into a cocktail glass. Garnish with a physalis fruit.

Southern Peach

The peach notes in America's classic whiskey liqueur are accentuated by its being mixed with peach brandy in this cream cocktail.

1 measure/1½ tbsp Southern Comfort
1 measure/1½ tbsp peach brandy
1 measure/1½ tbsp double (heavy) cream
dash Angostura bitters

Shake all the ingredients well with plenty of ice, and strain into a tumbler. Garnish with a wedge of ripe peach.

Sunburn

A dark and brooding combination of brandy and coffee liqueur is brightened up with fresh citrus juices. The effect is an unusual one, but you will find that you have grown to love it by the time you finish the drink.

1 measure/1½ tbsp cognac
1 measure/1½ tbsp Tia Maria
½ measure/2 tsp orange juice
½ measure/2 tsp lemon juice

Shake all the ingredients well with ice, and strain into a cocktail glass. Garnish with half-slices of orange and lemon.

Amsterdammer

Here is one of those bet-you-can't-drink-more-than-one-of-these recipes. I have never seen this on any cocktail list in Amsterdam. It seems more likely to be an American recipe.

1½ measures/6 tsp advocaat
1½ measures/6 tsp cherry brandy

Shake the ingredients very thoroughly with ice, and strain into a champagne saucer. Garnish with a cocktail cherry.

Milano

The assertive flavour of Galliano comes through strongly in this short, sour cocktail, which has a long aftertaste.

1 measure/1½ tbsp gin
1 measure/1½ tbsp Galliano

Duchess

This is a 1920s recipe in which the pungency of absinthe is tamed – if that's the right word – by a mixture of red and white vermouths.

1 measure/1½ tbsp absinthe
1 measure/1½ tbsp dry vermouth
1 measure/1½ tbsp sweet red vermouth

Shake all the ingredients well with ice, and strain into a cocktail glass. Add a small piece of lemon rind.

juice of half a lemon

Shake all the ingredients well with ice, and strain into a cocktail glass. Garnish with a cherry and slices of lemon and lime on a cocktail stick.

Saracen

This impeccably Scottish cocktail recalls the story of the Saracen's head, with which Glayva is associated. Good malt whisky is often matured in old sherry casks, so there is a Highland connection even in the use of dry sherry in the recipe.

1 measure/1½ tbsp Scotch
½ measure/2 tsp Glayva
½ measure/2 tsp pale dry (fino) sherry
dash orange bitters (or curaçao)
1 measure/1½ tbsp soda water

Shake all but the last ingredient well with ice, and pour without straining into a tumbler. Add the soda, and garnish with a piece of orange rind.

Bartending know-how
The tall fluted bottle in which Galliano is packaged is based on the classical design of Roman columns.

Strega Daiquiri

This is more or less a standard Daiquiri, in which the liqueur forms an additional element, rather than replacing the rum.

1 measure/1½ tbsp Strega
1 measure/1½ tbsp white rum
½ measure/2 tsp lemon juice
½ measure/2 tsp orange juice
2.5ml/½ tsp orgeat syrup (or sugar syrup)

Shake all the ingredients well with ice, and strain into a chilled cocktail glass. Garnish with a slice of lemon and a maraschino cherry.

Tuaca Cocktail

The combined flavours of vanilla, orange and lime in this heavenly mixture will test your moderate-drinking resolution to its limit. Once breached, you can then go on to enjoy another couple with a clear conscience.

1 measure/1½ tbsp vodka
1 measure/1½ tbsp Tuaca
½ measure/2 tsp lime juice

Shake well with ice, and strain into a cocktail glass. Garnish with orange rind.

Midori Sour

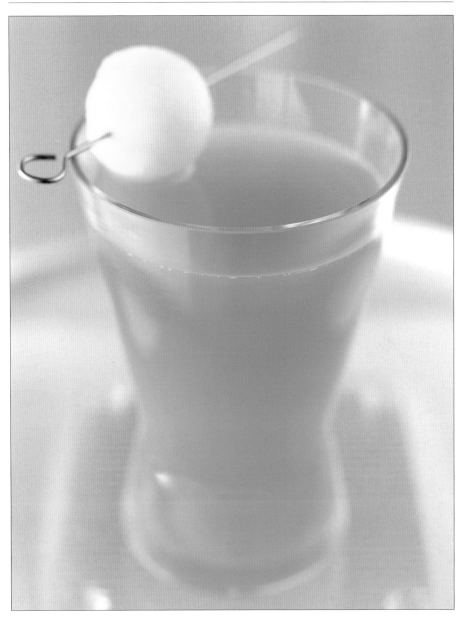

The standard Sour treatment works quite well with Midori, and certainly makes for a more exotic alternative to yet another Whisky Sour, but it's better shaken than stirred. You may well find it doesn't really need the sugar syrup.

2 measures/3 tbsp Midori
1 measure/1½ tbsp lemon juice
¼ measure/1 tsp sugar syrup

Shake well with ice, and strain into a tumbler. Garnish with a melon ball.

Café Kahlúa

This long, strong, creamy cocktail is pure self-indulgence. The addition of an optional cinnamon stick makes an imaginative alternative decoration to a plastic stirrer, and has the extra benefit of flavouring the drink as you swizzle it.

3 measures/4½ tbsp Kahlúa
1½ measures/6 tsp light rum
2 measures/3 tbsp whipping cream

Shake thoroughly with ice to incorporate the cream, and strain into a chilled tumbler. Add a stick of cinnamon.

Chrysanthemum

A 1920s recipe that, according to the *Savoy Cocktail Book*, was once popular in the bar of the Europa, one of the great passenger liners of the period.

1 measure/1½ tbsp Bénédictine
2 measures/3 tbsp dry vermouth
¼ measure/1 tsp absinthe

Shake all the ingredients well with ice, and strain into a cocktail glass. Squeeze a twist of orange rind over the surface of the drink and then drop it in.

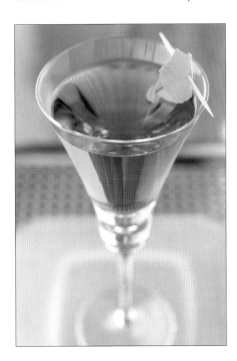

Bartending know-how
Among the many herbal and aromatic ingredients that go to make up the flavour of Bénédictine are: saffron, myrrh, aloes, hyssop, pine, cloves, nutmeg and tea.

Cara Sposa

Liqueurs and cream without the addition of a spirit base add up to a sweet, rich cocktail, and if that's your tipple, this luxurious creation is a well-nigh unbeatable one. Serve it at the end of dinner after a correspondingly light dessert.

1 measure/1½ tbsp Tia Maria
1 measure/1½ tbsp Cointreau
½ measure/2 tsp double (heavy) cream

Shake all the ingredients well with ice, and strain into a champagne saucer. Garnish with a twist of orange.

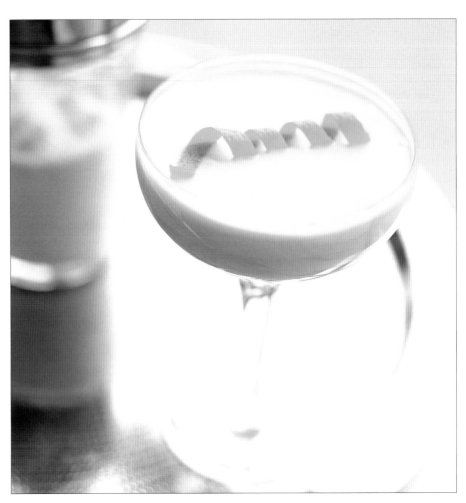

Viking

It has to be a thoroughly Scandinavian cocktail with that name, and so it is. The marriage of Swedish punsch and aquavit is, logically enough, a happy one.

1½ measures/6 tsp punsch
1 measure/1½ tbsp aquavit
1 measure/1½ tbsp lime juice

Shake all the ingredients well with ice, and strain into an Old-Fashioned glass or small tumbler. Garnish with lime.

Summertime

For the very sweet of tooth, this is a perfect way of livening up a dish of vanilla ice cream on a long, hot afternoon.

½ measure/2 tsp white crème de menthe
½ measure/2 tsp green crème de menthe
2 scoops vanilla ice cream

Process all the ingredients briefly in the blender, and then pour into a sundae glass. Sprinkle with grated dark chocolate.

Melon Patch

Another recipe for Midori, or indeed for any other melon liqueur you may have to hand.

1 measure/1½ tbsp Midori
½ measure/2 tsp Cointreau
½ measure/2 tsp vodka
4 measures/6 tbsp soda water

Shake the first three ingredients well with ice, and strain into a highball glass half-filled with cracked ice. Top up with soda, and garnish with a slice of orange.

Peugeot

This very French cocktail is intended, unexpectedly, as a tribute to the car manufacturer. Owners of their cars may justifiably drink it with pride, though not of course immediately before driving anywhere, as it's quite strong.

1½ measures/6 tsp Cointreau
¾ measure/3 tsp calvados
2 measures/3 tbsp orange juice

Shake well with ice and strain into a cocktail glass. Garnish with orange.

Kowloon

Coffee and orange make a successful partnership again in this recipe named after the Chinese district that faces Hong Kong Island.

1 measure/1½ tbsp Grand Marnier
1 measure/1½ tbsp Kahlúa
3 measures/4½ tbsp orange juice

Stir all the ingredients well with ice in a pitcher, and strain into a wine goblet half-filled with cracked ice. Add a slice of orange.

La Bomba

This explosive mixture has more than a touch of the Zombie about it.

1 measure/1½ tbsp light rum
½ measure/2 tsp orange curaçao
½ measure/2 tsp anisette
½ measure/2 tsp apricot brandy
½ measure/2 tsp lemon juice

Shake all the ingredients well with ice, and strain into a chilled cocktail glass. The drink could be garnished with a couple of chunks of pineapple and a cherry on a cocktail stick.

Bartending know-how
The variety of orange whose peel is used to flavour Grand Marnier is called *Citrus bigaradia*. It produces a bitter, orangey flavour that marries well with fine brandy.

Grand Hotel

This is a charming 1920s cocktail, the name of which may well refer to London's Savoy, one of the grandest of them all.

1½ measures/6 tsp Grand Marnier
1½ measures/6 tsp gin
½ measure/2 tsp dry vermouth
dash lemon juice

Shake all the ingredients well with ice, and strain into a large cocktail glass. Squeeze a twist of lemon over the surface and drop it into the glass.

Blue Lady

We have a Lemon Lady, a Scarlet Lady, a Pink Lady and a White Lady elsewhere, and here is their Blue sister. It's a sweet, creamy one that combines the flavours of orange and chocolate, but in a most peculiar hue.

Love

This sweet old 1920s cocktail is obviously made for sharing, so the recipe below serves two.

4 measures/6 tbsp sloe gin
1 measure/1½ tbsp lemon juice
1 egg white
¼ measure/1 tsp grenadine

Shake all the ingredients well with ice and then strain into two cocktail glasses. Garnish each with a pair of cherries joined at the stalk.

1½ measures/6 tsp blue curaçao
½ measure/2 tsp white crème de cacao
½ measure/2 tsp double (heavy) cream

Shake thoroughly with ice, and strain into a cocktail glass. Do not garnish.

Il Paradiso

Not to be confused with Paradise, this is a creamy, sumptuous, chocolate-orangey cocktail with a nice balance of sweet and bitter flavours.

1 measure/1½ tbsp Tuaca
1 measure/1½ tbsp orange curaçao
1 measure/1½ tbsp double (heavy) cream

Shake all the ingredients thoroughly with ice, and strain into a cocktail glass. Alternatively, whizz it up in the blender for an extra-frothy texture. Garnish with grated orange rind.

Bartending know-how

The credit for the formulation of the recipe on which the orangey Italian liqueur Tuaca is based is said to go to the Florentine politican Lorenzo de Medici in the 16th century – along with his many other achievements.

After-Dinner Coffee

This makes a superb Mexican-style way to end a meal. Kahlúa, the coffee liqueur used in this drink, is also delicious served in a liqueur glass topped with a thin layer of cream. This recipe serves four.

50g/2oz dark-roast ground coffee
475ml/16fl oz boiling water
120ml/4fl oz tequila
120ml/4fl oz Kahlúa
5ml/1 tsp natural vanilla essence (extract)
30ml/2 tbsp soft dark brown sugar
150ml/¼ pint double (heavy) cream

Put the ground coffee in a heatproof pitcher or cafetière, pour on the boiling water and leave until the coffee grounds settle at the bottom. Strain the coffee into a clean heatproof pitcher. Add the tequila, Kahlúa and vanilla essence to the coffee, and stir well to mix. Add the sugar and continue to stir until it has dissolved completely. Pour the mixture into small coffee cups or tall heat-resistant glasses. Hold a spoon just above the surface of each coffee. Pour the cream very slowly down the back of the spoon so that it forms a pool on top. Serve at once.

Highland Milk Punch

This is just the sort of thing to keep the cold at bay on cold nights in the frozen north, or anywhere else for that matter.

2 measures/3 tbsp Scotch
1 measure/1½ tbsp Drambuie
1 egg, beaten
250ml/8fl oz full-cream (whole) milk

Ski Lift

Here's another comforting hot drink for a rainy day. This gives ordinary drinking chocolate a real lift, and may well provide some compensation if the snow isn't good enough for skiing on.

1 measure/1½ tbsp peach schnapps
½ measure/2 tsp Malibu
hot chocolate

Make a pan of hot chocolate or cocoa in the normal way, but add the liqueurs to your mug before pouring it. Stir briskly, and top with a blob of whipped cream dusted with ground cinnamon.

Put all the ingredients into a small pan and heat gently, stirring all the time to incorporate the egg and prevent the milk from burning on the bottom of the pan. Just before the mixture boils, pour it into a mug and sprinkle the surface of the drink with powdered cinnamon.

Coffee Orloff

A John J. Poister recipe from the *New American Bartender's Guide*, this would make a very sexy after-dinner drink with a good, strong kick. Be sure to use the cream version of Grand Marnier.

¾ measure/3 tsp vodka
¾ measure/3 tsp Tia Maria
hot black coffee
¾ measure/3 tsp Crème de Grand Marnier

Add the vodka and Tia Maria to a large cup, and then top up with coffee. Pour the Crème de Grand Marnier over the back of a spoon so that it floats on top.

Café à l'Orange

This is one of numerous drink possibilities in which the flavours of orange and coffee are combined. The recipe serves four.

120ml/4fl oz whipping cream
30ml/2 tbsp icing (confectioners') sugar
5ml/1 tsp grated orange rind
600ml/1 pint hot black coffee
150ml/¼ pint any orange-flavoured liqueur, such as Grand Marnier, Cointreau, triple sec, etc
4 orange wedges, to garnish

In a clean bowl, whip the cream until stiff. Fold in the icing sugar and zest. Chill for 30 minutes, or until the cream mixture is firm enough to hold a wedge of orange on top. Divide the black coffee equally among tall glass mugs and stir about 30ml/2 tbsp liqueur into each. Top with chilled whipped cream and balance an orange wedge on top. Serve immediately.

Lisbon Flip Coffee

Here the coffee is not so much a main ingredient. It provides instead a subtle undertone to an interesting and profoundly satisfying cocktail. The recipe serves two.

4 measures/6 tbsp red port
2 measures/3 tbsp orange curaçao
1 measure/1½ tbsp very strong coffee
10ml/2 tsp icing (confectioners') sugar
2 eggs
20ml/4 tsp condensed milk
60ml/4 tbsp crushed ice
grated chocolate and orange rind shavings, to garnish

Place all the ingredients in a cocktail shaker, including the crushed ice. Shake vigorously and serve immediately in cocktail glasses. Top with the finely grated chocolate and orange rind.

African Coffee

In parts of Africa, coffee is often drunk with condensed milk. This recipe is an adaptation of an African brew with a luxurious liqueur finish.

250ml/8fl oz cold strong coffee (four generous espressos or cafetière coffee brewed using 70g/12 tbsp coffee per 1 litre/1¾ pints water)
40ml/8 tsp condensed milk
20ml/4 tsp brown crème de cacao

Shake well with ice, and strain into a tall glass half-filled with cracked ice.

Grasshopper Coffee

The name of this drink recalls the creamy crème de menthe cocktail we came across earlier, and the coffee will need to be good and strong to stand up to the flavours of the liqueurs. This recipe makes two servings.

dark and white chocolate mints
2 measures/3 tbsp green crème de menthe
2 measures/3 tbsp coffee liqueur, such as Tia Maria or Kahlúa
350ml/12fl oz hot strong black coffee
50ml/2fl oz whipping cream

Cut the dark and white chocolate mints diagonally in half. Divide the two liqueurs equally into two tall, strong latte glasses. Combine well. Fill each glass with the hot coffee and top them with whipped cream. Decorate with the chocolate mint triangles, dividing the white and dark chocolate evenly.

Easy Café Brûlot

This is a traditional coffee drink from New Orleans, where all the ingredients except the coffee are "flamed" in a bowl at the table. The flame is extinguished by pouring the coffee into the bowl. Except for the dramatic visual effects, this recipe achieves the same flavour with less fuss. It serves three to four.

3 measures/4½ tbsp brandy or rum
2 measures/3 tbsp Cointreau or other orange-flavoured liqueur
30ml/2 tbsp caster (superfine) sugar
6–8 cloves
2 sticks cinnamon
a strip of lemon and/or orange rind
700ml/24fl oz strong hot dark-roast coffee

Heat the brandy or rum, Cointreau, sugar, cloves, cinnamon sticks and lemon or orange rind in a large pan. Stir to dissolve the sugar. Pour the black coffee, brewed at about 65g/2½oz per 1 litre/1¾ pints water by the cafetière method, into the mixture. Stir and serve in coffee cups. Garnish with a cinnamon stick and orange rind.

Coffee Colada

This coffee cocktail is a riot of bold Caribbean flavours. A pitcher can be made up a couple of hours in advance, then allowed to freeze partially, before topping with plenty of whipped cream. This recipe serves four.

450ml/¾ pint cold, very strong coffee (filter/cafetière brewed using 80g/14 tbsp coffee per 1 litre/1¾ pints water)
2 measures/3 tbsp tequila (or white rum)
2 measures/3 tbsp Malibu
4 measures/6 tbsp coconut cream
2.5ml/½ tsp vanilla essence (extract)
350ml/12fl oz crushed ice
60ml/4 tbsp whipped cream and toasted coconut shavings, to garnish

Combine all the ingredients in a blender and process on a high speed. Serve in tall wine glasses. Garnish with whipped cream, topped with toasted coconut shavings.

White Hot Chocolate

This new spin on hot chocolate matches white chocolate with orange liqueur. The recipe serves four.

1.75 litres/3 pints milk
175g/6oz white chocolate, broken into small pieces
½ measure/2 tsp coffee powder
4 measures/6 tbsp Cointreau or other orange-flavoured liqueur
whipped cream and ground cinnamon, to serve

Heat the milk in a large heavy pan until almost boiling. Remove from the heat. Add the white chocolate, coffee powder and liqueur. Stir until all the chocolate has melted. Pour into four mugs. Top each with a spoonful of whipped cream and a sprinkling of ground cinnamon. Serve immediately.

Peanut Coffee

Fans of peanut butter will love this iced drink with a coffee flavour. It's rich and filling, like a sumptuous dessert.

1½ measures/6 tsp Kahlúa
3 measures/4½ tbsp full-cream (whole) milk
30ml/2 tbsp vanilla ice cream
10ml/2 tsp smooth peanut butter
3 measures/4½ tbsp 7-Up

Put all but the last ingredient into the blender with crushed ice, and combine. Pour into a cocktail glass, and add the 7-Up. Stir once more.

Wine and champagne

Table wines are used surprisingly seldom in cocktails. That may at first seem odd, but the reason is that their flavours are so hugely various that it is difficult to give recipes that are guaranteed to come out tasting the same each time. For the following recipes, where a dry white wine is specified, go for something like a light, unoaked Chardonnay from Chile, South Africa or the south of France, and where red is used, choose something like a Côtes du Rhône or other southern French blend. When it comes to sparkling wine recipes, it isn't really worth using champagne where lots of other flavours are involved. A less expensive sparkler from another region (Australia, New Zealand, South Africa or Spain) will do quite as well.

Spritzer

The most famous white wine cocktail is this simple fizzy creation. Everyone who drinks spritzers seems to have his or her own preferred proportions, but this recipe should be reliable. The point is that the drink is lower in alcohol than a standard glass of wine.

3 measures/4½ tbsp dry white wine
4 measures/6 tbsp soda water

Half-fill a highball glass with cracked ice, and add the wine and soda. Garnish with mixed berries if you like, but the drink doesn't really need them.

Operator

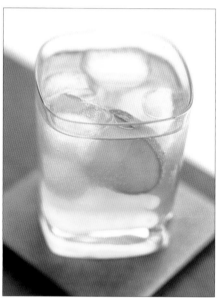

Another low-alcohol preparation, Operator is to my mind a rather more satisfying drink than basic Spritzer, although along the same lines. At least it tastes of something.

2 measures/3 tbsp dry white wine
2 measures/3 tbsp sparkling ginger ale
¼ measure/1 tsp lime juice

Half-fill a rocks glass with cracked ice, and then add all the ingredients. Stir, and garnish with a slice of lime.

Crimean

You might think this would have vodka in it with a name like that, but it's actually quite innocent of the stuff. It needs straining through something like a tea-strainer in order to remove the lemon rind as well as the used ice.

2 measures/3 tbsp dry white wine
⅔ measure/1 tbsp Cointreau
grated rind of one lemon
1 measure/1½ tbsp soda water

Stir the first three ingredients well with ice in a pitcher, and strain into a rocks glass. Add the soda and garnish with a half-slice of lemon.

Fantaisie

This appealing cocktail is best made with an off-dry or medium-dry white wine, rather than the very driest. An aromatic, floral-scented Gewurztraminer from Alsace would suit the recipe down to the ground.

4 measures/6 tbsp off-dry white wine
¾ measure/3 tsp apricot brandy

Pour the wine into a well-chilled goblet. Add the liqueur and stir well. No garnish is necessary.

Sonoma Cup

The Sonoma Valley in California produces some of the world's very best Chardonnays. However, a simpler white wine will do just as well.

3 measures/4½ tbsp dry white wine
½ measure/2 tsp Cointreau

Waltzing Matilda

A longer, stronger drink than most white wine cocktails, the name of this cocktail suggests that an Australian Chardonnay would be the best wine to use. If so, go for an unoaked one, as anything else will probably be too overwhelming for the mixture. Even the simplest wines should have a ripe, buttery flavour.

3 measures/4½ tbsp orange juice
4 measures/6 tbsp soda water

Shake all but the last ingredient well with ice, and strain into a highball glass. Add the soda, stir gently and garnish with a half-slice of orange.

4 measures/6 tbsp dry white wine
1 measure/1½ tbsp gin
1½ measures/6 tsp passion fruit juice
¼ measure/1 tsp orange curaçao
3 measures/4½ tbsp sparkling ginger ale

Shake all but the last ingredient well with ice, and strain into a highball glass. Add the ginger ale and a lemon slice.

Sangria

Testament to the Spanish influence on Mexican cooking, this popular thirst-quencher is traditionally served in large pitchers, with ice and citrus fruit slices floating on top. This recipe serves six.

750ml/1¼ pints red wine
juice of 2 limes
4 measures/6 tbsp orange juice
4 measures/6 tbsp brandy
50g/2oz caster (superfine) sugar
1 lime, sliced, to garnish

Combine the wine, lime juice, orange juice and brandy in a large glass pitcher. Stir in the sugar until it has dissolved completely. Serve in tall glasses with ice. Garnish each glass with a slice of lime.

English Christmas Punch

This old Victorian recipe for a red wine punch uses tea. It may not taste like any punch you've previously been used to, but it makes a properly festive tipple. It would once have contained about twice this quantity of sugar, so add more if you think the resulting mixture isn't sweet enough. The recipe makes about 24 servings.

2 bottles red wine
3 teacups strong tea
juice of an orange
juice of a lemon
225g/8 oz caster (superfine) sugar
a 700ml/1 pint bottle dark rum
orange and lemon slices, to garnish

Heat the wine, tea and fruit juices in a pan, without allowing them to boil. Simmer for about 5 minutes, and then add the sugar, stirring until it has all dissolved. Transfer to a punchbowl. Using the same pan, heat about a quarter of the rum until it starts seething and set it alight. Pour the flaming rum into the punchbowl, and then add the rest of the rum. Stir well, and throw in some orange and lemon slices.

Bordeaux Cocktail

A good way of disguising any harshness in a young red wine, this recipe is classically made with a young claret from Bordeaux. Wine-tasters claim to find the taste of blackcurrant in the Cabernet Sauvignon grape that most claret contains, but you can make sure of that by adding the blackcurrant liqueur, cassis.

2 measures/3 tbsp red Bordeaux
1 measure/1½ tbsp cognac
¾ measure/3 tsp crème de cassis

Stir all the ingredients well with ice in a pitcher, and strain into a large wine glass. Do not garnish.

Mulled Red Wine

This is an excellent warm drink to serve on a cold winter's evening (at Christmas, traditionally), as it will really get the party started. The word "mulled" is derived from an old English dialect word of the late 14th or early 15th century, meaning "mixed" or "muddled", which is how you may feel after over-indulging in it. Then again it might only mull you into a false sense of security. This recipe serves six.

1 bottle red wine
75g/3oz soft light brown sugar
2 cinnamon sticks
1 lemon, sliced
4 whole cloves
150ml/¼ pint brandy or port

Put all the ingredients, except the brandy or port, into a large pan. Bring the wine to the boil to dissolve the sugar. Remove immediately, cover the pan and leave it to stand for 5 minutes, allowing the flavours to infuse. Strain to remove the spices and lemon slices. Add the brandy and serve warm, with a fresh slice of lemon in each glass.

Royal Silver

A sparkling wine cocktail should always look grand, and this one benefits from the frosted red rim given to the glass.

½ measure/2 tsp Poire William
½ measure/2 tsp Cointreau
1½ measures/6 tsp pink grapefruit juice
champagne or sparkling wine

Frost the rim of a large wine goblet by dipping it into grenadine and then caster (superfine) sugar. Shake the first three ingredients well with ice, and strain into the prepared glass. Top up with champagne or sparkling wine, and garnish with a chunk of ripe pear and a half-slice of orange on a cocktail stick.

Champagne Cocktail

The original champagne cocktail probably dates from the 19th century, but nobody appears to know precisely when, or on which side of the Atlantic, it was first invented. It certainly makes a change from serving champagne straight, but I would only use a relatively inexpensive, non-vintage wine. As a rule, the very best stuff should never be mixed.

1 sugar cube
2 dashes Angostura bitters
¼ measure/1 tsp cognac
champagne

Drop the sugar cube into a champagne flute, and add the Angostura, rolling the sugar lump to soak it. Pour in the brandy, and then top the glass up with freshly opened champagne.

Marilyn Monroe

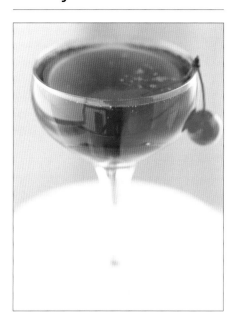

The drink named in honour of one of the great screen sirens of all time should really be made not just with champagne, but with the premium brand Dom Pérignon. It is fearfully expensive, though. Moet & Chandon Brut Impérial, made by the same house, might suffice instead.

4 measures/6 tbsp well-chilled champagne
1 measure/1½ tbsp applejack or calvados
¼ measure/1 tsp grenadine

Add all the ingredients to a champagne saucer, and give the drink the gentlest of stirs. Garnish with a couple of cocktail cherries.

Night and Day

This is an elegant recipe full of complementary flavours. The mixture should not be stirred, so that the layers of different drinks come at the drinker one by one.

3 measures/4½ tbsp champagne or sparkling wine
¾ measure/3 tsp cognac
½ measure/2 tsp Grand Marnier
¼ measure/1 tsp Campari

Add the ingredients in this order to a large wine goblet filled with crushed ice.

Sparkling Peach Melba

This refreshing fruit fizz is an excellent choice for summer celebrations. As with most soft fruit recipes, its success depends on using the ripest, tastiest peaches and raspberries available. This recipe serves four.

3 ripe peaches
90ml/6 tbsp orange juice
75g/3oz raspberries
10ml/2 tsp icing (confectioners') sugar
about 500ml/17fl oz raspberry sorbet
about 400ml/14fl oz medium sparkling
   wine, chilled

Put the peaches in a heatproof bowl and cover with boiling water. Leave for a minute, then drain and peel off the skins. Cut the fruit in half and remove the stones. Chop the peach halves roughly, and purée them with the orange juice in a blender until smooth. Transfer to a bowl.

Put the raspberries in the blender with the icing sugar, and process until smooth. Press the raspberry purée through a sieve into a separate bowl. Chill both purées for at least an hour.

Spoon the chilled peach purée into four tall glasses. Add scoops of sorbet to fill the glasses. Spoon the raspberry purée around the sorbet. Top up each glass with sparkling wine. Garnish with mint sprigs.

Buck's Fizz

Hugely popular in the 1980s, Buck's Fizz is a simple mixture of two-thirds champagne to one-third orange juice; it is not half and half, as is often suggested. It is a 1920s recipe invented at a club called Buck's in London. Some recipes add ¼ measure/1 tsp grenadine to it, to deepen the colour, but it isn't necessary. It is best served in flute glasses, but you can use a large wine goblet instead if you want to appear more generous.

Mustique

This rum drink was invented on the Caribbean island of Mustique.

1 measure/1½ tbsp light rum
1 measure/1½ tbsp orange juice
½ measure/2 tsp lemon juice
¼ measure/1 tsp grenadine
champagne or sparkling wine

Shake all but the last ingredient with ice, and strain into a large wine glass. Top with fizz, and garnish with a half-slice of lemon.

Blackberry and Champagne Crush

This sparkling blend makes a good brunch alternative to Buck's Fizz. For a party, divide the blackberry purée among six glasses and top up with champagne. This recipe, though, is just for two.

175g/6oz blackberries
15ml/1 tbsp icing (confectioners') sugar
30ml/2 tbsp cognac
250ml/8fl oz champagne or sparkling wine,
   chilled

Purée the blackberries in a food processor. Push the purée through a sieve, and then add the sugar. Pour the brandy into two glasses. Return the blackberry purée to the food processor, add the sparkling wine and blend for no more than two or three seconds. Pour into the glasses and serve immediately.

Bocuse Special

This recipe was created by the French master-chef Paul Bocuse at his restaurant in the south of France.

½ measure/2 tsp crème de cassis
½ measure/2 tsp crème de framboise
champagne

Mix the liqueurs together with ice in a small pitcher until well-chilled. Strain into a flute glass, and top up with champagne. Drop a raspberry into the glass if you have one to hand.

Southern Champagne

This is how they like a champagne cocktail in the southern states of America.

1 measure/1½ tbsp Southern Comfort
dash Angostura bitters
ice-cold champagne or sparkling wine

Add the liqueur and bitters to a champagne flute. Mix briefly and top up with champagne or sparkling wine. Squeeze a small twist of orange rind over the drink, and then drop it into the glass.

B2 C2

The story goes that American troops advancing through Germany in 1945 stumbled on a wine merchant's premises, and cobbled together their own cocktail from whatever came to hand. The name refers of course to the initials of the four ingredients.

1 measure/1½ tbsp brandy (cognac)
1 measure/1½ tbsp Bénédictine
1 measure/1½ tbsp Cointreau
4 measures/6 tbsp well-chilled champagne

Add the ingredients in this order to a large wine goblet. No garnish is necessary.

Pizzetti

This charming cocktail was created at a hotel in the Cortina region of Italy, and its name literally means "little pizzas". You work it out.

1 measure/1½ tbsp cognac
2 measures/3 tbsp orange juice
2 measures/3 tbsp grapefruit juice
champagne or sparkling wine

Shake the first three ingredients well with ice, and strain into a chilled wine goblet. Top up with champagne or sparkling wine, and stir gently. Garnish with a cherry.

Fortified wines

The most resourceful fortified wine of all for cocktail-making is vermouth. Whether in its dry white or sweet red version, its aromatic, herbal flavours equip it handsomely for mixing with any of the spirits and a fair few of the liqueurs. We shouldn't forget the other fortified wines, though: those that haven't had herbs infused in them, but are basically ordinary table wines boosted with the addition of grape spirit. Sherry and port are used quite widely, and I have even managed to track down a couple of recipes that use madeira and marsala.

Gin and It

The name of this drink is a shortened form of gin and Italian, so-called in the days when Italian vermouths were inaccurately thought to be always of the sweet red variety. (By the same token, gin and dry vermouth was known as Gin and French.) Proportions vary according to individual taste, and many recipes show the gin and vermouth in equal quantities. This is my preference.

2 measures/3 tbsp gin
1 measure/1½ tbsp sweet red vermouth

Add both ingredients to a rocks glass with a couple of ice cubes in it. Stir, and add a twist of lemon rind.

Bronx

An utterly satisfying mixture of gin and both vermouths, Bronx is basically a sort of gin Manhattan with a little orange juice. It is, naturally, a New York cocktail that dates back to the early years of the 20th century. Like all such mixtures, it makes a very effective aperitif.

1½ measures/6 tsp gin
¾ measure/3 tsp dry vermouth
¾ measure/3 tsp sweet red vermouth
juice of a quarter of an orange

Shake all the ingredients well with ice, and strain into a cocktail glass. Garnish with a half-slice of orange.

Bentley

Dubonnet has one of the most captivating flavours of all vermouth brands, derived in part from its long maturation in cask. Unless otherwise stated, these recipes call for the red version. Bentley is a fine aperitif mixture dating from the 1920s.

1½ measures/6 tsp calvados
1½ measures/6 tsp Dubonnet

Shake well with ice, and strain into a glass. Garnish with an orange twist.

Boston

This is another egg recipe containing a little sugar too, although the underlying mixture is quite dry.

1½ measures/6 tsp dry (sercial) madeira
1½ measures/6 tsp bourbon

Coronation

The Coronation for which this cocktail was created was that of George V in 1910. It's a strong, forthright mixture, much like King George himself.

1 measure/1½ tbsp sweet red vermouth
1 measure/1½ tbsp dry vermouth
1 measure/1½ tbsp calvados
¼ measure/1 tsp apricot brandy

Shake all the ingredients well with ice, and strain into a cocktail glass. Garnish with a half-slice of orange.

2.5ml/½ tsp caster (superfine) sugar
1 egg yolk

Shake all the ingredients with ice and strain into a small wine glass. Sprinkle with grated nutmeg.

Golf

This is an old 1920s recipe for a very short drink that is a distant relation of the Martini. It was indeed originally known as the Golf Martini, but is clearly for those who like a little more vermouth with their gin.

1 measure/1½ tbsp gin
½ measure/2 tsp dry vermouth
2 dashes Angostura bitters

Stir all the ingredients well with ice in a small pitcher, and strain into a tumbler. Garnish with a green olive.

Bartending know-how
Vermouth comes in a variety of styles. The red is made with red wine; the dry white gains an amber tinge from ageing in oak casks; bianco is sweetened-up dry white; the pink version is based on rosé wine.

Lily

Lillet is an aromatized, bittersweet, French fortified wine that comes in both red and white versions. It's hard to find now. It obviously bestowed its name (more or less) on this cocktail, but if you can't find it, use ordinary dry white vermouth instead.

1 measure/1½ tbsp gin
1 measure/1½ tbsp white Lillet or dry vermouth
1 measure/1½ tbsp crème de noyau
dash lemon juice

Shake all the ingredients well with ice, and strain into a wine glass. Garnish with a half-slice of lemon.

Midsummer Night

The orangey, quinine flavour of Italian Punt e Mes goes well with gin and a modest amount of blackcurrant liqueur in this modern recipe.

1 measure/1½ tbsp gin

1 measure/1½ tbsp Punt e Mes
½ measure/2 tsp crème de cassis

Shake all the ingredients well with ice, and strain into a cocktail glass. You could garnish with a twist of lemon.

Devil's Cocktail

For some reason, this old cocktail has come to be given the Spanish name, Diablo, in modern bar books, but the mixture remains essentially the same. It was probably originally made with red port, but white produces a more harmonious result.

1½ measures/6 tsp dry vermouth
1½ measures/6 tsp white port
2 dashes lemon juice

Shake all the ingredients well with ice, and strain into a cocktail glass. Garnish with a twist of lemon.

Breakfast

Save a tiny quantity of egg white before you scramble your breakfast eggs, and this cocktail might well make a good accompaniment to them. Then again, it would make a much better nightcap.

2 measures/3 tbsp red port
1 measure/1½ tbsp brown crème de cacao
¼ measure/1 tsp light rum
½ measure/2 tsp lemon juice
5ml/1 tsp egg white

Shake all the ingredients well with ice, and strain into a wine glass. Dust the surface with ground nutmeg.

Perfect Cocktail

Another gin and vermouths recipe from the 1920s, this is a little like Bronx, but without the orange juice. Then again, substitute Pernod for the gin and you have a Duchess.

1 measure/1½ tbsp gin
1 measure/1½ tbsp dry vermouth
1 measure/1½ tbsp sweet red vermouth

Shake all the ingredients well with ice, and strain into a cocktail glass. Garnish with a twist of lemon rind.

Bartending know-how
Use an LBV port if you can, in preference to plain ruby.

Bamboo

An exceedingly dry aperitif cocktail, with a slight bittering element, this makes a change from the usual neat dry sherry. One or two recipes add sweet red vermouth to it too, but that really is missing the point. If you have it, you could use orange bitters instead of the Angostura version.

2 measures/3 tbsp pale dry (fino) sherry
2 measures/3 tbsp dry vermouth
2 dashes Angostura bitters

Stir all the ingredients well with ice, and strain into a large, chilled cocktail glass. You could garnish the drink with a twist of lemon.

Sloppy Joe

Strong and exotic, this is an American recipe of the postwar years. Some suggest adding 2.5ml/½ tsp grenadine to the mixture, but it doesn't really make much difference.

1 measure/1½ tbsp red port
1 measure/1½ tbsp cognac
2 measures/3 tbsp pineapple juice
2 dashes Cointreau

Shake all the ingredients well with ice, and strain into a wine goblet. Garnish with a half-slice of orange.

First Avenue

A fine, slightly effervescent cocktail that uses one of the sweeter styles of sherry. Use decent oloroso, though, rather than cream sherry.

1½ measures/6 tsp sweet (oloroso) sherry
½ measure/2 tsp Cointreau
¾ measure/3 tsp soda water
¼ measure/1 tsp Campari

Half-fill a rocks glass with cracked ice. Add the first two ingredients and stir well. Add the soda, and then float the Campari on top. Do not garnish.

Prairie Oyster

I'm cheating a little by including this most challenging of hangover cures here, largely because it was once common in America to substitute sweet madeira for the brandy in a Prairie Oyster. If you're a stickler for tradition, use cognac, but you might find this a touch less aggressive if you are resorting to the drink medicinally.

1 measure/1½ tbsp sweet (malmsey)
   madeira, or cognac
¼ measure/1 tsp white wine vinegar
¼ measure/1 tsp Worcestershire sauce
pinch cayenne pepper
dash Tabasco
1 egg yolk

Add the first five ingredients to a small tumbler. Mix well without ice, and then spoon the yolk very gently on top. The preparation should then be swallowed in one gulp, without breaking the yolk.

Casanova

Marsala, from the island of Sicily, comes in various styles, but everyone seems agreed that the sweet version, dolce, is the best. That's what's used in this strong cream cocktail.

1 measure/1½ tbsp bourbon
½ measure/2 tsp marsala dolce

Downhill

The name of this drink reflects pretty much where you'll be going if you try to take more than one. It's a knee-trembling, all-alcohol cocktail for the truly intrepid.

1 measure/1½ tbsp sweet (oloroso) sherry
½ measure/2 tsp gin
½ measure/2 tsp dry vermouth
½ measure/2 tsp orange curaçao
¼ measure/1 tsp cognac

Stir the ingredients with ice in a pitcher to chill them, and strain into a rocks glass half-filled with cracked ice. Add an orange twist and a cherry.

½ measure/2 tsp Kahlúa
1 measure/1½ tbsp double (heavy) cream

Shake all the ingredients well with plenty of ice to amalgamate the cream, and strain into a cocktail glass. Sprinkle the top with ground nutmeg.

Third Rail

There isn't much call for the peppermint cordial that was once used in this American cocktail. If you can't get hold of it, use the white version of crème de menthe instead. It ups the alcohol ante of the drink, but only just.

3 measures/4½ tbsp dry vermouth
¼ measure/1 tsp orange curacao
¼ measure/1 tsp peppermint cordial

Stir all the ingredients well with ice in a pitcher, and strain into a chilled cocktail glass. Squeeze a piece of lemon rind over the drink, and then drop it into the glass.

Marsala Cocktail

This is my own preferred way of showing marsala to its best advantage if you don't want to drink it straight. The teaspoon of spirit and dash of acidity mingle very subtly with its toffee sweetness.

2 measures/3 tbsp marsala dolce
¼ measure/1 tsp cognac
dash lemon juice

Stir well with ice in a pitcher, and strain into a wine glass. Add a cube of ice.

Port Cocktail

Here is another very simple preparation that goes back a long way. Like the Sherry Cocktail, it uses a hint of orange.

2 measures/3 tbsp good red port (LBV)
dash cognac

Stir the ingredients well with ice in a small pitcher until quite cold, and strain into a wine glass. Squeeze a piece of orange rind over the drink so that plenty of its oil is released, but don't put it in.

Sherry Cocktail

This was very popular in the 1920s as a sophisticated aperitif, and deserves to be so now too.

2 measures/3 tbsp pale dry (fino or
    manzanilla) sherry
¼ measure/1 tsp dry vermouth
¼ measure/1 tsp orange bitters (or curaçao)

Stir all the ingredients with plenty of ice in a pitcher, and strain into a large wine glass. Do not garnish.

Dubonnet Cocktail

A quartet of recipes named after four of the basic fortified wine types concludes with this one using the French proprietary classic. Be sure to use the red version.

1½ measures/6 tsp gin
1½ measures/6 tsp Dubonnet

Shake both ingredients well with ice, and strain into a small wine goblet. Squeeze a twist of lemon rind over the drink and drop it in.

Adonis

If you don't care for the sweetness of sweet sherry, go for this 1920s recipe. A dry style is given the herbal sweetness of red vermouth instead.

2 measures/3 tbsp pale dry (fino) sherry
1 measure/1½ tbsp sweet red vermouth
2 dashes orange bitters (or curaçao)

Stir all the ingredients well with ice in a pitcher, and strain into a wine glass. Garnish with a twist of orange rind.

Sherry Flip

The recipe for a Flip would seem to go back to the 17th century, in that a mixture of alcohol, sugar and egg was being made then. In the pre-cocktail-shaker era, they were mixed by being repeatedly poured, or "flipped", between two glasses. A version using sweet sherry has proved the most enduringly popular of them all. The nutmeg is de rigueur.

Straight Law

This century-old recipe is as straight as they come. Both the ingredients are very dry and very strong in flavour. It's a real appetite awakener.

2 measures/3 tbsp pale dry (fino) sherry
1 measure/1½ tbsp gin

Stir both ingredients well with ice, and strain into a cocktail glass. Squeeze a piece of lemon rind over the surface and drop it into the drink.

2 measures/3 tbsp brown cream sherry
2.5ml/½ tsp caster (superfine) sugar
1 egg, beaten

Shake all the ingredients well with ice, and strain into a small wine glass. Sprinkle grated nutmeg on the surface. Alternatively, you can whizz it up in the blender if quite convenient.

Merry Widow

This is another 1920s recipe, this time at the bone-dry end of the spectrum, notwithstanding that splash of Bénédictine. It's a strong one too, all alcohol, which explains the merriness of the widow.

1 measure/1½ tbsp gin
1 measure/1½ tbsp dry vermouth
2 dashes absinthe
2 dashes Bénédictine
2 dashes Angostura bitters

Stir all the ingredients well with ice in a pitcher, and then strain into a large wine glass. Squeeze a twist of lemon rind over the drink, and then drop it in.

Havana Cobbler

This is an old-fashioned drink that is delightfully refreshing served in sultry, Caribbean-type weather, or in an English summer, at a push.

¼ measure/1 tsp sugar syrup
½ measure/2 tsp green ginger wine
1 measure/1½ tbsp light rum (preferably Cuban)
1 measure/1½ tbsp red port

Shake the first three ingredients well with ice, and strain into a chilled short tumbler. Tilt the glass, and slowly pour the port down the side to form a floating layer on top of the cocktail.

Bartending know-how
Stone's Special Reserve is the most gingery ginger wine of them all.

Parkeroo

This is a dry and rather startling mixture, which is worth trying at least once, just so you can say you have. I can't say it's one of my own favourites, but who's asking?

2 measures/3 tbsp pale dry (fino) sherry
1 measure/1½ tbsp tequila

Mix both ingredients in a pitcher with ice. Strain into a champagne flute filled with shaved ice, and add a twist of lemon rind.

Inigo Jones

Here is the only cocktail in this book to use rosé wine. Choose one from a southern-hemisphere country such as South Africa or Argentina. These wines tend to be much fruitier than the European ones, and you will of course have to finish the bottle straight after you've made this cocktail.

1 measure/1½ tbsp marsala dolce
1 measure/1½ tbsp dry rosé wine
1 measure/1½ tbsp cognac
dash orange juice
dash lemon juice

In a pitcher, stir together all the ingredients with plenty of ice. Strain into a tumbler half-filled with crushed ice. Garnish with a slice of orange.

Port in a Storm

I have always loved this poetically named cocktail, in which the port does indeed get buffeted by a storm of other ingredients.

2 measures/3 tbsp red wine
1½ measures/6 tsp red port
½ measure/2 tsp cognac

Stir all the ingredients with plenty of ice in a pitcher, and pour without straining into a large wine glass. You could garnish with a half-slice of orange.

Nightmare Abbey

Despite sounding like an adaptation of a Gothic novel starring Vincent Price, this mixture is perfectly sweet-natured.

1½ measures/6 tsp red Dubonnet
1 measure/1½ tbsp gin
1 measure/1½ tbsp orange juice
¾ measure/3 tsp cherry brandy

Shake all the ingredients well with ice, and strain into a bowl-shaped cocktail glass. Garnish with a twist of orange rind and a black cherry.

Soul Kiss

This fine American cocktail productively brings together three good fortified wines with orange to bind them.

1 measure/1½ tbsp red Dubonnet
1 measure/1½ tbsp sweet red vermouth
1 measure/1½ tbsp dry vermouth
1 measure/1½ tbsp orange juice

Shake all the ingredients well with ice, and strain into a large wine goblet. Garnish with a half-slice of orange.

Caffè Vermouth

Vermouth is not an obvious choice to partner coffee, but the resulting flavour is good: original and sophisticated. This recipe serves two.

4 measures/6 tbsp sweet red vermouth
60ml/4 tbsp very strong cold coffee (espresso strength or filter/cafetière brewed at 75g/3oz coffee per 1 litre/1¾ pints water)
250ml/8fl oz milk
10ml/2 tsp caster (superfine) sugar

Funchal Flip

This cocktail is named after Funchal, the capital of the island of Madeira, where some of the best fortified wines in the world are made.

1 measure/1½ tbsp sweet madeira
¾ measure/3 tsp cognac

Shake all the ingredients well with ice, and strain into cocktail glasses or tumblers. Garnish with a few roasted coffee beans.

Bartending know-how
Madeira is the hardiest of the fortified wines. An opened bottle will keep for years without declining.

½ measure/2 tsp Cointreau
¼ measure/1 tsp grenadine
1 egg yolk, beaten

Shake all the ingredients well with ice, and strain into a cocktail glass. Garnish with a half-slice of orange and a cherry.

Tinton

A traditional 1920s formula named after some long-forgotten worthy, this cocktail gives a sweet kick to apple brandy for those who find it too dry as it comes. It could be taken as an after-dinner digestif.

2 measures/3 tbsp calvados
1 measure/1½ tbsp red port

Shake both ingredients well with ice, and strain into a cocktail glass. There is no need for any garnish.

Dubonnet Fizz

This American recipe makes for a sweetly aromatic cocktail. High rollers might fill it up with champagne, but soda will do quite nicely, thank you.

4 measures/6 tbsp red Dubonnet
½ measure/2 tsp cherry brandy
2 measures/3 tbsp orange juice

1 measure/1½ tbsp lemon juice
soda water or champagne

Shake all but the last ingredient well with ice, and strain into a highball glass. Top up with soda water or champagne. You could garnish the drink with half-slices of orange and lemon.

Wine Collins

The wine named here is the fortified variety. Port, sweet madeira or marsala dolce can all be used as the base for this fizzy drink, but be generous.

4 measures/6 tbsp red port, malmsey
   madeira or marsala dolce
½ measure/2 tsp lime juice
sparkling lemonade

Add the first two ingredients to a highball glass half-filled with cracked ice, and stir well. Top up with lemonade, and garnish with a slice of lemon and a cherry.

Reform

Invented at the Reform Club at London in the 1920s, this cocktail is – as eagle-eyed drinkers will note – essentially a dry version of Adonis.

2 measures/3 tbsp pale dry (fino) sherry
1 measure/1½ tbsp dry vermouth
dash orange bitters (or curaçao)

Stir all the ingredients well with ice in a pitcher, and strain into a cocktail glass. Garnish with a cherry.

Bartending know-how
Pale dry sherry should always be treated with kid gloves. It needs drinking within a few days of the bottle being broached, and should always be served well-chilled. More than any other drink in this book, it is served in sub-standard condition in many bars and restaurants.

Beer and cider

Beer and cider are the least used of all alcoholic drinks in cocktails. They do come in handy for punches and mulled ale recipes, but as ingredients in short mixed drinks, they have only a limited number of applications. Probably the simplest beer "cocktail" of them all is shandy, which is roughly equal measures of beer and lemonade, and is always worth making for yourself, as opposed to resorting to one of the bottled proprietary brands. Good cider is one of the glories of the English brewing industry, as was once the now-forgotten perry, a refreshing sparkling drink made from pears.

Lamb's Wool

A kind of 17th-century punch, this was traditionally drunk on All Saints' Day, November 1. This recipe serves four.

1 litre/1¾ pints English bitter ale
4 baked apples
2.5ml/½ tsp ground nutmeg
2.5ml/½ tsp ground ginger
60g/2oz sugar

Heat the ale gently in a large pan without boiling it. When the apples have finished baking in the oven, peel them, remove the cores and mash the soft flesh with a potato masher. Stir the apple into the beer with the spices and sugar, and serve in warm glasses or mugs. It's a real treat that will warm you up on a dark autumn day.

Black Velvet

This simple but mightily effective drink was invented at Brooks' Club in London in 1861, following the death of Queen Victoria's husband, Prince Albert. It was considered an appropriate sign of mourning to dress the champagne up in black livery. As a popular mixture ever since, it has an appeal all its own.

Half-fill a tall, narrow beer glass with Guinness. Wait for the head to settle, and then without tilting the glass, gently top it up with good brut champagne.

Devon Gin

This is a short individual drink that will prove peculiarly potent on a cold winter's day. Tread warily.

3 measures/4½ tbsp strong sweet cider
¾ measure/3 tsp gin
¼ measure/1 tsp Cointreau

Half-fill a rocks glass with cracked ice, and add the first two ingredients, Stir gently, and then pour the Cointreau carefully on to the surface to form a float. Drink quickly.

Wassail Bowl

The wassail bowl was a wide-mouthed bowl from which hot punches were drunk. Cheer your Christmas carol-singers by offering them a bowl (or mug) each of this warming, festive drink. The recipe serves six.

2 litres/3½ pints strong bitter or brown ale
150ml/¼ pint brown cream sherry
90g/3oz caster (superfine) sugar
5ml/1 tsp ground nutmeg
5ml/1 tsp ground ginger
6 baked apples

Heat the beer, sherry, sugar and spices in a pan until gently simmering, stirring to dissolve the sugar. After about 5 minutes, decant the mixture into mugs or drinking bowls, each containing a whole mashed apple. Serve with spoons for stirring it up as it is drunk.

Cider Cup

A cup makes an excellent long and refreshing drink for an aperitif or party starter. It should be prepared shortly before serving so that the ice doesn't have time to melt. This recipe serves six.

rind of 1 lemon
slices of orange
5 measures/120ml/4fl oz pale dry (fino) sherry
3 measures/4½ tbsp cognac
3 measures/4½ tbsp white curaçao
2 measures/3 tbsp amaretto
600ml/1 pint good-quality strong dry cider

Partially fill a pitcher with cracked ice and stir in the lemon rind and the orange slices. Add the sherry, brandy, curaçao and amaretto, and stir well to mix. Pour in the cider and stir gently. Serve the cocktail in chilled tall glasses, including some of the citrus fruit in each one, and add a twist of cucumber rind.

Somerset Punch

This is a very appealing cider punch for serving at a garden party. The recipe makes around 14–16 servings.

1 litre/1¾ pints strong dry cider
150ml/¼ pint dry white wine
2 measures/3 tbsp cider brandy
150ml/¼ pint orange juice
2 measures/3 tbsp lemon juice
150ml/¼ pint pressed apple juice (not from concentrate)
300ml/½ pint sparkling ginger ale

Mix all the ingredients with ice in a punchbowl, and decant into wine glasses for serving. Garnish with thin slices of unpeeled apple.

Bartending know-how
The best ciders are those that come in a bottle with a champagne-style cork. They may be cloudy, but the quality is incomparable.

Non-alcoholic drinks

Not every cocktail session has to involve intoxication. There will be times, such as when dealing with a party of drivers, or in the course of a detox diet, or even in the middle of a raging hot day, when an alcoholic drink is not what's wanted. The non-alcoholic section of many cocktail books often has an air of "These are the also-rans" about it. That is not so here. There are enough recipes in the following pages to keep even the most determined mixologist going for a fair old time and, even more than their alcohol-based cousins, these drinks can be freely adapted as you see fit. Let your imagination off the leash.

Horse's Fall

This is a long drink to serve on a summer's day. The addition of strongly flavoured tea is a matter of taste.

1 lemon
dash Angostura bitters
2 measures/3 tbsp raspberry, Orange Pekoe
  or Assam tea, chilled (optional)
1 measure/1½ tbsp unsweetened apple juice
5 measures/120ml/4fl oz dry ginger ale or
  lemonade

Cut the rind from the lemon in one continuous strip and use it to line and decorate a long cocktail glass. Chill the glass until needed. Add a dash of Angostura to the bottom of the glass. Measure the tea, if using, into the cocktail shaker and add the apple juice. Shake for about 20 seconds. Strain into the prepared chilled glass. Finish with ginger ale or lemonade straight from the refrigerator, to taste.

Sunburst

Bursting with freshness and vitamins, this drink is a good early morning pick-me-up. This recipe makes two.

1 green apple, cored and chopped
3 carrots, peeled and chopped
1 mango, peeled and pitted
7 measures/150ml/¼ pint orange juice, chilled
6 strawberries, hulled

Place the apple, carrots and mango in a blender or food processor and process to a pulp. Add the orange juice and strawberries and process again. Strain well through a sieve, pressing out all the juice with the back of a wooden spoon. Discard any pulp left in the sieve. Pour into tumblers filled with ice cubes and serve immediately, garnished with a slice of orange on the side of the glass.

Virgin Prairie Oyster

This superior pick-me-up is a variation on the Bloody Mary. The tomato base can be drunk without the raw egg yolk if it does not appeal to you. Use only fresh free-range eggs.

175ml/6fl oz tomato juice
½ measure/2 tsp Worcestershire sauce
¼–½ measure/1–2 tsp balsamic vinegar
1 egg yolk
cayenne pepper, to taste

Measure the tomato juice into a large bar glass and stir over plenty of ice until well chilled. Strain into a tall tumbler half-filled with ice cubes. Add the Worcestershire sauce and balsamic vinegar to taste and mix with a swizzle-stick. Float the egg yolk on top and lightly dust with cayenne pepper.

Scarlet Lady

On the first sip, with its fruity and fresh tones, this drink could fool a fair few into thinking it was an alcoholic wine-based cocktail.

125g/4oz cubed melon, preferably Galia or Canteloupe
5 small red seedless grapes
3 measures/4½ tbsp unsweetened red grape juice

Put the melon and grapes in a blender and process until they form a smooth purée. Add the red grape juice and continue to process for another minute. Strain the juice into a bar glass of ice and stir until chilled. Pour into a chilled cocktail glass. Dip some red, seedless grapes in the lightly beaten white of an egg, and then into 15ml/1 tbsp sugar. Thread on to a cocktail stick to garnish.

Fruit and Ginger Ale

This is an old English mulled drink, served chilled over ice. Of course it can be made with ready-squeezed apple and orange juices, but roasting the fruit with cloves gives a much better flavour. This recipe makes four to six servings.

1 cooking apple
1 orange, scrubbed
1 lemon, scrubbed
20 whole cloves
7.5cm/3in piece fresh ginger, peeled
30g/1oz light brown sugar
375ml/13fl oz bitter lemon

Preheat the oven to 200°C/400°F/Gas 6. Score the apple around the middle and stud the orange and lemon with the cloves. Bake the fruits in the oven for about 25 minutes, until soft and completely cooked through. Quarter the orange and lemon, and mash the apple, discarding the peel and the core.

Finely grate the ginger. Place the fruit and ginger in a bowl with the light brown sugar. Add 300ml/½ pint boiling water. Using a spoon, squeeze the fruit to release more flavour. Cover and let sit for an hour until cool. Strain into a pitcher of cracked ice and use a spoon to press out all the juices from the fruit. Add the bitter lemon. Garnish with orange wedges and whole cloves.

Volunteer

This drink is ideal for a lazy summer afternoon. It's also a fine cocktail to serve the designated driver at a party. It was devised and drunk during a very rough Channel crossing in an undersized boat, a tribute to human resourcefulness!

2 measures/3 tbsp lime cordial
2–3 dashes Angostura bitters
7 measures/150ml/¼ pint chilled tonic water
decorative ice cubes, to serve

Pour the lime cordial into the bottom of the glass, and shake in the Angostura to taste. Add a few decorative ice cubes to the glass, if liked. Finish with tonic water and garnish with frozen lime slices.

Variation
Use fresh lime or grapefruit juice and a splash of sugar syrup instead of the lime cordial, and finish with ginger ale.

Blushing Piña Colada

This is good with or without the rum that is part of the original recipe. Don't be tempted to put whole ice cubes into the blender; the result won't be as smooth and you may ruin the blades. Make sure you crush it well first. The recipe serves two.

1 banana, peeled and sliced
1 thick slice pineapple, peeled
3 measures/4½ tbsp pineapple juice
1 scoop strawberry ice cream or sorbet
1 measure/1½ tbsp unsweetened coconut milk
30ml/2 tbsp grenadine

Roughly chop the banana. Cut two small wedges from the pineapple and set aside. Cut up the remainder of the pineapple and add it to the blender with the banana. Add the pineapple juice and process until smooth.

Add the ice cream or sorbet with the coconut milk and a little finely crushed ice, and process until smooth. Pour into two large cocktail glasses. Pour the grenadine syrup slowly on top of the drink; it will filter down, creating a dappled effect. Garnish each glass with a wedge of pineapple and a cherry.

Steel Works

This thirst-quenching drink can be served at any time of the day.

2 measures/3 tbsp passion fruit juice
dash Angostura bitters
3 measures/4½ tbsp soda water, chilled
3 measures/4½ tbsp lemonade, chilled
1 passion fruit

Pour the passion fruit juice into a tumbler. Add the Angostura, with some ice cubes. Finish the drink with the chilled soda water and lemonade and stir briefly. Cut the passion fruit in half; scoop out the seeds and flesh and add to the drink. Stir gently before serving.

Variation
For a Rock Shandy, pour equal parts of lemonade and soda over bitters or use your favourite variety of the naturally flavoured and unsweetened fruit drinks.

Bandrek

This is a rich and creamy version of a spicy Indonesian drink. Serve it either warm or chilled. If you like, add a very fresh egg to the syrup and mix in the blender, and you'll have something like an egg-nog.

3 whole cloves
3 juniper berries, bruised
1 cinnamon stick
6 green cardamom pods, bruised
4 whole black peppercorns
1 sugar cube
2 measures/3 tbsp unsweetened coconut milk
3 measures/4½ tbsp full-cream (whole) milk

Put the cloves, juniper berries, cinnamon, cardamom pods, peppercorns and sugar cube in a pan. Heat gently to release the aromas and flavours of the spices. Add 175ml/6fl oz water and bring to the boil over medium-high heat. Continue to boil for about ten minutes, or until reduced to 30–45ml/ 2–3 tbsp of spicy syrup. Remove from the heat and cool. Pour the syrup into a blender with the coconut milk and full-cream milk and process until smooth. Strain over cracked ice in a stemmed glass. Garnish with cinnamon sticks and a maraschino cherry.

St Clements

Oranges and lemons create a simple but thirst-quenching drink, which confirms that freshly squeezed fruit has a superior flavour to any of the ready-squeezed versions you can buy.

2 oranges
1 lemon
15ml/1 tbsp sugar, or to taste
75ml/5 tbsp water

Wash the oranges and lemons and then pare the rind off the fruit with a sharp knife, leaving the white pith behind. Remove the pith from the fruit and discard it. Put the orange and lemon rind in a pan with the sugar and water. Place over low heat and stir gently until the sugar has dissolved. Remove the pan from the heat and press the orange and lemon rind against the sides of the pan to release

Fennel Fusion

This hefty combination of raw vegetables and apples makes a surprisingly delicious juice. Cabbage has natural anti-bacterial properties, while apples and fennel can help to cleanse the system.

half a small red cabbage
half a fennel bulb
2 apples
⅔ measure/1 tbsp lemon juice

Roughly slice the cabbage and fennel and quarter the apples. Using a juice extractor, juice the vegetables and fruit. Add the lemon juice to the juice mixture and stir. Pour into a glass and serve.

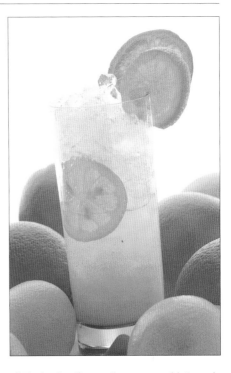

all their oils. Cover the pan and let cool. Remove and discard the rind. Purée the oranges and lemon and sweeten the fruit pulp by pouring the cooled citrus syrup over it. Set aside for 2–3 hours to allow the flavours to infuse. Strain the fruit pulp, pressing the solids in the sieve to extract as much of the juice as possible. Pour into a tall glass filled with finely crushed ice, and decorate with slices of orange and lemon.

Summer Tonic

The many nutrients in lettuce include betacarotene, iron and folic acid. This is a particularly appetizing way of getting your share of them.

3 large vine-ripened tomatoes
half a Little Gem (Bibb) lettuce
5cm/2in piece cucumber
1 small garlic clove
small handful fresh parsley, stalks
    included
⅔ measure/1 tbsp lemon juice

Halve the tomatoes and lettuce. Peel and chop the cucumber. Juice all the ingredients together and serve in a tall glass.

Raspberry and Orange Smoothie

This exquisite blend combines the sharp taste of raspberries and oranges with the creaminess of yogurt. It takes minutes to prepare, making it perfect for breakfast. Serves two to three.

250g/9oz raspberries, chilled
200ml/7fl oz natural (plain) yogurt, chilled
300ml/½ pint orange juice, chilled

Place the raspberries and yogurt in a food processor or blender, and process for about a minute until smooth and creamy. Add the orange juice to the raspberry and yogurt mixture and process for about 30 seconds, or until thoroughly combined. Pour into tall glasses and serve immediately.

Avocado and Lime Smoothie

Inspired by guacamole, this wonderfully thick smoothie combines mild and spicy flavours perfectly. It serves four.

3 ripe avocados
juice of 1½ limes
1 garlic clove, crushed
handful of ice cubes
400ml/14fl oz vegetable stock, chilled
400ml/14fl oz full-cream (whole) milk, chilled
150ml/¼ pint sour cream, chilled
few drops Tabasco
salt and ground black pepper
extra virgin olive oil, to serve

For the salsa:
4 tomatoes, peeled, seeded and finely diced
2 spring onions (scallions), finely chopped
1 green chilli, seeded and finely chopped
15ml/1 tbsp chopped fresh coriander (cilantro)

juice of half a lime
salt and ground black pepper

Prepare the salsa first. Mix all the ingredients and season to taste with salt and pepper. Chill while you prepare the smoothie. Halve and stone the avocados. Scoop out the flesh and place in a blender. Add the lime juice, garlic, a handful of crushed ice and about 150ml/¼ pint of the vegetable stock, and process until smooth. Pour the mixture into a large pitcher, and stir in the remaining stock, milk, sour cream, Tabasco and seasoning. Pour the smoothie into glasses and spoon a little salsa on to each. Add a splash of olive oil to each portion and garnish with fresh coriander leaves. Serve immediately, with a spoon.

Georgia 'n' Ginger

This is named after the US state of Georgia, which is famous for its peaches. The recipe serves six.

1 can (450–500g/1–1¼lb) sliced peaches in syrup
750ml/1¼ pints strong coffee
120ml/4fl oz whipping cream
25ml/1½ tbsp brown sugar
1.5ml/¼ tsp ground cinnamon
generous pinch ground ginger

Drain the peaches, retaining the syrup. In a blender, process half of the coffee and the peaches for 1 minute. In a clean bowl, whip the cream. Put 250ml/8fl oz cold water, the sugar, cinnamon, ginger and peach syrup in a pan and bring to the boil over a medium heat, then reduce the heat and simmer for 1 minute. Add the blended peaches and the remaining coffee to the pan and stir well. Serve, topped with whipped cream and decorated with orange rind.

Strawberry Soother

Relax with this comforting strawberry blend, which is rich in vitamin C and healing phytochemicals.

225g/8oz strawberries
1 peach or nectarine

Hull the strawberries, then quarter the peach or nectarine and pull out the stone. Cut the flesh into rough slices or chunks. Juice the fruit, using a juicer, or process in a food processor or blender for a thicker juice, and serve immediately.

Citrus Shake

This refreshing juice is great for boosting the immune system. Citrus fruits are a rich source of vitamin C.

1 pink grapefruit
1 blood orange
30ml/2 tbsp lemon juice

Peel the grapefruit and orange and cut them into rough segments. Juice the fruit, then stir in the lemon juice.

Lemonade on Ice

Home-made lemonade may not be fizzy, but it has a fresh, tangy flavour, unmatched by bought drinks. The basic lemonade will keep well in the refrigerator for up to 2 weeks and makes a thirst-quenching drink at any time of day. This recipe serves six.

6 lemons
225g/8oz caster (superfine) sugar
1.75 litres/3 pints boiling water

For each iced drink:
4 scoops lemon sorbet
thin lemon and lime slices
3 ice cubes, crushed

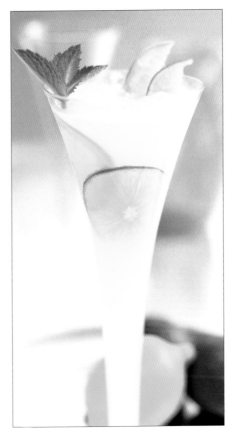

Tropical Soother

This reviving juice helps keep the liver and kidneys good and healthy. Melon is an especially good kidney tonic.

1 papaya
half a Cantaloupe melon
90g/3½oz white grapes

Start by making the lemonade. Wash the lemons and dry them thoroughly. Pare all the lemons thinly, avoiding the bitter white pith, and put the rind in a large heatproof bowl. Add the sugar. Squeeze the lemons and set the juice aside. Pour the measured boiling water over the lemon rinds and sugar. Stir until the sugar dissolves. Leave to cool, then stir in the lemon juice. Strain the lemonade into a large jug and chill.

For each glass of iced lemonade, place four scoops of sorbet in a tall glass and tuck some lemon and lime slices down the sides. Add the crushed ice. Top up each glass with about 200ml/7fl oz of the lemonade. Garnish with mint sprigs and half-slices of lemon and lime.

Halve and skin the papaya, then remove the seeds with a spoon and cut into rough slices. Cut open the melon and remove the seeds with a spoon. Cut into quarters and slice the flesh away from the skin, then cut into rough chunks. Juice all the fruit.

Melon Pick-Me-Up

This spicy blend of melon, pear and fresh root ginger will revive your body, stimulate your circulation and fire you into action.

half a Canteloupe melon
2 pears
2.5cm/1in piece fresh root ginger

Quarter the melon, remove the seeds and slice the flesh away from the skin, then quarter the pears. Using a juice extractor, juice all the ingredients, pour into a tall glass and serve immediately.

Apple Shiner

Enjoy radiant skin and instant energy with this cleansing fusion of fresh fruits and lemon juice.

1 apple
half a Honeydew melon
90g/3½oz red grapes
⅔ measure/1 tbsp lemon juice

Quarter the apple and remove the core. Cut the melon into quarters, remove the seeds and slice the flesh away from the skin. Using a juice extractor, juice the fruit. Alternatively, process the fruit in a food processor or blender for 2–3 minutes until smooth. Pour the juice into a chilled glass, stir in the lemon juice and serve.

Green Leaves

This healthy juice is exceptionally rejuvenating. Grapes are one of the most effective detoxifiers, and are used for alleviating many kinds of skin, liver and kidney disorders.

1 apple
150g/5oz white grapes

small handful fresh coriander (cilantro)
30g/1oz watercress
⅔ measure/1 tbsp lime juice

Quarter the apple. Juice the fruit, coriander and watercress, then stir in the lime juice. If you find this mixture too sour, use less lime.

Humzinger

This tropical cleanser will help boost the digestive system and the kidneys, making your eyes sparkle, your hair shine and your skin glow.

half a pineapple, peeled
1 small mango, peeled and pitted
half a small papaya, seeded and peeled

Use a sharp knife to remove any "eyes" left in the pineapple, and cut all the fruit into rough chunks. Using a juice extractor, juice the fruit. Alternatively, use a food processor or blender and process for 2–3 minutes until very smooth. Pour into a glass and serve immediately.

Cranberry, Cinnamon and Ginger Spritzer

Partially freezing fruit juice gives it a wonderfully slushy texture that is very refreshing. The combination of cranberry and apple juice contributes a tart, clean flavour that's not too sweet. Serves four.

600ml/1 pint chilled cranberry juice
150ml/¼ pint clear apple juice
4 cinnamon sticks
about 400ml/14fl oz chilled ginger ale

Pour the cranberry juice into a shallow freezerproof container and freeze for about two hours, or until a thick layer of ice crystals has formed around the edges. Mash with a fork to break up the ice, then return the mixture to the freezer for a further 2–3 hours until almost solid. Pour the apple juice into a small pan, add two cinnamon sticks and bring to just below boiling point. Pour into a pitcher and leave to cool, then remove the cinnamon sticks and set them aside with the other cinnamon sticks. Chill the juice until very cold. Spoon the cranberry ice into a food processor. Add the apple juice and blend very briefly until slushy. Pile into cocktail glasses or flutes, top up with chilled ginger ale and garnish with fresh or frozen cranberries. Put a long cinnamon stick into each glass to use as a swizzle-stick.

Super Clean

This delicious drink will really kick-start your system. Carrots are a key detox vegetable: they cleanse, nourish and stimulate the body.

3 carrots
30g/1oz young spinach
115g/4oz cooked beetroot in natural juice
2 celery sticks

Top and tail the carrots. Process all the ingredients in a blender until smooth, then pour into a glass and serve.

Bartending know-how

Beetroot is another key vegetable in cleansing the system. Like carrot, it is exceptionally good for the liver. Always use fresh beetroot (not the sliced pickled stuff that comes in jars). Not only does it add rich, lustrous colour to a vegetable juice blend, but it also contributes a pronounced degree of natural sweetness to the drink.

Iced Mango Lassi

Based on a traditional Indian drink, this is excellent with spicy food, or as a welcome cooler at any time of day. The recipe serves three to four.

For the yogurt ice:
175g/6oz caster (superfine) sugar
150ml/¼ pint water
2 lemons
500ml/17fl oz Greek yogurt

For each drink:
4 measures/6 tbsp mango juice

To make the yogurt ice, put the sugar and water in a pan and heat gently, stirring occasionally, until the sugar has dissolved. Pour the syrup into a pitcher. Leave to cool, then chill until very cold. Grate the lemons and squeeze them. Add the rind and juice to the chilled syrup and stir well to mix.

By hand: Pour the syrup mixture into a container and freeze until thickened. Beat in the yogurt, and return to the freezer until thick enough to scoop.

If using an ice cream maker: Churn the mixture until it thickens. Stir in the yogurt and churn for 2 minutes more until well mixed. Transfer to a plastic tub or similar freezerproof container and freeze.

To make each lassi, briefly blend the mango juice with three small scoops of the yogurt ice in a food processor or blender until just smooth. Pour the mixture into a tall glass or tumbler and add a few ice cubes. Top each drink with another scoop of the yogurt ice and garnish with fresh mint sprigs and mango wedges. Serve at once.

Tropical Fruit Soda

For many children, scoops of vanilla ice cream served in a froth of lemonade would make the perfect treat. This more elaborate version, with its tropical fruit content, will appeal to adults too. It serves four.

10ml/2 tsp sugar
1 papaya
1 small ripe mango
2 passion fruit
8 large scoops vanilla ice cream
8 large scoops caramel or toffee ice cream
about 400ml/14fl oz chilled lemonade or
   soda water

Line a baking sheet with foil. Make four small mounds of sugar on the foil, using about 2.5ml/½ tsp each time and spacing them well apart. Place under a medium grill (broiler) for about two minutes until the sugar mounds have turned to a pale golden caramel. Immediately swirl each pool of caramel with the tip of a cocktail stick or skewer to give a slightly feathery finish. Leave to cool.

Cut the papaya in half. Scoop out and discard the seeds, then remove the skin and chop the flesh. Skin the mango, cut the flesh off the stone and chop it into bitesize chunks. Mix the papaya and mango in a bowl. Cut each passion fruit in half, and scoop the pulp into the bowl of fruit. Mix well, cover and chill until ready to serve.

Divide the chilled fruit mixture among four large tumblers. Add one scoop of each type of ice cream to each glass. Peel the caramel decorations carefully away from the foil and press gently into the ice cream. Top up with lemonade or soda water and serve.

Yellow Pepper Revitalizer

This vibrant fresh fruit and vegetable combination will help to rejuvenate and revitalize your body. It is rich in immune-boosting vitamin C, protective betacarotene and energizing natural fruit sugars. As well as these handy attributes, it also tastes sensational – zesty, crisp, fresh and naturally sweet.

3 carrots
1 apple
1 yellow pepper

Scrub and trim the carrots and quarter the apple. Roughly chop the pepper. Using a juice extractor, juice all the ingredients, pour into a glass and serve immediately.

Revitalizer

This classic combination will benefit those suffering from constipation and arthritis. Natural fruit sugars will provide a boost of energy.

3 carrots
1 apple
1 orange

Top and tail the carrots, then quarter the apple. Peel the orange and cut into rough segments. Juice the carrots and fruit.

Licuado de Melon

Among the most refreshing drinks Mexicans make are fruit extracts mixed with honey and chilled water. This recipe is enough for four.

1 watermelon
1 litre/1¾ pints chilled water
juice of 2 limes
honey

Cut the watermelon flesh into chunks, discarding the black seeds. Cover with chilled water and leave for 10 minutes. Tip the mixture into a large sieve set over a bowl. Using a wooden spoon, press the fruit to extract all the liquid. Stir in the lime juice and sweeten with honey. Pour into a pitcher, add ice cubes and stir. Serve in tumblers.

Strawberry Kiss

A new spin on strawberries and cream, this makes a superb opener to a summer lunch.

12 strawberries
1½ measure/2 tsp lemon juice
½ measure/2 tsp whipping cream
2.5ml/½ tsp caster (superfine) sugar

Liquidize all the ingredients with a handful of crushed ice, and turn out into a wine glass. Garnish with a whole small strawberry.

Citrus Agua Fresca

These refreshing fruit juices are sold from street stalls in towns all over Mexico. The recipe serves four.

12 limes
3 oranges
2 grapefruit
600ml/1 pint water
75g/6 tbsp caster (superfine) sugar

Squeeze the juice from the fruits. Some fruit pulp should be used, but discard the seeds. Pour the mixture into a large pitcher. Add the water and sugar and stir until all the sugar has dissolved. Chill for at least an hour before serving with ice and extra fruit wedges. The drink will keep for up to a week in a covered container in the refrigerator.

Tamarind Agua Fresca

Sometimes referred to as the Indian date, tamarind is native to Asia and North Africa, and has now travelled to Mexico. It is used medicinally and as an antiseptic. The fruit has a sweet-sour taste and makes a drink similar to lemonade. This recipe serves four.

1 litre/1¾ pints water
225g/8oz tamarind pods
25g/2 tbsp caster (superfine) sugar

Pour the water into a pan and heat until warm. Remove from the heat and pour into a bowl. Peel the tamarind pods and add the pulp to the warm water. Soak for at least four hours. Place a sieve over a clean bowl. Pour the tamarind pulp and water into the sieve, then press the pulp through the sieve with the back of a wooden spoon, leaving the black seeds behind. Discard the seeds. Add the sugar to the tamarind mixture and stir well until dissolved. Pour into a pitcher and chill thoroughly before serving in tumblers filled with ice.

Bartending know-how
Jars of tamarind pulp or paste are available for buying at Indian and Asian food stores.

Pineapple and Lime Agua Fresca

The vivid colours of this fresh fruit drink give some indication of its wonderful flavour. It makes a delicious midday refresher or pick-me-up at the end of a hard day. The recipe serves four.

2 pineapples
juice of 2 limes
475ml/16fl oz still mineral water
50g/2oz caster (superfine) sugar

Peel the pineapples and chop the flesh, removing the core and "eyes" (see below). You should have about 450g/1lb flesh. Put this in a food processor or blender, and add the lime juice and half the mineral water. Purée to a smooth pulp. Stop the machine and scrape the mixture from the side of the goblet once or twice during processing. Place a sieve over a large bowl. Tip the pineapple pulp into the sieve and press it through with a wooden spoon. Pour the sieved mixture into a large pitcher, cover and chill in the refrigerator for about an hour. Stir in the remaining mineral water and sugar to taste. Serve with ice.

Bartending know-how
Remove pineapple skin with a deep spiral action to cut out the "eyes".

Granita di Caffè

This is basically coffee ice, or slush. The recipe serves four.

200ml/7fl oz strong coffee (about five generous cups of espresso or filter/cafetière brewed coffee using 80g/14 tbsp coffee per 1 litre/1¾ pints water)
400ml/14fl oz water
140g/5oz sugar
2.5ml/½ tsp vanilla essence (extract)
1 egg white (optional)
120ml/4fl oz whipped cream

Pour the brewed coffee into a large bowl and set aside. Boil half the water with the sugar, stirring to dissolve. Refrigerate. When the sugar syrup is cold, add it, the remaining water, and the vanilla to the coffee. Stir until well blended. If using, whisk the egg white and fold it into the mixture. Pour the mixture into a shallow freezerproof tin, such as an ice-cube tray or baking sheet, and freeze. About every 30 minutes, break the mixture up with a fork to create the traditional, grainy, shaved-ice consistency. When it is well frozen, serve in individual cups, and top them with a little whipped cream.

Mexican Coffee

The Aztec Indians were the first known chocolate aficionados, and chocolate is an ingredient in many Mexican recipes. Combined with coffee, it makes a rich, smooth drink. This recipe does four.

30ml/2 tbsp chocolate syrup
120ml/4fl oz whipping cream
1.5ml/¼ tsp ground cinnamon
25g/2 tbsp brown sugar
pinch ground nutmeg
475ml/16fl oz strong black coffee
whipped cream

Whip together the chocolate syrup, cream, cinnamon, sugar and nutmeg. Pour the hot coffee into the mixture and stir, before dividing among four mugs. Top with a dollop of whipped cream and garnish with shavings of cinnamon.

Coffee-Chocolate Soda

This is a fun, refreshing drink that tastes as good as it looks. The combination of chocolate ice cream and coffee-flavoured fizz makes for an unusually textured but thoroughly exciting cocktail. The recipe serves two.

250ml/8fl oz strong cold coffee
60ml/4 tbsp double (heavy) cream, or 30ml/2 tbsp evaporated (unsweetened condensed) milk (optional)
250ml/8fl oz cold soda water
2 scoops chocolate ice cream
chocolate-covered coffee beans, roughly chopped, to garnish

Pour the coffee into tall glasses. Add the cream or evaporated milk, if using. Add the soda water and stir. Gently place a scoop of ice cream into the mixture. Garnish with some of the roughly chopped chocolate-covered coffee beans. Serve with a long spoon or a straw.

Variation
Try also chocolate mint, vanilla, hazelnut or banana ice cream and sprinkle with chocolate shavings, fruit slices or even a few roughly chopped pieces of hazelnut.

Chilled Coffee Caribbean

Use coffee that is not too strong. Filter coffee gives a clean, clear texture. Serves two.

600ml/1 pint strong filter coffee, cooled for about 20 minutes
half an orange and half a lemon, thinly sliced
1 pineapple slice
sugar, to taste
1–2 drops Angostura bitters (optional)

Add the cooled coffee to the fruit slices in a large bowl. Stir and chill in the freezer for about an hour or until very cold. Remove from the freezer and stir again. Remove the fruit slices from the liquid. Add sugar to taste, and stir in the bitters, if using. Add three ice cubes per drink to tall glasses, or whisky tumblers, then pour over the chilled coffee drink. Garnish with half-slices of orange or lemon.

Cappuccino

There can be nothing more enjoyable than a steaming hot cup of coffee on a cold winter's day. This is the classic espresso and milk drink, to serve two.

160–250ml/5½–8fl oz very cold full-cream (whole) milk
about 15g/½oz dark-roast espresso coffee, finely ground

Pour very cold milk into a metal pitcher or frothing device, steam until a fine, smooth foam has formed, and set aside. Next, brew two cups of espresso, and pour into cappuccino or regular coffee cups. Pour the steamed milk over the coffee, holding back the froth with a spoon until last, when it can be spooned on to the surface.

The ideal cappuccino should be about one-third each espresso coffee, steamed milk and frothed milk. (After brewing the coffee you may need to re-steam the milk for just a moment if it has begun to "fall", or lose the froth.) Top with a sprinkle of chocolate or cocoa powder, if desired.

Caffè Latte

This is a very basic breakfast drink, as served in homes and bars throughout Italy and France. It can be made with only a manual espresso pot and a pan to heat the milk. Serves two.

2 parts espresso or very strong coffee
6 parts boiled milk
sugar (optional)
steamed, frothed milk for topping (optional)

Pour the brewed coffee into glasses or large French coffee bowls. Add the hot milk and sugar, if using, and stir well. Top each glass with a spoonful of steamed, frothed milk if desired.

Bartending know-how
If you are having a period of abstinence from caffeine, be assured that the decaffeinated versions of coffee are much improved these days. Carbonated water is now the only decaffeinating agent.

Café di Olla

This recipe is traditionally brewed in large quantities over a wood fire in a heavy earthenware Mexican cooking pot, called an *olla*. It serves four.

1 litre/1¾ pints water
150g/5oz dark brown sugar
5ml/1 tsp molasses
1 small cinnamon stick
50g/2oz dark-roast coffee, medium grind
aniseeds (optional)

Place the water, sugar, molasses, cinnamon and aniseeds, if using, in a pan and slowly bring to the boil. Stir thoroughly to dissolve the sugar and molasses. When the mixture reaches boiling point, stir in the dry coffee, remove from the heat, cover, and steep for 5 minutes. Strain into earthenware mugs and serve immediately. Add a few of the aniseeds, for that extra touch of spice.

Normandy Coffee

Like Washington State in the USA and England's West Country, Normandy is known for its apple orchards, and gives it name to many dishes made with apple juice or apple sauce. This recipe blends the flavour of apples with spices for a delicious, tangy coffee drink. It serves four.

475ml/16fl oz strong black coffee (espresso strength, or filter/cafetière brewed at 75g/13 tbsp coffee per 1 litre/1¾ pints water)
475ml/16fl oz apple juice
25g/2 tbsp brown sugar, to taste
3 oranges, thinly sliced
2 small cinnamon sticks
pinch ground allspice
pinch ground cloves

Bring all the ingredients to the boil over a medium heat, then reduce the heat and simmer for 10 minutes. Strain the liquid into a preheated flask or serving pitcher. Pour into cappuccino-style cups, adding a cinnamon stick to each, if you wish.

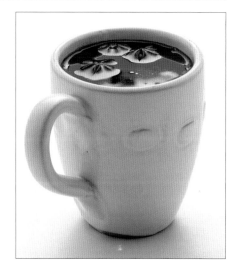

Bartending know-how
Use a French or Viennese roast coffee – dark but not as dark as for espresso, so that the spice and molasses aren't overwhelmed.

Café con Leche

Many Mexicans start the day with this spiced milky coffee, and those who have enjoyed a hearty midday meal will often opt for a cup of it with a pastry as the afternoon snack. This recipe serves four.

50g/2oz ground coffee
475ml/16fl oz boiling water
475ml/16fl oz full-cream (whole) milk
4 cinnamon sticks
sugar, to taste

Make up the coffee in a cafetière. Pour the milk into a heavy pan, add the cinnamon sticks and bring to the boil, stirring occasionally. Using a slotted spoon, lift out the cinnamon sticks and use a smaller spoon to press down on them to release any liquid they have absorbed. Set the cinnamon sticks aside for serving. Add the coffee to the hot milk, then pour into cups. Add a cinnamon stick to each cup. Drinkers should add sugar to taste.

Horchata

This delicious, aromatic rice drink tastes wonderfully creamy, yet does not contain a drop of milk. Mexicans swear by it as a means of settling stomach upsets or curing hangovers, and it is often served at breakfast. This recipe makes four.

450g/1lb long grain rice
750ml/1¼ pints water
150g/5oz blanched whole almonds
10ml/2 tsp ground cinnamon
finely grated rind of a lime
50g/2oz caster (superfine) sugar

Tip the rice into a sieve and rinse thoroughly under cold running water. Drain, tip into a large bowl and pour over the water. Cover and soak for at least two hours and preferably overnight. Drain the rice, reserving 600ml/1 pint of the soaking liquid. Spoon the rice into a food processor or blender and grind as finely as possible. Add the almonds to the processor or blender and continue to grind in the same way until finely ground. Add the cinnamon, grated lime rind and sugar to the ground rice and ground almonds. Add the reserved soaking water from the rice and mix until all the sugar has dissolved. Serve in tall glasses with ice cubes. Garnish with strips of lime rind.

Coffee Milkshake

This cold coffee drink does not require a blender. The recipe serves two.

200ml/7fl oz chilled strong coffee (four cups espresso, or filter/cafetière brewed using 70g/12 tbsps coffee per 1 litre/1¾ pints water)
2 eggs, well-beaten
450ml/¾ pint cold milk
100ml/3½fl oz single (light) or double (heavy) cream
15ml/1 tbsp sugar
pinch of salt
4 drops vanilla or almond essence (extract)

Mix the ingredients in a shaker. Serve at once, sprinkled with ginger cookies.

Atole

This drink, which is made from tehe white corn, *masa harina*, is traditionally flavoured with *piloncillo* (Mexican unrefined brown sugar) and ground cinnamon. It has the consistency of a thick milkshake. Fresh fruit purées are often added before serving and some recipes introduce ground almonds or milk. This one serves six.

200g/7oz white *masa harina*
1.2 litres/2 pints water
1 vanilla pod (bean)
50g/2oz *piloncillo*, or soft dark brown sugar
2.5ml/½ tsp ground cinnamon
115g/4oz fresh strawberries, chopped pineapple or orange segments (optional)

Put the *masa harina* in a heavy pan and gradually beat in the water to make a smooth paste. Place the pan over a medium heat, add the vanilla pod and bring the mixture to the boil, stirring constantly until it thickens. Beat in the sugar and ground cinnamon and continue to beat until the sugar has dissolved. Remove from the heat. If adding the fruit, purée it in a food processor or blender until smooth, and then press the purée through a sieve. Stir the purée into the corn mixture and return to the heat until warmed through. Remove the vanilla pod. Serve.

Champurrada

This popular version of Atole is made with Mexican chocolate. A special wooden whisk called a *molinollo* is traditionally used when making this frothy drink. The recipe serves six.

115g/4oz Mexican chocolate
1.2 litres/2 pints water or milk, or a mixture
200g/7oz white *masa harina*
25g/2 tbsp soft dark brown sugar

Put the chocolate in a mortar and grind with a pestle until it becomes a fine powder. Alternatively, grind the chocolate in a food processor. Put the liquid in a heavy pan and gradually stir in all the *masa harina* until a smooth paste is formed. Use a traditional wooden *molinollo* or a wire whisk for a frothier drink. Place the pan over a medium heat and bring the mixture to the boil, stirring all the time until the frothy drink thickens. Stir in the ground chocolate, then add the sugar. Serve immediately.

Mexican Hot Chocolate

This sumptuous version of hot chocolate relies on the beguiling flavours of almond, cloves and cinnamon for its sweetly spicy appeal. The recipe serves four.

1 litre/1¾ pints full-cream (whole) milk
1 cinnamon stick
2 whole cloves
115g/4oz plain dark chocolate, chopped into small pieces
2–3 drops almond essence (extract)

Heat the milk gently with the spices in a pan until almost boiling, then stir in the chocolate over a medium heat until melted. Strain into a blender, add the almond essence and whizz on high speed for about 30 seconds until frothy. Pour into warmed heatproof glasses and serve immediately.

Iced Mint and Chocolate Cooler

This makes a stimulating alternative to dessert, and is in a different class altogether to mint-choc-chip ice cream. The recipe serves four.

60ml/4 tbsp drinking chocolate
400ml/14fl oz full-cream (whole) milk
150ml/¼ pint natural (plain) yogurt
2.5ml/½ tsp peppermint essence (extract)
4 scoops chocolate ice cream

Place the drinking chocolate in a small pan and stir in about 120ml/4fl oz of the milk. Heat gently, stirring, until almost boiling, then remove the pan from the heat. Pour the hot chocolate milk into a heatproof bowl or large pitcher and whisk in the remaining milk. Add the yogurt and peppermint essence and whisk again. Pour the mixture into four tall glasses, filling them no more than three-quarters full. Top each drink with a scoop of ice cream. Garnish with mint leaves and chocolate shapes. Serve immediately.

Coffee Frappé

Similar to a milkshake, this frappé recipe is another long, cold coffee drink that is both refreshing and uplifting. The recipe serves two.

450ml/¾ pint cold strong coffee (brewed using about 80g/14 tbsp coffee per 1 litre/1¾ pints water)
8 drops vanilla essence (extract)
60ml/4 tbsp condensed milk
sugar, to taste

Add the cold brewed coffee to a large blender. Next, add the vanilla essence, a couple of handfuls of crushed ice and the condensed milk. Blend well until a smooth texture is obtained. Pour into tall, clear glasses, and stir in sugar to taste. Garnish with some whipped cream and banana slices, if you wish.

JUICES AND SMOOTHIES

Introduction

Juices, smoothies, shakes and blends have become extremely popular in recent years. They fit neatly into hectic modern lives, enabling you to incorporate healthy habits into your everyday routines. The main advantage of juices and smoothies is that they are easy to make, quick, convenient and packed with rejuvenating, healing and revitalizing nutrients. On top of all this, they are also delicious, and a luxurious blended drink can feel like a real treat.

The benefits of juicing

While you can buy ready-made juices and smoothies, nothing quite beats the taste of a blend made at home. Freshly made juices are also a more potent source of nutrients and certain combinations have specific health benefits. If you drink juices or blends on a regular basis, you'll enjoy clearer skin, better energy levels and balanced overall health. It is also well known that the antioxidants found in fruits and vegetables work most effectively when they are consumed together, and juicing encourages precisely this.

Combinations of specific different juices can be used to emphasize particular flavours or effects in the same way that you would in cooking – sweet and sour, savoury and spicy, warming or cooling – but you can afford to be

Above: Fresh flavours are whizzed up into nutrient-packed blends in minutes.

more adventurous than you might be with conventionally prepared foods. The juice of a fruit or vegetable often tastes much better than when the produce is cooked or even served raw. For instance, you may not particularly like celery as a vegetable, but juice it and combine the juice with pear and ginger and you get a completely different, more complex and utterly delicious taste sensation.

Even if you feel like going off the rails and indulging in extra ingredients, such as chocolate, alcohol or coffee, the very fact that the juice or smoothie is based on fresh fruits and vegetables means that you are still getting a wonderful boost of vitamins, antioxidants and minerals – healthy in anyone's book.

Preparing juices and blends also has a psychological benefit. The very act of making a juice or smoothie can make you feel good – you will feel you are nurturing and pampering yourself – and

Left: Let children get involved in juicing and watch them reap the benefits.

in addition, by using lots of fresh natural ingredients you will boost your own health and the health of your family. Juices and smoothies are great fun to make and to share: encourage your children to invent concoctions and join in the preparation, or share a juice instead of coffee with a friend.

The history of juicing and blending

As long ago as the 19th century, doctors and naturopaths were using fresh fruit and vegetable juices to improve the health of their patients. Many well-known pioneers were responsible for researching and creating the wealth of knowledge and evidence we now have about the therapeutic properties of juices. People such as Dr Kellogg, Father Kniepp, Dr Max Bircher-Bener and Dr Max Gerson all helped to popularize the notion of the "juice cure".

However, there is evidence to suggest that juicing is even older than this in the ancient practices of wine

Below: The process of making juices is as enjoyable as drinking them.

and scrumpy (apple cider) making. After extracting the fresh fruit juices, fermenting them into alcohol was simply a way of preserving the raw ingredients – and in those days drinking alcohol was safer than drinking water, which was often contaminated. The healing power of certain foods was even recognized by Hippocrates who said "Let food be your medicine." Indeed, since time immemorial, food, water and healing herbs have been the cornerstones of the healing arts.

The modern concept of blending drinks and making smoothies probably began with mixed drinks such as cocktails. For the more virtuous and health-conscious among us, however, non-alcoholic juices and blends have always sat comfortably alongside the bar choice.

We are going through a change in how we involve ourselves in our health. Reliance on prepared and fast foods has given way to a re-emergence of interest in healthy eating messages – the most familiar of these is that we need to eat five portions of fruit and vegetables every day. One convenient way of achieving this, in the context of

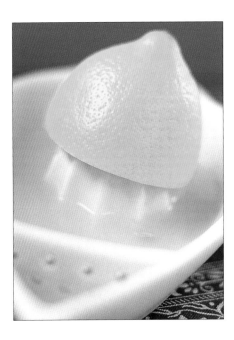

Above: Raw ingredients that can be juiced provide all the vitamins and minerals that you need to stay healthy.

our modern, fast-paced lives, is to embrace health drinks as easy-to-make snacks, quick breakfasts and fast energy boosters. The introduction of advanced kitchen technology, such as blenders, food processors and juicers, has made the preparation of blends and juices quick and easy.

In recent years, we have become more and more interested in natural ways of improving our health – echoing the thoughts and practices of the pioneering enthusiasts of earlier centuries. In addition to their more general health-boosting properties, juices and blends are also used for specific cleansing and detoxing, for helping speed recovery from illness and as part of anti-ageing regimes. There is also a school of thought that maintains that juices can help prevent some cancers, although this has yet to be proven. Nevertheless, freshly made fruit and vegetable juices provide many of the essential vitamins and minerals that are vital for a healthy life.

It is not often that something so healthy also tastes so good and is a pleasure to incorporate into daily life. Perhaps this is why juices, blended drinks, smoothies and shakes are standing the test of time.

ingredients & techniques

As you will discover in the following part of the book, you can make juices and smoothies with an incredible variety of ingredients – the fresher, the better. Great fruits to try include oranges and limes, apricots and plums, berries and currants, and of course exotic fruits such as pineapples, mangoes and lychees. You can also make juices and smoothies using vegetables, nuts and seeds, and not forgetting all-important additions such as eggs, honey, cream, chocolate and coffee. The chapter concludes with a step-by-step guide to basic juicing and blending techniques, with creative tips for decorating, serving and storing your delicious creations.

Buying produce

If you are really enthusiastic about making juices, blends and smoothies you may want to bulk buy some of the basic ingredients. Carrots, apples, bananas, pineapples and oranges are often used as base juices to which other ingredients are added. Additional ingredients, such as summer berries, are best used when really fresh and so should be juiced on the day of purchase.

Freshness

The produce you use for juices, smoothies and blends should be as fresh as possible to ensure that you will get the maximum nutrients from your drinks. It is not necessary to buy produce that looks perfect, but do avoid any that is bruised, damaged or overripe. Aim to buy fruit and vegetables that are in season if you can. By buying seasonally and locally, your produce will be bursting with health-boosting vitamins and minerals.

Ripeness

The riper the fruit, the more sugar it will contain and the sweeter it will be. It also means that the fruit contains more nutrients, especially if the produce has been ripened on the tree or plant. Fruits that are picked green and ripened in transit contain fewer nutrients.

Storage

All fruit and vegetables benefit from being stored in cool, dry conditions. However, if fruit is slightly underripe and too firm to be juiced, find a sunny windowsill on which to ripen it for a couple of days. Avoid wrapping produce in plastic bags as it cannot breathe. Ideally you should store ingredients in individual bowls or trays – for instance, one for citrus fruits, one for bananas and one for onions – as they all have different ripening times and one item can affect another, leading to premature rotting.

Above: Buy produce that is ripe if you can, but if it is needs further ripening, simply leave it on a sunny windowsill.

Organic produce

Food that is grown organically is slightly more expensive than regular produce, but there are some clear advantages in choosing it.

The levels of chemicals that you are exposed to via pesticides, fungicides and fertilizers will be significantly reduced if you choose organic produce. Advocates of organic fruit and vegetables also claim that they taste better because there is less water bulking out the produce. It is certainly true that if you taste an organic carrot and then compare it to the taste of a non-organic carrot, the former will usually have a more solid texture and a stronger, more intense carroty taste. This inevitably means that your blends will have more flavour, as there will be less water diluting the juice.

Even if you don't want to buy entirely organic produce, you may want to consider buying bulky base items, such as carrots and apples, from organic ranges.

Left: Organic fruits tend to contain less water so the taste is more intense, and they are exposed to fewer pesticides.

Above: It may be worth peeling the skin of non-organic produce, as this will remove any possible chemical residue.

Convenient options

For convenience, and because you can't always find fresh produce out of season, it is worthwhile keeping some dried, frozen, canned and bottled fruits or vegetables to hand in your store cupboard (pantry). Use these as substitutes whenever you run out of a fresh ingredient or if you find that an ingredient is unavailable or out of season. Choose fruits that are preserved in unsweetened fruit juice in preference to syrup, as this is a more natural state. Dried fruit is also a useful standby, especially dried apricots, dates and figs.

Frozen fruit such as strawberries, raspberries, blueberries and bags of frozen mixed summer fruits work very well in smoothies and blended drinks. If blended straight from the freezer, they turn smoothies into deliciously chilled slushes and you will not need to add any additional ice.

Whole nuts and seeds (for grinding into blends or for sprinkling on top of drinks as decoration) and dry ingredients such as wheatgerm should be kept in airtight jars or packets and stored in the refrigerator to keep them fresh once opened. However, because of their high fat content, nuts and seeds will become rancid if you keep them for too long. Make sure you buy from a supplier with a rapid turnover and always check the use-by date on the packet before you add them to drinks.

IRRADIATION
Most herbs and spices are irradiated (treated with radiation to delay spoiling) but this is forbidden with organic produce. If you wish to avoid irradiated herbs and spices you need to buy organic.

GM CROPS
Genetically modified foods are a recent innovation. If you have concerns about this type of produce, buy organic fruit and vegetables. Be aware that most soya products are GM-based, so look in your local health food shop and choose products that state they contain "non-genetically modified soya" on the packet.

Below: To avoid genetically modified produce, buy organic – it is worth spending a little bit more.

Citrus fruit

To juice citrus fruits you will need to use a citrus juicer, and the juice can then be added to other blends if desired. Oranges are available all year round and store well in cool, dry conditions. All citrus fruits are rich in vitamin C, and one large orange provides your recommended daily allowance (RDA). Oranges, tangerines, mandarins and other citrus fruits are also excellent sources of folic acid. As an alternative to using a citrus juicer, you could push the peeled fruit through a juicer to benefit from the fibre and pith. The pith is rich in two bioflavonoids, rutin and hesperidin, which aid the absorption of vitamin C and strengthen blood vessels. The rind is rich in limonene, which is very good for liver health. However, some people find that certain citrus fruits are too acidic for their digestive system.

Preparing and juicing citrus fruits

To juice citrus fruits, you will need a citrus juicer (handheld, electric or hydraulic), a chopping board and a sharp knife. If you are going to use the rind, you will also need a scrubbing brush, soap or washing-up liquid (dishwashing detergent), and a grater.

Juicing The simplest way to juice citrus fruits is to cut them in half and squeeze out the juice using a handheld juicer or a reamer. A hydraulic citrus press or citrus attachment on a citrus juicer is more efficient, however, and will produce more juice. Press the cut fruit against the cone of the juicer. Peeled fruits can also be juiced in a juicer or blended using a food processor or blender.

Grating rind If you wish to use rind in a juice, choose a non-waxed organic fruit to avoid chemical residue or scrub the skin with a firm brush using a little soap, then rinse. Grate on the fine mesh of your grater or use a zester.

Oranges

These are generally sweet, although some have a sharper flavour than others. Always choose eating oranges for juicing; Seville (Temple) oranges are too bitter. Blood oranges are sweeter than regular oranges and produce a lovely ruby-red juice.

Oranges are often used to make a base juice to which other juices can be added. To tone down the sweetness of orange juice, add grapefruit juice or dilute with water. Orange juice goes well with most other juices, particularly carrot, and can make a good base for smoothies too.

Therapeutic uses Orange juice is often used as a cold and flu remedy. It is rich in folic acid, which is good for cardiovascular health. It is recommended that women planning to conceive and those in the early stages of pregnancy have a good intake of folic acid in their diet (but supplements should also be taken to achieve the RDA at this time).

Grapefruits

Larger than oranges, grapefruits provide more juice. Their taste ranges from bitter/sour to sour/sweet. They add a mildly sour note to other sweeter juices, such as mango. Pink grapefruits are sweeter than yellow grapefruits.

Above: Vibrant pink grapefruits are sweeter than yellow ones.

Below: Buy oranges in bulk as they make a useful base juice.

Above: Refreshing clementines work as an effective digestive cleanser.

Therapeutic uses Grapefruit juice is thought to be useful in helping to lower cholesterol. It needs to be avoided if you are taking certain medications, particularly calcium-channel blockers and some chemotherapies. Consult your medical practitioner for advice.

Lemons and limes

These fruits have a sour/bitter taste so are used only in small quantities. They are good with tomato juice, made into lemonade or limeade, or in a hot toddy – honey and lemon juice with hot water (and brandy or whisky if you like). The delicious zesty flavour works well with almost any combination of ingredients.

Therapeutic uses Lemons have antiseptic and antibacterial properties, and are traditionally used to support liver and kidney health. They are an alkaline fruit and are often used to help calm digestive acid.

Right: Blends can be livened up with a fresh squeeze of lemon or lime juice.

Mandarins, tangerines, satsumas, clementines and tangelos

These are all different crosses of citrus fruit. They have individual mild, aromatic sweetness, which varies with the type of fruit. None of them is as tart as oranges. They make good base juices and combine well with tropical fruit.

Therapeutic uses These fruits have similar properties to oranges and are also good digestive cleansers.

Other citrus fruits

Kumquat These can be fairly bitter, so juice them with intensely sweet ingredients, such as apricots. Slices of kumquat may also be used to decorate glasses.

GIVE ME FIVE!

Most governments agree that we need to eat five portions of fruit and vegetables a day, but many people are not sure what constitutes a "portion". Put simply, the daily total should come to 400g/14oz, so a portion is 80g/just under 3oz. A portion can be:
• one apple, one orange, one banana or another similar-sized fruit or vegetable
• two small fruits, such as tangerines or kiwi fruit
• half a large fruit, such as a grapefruit, or a generous slice of melon
• a small bowl of salad or fruit salad
• one cup of chopped vegetables
• one wine-glass full of fruit or vegetable juice (but remember that juice only counts towards one portion, so you can't drink juice all day and count it as five).

Note Potatoes do not count as a portion of vegetables because they are a starchy food.

Mineola This fruit is distinguished by a bump at its stem end. It has very few pips (seeds) and is wonderfully sweet, so is perfect for juicing.

Pomelos These are a type of orange with a sharp grapefruit flavour. Their slightly dry texture renders less juice than oranges, lemons or grapefruits, but their juice makes a good addition to mixed drinks that need sharpening.

Ugli fruit Named for its appearance, this fruit is delicious, mild, acid-sweet and juicy.

Orchard and stone fruit

Apples and pears are the classic orchard fruits and they are excellent for juicing. They are available year round and are relatively cheap, making them ideal to use as base juices. Other stone and orchard fruit, such as apricots, cherries and plums, are restricted to the summer season and tend to be more expensive, but they make deliciously sweet juices. Apples and pears store well in cool, dry conditions, but it is best to keep soft fruit in the refrigerator. All of these fruits are rich in vitamins and minerals, with apricots being particularly high in betacarotene – a natural source of vitamin A.

Preparing and juicing orchard and stone fruits

To juice orchard and stone fruits, you will need either a juicer for hard fruits, such as apples and pears, or a blender or food processor for softer fruits, such as peaches or plums. You will also need a chopping board and a sharp knife. A cherry stoner is useful for removing stones (pits) from cherries.

Hard fruits Apples, hard pears and quinces are best prepared with a juicer (centrifugal or masticating). Using a brush, scrub the skin with soap or washing-up liquid (dishwashing detergent) and water. Quarter the fruits and remove stems, but leave the core intact (although you can remove this if you prefer). Push the quarters through the juicer. Firmer peaches, nectarines or plums can also be put through a juicer, although the yield is much less than if blended. Halve or quarter these fruits and remove the stones.

Soft fruits Ripe apricots, cherries, peaches, nectarines, plums and greengages are best prepared in a blender or food processor as they produce a deliciously thick pulp. Halve or quarter these fruits, removing the stems and stones. There is no need to peel these fruits, though leaving the peel on will give the blend a thicker texture. If you do not peel the fruit, wash it thoroughly first.

Cherries These need to be pitted and this is most easily done using a cherry pitter.

To use a blender Place the fruit in the goblet and add your choice of liquid – water, juice, milk or milk substitute. Cover and select the appropriate speed. For a thicker consistency, add banana, yogurt or cream.

To use a food processor Place the prepared fruit in the bowl, cover and select the appropriate speed. The resulting pulp can be diluted to drinking consistency by adding water, a liquid juice such as apple or orange juice, milk or a milk substitute. If your food processor can crush ice, add some cubes at the end to create a lovely fruit "slush" drink.

CLASSIC COMBINATIONS
In the late summer and autumn, there is often a glut of locally grown orchard fruit or berries. Buy plenty and either freeze them for use later in the year, or juice them, taking advantage of some of these classic flavour combinations.

- **Apple and blackberry** – the sweetness of the apples offsets the tart blackberries perfectly.
- **Apple and carrot** – this juice is packed full of healthy nutrients.
- **Pear, melon and ginger** – the warmth of ginger complements the cool melon in this exotic blend.
- **Peach and apricot** – this thick blend can be thinned with sparkling mineral water.
- **Nectarine and cherry** – a delicious sweet blend that children will love.
- **Pear and cranberry** – this refreshing juice should be served with plenty of crushed ice.
- **Pear and apricot** – the thick, sweet apricot juice complements the subtle, aromatic flavour of pear.

Above: Apples make juice that can be very sweet, tangy or sour.

Apple

Depending on the type of apple, the taste will range from sweet to tart or sour. For juicing purposes choose eating apples, not cooking or crab apples. Apples are available all year round, making them ideal as a base juice to which other juices can be added. Apple juice oxidizes quickly to a brown colour but a little lemon juice will slow down this process.

Some classic juice combinations are apple and cranberry, apple and blackcurrant, and apple and carrot. While it may seem that choosing sweet apples is best, sharper tasting eating varieties are often better, as juicing concentrates the sweetness. They also balance out sweeter ingredients – for instance, sharp green apples work well to counterbalance the flavour of intensely sweet watermelon.

Therapeutic uses Apples are a good all-round fruit. They contain malic acid, which aids digestion, and they are high in pectin, a soluble fibre that helps to lower cholesterol and may help in the treatment of constipation and diarrhoea. If you want to detox and generally clear out your system, apples are the perfect fruit. Some varieties are also very rich in vitamin C, so they can help to boost the immune system and stave off winter colds and flu.

Above: Aromatic pears make a subtle and refreshing juice.

Pears

These fruits have an aromatic scent and delicate flavour, which comes out particularly well when they are juiced. To fully enjoy their subtle flavour it is best not to mix them with other very strong tasting juices, although they can be used to tone down the sometimes overwhelming flavours of cabbage and celery, for example.

Therapeutic uses This is another detoxifying fruit, which also provides an energizing boost. The levulose sugar in pears is more easily tolerated by diabetics than other sugars.

Apricots

If you can, choose tree-ripened fruit as the betacarotene levels increase by 200 per cent in the final ripening period. When blended, apricots produce a thick, rich pulp that is best when diluted with other more liquid juices such as cucumber, apple or carrot. Alternatively,

Above: Apricots make a deliciously thick and nutritious blend, perfect for a healthy breakfast juice.

you could thin the juice with a splash of sparkling mineral water or add natural (plain) yogurt to make a delicious smoothie. Dried apricots can be prepared in a blender with some water.

Therapeutic uses Apricots are particularly rich in betacarotene, one of the most important antioxidants, while dried apricots are a useful source of iron, potassium and fibre.

Above: Fresh cherries have a short season so enjoy them while you can.

Cherries

Choose ripe, sweet cherries for juicing as they do not ripen further after picking. They should be plump and firm, but not hard. Cherries lend a rich, aromatic flavour to juices and smoothies. Preparing them can be extremely time-consuming, and it helps if you have a cherry stoner to pit them. They are best used in small quantities with other blends and they turn juices and drinks a vibrant pinky-red colour. Cherry juice combines well with most other fruits and vegetables.

Therapeutic uses Powerhouses of the phyto (plant) nutrients proanthocyanins, which derive from their red colour, cherries have potent antioxidant characteristics. They also have painkilling abilities, which some people find particularly useful for relieving rheumatism. The pain relief characteristics can also be useful for alleviating headaches – a portion of 20 cherries is reputed to be the equivalent of one aspirin in terms of painkilling ability. Fresh cherries are also traditionally used to alleviate gout by helping to moderate uric acid levels. If you cannot find fresh cherries, the canned variety make a good substitute.

Peaches and nectarines

These fruits produce similar thick, sweet juices, with peach juice being a little sweeter than that made with nectarines – but this difference is hardly noticeable once the juice has been blended.

Peaches have a fuzzy skin, which you may prefer to peel off before juicing, but this is not necessary. It is a bit of a waste putting peaches and nectarines

Above: Prunes add sweet flavour to juices when whizzed up in a blender.

through a juicer as a much better yield can be achieved using a blender or food processor. This process retains the fibre of the fruit, resulting in a much thicker, fruit purée, which can then be thinned if you like. If a recipe calls for fresh apricots but it is the wrong season and you cannot find them, peaches or nectarines make a good substitute.

Therapeutic uses Rich in vitamin C, betacarotene and other antioxidants, peaches and nectarines are excellent for skin, lung and digestive health, and are also particularly good for your eyes. One fresh nectarine contains an adult's entire recommended daily allowance of vitamin C. These fruits are very easy to digest but have a gentle laxative and diuretic effect, so should always be eaten in moderation.

Above: Juice from plums can be slightly sour if the fruit is underripe.

Left: Nectarines do not need to be peeled before blending, but the large stone must be removed.

Plums, greengages, damsons and prunes

Plums and greengages have a sweet, refreshing taste, although some varieties, especially if unripe, can be a little bit tart. Greengages are incredibly sweet and perfect for juicing, while damsons are fairly sour with a strong flavour, so are generally cooked with sugar before using. Prunes are dried plums and are intensely sweet – they can be blended with water to make a thick sweet juice, and they combine well with most citrus fruits.

As with other sweet, soft fruit, plums are best used with other fruits that are less sweet or with more liquid ingredients, such as slightly sour apple juice. If plums are a little underripe, they will work well with extremely sweet fruits, such as bananas, mangoes or even orange juice.

Therapeutic uses Plums and prunes are known for their laxative properties. They are also very rich in potent antioxidants, making them a good choice for general health. Plums are a rich source of vitamin E and are good for maintaining healthy skin.

Quinces

These are an old-fashioned fruit but they are now becoming increasingly available throughout the year. Apple or pear-like in shape, depending on the variety, and with a pale golden colour, they have a delightful scented taste when cooked, but when eaten raw the flavour can be very astringent.

Quinces are hard when grown in cooler climates but ripen to a much softer texture when grown in warm climates. Although they are most often used in jellies and jams, for juicing purposes quinces should be prepared like apples, and are juiced in the same way. They should ideally be combined with a very sweet juice, such as peach or apricot, to counteract their tart, slightly bitter taste.

Therapeutic uses Elixir of quince was traditionally used, many years ago, to help invalids through long periods of convalescence.

Above: If you find fresh quinces, prepare them as you would apples and juice them in the same way, then combine with very sweet fruit juices such as mango or peach.

DRIED FRUIT

These are widely available and include raisins, sultanas (golden raisins) and currants, apricots, prunes, figs, mangoes, papaya, banana, apple rings and dates. Dried fruits do not juice well because they are dehydrated; however, they can be rehydrated by soaking in hot water, tea (Earl Grey is delicious), warmed wine or fortified wine. Adding cinnamon or another spice, such as cloves, complements their flavour. Dried fruits provide more concentrated sources of nutrients – including iron, magnesium and antioxidants – than their fresh equivalents. They are very sweet, so a little goes a long way in juices and blended drinks.

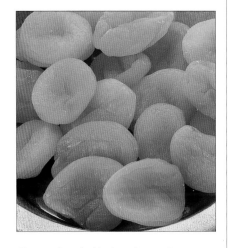

Above: Semi-dried apricots do not need soaking before use.

Above: Clockwise from top left, sultanas, currants and raisins don't juice well, but can be finely chopped and added to smoothies or fruit blends.

Berries and currants

Tiny delicious currants and ripe berries are ideal for making smoothies and shakes. You will need a blender or a food processor for this because soft fruits do not go through juicers well. Berries are mainly a summer fruit and this is when they not only taste their best but are also cheapest, although they are often available at other times of the year when they are imported. They must be stored in the refrigerator and used within two days of purchase at most. Berries need careful handling and you need to watch them as they can quickly become overripe. If you cannot find fresh berries and currants, frozen ones are a good option.

Weight for weight, strawberries, raspberries and blackcurrants contain as much vitamin C as citrus fruits. Dark red berries are also rich sources of proanthocyanins, which are powerful antioxidants. Some people have an allergic reaction to strawberries and other berries, especially if they eat too many, and this can result in a strawberry rash or even a fever.

FREEZING FRUIT
If there is a glut of berries you can freeze them for blending at other times of the year.

Remove the stalks and leaves, then place the fruit on a baking sheet in a single layer to freeze. Once frozen transfer to a freezerproof container or bag. When you want to use them, either defrost first or blend from frozen for an iced effect.

Preparing and blending berries and currants

To juice berries and currants, you will need either a blender or a food processor, a chopping board and a small, sharp knife.

Soft fruits These are easy to prepare for blending. Rinse, if you like, then discard any overripe or mouldy fruit. Remove any stems and leaves, either pulling them off by hand or using a sharp knife. Remove the calyx from strawberries, but remember there is no need to hull them when making juices.

To use a blender Place the prepared soft fruits in the flask, add liquid, such as water, fruit juice, milk or milk substitute, cover and select the appropriate speed. Add banana, other soft fruits, yogurt or cream to make a thicker consistency.

To use a food processor Place the prepared fruit in the bowl, cover and process. If you prefer a thinner consistency, the resulting pulp can be diluted by adding mineral water (still or sparkling, depending on your preference), a liquid juice such as orange juice, milk or a milk substitute.

Adding ice Create a delicious berry ice crush by adding plenty of ice to the blend. Before crushing ice in a blender of food processor, however, check the manufacturer's instructions.

MAKING A FRUIT COULIS
Coulis make delicious, jewel-coloured additions to trickle over a smoothie or milkshake, or even an ice cream, before serving.

1 Choose one fruit depending on the colour or flavour you want: raspberries or strawberries for dark red or pinkish red, peeled kiwi fruit for bright green or soaked dried apricots for a vibrant orange colour.

2 Put the fruit in a blender – approximately one small handful per person should be enough. Blend on high speed until puréed. If using dried apricots you will need to add 15–30ml/1–2 tbsp water before blending to achieve the correct consistency.

3 Strain the raspberry or strawberry coulis if you want a seedless purée.

Above: Buy plenty of strawberries for juicing when they are in season.

Strawberries, raspberries, blackberries and mulberries

Generally sweet but with a sharp undertone, strawberries are at their best and sweetest when perfectly ripe. Wild strawberries are much smaller than cultivated strawberries and have an intense, delicious flavour, but they are generally too expensive to blend unless you are lucky enough to have your own supply. Buy brightly coloured, plump berries and do not wash them until you are ready to use them.

Raspberries are a delicate berry so handle them with care, giving them just a light rinse, if necessary. They are more tart tasting than strawberries and they add a deeper reddish colour than the light pinky colour that strawberries give. Try a classic strawberry milkshake or a raspberry and peach smoothie to sample these fruits at their best.

Blackberries arrive later in the summer season than other berries, usually just as autumn is approaching. They grow wild in the countryside in abundance, but you can also find cultured blackberries in large supermarkets. They are very sweet and juicy when fully ripe.

Mulberries look a bit like blackberries in size and shape but they are less widely available. When ripe, their flavour is sweet but slightly sour and they are less aromatic than other berries.

Above: Raspberries add a delicious tart flavour and a vibrant red colour.

Right: Hunt for wild blackberry bushes, then pick your own.

When in season these fruits will be reasonably priced and you could use them as a base juice, but at other times, when the fruit is more expensive, just a few berries will add a really distinctive taste and colour to drinks. They blend well with bananas, orange juice, apples, melons, peaches and most other delicately flavoured fruits. Blackberries will dominate the colour of most other juices, turning the blend a deep, dark purple, but the taste is subtle enough to mix well with most fruit and vegetable combinations. Blackberries go particularly well with apples – a classic combination.

Therapeutic uses Strawberries are rich in pectin and ellagic acid, which makes them excellent for cleansing and detoxification. All four berries are good sources of proanthocyanins and have lots of vitamin C, both of which are good for boosting the immune system. As an antioxidant, vitamin C may even reduce the risk of developing certain cancers. Berries are a valuable source of calcium, which is important for healthy bones and teeth, and they are also soothing for the nervous system. People with cardiovascular health problems should include berries in their diet for their antioxidant properties. Raspberry juice is believed to cleanse the digestive system, and raspberries have traditionally been used in the treatment of diarrhoea, indigestion and rheumatism.

Above: The intense colour of blueberries will dominate any blend you add them to.

Blueberries

Also called bilberries, blueberries are very sweet when ripe, but rather tart when underripe. Generally, they have a short summer season, though in warm countries the season is prolonged. Buy plenty and freeze them in small bags.

As with blackberries, the dark juice of blueberries will dominate the blend; in this case the juice is a rich bluish-purple. They are a delicious addition to most fruit blends or, if you prefer simple juices, just add sparkling mineral water to a thick blueberry purée.

Therapeutic uses Blueberries are one of the most potent fruits in terms of antioxidant power. Primarily used to boost the immune system, they also play an important role in eye health. During World War II, pilots ate blueberries because they believed it would improve their night vision. As with cranberries, they are good for relieving urinary tract infections.

Blackcurrants, redcurrants and whitecurrants

The general flavour of blackcurrants is sour-sweet, depending on how ripe they are. They are best sweetened, although this is not necessary if you are mixing a small amount of blackcurrant juice with a sweeter fruit juice. They make ideal mixers but they are not good juiced on their own. Blackcurrants are more often made into cordials than into juices, and you could add some cordial to a juice made of other fruits.

Redcurrants and whitecurrants are available at the same time of the year as blackcurrants but are less abundant and can be more difficult to find. They are good mixed with less expensive blackcurrants in juices and smoothies.

Therapeutic uses Few fruits and vegetables have more vitamin C than blackcurrants, making them powerful allies in wintertime for fending off colds and flu. Blackcurrant pips (seeds) are a rich source of essential fatty acids (the same as those in evening primrose oil), which are helpful for female hormonal health, relieving symptoms of pre-menstrual syndrome and mastalgia (sore breasts).

Left: Whitecurrants are sweeter than other currants and less tart.

Left: Mix redcurrants with sweeter ingredients for a delicious blend.

Above: Tart blackcurrants contain more vitamin C than almost any other fruit, but are best used in small quantities.

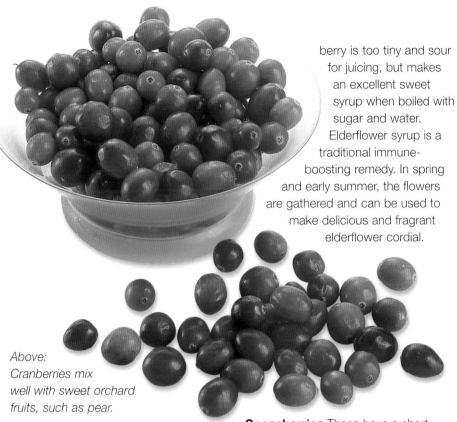

*Above:
Cranberries mix
well with sweet orchard
fruits, such as pear.*

Cranberries

These lovely berries are associated with the winter season as they are generally not available fresh at other times of the year. Buy them when available and keep them in your freezer until needed. Cranberries are fairly sour and need to be sweetened. They work well with juice made from sweet oranges, apples, pears or with carrot in a ratio of a quarter cranberry juice to three-quarters of the sweeter ingredient.

Therapeutic uses Cranberries are very successful at preventing or resolving cystitis and other urinary tract infections when drunk as a juice over several days. The antioxidants they contain specifically target the bacteria of the urinary tract and prevent them from adhering and causing damage. The quinine contained in cranberries is an effective liver detoxifier.

Other berries

Elderberries These are not generally available in the shops but must be gathered from the wild. The elder tree grows widely and can be found in many urban gardens. It is not uncommon for people to disregard it as a weed. The berry is too tiny and sour for juicing, but makes an excellent sweet syrup when boiled with sugar and water. Elderflower syrup is a traditional immune-boosting remedy. In spring and early summer, the flowers are gathered and can be used to make delicious and fragrant elderflower cordial.

Gooseberries These have a short summer season but can be frozen on baking sheets. They are widely available but not often used for juicing because they can be extremely sour. However, you could add a small number to a juice to gain the benefit of their immune-supporting effects.

Below: Instead of juicing raw, elderberries are first boiled with sugar to make a syrup.

Left: Freeze gooseberries to use all year round.

SUMMER SMOOTHIES

When there is a glut of surplus berries but you don't want to freeze them, try making some of these classic berry smoothies.

- **Raspberry and orange** – this smoothie has a delicious tart flavour and is perfect for breakfast.
- **Cranberry and pear** – sweet and juicy pear contrasts with the slightly dry flavour of cranberries.
- **Summer fruits** – simply redcurrants, raspberries, strawberries and blackberries.
- **Redcurrant and cranberry** – a tart and refreshing smoothie, perfect on a summer's day.
- **Raspberry and apple** – kids will love this combination with plenty of crushed ice.
- **Blueberry and orange** – this smoothie will take on a vibrant bluish-purple colour.
- **Blackberry and cinnamon** – a warm, spicy blend guaranteed to impress guests.

Exotic and other fruits

Most exotic fruits are now available year round. These fruits are mainly blended because, apart from melons and pineapples, they will not go through a juicer very well. Melons, pineapples and bananas produce enough juice to use as base ingredients, but the availability and yield of other exotic fruits mean that they are best used in smaller quantities. Orange-coloured fruits, such as mangoes, are excellent sources of betacarotene.

Preparing and juicing exotic and other fruits

You will need a blender or food processor, a juicer (centrifugal or masticating), a chopping board and a sharp knife. A spoon is useful for scooping the flesh out of some fruits.

Melons Cut a wedge and scoop out the pips (seeds). Cut away the flesh and purée in a blender or food processor. Firmer melons can be put through a juicer, particularly watermelon.

Bananas Peel and then break the flesh into chunks. Put the banana into a blender or food processor and blend to a pulp, then add other fruit juice until you get the right consistency.

Pineapples Lie the pineapple on its side on a chopping board, then, using a large sharp knife, slice off the base and the top. Cut the fruit into thick slices, then remove the skin. The flesh can be put in a blender or food processor, or pushed through a juicer.

Kiwi fruit, papaya and guava Cut the fruit in half. For papaya and guava, scoop out the seeds. For all three fruits, either scoop out the ripe flesh with a spoon or peel with a sharp knife. Put the flesh in a blender or food processor. None of these yields enough juice when put through a juicer.

Mangoes Slice down either side of the stone. Score the flesh into small squares, then push the skin from the outside and cut off the flesh into a blender or food processor.

Lychees The easiest way to peel lychees is by hand; the skin is slightly stiff and cracks easily. Ease the fruit out and remove the stone. Put the flesh in a blender or food processor. Lychees do not yield enough juice in a juicer.

RHUBARB

Traces of oxalic acid, which inhibits calcium and iron absorption and may exacerbate joint problems, can be found in many vegetables. The high levels of oxalic acid in rhubarb mean that it should not be used raw, and rhubarb leaves should never be eaten because they are poisonous. Rhubarb can, however, be added to drinks if it is cooked first. It contains high levels of calcium, potassium and thiamine (vitamin B_1).

Right: Add bananas to smoothies for a thick, creamy taste.

The enzymes also help to clear the blood and break down clots. Pineapple is thought to relieve arthritis and may help to reduce back pain. This fruit also helps to get rid of mucus build-up.

Kiwi fruit

Like the banana, kiwi fruit was once exotic but is now very easy to buy. If kiwi fruit are hard when bought they will ripen quickly on a windowsill. They taste sweet, zesty and aromatic when ripe and are inexpensive enough to use as a base juice. They combine well with other green fruits, such as apples or grapes, as well as tropical fruits.

Therapeutic uses Kiwi fruit is one of the richest sources of immune-boosting and collagen-building vitamin C.

Therapeutic uses Fresh pineapples contain one of the strongest protein-digesting enzymes, bromelain, making them valuable for all digestive complaints. They even "tidy up" the digestive tract by skimming off dead cells, and they can help to heal damaged digestive tracts.

Bananas

Once an exotic fruit, bananas are now a staple. Smaller and much more flavourful bananas are becoming generally available and they are well worth buying.

Bananas provide an excellent base for a smoothie and combine well with many different fruits, although they are not good when partnered with vegetables. They are a great way to thicken a blend and make it more filling, especially if you don't want to use dairy products.

Therapeutic uses
Bananas are very good energy boosters and they are full of bowel-supporting, gentle fibre.

Above: Kiwi fruit make a delicious, tangy base juice.

Pineapples

These are sweet to sweet-sharp tasting, often with an aromatic note. Pineapples do not ripen further once harvested, so make sure you buy a fruit that is ripe. Select a pineapple that is slightly soft to the touch, smells delicious and has a good colour with no green patches. The leaves should be crisp and green, with no sign of yellowing at the tips. Pineapple combines extremely well with most fruits and also with vegetable juices.

Above: Pineapples can be mixed with most fruits.

Left: Ripe mangoes have extremely soft flesh that is juicy and sweet.

Mangoes, papayas and guavas

These fruits are best bought ripe, when they yield slightly to gentle pressure, which is when they are at their sweetest. They are all aromatic, delicious and luxurious tasting. They combine well with banana and orange juice, apples or carrot to make tasty tropical smoothies.

Therapeutic uses Papaya is distinguished by its potent digestive enzyme, papain, which has all the advantages of bromelain (see pineapples). Papain also has a reputation for helping to restore healthy bowel flora (bacterial balance). All three fruits are rich in betacarotene and contain generous amounts of vitamin C as well as many minerals, making them excellent all-round sources of nutrition.

Lychees

These have a subtle, aromatic and sweet taste. They need to be combined with equally delicately flavoured fruits so that their flavour is not lost. Combine them in smoothie blends with melons, bananas, apples or strawberries.

Therapeutic uses Lychees are a good source of vitamin C.

Right: The juice from Galia melons is delicious when combined with either fruit or vegetables.

Melons

There are many different types of melon available, including cantaloupe, honeydew and watermelon. They are members of the gourd family, which also includes cucumbers and squashes. To choose a ripe melon (apart from watermelon), press the blossom end, which should yield slightly to gentle pressure. A ripe melon will have a sweet, perfumed aroma. For watermelon, tap the side of the fruit, which should sound hollow; the rind should barely give when pressed with a thumb.

Melons make a sweet, refreshing base juice that combines well with other fruits, such as tart apples or pears, or with slightly bitter vegetables such as cabbage.

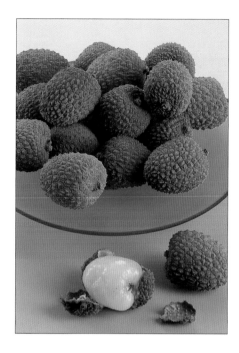

Above: Aromatic lychees contain significant amounts of vitamin C.

Therapeutic uses Melons have a diuretic and digestive cleansing action, and they are good for all problem skin conditions. The pips (seeds) are very rich in potassium, which helps to lower high blood pressure, and they are also valued for their zinc and vitamin E content, so it is worthwhile including a few. All of the orange-fleshed melons are rich in betacarotene, which is good for the immune system and for eye health in general. Watermelon also provides the phytonutrient lycopene, which is reputedly powerful in fighting against certain types of cancer, including prostate cancer. Lycopene must be consumed together with a small amount of fat to facilitate absorption, and supplements are recommended to gain its full benefit.

Grapes

Depending on the variety, grapes can be sweet or tart tasting. Black, red, green (or white) grapes are available, and you can choose from seeded or seedless varieties. They produce a light green or pink juice depending on the colour of the grape.

Grapes are fairly watery so they work well with fruits that produce thicker juice, such as mangoes, papayas, peaches or plums. They are a useful and delicious addition to most fruit and vegetable juices.

Therapeutic uses Dark-skinned grapes are rich in a compound called resveratrol, one of the most potent antioxidants, as well as proanthocyanins, and all colours of grapes have high levels of ellagic acid, which is a potent detoxifier. Grape juice is a traditional naturopathic rest cure and is also sometimes used as a nerve tonic. Grapes have been reported to help alleviate the symptoms of arthritis.

Right: There is no need to remove grape pips before blending as they will just be incorporated into the juice.

TROPICAL TOPPERS

Some tropical fruits are not good for juicing as they either yield too little juice or are too fiddly to prepare. Try using them as pretty decorations and toppings.

Figs Cut from the pointed end downwards but do not cut right through the base. Make a second cut at right angles to the first, creating a cross shape. Squeeze the fruit gently to open up into a "flower". This makes an attractive edible decoration – eat them with the skin on. Figs do not yield much juice but you can combine them with other juices. They have a strong laxative action, so should be consumed in moderation, and are useful for irritated bronchial tubes.

Star fruit (carambola) These pretty tropical fruits can be sliced very thinly into attractive star-shaped decorations.

Pomegranates Cut these in half and scoop out the scarlet pips (seeds), separating them from the pith. Sweet, refreshing and crunchy, the pips are ideal for sprinkling on top of juices and smoothies.

Passion fruit Cut in half and scoop out the pulp and pips (seeds). Sweet, aromatic and attractive, this pulp makes an ideal juice topping.

Dates Cut dates in half and discard the stone (pit). Although they cannot be juiced, they can be chopped and added to blends. Otherwise, slice thinly and serve as a side snack with a drink.

Root and tuber vegetables

These vegetables must be juiced using a centrifugal or masticating juicer. Carrot is the only root vegetable that is suitable to be used as a base juice, but others can be included in smaller proportions in juices and blends. Root vegetables are essentially autumnal and winter vegetables, but they are generally available year round. They all store best in cool, dry conditions, although beetroot (beet) is best kept in the refrigerator.

Preparing and juicing root and tuber vegetables

To juice root and tuber vegetables, you will need an electric juicer (centrifugal or masticating), a scrubbing brush or a vegetable peeler, a chopping board and a sharp knife.

Peeling When preparing root and tuber vegetables, decide first if you are going to peel them or just scrub off the dirt. With many fruits and vegetables it is a shame to peel them as a good proportion of the nutrients are just under the skin. Your decision will be, in part, influenced by how thin the skin is. You may want to peel old and gnarled carrots but leave small new carrots unpeeled. You do not usually need to peel carrots, beetroot (beet), celeriac, parsnips, radishes, swedes (rutabaga), turnips, sweet potatoes or yams. While you can include potato skin, you must be sure to cut away any peel or flesh that is sprouting or green in any way. This green colour indicates the presence of a highly toxic alkaloid called solanine, which could cause illness.

Juicing When root vegetables are juiced they tend to produce foam, which settles at the top of the juice. This can taste a bit earthy (even when the vegetables have been scrubbed clean). However, this taste indicates their high mineral content so the topping should be drunk for maximum benefit (you can mix it in with the rest of the juice). If you find the taste particularly unpleasant, just spoon it off, but do not strain the juice.

Carrot

When juiced, carrots are very sweet and the fresh juice has a much better flavour than commercial carrot juice. Because they yield a lot of mild-tasting juice, carrots provide the basis for many combinations. They work very well with both vegetables and fruit.

Therapeutic uses Rich in betacarotene, which is good for the immune system as well as for skin and eye health.

Nursing mothers are sometimes advised to drink carrot juice; it contains more easily assimilated calcium than cow's milk, which is essential to healthy growth in infancy. To ensure that betacarotene is converted to vitamin A (a fat-soluble vitamin) as needed, it helps to add 5ml/1 tsp flax seed oil or walnut oil to the carrot juice, or some full cream (whole) or semi-skimmed (low-fat) milk.

Beetroot

A rich ruby-red colour is imparted to drinks by the inclusion of beetroot (beet). Always used raw, they do not need to be peeled, just scrubbed. The juice is quite strong tasting, so use it sparingly: about one quarter beetroot juice to three-quarters other juice.

Beetroot greens enhance the nutritional value of the juice. However, they are fairly high in oxalic acid, which is poisonous if consumed in large quantities. Juiced beetroot and leaves work well in all vegetable combinations.

Therapeutic uses Beetroot is used as a blood fortifier and iron builder in traditional herbalism, particularly for heavy menstrual blood loss. It is very rich in immune-boosting beta-carotene, as well as many other minerals, including iron and manganese. It is also traditionally used during convalescence.

Above: Carrots make a sweet juice that works well as a base when combined with juice from other fruits or vegetables.

Right: Beetroot provides a stunning deep red juice.

Parsnip

This vegetable is high in sugar and so, like carrots, tastes fairly sweet. The juice is also quite creamy tasting. However, unlike carrot juice, parsnip juice should be added in smaller quantities – about one quarter parsnip to three-quarters other juice. It works best with other vegetable juices, especially slightly spicy, peppery ones.

Therapeutic uses Parsnips have a settling effect on the stomach and are mildly diuretic. Rich in silicon, they are also good for hair, skin and nails.

Radish

These attractive vegetables come in a variety of shapes and sizes. They have a distinctive peppery taste, so use them in small quantities as a flavouring for other vegetable juices. They are ideal for bringing a bland juice to life.

Therapeutic uses As with any peppery vegetable, radishes have a tonic effect on the liver and gall bladder. They also help to clear the sinuses.

Sweet potatoes and yams

Although these two vegetables look similar, they are not actually related and yams tend to be drier than sweet potatoes. There are many varieties of sweet potato, with flesh ranging from pale yellow to a vivid orange. Yam flesh varies from off-white, to yellow and pink, or even purple. Choose unblemished, smooth produce and store in a dark, cool, dry place.

Above: Peppery radishes should be juiced in small quantities only.

Therapeutic uses Both of these tubers are high in starch, with yams containing more natural sugar then sweet potatoes, but with a lower vitamin A and C content. They are both energizing and easier to digest than standard potatoes and they have an alkalizing effect on the body, which helps to curb over-acidity. Some people believe that they have anti-carcinogenic properties.

Celeriac, swedes and turnips

Celeriac has a mild celery taste; swede (rutabaga) is sweet and creamy but slightly earthy tasting; and turnips taste mild and peppery. Most of the nutrients in turnips are concentrated in the tops, so juice them along with the stems and leaves instead of discarding them. All of these vegetables work best when added to other vegetable blends, for example in a carrot-based juice with green leafy vegetables, but they do not combine particularly well with fruit.

Therapeutic uses Celeriac has a mildly astringent, diuretic action, while swede is energizing. Turnips, with their tops, provide a good source of calcium (without the limiting oxalic acid found in beetroot (beet) and spinach), making them a good nerve tonic, and they are also thought to be useful when you are feeling run down or depressed. By weight, turnip tops contain twice as much vitamin C as citrus fruit, and they also have an expectorant action, which is useful for chesty coughs.

Potatoes

Any type of potato can be used, but you must always use them raw in blended drinks. Potato is not a juice that anybody would drink on its own, but it has a slightly nutty flavour that is not unpleasant when mixed with other vegetable juices. It does, however, have good therapeutic effects, which makes it worth including. You only need a small quantity mixed with another juice, such as carrot, at a ratio of about one-eighth potato to seven-eighths other juice. (See the important note about preparation of potatoes opposite.)

Therapeutic uses Potato peel is high in potassium and may help to lower blood pressure, while the juice has traditionally been used to treat stomach ulcers and arthritis.

Above: The juice from potatoes is added to drinks for its therapeutic effect.

Leafy and brassica vegetables

Green leafy vegetables and brassicas need to be juiced using a juicer. The brassica family includes broccoli, cauliflower, and Brussels sprouts. Ideally these, and all leafy vegetables, should be stored in the refrigerator to avoid wilting, yellowing or browning, and they are best used as soon as possible after purchase as they quickly lose their nutritional value. They are all used in small quantities, to add flavour or for their nutritional or therapeutic properties, with other bulkier base juices. Generally you will add one quarter juice made from green leaves to three-quarters juice made from other ingredients.

All dark green leafy vegetables are good sources of magnesium and betacarotene, and many are also rich in iron. This group has important health qualities. They are all rich in compounds such as sulphurophanes, which are responsible for the vegetables' slightly bitter taste, and indole-3-carbinol, which is believed to have cancer-inhibiting properties.

Preparing and juicing leafy and brassica vegetables
To juice leafy and brassica vegetables, you will need a juicer (centrifugal or masticating), a chopping board and a sharp knife.

Loose, leafy vegetables Separate out the leaves and wash thoroughly. Cut away any that are discoloured but keep the outer leaves as they are richer in nutrients than the interior ones. Do not discard the cores of lettuce or any leaf stems.

Tightly packed leaves Vegetables, such as chicory (Belgian endive) or Chinese leaves (Chinese cabbage), should be washed, then quartered or chopped into an appropriate size to pass through the neck of the machine. Cut broccoli and cauliflower into florets and wash the pieces thoroughly. The cores can also be juiced.

To extract the maximum juice It is best to alternate putting leaves through the machine with a hard vegetable or fruit such as carrot or apple. This keeps the machine working efficiently to extract the maximum juice.

Cabbages and brussels sprouts
Dark green cabbage is the best choice for juicing as it is nutrient-rich. White cabbage is its poor relation, nutritionally speaking. Red cabbage generally tastes better when cooked, but if it is used for juicing the lovely purple colour will dominate your blend. Cabbage lends a surprisingly light, green taste to juices as long as the quantity of cabbage used does not overwhelm the blend. About one-eighth to one-quarter cabbage is the right quantity in any juice. Brussels sprouts, which are really just mini-cabbages, taste similar to cabbages when juiced but are slightly more nutty.

Therapeutic uses Using the dark green, outer leaves is important if you want to obtain the maximum level of nutrients. Along with the rest of the brassica family, cabbages are regarded as anti-cancer vegetables. Cabbage juice is also a powerful gut and ulcer healer. It should not be used excessively by people with underactive thyroids because cabbages are known to be goitrogenous and interfere with thyroid function.

These and other leafy vegetables should also be eaten in moderation by people on blood-thinning medication, as they are high in the blood-clotting factor, vitamin K. Cabbages and Brussels sprouts provide the richest vegetable sources of vitamin C.

Spinach
This has a mild, slightly peppery taste and lends a delightful green colour to juices. It is used in small quantities to add taste and nutrients to other sweeter bases, including some milder fruits such as apples or pears.

Therapeutic uses Spinach is very nutritious, high in betacarotene and folic acid, and rich in vitamins A and C. Its iron content is good although not as high as was once believed. It also contains the phytochemicals xeaxanthin and lutein, which are known to protect the eyes against ageing.

Above: Brussels sprouts should be juiced in small quantities only.

Above: Known as a superfood, broccoli is packed with iron and vitamin C.

Cauliflower and broccoli

These vegetables should have tightly packed, firm heads, showing no signs of wilt or discoloration. They are both available in more exotic forms, such as purple sprouting broccoli and cauliflower hybrids, and these can also be juiced, although these varieties can be expensive. Broccoli tastes slightly bitter while cauliflower is creamy. They are best used in small quantities with other milder flavours such as carrot or beetroot (beet).

Therapeutic uses Along with cabbage and Brussels sprouts, these are thought to be anti-cancer foods, and they are powerful additions to juices. They are not goitrogenous but are high in vitamin K. Broccoli is a good source of vitamin C.

Lettuce

There are many types of lettuce available. It is easier to juice firm rather than softer leaves. Most varieties lend a slightly bitter taste to juices, so should only be used in small quantities. It works well in either vegetable or fruit blends.

Therapeutic uses Lettuce is well known for its soporific, calming and sleep-inducing qualities. Very rich in asparagine, which is also found in asparagus, it has a slight laxative and digestive cleansing effect.

Kale and watercress

Both of these vegetables are strong tasting; kale is slightly bitter while watercress has a peppery flavour, so add only small amounts to juices. They are best used alongside other vegetable juices.

Therapeutic uses Watercress and kale are nutrient powerhouses, and are used extensively in therapeutic juicing. Excellent sources of magnesium, calcium and iron, watercress is also rich in sulphur, which is good for the hair and nails.

Other leafy vegetables

There are many different types of leafy vegetables. Slightly bitter or peppery leaves include radicchio, rocket (arugula), Swiss chard, chicory (Belgian endive) and endive (US chicory). These are best when used in small quantities and mixed with other vegetable juices. Sweeter tasting leaves include Chinese leaves (Chinese cabbage) and pak choi (bok choy) – these combine well with both vegetable and fruit juices.

Above: All green-leafed vegetables are full of minerals and nutrients but should be mixed with other vegetables.

SUPERTASTERS

It has been identified that at least one quarter of people are "supertasters" and have a very acute sense of taste, particularly for bitter and sour flavours. These people find that foods such as grapefruit, broccoli and Brussels sprouts are so bitter that they are unpleasant.

The result is that "supertasters" eat fewer vegetables to the point where it might impact on their health. Juicing is ideal for this group, as bitter tastes can be masked by sweeter and milder flavours from healthy sources.

Therapeutic uses Leaves are excellent sources of minerals, and darker ones contain lots of carotenoids, which help to neutralize free radicals. Bitter-tasting leaves contain chemicals that are thought to have liver, gall bladder and digestive cleansing properties.

Wild greens

Look around when you are out on a walk and you will be able to identify a number of wild greens. In times gone by everyone was familiar with these free foods and they were incorporated into many dishes. It is fairly easy to find dandelion, sorrel and nettles, and watercress can also be found in some areas. Before gathering these plants make sure you have identified them correctly and check that they have not been sprayed with weed killers.

Therapeutic uses Wild greens are traditionally used in tonics to cure anaemia. Dandelion leaves are used as a nerve tonic and also help to balance acid/alkaline levels, which makes them useful in arthritic conditions. Nettles are believed to be useful in combating the symptoms of hay fever, and they are also thought to be helpful in relieving rheumatism and settling nervous eczema.

Vegetable fruits

Some vegetables are actually the fruit of the plant, although they are not sweet in the way that we usually think of fruit. If allowed to ripen on the vine they are all exceptionally rich in various nutrients.

Preparing and juicing vegetable fruits

You will need a chopping board, a sharp knife, a spoon, a fork, a blender or food processor and a juicer (masticating or centrifugal).

Preparing avocados Make sure the avocado is ripe and yields slightly to pressure applied to the skin. Cut the avocado in half lengthways, ease the two halves apart and scoop out the stone (pit) with a spoon. Scoop out the flesh and place it in a blender or food processor with other ingredients. (Avocados are too soft to put in a juicer.)

You could also mash the flesh using a fork and stir it into a blend by hand.

Juicing (bell) peppers Cut the pepper in half lengthways, then cut away the stem, pips (seeds) and pith. Wash under running water to remove any remaining pips, then push the flesh through a juicer.

Skinning tomatoes These can be juiced whole or skinned first. To skin tomatoes, place them in a heatproof bowl and pour boiling water over them. Leave to soak for 2–3 minutes. Lift the tomatoes out, nick the skin with the point of a knife and it should begin to peel back. Peel off the loosened skin. Blend the tomatoes in a blender or food processor.

Avocados

When properly ripe, avocados are rich and slightly nutty tasting. They lend a creamy texture to juices and can be used to thicken a blend as an alternative to milk. They combine well with most vegetable juices – adding a little lemon juice will help cut through the richness and will slow down discoloration.

Therapeutic uses Avocados are an excellent source of oleic acid, which is associated with heart health. They are also full of vitamin E, which is essential for healthy skin.

Peppers

Although they come in a variety of colours, (bell) peppers are all the same vegetable – green peppers are simply unripe red peppers. Peppers do not ripen much after picking, so they don't change colour or become sweeter. The taste of yellow, orange and red peppers is similarly sweet, while green ones have a slightly more bitter flavour.

Peppers can dominate a juice and so are best used in small quantities. They are ideal combined with tomato juice.

Therapeutic uses Peppers are one of the richest sources of vitamin C, so they provide support for the immune system. Yellow, orange and red peppers also contain high levels of the antioxidant betacarotene.

Below: Avocados contain plenty of vitamin E, making them good for the skin.

Tomatoes

Mild-tasting tomatoes are sweet when ripe and acidic when unripe. Select vine-ripened tomatoes for the best flavour. Tomatoes mix well with most other vegetables and fruits. They are often used as a base juice as they are abundant and versatile.

Therapeutic uses Tomatoes are a rich source of lycopene, which has stronger antioxidant properties than betacarotene. They are also thought to have anti-cancer properties.

Left: For the best flavour, store tomatoes at room temperature.

Squash vegetables

The high water content of these vegetables makes them ideal for juicing in a centrifugal or masticating juicer. Cucumbers are available all year round and the best variety to use for juicing is the English (hothouse) cucumber. Courgettes (zucchini) are also available all year round, but are at their best in the summer, and other squashes only appear in the autumn. Cucumbers and courgettes should be stored in the refrigerator, but other squashes may be kept for up to a week or two in cool, dry conditions.

Preparing and juicing squash vegetables
To juice squash vegetables, you will need a juicer (either centrifugal or masticating), a clean chopping board and a sharp knife.

Preparing cucumbers and courgettes
Wash the skin, using a scrubbing brush if the vegetables are waxed. There is no need to peel or seed them, but do so if you prefer. Cut into large chunks and push through the juicer. You could also blend cucumbers in a blender or food processor as they contain so much water.

Right: Courgette skin contains valuable nutrients so don't peel before juicing.

Juicing squashes Cut large squashes, such as butternut and pumpkin, in half and scoop out most of the pips (seeds), leaving some to go through the juicer, if you like. Slice away the peel, then cut the flesh into large chunks and push through the juicer.

Cucumber and courgette
When juiced, all cucumbers are mild and tasty, although small cucumbers have the best flavour. Ideal for using as a base juice, they mix well with both vegetables and fruit. Courgettes (zucchini) are similar to cucumbers when juiced, but not quite as sweet.

Therapeutic uses The nutrients of cucumbers and courgettes are mainly concentrated in the skin, which is why you should leave it on. If this is too bitter, experiment with peeling half the skin. These vegetables have a strong diuretic action and help to lower high blood pressure. They support healthy hair and nail growth, and also help relieve the symptoms of rheumatism.

> **JUICY SOUP**
> Raw vegetable juices can be used very successfully as soups. Either enjoy them cold in the summer, garnished with a dollop of cream or yogurt and chopped fresh herbs, or warm them through (but do not boil) in the winter months.
>   Gazpacho, which is made with raw tomatoes, cucumber and (bell) peppers, is the classic soup made in this way.

Pumpkin and butternut squash
Both of these squashes produce a juice with a surprisingly sweet and nutty taste, but it is not a juice that you would want to drink on its own. Mix one-quarter pumpkin or squash juice with three-quarters other vegetable juice, such as carrot or cucumber, along with something else to give it a bit of a zing – perhaps a bit of onion.

Therapeutic uses Be sure to include some of the pips in the juice as they are high in zinc and iron. As with all the vegetables in this family they have a kidney-supporting and anti-water-retention action and are also powerhouses of carotenoid antioxidants.

Above: Pumpkins produce a sweet, nutty juice that is best mixed with other flavours.

Pod, shoot and bulb vegetables

All of these vegetables need to be put through a juicer. They all produce fairly strong tasting juices which should be combined with other vegetables. Pods and bulbs share the common trait that they, along with seeds, are potential plants. This means that all the goodness for the growing plant is stored in the pod or bulb ready for use, so you get many extra nutritional benefits. Shoots are also highly nutritious because they are at the stage of growth before a fully-fledged plant develops – they are fantastically rich in nutritional power for the growing plant.

Preparing and juicing pod, shoot and bulb vegetables

To juice pod, shoot and bulb vegetables, you will need a juicer (centrifugal or masticating), a chopping board and a sharp knife.

Preparing pods French (green) beans, broad (fava) beans, runner beans and mangetout (snow peas) do not need any preparation other than ensuring that they are clean. They do not require stringing or trimming as the juicer will simply turn the undesirable parts of the vegetables into pulp.

Preparing bulbs Pull off the outer leaves and wash these vegetables thoroughly before juicing, then cut into chunks the right size for your machine. It is not essential to remove the outer leaves or skin from onions, spring onions (scallions), leeks, fennel and celery, but they must be washed thoroughly as they tend to get quite dirty.

Juicing shoots Except for globe artichokes, all of these vegetables can simply be cleaned and juiced as they are. For alfalfa and cress, this will probably mean cutting the shoots from the root as the roots are likely to be embedded in soil. You will need to alternate shoot vegetables with hard vegetables, such as carrots, otherwise no juice will come out.

Preparing globe artichokes Remove the woody stem, then cut the rest of the flower into chunks and push through the juicer.

Beans and mangetout

Choose firm, crisp beans – choices include broad (fava), runner and French (green) beans. Avoid any that have been pre-trimmed or that are going soft. Buying local produce in season is the best option, because out of season beans are usually imported from countries where there might not be any regulations regarding chemical sprays. With the exception of mangetout (snow peas), which make a fairly mild and sweet juice, beans do not taste great when juiced – you will want to mix them with other vegetables.

Therapeutic uses Traditional herbal uses of pod vegetables are as a stimulant for the nervous system, for convalescence, to treat gout and to help support the insulin-producing ability of the pancreas.

Fennel and celery

These two bulb vegetables make very useful juices. Their tastes are fairly strong so they are best added to other juices, such as carrot, apple or pear, at a ratio of about one-fifth fennel or celery to four-fifths other juice. Fennel tastes of aniseed, and juiced celery, when combined with other juices, does not taste nearly as strong as the raw vegetable. Buy firm, pale green produce for the best flavours.

Therapeutic uses The cleansing actions of these two bulb vegetables are similar, and they are excellent for supporting the liver and gall bladder. Celery also has a strong diuretic action and is often used to calm the nervous system, while fennel is used to manage flatulence and nausea. When combined with carrot juice, fennel is a traditional remedy for failing eyesight. It is also used to ward off headaches and migraines, and some people believe it is helpful in alleviating menstrual and menopausal symptoms.

Onions and leeks

All onions, including shallots, spring onions (scallions) and even red (Italian) onions, produce strong tasting juices. You only need to add a tiny quantity to a general vegetable juice. Leek juice is not as strong as onion juice but has a similar taste. One of the

Left: Fennel produces a strong aniseed juice that can be overpowering.

Left: Leeks are a member of the onion family with similar healing properties.

problems with onions, as with garlic, is that they can leave a residual taste on the mesh of the machine, meaning that extra cleaning is needed. Running half a lemon through the machine can help to mop up the scent.

Therapeutic uses These bulb vegetables have renowned healing qualities. Onions are recommended for their immune-boosting qualities whenever you have a cold or the flu. They are also antibacterial and antiseptic – leeks have similar but milder actions.

Asparagus

A shoot vegetable, asparagus is available in the spring. It combines well with other vegetables but is not suitable to drink on its own.

Therapeutic uses Asparagus is used as a traditional remedy for kidney problems. The alkaloid asparagine, which is also found in potatoes and beetroot (beet), stimulates the kidneys but also turns urine a dark colour with a distinctive smell. This is not something to worry about, it is simply an indication of its successful diuretic effect.

Beansprouts, cress and alfalfa

You can buy beansprouts and cress in most large supermarkets, and alfalfa may be sourced in health food shops. Otherwise you can buy seeds and sprout them yourself (see right). They all give fairly strong tasting, peppery juices, so need to be mixed with other vegetable juices to tone down their flavour. They are probably easier to use in salads than in juices, but some people like to juice them for their distinctive taste.

Therapeutic uses These shoot vegetables have lots of nutritional benefits. Beansprouts are high in many minerals and vitamins, while cress is a member of the brassica family and therefore is believed to provide the same anti-cancer health benefits. Alfalfa has high levels of vitamins A, C and K, but should not be used often because it is high in a compound called canavanine, which is believed to aggravate rheumatoid arthritis.

Below: Beansprouts produce a distinctive, peppery juice.

Below: Mix asparagus juice with other vegetables for the best flavour.

SPROUT YOUR OWN
Leguminous beans, pulses, lentils and peas are not suitable for juicing, but they can be soaked and sprouted and then juiced.

1 Put one type of pulse in a large glass jar. Pour in a generous amount of cold water and leave to soak for 24 hours. Discard the water, rinse the beans under cold running water and drain in a sieve.

2 Put the damp beans back in the jar. Cover with a square of cloth, securing with an elastic band.

3 Leave the beans in a dark, warm place and repeat the rinsing and draining twice a day for 3–4 days.

4 When the beans have sprouted, put them on a windowsill for 24 hours until the shoots turn green. They are now ready for juicing.

Globe artichoke

The globe artichoke is actually a flower related to the thistle. The heart of the globe and the soft part of the petals attached to the middle are the parts that are normally eaten, but you can juice the whole vegetable, minus any woody parts.

Therapeutic uses The globe artichoke has cleansing and diuretic actions, and is often used to help with liver complaints. It can be used as an effective pick-me-up after festive occasions or parties.

Natural flavourings and health supplements

Herbs and spices have been used for many years for flavouring food, as well as for health and healing purposes. Some of the traditional herbal remedies that have developed over the centuries are now being confirmed as active compounds, and treatments are being refined.

Culinary herbs

They are so familiar in our everyday cuisine, it is easy to forget that culinary herbs have important health properties. Most fresh herbs go well with vegetable juices; they should be put through a juicer with hard ingredients so the machine does not become clogged up. Alternatively, they can be steeped in the juice, but don't wait too long to drink it or the value of the juice's nutrients will begin to decrease. Fresh herbs can also be finely chopped and added as a garnish. Mint and lemon balm work very well with fruit juices. Lavender flowers, borage and fresh rosemary may also be used in some fruit blends.

Above: If possible, pick fresh mint from your garden for the best flavour.

Basil Fresh basil has a pungent, peppery flavour and a sweet aroma. It is known as a soporific herb because it is very relaxing. Put it through a juicer, followed by a hard vegetable, or crush the leaves using a mortar and pestle. Alternatively, make a tisane with hot water and add this to a juice or blend.

Mint There are many varieties of this prolific herb, which is also a potent digestive aid. Flavours vary but all mints have a strong, sweet aroma and cool aftertaste. Make a tisane and use it to dilute juices.

Left: Basil can either be juiced or used as a tasty garnish.

Right: Dill works well with carrot juice and aids digestion.

Parsley There are two basic varieties of parsley – curly and flat leaf, the latter having the stronger flavour. Use it sparingly. This herb is very rich in a number of nutrients including calcium and betacarotene. It can be put through a juicer, but it must be followed by a hard vegetable, such as carrot.

Chives These are a member of the onion family, and they provide a mild onion flavour. They have the same immune-supporting benefits as all types of onion and leeks.

Rosemary This herb acts as a stimulant to the nervous and circulatory systems and is also thought to relieve indigestion. As an infusion, it is traditionally used to relieve colds and headaches.

Sage Fresh sage has a pungent, slightly bitter aroma. It is an effective alleviator of sweating as a side effect of menopausal hot flushes. Make a tisane with hot water and use to dilute juices. Do not use sage if breastfeeding as it can reduce milk flow.

Dill With its distinctive yet mild caraway-like flavour, dill marries well with all green juices and carrot juice. It is a calming herb and is known to be a soporific. It also aids digestion.

Juniper berries These have antiseptic properties and can be used to treat urinary tract infections such as cystitis. Juniper berries should not be used if you are pregnant or suffer from kidney infections, as they can cause the uterus to contract.

Culinary spices

As with culinary herbs, these are easy to overlook because they are used in such small quantities in cooking. However, they add wonderful flavourings to many juices and blends and have extremely important therapeutic benefits too.

Horseradish
This pungent root is a potent sinus clearer. Grate a little and add as required to juices but do not put horseradish through a juicer.

Chilli Ranging from fairly mild to fiery hot, it is believed that chilli spices help to build up a strong immune system and may chase off imminent colds and fevers. Use only a tiny amount in vegetable juices and do not put through a juicer or you may end up with chilli-flavoured fruit juices. Grind in a mortar using a pestle, and avoid using the seeds unless you have a very strong constitution.

Above: Remove the seeds from chillies before juicing, unless you are a real fan of hot and spicy blends.

Cumin Strong and nutty, yet slightly bitter, cumin is emerging as one of the most potent antioxidant-rich "super-spices" around. The active compound is curcumin. Dry-roast the seeds, then grind in a mortar using a pestle and add to drinks.

Left: Grate a little horseradish into a juice to add extra spice.

Ginger Fresh or ground ginger is pungent and quite hot. It is a warming spice that naturally lends itself to both fruit and vegetable juices, complementing citrus fruits particularly well. Use the fresh root if you can, otherwise add ground ginger or a supplement.

Above: Root ginger is hot and spicy so use small quantities.

Nutmeg Sweet and aromatic, this is a warming spice, but do not use too much as it can have very unpleasant hallucinogenic effects.

Cardamom These pods can help to relieve vomiting and indigestion. Cardamom sweetens the breath when chewed and is also used to treat colds.

GARLIC
This pungent bulb is regarded as a "super-herb" by juicing fans.

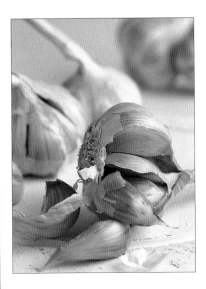

It is a potent blood thinner and immune-system supporter. It is best not to put it through the juicer as you will never get rid of the taste. Instead, pulverize it using a mortar and pestle and add just a tiny bit directly to the juice.

Star anise With a distinct aniseed flavour, star anise is useful for treating inflammation of the respiratory tract, loosening phlegm and calming peptic ulcers. It is also used to treat cramps. Grind the seed and add to a juice.

Cloves The oil from cloves is potent and is traditionally used to numb the gums during dental treatment or to relieve the pain for young children who are teething. Its strong antibacterial properties can be harnessed by making a tisane and adding to drinks, although the flavour of cloves will dominate any other ingredients.

Cinnamon A tree bark, cinnamon helps to soothe unsettled stomachs, can be used to revive your appetite, eases digestive tract spasms and alleviates flatulence. Grind the fresh spice and add half a teaspoon to juices or smoothies – the flavour complements banana, pear and carrot.

Other useful herbs, spices and supplements

It is easy to add medicinal herbs to blends and juices. Before you do so, however, make sure there are no contra-indications or interactions with any medications you are currently taking – check with your medical practitioner.

Chamomile This herb has an apple-like scent that belies its pungent, rather bitter flavour. It is a calming herb and is very safe even for children. Use a chamomile teabag, available from larger supermarkets and health food shops, or simply infuse 4–5 fresh flower-heads, then add the infusion to your juice. Chamomile should not be used by anybody who has an allergy to ragwort.

Ginkgo This is excellent for the circulation and is thought to be good for boosting memory. Simply empty a capsule into your blend and mix thoroughly.

Above: Rosehips are usually made into powder or tablets.

Rosehip The reddish-orange fruit of the rose has extremely high levels of vitamin C. Rosehips are usually sold in powdered form or as tablets. Add a small amount of powder to your blend (check the packet for quantities), crumble a tablet in, or make a rosehip tisane and add it to your juice.

Ginseng A sweet liquorice-flavoured root, this is used as an energy booster, and some people even believe it is a libido enhancer. It is also reputed to help with the treatment of high blood pressure. Available in health food shops, simply empty a capsule or sprinkle some of the powder (according to instructions) into your blend.

Milk thistle This is an important liver-supporting herb which marries well with globe artichoke. It can help prevent damage to the liver from alcohol. Empty one or two capsules into your blend.

Liquorice This root has a mild steroid effect and can help relieve the symptoms of most allergies. However, it should not be used alongside steroid medication or by anyone who suffers from high blood pressure as it can cause the retention of sodium and the depletion of potassium. Liquorice is available as a root from most health food shops. Grind the root with a mortar and pestle and sprinkle a little into your blend.

Left: Liquorice can help to relieve allergies.

Echinacea This is a classic immune-boosting herb often found as a supplement in fruit or herbal teas. It is usually taken in the winter to stave off cold and flu symptoms. Echinacea is widely available in tincture form and it is easy to add a few drops to your blend according to instructions, or you could make a tisane with hot water and add this to your drink.

A NATURAL HEALER

Grown from the wholewheat grain, wheatgrass has been recognized for centuries for its general healing qualities. It is a powerful detoxifier and cleanser and a rich source of B vitamins and vitamins A, C and E, as well as all the known minerals. Its vibrant green colour comes from chlorophyll (known as nature's healer), which works directly on the liver to eliminate harmful toxins. Once it is juiced, wheatgrass should be consumed within 15 minutes, preferably on an empty stomach. Wheatgrass juice can be powerful in its effect, and some people may feel dizzy or nauseous the first time they drink it. Sip small amounts until your body gets used to it.

Left: Kelp is a form of seaweed and is packed full of vitamins and minerals.

Other health ingredients

Once you realize that supplements can be added to juices, checking for contraindications first, you can become quite adventurous. It is easy to do and beats popping endless vitamin and supplement pills every day.

Brewer's yeast Very rich in B-vitamins and minerals such as iron, zinc, magnesium and potassium, Brewer's yeast also supplies a form of protein. It has a very strong flavour but this becomes a pleasant nutty taste when blended with fruits or vegetables.

Bee pollen This is a useful immune booster and can also help relieve the symptoms of hay fever.

Spirulina and wheatgrass One of the main superjuice ingredients, spirulina is rich in a wide variety of nutrients and vitamins. Both spirulina and wheatgrass are often used as an ingredient in supercharged, healthy juices. They are readily available in powdered form and can easily be added to juices, but you could create your own free supply by growing it at home.

Vitamin C It is extremely easy to add a little vitamin C to your daily juice, whether you use a squeeze of lemon or lime juice, a powder sprinkled into your blend or a tablet crumbled in. A non-acidic version of vitamin C, such as magnesium ascorbate, is gentler on the stomach than most others. Make sure you choose one with bioflavonoids for maximum effect.

Kelp This form of seaweed is naturally very rich in minerals, such as calcium, copper, iron, magnesium, potassium and zinc, B vitamins and betacarotene. It also contains high levels of iodine, which is vital for encouraging the normal functioning of the thyroid gland, but it should not be taken by those with an overactive thyroid. Seaweeds, such as kelp, have long been used to treat those suffering from common colds, constipation, arthritis and rheumatism.

Sambucol (elderberry extract) During the winter when berries are not readily available or are too expensive, simply add a teaspoonful of sambucol to your juices. This is a rich source of proanthocyanins and will give your immune system a well-deserved boost.

Aloe vera The fleshy succulent plant called aloe vera provides two main products: aloe vera gel, which is used externally for soothing skin irritations and sunburn, and aloe vera juice, which can be added to your juices and blends. Aloe vera juice is reputed to help relieve the symptoms of arthritis, ME and eczema, and is also renowned for soothing and rebuilding the digestive tract. Make sure you choose a certified product with a guaranteed amount of active compounds and add a dose, according to the instructions on the packet, to your blend.

FATS AND OILS

Healthy fats are good sources of essential fatty acids, which can help to clear up a range of complaints including dry skin, listless hair and low energy levels.

Lecithin This is an emulsifier derived from soya, which is ideal to add to a juice or blend before any fats. Add 5–10ml/1–2 tsp to the ingredients in a blender. It tastes pleasant and helps fat digestion.

Evening primrose oil This can be helpful in alleviating pre-menstrual problems and for allergies. Pierce a capsule with a pin and squeeze into your juice or blend.

Walnut oil This oil has a pleasant nutty taste and is light so it does not overwhelm juices. It is a good source of both omega-3 and omega-6 fatty acids, which are useful for nervous and hormonal health. Add 5–10ml/1–2 tsp to a glass of juice. Store in the refrigerator.

Flax seed oil A "super-oil", this has high levels of omega-3 fatty acids. Add 5–10ml/1–2 tsp to your juice. Store in the refrigerator.

Above: Walnut oil has a nutty flavour that works well in most juices.

Nuts and seeds

These powerhouses of nutrition are excellent sources of protein, fibre, vitamin E, and the minerals zinc, iron, selenium, magnesium and calcium. They also provide the vitamin-like oils called essential fatty acids, which are required for a healthy nervous system, hormone balance and cell structure as well as having potent anti-inflammatory effects which help to control a number of diseases. However, for all their health benefits, some people are allergic to nuts and seeds – peanuts and sesame seeds being the main culprits – so check before offering a blend to someone. Particular care needs to be taken when making drinks for children, who may not be aware that they are allergic.

Below: Pistachio nuts add a delicate green colour to blends, while pecan nuts combine particularly well with banana.

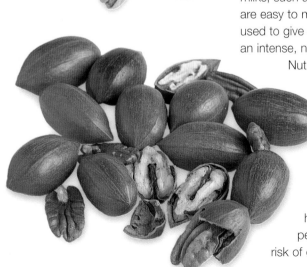

You can use nuts and seeds in juices and blends in a number of ways. They can be ground in a small nut grinder (available separately or as an attachment for food processors). Or you could use a mortar and pestle to grind them. Add them to creamy drinks and juices and mix well. Chopped nuts and seeds also make a pretty decoration when sprinkled on top of smoothies or milkshakes.

Nuts

Choose whole unsalted nuts for making blends and smoothies, and always check the expiry date on packets. After opening a packet of nuts, store any that are left over in a glass jar with a screwtop lid in the refrigerator to keep them fresh. Choose from walnuts, Brazil nuts, pistachio nuts, pecan nuts, hazelnuts or almonds to add flavour and crunch to blended drinks. Peanuts are not really nuts but legumes, a member of the bean family, which is a part of the reason why some people are allergic to them.

You could use various smooth nut butters, which are available from supermarkets or health food shops, to flavour drinks instead of whole nuts. Add them directly to the blend and mix thoroughly. Delicious nut and seed milks, such as almond milk (see right) are easy to make at home and can be used to give smoothies or milkshakes an intense, nutty taste.

Nuts have been shown to have important therapeutic benefits when used to replace other fatty ingredients in the diet. For instance, if you eat walnuts regularly, this can help to reduce the risk of heart disease, while eating peanuts could reduce the risk of contracting diabetes.

MAKING ALMOND MILK

This method can be used for almost any other nuts and seeds as well as almonds.

1 In a heatproof bowl, cover 115g/4oz/1 cup whole almonds with boiling water and leave to stand for 5 minutes. Drain, discarding the water.

2 The skins will now be loose. Squeeze the almonds gently out of their skins.

3 Place the skinned almonds in a blender with 250ml/8fl oz/1 cup water and blend roughly.

4 Add another 250ml/8fl oz/1 cup water and continue blending until you have a thick paste.

5 Gradually add more water until you achieve the consistency you require, somewhere between cream and milk.

6 Blend until no residue remains or strain the almond milk to remove any residue.

Seeds

Buy seeds ready hulled in small packets and keep them as you would nuts. Choose from pumpkin seeds, sunflower seeds, pine nuts, linseeds (flax seeds) and sesame seeds.

Coconut is not really a nut, but a huge seed. It is high in saturated fats so it is best to limit the amount of coconut flesh or milk you use. Linseeds (flax seeds) are particularly rich in an important member of the omega-3 family of fatty acids. The culinary oil derived from linseeds is called flax seed oil. Sesame seeds are made into a thick, rich-tasting purée called tahini, which can be added in small amounts to blended drinks. Dark tahini, which uses the whole seed including the husk, is about ten times richer in calcium than light tahini, and turns it into a calcium-match for milk.

Above: Despite their name, pine nuts are actually a seed.

GRAINS AND FIBRE

When making juices and blends it is easy to sneak in extra healthy ingredients. Grains are excellent sources of B-complex vitamins, vitamin E, calcium, magnesium, iron, zinc and essential fatty acids.

Wheatgerm This comes as a coarse powder and it is easy to add 5ml/1 tsp to a smoothie blend.

Above: Add wheatgerm powder to your blends in small quantities.

Oatmeal Choose fine-ground oatmeal and add 10–15ml/2–3 tsp to a blend, or to milk with some honey for a night-time drink. Oatmeal provides gentle soluble fibre, which is important for reducing cholesterol levels.

Above: Pudding rice works well as a thickener for blended drinks.

Rice Choose rice as a thickener for smoothies or shakes if you are allergic to wheat. Cooked pudding rice works well.

Bran and psyllium Bran is widely available, while psyllium can be bought from health food shops. Oatbran contains soluble fibre, which can help to reduce cholesterol levels. If you suffer from constipation, however, you may be tempted to try wheat bran. Many people with digestive problems find bran too abrasive, so a better option is to add 5–10ml/ 1–2 tsp of psyllium to a blend.

Above: Coconut is delicious but extremely high in saturated fat.

Dairy and dairy alternatives

Adding milk, yogurts, dairy or milk substitutes to blended drinks results in a more luxurious and creamy, though not necessarily more fattening, treat. Milk is calcium-rich (even skimmed milk) and many alternative milks are also now enriched with calcium. You can keep a lid on calorie and fat counts by choosing low-fat versions. Dairy substitutes are useful for people with dairy intolerances, meaning they can still add creamy texture to smoothies and milkshakes.

Milk

For a rich and creamy taste choose full cream (whole) milk. Most people, however, need to avoid too much saturated fat in their diet and would be better advised to use skimmed or semi-skimmed (low-fat) milk.

Therapeutic uses Milk is one of the richest sources of calcium available. Full cream milk is only usually advised for young children, who need the calories it provides to promote growth and bone health.

Below: Yogurt is available in many forms, both low-fat and full-fat. Natural yogurt is ideal, but you could experiment with low-fat flavoured yogurts.

Cream

For extra indulgence, use double (heavy) or single (light) cream, crème fraîche, mascarpone, smetana or, for a different taste, sour cream.

Therapeutic uses Cream is an excellent source of vitamin E, which helps to maintain healthy skin, but it is very high in calories so should be used in moderation.

Yogurt

For making shakes or smoothies thicker, yogurts are an extremely useful ingredient. Greek (US strained plain) yogurt is much thicker than standard varieties but has almost as many calories as cream, so it should not be used on a regular basis. Low-fat yogurts, including low-fat Greek yogurt, are readily available instead, so you can still indulge yourself without feeling too guilty. Fruit yogurts can add interesting flavours to fruity blends.

Therapeutic uses Yogurt is rich in calcium and it is often suitable even for people who have a milk intolerance. Choosing live "bio" yogurt can help improve digestive tract health by providing healthy bacteria. High-fibre yogurts that have cholesterol-lowering properties are now available.

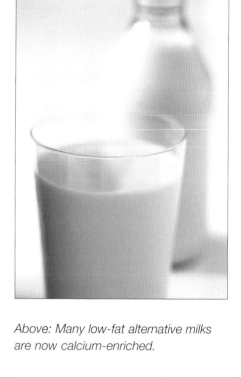

Above: Many low-fat alternative milks are now calcium-enriched.

ALTERNATIVE MILKS

Often used by people who have a dairy allergy, alternative milks are a good low-calorie option. The fats in most nut milks, except for coconut, are healthy polyunsaturated fats.

Soya milk Choose the calcium-enriched variety of soya milk if you are using it instead of cow's milk on a regular basis.

Rice milk This has a thinner and lighter consistency than cow's milk, but a deliciously sweet flavour. Vanilla- and chocolate-flavoured rice milks are also available.

Oat milk This alternative to cow's milk is extremely rich and has a creamy, smooth taste.

Nut milks Coconut milk is delicious but, because it has a very rich flavour, it is best if you either dilute it or use just a small amount. You can now buy almond milk and various other nut milks from most large supermarkets or health food shops.

Above: Use real strawberry ice cream to make a traditional milkshake.

Frozen ingredients

Ice creams, sorbets (sherbets), frozen yogurts and soya ices can all be scooped straight from the freezer to make a delicious old-fashioned shake.
Therapeutic uses Dairy ice cream is a good source of calcium, although it is high in calories, but non-dairy ice creams and sorbets do not have the benefit of calcium.

Low-fat creamy ingredients

Fromage frais (cream cheese) and plain cottage cheese can both be bought in low-fat versions and used as creamy thickeners, as can buttermilk which is slightly sour tasting.
Therapeutic uses These are perfect for anybody on a calorie-controlled diet.

Tofu

Also known as soya bean curd and beancurd, tofu is available in three different textures: firm, medium-firm and silken. Naturally a fairly bland food with a slight nutty taste, it will affect the texture of drinks, but not the taste. Soft, silken tofu has the best texture for blending and adds a creamy thickness to the blend.
Therapeutic uses Tofu is an all-round healthy food – high in protein, low in saturated fats and calories, easy to digest and cholesterol-free. It has high levels of calcium and lots of vitamin E, which is important for maintaining healthy skin and helps protect against heart disease.

Below: Tofu is rich in hormone-balancing phytoestrogens, which can help protect against some cancers.

EGGS

Raw eggs contain high levels of vitamin B_{12}, which is vital for the nervous system. Eggs are often used as the basis of protein shakes by sports enthusiasts or in hangover remedies to kick-start the system. Before using raw eggs in a blend, you should be aware of the following:

• Raw egg white binds with the B-vitamin biotin and, if overused, can lead to a deficiency of this nutrient.
• Pregnant women, children, the sick or elderly, or those with an impaired immune system should not consume raw eggs, because of the risk of salmonella. (While chickens are often routinely vaccinated for salmonella in some countries, there is still a residual risk from unvaccinated flocks.)
• Eggs have a high cholesterol content, contained in the yolk. People who have high cholesterol levels may benefit from limiting their egg intake to five a week. However, as we make most of the cholesterol in the body (cholesterol is needed for cell maintenance) and this is adversely affected by a high saturated fat intake, it is more beneficial to reduce saturated fats from butter, cheese and meat.
• Eggs that have been produced to contain high levels of omega-3 fatty acids are now widely available and these could make an important contribution to heart health.

Above: Raw eggs can thicken blends nicely but it is not safe for everybody to eat them.

Sweeteners and other flavourings

We are all naturally attracted to sweet-tasting foods. The advantage of juices and smoothies is that it is possible to give in to that craving occasionally, with some indulgent additions, and yet still know that you are benefiting from the healthy basic ingredients.

Many juices, whether made from fruit or vegetables, are naturally sweet, so you may find that you need to dilute them slightly to reduce their sweetness. This can easily be done by adding one-third to one-half water – either still or sparkling, according to taste. You could also add a variety of milky ingredients. Adding water or milk will ensure that blood sugar levels rise more slowly. Children should always drink juices that are diluted to reduce the impact on their teeth.

If a juice, smoothie or milkshake is not sweet enough, you could simply add some sugar – white, brown or muscovado (molasses) – or flavoured syrups, such as vanilla, or fruit cordials. There are, however, many other sweeteners that can be used.

Honey
Different honeys have varying tastes, depending on which type of pollen the bees have gathered. Popular choices are lavender or apple blossom honey, which have a fragrant sweetness. Manuka honey is renowned for its health-promoting properties; it is anti-bacterial, making it ideal for sore throats. Honey should not be fed to children under the age of 12 months as it could cause botulism, a type of food poisoning that can be fatal.

Fructose
Instead of using table sugar (sucrose) you could use fructose (a totally natural fruit sugar). This has a lower Glycaemic Index (GI) score than sucrose so can be used in moderation by diabetics. (The GI is a measure of how fast a carbohydrate enters the blood stream as sugar. The higher the score, the less healthy the carbohydrate.) Fructose is sweeter than table sugar so do not use as a direct substitution in drinks.

Blackstrap molasses
During the refining of sugar, the juice squeezed from the cane or beet is boiled until syrupy and then the sugar crystals are extracted. There are three boilings, resulting in light molasses, then dark and finally blackstrap molasses, which is thick, dark and rather bitter. It is a rich source of calcium, iron and magnesium but only a little should be used.

Above: Blackstrap molasses is intensely sweet and so only a tiny bit is needed.

Above: Choose from many different flavours and types of honey.

Above: Liven up parties by adding a few shots of alcohol to your punchbowl.

Above: Try crumbling brownies on top of your favourite chocolate milkshake.

Above: When added to your blends, meringues give an irresistible crunch.

FOS (fructooligosaccharide)

This is a natural fibre found in bananas, Jerusalem artichokes, tomatoes, onions and many other fruits and vegetables. It looks like sugar and is almost as sweet but it has no effect on blood sugar levels. It can be found in health food shops. Using a moderate amount has a beneficial effect on digestive tract health as it promotes the growth of good bacteria, but too much FOS can lead to bloating.

Other flavourings

Many other ingredients and sweet additions can be included in smoothies. Health-promoting properties become less important here – everyone deserves to indulge themselves occasionally.

Coffee Freshly ground or instant, coffee is just the thing if you need a wake-up call with your morning blend. Try adding it to creamy blends to make a coffee-flavoured smoothie or shake. Use decaffeinated coffee if you are caffeine sensitive and, if you are feeling particularly virtuous, try using dandelion coffee, which is reputed to have liver-cleansing properties.

Chocolate This is an irresistible ingredient, whether melted, grated or in powder form. Dark (bittersweet) chocolate is the best for you as it is rich in iron and antioxidants, but for a milder flavour you should use milk chocolate. For a decadent finish, grate or shave chocolate on top of your smoothie – dark, plain (semisweet), milk or white, whichever you prefer.

Sweets (candies) Try adding sweets to the side of the glass as a decoration that is guaranteed to impress at a kid's party, or add them to the blender and blend them into the drink. Turkish delight or nougat are good choices, or you could serve a smoothie with an edible swizzle stick in the shape of a chocolate wand.

Cakes and cookies Brownies or meringues can be crumbled on top of smoothies or added to the blend for texture, and any other cakes or cookies can be used instead if they complement the drink you are serving. Amaretti provide a lovely almond accent, for example, which would be delicious with strawberry, apricot or peach-based blends, or try crunchy coconut macaroons sprinkled on top of a tropical fruit blend.

Alcohol Add a splash of alcohol to your favourite drinks when you just want to relax with a smoothie at the end of the day, or give your party juices a boost. Choose different drinks for their flavours, such as coffee, mint or orange liqueurs, or give your blend a real kick by adding a shot (or two) of brandy or whisky.

Above: Create a traditional, decadent milkshake with rich, dark chocolate.

Juicing and blending in a healthy diet

Following a healthy diet is one of the most fundamental ways in which you can ensure optimal energy levels, balanced moods, a zest for life and, of course, good general health. For overall wellbeing, it is also important to take sufficient exercise and to maintain a positive attitude to life.

What constitutes a healthy diet? Fresh fruit and vegetables are the most essential aspect – at least five portions a day – and drinking juices will keep you rehydrated as well as ensuring that you get the recommended amounts. These four easy-to-follow rules could help you develop a regime that will set you up for life.

1 Eat a wide variety of fresh foods to make sure you get all the vitamins and minerals you need.
2 Base your diet on fruits, vegetables, grains, legumes, nuts, seeds and eggs. If you are a meat-eater, always select lean cuts and restrict your intake of red meats. Fresh, unprocessed fish is always a healthier option.
3 Keep processed, salty, sugary or fatty foods to a minimum.
4 Drink sufficient water to stay hydrated: 1.5–2 litres/2½–4 pints/1½–2 quarts per day is the usual recommendation.

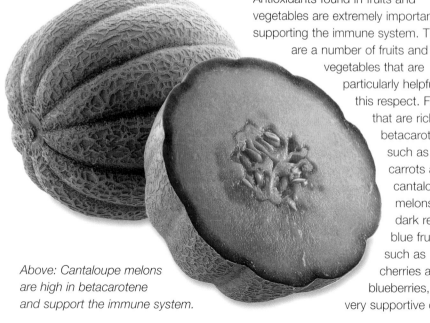

Above: Cantaloupe melons are high in betacarotene and support the immune system.

Therapeutic juicing

In order to receive the therapeutic benefits from juices, you will need to incorporate the suggested juice on a regular basis – daily, if possible. However, remember that therapeutic juicing is not intended to take the place of eating balanced, healthy meals, but should always be an addition to your health routine.

Juices have been used by herbalists, naturopaths and nutritionists for centuries to prevent illness and alleviate ailments. However, self-diagnosis and treatment of any serious condition is not really advisable, and you should always check with your health practitioner if any symptoms persist.

Their acidity and sugar levels mean that juices can have an eroding effect on teeth. To minimize this, it is best to consume them alongside meals. You can also reduce the effect by adding milk and dairy substitutes, which are more alkaline and so temper the acidic effect – calcium-rich choices are also tooth-friendly. Avoid brushing your teeth for an hour after drinking a juice as the enamel on the teeth needs time to harden again.

Immune system health and allergies

Antioxidants found in fruits and vegetables are extremely important in supporting the immune system. There are a number of fruits and vegetables that are particularly helpful in this respect. Foods that are rich in betacarotene, such as carrots and cantaloupe melons, and dark red or blue fruits, such as cherries and blueberries, are very supportive of the

THE POWER OF ANTIOXIDANTS

Antioxidants protect you against a number of diseases which are caused by free radicals. The plants actually make these antioxidants to protect themselves but when we eat those plants, we enjoy the benefits. Free radicals are largely a by-product of oxidization, such as when iron rusts or a cut apple turns brown. In humans this damage results in cataracts, inflammation, damage to blood vessels and cancer. Vitamins A, C and E are antioxidants but there are also thousands of phytonutrients, which are highly protective as well. Only plant foods give us these valuable nutrients and juicing is a way of ensuring that you give yourself a good level of protection.

immune system. Foods rich in vitamin C, such as blackcurrants and kiwi fruit, are also important. Additionally, specific compounds, such as resveratrol in grapes and lycopene in watermelons and tomatoes, are thought to help keep the immune system healthy.

The brassica family, which includes broccoli, cabbage, Brussels sprouts and cauliflower, are thought to be potent cancer fighters. Garlic, onions and leeks are all good weapons for fighting off colds, coughs and flu. If you find raw onion or garlic in juice a little too strong, try a delicious warm onion and garlic broth instead. Quince was traditionally used to help people through periods of convalescence, and it is still recommended by many people today.

Anyone with allergies, unless they are allergic to a particular fruit or vegetable, will benefit from at least five portions daily to strengthen their immune system and raise the threshold at which allergic reactions are triggered. Dark red and purple berries seem to be particularly effective in this respect.

*Right:
Quercitin,
found in onions,
is good for the lungs.*

Respiratory health

The delicate tissues of the respiratory tract can be strengthened and supported by using particular fruits and vegetables. Quercitin, which is found in apples and onions, has a strengthening effect on the lungs, and dark red and purple berries have potent lung supporting properties, which result from the high levels of proanthocyanins they contain.

Catarrh can often be reduced by avoiding dairy products, while the inclusion of garlic in juices and blends – and in your diet generally – will also help to reduce the build up of catarrh. Turnips have expectorant properties, and radish and horseradish, used in very small amounts, can also help to clear the sinuses.

People who suffer badly from hay fever may find that nettles are useful in helping to alleviate their symptoms.

Cleansing and urinary tract health

Keeping the body cleansed of toxins is an obvious way to maintain good health. General detoxing effects can be helped along by juicing fruits that are naturally high in pectin and/or ellagic acid, such as apples, strawberries and grapes.

Liver-supporting ingredients include globe artichoke, lemon and cranberry. Fennel juice helps to detoxify the liver,

and is also useful in helping to restore a general feeling of wellbeing. Radish helps to support the gall bladder, which is where bile is stored before being discharged into the duodenum, where it aids the emulsification and absorption of fats.

Juices that have a diuretic action, reducing water retention and stimulating the kidneys, include celery, cucumber, cranberry, dandelion, celeriac, fennel, strawberry, peach and watermelon. In the last case, leave the pips (seeds) in for extra potassium when juicing and throw in a piece of the rind for some extra nutrients. Asparagine, found in asparagus, also stimulates the kidneys and helps to purify the blood. It makes the urine turn a dark colour, with a distinctive smell, but this is not harmful and is actually an indication that it is doing its job properly.

If you suffer from cystitis or other urinary infections, drink plenty of fresh cranberry or blueberry juice. These juices are known to help prevent bacteria from adhering to the urinary tract. Garlic is also a potent antibacterial ingredient and may be useful in treating this unpleasant and painful condition.

Digestive health

A healthy digestive system is vital for optimal health and to ensure the maximum absorption of nutrients from foods. For both constipation and diarrhoea, add 5–10ml/1–2 tsp ground linseeds (flax seeds) or 5ml/1 tsp psyllium husks to a drink daily. Laxative effects can also be induced with plums, prunes, peaches, nectarines, figs or pears. Ginger is a traditional remedy for nausea, including morning sickness in early pregnancy.

Apples are high in pectin, malic acid and tannic acid, all of which help to normalize digestive function (and improve liver function). Fennel juice is excellent for most digestive conditions,

Above: Cranberry juice can help to relieve urinary tract infections.

Below: Apples are useful for aiding digestion and cleansing the liver.

Below: Cucumbers are full of the valuable mineral potassium.

while indigestion, impaired digestion and stomach ulcers respond well to pineapples or papayas. Cabbagin, a compound in cabbages, helps to heal the gut wall and, along with potato juice, is a useful remedy for ulcers. All fruits and vegetables are good sources of fibre, which helps to keep the bowels in good general health. Drinking smoothies rather than juices will increase your fibre intake, as the fibrous, pulpy part of the fruit is preserved in the drink.

Circulation and blood health

A healthy blood supply will deliver oxygen, the primary nutrient, to all of your cells. For general circulation and blood health, including arterial health, be sure to eat plenty of dark green leafy vegetables. These are rich in folic acid, which helps to lower levels of homocysteine, a substance that may be a contributor to osteoporosis. The bioflavonoids in citrus fruits, known as rutin and hesperidin, also support healthy blood vessels and so help to prevent varicose veins.

Raw beetroot (beet) and dandelion juices, along with dark green leafy vegetables, are traditionally used to combat anaemia, and if you combine these with citrus juice or tomato juice, this will serve to improve iron absorption. Potassium, which is found at fairly high levels in all fruit and vegetables, helps to lower blood pressure – watermelon, cucumber, grapes and bananas are especially good sources.

Reproductive and sexual health

The health of the next generation depends upon healthy parents. It is now recognized that both parents should ensure that they are in optimum health before conception. This can cause problems, because many women do not realize they are pregnant until a number of weeks after they have conceived, yet the very early stages of pregnancy are the most important for the development of a healthy baby.

For men, zinc is essential for healthy sperm and can be found in nuts and seeds. For women, folic acid is vital preconceptually and in the first trimester. It is used to help form the baby's cells, and there is now a proven link between folic acid deficiency and the incidence of neural tube defects in babies, such as spina bifida. Folic acid can be found in green leafy vegetables and in citrus fruit.

For older generations, a flagging libido may be revitalized by adding warming ginger and ginseng to juices or blends. Women with perimenopausal symptoms can try adding 50–90g/ 2–3½oz silken tofu or 300ml/ ½ pint/1¼ cups soya milk to drinks on a daily basis for their valuable phytoestrogens, as these mimic the action of the female hormone oestrogen.

Skeletal and muscular health

Looking after your bones is most important in your youth, when you build up maximum density, and in old age, when this density is declining. Weight-bearing exercise is extremely helpful in maintaining healthy bones.

Magnesium-rich foods are needed to help calcium utilization in bones – these include all types of green leafy vegetables, nuts and seeds. They are also good for alleviating muscular cramps, including menstrual cramps. Magnesium-rich juices or blends, taken on a daily basis, will help to improve bone health considerably.

Cucumber juice helps combat rheumatoid arthritis and many other juices are also useful in this respect, including cherry, grape, pineapple and dandelion. Rheumatic pain may be eased by adding some elderberry juice.

Milk, yogurt or calcium-enriched alternative milks added to blends or smoothies is an easy and delicious way to make sure you get enough calcium in your diet. Vitamin D, which is made in the skin, is vital for calcium use by bones and the best source is half an hour of sunlight exposure each day during spring and summer – although this is not always possible in some climates. If you are convalescing or susceptible to osteoporosis, add the contents of a vitamin D supplement to a juice every day.

Above: Seeds are rich in magnesium, which helps maintain healthy bones.

Above: Juice seedless black grapes when you want to unwind.

General health

Juices help to bring a healthy glow to your skin, a sparkle to your eyes and a glossy sheen to your hair, as well as putting a spring in your step.

Fruit and vegetables that are rich in vitamin C, such as citrus fruits, strawberries, blackcurrants, green (bell) peppers and cabbage, help to build collagen for general skin health, so add these to your juices regularly. A healthy intake of vitamin C has also been proven to prevent the damage that leads to cataracts forming in the lens of the eye. To help alleviate the symptoms of eczema, try adding a tablespoon of flax seed oil to your blends each day – you can help to emulsify it into the blend by adding a teaspoon of lecithin.

Eyes need betacarotene to maintain good health, and this antioxidant can be derived in large quantities from such ingredients as blueberries and spinach. Watercress is rich in sulphur, which helps with the healthy growth of hair and nails, while cucumbers and courgettes (zucchini) are also great for healthy nails.

Grapes have long been used as a traditional rest-cure, but if you want to boost your energy levels, pears, bananas, yams and sweet potatoes are all good choices to add to your blends – try them first thing in the morning to kick-start your system. Betacarotene-rich fruit and vegetables, such as apricots, carrots, cantaloupe melons, red peppers, squashes and spinach help to protect the skin against sun damage.

If you are on a calorie-controlled diet to aid weight loss, this can be speeded up by including filling, nutrient-rich, but low calorie juices based on fruits and vegetables. Drinking juices should help prevent you snacking through-out the day. Use fat-free dairy products instead of half-fat or full-fat ones – you will still get the same amount of calcium from these. However, if blood-sugar swings are a problem for you, dilute your juices or blends by half with water, always drink them with meals and sip slowly.

Mental and nervous health

A balanced mood depends, in part, on a balanced diet. The saying "You are what you eat" is equally applicable to mental health as it is to physical health.

If you are feeling lethargic, turnip and dandelion are traditional nerve tonics, while beans also stimulate the nervous system. On the other hand, if you are feeling tense, celery can have a truly restful effect, while lettuce juice has a sedative action and helps to promote sleep. Oatmeal is another traditional calming remedy.

Lavender is thought to reduce headaches; try making a tisane with a few lavender spikes and adding it to a juice. Fennel is also a traditional remedy for headaches and migraines. Nervous eczema can be a recurrent problem for some people when they're not feeling 100 per cent. This can sometimes be relieved with small quantities of potato juice. Memory and moods are helped by a good intake of B-vitamins, which are found in

wheatgerm, brewer's yeast, yogurt, vegetable extract, molasses, peanut butter, oranges and other citrus fruits, sweet potatoes and broccoli.

Anti-stress nutrients that help to support the adrenal glands, which produce stress hormones, are magnesium, found in green leafy vegetables, nuts and seeds, B-vitamins and vitamin C, found in blackcurrants, citrus fruit, strawberries, Brussels sprouts and peppers.

> **SYNDROME X**
> This is the term for a condition that could also be described as pre-diabetes, when cells become resistant to the effects of insulin. Insulin is produced by the body in response to the sugar and carbohydrates in your diet. If you tend to suffer from sugar and carbohydrate cravings, tiredness, difficulty concentrating (especially mid-afternoon), and have problems controlling your weight, then you could be suffering from difficulty in managing your blood-sugar levels. If this is the case, make sure that you dilute juices with water by half and sip them slowly instead of drinking them down in one go. Alternatively, add milk, yogurt or soya milk to the mix to slow down the effect on blood sugar.

Above: Celery is known to have a restful, calming effect.

Vitamins and minerals

These nutrients are needed in the diet in tiny amounts, but they are essential for health. It has been established that many people do not get their recommended daily allowances (RDAs) of many of these nutrients. Drinking fresh juices and blends made from fruits and vegetables naturally boosts the quantity of vitamins and minerals that you intake daily.

VITAMINS
Vitamin A – Retinol
This vitamin is needed for healthy eyes, skin and mucus membranes (lungs, digestive tract and immune system). Retinol is available only from animal sources such as full cream (whole) dairy produce, oily fish, egg yolks and liver. Large amounts of vitamin A in the diet can be toxic. Betacarotene converts to vitamin A only as it is needed, and so is non-toxic.
Juicing it Betacarotene is found in orange-coloured fruit and vegetables. It is also present in dark green, leafy vegetables. As vitamin A needs fat for absorption, conversion and use, adding a little flax seed oil or similar to betacarotene-rich juices will help.

Vitamin B1 – Thiamine
This is needed to produce energy and to support the nervous system. It is mainly found in cereals and wholegrains, but other non-juicing sources include legumes and meat.
Juicing it Cauliflower, pineapple, orange, leek, brewer's yeast and peanuts are all good sources of vitamin B1.

Vitamin B2 – Riboflavin
Also needed for energy production, it supports the growth of healthy skin, hair and nails. It is mainly supplied by cereals and wholegrains, but other non-juicing sources are fish and liver.
Juicing it Try juicing broccoli, apricots, spinach and watercress for plenty of vitamin B2, or add small amounts of brewer's yeast to juices and blends. Milk, yogurt and cottage cheese are also very good sources, and these can be used in smoothies.

Vitamin B3 – Niacin
Niacin is needed for energy production and it helps promote a feeling of calm. Mainly found in fortified cereals, the niacin equivalent, tryptophan, is also in meat, milk and eggs.
Juicing it Juice potatoes, beansprouts, strawberries, parsley, (bell) peppers, avocados, figs and dates. Add wheatgerm to juices and blends.

Vitamin B5 – Pantothenic acid
Needed for energy production and to control the effects of stress, this vitamin is widely available.
Juicing it Broccoli, berries, watermelon, celery and sweet potatoes all provide pantothenic acid, as well as wheatgerm, brewer's yeast, vegetable extract, molasses and nuts.

Vitamin B6 – Pyridoxine
Needed for processing protein, vitamin B6 is also used for supporting the nervous and immune systems, and is necessary for healthy skin. It is found in fish, meat, poultry, eggs and wholegrains.
Juicing it Oranges, brassicas, bananas, potatoes and yam provide pyridoxine. Also add watermelon and pumpkin seeds or wheatgerm to drinks.

Vitamin B12 – Cobalamine
Needed to metabolize iron and for a healthy nervous system, this vitamin is found in animal sources or yeast.
Juicing it Vegetable extract is a good source, and can be added to tomato or other vegetable juices. Milk, yogurt and cottage cheese, used in smoothies, provide some vitamin B12.

Folic acid
This is essential preconceptually and in early pregnancy for healthy foetal development. It works best when combined with vitamins B12 and B6. Fortified cereals are an excellent source.
Juicing it Citrus fruits, broccoli, Brussels sprouts, lettuce, potato, beetroot (beet), apricots, pumpkin, peanuts and almonds are all valuable sources.

Above: Broccoli juice is packed with essential minerals and vitamins.

Vitamin C – Ascorbic acid
This vitamin supports immunity and bone health. It is needed for skin repair and aids recuperation. It also helps in the absorption of iron, and protects against heart disease and cancer.
Juicing it Raspberries, strawberries, blackcurrants, citrus fruits, papaya and kiwi fruit are good sources of vitamin C. Also try adding beetroot (beet), tomatoes, (bell) peppers, cabbage, cauliflower, watercress and potatoes to juices and smoothies.

Vitamin D
Vital in helping calcium build healthy bones and teeth, vitamin D also protects against breast and prostate cancer. It is mainly made by the skin on exposure to the sun. Half an hour per day is needed on the face, hands and arms during sunny months. The most useful dietary source is oily fish, such as mackerel and salmon, and vitamin D is also added to margarines.
Juicing it There are no food sources of vitamin D to add to juices. Vitamin drops can help to make up a shortfall, but follow the manufacturer's instructions as an excess can be toxic.

Vitamin E

This antioxidant protects against heart disease and ageing, and it also thins the blood. Wholegrains are a valuable source.
Juicing it Vitamin E is found in all nuts and seeds and their oils (it is there to protect them from going rancid). Other sources include dark green leafy vegetables, cream and wheatgerm.

Vitamin K

This is essential for healthy blood clotting and wound repair, and is also needed to maintain healthy bones.
Juicing it Leafy vegetables are a good source of vitamin K, but cauliflower is the richest source. Yogurt supports healthy gut flora, which make vitamin K.

MINERALS
Calcium

Essential for healthy bones, calcium is also important for muscle and heart health and blood clotting. Non-juicing sources include canned fish with bones (sardines and salmon) and wholegrains.
Juicing it Good juicing sources include green leafy vegetables, broccoli and cabbage. Kale contains as much calcium as milk. It is also found in dairy produce (but not butter or cream) and in calcium-fortified dairy substitutes, such as soya milk or rice milk, as well as tofu.

Chromium

This mineral is used in glucose-tolerance factor, a dietary compound that is used for regulating blood sugar levels. Shellfish, mushrooms and chicken are non-juicing sources.
Juicing it Carrots, cabbage, lettuce, oranges, apples and bananas are all good sources, and chromium is also found in milk.

Iodine

This is needed for thyroid health, metabolism, energy and mental function. Non-juicing sources include fish, white rice and iodized salt.
Juicing it Vegetables contain iodine, but only if they have been grown in iodine-rich soil. Seaweed (kelp) is a good source and milk also contains some iodine.

Iron

Needed to make blood and deliver oxygen to cells, iron deficiency can result in lethargy and slowed mental function. Meat is the source of the most easily absorbed form of iron. Vegetarian protein substitutes, such as beans and lentils, are also important sources.
Juicing it Dark green leafy vegetables and dried fruit are good juicing sources. Nuts and seeds, molasses and dark (bittersweet) chocolate can also provide extra iron. Uptake of iron from plant sources is doubled when taken with juices that contain plenty of vitamin C.

Magnesium

Needed for healthy bones, magnesium works in synergy with calcium.
Juicing it Juicing sources include green leafy vegetables, potatoes, citrus fruits and dried fruit. Nuts and seeds also contain magnesium.

Manganese

Involved in the metabolism of fats and carbohydrates, non-juicing sources are eggs and wholegrain cereals.
Juicing it Juice green leafy vegetables, peas and beetroot (beet) for manganese. Add nuts to blends and smoothies.

Phosphorus

Important for bones and teeth, as well as for kidney health.
Juicing it Celery, broccoli, melon, grapes, kiwi fruit and blackcurrants are all good juicing sources, as well as milk.

Potassium

This mineral is needed for healthy nerves, brain health and good kidney function. It counterbalances sodium from salt and helps to lower blood pressure.
Juicing it Juicing sources include all fruit and vegetables.

Selenium

This has antioxidant properties and is good for liver and cardiovascular health. Sources include fish, wholegrains and rice.
Juicing it Brazil nuts are the richest source, along with green vegetables, garlic, onions, tomatoes and wheatgerm.

Sodium

This is needed for healthy nerve function. However, we get too much of the sodium in our diet from salt, which contributes to high blood pressure and heart disease.
Juicing it Sodium is present in small quantities in all fruit and vegetables and is balanced by potassium and water. Seaweeds are alternative sources.

Sulphur

This mineral is needed to maintain healthy skin, hair and nails.
Juicing it Good juicing sources are cabbage, garlic, onion, radish, cucumber, watercress, grapes and berries.

Zinc

Involved in all protein metabolism, zinc is very important for growth and healing, reproduction, immunity and digestion. Meat and fish are the richest sources available, but other non-juicing sources include vegetarian proteins, such as beans and pulses. Zinc is also found in brown rice and wholegrains.
Juicing it Broccoli, cauliflower, carrots, cucumbers and raspberries are the best juicing sources of zinc. Also, try adding nuts and seeds, wheatgerm and brewer's yeast to drinks, as these are also good sources.

Below: Drinks made from grapes and berries provide sulphur for healthy skin.

Juicing and blending techniques

Once you have purchased the necessary equipment for juicing or blending you will want to get started as soon as possible. For maximum freshness and flavour, prepare the fruit and vegetables just before you are ready to juice them. There are slightly different requirements for preparing produce for each type of machine. Always read the equipment manufacturer's instructions first.

Centrifugal and masticating juicers

Although centrifugal and masticating juicers function in different ways, the preparation of fruits and vegetables, and the basic principles for using the machines, are much the same.

1 Always choose firm produce as soft fruits will not give successful results. For instance, firm, underripe pears work well, but soft, ripe pears are best prepared in a blender or food processor.

2 Prepare the produce. Most fruit and vegetables do not need to be cored or peeled – although you might prefer to core fruit – as peel, pips (seeds) and core will simply be turned into pulp in the machine.

3 Scrub any produce you are not going to peel with a hard brush under cold running water to get rid of any dirt. If there is a waxy residue, then use a little bit of soap or washing-up liquid (dishwashing detergent) to help dissolve this, then rinse the produce thoroughly under cold running water.

4 Large stones (pits) of fruit such as peaches and plums need to be removed. Cut round the middle of the fruit, using a small, sharp knife, then twist to break into two halves. Carefully ease out the stone with the knife. Mangoes have a large, flat stone. Peel the fruit, then cut the flesh away from either side of the stone, then remove as much flesh as possible from the stone.

5 All leafy vegetables, such as cabbages and lettuces, can be put through a juicer. Include the outer leaves, which are nutritionally superior, although these must be washed thoroughly first.

6 Citrus fruit can be put through a juicer. Ensure that you remove all the peel, but there is no need to remove the pips or pith.

7 When pushing the produce through the feeder tube of the machine, it is very important that you use the plunger provided. Remember to position a jug (pitcher) or glass under the nozzle of the machine to catch the juice, otherwise it will spray all over the work surface.

8 Put the ingredients through the machine in manageable quantities. Cut pears and apples into quarters, for example, and alternate them if possible to ensure that the juices mix well. If you push too many pieces of fruit or vegetable through in one go, or push through pieces that are too large, the machine will clog up.

9 Push through a hard ingredient, such as a carrot, after softer ingredients, such as cabbage. This will keep the juice flowing freely and will prevent blockages.

Cleaning juicers, blenders and food processors

The one and only dreary thing about making delicious juices and blends is that the equipment needs to be cleaned soon afterwards. However, there are some simple, no-fuss ways of making this chore much easier.

Cleaning a juicer, blender or food processor thoroughly is important if you want to avoid unwanted and unhealthy bacteria, and the best time to do this is straight after you have made the juice or smoothie and poured it into glasses or a jug (pitcher). If you clean the parts of a juicer, blender or food processor immediately (or at least put them in to soak), the pulp and residue should just rinse off easily.

1 To clean a centrifugal or masticating juicer, blender or food processor, fill a sink with cold water and carefully take the equipment apart, following the manufacturer's instructions.

2 Using a plastic spatula or spoon, scoop off any large pieces of residue (such as the fruit and vegetable pulp that collects inside the spout of the juicer or around the blades) and discard it. Better still, if you have a compost heap in the garden, add the fruit or vegetable residue to it.

3 Plunge the non-electrical, removable machine parts of the juicer, blender or food processor into the sink full of cold water and leave them to soak until you are ready to clean them – this will probably be after you've sat back and enjoyed your freshly made juice or blend. Soaking the machine parts will help to loosen any remaining fruit and vegetable pulp and will make cleaning them much easier.

4 After soaking, either carefully handwash the non-electrical, removable machine parts or put them into a dishwasher on a normal setting.

5 Scrub any attachments that you have used with a firm brush to loosen any residue that remains. Take care when handling grating attachments as they are extremely sharp.

6 The removable components of your juicer, blender or food processor may occasionally get stained, especially if you regularly make juices with vibrantly coloured ingredients such as blackberries or beetroot. Soak these stained components every now and then in plenty of cold water with a little bleach added. Be sure to rinse the parts thoroughly afterwards, then leave them until they are completely dry before putting the machine back together.

TROUBLESHOOTING

If you experience any problems using your juicer, or if the resulting drink is not quite what you imagined, the following may help.

The machine gets clogged up

Push a hard fruit or vegetable, such as carrot or apple, through the machine to keep the juice flowing.

The taste of one ingredient is overwhelming the juice

Increase the quantity of another ingredient, use a base juice to dilute the flavours or add a splash of lemon or lime juice to help rescue the juice.

The blend is too thin

Add an ingredient to thicken the drink, such as yogurt, cream, banana or avocado.

TROUBLESHOOTING

If you experience any problems using a blender or food processor, or if the resulting drink is not quite what you imagined, the following may help.

The blend is too thick

Thin it using water or the juice of a watery fruit. For a pure taste, use fruit juice to dilute a fruit purée made in a blender.

The blend is too pulpy

Strain the mixture through a sieve, pressing the pulp down with the back of a spoon.

The ingredients get stuck to the side of the bowl

Scrape down the mixture with a plastic spatula to ensure that all ingredients are mixed thoroughly.

Blenders and food processors

These machines work in fairly similar ways, and the preparation of fruit is the same for both types of equipment. The main difference is the point at which you add liquid. Blenders and food processors are best used for soft fruits.

1 Fruits with inedible skins, such as bananas, mangoes and papayas, should be peeled.

2 Fruits with edible skins, such as peaches or plums, do not need to be peeled but should be washed thoroughly. If you prefer a juice with a finer, smoother texture, peel the fruits before blending.

3 Fruits with large stones (pits), cores or pips (seeds), such as mangoes, plums, cherries and apples, should be stoned (pitted), cored or seeded.

4 Fruits with tiny seeds, such as raspberries, strawberries or kiwis, can be used whole, when the seeds add texture and a pretty speckled effect. However, if you prefer a smooth drink, the pulp can be pushed through a fine sieve, using a plastic spatula, to remove the seeds.

5 When using berries and currants, remove the stalks and leaves and wash the fruit thoroughly. An easy way to detach, or string, redcurrants, blackcurrants or whitecurrants from their stalks is to hold the bunch firmly at the top, then slowly draw the tines of a fork through the fruit so that the currants fall away.

6 To blend fruit in a food processor, place it in the bowl of the machine and process to a thick pulp. Add any liquid or creamy ingredient, such as water, fruit juice, milk or yogurt, and process again.

7 To blend fruit in a blender, it is important to add the liquid ingredients and the soft fruit at the same time, then process altogether, otherwise the blades will not be able to blend the fruits effectively.

8 If using a handheld electric wand, remember that this piece of equipment is not as powerful as other juicers or blenders. Use only very soft fruits, such as bananas, peaches and berries, as it cannot cope with anything firmer.

Citrus juicers

1 First, cut the citrus fruit in half using a sharp knife.

2 To use a traditional handheld juicer, press the cut half over the cone of the juicer and, using an even pressure all round, twist the fruit to squeeze out as much juice as possible. The rim of the squeezer will catch any pips (seeds) but you may need a bowl to catch the juice.

3 To use a juicer with a citrus attachment or an electrically operated citrus juicer, firmly press the halved fruit over the spinning cone of the juicer. The motor will turn the cone under the fruit, and this will extract more juice than a handheld juicer would usually produce.

4 To use a manual hydraulic press, place a container under the juice nozzle to collect the juice (unless one is supplied as part of the juicer) and place the halved citrus fruit in the press. Pull the lever forwards to apply pressure and squeeze out the juice.

5 To use a centrifugal or masticating juicer, remove the citrus peel with a sharp knife (there is no need to worry about removing the pips or the white pith that remains). Cut the fruit into similar-sized chunks or break into segments, then press the fruit through the juicer funnel.

QUICK START TIPS

If you are impatient to get going, you can achieve some delicious instant results with one of these simple basic blends.

Banana and Berry Milkshake
1 banana
generous handful of strawberries, raspberries or other soft berries
1 glass cold milk or soya milk

Peel the banana and chop into chunks. Put all the ingredients in a blender or food processor. Blend, pour into a glass and serve.

Carrot and Apple Juice
2 large carrots
1 apple

Wash the carrots and apple, cut into chunks and push through a juicer. Spoon off any foam, if you prefer, and serve.

Lemon and Orange Refresher
1 orange
½ lemon
sparkling water
5ml/1 tsp sugar (optional)
ice cubes and/or fresh mint leaves

Juice the fruit in a juicer. Add the sparkling water and sugar, if using. Pour into a glass, add ice cubes and/or mint leaves, then serve.

Tomato and Pepper Boost
½ red (bell) pepper
150g/5oz tomatoes
juice of ½ lime
ice cubes

Soak the tomatoes in boiling water, then peel off the skin and chop into chunks. Halve the red pepper, remove the seeds and chop into similar-sized chunks. Add the pepper and tomatoes to a blender or food processor and blend well. Add a squeeze of lime juice and some ice cubes, then serve.

Serving and storing juices, smoothies and blends

The ideal way to enjoy juices, blends and smoothies is to drink them immediately. This way you benefit from the full flavour and nutritional benefits, because time and exposure to oxygen take their toll on the nutrient content of most prepared fruits and vegetables. For instance, when you make carrot juice, it is a bright orange colour, but if you leave it for an hour it will turn brown as it oxidizes. Likewise, the flesh of apples or avocados turns brown as it oxidizes and loses nutritional value.

Serving and decorating juices and drinks

There are many attractive and quirky ways to serve fresh drinks. With a little forethought and imagination, you can present friends and family with gorgeous-looking concoctions – whatever the occasion.

Adding ice Ice is a wonderful vehicle for serving, cooling and decorating drinks. Cubes are best for cooling drinks, and these can be decorated or flavoured in different ways. A handful of ice can be added to a drink, or you can add crushed ice to drinks in glasses to cool them quickly.

Juicy ice cubes Make cubes from orange, cranberry or diluted lime juice in an ice-cube tray. Thse will create a rainbow effect in your drinks and will also alter the taste as they melt.

Right: Suspend sprigs of currants over your drinks for a stunning effect.

Fruit ice cubes Place raspberries or other small fruits in an ice-cube tray and add water.

Flower and petal ice cubes Choose flowers that will be attractive even when the ice has melted – rose petals, carnation pinks or borage flowers.

Sugar-rimmed glasses Moisten the rim of a glass with water, dip into grated lemon or lime rind and then into icing (confectioners') sugar.

Fruit purée drizzle For a striped effect, pour fruit purée down the inside of glasses before adding the drink.

Edible swizzle sticks These can be fun and celery sticks are a natural choice for savoury drinks. Finely slice one end of the stick then soak in iced water for about 15 minutes – a fanned out fringe will develop.

Fruit skewers Place fruit segments or currants on a skewer and use as a swizzle stick. Bruised lemon grass stalks, lavender or rosemary stems, or cinnamon sticks can also be used.

Glass decorations Place fruit slices on the rim of a glass or skewer small pieces of fruit on to cocktail sticks (toothpicks) and balance these across the tops of glasses. Experiment with herb leaves and pared citrus rind.

Ice lollies Fruit juices make healthy ice lollies (popsicles) for children. All you need is an inexpensive mould, available from kitchenware shops. This is a fun way to serve drinks at parties.

Storage of juices and drinks

While it is definitely best to serve juices and smoothies when they are just freshly made, you may want to store them for one reason or another. Perhaps you have made too much to drink in one go, maybe you have a glut of berries or some other produce that you need to use up before it over-ripens, or you might simply want to take a juice or smoothie into work for a healthy mid-morning snack.

One way to minimize the oxidization of juices is to add some vitamin C. Either squeeze in a little fresh lemon or orange juice or add 2.5ml/½ tsp of powdered vitamin C, which is available from health food shops. Juices can then be stored in the refrigerator for a few hours and won't discolour – make sure you chill them as soon as possible after making.

Above: To make children's parties fun, try serving fresh juices frozen into lollies.

To store a juice or smoothie pour it into a jar or jug (pitcher), filling it right to the brim. Seal with clear film (plastic wrap) or, alternatively, use a screw-top jug or vacuum flask.

Most juices can be frozen for use at a later date and this will preserve almost all of their full nutritional value. Try freezing different flavoured juices in ice-cube trays – the ice cubes can then simply be removed and added to drinks. Otherwise, try to freeze the juice in fairly small amounts (glassfuls). Any juice or blended drink can be frozen successfully, but it is a good idea to make single ingredient base juices to freeze, because you can then add different flavourings when the juice is thawed. Make sure you label and date the containers clearly.

making juices & smoothies

The final part of the book consists of a fantastic range of recipes for juices and smoothies. It is divided into twelve chapters, each covering a different type of drink: from super healthy juices through to perfect party drinks, there is a recipe for every type of drink and using every ingredient imaginable. There are easy breakfast blends made with oatmeal and muesli, creamy shakes made with banana and cinnamon, and fun drinks that kids will love to make themselves. Whether you fancy a creamy, indulgent smoothie, a healthy vegetable juice, a fruity, aromatic blend or a refreshing alcoholic punch, you'll find the perfect recipe here.

super
healthy
juices

This chapter contains a selection of fabulous
juices that have wonderful health benefits.
Highly nutritious, natural additives such as
wheatgrass, sprouting beans, echinacea and kelp
are combined with everyday fruit and vegetables
to make a range of feel-good juices for the
seriously health-conscious.

Parsnip Pep

Although parsnips yield a relatively small amount of juice, the juicer produces an amazingly thick, sweet and creamy drink, perfect for adding body to any raw fruit and vegetable blend. Refreshing fennel, apple and pear are the perfect foils for the intense sweetness of parsnip and together produce the most tantalizing power-pack of a fresh juice.

Makes 2 glasses

115g/4oz fennel
200g/7oz parsnips
1 apple
1 pear
a small handful of flat leaf parsley
crushed ice

Cook's tip

Parsnips are at their sweetest a few weeks after the first frost, so try a shot of this wonderful juice when you are most in need of a little winter boost.

1 Using a sharp knife, cut the fennel and parsnips into large similar-sized chunks. Quarter the apple and pear, carefully removing the core, if you like, then cut the quartered pieces in half.

2 Push half the prepared fruit and vegetables through a juicer, then follow with the parsley and the remaining fruit and vegetables.

3 Fill short glasses with ice and pour the juice over. Serve immediately.

Clean Sweep

This juice is so packed with goodness, you can almost feel it cleansing and detoxing your body. As well as valuable vitamins, the carrots and grapes provide plenty of natural sweetness, which blends perfectly with the mild pepperiness of the celery and fresh scent of parsley. Drink this juice on a regular basis to give your system a thorough clean-out.

Makes 1 large or 2 small glasses

1 celery stick
300g/11oz carrots
150g/5oz green grapes
several large sprigs of parsley
celery or carrot sticks, to serve

1 Using a sharp knife, roughly chop the celery and carrots. Push half of the celery, carrots and grapes through a juicer, then add the parsley sprigs. Add the remaining celery, carrots and grapes in the same way and juice until thoroughly combined.

2 Pour into one or two glasses and serve with celery or carrot stick stirrers.

Cook's tip
When juicing herbs, do not remove their individual stalks because it is the stalks that contain all the goodness and flavour – and they go through the juicing machine really easily. Parsley contains calcium, vitamins and iron and also works as a natural cleanser and breath freshener.

Bean Good

Beansprouts are a highly nutritious food, bursting with vitamins B and C, and they are one of the few vegetables that actually increase in goodness after they are picked. Although mild in flavour, their juiciness works well in any nourishing blend. Mixed with broccoli, another superfood, and naturally sweet fruits, this blend is a real tonic for your skin, hair and general health.

Makes 1 large or 2 small glasses

90g/3½oz broccoli
1 large pear
90g/3½oz/scant ½ cup beansprouts
200g/7oz green grapes
ice cubes and sliced green grapes

3 Push all the ingredients through the juicer. Pour into glasses and serve with ice cubes and sliced green grapes.

Cook's tip

When juicing fruits and vegetables, always use the freshest ingredients you can find; that way the juice will have maximum flavour and you'll get additional health benefits. If at all possible, use organic produce. This is a bit more expensive but is definitely worth it – you can really taste the difference and your body will reap the rewards.

1 Using a small, sharp knife cut the broccoli into pieces small enough to fit through a juicer funnel.

2 Quarter the pear and carefully remove the core, then roughly chop the flesh into small chunks.

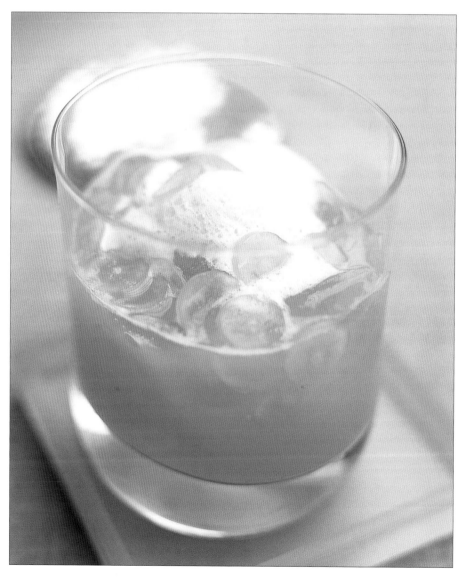

Wheatgrass Tonic

The nutritional benefits of wheatgrass are enormous. It is grown from wheat berries and is a concentrated source of chlorophyll, which combats tiredness and fatigue, and also provides enzymes, vitamins and minerals. It has a distinctive flavour so in this juice it is blended with mild white cabbage, but it is just as tasty combined with other vegetables instead.

Makes 1 small glass

50g/2oz white cabbage
90g/3½oz wheatgrass

1 Using a small, sharp knife, roughly shred the cabbage.

2 Push through a juicer with the wheatgrass. Pour the juice into a small glass and serve immediately.

Immune Zoom

Red- and orange-coloured fruits and vegetables are particularly good for protecting against or fighting off colds or flu, and are full of powerful antioxidants that are known to protect against many more serious illnesses. This refreshing, fruity drink also contains a herbal blend called echinacea, which helps to relieve the symptoms of colds and flu.

Makes 2 glasses

1 small mango
1 eating apple
2 passion fruit
juice of 1 orange
5ml/1 tsp echinacea
mineral water (optional)
ice cubes (optional)

Cook's tip

If you are suffering from a cold or flu, or can sense its imminent arrival, echinacea can be taken in about 5ml/1 tsp servings, which can be repeated throughout the day. Check the recommended dosage on the manufacturer's packaging before use, however.

1 Halve the mango, cutting down one side of the flat stone (pit). Remove the stone and scoop the flesh from the skin. Roughly chop the flesh and place in a blender or food processor.

2 Peel, core and roughly chop the apple. Add to the blender and process together until smooth, scraping the mixture down from the side of the bowl, if necessary.

3 Halve the passion fruit and scoop the pulp into the mango and apple purée. Add the orange juice and echinacea, then blend briefly.

4 Thin with a little mineral water, if you like, pour into two glasses and serve. Otherwise, transfer the juice into a jug (pitcher) and chill in the refrigerator, then serve in large glasses with ice cubes and slices of mango to decorate.

Ginseng Juice

This vibrantly coloured, deliciously tangy juice is also an excellent boost for the immune system. Ginseng is a natural cure-all that is claimed to stimulate digestion, reduce tiredness, alleviate stress, strengthen the immune system and even revive a flagging libido. Here it is added to the juice as a powder but it can also be taken as a dietary supplement in tablet form.

Makes 1 glass

1 red or orange (bell) pepper
200g/7oz pumpkin
1 large apricot
squeeze of lemon juice
5ml/1 tsp ginseng powder
ice cubes

Cook's tip

When seeding peppers, halve them, then cut around the stalk. Give the stalk a sharp pull and the core will come away easily.

1 Using a sharp knife, discard the core from the pepper and roughly chop the flesh. Slice the pumpkin in half. Scoop out the pips (seeds) with a spoon and then cut away the skin. Chop the flesh. Halve and stone (pit) the apricot.

2 Push the pumpkin, pepper and apricot pieces through a juicer. Add a squeeze of lemon juice and the ginseng powder, and stir well to mix together. Pour the juice over ice cubes in a tall glass and serve.

Red Alert

This juice is perfect for those times when you're not thinking straight or you need to concentrate. Beetroot, carrots and spinach all contain folic acid, which is known to help maintain a healthy brain, while the addition of fresh orange juice will give your body a natural vitamin boost. This delicious and vibrant blend is guaranteed to set your tastebuds tingling.

Makes 1 large or 2 small glasses

200g/7oz raw beetroot (beets)
1 carrot
1 large orange
50g/2oz spinach

1 Using a sharp knife, cut the beetroot into wedges. Roughly chop the carrot, then cut away the skin from the orange and roughly slice the flesh.

2 Push the orange, beetroot and carrot pieces alternately through a juicer, then add the spinach. Pour into glasses.

Cook's tip
Only use fresh, raw, firm beetroot for juicing, rather than the cooked variety – and most definitely avoid the pickled type in jars. Beetroot juice is a stunning, vibrant red and is surprisingly sweet, especially when mixed with carrot and orange juice.

Vitality Juice

Fresh pears are a great energizer and can help give you a kick-start in the morning if you have a long, busy day ahead or a looming deadline to meet. This nutritious blend of ripe, juicy fruit, wheatgerm, yogurt, seeds and watercress makes a great-tasting tonic. If you would prefer a non-dairy version, use yogurt made from goat's milk, sheep's milk or soya.

Makes 1 large glass

25g/1oz watercress
1 large ripe pear
30ml/2 tbsp wheatgerm
150ml/¼ pint/⅔ cup natural (plain) yogurt
15ml/1 tbsp linseeds (flax seeds)
10ml/2 tsp lemon juice
mineral water (optional)
ice cubes

1 Roughly chop the watercress (you do not need to remove the tough stalks). Peel, core and roughly chop the pear.

2 Put the watercress and pear in a blender or food processor with the wheatgerm and blend until smooth. Scrape the mixture down from the side of the bowl if necessary.

Cook's tip
If you never have time for breakfast, prepare this juice in the evening and chill overnight. You can drink the juice on your journey into work and you'll then feel the benefits kick in throughout the day.

3 Add the yogurt, seeds and lemon juice and blend until evenly combined. Thin with a little mineral water if the mixture is too thick and pour over ice cubes. Decorate with watercress.

Iron Crazy

This energizing drink contains spinach, apricots, carrots and pumpkin seeds, which are all rich in iron, as well as kelp, a type of seaweed, to give you an invigorating lift. Iron is essential for carrying oxygen in the blood and a shortage can quickly lead to tiredness and anaemia.

Makes 1 small glass

50g/2oz/¼ cup ready-to-eat dried apricots
15ml/1 tbsp pumpkin seeds
250g/9oz carrots
50g/2oz spinach
15ml/1 tbsp lemon juice
10ml/2 tsp kelp powder
mineral water
spinach leaf and pumpkin seeds, to decorate

Cook's tip
Sea vegetables are packed with minerals, protein and other valuable nutrients. Kelp is often sold in powder form, along with spirulina, a similarly nutrient-packed seaweed.

1 Chop the apricots finely, cover with 100ml/3½fl oz/ scant ½ cup boiling water and leave for 10 minutes.

2 Using a large, sharp knife, carefully chop the pumpkin seeds into small pieces. (Take it slowly at first as the whole seeds have a tendency to scatter.) Roughly chop the carrots.

3 Drain the apricots. Push the spinach through a juicer, followed by the apricots and carrots. Stir in the lemon juice, pumpkin seeds and kelp powder.

4 Pour the juice into a glass, top up with a little mineral water, decorate with a spinach leaf and pumpkin seeds, then serve immediately for maximum benefit.

Body Builder

Wheatgerm, the most nutritious part of the wheat grain, is packed with B and E vitamins, protein and minerals. Combined with bananas, it makes a great carbohydrate-rich drink that is boosted by the goodness of orange juice and linseeds and is perfect before exercise. Like all seeds, linseeds contain essential fatty acids that are good for the heart.

Makes 1 large glass

30ml/2 tbsp wheatgerm
1 large banana, chopped
130g/4½oz/generous ½ cup soya yogurt
15ml/1 tbsp linseeds (flax seeds)
juice of 1 lime
juice of 1 large orange
mineral water (optional)
linseeds and grated lime zest, to decorate

Cook's tip
Brewer's yeast is another healthy supplement that can be added to energy-boosting drinks. Rich in B vitamins and minerals, it is great for increasing vitality.

1 Put the wheatgerm, two-thirds of the banana, the yogurt and linseeds in a blender or food processor. Blend until smooth then, using a plastic spatula or spoon, scrape down the side of the bowl if necessary. Stir well.

2 Add the lime and orange juice to the yogurt mixture and blend again until evenly mixed. Pour the juice into a large glass and top up with mineral water. Decorate with linseeds, lime zest and the remaining banana, then serve.

Ginger Juice

Fresh root ginger is one of the best natural cures for indigestion and it helps to settle upset stomachs, whether caused by food poisoning or motion sickness. In this unusual fruity blend, it is simply mixed with fresh, juicy pineapple and sweet-tasting carrot, creating a quick and easy remedy that can be juiced up in minutes – and tastes delicious too.

Makes 1 glass

½ small pineapple
25g/1oz fresh root ginger
1 carrot
ice cubes

Cook's tip
Before preparing the pineapple, turn it upside down and leave for half an hour – this makes it juicier.

1 Using a sharp knife, cut away the skin from the pineapple, then halve and remove the core. Roughly slice the pineapple flesh. Peel and roughly chop the ginger, then chop the carrot.

2 Push the carrot, ginger and pineapple through a juicer and pour into a glass. Add ice cubes and serve immediately.

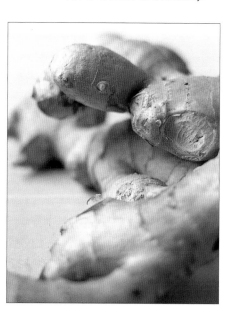

Sleep Easy

Some herbal teas are known for their purely soporific qualities, but this concoction is slightly more substantial – the last thing you want is to go to bed hungry. Blended bananas provide slow-release carbohydrates to sustain you through the night and lettuce is renowned for its sleep-inducing properties. It's just what you need when you want to relax.

1 Cover the teabag with 150ml/¼ pint/ ⅔ cup boiling water and leave to steep for 10 minutes. Meanwhile, chop the lettuce. Drain the teabag.

2 Chop the banana into a blender or food processor, add the lettuce and blend well until smooth, scraping the mixture down from the sides of the bowl, if necessary. Add the lemon juice and chamomile tea and blend briefly until smooth. Serve immediately.

Makes 1 large glass

1 chamomile teabag
90g/3½oz iceberg lettuce
1 small banana
juice of ½ lemon

Cook's tip

If you have chamomile in the garden, use three or four flower-heads instead of the chamomile teabag. Let them steep in the boiling water for a few minutes, but don't leave them for too long or the flavour will become bitter.

vital veggie blends

When your energy levels are flagging, these drinks are guaranteed to perk you up. Made using pure vegetables with no additional additives, they serve a variety of purposes from detoxing and cleansing the body to healing and energizing the mind. Ready in minutes, blends including carrot, celery, tomato and spinach are a sure-fire way to drink yourself healthy.

Bright Eyes

Thin-skinned citrus fruits like clementines can be put through the juicer without peeling, adding a zesty kick to the final mix – and saving time when you're in a hurry. This vibrant, intensely flavoured carrot and clementine combination is packed with vitamin A, which is essential for healthy vision, and vitamin C to give an extra boost to the whole system.

1 Scrub the carrots and, using a sharp knife, chop them into large chunks of a similar size. Quarter the clementines, discarding any pips (seeds).

2 Push the clementine quarters through a juicer, then repeat the procedure with the carrot chunks.

3 Pour the juice over ice cubes in tall glasses and decorate each glass with a wedge or slice of clementine, if you like.

Makes 2 glasses

200g/7oz carrots
6 clementines, plus extra wedges or slices
   to decorate
ice cubes

Cook's tip

Take the tingle factor up a notch and add some extra zing by spicing up the mix a little. Peel and slice some fresh root ginger and push through the juicer with the clementines and carrots.

Smooth yet sassy, with all the colour of a brilliant golden sunrise, this mouthwatering juice will make waking up worthwhile – even on the most sluggish mornings.

Veggie Boost

This simple blend makes a great juice boost. It has pure clean flavours and a chilli kick that is guaranteed to revitalize flagging energy levels. Tomatoes and carrots are rich in the valuable antioxidant betacarotene, which is reputed to fight cancer, and they contain a good supply of vitamins A, C and E, all of which are essential for good health.

Makes 2 glasses

3 tomatoes
1 fresh red or green chilli
250g/9oz carrots
juice of 1 orange
crushed ice

Cook's tip

Non-organic carrots often contain a lot of chemicals in their skins. If you use these, scrub them well or wash and peel them before use.

1 Quarter the tomatoes and roughly chop the chilli. (If you prefer a milder juice, remove the seeds and white pith from the chilli before chopping.) Scrub the carrots and chop them roughly.

2 Push the carrots through a juicer, then follow with the tomatoes and chilli. Add the orange juice and stir well to mix. Fill two tumblers with crushed ice, pour the juice over and serve.

Gazpacho Juice

Inspired by the classic Spanish soup, this fabulous juice looks and tastes delicious. Fresh salad vegetables can be thrown into a blender or food processor and whizzed up in moments to create a refreshing, invigorating drink. If you are planning to invite friends for a relaxing al fresco lunch, serve this cooling juice as an appetizer; it is perfect for a hot summer's day.

Makes 4–5 glasses

½ fresh red chilli
800g/1¾lb tomatoes, skinned
½ cucumber, roughly sliced
1 red (bell) pepper, seeded and cut
  into chunks
1 celery stick, chopped
1 spring onion (scallion), roughly chopped
a small handful of fresh coriander (cilantro),
  stalks included, plus extra to decorate
juice of 1 lime
salt
ice cubes

1 Using a sharp knife, seed the chilli. Add to a blender or food processor with the tomatoes, cucumber, red pepper, celery, spring onion and coriander.

2 Blend well until smooth, scraping the vegetable mixture down from the side of the bowl, if necessary.

Cook's tip
Stir in a little extra tomato juice or mineral water if the juice is still thick after blending. A splash of red wine vinegar will intensify the flavour.

Juices made from fresh salad vegetables, packed full of valuable nutrients, are the ultimate thirst quenchers on a hot day, providing wonderfully fresh flavours and refreshing the palate instantly.

3 Add the lime juice and a little salt and blend. Pour into glasses. Add ice cubes and a few coriander leaves to serve.

Ruby Roots

Beetroot has the highest sugar content of any vegetable and, not surprisingly, makes one of the most delicious, sweet juices, with a vibrant red colour and a rich yet refreshing taste. Despite its firm texture, beetroot can be juiced raw and its intense flavour combines wonderfully with tangy citrus fruits and fresh root ginger. Enjoy this juice as a natural cleanser.

Makes 1 large glass

200g/7oz raw beetroot (beets)
1cm/½in piece fresh root ginger, peeled
1 large orange
ice cubes

Cook's tip
Blood-red beetroot produces a vibrant, shockingly intense, jewel-coloured juice that is packed with vitamins and minerals, making it the perfect tonic and the ultimate health juice.

1 Trim the beetroot and cut into quarters. Push half through a juicer, followed by the ginger and remaining beetroot.

2 Squeeze the juice from the orange and mix with the beetroot juice.

3 Pour the juice over ice cubes in a glass or clear glass cup. Serve immediately.

Mixed Salad

Despite their reputation as being full of water, lettuce and cucumber contain important minerals such as calcium and zinc, alongside other crucial nutrients like vitamin K. Spinach contains plenty of betacarotene and has cancer-fighting properties. Juiced with ripe pears for maximum sweetness, a regular dose of this super juice can only enhance your health.

Makes 2–3 glasses

½ cucumber
½ iceberg, cos or romaine lettuce
2 large, ripe pears
75g/3oz fresh spinach
6–8 radishes
crushed ice
sliced radishes and cucumber, to decorate

Cook's tip
Although it can taste fairly bland in a salad, unpeeled cucumber has a surprisingly intense flavour when it is juiced. If you prefer a lighter taste, peel the cucumber with a sharp knife before juicing.

1 Using a small, sharp knife, chop the cucumber into chunks. Roughly tear the lettuce into pieces. Quarter the pears and remove the core.

2 Push all the ingredients through a juicer. Pour over crushed ice in tall glasses and serve with sliced radishes and cucumber swizzle sticks.

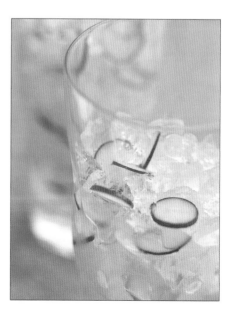

Orange Blossom

Avocados are extremely good for the skin, mainly because of their high vitamin E content. Combined with parsley, asparagus and orange, this juice makes a great cleanser and skin tonic. If you have a particular skin problem, drinking this juice regularly should really make a difference – it is extremely effective and much cheaper than many skin creams on the market.

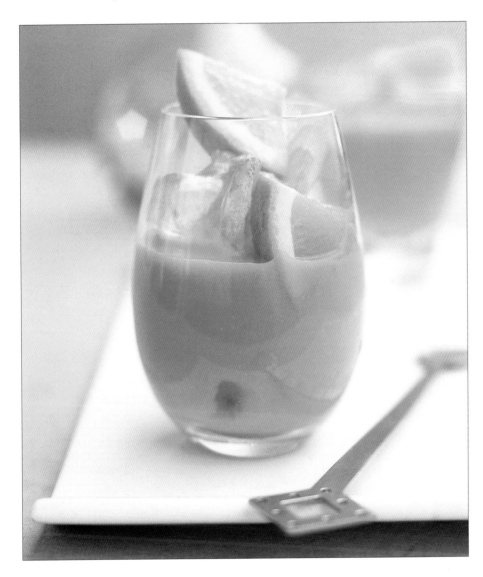

2 Roughly chop the asparagus and add to the avocado. Blend thoroughly until smooth, scraping the mixture down from the side of the bowl, if necessary.

3 Juice the oranges and add to the mixture with the lemon juice. Blend briefly until the mixture is very smooth. Pour the juice into two glasses until two-thirds full, then add ice cubes and mineral water. Decorate with chunky orange wedges.

Cook's tip

The orange and lemon juice in this blend means that the avocados will not discolour, so you might want to refrigerate a glass for later on. If it has thickened slightly, stir in a little extra mineral water.

Makes 2 glasses

1 small avocado
small handful of parsley
75g/3oz tender asparagus spears
2 large oranges
squeeze of lemon juice
ice cubes
mineral water
orange wedges, to decorate

1 Halve the avocado and discard the stone (pit). Scoop the flesh into a blender or food processor. Remove any tough stalks from the parsley and add.

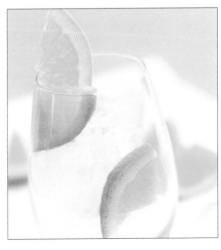

Sugar Snap

Sweet and juicy sugar snap peas are one of the most delicious vegetables to serve raw and they taste just as good when put through a juicer. The sweetness of the peas and the melon intensifies when they are juiced and the fresh root ginger adds a certain edge to this mellow, cooling juice. Keep the melon in the refrigerator so that it's well and truly chilled when you come to blend the juice – you won't need to add ice.

Makes 1 large glass

1cm/½in piece fresh root ginger, peeled
¼ honeydew or Galia melon
200g/7oz sugar snap peas, including pods
melon chunks and peas, to decorate

Cook's tip
Use a fresh, plump-looking piece of ginger. If it is too old, it may have started to shrivel and won't produce the necessary juice and flavour.

1 Using a sharp knife, chop the ginger. Scoop out the seeds from the melon and cut it into wedges. Cut away the skin, then chop the flesh into chunks.

2 Push the sugar snap peas through a juicer, followed by the chunks of melon and the slices of ginger. Serve chilled, with melon chunks and peas.

Celery Sensation

Savoury, almost salty, celery and sweet, green grapes make an astoundingly effective twosome when combined in a blended juice. A small handful of peppery watercress adds an extra punch, but be careful not to add too much because its flavour intensifies considerably when the leaves are juiced. Celery has one of the lowest calorie contents of all vegetables, so this is a particularly useful juice for anyone on a low-calorie diet.

Makes 1 large glass

2 celery sticks
a handful of watercress
200g/7oz/1¾ cups green grapes
1 leafy celery stick, to serve
crushed ice

1 Push the celery sticks through a juicer, followed by the watercress and the green grapes.

2 Put a leafy celery stick in a large glass to act as an edible swizzle stick and half-fill with crushed ice. Pour the juice over the ice and serve.

Broccoli Booster

Hailed as a cure-all superfood and a vital ingredient in a healthy diet, broccoli's strong taste does, however, need a bit of toning down when juiced. Sweet and tangy apples and lemon juice soften its flavour, making a drink that's thoroughly enjoyable.

Makes 1 large glass

125g/4¼oz broccoli florets
2 eating apples
15ml/1 tbsp lemon juice
ice cubes

1 Cut the broccoli florets into small pieces and chop the apples.

2 Push both through a juicer and stir in the lemon juice. Serve in a tall glass with plenty of ice.

Cook's tip

Don't use the tough broccoli stalks as they provide little juice and don't have as good a flavour as the delicate florets. Broccoli is packed with antiviral and antibacterial nutrients and contains almost as much calcium as milk. It is also thought to prevent some cancers, so this juice is definitely worth drinking for its health benefits as well as its wonderful flavour.

Basil Blush

Some herbs just don't juice well, losing their aromatic flavour and turning muddy and dull.
Basil, however, is an excellent juicer, keeping its distinctive fresh fragrance. It makes the perfect
partner for mild, refreshing cucumber and the ripest, juiciest tomatoes you can find.

Makes 1–2 glasses

½ cucumber, peeled
a handful of fresh basil, plus extra to decorate
350g/12oz tomatoes
ice cubes

Cook's tip
You don't have to peel the cucumber,
but the juice will have a fresher, lighter
colour without peel.

1 Quarter the cucumber lengthways –
do not remove the seeds. Push it
through a juicer with the basil, then do
the same with the tomatoes.

2 Pour the blended tomato, basil and
cucumber juice over cubes of ice in one
or two glasses and serve decorated
with a few fresh sprigs of basil.

fresh
&
fruity

Ripe, juicy fruits make fabulous drinks, whatever the combination of ingredients but, if you're looking for guidance, this stunning assortment of recipes will set you off in a frenzy of fruity blending. Whether using blackcurrants, bananas or exotic papayas, make sure you use the pick of the crop so your juices are both highly nutritious and tantalizingly tasty.

Pink and Perky

This deliciously refreshing, rose-tinged blend of grapefruit and pear juice will keep you bright-eyed and bushy-tailed. It's perfect for a quick breakfast drink or as a pick-me-up later in the day when energy levels are flagging. If the grapefruit is particularly tart, serve with a little bowl of brown sugar to sweeten, or use brown sugar stirrers.

Makes 2 tall glasses

1 pink and 1 white grapefruit, halved
2 ripe pears
ice cubes

1 Take a thin slice from one grapefruit half and cut a few thin slices of pear. Roughly chop the remaining pear and push through a juicer.

2 Squeeze all the juice from the grapefruit halves. Mix the fruit juices together and serve over ice. Decorate with the grapefruit and pear slices.

Sweet, Sharp Shock

The taste-tingling combination of sweet red grape and tart apple is quite delicious. Grapes are full of natural sugars and, mixed with apple juice, they'll create a juice that's full of pep and zing. Grapes are also renowned for their cleansing properties, making this an ideal addition to any detox regime. For a longer, more refreshing drink, top up with sparkling mineral water.

1 Slice some grapes and a sliver or two of apple for the decoration. Roughly chop the remaining apples. Push through a juicer with the grapes.

2 Pour over crushed ice, decorate with the sliced fruit and serve immediately.

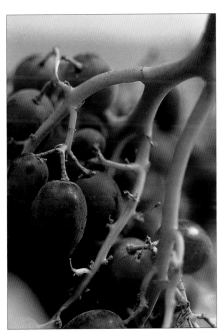

Makes 1 large glass

150g/5oz/1¼ cups red grapes
1 red-skinned eating apple
1 small cooking apple
crushed ice

Cook's tip
The simplest flavour combinations are often the most delicious. Sugary grapes together with mouth-puckeringly tart apples is one of those perfect pairings that simply cannot be beaten.

Red Defender

Boost your body's defences with this delicious blend of red fruits. Watermelon and strawberries are a good source of vitamin C and the black watermelon seeds, like all other seeds, are rich in essential nutrients. If you really don't like the idea of blending the seeds, remove them first.

1 Hull the strawberries and halve them if they are large. Pull the grapes from their stalks. Cut away the skin from the watermelon.

2 Put the watermelon in a blender or food processor and blend until the seeds are broken up. Add the strawberries and grapes and blend until completely smooth, scraping the mixture down from the side of the bowl, if necessary. Serve in tall glasses.

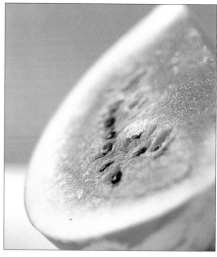

Makes 2 glasses

200g/7oz/1¾ cups strawberries
small bunch red grapes, about 90g/3½oz
1 small wedge of watermelon

Cook's tip
Decorate this juice with chunks of watermelon or strawberry halves.

Apricot Squash

The availability of fresh apricots can be rather erratic, so buy lots when you see them and make delicious apricot-based juices like this one. Choose sweet and juicy, ripe apricots, as they will act as a perfect foil to the tangy limes in this refreshing drink.

Makes 2 glasses

2 limes
3 oranges
4 ripe apricots
several sprigs of lemon balm, plus extra
   to decorate

Cook's tip
This makes a tangy, invigorating blend to wake up your senses. Stir in a little honey or sugar if you find it a bit too tart.

1 Squeeze the limes and oranges, either by hand or using a citrus juicer. Halve and stone (pit) the apricots.

2 Put the apricots in a blender or food processor with a little of the citrus juice and the lemon balm, and blend until smooth, scraping the mixture down from the side of the bowl, if necessary. Add the remaining juice and blend until completely smooth.

3 Pour into medium glasses and serve decorated with extra lemon balm.

Blue Lagoon

Blueberries are not only an excellent source of betacarotene and vitamin C, they are also rich in flavonoids, which help to cleanse the system. Mixed with other dark red fruits, such as blackberries and grapes, they make a highly nutritious and extremely delicious blend that can be stored in the refrigerator and relished throughout the day.

1 Pull the blackcurrants, if using, and grapes from their stalks.

2 Push the fruits through a juicer, saving a few for decoration. Place the ice in a medium glass and pour over the juice. Decorate with the remaining fruit and serve.

Makes 1 glass

90g/3½oz/scant 1 cup blackcurrants
  or blackberries
150g/5oz red grapes
130g/4½oz/generous 1 cup blueberries
ice cubes

Cook's tip

This is a really tangy wake-up drink that you might find a bit too sharp. Add a dash of sugar or honey, or top up with mineral water to dilute it slightly, if you like.

Pomegranate Plus

Sometimes difficult to find, pomegranates are worth buying when you see them because their exotic and distinctive flavour is quite delicious. A reddish skin is usually a sign that the seeds inside will be vibrant and sweet. Pomegranate juice makes a delicious base for this treat of a juice, which is mildly spiced with a hint of fresh ginger.

Makes 2 glasses

2 pomegranates
4 fresh figs
15g/½oz fresh root ginger, peeled
10ml/2 tsp lime juice
ice cubes and lime wedges, to serve

Cook's tip
Pomegranates are refreshing in hot weather, especially when juiced with figs, ginger and lime juice. Serve ice-cold to quench a summer thirst.

1 Halve the pomegranates. Working over a bowl to catch the juices, pull away the skin to remove the jewel-like clusters of seeds.

2 Quarter the figs and roughly chop the ginger. Push the figs and ginger through a juicer. Push the pomegranate seeds through, reserving a few for decoration. Stir in the lime juice. Pour over ice cubes and lime wedges, then serve.

Minty Melon Cooler

The wonderfully juicy flesh of ripe melon seems somehow more fragrant and sweet when juiced. A dash of lime cuts through the sweetness perfectly and zips up the flavour, while refreshing, peppery mint makes a classic, cool companion to both. This mellow soother is equally calming and stimulating – what a combination.

Makes 3–4 glasses

1 Galia or cantaloupe melon
several large mint sprigs
juice of 2 large limes
ice cubes
extra mint sprigs and lime slices, to decorate

1 Halve and seed the melon and cut into wedges. Cut one wedge into long, thin slices and reserve for decoration.

2 Cut the skin from the remaining melon wedges and push half the melon through a juicer. Strip the mint leaves from the sprigs, push them through the juicer, then juice the remaining melon.

3 Stir in the lime juice and then pour the juice over ice cubes in glasses. Decorate with mint sprigs and lime slices. Add a slice of melon to each glass and serve.

Cherry Berry Trio

Strawberries and grapes have long been reputed to cleanse and purify the system, while cherries and strawberries are rich in vitamin C. This trio of plump, ripe fruits is packed with natural fruit sugars and needs absolutely no sweetening. To really spoil yourself (and undo all that cleansing power), try adding a splash of your favourite orange liqueur.

Makes 2 large glasses

200g/7oz/1¾ cups strawberries
250g/9oz/2¼ cups red grapes
150g/5oz/1¼ cups red cherries, pitted
ice cubes

Cook's tip
Each year, the cherry season passes all too swiftly, so enjoy them in their full glory in this refreshing blend of sweet, fruity, fragrant red juices.

1 Halve two or three strawberries and grapes and set aside with a few perfect cherries for decoration. Cut up any large strawberries, then push through a juicer with the remaining grapes and cherries.

2 Pour into glasses, top with the halved fruits, cherries and ice cubes, and serve immediately. To make a fun decoration, skewer a halved strawberry or grape on a cocktail stick (toothpick) and hang a cherry by its stem.

No Gooseberry Fool

Combine a sharp, tangy fruit like gooseberries with the sweetness of apples, greengages and kiwi fruit for a perfect blend of flavours – not too sweet, not too sharp, in fact just perfect. Even better, this drink is 100 per cent natural and is loaded with vital vitamins and minerals, meaning you can enjoy this delicious healthy tonic at any time of the day – guilt-free.

1 Peel the kiwi fruit, then halve and stone (pit) the greengages. Core and roughly chop the apple.

2 Push the kiwi fruit, greengages, apple and gooseberries through a juicer and pour over ice cubes into a glass. Add one or two gooseberries to decorate.

Makes 1 glass

1 kiwi fruit
2 greengages
1 eating apple
90g/3½oz/scant 1 cup gooseberries, plus
 extra to decorate
ice cubes

Cook's tip
Pink-tinged dessert gooseberries tend to be sweeter than the green ones, but both taste good in this refreshing drink. You might want to freeze a punnet of gooseberries so that you have a handy supply.

Golden Wonder

Ripe plums make delicious juices and work really well with the banana and passion fruit in this unconventional blend. Use yellow plums if you can find them, as they are irresistibly sweet and juicy, but red ones can easily be substituted as long as they're really soft and ripe. Vitamin-rich and energizing, this drink is sure to set you up for the day.

Makes 1 large glass

2 passion fruit
2 yellow plums
1 small banana
about 15ml/1 tbsp lemon juice

Cook's tip
Passion fruit seeds might look pretty in a fruit juice, but they are not to everyone's taste. If you prefer a juice without seeds, press the pulp through a small sieve before adding to the blender.

1 Halve the passion fruit and, using a teaspoon, scoop the pulp into a blender or food processor. Using a small, sharp knife, halve and stone (pit) the plums and add to the blender or food processor.

2 Add the banana and lemon juice and blend the mixture until smooth, scraping the mixture down from the side of the bowl, if necessary. Pour into a large glass and check the sweetness. Add a little more lemon juice, if you like.

extra
exotic
coolers

Take juicing and blending into another league altogether with these enticing, adventurous and utterly irresistible creations. Try delicious sun-dried tomatoes with orange and tarragon or fabulous ripe pomegranates with Asian pears. Start experimenting and you'll soon discover that the possibilities are endless.

Apple Infusion

East meets West in this fabulous fusion of fresh apple and fragrant spices. Ginger is combined with apple juice and exotic, fragrant lemon grass to make a deliciously refreshing cooler. As with many of these juices, it is well worth making double the quantity and keeping a supply in the refrigerator – as you will undoubtedly be back for more.

2 Roughly chop the root ginger and cut the apples into chunks. Push the ginger and then the apples through a juicer.

3 Pour the juice into the jug and place in the refrigerator for at least 1 hour to let the flavours infuse.

4 Half-fill two or three tall glasses with ice cubes and red apple slices, if you like, and pour in the juice until it just covers the ice. Top up with sparkling water or lemonade, if you prefer, and serve immediately.

Makes 2–3 glasses

1 lemon grass stalk
15g/½oz fresh root ginger, peeled
4 red-skinned eating apples
ice cubes
sparkling water or real lemonade
red apple slices, to decorate

Cook's tip
Bruising the lemon grass stalk releases the subtle flavour, which pervades this cooler and provides a fragrant hint of the East.

1 Bruise the lemon grass stalk by pounding it with the tip of a rolling pin. Make several lengthways cuts through the stalk to open it up, keeping it intact at the thick end. Put the bruised stem into a small glass jug (pitcher).

Lavender Orange Lush

This fragrant, lavender-scented juice is guaranteed to perk up a jaded palate in no time at all. Its heavenly aroma and distinct yet subtle taste is quite divine. Make plenty and keep it in the refrigerator, adding a few extra lavender sprigs to intensify the flavour, if you like. Additional sprigs of lavender make fun stirrers or a pretty garnish if serving at a party.

Makes 4–6 glasses

10–12 lavender flowers, plus extra to serve
45ml/3 tbsp caster (superfine) sugar
8 large oranges
ice cubes

Cook's tip
This is an ideal drink to prepare for friends on a summer evening. Just pour into ice-cold glasses and then sit back and relax.

1 Pull the lavender flowers from their stalks and put them in a bowl with the sugar plus 120ml/4fl oz/½ cup boiling water. Stir until the sugar has dissolved, then leave to steep for 10 minutes.

2 Squeeze the oranges using a citrus juicer and pour the juice into a jug (pitcher). Strain the lavender syrup into the juice and chill.

3 Put a few ice cubes and a couple of lavender stirrers in some glasses, top up with the juice and serve.

Fragrant Fruits

This blend of sweet and subtle fruits packs a surprising punch. It combines a splash of lemon and a hint of fresh root ginger to add zest and bite without overpowering the delicate, fragrant flavours of lychee, cantaloupe and pear. Other types of melon can be used in place of the cantaloupe, but you will lose the pretty colour that is part of this juice's appeal.

Makes 2 tall glasses

10 lychees
1 large pear
300g/11oz wedge cantaloupe melon,
   rind removed
2cm/¾in piece fresh root ginger,
   roughly chopped
squeeze of lemon juice
crushed ice
mint sprigs, to decorate

1 Peel and stone (pit) the lychees and, using a sharp knife, cut both the pear and the melon into large chunks.

2 Push the ginger through a juicer, followed by the lychees, pear and melon. Sharpen the flavour with a little of the lemon juice to taste.

3 Place the crushed ice and one or two mint sprigs in tall glasses and pour over the juice. Place some more mints sprigs on top to decorate, then serve the juice immediately – before the ice melts.

Cook's tip
Sweet, scented lychee and perfectly ripe cantaloupe melon shine through in this gloriously fragrant, delicately coloured blend of fresh fruits. To say that this drink is simply delicious is understating its qualities – not only is it subtle and refreshing, it is also extremely good for you. If you want to be a little wicked, however, add a dash of vodka – it will add an extra special kick.

Pink Gin

Juniper berries are a vital ingredient in the making of gin and, not surprisingly, they exude distinct gin-like aromas in this fabulous drink. For a good colour, this is best made using early, forced rhubarb, which gives the juice a characteristic pink blush. Top up the gin with chilled sparkling water, or use real lemonade for a delicious, tangy taste.

Makes 4 glasses

600g/1lb 6oz rhubarb
finely grated rind and juice of 2 limes
75g/3oz/6 tbsp caster (superfine) sugar
15ml/1 tbsp juniper berries, lightly crushed
ice cubes
lime slices, quartered
sparkling mineral water, soda water (club
    soda) or real lemonade

1 Using a sharp knife, chop the rhubarb into 2cm/¾in lengths and place in a pan with the lime rind and juice.

2 Add the sugar, crushed juniper berries and 90ml/6 tbsp water. Cover with a tightly fitting lid and cook for 6–8 minutes until the rhubarb is just tender. (Test by prodding the rhubarb with the tip of a knife.)

3 Transfer the rhubarb to a food processor or blender and process to form a smooth purée. Press the mixture through a coarse sieve into a bowl and set the strained juice aside until completely cooled.

4 Half-fill medium glasses with the juice. Add ice cubes and lime slices and top up with sparkling mineral water, soda water or lemonade. Serve immediately.

Cook's tip

If the rhubarb syrup is stored for a couple of days in the refrigerator after straining, the juniper flavour will become more pronounced. The overall intensity is better if the drink is made with just rhubarb, but you could use a mixture of apple and rhubarb, if you prefer.

Watermelon and Star Anise Fizz

The delicate taste of watermelon becomes surprisingly intense when juiced, so to balance it, additional flavours need to be equally pronounced. A light syrup infused with scented star anise is the perfect choice. For maximum impact, make sure the star anise is really fresh as its liquorice-like flavour and aroma tend to fade with age.

1 Roughly crush the star anise in a mortar using a pestle, or place it in a small metal bowl and pound with the end of a rolling pin.

2 Tip the crushed spice into a small pan and add the sugar and 90ml/ 6 tbsp water. Bring to the boil, stirring, then let it bubble for about 2 minutes. Remove the pan from the heat and leave to steep for 10 minutes.

3 Cut off and discard the rind from the watermelon and, using a small, sharp knife, cut the flesh into chunks of roughly the same size, removing all of the hard black seeds.

4 Push the melon chunks through a juicer. Strain the anise syrup through a fine sieve and pour it into the melon juice. Stir well to mix the flavours together thoroughly.

5 Fill two glasses two-thirds full with the juice, then top up with sparkling water and serve immediately.

Makes 2 tall glasses

15g/½oz star anise
15ml/1 tbsp caster (superfine) sugar
500g/1¼lb wedge of watermelon
sparkling mineral water

Cook's tip
Sweet, scented, frothy pink bubbles make this heavenly juice perfect as a non-alcoholic cocktail to serve at parties. Or enjoy it as a cooling thirst-quencher on a long, hot summer afternoon.

Kiwi and Stem Ginger Spritzer

The delicate, refreshingly tangy flavour of kiwi fruit becomes sweeter and more intense when the flesh is juiced. Choose plump, unwrinkled fruits that give a little when gently pressed as under-ripe fruits will produce a slightly bitter taste. A single kiwi fruit contains more than one day's vitamin C requirement, so this juice will really boost the system.

Makes 1 tall glass

2 kiwi fruit
1 piece preserved stem ginger, plus 15ml/
    1 tbsp syrup from the ginger jar
sparkling mineral water

1 Using a sharp knife, roughly chop the kiwi fruit and the ginger. (For a better colour you can peel the kiwi fruit first, but this is not essential.)

2 Push the ginger and kiwi fruit through a juicer and pour the juice into a jug (pitcher). Stir in the ginger syrup.

3 Pour the juice into a tall glass, then top up with sparkling mineral water and serve immediately.

Cook's tip

Kiwis are a subtropical fruit, not a tropical one, so it is best to store them in the refrigerator before using. If you want them to ripen quickly, store in a closed plastic bag with an apple, pear or banana.

Spiced Pomegranate and Asian Pear Fizz

Sweet but with a milder flavour than traditional pears, Asian pears make a good partner for the fresh tang of pomegranates. Juice the fruits in advance if you have the time, so the spice can mellow into the fruits, all ready for topping up with fizzy tonic water.

Makes 2 glasses

2 Asian pears
1.5ml/¼ tsp ground allspice
1 pomegranate
5–10ml/1–2 tsp clear honey
ice cubes
tonic water
pear wedges and pomegranate seeds,
   to decorate

Cook's tip
Ideal for slimmers, pears are virtually fat-free and contain absolutely no cholesterol or sodium. They also provide significant amounts of vitamin C and potassium.

1 Using a small, sharp knife, chop the pears into large chunks. Mix the allspice in a jug (pitcher) with 15ml/ 1 tbsp boiling water.

2 Halve the pomegranate. Working over the jug to catch the juices, peel away the skin and layers of pith to leave the clusters of seeds.

3 Push the pears and pomegranate seeds through a juicer and mix together in the jug with the allspice. Stir in a little honey to sweeten, then chill.

4 Pour the juice into glasses until two-thirds full. Serve with ice cubes, pear wedges and pomegranate seeds to decorate. Top up with tonic water.

Elderflower, Plum and Ginger Juice

Captured in cordials and juices, the aromatic flavour of elderflowers can be enjoyed all year round. Here it is used with fresh root ginger to give an exotic boost to sweet, juicy plums. Serve this juice just as it is over plenty of crushed ice or top up with sparkling water, if you prefer a more diluted drink. It is an utterly delicious and wonderfully uplifting blend.

Makes 2–3 glasses

15g/½oz fresh root ginger
500g/1lb 2oz ripe plums
125ml/4½fl oz/generous ½ cup sweetened
   elderflower cordial
ice cubes
sparkling water or tonic water
mint sprigs and plum slices, to decorate

Cook's tip
The elder is a tree or bush with perfumed, yellowish-white flowers and tiny black-violet berries, both of which are thought to be medicinal.

1 Roughly chop the ginger without peeling. Halve and stone (pit) the plums.

2 Push half the plums through a juicer, followed by the ginger then the remaining plums. Mix the juice with the elderflower cordial in a jug (pitcher).

3 Place the ice cubes into two large or three medium-sized glasses. Pour over the juice until the glasses are two-thirds full. Place the mint sprigs and plum slices on top to decorate and top up with sparkling mineral water or tonic water. Serve immediately.

Thyme-Scented Plum Lush

Make this divine drink in the early autumn when plums are at their sweetest and best. Their silky smooth flesh blends down to produce the most wonderfully textured smoothie, while delicately scented lemon thyme and honey complement the flavour perfectly. This luxurious juice is easy to make and has an irresistible fragrance that is at once warming and refreshing.

Makes 2–3 glasses

400g/14oz red plums
30–45ml/2–3 tbsp clear honey
15ml/1 tbsp chopped fresh lemon thyme,
   plus extra thyme sprigs to decorate
100g/3¾oz crushed ice

Cook's tip
Dark, purplish-red plums, with their almost violet bloom and sweet, intense flavour, juice well and make some of the most tempting and vibrant fruit drinks.

1 Using a sharp knife, halve and stone (pit) the plums and put in a blender or food processor. Add 30ml/2 tbsp of the honey and the lemon thyme and blend until smooth, scraping down the side of the bowl, if necessary.

2 Add the ice and blend until slushy. Taste for sweetness, adding a little more honey if necessary. Pour into glasses and serve immediately, decorated with a sprig of thyme.

Iced Pear Aniseed

Aniseed is a spice widely used in cooking, not only in sweet and savoury dishes but as the dominant flavour in many alcoholic drinks like pastis, ouzo and raki. If these flavours appeal to you – without the alcohol, though – you'll love this deliciously spicy pear-based infusion. Serve in small glasses over plenty of crushed ice. Add a slice or two of fresh pear, if you like.

Makes 2–3 glasses

30ml/2 tbsp aniseeds
30ml/2 tbsp caster (superfine) sugar
3 soft, ripe pears
10ml/2 tsp lemon juice
crushed ice

1 Using a mortar and pestle, lightly crush the aniseeds. (Alternatively, use a small bowl and the end of a rolling pin to crush the seeds.) Put in a small pan with the sugar and 100ml/3½fl oz/ scant ½ cup water. Heat very gently, stirring until the sugar has dissolved. Bring to the boil and boil for 1 minute. Pour the syrup into a small jug (pitcher) and leave to cool completely.

2 Quarter the pears and remove the cores. Push through a juicer. Add the lemon juice. Strain the syrup into the pear juice and chill until ready to serve. Pour over crushed ice in small glasses.

Cook's tip

For a great-tasting juice that really packs a punch, make sure you use fresh, sweet pears as underripe ones will result in a disappointing and almost bland juice.

It is also important to use fresh and aromatic aniseed. Like all herbs and spices, aniseed loses its flavour extremely quickly and, when it turns stale, it lacks flavour and has a slightly musty aroma, which could ruin your drink.

Red Hot Chilli Pepper

Sweet red peppers make a colourful, light juice that's best mixed with other ingredients for a full flavour impact. Courgettes add a subtle, almost unnoticeable body to the drink, while chilli and radishes add a wonderful kick of peppery heat. Freshly squeezed orange juice gives a delicious underlying zest to this extremely drinkable beverage.

1 Halve the red peppers, remove the cores and seeds, quarter the pieces and push them through a juicer with the chilli. Cut the courgettes into chunks, halve the radishes and push them through the juicer.

2 Squeeze the orange and stir the juice into the vegetable juice. Fill two or three glasses with ice, pour over the juice and serve immediately.

Makes 2–3 glasses

2 red (bell) peppers
1 fresh red chilli, seeded
150g/5oz courgettes (zucchini)
75g/3oz radishes
1 orange
ice cubes

Cook's tip
When working with chillies, always wash your hands thoroughly after chopping them. Avoid touching your eyes or any other delicate area because it really will sting.

Tarragon, Orange and Sun-Dried Tomato Juice

Lovers of tomato juice are sure to get hooked on this flavour-packed, vitalizing blend. Fresh orange makes it irresistibly moreish and adds extra vitamin C, while tarragon adds a lovely aromatic note. Add a dash of Tabasco or chilli sauce instead of the ground black pepper if you simply cannot resist the classic combination of chilli and tomato.

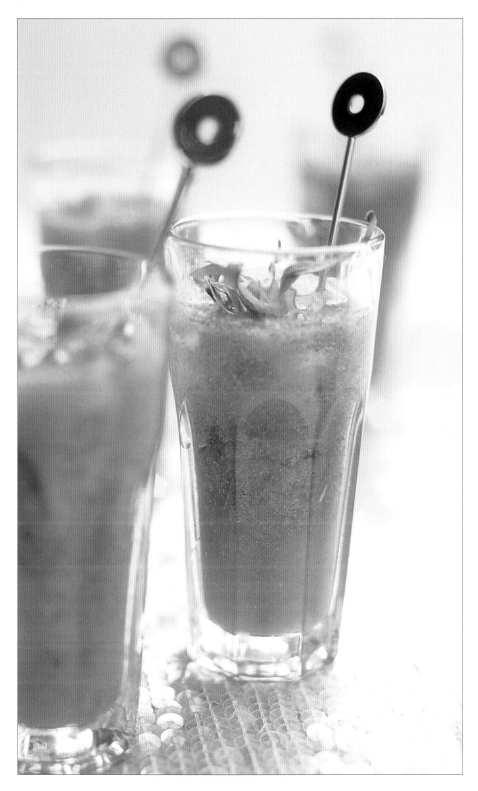

Makes 2 glasses

4 large sprigs of tarragon, plus extra to garnish
500g/1lb 2oz tomatoes
2 large oranges
15ml/1 tbsp sun-dried tomato paste
ice cubes
ground black pepper

1 Pull the tarragon leaves from their stalks. Roughly chop the tomatoes. Push them through a juicer, alternating with the tarragon leaves.

2 Squeeze the juice from the oranges by hand or using a citrus juicer. Stir into the tomato and tarragon juice. Add the sun-dried tomato paste and stir well to mix all the ingredients together.

3 Place ice cubes into two glasses and pour over the juice. Serve immediately with pretty stirrers (if you have them), a sprinkling of black pepper to taste and tarragon sprigs to garnish.

easy breakfast blends

Breakfast is the most important meal of the day but also the most neglected, so give yourself a kick-start with these fuel-packed, imaginative drinks. Made in minutes and easier to digest than a bowl of cereal, fabulous fresh fruit juices and decadent mocha smoothies provide the perfect early-morning boost.

Citrus Tingler

With a reliable abundance of oranges available throughout the year, it is all too easy to overlook the more unusual citrus fruits. This citrus trio combines the sharp, grapefruit-like fragrance of pomelos, the mild sweetness of Ugli fruit and the vibrant colour of flavour-packed mandarins.

1 Halve the fruits and squeeze the juice using a citrus juicer. Add a little squeeze of lemon or lime juice, if you like, to create a sharper flavour.

2 Pour the juice into a tall glass and add ice cubes and a few citrus fruit slices to decorate. Serve immediately.

Makes 1 glass

1 pomelo
1 Ugli fruit
1 mandarin
squeeze of lemon or lime juice (optional)
ice cubes
citrus fruit slices, to decorate

Cook's tip

If you are making breakfast for your partner or the family, simply multiply the ingredients by the number of people that you are serving – or even better, let them make their own.

Morning After

A Bloody Mary is a traditional hangover cure with a reputation for actually working. Spicy, refreshing and mildly alcoholic – if you can face it – this version will invigorate sluggish energy levels with a generous dose of vitamin C and antioxidants to cleanse your system.

Makes 1 glass

300g/11oz ripe tomatoes
5ml/1 tsp Tabasco or Worcestershire sauce
5ml/1 tsp lemon juice
15–30ml/1–2 tbsp vodka (optional)
crushed ice
celery leaves, to decorate

Cook's tip
You don't need to have a hangover to enjoy this rich, refreshing drink, but if you want to have it for breakfast on a regular basis, it's best to leave out the vodka.

1 Roughly chop the tomatoes and push through a juicer.

2 Add the Tabasco or Worcestershire sauce, lemon juice and vodka, if using. Pour over plenty of crushed ice in a large glass. Add a few celery leaves and serve immediately.

Creamy Banana Boost

Bananas are a great energy food. They are packed with valuable nutrients and healthy carbohydrates, and they also fill you up – which is definitely a bonus. Blended with the additional fruits – pineapple, dates and lemon juice – and creamy milk, this delicious concoction will keep you going for hours. If you're prone to snacking throughout the day, try this and you'll feel all the better for it. Any leftover drink can be stored in the refrigerator for up to a day.

Makes 2–3 tall glasses

½ pineapple
4 Medjool dates, pitted
1 small ripe banana
juice of 1 lemon
300ml/½ pint/1¼ cups very cold full cream (whole) milk or soya milk

Cook's tip
The Medjool date is considered to be the jewel of all dates because of its size, texture and sweetness. It originates from Morocco, where it was reserved for royal hosts and other dignitaries centuries ago. Nowadays we can all enjoy them.

1 Using a small, sharp knife, cut away the skin and core from the pineapple. Roughly chop the flesh and put it in a blender or food processor, then add the pitted dates.

2 Peel and chop the banana and add it to the rest of the fruit together with the lemon juice.

3 Blend thoroughly until smooth, stopping to scrape the mixture down from the side of the bowl with a rubber spatula, if necessary.

4 Add the milk to the blender or food processor and process briefly until well combined. Pour the smoothie into tall glasses and serve immediately.

Zesty Soya Smoothie

Whizzed up with freshly squeezed orange juice, a splash of tangy lemon and a little fragrant honey, tofu can be transformed into a drink that's smooth, creamy, nutritious and delicious. Most people would not think to add tofu to a blended drink, but please do try it – you will be genuinely surprised. If possible, try to get hold of some silken tofu for this smoothie, as it has a wonderful satiny texture that blends particularly well.

Makes 1 large glass

2 oranges
15ml/1 tbsp lemon juice
20–25ml/4–5 tsp sunflower honey or herb honey
150g/5oz tofu
long, thin strips of pared orange rind, to decorate

Cook's tip
If you prefer a smooth drink, strain the liquid through a sieve after blending to remove the orange rind.

1 Finely grate the rind of one orange and set aside. Use a citrus juicer to juice both oranges and pour the juice into a food processor or blender. Add the grated orange rind, lemon juice, sunflower or herb honey and tofu.

2 Whizz the ingredients until smooth and creamy, then pour into a glass. Decorate with the pared orange rind and serve.

Opposite: Creamy banana boost (left) and Zesty soya smoothie (right)

Dairy-Free Deluxe

Prunes, apples, oranges and soya milk may seem like an unusual combination but the results are absolutely fabulous. Sweet, caramel-rich and very drinkable, this is a great milkshake for both adults and children, and, of course, for anyone on a dairy-free diet. Regular cow's milk can be used, if you prefer, but if you are watching the calories, use skimmed milk. The resulting drink will not be quite as creamy, but it will still be delicious.

Makes 1 tall glass

2 small eating apples
5 ready-to-eat pitted prunes
juice of 1 orange
60ml/4 tbsp soya milk
ice cubes

Cook's tip

Any eating apples can be used for this drink. If you prefer a tart flavour opt for a Granny Smith or a Cox's Pippin; if not, go for a sweet apple like the Royal Gala.

1 Using a small, sharp knife, remove the core from the apples and chop into chunks – but do not peel them. Push half the chopped apple through a juicer, followed by the prunes and the remaining chopped apple.

2 Pour the apple and prune juice into a jug (pitcher) and add the orange juice and soya milk. Whisk lightly until smooth and frothy. Pour into a chunky glass and serve immediately, adding a few cubes of ice.

Pear Flair

For a truly refreshing combination, you can't do much better than a mixture of juicy pears and grapes. Wheatgerm adds body for a sustained energy fix and soya yogurt turns the juice into a protein-packed milkshake with a lusciously light and frothy topping. This really is quite a filling drink and is a great choice for those who feel that their life is too busy to prepare really nutritious food. A quick and easy drink that is good for you too – what could be better?

Makes 1 large glass

1 large pear
150g/5oz/1¼ cups green grapes
15ml/1 tbsp wheatgerm
60ml/4 tbsp soya yogurt
ice cubes

Cook's tip

If you would prefer to use a dairy yogurt rather than the soya variety, substitute with the type of your choice. It is better that you stick with a natural (plain) yogurt as plenty of fruity flavour is gained from the pear and the grapes. Look for the 0 per cent fat varieties.

1 Using a vegetable peeler, peel the pear and chop the flesh into large chunks of roughly the same size.

2 Push half the pear chunks through a juicer, followed by the grapes and then the remaining chunks of pear. Transfer the juice to a small jug (pitcher).

3 Add the wheatgerm to the yogurt and stir to mix thoroughly.

4 Pour into the pear and grape juice, whisking until it is light and frothy. Pour the milkshake over ice cubes and serve.

Opposite: Dairy-free deluxe (left) and Pear flair (right)

Passion Fruit and Orange Crush

The scent and taste of this juice achieves that perfect balance of aromas and flavours. Sweet, zesty orange juice sits in perfect harmony with aromatic cardamom and intensely fragrant passion fruit to make the most heavenly juice imaginable. And, as well as the fabulous flavour and glorious colour, you get a generous shot of valuable vitamin C.

Makes 2 glasses

15ml/1 tbsp cardamom pods
15ml/1 tbsp caster (superfine) sugar
2 passion fruit
4 large oranges
ice cubes
halved orange slices, to decorate

1 Crush the cardamom pods in a mortar with a pestle or place them in a small, metal bowl and pound with the end of a rolling pin until the seeds are exposed.

2 Tip the cardamom pods, with any stray seeds, into a small pan. Add the sugar and stir in 90ml/6 tbsp water. Cover and simmer for 5 minutes.

3 Halve the passion fruit and scoop the pulp into a small jug (pitcher). Squeeze the oranges in a citrus juicer or by hand and tip the juice into the jug. Strain the cardamom syrup through a fine sieve into the fruit juice and whisk the mixture to distribute the passion fruit and make a light froth.

4 Half-fill tall glasses with ice cubes and pour over the juice. Slip the orange slices into the glasses to serve as edible decoration.

Cook's tip
The dark seeds in passion fruit look pretty when suspended in the juice and are perfectly edible, but they do not offer any nutrition and can get stuck between your teeth. If you don't want them in the drink, press the pulp through a small sieve with the back of a wooden spoon and just use the juice.

Sweet yet sharp, delicate yet robust, mouth-puckering yet refreshing – each and every sip of this unbelievably delicious blend will delight you.

Mango and Lime Lassi

Inspired by the classic Indian drink, this tangy, fruity blend is great for breakfast or as a delicious pick-me-up at any time of day. Soft, ripe mango blended with yogurt and sharp, zesty lime and lemon juice makes a wonderfully thick, cooling drink that's packed with energy. It can also be enjoyed as a mellow soother when you need to unwind.

Makes 2 tall glasses

1 mango
finely grated rind and juice of 1 lime
15ml/1 tbsp lemon juice
5–10ml/1–2 tsp caster (superfine) sugar
100ml/3½fl oz/scant ½ cup natural
   (plain) yogurt
mineral water
1 extra lime, halved, to serve

1 Peel the mango and cut the flesh from the stone (pit). Put the flesh into a blender or food processor and add the lime rind and juice.

2 Add the lemon juice, sugar and natural yogurt. Whizz until completely smooth, scraping down the sides of the bowl, if necessary. Stir in a little mineral water to thin it down.

3 Serve immediately, with half a lime on the side of each glass so that more juice can be squeezed in, if desired.

Peachy Pleasure

When juiced together, apricots, peaches and kumquats produce the most amazingly vibrant orange-coloured juice with a flavour that has just as big a kick – and it is utterly delicious. The natural sugar content of apricots and peaches can vary enormously so you will need to add some honey to get the taste just right. Add a little at a time, then stir and, of course, keep tasting the juice until you find exactly the right flavour for you.

Makes 2 glasses

4 kumquats
6 ripe apricots, stoned (pitted)
2 peaches, stoned (pitted)
clear honey, to taste
ice cubes

Cook's tip

This drink is ideal for informal parties as well as a quick breakfast. If you are having friends round for dinner or drinks, make some funky New York cocktail-style stirrers. Simply halve some apricots, thread them on to long wooden skewers and place a skewer in each glass.

1 Using a small, sharp knife, roughly chop the kumquats and cut the apricots and peaches into large chunks. (There is no need to peel the fruit.)

2 Push the kumquat pieces through a juicer, followed by the apricot and peach chunks, alternating the fruit as you go to ensure they mix well.

3 Fill 2 large glasses with ice cubes and pour the fruit juice over the ice.

4 Stir in a little honey to the juice and taste. Add a little more honey if the juice is not sweet enough. (Be careful not to add too much honey, however, or it will overpower the other flavours and spoil the drink.) Serve immediately.

Tropicana

Even in winter this drink can brighten your day with its lively colour and deliciously tropical, fruity flavour. Any blend of tropical fruits will make a fabulous tasty juice as long as they are really ripe and ready for use. Persimmon and guavas can both be quite bitter if juiced when underripe so, if necessary, leave the fruits in the fruit bowl to ripen for a few days before using – the resulting juice will definitely be well worth the wait.

Makes 2–3 glasses

1 large papaya
1 persimmon
1 large guava
juice of 2 oranges
2 passion fruit, halved

Cook's tip

When chopping the fruit, cut some into chunky slices and reserve for decoration, if you like. Otherwise throw in some fruit chunks at the end to add some texture.

1 Halve the papaya, then scoop out and discard the black seeds. Using a small, sharp knife, cut the papaya, persimmon and guava flesh into large chunks of roughly the same size. (There's no need to peel them.)

2 Push the papaya through a juicer, followed by the persimmon and the guava. Pour the juice into a jug (pitcher), then add the orange juice and scoop in the passion fruit pulp. Whisk and chill until ready to serve.

Sweet Dream

A soothing blend guaranteed to wake you up slowly, this fruity threesome is naturally sweet so there is no need for any additional sugar. Fresh grapefruit juice marries brilliantly with the dried fruits, and rich creamy yogurt makes a delicious contrast of colour and flavour – simply perfect to sip over a leisurely breakfast while reading the newspaper.

Makes 2 glasses

25g/1oz/scant ¼ cup dried figs or
   dates, stoned (pitted)
50g/2oz/¼ cup ready-to-eat prunes
25g/1oz/scant ¼ cup sultanas (golden raisins)
1 grapefruit
350ml/12fl oz/1½ cups full cream
   (whole) milk
30ml/2 tbsp Greek (US strained plain) yogurt

Cook's tip
For a dairy-free version of this drink, omit the yogurt and use soya or rice milk instead of ordinary milk. The consistency of the smoothie will not be as creamy but it will still be delicious – and perhaps better for those who prefer a lighter drink.

1 Put the dried fruits in a blender or food processor. Squeeze the grapefruit juice and add to the machine. Blend until smooth, scraping the mixture down from the side of the bowl, if necessary. Add the milk and blend until completely smooth.

2 Using a teaspoon, tap a spoonful of the yogurt around the inside of each of two tall glasses. Pour in the fruit mixture and serve immediately.

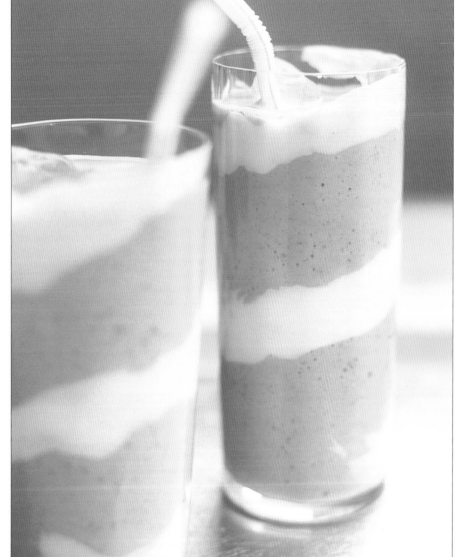

Raspberry and Oatmeal Smoothie

Just a spoonful or so of oatmeal gives substance to this tangy, invigorating drink. If you can, prepare it ahead of time because soaking the raw oats helps to break down the starch into natural sugars that are easy to digest. The smoothie will thicken up in the refrigerator so you might need to stir in a little extra juice or mineral water just before serving.

Makes 1 large glass

25ml/1½ tbsp medium oatmeal
150g/5oz/scant 1 cup raspberries
5–10ml/1–2 tsp clear honey
45ml/3 tbsp natural (plain) yogurt

1 Spoon the oatmeal into a heatproof bowl. Pour in 120ml/4fl oz/½ cup boiling water and leave to stand for about 10 minutes.

2 Put the soaked oats in a blender or food processor and add all but two or three of the raspberries, the honey and about 30ml/2 tbsp of the yogurt. Process until smooth, scraping down the side of the bowl if necessary.

Cook's tip

If you don't like raspberry pips (seeds) in your smoothies, press the fruit through a sieve with the back of a wooden spoon to make a smooth purée, then process with the oatmeal and yogurt as before. Alternatively, try using redcurrants instead of the raspberries.

Although a steaming bowl of porridge can't be beaten as a winter warmer, this smooth, oaty drink makes a great, light alternative in warmer months. It is a good way to make sure you get your fill of wholesome oats for breakfast.

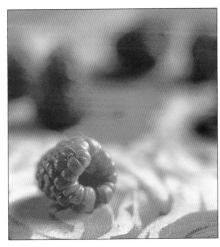

3 Pour the raspberry and oatmeal smoothie into a large glass, swirl in the remaining yogurt and top with the reserved raspberries.

Big Breakfast

Easy to prepare and even easier to drink, this energy-packed smoothie makes a great start to the day. Bananas and sesame seeds provide the perfect fuel in the form of slow-release carbohydrate that will keep you going all morning, while fresh and zesty orange juice and sweet, scented mango will set your tastebuds tingling first thing.

Makes 2 glasses

½ mango
1 banana
1 large orange
30ml/2 tbsp wheat bran
15ml/1 tbsp sesame seeds
10–15ml/2–3 tsp honey

Cook's tip
Mango juice is naturally very sweet so you may wish to add less honey or leave it out altogether. Taste the drink to decide how much you need.

1 Using a small, sharp knife, skin the mango, then slice the flesh off the stone (pit). Peel the banana and break it into short lengths, then place it in a blender or food processor with the mango.

2 Squeeze the juice from the orange and add to the blender or food processor along with the bran, sesame seeds and honey. Whizz until the mixture is smooth and creamy, then pour into glasses and serve.

Muesli Smoothly

Another great breakfast booster, this store-cupboard smoothie can be a lifesaver if you've run out of fresh fruit. It's also a perfect option for breakfast in bed without the crumbs. Any extra drink can be covered and stored overnight in the refrigerator, although you'll probably need to add more milk in the morning as it will undoubtedly thicken on standing.

Makes 2 glasses

1 piece preserved stem ginger, plus
   30ml/2 tbsp syrup from the ginger jar
50g/2oz/¼ cup ready-to-eat dried apricots,
   halved or quartered
40g/1½oz/scant ½ cup natural
   muesli (granola)
about 200ml/7fl oz/scant 1 cup
   semi-skimmed (low-fat) milk

Cook's tip
Apricot and ginger are perfect partners in this divine drink. It makes an incredibly healthy, tasty breakfast, but is so delicious and indulgent that you could even serve it as a dessert after a summer meal.

1 Chop the preserved ginger and put it in a blender or food processor with the syrup, apricots, muesli and milk.

2 Process until smooth, adding more milk if necessary. Serve in wide glasses.

Late Breakfast

This energizing blend is simply bursting with goodness, just what you need when the morning has got off to a slow start. Not only is tofu a perfect source of protein, it is also rich in minerals and contains nutrients that protect against dangerous diseases. Blended with seeds and vitamin-rich strawberries, this creamy blend should see you through until lunchtime. Store any leftovers in the refrigerator for later in the day or the following morning.

Makes 2 glasses

250g/9oz firm tofu
200g/7oz/1¾ cups strawberries
45ml/3 tbsp pumpkin or sunflower seeds,
   plus extra for sprinkling
30–45ml/2–3 tbsp clear honey
juice of 2 large oranges
juice of 1 lemon

Cook's tip
Almost any other fruit can be used instead of the strawberries. Those that blend well, such as mangoes, bananas, peaches, plums and raspberries, work particularly well as a substitute.

1 Roughly chop the tofu, then hull and roughly chop the strawberries. Reserve a few strawberry chunks.

2 Put all the ingredients in a blender or food processor and blend until completely smooth, scraping the mixture down from the side of the bowl, if necessary.

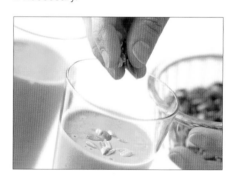

3 Pour into tumblers and sprinkle with extra seeds and strawberry chunks.

A Good Fix

While some people thrive on a glass of freshly juiced fruits first thing in the morning, others can't quite get going without their daily caffeine fix in the form of strong coffee. This gorgeous mocha smoothie combines decadent dark chocolate and caffeine-rich coffee in a deliciously frothy energizing mix. This is an intensely sweet and indulgent way to start the day – so don't treat yourself too often.

Makes 1 large glass

40g/1½oz plain (semisweet) chocolate,
 plus extra for decoration
5–10ml/1–2 tsp instant espresso powder
300ml/½ pint/1¼ cups full cream (whole) milk
30ml/2 tbsp double (heavy) cream (optional)
ice cubes
cocoa powder (unsweetened), for dusting

1 Chop the chocolate into pieces and place in a small, heavy pan with the espresso powder and 100ml/3½ fl oz/ scant ½ cup of the milk. Heat very gently, stirring with a wooden spoon, until the chocolate has melted. Remove from the heat and pour into a bowl. Leave to cool for 10 minutes.

2 Add the remaining milk and cream, if using, and whisk the mixture together until smooth and frothy – you could use a handheld blender wand. Pour the smoothie over ice cubes in a large glass or mug and serve sprinkled with cocoa powder and chocolate shavings.

smooth
&
simple

Refreshingly tangy or as smooth as silk, super smoothies have earned their place as one of our favourite drinks. Keep them simple with pure fruit blends, or try something a little different by adding creamed coconut, fruit tea, herbs or spices. Let the irresistible ideas in this chapter inspire you to experiment with all kinds of combinations.

  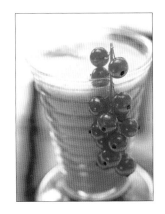

Ruby Dreamer

Figs have a distinctive yet delicate taste and are best used in simple combinations, with ingredients that enhance, rather than mask, their flavour. Like most fruits, fresh figs are now available most of the year round but they are often at their best in winter when ruby oranges are also in season – giving you the perfect excuse to make this veritable treat of a smoothie.

1 Cut off the hard, woody tips from the stalks of the figs, then use a sharp knife to cut each fruit in half.

2 Squeeze the oranges, using a citrus juicer or by hand. Pour the juice into a blender or food processor and add the figs and sugar. Process well until the mixture is really smooth and fairly thick, scraping the fruit down from the side of the bowl, if necessary.

3 Add lemon juice and blend briefly. Pour over crushed ice and serve.

Makes 2 glasses

6 large ripe figs
4 ruby oranges
15ml/1 tbsp dark muscovado (molasses) sugar
30–45ml/2–3 tbsp lemon juice
crushed ice

Cook's tip
If you cannot find ruby oranges, use any other type of orange. The colour of the juice, however, will not be quite so vibrant.

Mango Mania

Even people on a dairy-free diet can enjoy rich, creamy, indulgent drinks. This one is made using soya milk, which is particularly good in milkshakes and smoothies. It has a lovely caramel flavour that blends brilliantly with fruit purées, especially those made from fruits with an intense, naturally sweet taste like mangoes.

Makes 2 tall glasses

1 medium mango
300ml/½ pint/1¼ cups soya milk
finely grated rind and juice of 1 lime,
    plus extra rind for garnish
15–30ml/1–2 tbsp clear honey
crushed ice

Cook's tip
If you like very sweet drinks, choose soya milk sweetened with apple juice for this recipe. It is readily available in supermarkets and has a really rich flavour.

1 Using a sharp knife, peel the mango and cut the flesh off the stone (pit). Place the chopped flesh in a blender or food processor and add the soya milk, lime rind and juice and a little honey. Blend until smooth and frothy.

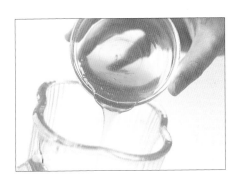

2 Taste the mixture and add more honey, if you like, blending until well mixed. Place some crushed ice in two glasses, then pour over the smoothie. Sprinkle with lime rind and serve.

Smooth and Simple

Pre-packed and ready to use, a mixed bag of summer fruits (which can be bought from the freezer section in most large supermarkets) makes an unbelievably simple, fruity base for drinks. The frozen fruits mean that the final blend is perfectly chilled as well, so you don't need to add ice. Mixed with orange juice and enriched with a tempting swirl of cream, this smoothie is made in a flash – the perfect accompaniment to a relaxing afternoon in the sunshine.

Makes 3 glasses

500g/1lb 2oz frozen mixed summer fruits, partially thawed
30ml/2 tbsp caster (superfine) sugar
about 300ml/½ pint/1¼ cups freshly squeezed orange juice
60ml/4 tbsp single (light) cream

Cook's tip
If you do not want to squeeze the oranges, you can buy juice – but avoid the concentrated types.

1 Tip all but a few of the summer fruits into a blender or food processor and add the sugar and orange juice. Blend until smooth, adding a little more orange juice if the mixture is too thick.

2 Pour the smoothie into 3 tall glasses and, using a teaspoon, swirl a little cream into each glass. Top with the reserved fruits and serve with long spoons to mix in the cream.

Fruit-Tea Smoothie

Depending on your preference you can use any of the varied assortment of fruit teas, now readily available in most large supermarkets, for this thick, creamy blend. This recipe uses dried apricots and apples but you could easily replace these with dried pears, peaches or tropical dried fruits. From start to finish, this smoothie takes about one hour to prepare, so make sure you don't leave this one until the last minute.

Makes 2 glasses

50g/2oz dried apples
25g/1oz dried apricots
2 fruit teabags
juice of 1 lemon
30ml/2 tbsp crème fraîche or natural (plain) yogurt
mineral water (optional)

Cook's tip
Apple and lemon, apple and mango, forest berries and strawberry and raspberry fruit teas are just a few that are readily available. When choosing the dried fruit, pick the types that will work best with the flavours in your tea.

3 Put the fruit and tea mixture into a blender or food processor and add the lemon juice. Blend well until smooth, scraping the mixture down from the side of the bowl, if necessary.

1 Using a small, sharp knife, roughly chop the dried apples and apricots. Steep the teabags in 300ml/½ pint/ 1¼ cups boiling water for 5 minutes, then remove the teabags.

2 Add the chopped fruit to the tea and leave to stand for 30 minutes. Chill in the refrigerator for about 30 minutes until the tea is completely cold.

4 Add the crème fraîche or yogurt and blend briefly, adding a little mineral water if the smoothie is too thick. Serve in tall glasses.

Very Berry

Fresh and frozen cranberries are often in short supply, but dried berries are available all year round and make a tasty dairy-free shake when combined with soya milk. Tiny crimson redcurrants make the perfect partner for the dried cranberries in this refreshingly tart, sparkling smoothie, and this low-fat blend is packed with natural sugars, essential nutrients and vitamins.

Makes 1 large glass

25g/1oz/¼ cup dried cranberries
150g/5oz/1¼ cups redcurrants, plus extra
   to decorate
10ml/2 tsp clear honey
50ml/2fl oz/¼ cup soya milk
sparkling mineral water

1 Put the cranberries in a small bowl, pour over 90ml/6 tbsp boiling water and leave to stand for 10 minutes.

2 String the redcurrants by drawing the stems through the tines of a fork to pull off the delicate currants.

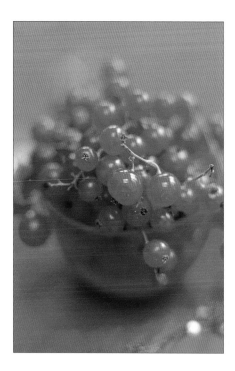

3 Put the currants in a food processor or blender with the cranberries and soaking water. Blend well until smooth.

4 Add the honey and soya milk and whizz briefly to combine the ingredients.

5 Pour the berry shake into a large glass, then top with a little sparkling mineral water to lighten the drink. Drape the redcurrants decoratively over the edge of the glass and serve the smoothie immediately.

Cook's tip
Allowing time for the dried cranberries to rehydrate means they will become plump and juicy – making them much easier to blend and maximizing their flavour.

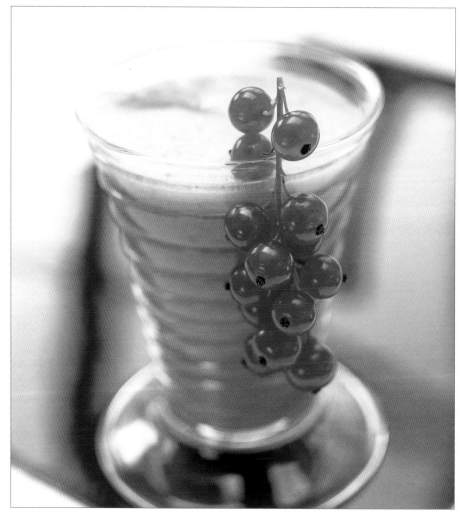

Purple Haze

Thick, dark blueberry purée swirled into pale and creamy vanilla-flavoured buttermilk looks stunning and tastes simply divine. Despite its creaminess, the buttermilk gives this sumptuous smoothie a delicious sharp tang. If you do not like buttermilk or cannot find it in your local supermarket, you could use a mixture of half natural yogurt and half milk instead.

Makes 2 tall glasses

250g/9oz/2¼ cups blueberries
50g/2oz/¼ cup caster (superfine) sugar
15ml/1 tbsp lemon juice
300ml/½ pint/1¼ cups buttermilk
5ml/1 tsp vanilla essence (extract)
150ml/¼ pint/⅔ cup full cream (whole) milk

1 Push the blueberries through a juicer and stir in 15ml/1 tbsp of the sugar and the lemon juice. Stir well and divide between two tall glasses.

2 Put the buttermilk, vanilla essence, milk and remaining sugar in a blender or food processor and blend until really frothy. (Alternatively, use a hand-held electric blender and blend until the mixture froths up.)

3 Pour the buttermilk mixture over the blueberry juice so the mixtures swirl together naturally – there is no need to stir them together as it tastes and looks better if they remain separate to a certain degree. Serve immediately.

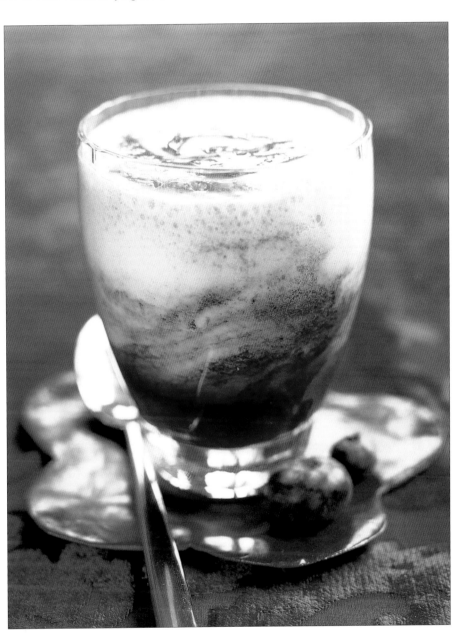

Cook's tip
Deep violet blueberry juice makes a fantastic contrast in both colour and flavour to the buttermilk. If you cannot get hold of blueberries, other slightly tart fruits such as raspberries or blackberries would also work in this creamy combination.

Berry Smooth

This simple recipe uses oat milk, a cholesterol-free, calcium-rich alternative to cow's milk, and a good partner to sweet summer fruits. Although a good store-cupboard stand-by, you might prefer to keep the oat milk in the refrigerator, ready for an impromptu milkshake whenever you're in the mood. For a really chilled, extremely refreshing flavour, use a mixed bag of semi-thawed frozen fruits, which will blend to a fabulously thick consistency.

Makes 2 glasses

250g/9oz frozen mixed summer fruits,
   partially thawed, plus extra to garnish
130g/4½oz/generous ½ cup soya yogurt
45ml/3 tbsp vanilla syrup
350ml/12fl oz/1½ cups oat milk

Cook's tip

Vanilla syrup is really sweet and full of flavour, great for giving drinks and desserts a deep, mellow flavour. If you cannot find any, use 45ml/3 tbsp caster (superfine) sugar and 5ml/1 tsp good quality vanilla essence (extract).

1 Put the partially thawed mixed summer fruits in a blender or food processor. Add the soya yogurt and blend thoroughly to make a thick purée. Scrape the mixture down from the side of the bowl with a rubber spatula, if necessary, and blend again, briefly, to incorporate into the mixture.

2 Add the vanilla syrup and oat milk to the fruit purée and blend the mixture again until smooth.

3 Transfer the smoothie to a small jug (pitcher) and chill, or pour it into two tall glasses and serve immediately, decorated with the extra fruits.

Pear, Rhubarb and Cranberry Cooler

For best results this delicious smoothie should be made with really ripe and extremely juicy pears, so if the ones you buy are hard, leave them in the fruit bowl for several days before making this fresh and fruity treat. Do not forget to cook the rhubarb well in advance so that it has plenty of time to cool down before you start blending.

Makes 3–4 glasses

400g/14oz early rhubarb
2 large ripe pears
130g/4½oz/generous 1 cup fresh or
   frozen cranberries
90g/3½oz/½ cup caster (superfine) sugar
mineral water (optional)

Cook's tip

If you are using frozen cranberries, don't bother to thaw them first. They'll still blend, and their icy coolness will chill the smoothie to just the right temperature.

1 Using a small, sharp knife, trim the rhubarb and cut into 2cm/¾in lengths.

2 Place the rhubarb slices in a pan with 90ml/6 tbsp water and cover with a tight-fitting lid. Cook gently for about 5 minutes or until tender. Transfer to a bowl and leave to cool, putting several pieces aside for garnish.

3 Peel, quarter and core the pears and tip into a blender or food processor with the cranberries, the rhubarb and its cooking juices and the sugar.

4 Blend until smooth, scraping down the side of the bowl, if necessary. Thin with mineral water, if you like, then serve, garnished with the rhubarb pieces.

Rosemary Nectar

This is one of those smoothies that's only worth making if you've got the perfect, ripe ingredients. The fabulously aromatic fragrance of fresh rosemary reacts with the sweet, scented flavour of juicy nectarines to produce a delicious blend with a mouthwatering taste that will almost explode on your tongue – make plenty as you're sure to want more.

Makes 3 glasses

4 long rosemary sprigs, plus extra
  to decorate
15ml/1 tbsp golden caster (superfine) sugar
2.5ml/½ tsp ground ginger
2 oranges
4 nectarines
ice cubes

1 Put the rosemary sprigs in a small pan with the sugar, ground ginger and 150ml/¼ pint/⅔ cup water. Heat gently until the sugar dissolves, then simmer for 1 minute. Remove from the heat, transfer the sprigs and syrup to a bowl and leave to cool.

2 Squeeze the oranges. Halve and stone (pit) the nectarines and put in a food processor or blender with the orange juice. Process until smooth but don't worry if there are a few specks of nectarine skin dotting the juice.

3 Remove the rosemary from the syrup and pour into the juice. Blend briefly.

4 Put a few ice cubes in each glass and fill with the juice. Serve immediately, with extra rosemary sprigs to decorate.

Cook's tip
If you've bought nectarines only to find that they're as hard as bullets, leave them in the fruit bowl for a couple of days – they should ripen fairly quickly.

Vanilla Snow

While a good quality vanilla essence is perfectly acceptable for flavouring drinks, a far more aromatic taste will be achieved using a vanilla pod. This simple smoothie is deliciously scented, creamy and thick, and well worth the extravagance of using a whole vanilla pod. Its lovely, snowy whiteness is delightfully speckled with tiny black vanilla seeds.

Makes 3 glasses

1 vanilla pod (bean)
25g/1oz/2 tbsp caster (superfine) sugar
3 eating apples
300g/11oz/1⅓ cups natural (plain) yogurt

1 Using the tip of a sharp knife, split open the vanilla pod lengthways. Put it in a small pan with the sugar and 75ml/5 tbsp water. Heat until the sugar dissolves, then boil for 1 minute. Remove from the heat and leave to steep for 10 minutes.

2 Cut the apples into large chunks and push through the juicer, then pour the juice into a large bowl or jug (pitcher).

3 Lift the vanilla pod out of the pan and scrape the tiny black seeds back into the syrup. Pour into the apple juice.

4 Add the yogurt to the bowl or jug and whisk well by hand or with an electric mixer until the smoothie is thick and frothy. Pour into glasses and serve.

Cook's tip
Like most smoothies, this one should ideally be served well chilled. Either use apples and yogurt straight from the refrigerator, or chill briefly before serving. To make a thick, icy version, you could try using frozen yogurt.

Raspberry, Apple and Rose Water Smoothie

Although usually put through the juicer for drinking, apples can be blended as long as you process them well to ensure a really flavour-packed smoothie. This recipe is thinned with fresh apple juice, which can be either shop-bought (make sure it is good quality) or home-made.

Makes 2 glasses

2 eating apples
10ml/2 tsp caster (superfine) sugar
15ml/1 tbsp lemon juice
130g/4½oz/¾ cup fresh or frozen raspberries
150ml/¼ pint/⅔ cup apple juice
15–30ml/1–2 tbsp rose water
whole raspberries and rose petals,
   to decorate (optional)

Cook's tip

If you prefer raspberries without the pips (seeds), blend them first and then push the purée through a sieve to remove the pips before mixing it with the apples.

1 Peel and core the apples and put in a blender or food processor with the sugar and lemon juice. Blend well until smooth, scraping the mixture down from the side of the bowl, if necessary.

2 Add the raspberries and apple juice to the apple purée and blend until completely smooth.

3 Add the rose water to the smoothie and blend briefly to combine.

4 Pour the smoothie into two medium glasses and place whole raspberries and rose petals on top of the drinks to decorate, if you like. Serve the smoothie immediately, or chill in the refrigerator until ready to serve.

Coconut and Hazelnut Smoothie

This intensely nutty, rich and creamy drink is one to sip at your leisure. Leftovers can be put in the refrigerator for up to a couple of days, in which time the flavour of the hazelnuts will develop.

Makes 2 glasses

90g/3½oz/scant 1 cup whole
   blanched hazelnuts
25g/1oz/2 tbsp golden caster
   (superfine) sugar
2.5ml/½ tsp almond essence (extract)
200ml/7fl oz/scant 1 cup coconut cream
30ml/2 tbsp double (heavy) cream (optional)
150ml/¼ pint/⅔ cup mineral water
crushed ice

Cook's tip

If you want a frothy topping on this creamy smoothie, whisk it using a handheld electric wand after adding the mineral water, before pouring into the glasses.

1 Roughly chop the hazelnuts and lightly toast them in a small frying pan, turning frequently. Leave to cool, then tip the nuts into a blender or food processor with the caster sugar and blend well until very finely ground.

2 Add the almond essence, coconut cream and double cream, if using, and blend thoroughly until smooth.

3 Strain the mixture through a sieve into a jug (pitcher), pressing the pulp down with the back of a spoon to extract as much juice as possible. Stir in the mineral water.

4 Half-fill two glasses with crushed ice and pour over the nut smoothie. Serve the drinks immediately, or chill in the refrigerator until ready to serve.

Cinnamon Squash

Lightly cooked butternut squash makes a delicious smoothie. It has a wonderfully rich, rounded flavour that is lifted perfectly by the addition of tart citrus juice and warm, spicy cinnamon. Imagine pumpkin pie as a gorgeous smooth drink and you're halfway to experiencing the flavours of this lusciously sweet and tantalizing treat.

2 Put the cooled squash in a blender or food processor and add the ground cinnamon.

3 Squeeze the lemons and grapefruit and pour the juice over the squash, then add the muscovado sugar.

4 Process the ingredients until they are very smooth. If necessary, pause to scrape down the side of the food processor or blender.

5 Put a few ice cubes in two or three short glasses and pour over the smoothie. Serve immediately.

Makes 2–3 glasses

1 small butternut squash,
   about 600g/1lb 6oz
2.5ml/½ tsp ground cinnamon
3 large lemons
1 grapefruit
60ml/4 tbsp light muscovado (brown) sugar
ice cubes

Cook's tip
If you can only buy a large squash, cook it all and add the leftovers to stew or soup.

1 Halve the squash, scoop out and discard the seeds and cut the flesh into chunks. Cut away the skin and discard. Steam or boil the squash for 10–15 minutes until just tender. Drain well and leave to stand until cool.

Green Devil

Choose a well-flavoured avocado, such as a knobbly, dark-skinned Haas, for this slightly spicy, hot and sour smoothie. Cucumber adds a refreshing edge, while lemon and lime juice zip up the flavour, and the chilli sauce adds an irresistible fiery bite. This is one little devil that is sure to liven up even the most lethargic days.

Makes 2–3 glasses

1 small ripe avocado
½ cucumber
30ml/2 tbsp lemon juice
30ml/2 tbsp lime juice
10ml/2 tsp caster (superfine) sugar
pinch of salt
250ml/8fl oz/1 cup apple juice or
   mineral water
10–20ml/2–4 tsp sweet chilli sauce
ice cubes
red chilli curls, to decorate

2 Process the ingredients until smooth and creamy, then add the apple juice or mineral water and a little of the chilli sauce. Blend once more to lightly mix the ingredients together.

3 Pour the smoothie over ice cubes. Decorate with red chilli curls and serve with stirrers and extra chilli sauce.

1 Halve the avocado and use a sharp knife to remove the stone (pit). Scoop the flesh from both halves into a blender or food processor. Peel and roughly chop the cucumber and add to the blender or food processor, then add the lemon and lime juice, the caster sugar and a little salt.

Cook's tip

To make chilli curls, core and seed a fresh red chilli and cut it into very fine strips. Put the strips in a bowl of iced water and leave to stand for 20 minutes or until the strips curl. Use them to decorate this smoothie.

Seductively smooth avocados are as good for you as they taste. Their fresh vitamin- and mineral-rich flesh is reputed to be fantastic for healthy hair and skin.

cool
creamy
shakes

Milkshakes can be either refreshing and fruity or smooth and creamy, but they are always a treat. Inspiring ingredients include brownies and garden mint, and there are several shakes made with more traditional flavours such as vanilla or banana. Fun for kids and nostalgically appealing for adults, comfort drinks never looked or tasted so good.

Real Vanilla Milkshake

This is a milkshake for connoisseurs: it is the cream of the crop and definitely one to linger over. Nothing beats the flavour achieved by infusing a vanilla pod in the milk beforehand, but if you just cannot wait for the milk to cool, use a teaspoon of good quality vanilla essence instead.

Makes 2 glasses

1 vanilla pod (bean)
400ml/14fl oz/1⅔ cups full cream
   (whole) milk
200ml/7fl oz/scant 1 cup single (light) cream
4 scoops vanilla ice cream

1 Using a sharp knife, score the vanilla pod down the centre. Place in a small pan, pour the milk over and bring slowly to the boil.

2 Remove the pan from the heat but leave the pod in the milk. Leave to stand until the milk has cooled.

3 Remove the vanilla pod from the cooled milk and scrape out the seeds with the tip of a knife. Put the seeds in a blender or food processor with the milk and cream. Blend until combined.

4 Add the vanilla ice cream to the mixture and blend well until it is deliciously thick and frothy. Pour the smoothie into two large glasses and serve immediately with stirrers and straws to decorate, if you like.

Cook's tip
This classic milkshake is extremely rich and creamy, but if you'd prefer a lighter consistency, replace half the cream with the same quantity of extra milk.

Simply Strawberry

Nothing evokes a sense of summer wellbeing more than the scent and flavour of sweet, juicy strawberries. This recipe uses an abundance of these fragrant fruits so, if possible, make it when the season is right and local ones are at their most plentiful.

Makes 2 glasses

400g/14oz/3½ cups strawberries, plus extra to decorate
30–45ml/2–3 tbsp icing (confectioners') sugar
200g/7oz/scant 1 cup Greek (US strained plain) yogurt
60ml/4 tbsp single (light) cream

Cook's tip
You can replace the strawberries with other fruits if they are not in season. Try using fresh bananas instead to make another very popular milkshake.

1 Hull the strawberries and place them in a blender or food processor with 30ml/2 tbsp of the icing sugar. Blend to a smooth purée, scraping the mixture down from the side of the bowl with a rubber spatula, if necessary.

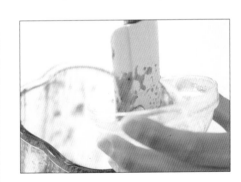

2 Add the yogurt and cream and blend again until smooth and frothy. Check the sweetness, adding a little more sugar if you find the flavour too sharp. Pour into glasses and serve decorated with extra strawberries.

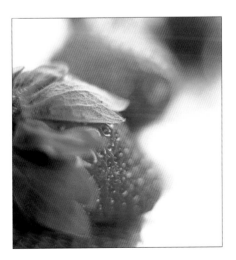

Rose Petal and Almond Milk

If you're lucky enough to have a mass of roses in the garden, it's well worth sacrificing a few to make this delicately scented summer smoothie. Thickened and flavoured with ground ratafia biscuits, this fragrant drink is the perfect way to relax on a hot lazy afternoon.

Makes 2 glasses

15g/½oz scented rose petals (preferably pink), plus extra to decorate
300ml/½ pint/1¼ cups milk
25g/1oz ratafia biscuits (almond macaroons)
ice cubes

Cook's tip

If you have bought roses, or even if you have picked them from your own garden, make sure you wash the petals thoroughly before you use them for cooking. This will help to remove any chemicals or pesticides that may have been sprayed on to the flowers.

1 Put the rose petals in a small pan with half the milk and bring just to the boil. Put the ratafia biscuits in a bowl, pour over the hot milk and leave to stand for 10 minutes.

2 Transfer the mixture to a blender or food processor with the remaining milk, and blend until smooth.

3 Strain the milk through a sieve into a wide jug (pitcher) to remove any lumps of biscuit or rose petals that have not been blended properly, and chill for at least 1 hour.

4 When the milk is well chilled, pour over ice cubes and serve immediately, decorating with rose petals, if you like.

Banana and Maple Crunch

Brilliant for making quick and easy blended drinks, bananas have a natural affinity with maple syrup and pecan nuts – what a combination. Serve this creamy, syrupy smoothie over ice and, if you are feeling decadent, dunk in some chunky chocolate cookies to scoop up a mouthful. It is best to serve this smoothie as soon as it is ready because it will not keep well. Finishing it off in one sitting should not be too difficult.

Makes 2 glasses

2 large bananas
50g/2oz/½ cup pecan nuts, plus extra to serve
150ml/¼ pint/⅔ cup full cream (whole) milk
60ml/4 tbsp pure maple syrup
crushed ice

Cook's tips

It is important to use ripe bananas in this recipe and, although you could replace the nuts with another variety such as hazelnuts, the combination of pecans, bananas and maple syrup is such a classic that any variation won't be as good.

1 Put the bananas in a blender or food processor and process until smooth. Add the nuts and blend again until thoroughly combined.

2 The nuts must be finely ground so stop and scrape down the side of the bowl once or twice, if necessary.

3 Add the maple syrup, then pour the milk over the banana paste and blend again until creamy.

4 Half-fill two large glasses with crushed ice and pour the smoothie over the top. Serve sprinkled with extra pecan nuts, if you like.

Honey and Banana Milkshake

This delicious drink demonstrates just how smooth and creamy a milkshake can be, even without using dairy produce. Make it using either soya or rice milk together with a vanilla-flavoured, iced non-dairy dessert to achieve a surprisingly rich and creamy flavour. Bananas make a nutritious, energy-boosting addition to drinks – this one is almost a meal in itself.

Makes 2 glasses

2 bananas
30ml/2 tbsp clear honey
15ml/1 tbsp lemon juice
300ml/½ pint/1¼ cups soya or rice milk
4 scoops vanilla iced non-dairy dessert

Cook's tip
If you are happy to use dairy produce, simply use ordinary milk and vanilla ice cream in place of the non-dairy ingredients.

1 Break the bananas into pieces and put in a blender or food processor with the honey and lemon juice. Blend until very smooth, scraping the mixture down from the side of the bowl with a rubber spatula, if necessary.

2 Add the soya or rice milk and two scoops of iced non-dairy dessert, then blend until smooth. Pour into tall glasses and add another scoop of dessert to each. Serve immediately.

Stem Ginger and Pear Shake

Although fresh fruit cannot be beaten for its flavour and nutritional value, canned varieties are a good store-cupboard stand-by for when you've run out of fresh. They are still nutritionally sound, particularly if packed in natural, unsweetened fruit juice. Preserved stem ginger makes the perfect partner to pears in this taste-tingling, creamy creation.

1 Shave off some wafer-thin slices from one of the pieces of ginger and reserve. Roughly chop the remaining ginger. Drain the pears, reserving about 150ml/¼ pint/⅔ cup of the juice.

2 Put the pears, measured juice and chopped ginger in a blender or food processor and blend until smooth, scraping the mixture down from the side of the bowl, if necessary.

3 Strain through a sieve into a jug (pitcher). Whisk in the milk, cream and ginger syrup and pour into two glasses. Serve scattered with the ginger shavings.

Makes 2 glasses

3 pieces (about 65g/2½oz) preserved stem ginger, plus 30ml/2 tbsp ginger syrup from the jar
400g/14oz can pears in natural fruit juice
150ml/¼ pint/⅔ cup full cream (whole) milk
100ml/3½fl oz/scant ½ cup single (light) cream
ice cubes

Cook's tip

If you like your milkshake really smooth, strain the pear mixture through a sieve to remove any bits of fibre that might remain in the pears. However, if you like the consistency of the stringy bits, skip this part of the recipe.

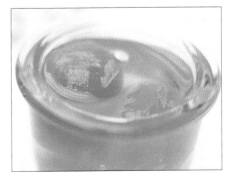

Lemon Meringue

Just as lemon meringue pie is a favourite dessert, this wonderful milkshake is sure to become a favourite drink. The blend of sweet meringue and lemon is carefully balanced in a velvety smooth, ice-cool drink that is not too rich and surprisingly refreshing. This really is a dessert in a glass and will undoubtedly go down well at your next dinner party.

2 Coarsely crush 15g/½oz of the meringues and reserve for decoration. Break the remainder into a blender or food processor. Add the lemon syrup and blend until smooth.

3 With the machine still running, gradually pour in the milk until the mixture is pale and frothy. Add the ice cream and blend again until smooth.

4 Pour the milkshake into tall glasses and decorate the sides with lemon slices or twists of lemon peel. Scatter the reserved meringue on top and serve immediately with spoons.

Makes 2 glasses

30ml/2 tbsp caster (superfine) sugar
3 lemons
50g/2oz crisp white meringues
300ml/½ pint/¼ cups full cream (whole) milk
2 scoops vanilla ice cream
lemon slices or twists of peel,
  to decorate

Cook's tip

When shopping for the lemons to decorate this drink, be sure to buy the unwaxed variety.

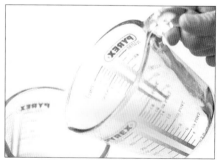

1 Put the sugar in a small pan with 100ml/3½fl oz/scant ½ cup water and heat gently until the sugar dissolves. Pour into a jug (pitcher). Squeeze the lemons using a citrus juicer and add the juice to the syrup. Leave to cool.

Garden Mint Milkshake

If you have mint growing in your garden, pick some for this recipe, as the fresher the mint, the better the flavour will be. The mint is infused in a sugar syrup, then left to cool before being blended to an aromatic, frothy shake with yogurt and creamy milk. The final milkshake is speckled with tiny green flecks, but if you prefer a completely smooth texture, you can strain these out.

Makes 2 tall glasses

25g/1oz/1 cup fresh mint
50g/2oz/¼ cup caster (superfine) sugar
200g/7oz/scant 1 cup natural
 (plain) yogurt
200ml/7fl oz/scant 1 cup full cream
 (whole) milk
15ml/1 tbsp lemon juice
crushed ice cubes
icing (confectioners') sugar, to decorate

2 Heat the mixture, stirring occasionally, until the sugar dissolves, then boil for 2 minutes. Remove the pan from the heat and set aside until the syrup is completely cool.

3 Strain the cooled syrup through a sieve into a jug (pitcher), pressing the mint against the side of the sieve with the back of a spoon. Pour into a blender or food processor.

4 Add the yogurt and milk to the syrup and blend until smooth and frothy. Add two of the reserved mint sprigs and the lemon juice and blend until the milkshake is specked with tiny green flecks.

5 Put the crushed ice in tall glasses or tumblers and pour over the milkshake. Dust the mint sprigs with icing sugar and use to decorate the glasses. Serve.

1 Pull out four small mint sprigs and set aside. Roughly snip the remaining leaves into a small pan. Add the sugar and pour over 105ml/7 tbsp water.

Rosemary and Almond Cream

This delightful concoction is definitely one to choose if you are looking for something a little different. Fresh sprigs of rosemary, infused in milk, provide a gentle fragrance and flavour that blends deliciously with the sweet ratafia biscuits. Frothed up with creamy, melting vanilla ice cream, this velvety smooth creation is quite simply superb.

Makes 2 glasses

4 long sprigs of fresh rosemary
400ml/14fl oz/1⅔ cups full cream (whole) milk
50g/2oz ratafia biscuits (almond macaroons)
  or amaretti, plus extra to decorate
3 large scoops vanilla ice cream
frosted rosemary sprigs, to decorate

Cook's tip
To make frosted rosemary sprigs, lightly coat the sprigs in a little beaten egg white. Dip in caster (superfine) sugar and leave to dry.

1 Put the rosemary sprigs in a small pan. Add 150ml/¼ pint/⅔ cup of the milk and heat very gently until the milk begins to boil. Remove the pan from the heat and tip the mixture into a bowl. Leave to cool for 10 minutes.

2 Remove the rosemary sprigs and carefully pour the still warm milk into a blender or food processor. Add the ratafia biscuits and blend until smooth and creamy. Add the remaining 250ml/8fl oz/1 cup milk and blend the mixture thoroughly.

3 Scoop the vanilla ice cream into the milk and biscuit mixture and blend until it is fully incorporated. Pour into large glasses and serve the milkshake immediately, decorating the top of each glass with delicate frosted rosemary sprigs and a few pieces of crumbled ratafia biscuits.

Pistachio Thick-Shake

Don't be put off by the presence of rice in this lovely, layered dairy-free milkshake. Blended with soya milk, pistachio nuts and non-dairy ice cream, it makes a dreamy, creamy blend that can be sipped, layer by layer, or swirled together with a pretty stirrer. As its name suggests, this shake is wonderfully rich and decadent; serve it in tall narrow glasses.

Makes 3–4 small glasses

550ml/18fl oz/2½ cups soya milk
50g/2oz/generous ¼ cup pudding rice
60ml/4 tbsp caster (superfine) sugar
finely grated rind of 1 lemon
75g/3oz/¾ cup shelled pistachio nuts, plus
  extra to decorate
300ml/10fl oz vanilla iced non-dairy dessert
5ml/1 tsp almond essence (extract)

1 Put the soya milk in a large, heavy pan with the rice, sugar and lemon rind. Bring slowly to the boil, then reduce the heat to simmer. Partially cover the pan with a lid and cook on the lowest heat for about 30 minutes, or until the rice is completely tender.

2 Transfer the rice to a heatproof bowl and leave to stand until completely cold.

3 Put the pistachio nuts in another heatproof bowl and cover with boiling water. Leave to stand for about 2 minutes and then drain.

4 Rub the pistachio nuts between several layers of kitchen paper to loosen the skins, then peel them away. (Don't worry about removing every bit of skin, but getting most of it off will make a prettier coloured milkshake.)

5 Tip the cold rice into a blender or food processor and blend until smooth. Put half the mixture in a bowl. Add the non-dairy dessert to the blender and blend until smooth. Pour into a separate bowl. Add the nuts, the reserved rice and the almond essence to the blender and process until the nuts are finely ground.

6 Layer the two mixtures in glasses and serve decorated with extra pistachios.

Marzipan and Orange Crush

The wintry scents and flavours of juicy oranges and marzipan make an interesting combination and the citrus juice adds a delicious refreshing tang to an otherwise very rich, creamy drink. It's a great blend to make if you are entertaining friends as its unusual blend of ingredients is sure to be a talking point. Make plenty of this irresistible shake and chill whatever you don't use in the refrigerator for another time.

Makes 3–4 glasses

130g/4½oz marzipan
finely grated rind and juice of 2 large oranges
juice of 1 lemon
150ml/¼ pint/⅔ cup mineral water
150ml/¼ pint/⅔ cup single (light) cream
ice cubes
orange wedges, to decorate (optional)

Cook's tip
Give this drink a whisk before serving, as it may have settled.

1 Break the marzipan into small pieces and put in a blender or food processor. Add the orange rind and juice along with the lemon juice. Blend the mixture thoroughly until smooth.

2 Add the mineral water and cream and blend again until smooth and frothy. Pour over ice cubes in glasses and serve decorated with the orange wedges, if you like.

Cherry and Coconut Shake

The season for fresh cherries is all too short, but canned cherries make a very good and surprisingly delicious stand-by. Here they are combined in a classic partnership with creamy coconut milk to make a rich, fruity drink that is perfect for people who are not too keen on really sweet, thick milkshakes. Make sure you buy pitted cherries, otherwise you will have to carefully stone them yourself before tipping them into the blender.

Makes 2 glasses

425g/15oz can pitted black cherries
    in syrup
200ml/7fl oz/scant 1 cup coconut milk
15ml/1 tbsp light muscovado (brown) sugar
150ml/¼ pint/⅔ cup black cherry-flavour
    yogurt
100ml/3½fl oz/scant ½ cup double
    (heavy) cream
lightly toasted shredded coconut,
    to decorate

Cook's tip
If you can't get black cherry flavour yogurt, use a vanilla or natural (plain) yogurt instead and add a little extra sugar when blending.

1 Tip the canned cherries into a sieve over a bowl to drain. Reserve the syrup for later.

2 Put the drained cherries in a blender or food processor with the coconut milk and sugar and blend briefly until fairly smooth. (Do not be tempted to over-blend the mixture or it may begin to separate.)

3 Pour the mixture through a sieve into a jug (pitcher), pressing the pulp down into the sieve with the back of a spoon to extract as much juice as possible.

4 Add the reserved cherry syrup, yogurt and cream and whisk lightly until smooth and frothy. Pour into glasses and scatter with shredded coconut.

Passionata

The combination of ripe passion fruit with sweet caramel is gorgeous in this dreamy milkshake. For convenience, you can easily make the caramel syrup and combine it with the fresh passion fruit juice in advance, so it's all ready for blending with the milk. For the best results make sure you use really ripe, crinkly passion fruit.

Makes 4 glasses

90g/3½oz/½ cup caster (superfine) sugar
juice of 2 large oranges
juice of 1 lemon
6 ripe passion fruit, plus extra for garnish
550ml/18fl oz/2½ cups full cream
   (whole) milk
ice cubes

1 Put the sugar in a small, heavy pan with 200ml/7fl oz/scant 1 cup water. Heat gently, stirring with a wooden spoon until the sugar has dissolved.

2 Bring the mixture to the boil and cook, without stirring, for about 5 minutes until the syrup has turned to a deep golden caramel. Watch closely towards the end of the cooking time as caramel can burn very quickly. If this happens, let the caramel cool, then throw it away and start again.

3 When the caramel has turned deep golden, immediately lower the base of the pan into cold water to prevent it from cooking any further.

4 Carefully add the orange and lemon juice, standing back slightly as the mixture will splutter. Return the pan to the heat and cook gently, stirring continuously, to make a smooth syrup. Transfer the syrup to a small heatproof bowl and set aside until it has cooled completely.

5 Halve the passion fruit and scoop the seeds into a blender or food processor. Add the caramel and milk and blend until smooth and frothy. Pour over ice and serve with a passion fruit garnish.

Rocky River

This rich, sweet milkshake combines chilled custard with decadent chocolate, chunky nuts and delicious marshmallows. It is great fun to make with children, who will enjoy its sticky, indulgent sweetness almost as much as the adults. Prepare this shake whenever you're really in need of a treat or when relaxing in the garden on a hot afternoon.

Makes 3 glasses

75g/3oz plain (semisweet) chocolate
40g/1½oz/scant ½ cup blanched almonds
50g/2oz pink and white marshmallows
600ml/1 pint/2½ cups good quality
   ready-made custard
300ml/½ pint/1¼ cups milk
30ml/2 tbsp caster (superfine) sugar
5ml/1 tsp vanilla essence (extract)

4 Pour into big glasses and serve immediately, sprinkled with the reserved marshmallows and grated chocolate.

Cook's tip

Very cold chocolate can be difficult to grate. You might find it easier if you microwave it, very briefly, as this will make the chocolate less brittle for grating.

1 Coarsely grate the chocolate. Lightly toast the almonds, then chop them. Cut the marshmallows roughly into pieces, using scissors, reserving a few pieces for decoration.

2 Tip the custard into a blender or food processor and add the milk, sugar and vanilla essence. Blend briefly to combine.

3 Reserve a little chocolate for sprinkling, then add the remainder to the blender with the almonds and marshmallows. Blend until the marshmallows are chopped into small pieces.

Cinnamon Iced Coffee

When the weather warms up, swap mugs of hot coffee for this treat of a summer cooler. Lightly flavoured with cinnamon and served icy cold, it's a smooth relaxing drink for when you need to unwind – and it's well worth keeping a jug in the refrigerator.

Makes 2 large glasses

5ml/1 tsp ground cinnamon
400ml/14fl oz/1⅔ cups full cream
  (whole) milk
40g/1½oz/3 tbsp caster (superfine) sugar
300ml/½ pint/1¼ cups strong cold
  espresso coffee
ice cubes
cinnamon sticks, to serve

Cook's tip
For a dinner party, why not spice things up and serve these shakes with a large dash of Bailey's or Tia Maria. These types of alcohol work particularly well with this drink's creaminess and its subtle cinnamon tones.

1 Put the cinnamon and 100ml/3½fl oz/ scant ½ cup of the milk in a small pan with the sugar. Bring the milk slowly to the boil then remove from the heat and leave to cool.

2 Turn the cinnamon milk into a large jug (pitcher) or bowl. Add the remaining milk and the coffee and whisk well, using a hand-held electric wand, until frothy. Pour into glasses with ice and serve with cinnamon sticks for stirrers.

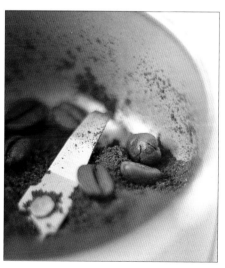

Chocolate Brownie Milkshake

For a truly indulgent flavour, use home-made chocolate brownies in this fabulously tasty milkshake. It is very rich – and incredibly decadent – so sit back, relax and just enjoy a totally luxurious moment on your own – well, you wouldn't want to share it.

1 Crumble the chocolate brownies into a blender or food processor and add the milk. Blend until the mixture is a pale chocolate colour.

2 Add the ice cream and blend until smooth and frothy. Pour into a tall glass and spoon over a little whipped cream. Serve scattered with chocolate shavings or a dusting of cocoa powder.

Makes 1 large glass

40g/1½oz chocolate brownies
200ml/7fl oz/scant 1 cup full cream
 (whole) milk
2 scoops vanilla ice cream
a little whipped cream
chocolate shavings or cocoa powder
 (unsweetened), to decorate

Cook's tip
If you fancy treating yourself to a milkshake that's even more chocolatey than this one, replace the vanilla ice cream with the same amount of a chocolate or chocolate-chip variety.

drinks
for
kids

Drinks for breakfast, after school or even kids' parties are transformed with these delicious concoctions. There are fresh fruit squashes, fun fizzes and shakes, and some real teatime treats that could quite easily take the place of an ordinary dessert or pudding. Let the kids help prepare them and they'll enjoy these blends even more.

Fresh Orange Squash

Pushing oranges through a juicer rather than squeezing out the juice means you maximize the fruits' goodness and reduce the amount of wastage. Although this squash uses a significant amount of sugar in the syrup, at least you can rest assured that there are no secret colourings, flavourings and preservatives, making it a far healthier alternative to shop-bought versions – perfect for children who get through gallons of squash every day.

Makes about 550ml/18fl oz/2½ cups, before diluting

90g/3½oz/½ cup caster (superfine) sugar
6 large oranges
still or sparkling mineral water, to serve

1 Put the sugar in a small, heavy pan with 100ml/3½fl oz/scant ½ cup water. Heat gently, stirring until the sugar has dissolved. Bring to the boil and boil rapidly for 3 minutes until the mixture is syrupy. Remove from the heat.

2 Cut away the skins from three of the oranges and chop the flesh into pieces small enough to fit through a juicer funnel. Chop the remaining oranges, with skins on, into similar-size pieces.

3 Push the orange pieces through the juicer, then mix with the sugar syrup. Pour into a bottle or jug (pitcher) and store in the refrigerator. To serve, dilute the orange squash to taste with still or sparkling mineral water.

Ruby Red Lemonade

Use blackberries or blueberries, or a mixture of the two, in this quick and easy fruit cordial.
A far healthier alternative to ready-made drinks, it's made in minutes and can be kept in the
refrigerator for several days. If you have a glut of summer fruits, it makes sense to prepare extra
and freeze it, preferably in single portions in ice-cube trays, so that children can easily pick
them out, then all they need do is drop them into a glass and top up with water.

3 Put the sugar in a small, heavy pan
with 100ml/3½fl oz/scant ½ cup water.
Heat gently until the sugar dissolves,
stirring with a wooden spoon, then
bring to the boil and boil for 3 minutes
until syrupy. Reserve until cool.

4 Mix the fruit juice with the syrup in
a jug (pitcher). For each serving pour
about 50ml/2fl oz/¼ cup fruit syrup into
a tumbler and add ice. Serve topped
up with sparkling mineral water.

**Makes about 350ml/12fl oz/1½ cups,
before diluting**

350g/12oz/3 cups blackberries or blueberries
130g/4½oz/scant ¾ cup golden caster
(superfine) sugar
ice cubes
sparkling mineral water, to serve

1 Examine the blackberries or
blueberries carefully, removing any
tough stalks or leaves from the fruit,
and then wash them thoroughly. Allow
the fruit to dry.

2 Push handfuls of the fruit through
a juicer.

Strawberry and Apple Slush

Sweet, juicy strawberries make wonderfully fragrant juices, especially when they are grown outside in the summer. The juice has an almost perfect consistency that's not too thick and not too thin. The addition of apple juice and just a hint of vanilla creates a tantalizing, fruity treat that's ideal for children spending a lazy summer afternoon in the garden.

1 Pick out a couple of the prettiest strawberries and reserve for the decoration. Hull the remaining strawberries and roughly chop the apples into large chunks.

2 Push the fruits through a juicer and stir in the vanilla syrup.

3 Half-fill two tall glasses with ice. Add straws or stirrers and pour over the juice. Decorate with the reserved strawberries (slicing them, if you like) and serve immediately.

Makes 2 tall glasses

300g/11oz/2½ cups ripe strawberries
2 small, crisp eating apples
10ml/2 tsp vanilla syrup
crushed ice

Cook's tip
Vanilla syrup can be bought in jars from supermarkets and delicatessens. As an alternative, you could add a few drops of vanilla essence (extract) and a sprinkling of sugar, if necessary.

Lemon Float

Old-fashioned lemonade made with freshly squeezed lemons is a far cry from the carbonated, synthetic commercial varieties. Served with generous scoops of ice cream and soda water, it makes the ultimate refreshing dessert drink. The lemonade can be stored in the refrigerator for up to two weeks, so it is well worth making a double batch.

Makes 4 large glasses

6 lemons, plus wafer-thin lemon slices,
   to decorate
200g/7oz/1 cup caster (superfine) sugar
8 scoops vanilla ice cream
soda water (club soda)

1 Finely grate the rind from the lemons, then squeeze out the juice using a citrus juicer or by hand.

2 Put the rind in a bowl with the sugar and pour over 600ml/1 pint/2½ cups boiling water. Stir until the sugar dissolves, then leave to cool.

3 Stir in the lemon juice. Strain into a jug (pitcher) and chill for several hours.

4 Put a scoop of the vanilla ice cream in each of the glasses, then half-fill with the lemonade and add plenty of lemon slices to decorate. Top up each glass with soda water, add another scoop of ice cream to each one and serve immediately with long-handled spoons.

Puppy Love

Rather like bought slushy drinks, this sweet, semi-frozen fruit treat will be enjoyed by children of all ages. Make the fruit syrup and freeze it for an hour or two so it is ready to blend to a slushy consistency. If you forget about it and the syrup freezes solid, let it thaw a little at room temperature or simply heat it for a few seconds in a microwave.

Makes 2–3 glasses

2 oranges
250g/9oz/2¼ cups blueberries
50g/2oz/4 tbsp caster (superfine) sugar

1 Using a small, sharp knife, carefully cut away the majority of the skin from the oranges, then cut the oranges into 8–10 chunky wedges of roughly the same size.

2 Reserve a few blueberries for decoration, then push the rest through a juicer, alternating them with the orange wedges.

3 Add the sugar and 300ml/½ pint/ 1¼ cups cold water to the juice and stir until the sugar has dissolved. Pour into a shallow, non-metallic freezer container and freeze for 1–2 hours or until the juice is beginning to freeze all over.

4 Use a fork to break up any solid areas of the mixture and tip into a blender or food processor. Blend until smooth and slushy. Spoon the drink into glasses and serve, topped with blueberries or other fruit.

Rainbow Juice

Brightly coloured layers of pure fruit juice give this smoothie extra child-appeal. Strawberry, kiwi fruit and pineapple provide plenty of colour contrast but you can use almost any other fruits that blend to a fairly thick consistency, and create your own rainbow. Check the sweetness of each juice before layering up the fruits, stirring in a little sugar if necessary.

Makes 3 glasses

4 kiwi fruit
½ small pineapple
130g/4½oz/generous 1 cup strawberries

3 Add the kiwi fruit to the blender and blend until smooth. Tip into a separate bowl. Finally, blend the strawberries until smooth.

1 Using a sharp knife, peel the kiwi fruit. Cut away the skin from the pineapple, then halve and remove the core. Roughly chop the pineapple flesh.

2 Put the pineapple in a blender or food processor and add 30ml/2 tbsp water. Process to a smooth purée, scraping the mixture down from the side of the bowl with a rubber spatula, if necessary. Tip into a small bowl.

4 Pour the strawberry purée into three glass tumblers. Carefully spoon the kiwi fruit purée into the glasses to form a separate layer. Spoon the pineapple purée over the kiwi fruit and serve with spoons or thick straws.

Raspberry, Banana and Peach Smoothie

Children will love this naturally sweet fruit drink. Whizzed up in just minutes, this thick, slightly tart smoothie makes a good stop-gap between meals, a brilliant, easy-to-eat breakfast or serves as a healthy – and very tasty – dessert.

1 Halve, stone (pit) and roughly chop the peach, break the banana into pieces and put both fruits in a blender or food processor. Blend until smooth, scraping the mixture down the side of the bowl if necessary.

2 Add the raspberries and blend until smooth. Pour into glasses and top up with mineral water, if using. Add ice cubes, decorate with extra raspberries and serve with straws or spoons.

Makes 2 small glasses

1 large ripe peach
1 small banana
130g/4½oz/¾ cup fresh or frozen
   raspberries, plus extra to decorate
still or sparkling mineral water (optional)
ice cubes

Cook's tip
If your children are fussy about the pips (seeds) in raspberries, blend them first and push the mixture through a fine sieve to remove the seeds, then return the purée to the blended banana mixture.

Top Pops

Chunky ice-lolly stirrers give this fruit-packed smoothie plenty of child-appeal. It's great for a party or as an after-school treat on a hot day. The lollies can be frozen ahead and stored so they're ready on demand, and the juice takes just moments to prepare.

Makes 2 glasses

1 apple
300ml/½ pint/1¼ cups apple juice
2 kiwi fruit
90g/3½oz/generous ½ cup raspberries
10ml/2 tsp caster (superfine) sugar
150g/5oz/1 cup red grapes
150g/5oz/1¼ cups blackcurrants or
  blackberries
1 large banana

1 Peel, core and roughly chop the apple. Place in a food processor or blender with 100ml/3½fl oz/ scant ½ cup of the apple juice and blend to a smooth purée. Pour into a third of the sections of an ice-cube tray.

2 Peel and roughly chop the kiwi fruit and blend until smooth with 100ml of the apple juice. Pour into another third of the ice-cube tray sections.

3 Blend the raspberries with the sugar and the remaining apple juice and spoon into the final sections. Freeze the tray for about 30 minutes then push a wooden ice-lolly (popsicle) stick into each. Freeze until solid.

4 Put the grapes, blackcurrants or blackberries, and banana into the blender or food processor and blend until smooth. If you like, push the mixture through a coarse sieve after blending to remove the seeds and skins.

5 Push several of the fruit lollies out of the tray and place on separate plates for each child. Pour the fruit juice into two glasses and place on plates with the lollies. Serve immediately as the lollies will start to melt very quickly – and don't forget to supply the children with plenty of napkins.

Tropical Fruit Shake

Sweet, fruity and packed with vitamin C, this is a brilliant way to get children to enjoy healthy drinks. If you use really ripe fruit, it shouldn't need any additional sweetening, but taste it to check before serving. Mango makes a thick purée when blended, so top it up with mineral water – or try a good quality lemonade instead.

Makes 2 glasses

½ small pineapple
small bunch seedless white grapes
1 mango
mineral water or lemonade (optional)

1 Using a sharp knife, cut away the skin from the pineapple and halve the fruit. Discard the core and roughly chop the flesh of one half. Add to a blender or food processor with the grapes. Halve the mango either side of the flat stone (pit). Scoop the flesh into the blender.

2 Process thoroughly until really smooth, scraping the mixture down from the side of the bowl, if necessary. Pour into glasses and top up with mineral water or lemonade, if using. Serve immediately.

Cook's tip

For really fussy children, you might want to strain the mixture first. To do this, push it through a fine sieve, pressing the pulp in the sieve with the back of a spoon to extract as much juice as possible. Follow the recipe as normal, topping up the glasses with mineral water or lemonade if your children prefer it. To make a novelty decoration, thread pieces of fruit on to straws before you serve the shake.

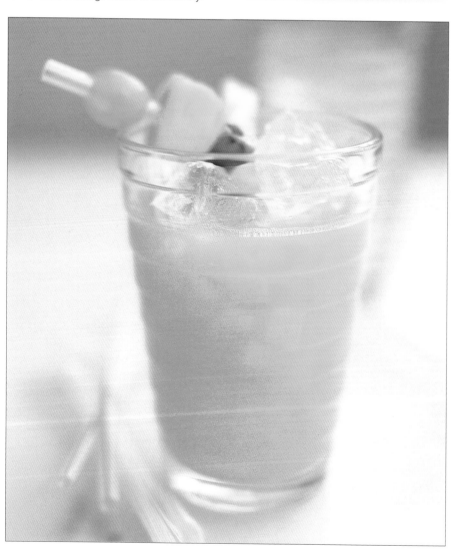

Raspberry Rippler

Colourful ripples of raspberry and mango give instant child appeal to this fruit-packed smoothie. Soya milk is so delicious and such a healthy alternative to cow's milk in drinks that it's worth trying, even for children who are not on a dairy-free diet. Here it's blended with mango to create a smooth, thick contrast to the tangy raspberries. For best results, use only really ripe, sweet mango.

Makes 2 glasses

90g/3½oz/generous ½ cup fresh or frozen
    raspberries, plus a few extra to decorate
15–30ml/1–2 tbsp clear honey
1 mango
100ml/3½fl oz/scant ½ cup soya milk

1 Process the raspberries in a blender or food processor until smooth. Add 15ml/1 tbsp water and 5–10ml/1–2 tsp of the honey to sweeten. Transfer to a small bowl and rinse out the blender or food processor bowl.

2 Halve the mango either side of the flat stone (pit). Scoop the flesh from the two halves and around the stone into the clean blender or food processor and process until smooth. Add the soya milk and 10–20ml/2–4 tsp honey to sweeten.

Cook's tip

It will make such a difference to your children's health, and to their general appreciation of food, if they can enjoy fresh, naturally sweet drinks like this. Try serving this smoothie as a refreshing dessert after a barbecue or a family meal – it makes a delicious alternative to the similarly named, but slightly less healthy, raspberry ripple ice cream.

3 Pour a 2.5cm/1in layer of the mango purée into two tumblers. Spoon half the raspberry purée on top. Add the remaining mango purée, then finish with the remaining raspberry purée. Using a teaspoon, lightly swirl the two mixtures together. Serve decorated with extra raspberries.

Candystripe

This wickedly indulgent drink combines freshly blended strawberries with a marshmallow flavoured cream, making a milkshake that adults as well as kids will find totally irresistible. There's no point even trying to resist the melting marshmallow sweetness of this cheeky little strawberry confection – just sit back and give yourself up.

Makes 4 large glasses

150g/5oz white and pink marshmallows
500ml/17fl oz/generous 2 cups full cream (whole) milk
60ml/4 tbsp redcurrant jelly
450g/1lb/4 cups strawberries
60ml/4 tbsp double (heavy) cream
extra strawberries and marshmallows, to decorate

1 Put the marshmallows in a heavy pan with half the milk and heat gently, stirring frequently until the marshmallows have melted. Leave to stand until it has cooled.

2 Heat the redcurrant jelly in a small pan until melted. Put the strawberries in a blender or food processor and process until smooth, scraping down the side of the bowl with a rubber spatula as often as is necessary.

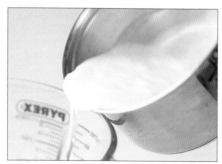

3 Stir 10ml/2 tsp of the strawberry purée into the melted jelly. Set aside the strawberry syrup. Pour the remaining purée into a jug (pitcher) and add the marshmallow mixture, the cream and the remaining milk. Chill the milkshake and four large glasses for about 1 hour.

4 To serve, use a teaspoon to drizzle lines of the strawberry syrup down the insides of the glasses – this creates a candystripe effect when filled. Fill the glasses with the milkshake. Serve topped with the extra marshmallows and strawberries and drizzle with any leftover strawberry syrup.

Cook's tip
If you can convince the children to wait long enough, this blend will really benefit from being chilled in the refrigerator for a couple of hours before serving.

Peppermint Crush

The next time you see seaside rock or the peppermint candy canes that are around at Christmas time, buy a few sticks for this incredibly easy, fun drink for children. All you need to do is whizz it up with some milk and freeze until slushy, so it's ready and waiting for thirsty youngsters. This shake could almost pass as a dessert, so try serving it after a meal.

Makes 4 glasses

90g/3½oz pink peppermint rock (rock candy)
750ml/1¼ pints/3 cups full cream (whole) or
  semi-skimmed (low-fat) milk
a few drops of pink food colouring (optional)
pink candy canes, to serve

Cook's tip

If you cannot find pink candy canes to use as novelty stirrers for this drink, buy peppermint lolly pops instead.

1 While the rock is still in its wrapper, hit with a rolling pin to break into small bits. (If unwrapped, put the rock in a polythene bag to crush it.) Tip the pieces into a blender or food processor.

2 Add the milk and a few drops of pink food colouring, if using, to the crushed rock and process until the rock is broken up into tiny pieces.

3 Pour the mixture into a shallow freezer container and freeze for about 2 hours or until turning slushy around the edges. Beat the mixture with a fork, breaking up the semi-frozen areas and stirring them into the centre.

4 Re-freeze and repeat the process once or twice more until the mixture is slushy. Spoon into glasses and serve with candy cane stirrers.

Custard Cream Float

This fabulously frothy dessert drink makes a wonderful treat that rounds off any meal brilliantly, or you could serve it to your children as a special snack mid-morning or at teatime.

Makes 3 glasses

75g/3oz custard cream biscuits (cookies)
1 large banana
5ml/1 tsp vanilla essence (extract)
200ml/7fl oz/scant 1 cup full cream
  (whole) milk
6 scoops vanilla ice cream
banana slices and crumbled biscuit
  (cookie), to decorate
drinking chocolate or cocoa powder
  (unsweetened), for dusting

Cook's tip
For an extra burst of banana flavour, use banana ice cream.

1 Put the custard cream biscuits in a blender or food processor and blend well until finely ground. Break the banana into chunks and add to the ground biscuits. Process thoroughly until a smooth, thick paste forms, scraping down the side of the bowl with a rubber spatula, if necessary.

2 Add the vanilla essence, milk and three scoops of the ice cream and process again until smooth and foamy. Pour into tumblers and top with the remaining scoops of ice cream. Decorate with banana slices and crumbled biscuit and serve dusted with a little drinking chocolate or cocoa powder.

Chocolate Nut Swirl

Children everywhere will be captivated by this fabulous chocolatey concoction. It is a mixture of melted milk chocolate, chocolate nut spread and creamy milk, marbled together to make an attractive and delicious drink. Adults who like chocolate will love it too.

Makes 2 tall glasses

40g/1½oz/3 tbsp chocolate hazelnut spread
400ml/14fl oz/1⅔ cups full cream
  (whole) milk
90g/3½oz milk chocolate
30ml/2 tbsp extra thick double (heavy)
  cream (optional)
a little crushed ice
2 chocolate flake bars, to serve

Cook's tip
This drink is extremely rich and filling and should probably be reserved for special occasions, but if you feel that using chocolate flakes as novelty stirrers is a bit too much chocolate for your children, serve the drink with multi-coloured straws or plastic stirrers instead.

1 Put the chocolate spread in a small bowl with 10ml/2 tsp of the milk. Stir well until smooth and glossy.

2 Chop the chocolate. Put 100ml/ 3½fl oz/scant ½ cup of the remaining milk in a small pan and add the chocolate pieces. Heat gently, stirring until the chocolate has dissolved. Remove from the heat and pour into a jug (pitcher). Leave to cool for 10 minutes, then stir in the remaining milk.

3 Using a teaspoon, dot the chocolate hazelnut mixture around the sides of two tall glasses, rotating them so that each glass is randomly streaked with chocolate. Dot the cream around the glasses in the same way, if using.

4 Put a little crushed ice in each glass and pour over the chocolate milk. Serve immediately with flake bar stirrers that can be used to swirl the hazelnut mixture into the chocolate milk.

crushes
&
slushes

What could be better than relaxing in the garden
on a hot afternoon enjoying an ice-cool, refreshing
blend? This chapter offers a fabulous fusion of
flavours, whether you prefer fat-free, refreshing
slushes made with blackcurrants or strawberries,
or luxurious, creamy blends with white chocolate,
ice cream and hazelnuts.

Cool as a Currant

Tiny, glossy blackcurrants are a virtual powerhouse of nutrients, packed with vitamins C and E, as well as essential iron, calcium and magnesium. Whizzed in a blender with plenty of crushed ice, they make a drink so deliciously thick and slushy that you might want to serve it with long spoons so that you can scoop up every last drop.

Makes 2 tall glasses

125g/4¼oz/generous 1 cup blackcurrants,
  plus extra to decorate
60ml/4 tbsp light muscovado (brown) sugar
good pinch of mixed (apple pie) spice
  (optional)
225g/8oz/2 cups crushed ice

1 Put the blackcurrants and sugar in a pan. (There is no need to string the blackcurrants first.) Add the mixed spice, if using, and pour in 100ml/ 3½fl oz/scant ½ cup water. Bring to the boil and cook for 2–3 minutes until the blackcurrants are completely soft.

2 Press the mixture through a sieve into a bowl, pressing the pulp with the back of a wooden spoon to extract as much juice as possible. Leave to stand until it has completely cooled.

Cook's tip

This is a great juice to make if you have plenty of blackcurrants in the freezer – they will thaw quickly in the pan. Redcurrants, or a mixture of redcurrants and blackcurrants, could also be used.

  Make a double quantity of this juice and store it in the refrigerator for up to a week – then it can be quickly blended with ice whenever you like.

3 Put the crushed ice in a blender or food processor with the cooled juice and blend for about 1 minute until slushy. Pour into glasses, decorate with blackcurrants and serve immediately.

Frosty Fruits

Long after summer is over you can still summon up the glorious flavours of the season by making this fruity and refreshing drink from frozen summer fruits. This purple, slushy, fruity delight will pep up even the darkest mornings. Revitalize yourself with this blend before you leave for work in the morning to give your body a well-deserved boost.

1 Take the frozen fruits straight from the freezer and tip them into a blender or food processor. Blend until finely crushed, scraping down the side of the bowl, if necessary.

2 Add the yogurt and cream to the crushed fruit, then spoon in 30ml/ 2 tbsp of the sugar. Blend again until the mixture is smooth and thick. Taste and add the extra sugar if necessary. Serve immediately, decorated with fruit.

Makes 2–3 glasses

250g/9oz/2 cups frozen summer fruits, plus extra to decorate
200g/7oz/scant 1 cup natural (plain) yogurt
45ml/3 tbsp double (heavy) cream
30–45ml/2–3 tbsp caster (superfine) sugar

Cook's tip
This drink takes only moments to whizz up and you can use any mixture of fruits, whether you've grown your own berries or bought them frozen in bags.

Strawberries and Cream

Real strawberries and cream are really only worth eating when fresh strawberries are at their best, and the same goes for this delectable drink. Use small, vibrantly red and thoroughly ripe fruit. Frozen whole, they serve as flavour-packed ice cubes that will chill the drink.

Makes 2 tall glasses

275g/10oz/2½ cups small strawberries
15ml/1 tbsp lemon juice
5ml/1 tsp vanilla sugar
cream soda

Cook's tip
If you cannot find vanilla sugar in the supermarket, make your own. Fill a jar with caster (superfine) sugar and press a whole vanilla pod (bean) into the centre. Seal and leave for 2–3 weeks. As the sugar is used, simply top up the jar with more.

1 Hull the strawberries. Freeze about 130g/4½oz/generous 1 cup of the smallest strawberries for about 1 hour, or until firm. Process the remainder in a blender or food processor with the lemon juice and sugar until smooth, scraping the mixture down from the side of the bowl, if necessary.

2 Divide the frozen strawberries between two tall glasses and pour in the strawberry purée. Top up with cream soda and serve immediately with long-handled spoons so your guests can scoop out the delicious frozen strawberries and eat them – once they have defrosted slightly.

Apple Refresher

Made using freshly juiced apples, this vibrant blend has a wonderfully crisp, thirst-quenching flavour. The really sweet, ripe fruits are juiced and then frozen until slushy. Served with additional apples and topped up with sparkling water, this drink couldn't be simpler.

Makes 3 glasses

6 large red eating apples
10ml/2 tsp lemon juice
a little clear honey (optional)
sparkling mineral water

1 Reserve one of the apples. Quarter and core the remainder and cut the flesh into small pieces. Juice the apple pieces and stir in the lemon juice.

3 Using a fork, break up the frozen apple juice, pushing it into the centre of the container. Re-freeze for 1 hour or until slushy all over. Again, break up the mixture with a fork.

4 Quarter and core the remaining apple and cut into thin slices. Spoon the slush into three glasses until two-thirds full and tuck the apple slices down the sides. Top up with sparkling water to serve.

Cook's tip
Green and red apples produce quite different flavours in juices. Red apples are better for this recipe because the colour is pretty and the flavour light and fragrant. Crisp, green apples will give a sweeter, tangier and denser flavour.

2 Check for sweetness, adding a little honey, if using. (Remember that the flavour will be less sweet once frozen.) Pour into a shallow freezer container, cover and freeze until a band of slush has formed around the edges.

Fire and Ice

Tickle your tastebuds with this unconventional frozen yogurt drink that is flavoured with fresh orange juice and specks of hot red chilli. It's great on a hot summer's day, after lunch or any other time when you're in need of a refreshing boost. If you've plenty of time on your hands, add an alcoholic kick to the drink by drizzling each glass with a splash of orange liqueur before serving.

Makes 2–3 tall glasses

90g/3½oz/½ cup caster (superfine) sugar
1 lemon
300ml/½ pint/1¼ cups freshly squeezed
   orange juice
200g/7oz/scant 1 cup Greek (US strained
   plain) yogurt
1 red chilli, seeded and finely chopped
60ml/4 tbsp Cointreau or other orange-
   flavoured liqueur (optional)
orange slices and extra chillies, to decorate

1 Put the sugar in a pan with 100ml/ 3½fl oz/scant ½ cup water and heat gently, stirring with a spoon until the sugar has dissolved. Pour into a freezer container and leave to cool. Finely grate the rind of the lemon and juice.

2 Add the lemon rind and juice and 100ml/3½fl oz/scant ½ cup of the orange juice. Freeze for 2 hours or until a band of ice has formed around the edges. Turn into a bowl and add the yogurt and chopped chilli. Whisk until thick. Freeze for 1–2 hours until almost solid.

3 To serve, scoop the frozen yogurt into a blender or food processor and add the remaining orange juice. Process until very thick and smooth. Pour into tall glasses and drizzle with a little liqueur, if using. Serve with straws and decorate with orange slices and fresh chillies.

Cook's tip
Don't worry if you forget to remove the chilli yogurt from the freezer before it has frozen solid. Leave it at room temperature for a while to soften or simply heat it briefly in a microwave.

Pineapple and Yogurt Ice

Cooling and delicious yogurt ice can be bought in several flavours, including vanilla, orange and lemon, and is perfect in summer drinks as a lighter alternative to traditional ice cream. Use a really sweet, juicy pineapple and fresh, pungent basil to add plenty of vibrant colour and exotic flavour to this refreshing iced drink.

1 Remove the basil leaves from the stems and tear them into small pieces. Cut away the skin from the pineapple, then halve the fruit and remove the core. Chop the flesh into chunks. Push the pineapple through a juicer with the basil. Chill until ready to serve.

2 Pour the juice into tall glasses and add two scoops of yogurt ice to each. Decorate with basil sprigs and dust lightly with icing sugar.

Makes 2 glasses

25g/1oz fresh basil, plus extra sprigs to decorate
1 pineapple
4 large scoops vanilla-, lemon- or orange-flavoured yogurt ice
icing (confectioners') sugar, for dusting

Cook's tip
Fresh mint makes an equally refreshing alternative to basil if you have plenty growing in the garden, or try other soft-leaved herbs, such as lemon balm.

White Chocolate and Hazelnut Cream

This luxurious combination of smooth, creamy white chocolate and crunchy hazelnut is simply irresistible. To get the maximum flavour from the hazelnuts, it is always best to use whole ones, toasting them first to develop their nuttiness and then grinding them fresh, rather than using ready chopped or ground nuts.

Makes 3 glasses

90g/3½oz/scant 1 cup blanched hazelnuts
150g/5oz white chocolate
300ml/½ pint/1¼ cups full cream
   (whole) milk
4 large scoops white chocolate or vanilla
   ice cream
a little freshly grated nutmeg (optional)

1 Roughly chop the hazelnuts using a large, sharp knife, then toast them lightly in a dry frying pan, turning continuously to ensure that they are toasted evenly. Reserve 30ml/2 tbsp for decoration, then tip the remainder into a blender or food processor. Blend until very finely ground.

2 Finely chop the chocolate and reserve 30ml/2 tbsp for decoration. Put the remainder in a small, heavy pan with half of the milk and heat very gently until the chocolate has melted thoroughly. Stir until smooth, then pour the chocolate into a bowl. Add the remaining milk, stir and leave to cool.

3 Add the melted chocolate mixture to the blender with the ice cream and a little grated nutmeg, if using. Blend until the mixture is smooth. Pour into glasses and sprinkle with the reserved hazelnuts and chocolate. Grate over a little extra nutmeg, if you like, and serve immediately.

Ice Cool Coconut

This fabulously cooling, dairy-free drink is just about as silky smooth as they come. Rather than using coconut milk, this recipe opts for desiccated coconut, steeped in water, which is then strained to extract the flavour. Without the nutty texture, this delicious coconut feast slides down very nicely on a summer's evening. If it's the weekend – or even if it's not – and you fancy a bit of a treat, add a splash of Malibu or coconut-flavoured liqueur.

Makes 2–3 glasses

150g/5oz/2½ cups desiccated (dry
   unsweetened shredded) coconut
30ml/2 tbsp lime juice
30ml/2 tbsp icing (confectioners') sugar, plus
   extra for dusting
200g/7oz vanilla iced non-dairy dessert
lime slices, to decorate

Cook's tip
Desiccated coconut can be bought ready sweetened. If using this, you may wish to omit the sugar that's added with the lime juice.

1 Put the coconut in a heatproof bowl and add 600ml/1 pint/2½ cups boiling water. Leave to stand for 30 minutes. Strain the coconut through a sieve lined with muslin (cheesecloth) into a bowl, pressing the pulp with a spoon to extract as much juice as possible. Discard the pulp and chill the coconut milk.

2 Pour the coconut milk into a blender or food processor with the lime juice, sugar and non-dairy dessert. Blend thoroughly until completely smooth. Pour into glasses and decorate with lime slices. Lightly dust the lime slices and edges of the glasses with icing sugar and serve immediately.

Rum and Raisin Thick-Shake

This rich and creamy milkshake, based on the classic combination of rum and raisins, is remarkably easy to prepare. Use a good quality ice cream, leave it to soften slightly in the refrigerator before scooping, and you simply can't go wrong. If the raisins are a little dry, leave them to soak in the rum for a few minutes to soften and plump up before you blend them.

1 Put the raisins, rum and a little of the milk into a blender or food processor and process for about 1 minute, or until the raisins are finely chopped.

2 Spoon two large scoops of the vanilla ice cream into two tall glasses and put the remaining ice cream and milk into the blender. Process until creamy.

3 Pour the milkshake into glasses and serve immediately with straws and long spoons for scooping up the raisins.

Makes 2 tall glasses

75g/3oz/generous ½ cup raisins
45ml/3 tbsp dark rum
300ml/½ pint/1¼ cups full cream
   (whole) milk
500ml/17fl oz/2¼ cups good quality vanilla
   ice cream

Cook's tip
As an alternative, replace the vanilla ice cream with a good quality chocolate-flavoured ice cream – this will taste exceptionally good with rum and raisins.

Espresso Crush

A fresh update on iced coffee, this creatively layered treat combines slushy frozen granita with a thick vanilla ice cream layer, and is perfect for rounding off a lazy summer lunch or as a late afternoon refresher. The granita needs several hours in the freezer but will then keep for weeks so it is ready and waiting whenever you fancy a burst of ice-cold espresso.

Makes 4 glasses

75ml/5 tbsp ground espresso coffee
75g/3oz/scant ½ cup caster (superfine) sugar
300g/11oz vanilla ice cream or
    vanilla iced non-dairy dessert
75ml/5 tbsp milk or soya milk

1 Put the coffee in a cafetière (press pot), add 750ml/1¼ pints/3 cups boiling water and leave to infuse for 5 minutes. Plunge the cafetière and pour the coffee into a shallow freezer container. Stir in the sugar until dissolved. Leave to cool completely, then cover and freeze for about 2 hours or until the mixture starts to turn slushy around the edges.

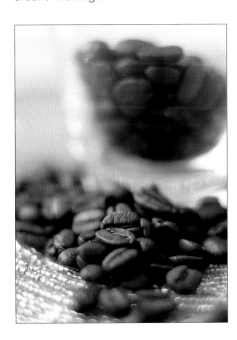

2 Using a fork, break up the ice crystals, stirring them into the centre of the container. Re-freeze until the mixture is slushy around the edges again. Repeat forking and stirring once or twice more until the mixture is completely slushy and there is no liquid remaining. Re-freeze until ready to use.

Cook's tip
The softened ice cream will melt quickly once you start layering it up in the glasses, so a good trick is to thoroughly chill the glasses before using them.

3 Put the ice cream or iced dessert and milk in a blender or food processor and process until thick and smooth. To serve, spoon a little into the base of each glass and sprinkle with a layer of the granita. Repeat layering until the glasses are full. Serve immediately.

tempting dessert drinks

Irresistible blends that imitate popular desserts are cleverly transformed into stunning drinks you can sip leisurely or, in some cases, scoop with a spoon. Be tempted by true classics such as peach Melba and Turkish delight or, for something a bit different, try a spicy rhubarb milk and an unusual take on traditional banoffee pie.

Sparkling Peach Melba

Serve this delightfully fresh and fruity drink during the summer months when raspberries and peaches are at their sweetest and best. Traditional cream soda gives this drink a really smooth flavour and a lovely fizz, while the optional shot of Drambuie or brandy gives it a definite kick. Serve with long spoons for scooping up any fruit left in the glasses.

Makes 2 glasses

300g/11oz/scant 2 cups raspberries
2 large ripe peaches
30ml/2 tbsp Drambuie or brandy (optional)
15ml/1 tbsp icing (confectioners') sugar
cream soda, to serve

1 Pack a few raspberries into six tiny shot glasses, or into six sections of an ice cube tray, and pour over water to cover. Freeze for several hours.

2 Using a small, sharp knife, halve and stone (pit) the peaches and cut one half into thin slices. Reserve 115g/4oz/ ⅔ cup of the raspberries and divide the rest, along with the peach slices, between two tall stemmed glasses. Drizzle with the liqueur, if using.

3 Push the reserved raspberries and the remaining peach flesh through the juicer. Stir the icing sugar into the juice and pour the juice over the fruits.

Cook's tip

If using shot glasses, dip these into a bowl of warm water for a few seconds to loosen the blocks of frozen raspberries. If using ice cube trays, turn these upside down and hold under warm running water for a few seconds. The ice cubes should then pop out easily.

4 Turn the raspberry-filled ice cubes out of the shot glasses or ice cube tray and add three to each glass. Top up with cream soda and serve immediately.

Super Sorbet Fizz

Freshly blended pineapple and cool, tangy lemon sorbet, topped up with sparkling ginger ale, makes a tastebud-tingling, fantastically mouthwatering drink. This semi-frozen blend is perfect after a summer lunch as a light alternative to more conventional desserts, or as a drink that can be whizzed up to allow you to chill out whenever the mood takes you.

Makes 4 glasses

30ml/2 tbsp muscovado (molasses) sugar
15ml/1 tbsp lemon juice
½ pineapple
1 piece preserved stem ginger,
   roughly chopped
200ml/7fl oz/scant 1 cup lemon sorbet,
   slightly softened
wafer thin pineapple and lemon slices,
   to decorate
ginger ale, to serve

3 Add the sorbet and process briefly until smooth. Spoon the muscovado syrup into four tumblers, then pour in the pineapple mixture.

4 Decorate the edge of the glasses with the pineapple and lemon slices. Top up each glass with ginger ale and serve immediately.

Cook's tip
The easiest way to prepare a pineapple is to chop off the top and base, then slice off the skin. Use the tip of a sharp knife to remove the "eyes" and then roughly chop into chunks.

1 Mix the sugar with the lemon juice in a small bowl and leave to stand for about 5 minutes until it turns syrupy.

2 Discard the skin and core from the pineapple and cut the flesh into chunks. Put the chunks in a blender or food processor with the ginger and whizz until smooth, scraping down the side of the bowl once or twice, if necessary.

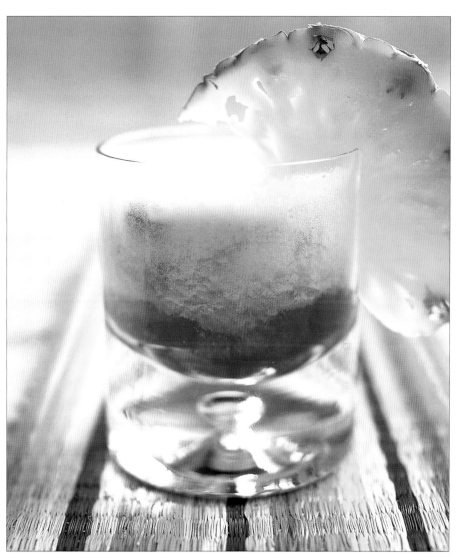

Black Beauty

This refreshing drink celebrates the perfect, classic partnership of apples and tart blackberries. The sweetness of the apples is balanced deliciously by the sharp tang and vibrant colour of the ripe berries. If you cannot find fresh blackberries, other deep red fruits such as mulberries or loganberries can be used as an equally irresistible substitute.

Makes 2–3 tall glasses

30ml/2 tbsp golden sugar
2.5ml/½ tsp ground cinnamon
3 eating apples
200g/7oz/1¾ cups blackberries
ice cubes
borage, to decorate (optional)

Cook's tip
This drink will taste best if you've picked the blackberries yourself. If you can't find them, however, other fruits will work just as well, or you could use frozen blackberries.

1 Put the golden sugar in a small bowl. Add the cinnamon and 60ml/4 tbsp boiling water and stir until the sugar dissolves to form a syrup.

2 Roughly chop the apples. Push the blackberries through a juicer and follow with the apples. Pour in the sugar syrup and stir well to mix.

3 Pour the juice into tall glasses and add several ice cubes to each one. Decorate the drinks with sprigs of borage or individual borage flowers, if using, and serve immediately.

Blueberry Meringue Crumble

Imagine the most appealing flavours of a blueberry meringue dessert – fresh tangy fruit, crisp sugary meringue and plenty of vanilla-scented cream. This drink combines all of these in one delicious milkshake. Iced yogurt is used to provide a slightly lighter note than ice cream, but there's nothing to stop you using ice cream instead for an even greater indulgence.

1 Put the blueberries and sugar in a blender or food processor with 60ml/ 4 tbsp water and blend until smooth, scraping the mixture down from the side once or twice, if necessary.

2 Transfer the purée to a small bowl and rinse out the blender or food processor bowl to get rid of any remaining blueberry juice.

3 Put the iced yogurt, milk and lime juice in the blender and process until thoroughly combined. Add half of the crushed meringues and process again until smooth.

4 Carefully pour alternate layers of the milkshake, blueberry syrup and the remaining crushed meringues into tall glasses, finishing with a few chunky pieces of meringue.

5 Drizzle any remaining blueberry syrup over the tops of the meringues and decorate with a few extra blueberries. Serve immediately.

Makes 3–4 tall glasses

150g/5oz/1¼ cups fresh blueberries, plus extra to decorate
15ml/1 tbsp icing (confectioners') sugar
250ml/8fl oz/1 cup vanilla iced yogurt
200ml/7fl oz/scant 1 cup full cream (whole) milk
30ml/2 tbsp lime juice
75g/3oz meringues, lightly crushed

Cook's tip
The easiest way to crush the meringues is to put them in a plastic bag on a work surface and tap them gently with a rolling pin. Stop tapping the meringues as soon as they have crumbled into little bitesize pieces otherwise you'll just be left with tiny crumbs.

Raspberry Brûlée Cream

This recipe, based on a classic French dessert, takes a little more preparation than most drinks but is well worth the extra effort. Like all the best brûlée recipes it starts with a home-made custard, so you'll need to be patient and allow time for it to thicken and chill.

Makes 4 glasses

800ml/1⅓ pints/3½ cups full cream (whole) milk
3 large egg yolks
130g/4½oz/scant ¾ cup caster (superfine) sugar
5ml/1 tsp vanilla essence (extract)
15ml/1 tbsp cornflour (cornstarch)
250g/9oz/1½ cups fresh or frozen raspberries
extra raspberries and mint or lemon balm sprigs, to decorate

1 Pour 300ml/½ pint/1¼ cups of milk into sections of an ice-cube tray and freeze for 1 hour. Put the egg yolks in a bowl with 50g/2oz/¼ cup of the sugar, the vanilla essence and cornflour. Beat until smooth. Bring the remaining milk to the boil in a pan. Pour the milk over the yolk mixture, whisking until smooth.

2 Return the custard to the pan and cook over the lowest heat, stirring until slightly thickened. (The custard should start to thicken as the steam rises; take care not to overheat it or it may curdle.)

3 Pour the custard into a jug (pitcher), cover the surface with a round of greaseproof (waxed) paper to prevent a skin forming and leave to cool. Once cool, chill until ready to serve.

4 Line a baking sheet with baking parchment. Heat the remaining sugar in a pan with 60ml/4 tbsp water until the sugar has dissolved. Bring to the boil and boil for 3–5 minutes until the syrup turns a golden caramel colour. Plunge the base of the pan in cold water to prevent further cooking.

5 Using a dessertspoon, "scribble" the caramel on to the baking sheet to make four decorative circles. Leave to set.

6 Divide the raspberries among the glasses and mash lightly. In a blender or food processor, blend the custard with the milk ice cubes until lightly broken. Ladle the mixture over the fruit. Balance the caramel on top of the glasses and decorate with extra raspberries, mint or lemon balm sprigs.

Strawberry Trifle

This wonderfully indulgent recipe takes the tastiest components of a classic trifle – the fruit, cream, nuts and a dash of liqueur – and combines them with ice cream to make a positive feast of a drink. Serve this blend as soon as it is assembled because the ingredients will swirl together in the glass fairly quickly and the pretty marbling effect will be lost.

Makes 4 glasses

2 eating apples
500g/1¼lb/5 cups strawberries
15ml/1 tbsp caster (superfine) sugar
60ml/4 tbsp sherry or Marsala
150ml/¼ pint/⅔ cup double (heavy) or whipping cream
60ml/4 tbsp flaked (sliced) almonds, lightly toasted
4 large scoops of vanilla ice cream

Cook's tip
As an alternative to vanilla ice cream use strawberry ice cream.

1 Quarter and core the apples then roughly chop the flesh. Hull and halve 200g/7oz/1¾ cups of the strawberries and set aside. Push the remaining strawberries and the apples through the juicer and stir in the sugar and sherry or Marsala. Chill until ready to serve.

2 Lightly whip the cream until it is barely holding its shape. Put the strawberries into chilled glasses and sprinkle with half the nuts. Add a scoop of ice cream to each. Pour over the strawberry juice and top with the whipped cream. Decorate with the remaining nuts and serve.

Rhubarb and Allspice Cream

Pale shoots of young rhubarb, poached with sugar and spice, and blended with cream, make a truly dreamy concoction. Make this delicious blend early in the season otherwise the rhubarb stalks will be tougher, possibly stringy, and so acidic that you'll need heaps of sugar to make this the indulgent treat that it should be. Serve with a spoon to scoop up every last drop.

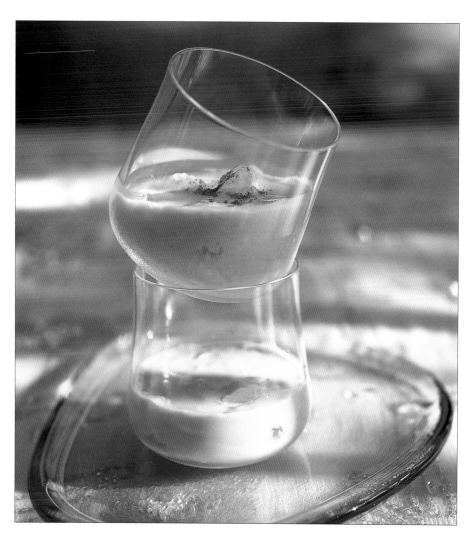

2 Transfer the rhubarb and cooking juice to a blender or food processor and process in short bursts until smooth, scraping down the mixture from the side of the bowl, if necessary.

3 Add the cream and milk to the rhubarb purée and blend again until combined. Transfer to a jug (pitcher) and chill until ready to serve.

4 Half-fill glasses with crushed ice, if using, pour over the juice, sprinkle with allspice and serve immediately.

Cook's tip

If you don't have fresh oranges to squeeze for this drink, you can use orange juice from a carton instead, or try a mix of citrus juices.

Makes 4 glasses

500g/1¼lb early rhubarb
100ml/3½fl oz/scant ½ cup freshly squeezed orange juice
75g/3oz/scant ½ cup caster (superfine) sugar
2.5ml/½ tsp ground allspice, plus extra to decorate
100ml/3½fl oz/scant ½ cup double (heavy) cream
200ml/7fl oz/scant 1 cup full cream (whole) milk
crushed ice (optional)

1 Trim the rhubarb and cut it into chunks. Put in a pan with the orange juice, sugar and allspice and bring to the boil. Cover and simmer gently for 6–8 minutes until tender. Remove the pan from the heat and leave to cool.

Turkish Delight

If you like Turkish delight, you'll love this fabulously indulgent drink. With the scented aroma of rose water and the delicious icy sweetness of vanilla ice cream, it is difficult to imagine a more decadent, or delicious, combination of ingredients.

Makes 3–4 glasses

125g/4¼oz rose-flavoured Turkish delight
475ml/16fl oz/2 cups semi-skimmed
   (low-fat) milk
250ml/8fl oz/1 cup good quality vanilla
   ice cream
a little finely grated plain (semisweet)
   chocolate, or drinking chocolate powder, for
   sprinkling (optional)

Cook's tips

For an even frothier top on this drink, pour the milkshake into a large bowl and whisk with a hand-held electric mixer.

   If the Turkish Delight is very sticky, you'll find it easier to cut it with scissors instead of a knife.

1 Roughly chop the Turkish delight and reserve a few pieces for decoration. Put the rest in a pan with half the milk. Heat gently until the pieces begin to melt. Remove the pan from the heat and leave to cool.

2 Spoon the mixture into a blender or food processor and add the remaining milk. Process until smooth, then add the ice cream and blend briefly to combine. Pour into glasses, top with the reserved Turkish delight and serve, sprinkled with chocolate or drinking chocolate, if using.

Nutty Nougat

For the best results, chill this glorious milkshake for a few hours until it is icy cold and the jumble of ingredients has had time to merge into a hedonistic fusion of flavours. Skinning the pistachio nuts is not essential, but it makes a fabulous visual impact, transforming the specks of nut from a dull green to a gorgeous, vivid emerald colour.

Makes 3 glasses

90ml/6 tbsp sweetened condensed milk
300ml/½ pint/1¼ cups semi-skimmed
    (low-fat) milk
100ml/3½fl oz/scant ½ cup crème fraîche
15ml/1 tbsp lemon juice
25g/1oz/¼ cup skinned pistachio nuts
25g/1oz/¼ cup blanched almonds
25g/1oz/3 tbsp candied peel, finely chopped,
    plus a few extra slices for decoration
ice cubes

1 Put the condensed milk and the semi-skimmed milk in a blender or food processor. Add the crème fraîche and blend until combined.

2 Add the lemon juice, pistachio nuts, almonds and chopped peel to the blender or food processor and blend until chopped into tiny pieces. Pour over ice cubes in glasses, add a few slices of candied peel and serve.

Cook's tip

Pretty, emerald-green flecks of pistachio nut pepper this rich, nougat-flavoured milkshake, giving it the subtlest hint of colour and the most wonderful texture.

To skin the pistachio nuts, put them in a heatproof bowl, cover with boiling water and leave for about 2 minutes. Drain the nuts and rub them between layers of kitchen paper to loosen the skins. Pick out the nuts, carefully peeling off the remaining skin.

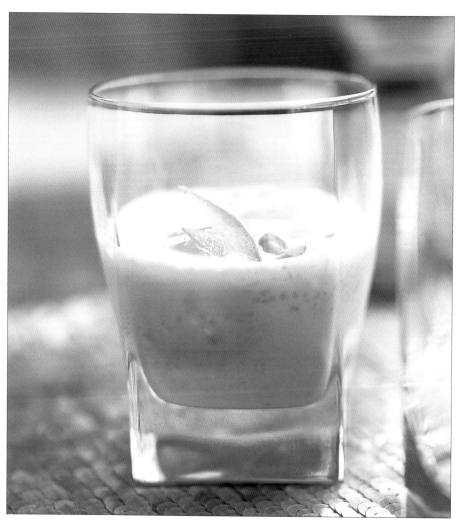

Banoffee High

Make plenty of this outrageous, lip-smacking milkshake because everyone will love it.
Nobody is pretending this is a health drink, but it is guaranteed to give you an energy rush of
astronomic proportions. Keep any leftover syrup in the refrigerator to use as a quick and
delicious toffee sauce for spooning over ice cream.

1 To make the toffee syrup, put the
sugar in a small heavy pan with 75ml/
5 tbsp water. Heat gently, stirring until
the sugar dissolves, then add 45ml/
3 tbsp of the cream and bring to the
boil. Let the syrup simmer for about
4 minutes until thickened. Remove
from the heat and leave to cool for
about 30 minutes.

2 Peel the bananas, break into pieces
and put into a blender or food processor
with the milk, vanilla sugar, ice cubes
and a further 45ml/3 tbsp of the cream.
Blend until smooth and frothy.

3 Pour the remaining cream into a
bowl and whip lightly with a whisk or
hand-held electric mixer until it just
holds its shape.

4 Add half the toffee syrup to the
milkshake and blend, then pour into
glasses. Drizzle more syrup around
the insides of the glasses. Spoon the
whipped cream over and drizzle with
any remaining syrup. Serve immediately.

Makes 4 tall glasses

75g/3oz/scant ½ cup light muscovado
   (brown) sugar
150ml/¼ pint/⅔ cup double (heavy) cream
4 large bananas
600ml/1 pint/2½ cups full cream (whole) milk
15ml/1 tbsp vanilla sugar
8 ice cubes

Cook's tips
If you use a blender, read the
instructions to check whether it is
powerful enough to cope with
crushing ice cubes.
   Make the syrup a little in
advance so it has time to thicken.

Coconut and Passion Fruit Ice

Few things beat the unadulterated, pure flavour of freshly juiced coconut. Whizzed with plenty of crushed ice and teamed with sharp, intensely flavoured passion fruit, it produces a milkshake that tastes indulgently good but is still refreshingly natural and wholesome.

Makes 2–3 tall glasses

1 coconut
75ml/5 tbsp icing (confectioners') sugar
3 passion fruit
150g/5oz crushed ice
60ml/4 tbsp double (heavy) cream

Cook's tip

This tropical, icy, passionately luxurious drink is heavenly on a summer's evening. You don't have to be on holiday to enjoy this type of decadence as this drink can be made quickly and easily at any time. Make a jug full and share with friends or family – if you feel that you are able to share it.

1 Drain the milk from the coconut and put to one side. Break open the coconut, remove the flesh, then pare off the brown skin. Push the coconut pieces through a juicer along with 150ml/¼ pint/⅔ cup water. Stir the icing sugar into the juice and reserve.

2 Halve the passion fruit and scoop the pulp into a small bowl. Set aside.

3 Put the crushed ice in a blender or food processor and blend until slushy. Add the juiced coconut, any drained coconut milk and the cream. Process to just blend the ingredients.

4 Pour the mixture into tall stemmed glasses, then, using a teaspoon, spoon the passion fruit on top of the drink. Add stirrers, if you like, and serve.

Death by Chocolate

There are only two ingredients used in this decadently rich smoothie: creamy milk and the best chocolate you can buy. Blended together, they make the frothiest, smoothest and most deliciously chocolatey drink you will ever taste. Once you've tried this recipe, you will never view a chocolate smoothie in the same light again.

Makes 2 large glasses

150g/5oz good quality chocolate
350ml/12fl oz/1½ cups full cream (whole) milk
ice cubes
chocolate curls or shavings, to serve

Cook's tip

Depending on personal taste, use dark (bittersweet) chocolate with 70 per cent cocoa solids, or a good quality milk chocolate. If you like the intensity of dark chocolate but the creaminess of milk, try using half of each type.

1 Break the chocolate into pieces and place in a heatproof bowl set over a pan of simmering water, making sure that the bowl does not rest in the water.

2 Add 60ml/4 tbsp of the milk and leave until the chocolate melts, stirring occasionally with a wooden spoon.

3 Remove the bowl from the heat, pour the remaining milk over the chocolate and stir to combine.

4 Pour the mixture into a blender or food processor and blend until frothy. Pour into glasses, add ice and chocolate curls or shavings, then serve.

Coffee Ice Cream Frappé

This creamy, smooth creation, which is strictly for adults (because of the alcoholic content), makes a wonderful alternative to a dessert on a hot summer's evening – or indeed at any time when you feel you need to indulge yourself. Serve in small glasses or little cappuccino cups for a glamorous touch, and provide your guests with both straws and long-handled spoons to allow them to scoop out every last bit of this delicious drink.

Makes 4 glasses

8 scoops of classic coffee ice cream
90ml/6 tbsp Kahlúa or Tia Maria liqueur
150ml/¼ pint/⅔ cup single (light) cream
1.5ml/¼ tsp ground cinnamon (optional)
crushed ice
ground cinnamon, for sprinkling

Cook's tip
To make a non-alcoholic version of this drink, simply substitute strong black coffee for the Kahlúa or Tia Maria.

1 Put half the coffee ice cream in a food processor or blender. Add the liqueur, then pour in the cream with a little cinnamon, if using, and blend. Scoop the remaining ice cream into four glasses or cappuccino cups.

2 Using a dessertspoon, spoon the coffee cream over the ice cream in each glass, then top with a little crushed ice. Sprinkle the top of each frappé with a little ground cinnamon and serve immediately.

Cool Chocolate Float

Frothy, chocolatey milkshake and scoops of creamy sweet chocolate and vanilla ice cream are combined here to make the most meltingly delicious drink ever, which is sure to prove a big success with children and adults alike. If you simply adore chocolate and you love ice cream, this may be the perfect drink for you. As this is such a rich, indulgent blend, however, try and resist temptation and don't indulge too often – save it for very special occasions.

Makes 2 tall glasses

115g/4oz plain (semisweet) chocolate, broken
  into pieces
250ml/8fl oz/1 cup milk
15ml/1 tbsp caster (superfine) sugar
4 large scoops of classic vanilla ice cream
4 large scoops of dark (bittersweet) chocolate
  ice cream
a little lightly whipped cream
grated chocolate or chocolate curls,
  to decorate

Cook's tip
Try substituting banana, coconut or toffee ice cream for the chocolate and vanilla ice cream if you prefer.

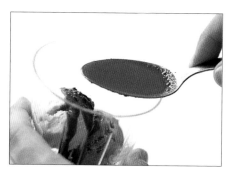

1 Put the chocolate in a heavy pan and add the milk and sugar. Heat gently, stirring with a wooden spoon until the chocolate has melted and the mixture is smooth. Leave to cool.

2 Blend the cooled chocolate mixture with half of the ice cream in a blender or food processor.

3 Scoop the remaining ice cream alternately into two tall glasses: vanilla then chocolate. Using a dessertspoon, drizzle the chocolate milk over and around the ice cream in each glass. Top with lightly whipped cream and sprinkle over a little grated chocolate or some chocolate curls to decorate. Serve immediately.

real boozy blends

If you're entertaining friends or simply relaxing
after a hard day's work, try one of these
tasty tipples, which are guaranteed to put
everyone in a mellow mood. Some are fruity and
only mildly alcoholic, while others are spirit-based
and pack a real punch – there's something
here to suit every occasion.

Iced Strawberry Daiquiri

The classic daiquiri cocktail is named after a village in Cuba that lies near the Bacardi processing plant. The original version was an incredibly potent blend of rum and whisky but the fruit versions, which are so popular today, are slightly less alcoholic. This one combines sweet and fragrant strawberries with white rum and refreshingly tangy lime juice.

Makes 4 small glasses

4 limes
60ml/4 tbsp icing (confectioners') sugar
200ml/7fl oz/scant 1 cup white rum
275g/10oz/2½ cups strawberries
300g/11oz crushed ice

Cook's tip
To make a really slushy, thick iced daiquiri, use frozen strawberries. There's no need to leave them to thaw, just use them as they are.

To make a banana version of this drink, replace the strawberries with two bananas. Peel the bananas, break them into pieces and add with the rum and icing sugar.

1 Squeeze the limes and pour the juice into a blender or food processor. Add the icing sugar, rum and all but two of the strawberries. Process until really smooth and frothy.

2 Add the crushed ice to the blender or food processor and blend until slushy. Pour the daiquiri into glasses, add a strawberry half to each glass and serve.

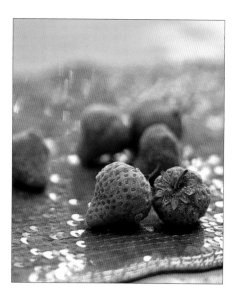

Frozen Margarita

For the serious cocktail connoisseur, a margarita sipped with a slice of lime from the salt-crusted rim of a glass is simply the best choice. A classic citrus juicer will help you to get the maximum juice from limes, but if the fruits are very firm and don't yield much juice, you could try giving them a brief blast in the microwave first.

1 To coat the glass rims with salt, put 30ml/2 tbsp of the lime juice into a saucer and plenty of salt flakes in another. Turn the glasses upside down and dip the rim of each glass in the lime juice, then in the salt. Invert the glasses again and put to one side.

2 Put the remaining lime juice in a blender or food processor with the Cointreau or Grand Marnier, tequila and ice. Process until the mixture is slushy.

3 Pour the margarita mixture into the salt-rimmed glasses, add a slice of lime to each glass and serve immediately.

Makes 8 small glasses

150ml/¼ pint/⅔ cup lime juice, from about
   6 large limes
sea salt flakes
120ml/4fl oz/½ cup Cointreau or
   Grand Marnier
200ml/7fl oz/scant 1 cup tequila
150g/5oz crushed ice
1 lime, thinly sliced, to decorate

Cook's tip
Gold tequila has aged in casks for longer than white and has a slightly golden tinge to it. Try to use clear tequila for this recipe as it will result in a fresh, clear cocktail in which the colour of the lime really shows through.

Raspberry Rendezvous

Pink, raspberry-flavoured bubbles and a suspicion of brandy make this the ultimate in sippable sophistication. A splash of sweet, sugary grenadine added to the jewel-coloured raspberry juice will smooth out any hint of a sharp tang that there might be from slightly underripe fruit.

Makes 6 tall glasses

400g/14oz/2⅓ cups raspberries, plus extra
   raspberries, to serve
100ml/3½fl oz/scant ½ cup grenadine
100ml/3½fl oz/scant ½ cup brandy or
   cherry brandy
ice cubes
1 litre/1¾ pints/4 cups ginger ale

Cook's tip
Grenadine is a sweet, ruby-coloured syrup made from pomegranates. It is popularly used to enhance fruit juices and cocktails. True grenadine contains no alcohol, but there are alcoholic versions around.

1 Push handfuls of the raspberries through a juicer and transfer the juice into a jug (pitcher).

2 Stir the grenadine and brandy or cherry brandy into the raspberry juice and chill (preferably overnight, but for at least 1 or 2 hours) until you are ready to serve it.

3 Prepare six tall glasses: add plenty of ice cubes to each and place a few extra raspberries in the bottom of the glasses.

4 Pour the raspberry mixture into each of the prepared glasses and then top up with the ginger ale. Serve the cocktails immediately.

Scent Sensation

Orange flower water, which is distilled from the delicate white blooms of the orange blossom tree, gives delicious sweet pear and redcurrant juices a delicate fragrance and a subtle, barely there flavour. Like rose water, it is often associated with Middle Eastern cooking and goes really well with warm-flavoured spices such as cinnamon.

Makes 4–5 glasses

4 pears
300g/11oz/2¾ cups redcurrants
2 cinnamon sticks
45ml/3 tbsp orange flower water
about 25g/1oz/¼ cup icing (confectioners')
   sugar
tonic water
cinnamon sticks and extra redcurrants, to
   decorate (optional)

Cook's tip
If you like, add a splash of alcohol; try an almond liqueur, such as Disaronno, as the almondy edge goes well with the scented flavours.

1 Using a small, sharp knife, cut the pears into chunks of roughly the same size and push the chunks through a juicer with the redcurrants.

2 Crumble the 2 cinnamon sticks, using your fingers, and add to the redcurrant juice. Cover and leave to stand for at least 1 hour.

3 Strain the juice through a sieve into a bowl, then whisk in the orange flower water and a little icing sugar to taste.

4 To serve, put one or two cinnamon sticks in each glass, if using. Pour the juice into glasses, then top up with tonic water and decorate with the extra redcurrants, if you like.

Watermelon Gin

The fabulously red, juicy flesh of the watermelon makes a perfect partner for the strong, heady scent and flavour of gin. The juice is so sweet and delicate, and this sparkling drink is so stunningly pretty, that you'll be hard-pressed to resist its appeal. For a party, just make up a large jug of the juice, top up with tonic water and pour out for guests as they arrive.

1 Cut off the skin from the watermelon and chop the flesh into large chunks, removing the seeds. Push the flesh through the juicer and pour into a large jug (pitcher). Stir in the lime juice and sugar and chill.

2 Half-fill glasses with crushed ice. Stir the gin into the juice and pour over the ice. Add the lime slices and top up with tonic water. Serve immediately.

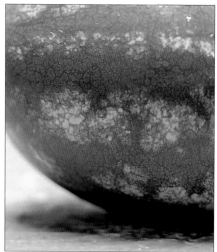

Makes 4 large glasses

500g/1¼lb wedge watermelon
juice of 1 lime
10ml/2 tsp caster (superfine) sugar
crushed ice
150ml/¼ pint/⅔ cup gin
lime slices
tonic water

Cook's tip
This recipe makes a cocktail that is not too alcoholic. If you would prefer a slightly stronger drink, however, add up to 75ml/2½fl oz/ ⅓ cup more gin to the mix before you pour it over the ice.

Blackcurrant Cassis

Cassis is an intensely flavoured blackcurrant liqueur, and is generally used to add just a hint of colour and flavour to Champagne and sparkling wines. This home-made variation is so packed with the summer freshness of juicy blackcurrants that you'll want to ensure it is the predominant flavour in any cocktail.

Makes 6–8 glasses

225g/8oz/2 cups blackcurrants
50g/2oz/¼ cup caster (superfine) sugar
75ml/5 tbsp vodka
sparkling wine or Champagne

Cook's tip
For a less alcoholic version, either leave out the vodka from the syrup or top up the glasses with chilled sparkling mineral water instead of the wine or Champagne.

1 Using a fork, strip the blackcurrants from their stems. Scatter 50g/2oz/ ½ cup of the fruit into the sections of an ice-cube tray. Top up with cold water and freeze for about 2 hours.

2 Put the sugar in a small, heavy pan with 60ml/4 tbsp water and heat gently until the sugar has dissolved. Bring to the boil, remove from the heat, then pour into a jug and leave to cool. Push the remaining blackcurrants through a juicer and mix with the syrup. Stir in the vodka and chill until ready to serve.

3 Put two or three of the blackcurrant ice cubes into each tall-stemmed glass. Add 15–30ml/1–2 tbsp of the syrup to each glass and top up with sparkling wine or Champagne. Serve immediately.

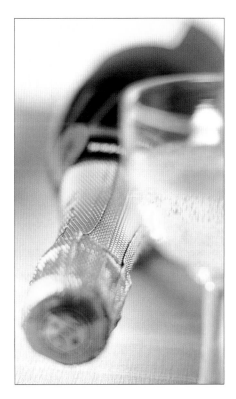

Mulled Plums in Marsala

You needn't confine mulled drinks to the festive season. This fruity version, distinctively spiced and laced with Marsala, is served chilled, so is perfect for drinks parties at any time of the year. This is a delicious and practical way of using an abundance of sweet, juicy plums to make an exotic drink that is guaranteed to impress your guests.

Makes 4 glasses

500g/1¼lb ripe plums
15g/½oz fresh root ginger, sliced
5ml/1 tsp whole cloves
25g/1oz/2 tbsp light muscovado (brown) sugar
200ml/7fl oz/scant 1 cup Marsala
ice cubes

3 Push the remaining plums through a juicer. Strain the syrup and mix with the plum juice and Marsala.

4 Put ice cubes and plum halves in four glasses and pour over the syrup. Serve with stirrers, if you like.

Cook's tip
If you are having a party, make a large batch of this drink. It can be transferred to a large punch bowl with a ladle so that your guests can help themselves and fish out the marsala-soaked plums.

1 Halve two of the plums and discard the stones (pits). Roughly chop the remainder. Put the ginger, cloves and sugar in a small pan with 300ml/ ½ pint/1¼ cups water. Heat gently until the sugar has dissolved then bring to the boil and add the halved plums.

2 Reduce the heat and simmer gently for 2–3 minutes until the plums have softened but still retain their shape. Using a slotted spoon, lift out the plums and leave the plums and syrup to cool.

Berried Treasure

The combination of cranberries and raspberries is fast becoming a juice classic, despite the fact that these fruits are at their best during different seasons. This needn't hinder you though, just use one in frozen form – the fruit will thaw quickly and save you adding ice. This recipe uses raspberry conserve in place of the more usual sugar or honey to add sweetness.

1 Push all the raspberries through a juicer, followed by the raspberry conserve and then the cranberries.

2 Pour the juice into tall glasses, top up with soda water or sparkling mineral water and serve immediately.

Makes 2 tall glasses

250g/9oz/1½ cups raspberries
45ml/3 tbsp raspberry conserve
250g/9oz/1½ cups cranberries
soda water (club soda) or sparkling
    mineral water

Cook's tip
For a pretty presentation, thread a few of the berries on to wooden cocktail sticks (toothpicks) and rest them across the rim of the glasses. (To balance the sticks successfully, you'll need to use relatively narrow glasses.)

Brandy Mint Julep

Traditionally, a julep is a sweetened, iced drink made using brandy or whisky and flavoured with fresh mint leaves. This stunning version infuses the mint in sugar syrup to colour it a cooling shade of green. Zipped up with brandy, or delicious peach brandy, and poured over ice, this makes a refreshingly good summertime tipple.

Makes 4 small glasses

25g/1oz/2 tbsp caster (superfine) sugar
25g/1oz fresh mint, plus extra mint sprigs, to decorate
crushed ice
100ml/7 tbsp brandy or peach brandy

Cook's tip
This sexy little number would be well placed in any cosmopolitan New York cocktail bar. To bring a little bit of that New York ambience into your home, prepare a large batch and invite plenty of friends round to help you drink it.

1 Put the sugar in a small, heavy pan with 200ml/7fl oz/scant 1 cup water. Heat gently until the sugar dissolves, then bring to the boil and boil for 1 minute to make a syrup. Pour into a small bowl. Pull the mint leaves from the stalks and add to the hot syrup. Leave the syrup to stand for about 30 minutes or until cool.

2 Strain the syrup into a blender or food processor, add the mint and blend lightly until it is finely chopped.

3 Half-fill four small glasses with crushed ice, packing one or two mint sprigs into each glass. Mix the brandy with the mint syrup and pour over the ice. Serve immediately.

Lime Mojito

Cuba and the Caribbean islands have invented some of the most delicious lime- and rum-based cocktails, from tangily refreshing shorts to thick, creamy concoctions that are almost a meal in themselves. This recipes fits the first category, but beware, you're bound to find it irresistibly moreish – which could prove dangerous.

Makes 4 glasses

4 lemon balm sprigs
40ml/8 tsp caster (superfine) sugar
4 limes
130ml/4½fl oz/generous ½ cup white rum
ice cubes
strips of pared lime rind, to decorate
sparkling mineral water, to serve

Cook's tip
To ensure you get the maximum juice from the limes, microwave them for approximately 20–30 seconds on medium (50 per cent power).

1 Pull the lemon balm leaves from their stems. Put 10ml/2 tsp of the sugar into each small glass.

2 Add several lemon balm leaves to each glass and lightly rub the leaves into the sugar, using the back of a teaspoon, to release their fragrance.

3 Squeeze the limes using a citrus juicer, or by hand, and then pour the juice into the glasses with the rum.

4 Add plenty of ice to each glass and decorate with pared lime rind. Serve immediately, topped up with sparkling mineral water.

Tropical Fruit Royale

This recipe is a fresh and fruity variation of a kir royale, in which Champagne is poured over crème de cassis. Made with tropical fruits and sparkling wine, this cocktail is a lot less expensive than the Champagne version but still has a wonderfully elegant feel. Remember to blend the fruits ahead of time to give the mango ice cubes time to freeze.

Makes 6 glasses

2 large mangoes
6 passion fruit
sparkling wine

Cook's tip
Delight your guests with this delicious thirst-quencher. With its taste of the tropics, it makes the perfect choice for garden parties on balmy summer evenings, wherever in the world you are.

1 Peel the mangoes, cut the flesh off the stone (pit), then put the flesh in a blender or food processor. Process until smooth, scraping the mixture down from the side of the bowl, if necessary.

2 Fill an ice-cube tray with half of the purée and freeze for 2 hours.

3 Cut six wedges from one or two of the passion fruit and scoop the pulp from the rest of the passion fruit into the remaining mango purée. Process until well blended.

4 Spoon the mixture into six stemmed glasses. Divide the mango ice cubes among the glasses, top up with sparkling wine and add the passion fruit wedges. Serve with stirrers, if you like.

Pineapple and Coconut Rum Crush

This thick and slushy tropical cooler is unbelievably rich thanks to the combination of coconut milk and thick cream. The addition of sweet, juicy and slightly tart pineapple, and finely crushed ice, offers a refreshing foil, making it all too easy to sip your way through several glasses.

1 Trim off the ends from the pineapple, then cut off the skin. Cut away the core and chop the flesh. Put the chopped flesh in a blender or food processor with the lemon juice and whizz until very smooth.

2 Add the coconut milk, cream, rum and 30ml/2 tbsp of the sugar. Blend until thoroughly combined, then taste and add more sugar if necessary. Pack the ice into glasses and pour the drink over. Serve immediately.

Makes 4–5 large glasses

1 pineapple
30ml/2 tbsp lemon juice
200ml/7fl oz/scant 1 cup coconut milk
150ml/¼ pint/⅔ cup double (heavy) cream
200ml/7fl oz/scant 1 cup white rum
30–60ml/2–4 tbsp caster (superfine) sugar
500g/1¼ lb finely crushed ice

Cook's tip
This is a great cocktail for making ahead of time. Blend the drink in advance and chill in a jug (pitcher). Store the crushed ice in the freezer ready for serving as soon as it's required.

Foaming Citrus Eggnog

For most of us, eggnog is inextricably associated with the festive season. This version, however, pepped up with orange rind and juice for a lighter, fresher taste, has a much wider appeal. Whether you sip it as a late-night soother, serve it as a wintry dessert or enjoy it as a cosy tipple on a wet afternoon, it's sure to bring a warm, rosy glow to your cheeks.

Makes 2 glasses

2 small oranges
150ml/¼ pint/⅔ cup single (light) cream
plenty of freshly grated nutmeg
2.5ml/½ tsp ground cinnamon
2.5ml/½ tsp cornflour (cornstarch)
2 eggs, separated
30ml/2 tbsp light muscovado (brown) sugar
45ml/3 tbsp brandy
extra nutmeg, for sprinkling (optional)

1 Finely grate the rind from the oranges, then squeeze out the juice and pour it into a jug (pitcher).

2 Put the rind in a small heavy pan with the cream, nutmeg, cinnamon and cornflour. Heat gently over a low heat, stirring frequently until bubbling.

3 Whisk the egg yolks with the sugar, using a handheld whisk.

4 Stir the hot citrus cream mixture into the egg yolks, then return to the pan. Pour in the orange juice and brandy and heat very gently, stirring until slightly thickened.

5 Whisk the egg whites in a large, clean bowl until foamy and light.

6 Strain the cream mixture through a sieve into the whisked whites. Stir gently and pour into heatproof punch cups, handled glasses or mugs. Sprinkle over a little extra nutmeg before serving, if you like.

Cook's tip
Note that this recipe contains almost raw egg.

Amaretto Apricot Dream

This really is a dream of a drink, combining fresh, ripe apricots, oranges and delicious maple syrup with creamy cool yogurt. Light and fruity, it is a wonderful choice for a breezy, sunny day in the garden, and the addition of almond liqueur and amaretti biscuits gives it a wonderfully complex flavour. Once you've tasted one you'll surely be back for more.

Makes 4 glasses

3 large oranges
600g/1lb 6oz small fresh apricots
60ml/4 tbsp maple syrup, plus extra
   to serve
50g/2oz amaretti
200g/7oz/scant 1 cup Greek (strained
   plain) yogurt
30ml/2 tbsp amaretto liqueur
mineral water (optional)
ice cubes

2 Put half the fruit, the strained juice, maple syrup and amaretti in a food processor or blender and blend until smooth. Arrange the remaining fruit halves in the bases of four glasses.

3 Stir the yogurt until smooth and spoon half over the fruits. Add the amaretto, and a little mineral water to the blended mixture (if the juice is too thick), and pour into the glasses. Add the remaining yogurt and one or two ice cubes to each glass. Drizzle with maple syrup to serve.

Cook's tip
To impress guests at parties, use two teaspoons to delicately place a spoonful of yogurt on top of this apricot drink.

1 Grate the rind from one of the oranges and squeeze the juice from all three. Halve and stone (pit) the apricots and put them in a pan. Add the orange juice and zest then heat slowly. Cover with a lid and simmer very gently for 3 minutes or until the apricots are tender. Strain through a sieve, reserving the juice, and leave to cool completely.

perfect
party
drinks

If you're entertaining a large crowd, whizzing up a choice of interesting party brews is a sure-fire way to get the occasion off to a lively start. From long and refreshing spritzers to short, punchy tipples, this chapter offers a feast of innovative choices that include a couple of fresh fruit blends for partygoers who prefer not to drink alcohol.

Lemon Vodka

Very similar to the deliciously moreish Italian liqueur, Limoncello, this lemon vodka should be drunk in small quantities due to its hefty alcoholic punch. Blend the sugar, lemons and vodka and keep in a bottle in the refrigerator, ready for pouring over crushed ice or topping up with soda or sparkling water. It is also delicious drizzled over melting vanilla ice cream.

1 Squeeze the lemons using a citrus juicer. Pour the juice into a jug (pitcher), add the sugar and whisk well until all the sugar has dissolved.

2 Strain the sweetened lemon juice into a clean bottle or narrow-necked jar and add the vodka. Shake the mixture well to combine, and chill for up to 2 weeks.

3 To serve, fill small glasses with ice and pour the lemon vodka over.

Makes 12–15 small glasses

10 large lemons
275g/10oz/generous 1¼ cups caster (superfine) sugar
250ml/8fl oz/1 cup vodka
ice cubes

Cook's tip
Pure, clear vodka and zesty lemon juice make a tantalizing spirit that tastes like bottled sunshine. If you like, bruise a couple of mint leaves and add to the glass before pouring the vodka – this will add a delicious freshness to the drink.

Apple-Tice

Even the dullest of eating apples seem to juice well. With the addition of a fresh mint syrup and sparkling cider, any apple juice can be transformed into a distinctly exciting, mildly alcoholic blend that makes an excellent party drink. The recipe allows you to choose how much cider you add to each glass, which makes it easier to control your alcohol consumption.

Makes 6–8 glasses

25g/1oz/1 cup mint leaves, plus extra mint
　sprigs, to decorate
15g/½oz/1 tbsp caster (superfine) sugar
6 eating apples
ice cubes
1 litre/1¾ pints/4 cups dry (hard) cider

1 Using a pair of kitchen scissors, roughly snip the mint into a heatproof jug (pitcher). Add the sugar to the jug, then pour over 200ml/7fl oz/scant 1 cup of boiling water. Stir well until the sugar has dissolved, then leave to stand until cool.

2 Drain the mint from the syrup and discard the mint leaves. Using a small, sharp knife, core the apples, chop them into chunks of roughly the same size and push them through a juicer.

3 Mix the apple juice and mint-flavoured syrup in a large jug and chill (preferably overnight, but for at least 1–2 hours) until ready to serve.

4 To serve, add ice cubes and mint sprigs and top up with cider.

Cook's tip
If you'd prefer a non-alcoholic version of this drink, top up the glasses with sparkling mineral water, ginger ale or lemonade instead of cider.

Cranberry and Apple Spritzer

Don't forget to look after the non-drinkers at your party – all too often they're left with just the mixers, fizzy drinks or tap water. This colourful, zingy cooler combines tangy cranberries with fresh juicy apples and a subtle, fragrant hint of vanilla. Topped up with sparkling mineral water, this is one spritzer that's sure to keep everyone happy.

Makes 6–8 glasses

6 red eating apples
375g/13oz/3½ cups fresh or frozen
    cranberries, plus extra to decorate
45ml/3 tbsp vanilla syrup
ice cubes
sparkling mineral water

Cook's tip

To make vanilla syrup, heat a vanilla pod (bean) with sugar and water in a pan until the sugar dissolves. Simmer for 5 minutes then leave to cool.

1 Quarter and core the apples then cut the flesh into pieces small enough to fit through a juicer. Push the cranberries and apple chunks through the juicer. Add the vanilla syrup to the juice and chill until ready to serve.

2 Pour the juice into glasses and add one or two ice cubes to each. Top up with sparkling mineral water and decorate with extra cranberries, threaded on to cocktail sticks (toothpicks). Serve immediately.

Pink Perfection

Make plenty of freshly juiced blends like this gorgeous combination and your guests will keep coming back for more. Raspberry and grapefruit juice make a great partnership, particularly if you add a little cinnamon syrup to counteract any tartness in the fruit.

Makes 8 tall glasses

1 cinnamon stick
50g/2oz/¼ cup caster (superfine) sugar
4 pink grapefruits
250g/9oz/1½ cups fresh or frozen raspberries
wedge of watermelon
crushed ice
borage flowers, to decorate (optional)

Cook's tip

Make non-alcoholic drinks more interesting by dressing them up with extra fruits and decorations. As an alternative to watermelon, serve other stirrers such as cinnamon sticks, or provide sugar stirrers so guests can sweeten their drinks to suit their own personal preference.

1 Put the cinnamon stick in a small pan with the sugar and 200ml/7fl oz/scant 1 cup water. Heat gently until the sugar has dissolved, then bring to the boil and boil for 1 minute. Reserve to cool.

2 Cut away the skins from the pink grapefruits. Cut the flesh into pieces small enough to fit through a juicer funnel. Juice the grapefruits and raspberries and pour into a small glass jug (pitcher).

3 Remove the cinnamon from the syrup and add the syrup to the grapefruit and raspberry juice in the jug.

4 Carefully slice the watermelon into long thin wedges and place in eight tall glasses. Half-fill the glasses with the crushed ice and sprinkle with borage flowers, if you like. Pour over the pink fruit juice and serve immediately with plenty of napkins to allow your guests to eat the watermelon wedges.

Peach Bellini

Serve this classic, fabulous cocktail when peaches are at their most delicious and best. Preserved stem ginger and peach juice ice cubes make an unusual twist, so allow plenty of time for them to freeze before serving. If using both brandy and sparkling wine is a little too alcoholic for your taste, top up the cocktail with sparkling mineral water instead of the wine, or alternatively omit the brandy. In fact, any combination would be equally delicious.

Makes 8–10 glasses

75g/3oz preserved stem ginger (about 5 pieces), sliced
6 large ripe peaches
150ml/¼ pint/⅔ cup peach brandy or regular brandy
1 bottle sparkling wine

Cook's tip

When the ice cubes start to melt you will get an extra hit of peach and ginger juice in your drink. Drink this cocktail slowly to allow all of the flavours to merge.

1 Place one or two slices of ginger in all the sections of an ice-cube tray. Halve and stone (pit) the peaches then push through a juicer. Make 200ml/7fl oz/ scant 1 cup of the peach juice up to 300ml/½ pint/1¼ cups with water. Pour into the ice-cube tray. Freeze.

2 When frozen solid, carefully remove the ice cubes from the tray and divide among eight to ten wine glasses. Stir the brandy into the remaining peach juice, mix well and pour over the ice cubes. Top up with the sparkling wine and serve immediately.

Tropical Storm

Whisky and ginger makes a popular flavour combination in party drinks and cocktails, either served neat or blended with other ingredients to dilute the intense flavour. This incredibly refreshing creation with mango and lime has, not surprisingly, plenty of kick.

Makes 8 tall glasses

2 large ripe mangoes
2 papayas
2 limes
150ml/¼ pint/⅔ cup ginger wine
105ml/7 tbsp whisky or Drambuie
ice cubes
lime slices and mango and papaya wedges, to decorate
soda water (club soda)

Cook's tip

Mango and papaya sometimes collects inside the juicer rather than flowing easily into the container. If this happens, pour a little cold water through the juicer funnel.

1 Halve the mangoes either side of the flat stone (pit). Using a spoon, scoop out the flesh from the halves and cut from around the stone using a small, sharp knife. Chop roughly.

2 Halve the papaya and discard the pips (seeds). Remove the skin and roughly chop the flesh. Cut away the skins from the limes and halve.

3 Push the mangoes, papayas and limes through a juicer. Pour into a jug (pitcher), add the ginger wine and whisky or Drambuie and chill until ready to serve.

4 Place plenty of ice cubes and long wedges of mango and papaya and slices of lime into tall glasses. Pour over the juice until the glasses are two-thirds full. Top up with soda water and serve.

Happy Days

Set a midsummer drinks party off to a good start with this fabulously fruity blend. It's packed with summer fruits and flavoured with refreshingly light, but highly intoxicating, Limoncello – a welcome alternative to the more traditional spirits used in party blends.

1 Using a fork, strip the redcurrants from their stalks. Reserve 50g/2oz/ ½ cup. Hull the strawberries and reserve 200g/7oz/1¾ cups. Push the remainder through a juicer with the redcurrants. Pour into a glass punch bowl or jug (pitcher) and stir in the liqueur. Chill until ready to serve.

2 Halve the reserved strawberries and add to the juice with the redcurrants, plenty of ice cubes and the mint or lemon balm. Top up with lemonade or cream soda, and serve.

Makes 8 glasses

250g/9oz/generous 2 cups redcurrants
675g/1½ lb/6 cups strawberries
200ml/7fl oz/scant 1 cup Limoncello liqueur
ice cubes
small handful of mint or lemon balm
l litre/1¾ pints/4 cups lemonade or
   cream soda

Cook's tip
Limoncello is an intensely tangy, very alcoholic Italian lemon liqueur. It's great served on its own over plenty of crushed ice or, more unusually, in this fruity punch. If you can't find it, use a well-flavoured orange liqueur such as Cointreau or Grand Marnier instead.

Grand Marnier, Papaya and Passion Fruit Punch

The term "punch" comes from the Hindu word *panch* (five), relating to the five ingredients traditionally contained in the drink – alcohol, lemon or lime, tea, sugar and water. The ingredients may have altered somewhat over the years but the best punches still combine a mixture of spirits, flavourings and an innocent top-up of fizz or juice.

Makes about 15 glasses

2 large papayas
4 passion fruit
300g/11oz lychees, peeled and pitted
300ml/½ pint/1¼ cups freshly squeezed
  orange juice
200ml/7fl oz/scant 1 cup Grand Marnier or
  other orange-flavoured liqueur
8 whole star anise
2 small oranges
ice cubes
1.5 litres/2½ pints/6¼ cups soda water
  (club soda)

1 Halve the papayas and discard the seeds. Halve the passion fruit and press the pulp through a sieve into a small punch bowl or a pretty serving bowl.

2 Push the papayas through a juicer, adding 100ml/7 tbsp water to help the pulp through. Juice the lychees. Add the juices to the bowl with the orange juice, liqueur and star anise. Thinly slice the oranges and add to the bowl. Chill for at least 1 hour or until ready to serve.

3 Add plenty of ice cubes to the bowl and top up with soda water. Ladle into punch cups or small glasses to serve.

Apple-Spiced Beer

Lager takes on a whole new dimension in this fun and fruity cooler. Diluted with freshly squeezed apple juice and flavoured with ginger and star anise, it's a great drink for anyone who wants to pace themselves through a party. The spiced apple juice can be made several hours in advance and chilled in a serving jug, ready for topping up at the last minute.

Makes 8–10 tall glasses

8 eating apples
25g/1oz fresh root ginger
6 whole star anise
800ml/1⅓ pints/3½ cups lager
crushed ice

1 Quarter and core the apples and, using a small, sharp knife, cut the flesh into pieces small enough to fit through a juicer. Roughly chop the ginger. Push half the apples through the juicer, then juice the ginger and the remaining apples.

2 Put 105ml/7 tbsp of the juice in a small pan with the star anise and heat gently until almost boiling. Add to the remaining juice in a large jug (pitcher) and chill for at least 1 hour.

3 Add the lager to the juice and stir gently to help disperse the froth. Pour over crushed ice in tall glasses and serve immediately.

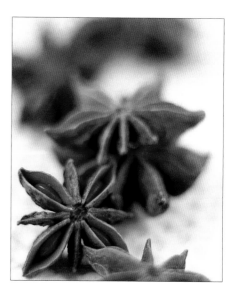

Cucumber Pimm's Punch

This tangy blend of freshly juiced cucumber, ginger and apples isn't as innocent as it looks – or tastes. It's lavishly topped with alcohol, so is definitely a drink to enjoy on a lazy summer afternoon. To enjoy on a picnic, just chill the juice really well, pour into a vacuum flask and top up with chilled ginger ale when you reach your destination.

2 Peel the remaining cucumber and cut it into large chunks. Roughly chop the ginger and apples. Push the apples, then the ginger and cucumber through a juicer and pour the juice into a large jug (pitcher) or bowl.

3 Stir the Pimm's into the juice, add the cucumber, lemon slices and mint and borage sprigs, then chill.

4 Just before serving, add the ice cubes and borage flowers to the punch and top up with ginger ale. Ladle into glasses or glass cups.

Makes 12 small glasses

1 cucumber
1 lemon
50g/2oz fresh root ginger
4 eating apples
600ml/1 pint/2½ cups Pimm's
sprigs of mint and borage
ice cubes
borage flowers
1.5 litres/2½ pints/6¼ cups ginger ale

1 Cut off a 5cm/2in length from the cucumber and cut into thin slices. Slice the lemon and set both aside.

GLOSSARY

What follows is a list of the specialist terms most frequently encountered in the cocktail world.

ABV: Stands for "alcohol by volume", and shows the total percentage within the drink that is accounted for by pure ethyl alcohol. All alcoholic products must, by law, give this information.

Aperitif: Any drink taken before eating as a stimulant to the appetite. Can be as simple as a glass of dry white wine, champagne or sherry. Can also be a dry or sour cocktail.

Cobbler: A long drink consisting of spirit with sugar and ice, served with plenty of fruit to garnish. American in origin, it is the forerunner of all lavishly garnished cocktails.

Chaser: A longer drink that is taken immediately after a small one, typically a glass of beer to follow a shot of neat spirit. It soothes the throat after the high alcohol of its predecessor.

*Below: Champagne is an excellent **aperitif** for whetting the appetite.*

*Above: A **cup** makes a refreshing, long drink as a party starter. They are generally lavishly garnished with fruit.*

Collins: A long drink originally called the Tom Collins after a particular variety of gin. A Collins is now any spirit mixed with lemon juice and sugar, and topped up with soda. It is basically a long version of the Sour.

Cooler: An indeterminate long drink that consists of any spirit with fruit juice (usually citrus), sugar and a sparkling topper (which may be soda, lemonade or ginger ale). Classically decorated with a spiral citrus twist.

Crusta: Any drink that comes in a glass with a frosted rim, usually of sugar (although the salt-rimmed Margarita is theoretically a Crusta too). Should also technically be served with a continuous twist of lemon rind lining the glass.

Cup: Essentially the cold version of Punch, a Cup is a mixture of wine or cider with spirits and fruit juices, served from a large bowl full of fruit garnishes and ice. Best served in summer.

Daisy: A soured spirit that also contains a measure of fruit syrup such as grenadine, topped up with soda.

Egg-nog: A long mixture of spirit or fortified wine with whole egg, sugar and milk, served cold and usually seasoned with nutmeg. Traditional as a Christmas drink in the USA.

Fix: Virtually the same thing as a Daisy. Consists of spirit, lemon juice, a fruit syrup and a sparkling topper, but with the Fix, it is essential to put the squeezed lemon rind into the drink.

Fizz: Almost any long drink topped up with soda, but classically just spirit, lemon juice, sugar and soda, perhaps with a drop of egg white to help the texture. Buck's Fizz, a champagne drink, marked a radical departure for the Fizz.

Flip: A short drink containing egg, sugar and either spirit or fortified wine, usually seasoned with nutmeg. Similar to an egg-nog, but without the milk.

Frappé: Any drink that is served over a snow of finely crushed ice.

*Below: A gin and lemon **fizz** topped with fruit and flower ice cubes.*

*Above: A tall glass can be used for fruity drinks served **on the rocks**.*

Highball: Simply spirit with ice, topped up with soda or some other sparkling mixer, but with no other ingredient.

Julep: A hot-weather American drink, served in a tall glass. Consists of spirit (classically bourbon) and plenty of crushed ice, on a base of mint leaves pressed with sugar. As the ice melts, it becomes a long drink.

Mulling: The technique of gently heating wine, beer or cider with spices, fruit and perhaps a shot of spirit. To be served hot during the British Christmas season.

Neat: Any spirit drunk on its own without ice or mixer. "As it comes" is the synonymous phrase.

On the rocks: Any drink served over ice cubes or cracked ice, usually in a tumbler or Old-Fashioned glass.

Pick-me-up: Any drink whose purpose is to revive the drinker, whether in mid-morning or to counteract the effects of over-indulgence. It is a bit of a loaded term, since it shouldn't be forgotten that all alcohol depresses the central nervous system, rather than "picks it up".

Pousse-café: A small cocktail in which two or more ingredients are poured slowly into the glass one by one to create a layered effect. Must be served without ice or garnishes.

Punch: An old British colonial drink consisting of spirits and wine, heated up with spices and fruit, and served from a large bowl. Similar to mulled wine, and likewise traditionally served at Christmas.

Rickey: A unsweetened measure of spirit with lime juice and ice, topped up with soda.

Sangaree: May be based on a spirit, but is usually fortified wine with sugar, soda and a nutmeg topping.

Shooter: A small, strong cocktail served in a shot glass, intended to be downed in one. Historically, any tot of neat spirit taken in the same way.

*Below: A **pousse-café** layered with Kahlúa, Bailey's Irish Cream and Grand Marnier.*

*Above: A **sour** made from gin, fresh lemon juice and a pinch of sugar.*

Shrub: A drink consisting of spirit (usually brandy or rum) bottled with fruit juices and loaf (or lump) sugar, and left for several weeks.

Sling: A long drink consisting of spirit with lemon juice, sugar and soda. Similar to a Collins, it now generally contains a shot of some liqueur as well.

Smash: An undersized version of the Julep, made with crushed mint, sugar and spirit, but served in a small glass and with not as much ice.

Sour: Any spirit mixed with lemon juice and a pinch of sugar, sometimes taken with a small splash of soda, but always as a short drink.

Swizzle: Cocktail of Caribbean origin involving spirit, lime juice, bitters, sugar and ice, frothed up by being vigorously stirred with a swizzle-stick held between the palms of the hands. Must be served Antarctically cold.

Toddy: A cold-weather drink consisting of spirit, lemon juice and sugar (or perhaps honey), to which hot water is added. Implicitly believed in as a cold remedy by previous generations.

INDEX

Acknowledgements

The publisher would like
to thank Danes Ltd
(tel. 01273 674 022;
www.danesltd.co.uk)
for supplying Kikor, Poncino
Livornese and Monasterium
bottles for photography.

The publisher would also like to
thank the following for the use of
their pictures in the book (l=left,
r=right, t=top, b=bottom).
AKG: 6, 7t and b, 8t and b;
Album Archivo Fotográfico:
15t; **Cephas**: 9b, 42b, 65t, 95t
and b; **Tim Ellerby**: 9t, 42t,
43bl, 94tl and b.